NEWSWEEK CONDENSED BOOKS

TIM JEAL

JANE HOWARD

JOHN BROOKS

HOWARD COSELL

LIVINGSTONE

A DIFFERENT WOMAN

THE GO-GO YEARS

COSELL

NEWSWEEK BOOKS, New York

NEWSWEEK CONDENSED BOOKS

Kermit Lansner, Editor

Barbara Graustark, Copy Editor

The condensations in this volume have been created
by Newsweek, Inc., and are used by permission of
and special arrangement with the publishers
and the holders of the respective copyrights.

The original editions of the books in
this volume are published and copyrighted
as follows:

Livingstone
Published by G. P. Putnam's Sons
Copyright © 1973 by Tim Jeal

A Different Woman
Published by E. P. Dutton & Co., Inc.
Copyright © 1973 by Jane Howard

The Go-Go Years
Published by Weybright & Talley
Copyright © 1973 by John Brooks

Cosell
Published by The Playboy Press
Copyright © 1973 by Howard Cosell

CONTENTS

LIVINGSTONE

THE BIBLE

JOURNAL

TRAVELS

LIVINGSTONE

A condensation of the book by

TIM JEAL

A CONTRADICTORY HERO

On April 18, 1874, Dr. Livingstone's body was buried in Westminster Abbey. The Prime Minister and the Prince of Wales attended, thick crowds lined Pall Mall and Whitehall, and many people wept.

During his last wanderings in Africa four search parties had been sent out in as many years, and the most expensive journalistic venture of all time had been instigated by the *New York Herald* when they sent Stanley to find him. Three years later Livingstone's body, disguised as a bale of cloth, had been carried by his native followers from the heart of Africa to the coast: a journey of fifteen hundred miles taking over eight months.

Today such excessive adulation and reverence are hard to understand, for Livingstone appears to have failed in all he most wished to achieve. He failed as a conventional missionary, making but one convert, who subsequently lapsed. His first great journey across Africa from coast to coast was an outstanding achievement, but even this was marred by his discovery that Portuguese and Arab traders had already reached the center of the continent. The abrupt ending of his optimistic dream that the Zambesi would prove a navigable river was not offset by the discovery of Lake Nyassa—a lake which, in all probability, had been reached by the Portuguese some years before. Livingstone was considered the greatest geographer of his age, yet a series of miscalculations deceived him into believing that he had found the source of the Nile when he was in fact on the upper Congo. There were other failures too: failure as a husband and a father, failure to persuade the British government to advance into Africa—yet, almost unbelievably, failures that did nothing to impair his influence.

9

Livingstone's fame was not due so much to what he had done, nor even to what he had been; the crucial factor was what he had come to represent. He could be admired as exemplifying bravery, endurance, modesty, and self-sacrifice—all the virtues Victorians wished to possess—but, more than that, he had told his countrymen that they were the most philanthropic and freedom-loving in the world, and that on them, above all others, was laid the sacred trust of bringing progress and liberty to the benighted.

CHAPTER 1

FACTORY BOYS

The harsh conditions which David Livingstone endured during his childhood wore down and destroyed all but a handful of those who experienced similar early hardships. With Livingstone the effect was to be a lasting sense of personal isolation and an incapacity to live with or tolerate less exceptional people.

Scotland, at the end of the eighteenth and the beginning of the nineteenth century, was going through a period of intense social change. Landowners had discovered that they could make more money from their estates by expelling their tenants and devoting the land to sheep grazing, and the dispossessed crofters poured into the already crowded industrial cities. David Livingstone's grandfather, Neil, formerly a tenant farmer on the small island of Ulva, came to Glasgow in 1792 where he found work in a cotton mill at Blantyre, eight miles southeast of the city.

Livingstone's father, also called Neil, was one of five sons in a poor family. He was put to work in the mills as a child, but was then apprenticed to a local tailor. Young Neil stuck at the job long enough to meet and subsequently marry the tailor's daughter, Mary Hunter. The couple moved to Glasgow for a while and Neil gave tailoring a last chance, but the wages were low, the rents were high, and he grew disgusted with the language and behavior of his workmates. So the Livingstones returned to Blantyre where Neil became a traveling tea salesman, a job which paid little but gave his religious interests greater scope, enabling him to distribute tracts to his customers. It was in Blantyre on March 19, 1813 that David Livingstone was born, the second of seven children, two of whom died in infancy.

Although Neil Livingstone had a great admiration for learning, the size of his family and the small financial rewards of tea selling forced him to put his three sons to work in the mills while still children. David started at the age of ten. All employees at Blantyre Mills, adults and children, worked six days a week from six in the morning till eight at night.

Three-quarters of the work force at Blantyre were children, and most of these, like Livingstone, were employed as "piecers," their job being to piece together threads on the spinning frames if they looked like breaking. Each adult spinner had three piecers attending to his machines and, since he was paid in proportion to what he produced, it was in his interest to force the children on. Often towards evening they started to fall asleep on their feet, but a beating with a leather strap or a dousing with a bucket of water generally renewed their energies.

By the end of the working day most piecers were too tired to play, and certainly in no frame of mind to learn. But David Livingstone and a handful of other children were made of sterner stuff, for they made their way to the company school to spend two hours learning to read and write. Already taught these skills by his father, Livingstone started Latin during his first year of evening school. During the next few years he spent what little money he did not give to his mother on classical textbooks.

The dominant figure in David's early life was his father. Neil's disapproval of alcohol was expressed by total abstinence, while he labeled all literature not of a religious nature as "trashy novels." About the use of bad language he was fanatical. David preferred reading travel books and scientific manuals to the religious tracts which his father pushed at him, and once he was thrashed for refusing to read Wilberforce's *Practical Christianity*. But while he was ready to laugh at his sister for being afraid of divine punishment, he was still terrified by the possibility of his personal damnation.

This religious fear was to last throughout Livingstone's boyhood and was only to be resolved when he was almost twenty, when by chance he purchased a book by a Scottish nonconformist minister and amateur astronomer, Dr. Thomas Dick. Science, the elderly astronomer assured his readers, was in no way opposed to Christian beliefs and did not in any sense render God obsolete. Far from it; a greater awareness of the complexity and variety of creation only confirmed Christians in the necessity of there being a Maker.

In 1832, the same year that Livingstone read Dick for the first time, his father was persuaded by friends to go and listen to Henry Wilkes, a young Canadian preacher. His withering attack on the Established Kirk and on orthodox Calvinist theology proved a turning point in Neil Livingstone's life. He had heard this sermon in the independent church at Hamilton, near Blantyre, and shortly afterwards he applied for membership there. The independent churches had no unified approach to theology but reserved the right to govern their own affairs, the congregation electing their own elders and making their own decisions about church discipline.

Neil Livingstone's change of heart brought him closer to David and the old rifts were completely healed. His father's membership in the Hamilton Church was important to Livingstone in another way too. It brought him in touch with a far wider social circle; several members of the congregation were relatively wealthy and well-educated men who corresponded with theologians in America, where a simultaneous religious revival was taking place.

It is hard to describe the intense pride that Livingstone and like-minded men felt in their more liberal faith. They believed themselves to be in the vanguard of contemporary thought, pioneers of a new and stronger truth. This great revival was closely linked with the anti-slavery movement, which in 1833 recorded its greatest triumph; in that year slavery was abolished throughout the British Empire by Act of Parliament. This victory spurred on the missionary societies, whose members considered freeing the slaves to be the first step towards spiritual freedom; the heathen must next be given the gospel. And 1832 was the year of the Reform Bill, which stimulated rather than abated demands for social and educational reform. The confident optimism of the 1830's was to stay with Livingstone long after he had left Britain.

Optimist or not, at twenty-one Livingstone was still working in the mills. He had expressed interest in medicine, but his father opposed any medical training unless his son was to put it to a specifically religious end. Then, in the middle of 1834, he read a pamphlet from the Hamilton Church, an appeal for medical missionaries to be sent from Britain and America to China. Medical missionaries were a comparatively new phenomenon but Livingstone saw at once that if his father could be made to see how medicine could serve a religious purpose—for gratitude inevitably followed the relief of physical suffering—he could leave the mills and train as a doctor.

12

Neil Livingstone was duly convinced but a medical education still remained the first requirement; the main obstacle to becoming a university student was financial. The fees for each session came to £12 and, since Livingstone for much of his working life had been earning less than four shillings a week, this was an enormous sum. But, with his father's encouragement and his own determination, he saved most of the money during the next year and a half, and with a little help from his brother John the goal appeared attainable.

CHAPTER 2

MEDICAL STUDIES AND MISSIONARY TRAINING

The medical training Livingstone received so eagerly, between 1836 and 1838, was primitive. Surgical operations were performed at hazardous speed because of the lack of anaesthetics. Chloroform and ether were not introduced till seven years later and the discovery of antisepsis lay twenty-five years ahead. The study of chemistry was growing, but that of physics had hardly started and biochemistry and bacteriology were unknown. Knowledge of the origins of diseases was limited and largely inaccurate. Nothing at all was known about the tropical diseases he was to encounter, like malaria and blackwater fever, and the role played by insects in their transmission was not even guessed at till the end of the century.

During the next two years, as well as studying medicine, Livingstone went to Greek classes at Glasgow University and attended theology lectures. He also made a range of new contacts which would have been inconceivable at Blantyre. The most important of these was James Young, a chemist who was soon to invent a process for distilling oil from shale. Young was to remain a lifelong friend and correspondent, and thirty years later his generosity offset the government's stinginess and enabled Livingstone to depart on his final journey.

During his second year at Anderson's College, Livingstone began to think seriously about which missionary society he ought to approach. In the end he chose the London Missionary Society, largely because of its sympathies for congregational church government and its acceptance of candidates from all Protestant denominations; the Society's operations were worldwide and included missions in

China, the South Seas, the West Indies, India, Sierra Leone, and South Africa. After two personal interviews with the Directors in August 1838, Livingstone was accepted on probation.

The plan was that Livingstone's probation should be spent under the tuition of the Rev. Richard Cecil at the small market town of Chipping Ongar in Essex. Then, if he proved competent in Latin, Greek, and theology, he would go on to a theological college, and after that complete his medical training in London. He must have impressed at his interviews, for this treatment was reserved only for the pick of London Missionary Society recruits.

In Chipping Ongar, Livingstone lodged with six other students in a long, low building where they did their own cooking and washing. It would be hard to think up a worse training for aspiring missionaries than the rigid diet of Greek, Latin, Hebrew, and theology meted out to the young men at Ongar with Livingstone. Their new knowledge would have been excellent if they were destined for work as ministers in British university towns or in affluent areas of major cities, but for practical assistance in converting Indians, Africans or Chinese it was useless.

In 1839 world events altered Livingstone's subsequent career. In September of that year Britain and China drifted into the inglorious Opium War that was to last till August 1842, and the Directors of the London Missionary Society decided that no more missionaries ought to be risked in China till the war was over. Livingstone therefore had to think of somewhere else to begin his missionary life and suggested South Africa, which the Directors accepted.

His move to London took place on January 2, 1840, and he stayed in a boarding house for young missionaries where he met the famous South African missionary, Robert Moffat and his wife. Their warnings that he would be lonely and wretched in South Africa without a wife did nothing to help him find one and only left him feeling confused. The pressure of work in London left him no time to make friends with likely ladies and within a few months the strain had made him take to his bed. After his illness, he returned to Scotland, and in November, after sitting the relevant exams, gained the license of the Faculty of Physicians and Surgeons, Glasgow.

Unrelated to his medical studies, but of far greater importance for his subsequent thinking, was his attendance, on June 1, 1840, of the vast public meeting mounted by the Society for the Extinction of the

Slave Trade and for the Civilization of Africa. Livingstone heard for the first time Thomas Fowell Buxton, Wilberforce's successor, propound his panacea for the remedy of every African evil. Africans would only be saved from the slave-trade if they were woken up to the possibilities of selling their own produce; otherwise chiefs would continue to sell their own people to pay for the European beads, cloth, guns, and trinkets they coveted. Commerce and Christianity could achieve the miracle, not Christianity alone. These were ideas which Livingstone would one day publicize.

On November 20, 1840 Dr. Livingstone was ordained a nonconformist minister, not affiliated to any church or establishment, but within the voluntary Congregational Union of England and Wales. Livingstone's academic preparation for ordination had not been very different from that of a contemporary Anglican, with the exception of some crucial points of theology, and the major difference of church organization would have been recognized by all nonconformists, but not by Anglicans or Catholics who would not have allowed him to preach in their churches.

When Livingstone sailed from London on December 8, 1840, on the *George,* he must have known that many humanitarians disapproved of missionary work abroad. But Livingstone would have brushed aside such arguments with scorn. All men had the right to hear God's word. No anti-missionary arguments nor any fears of the discomforts ahead would have troubled Livingstone as he watched the London docks fall astern.

On March 15, 1841, after a voyage of over three months, the *George* anchored in Simon's Bay, and Livingstone went ashore. A few days later he was in Cape Town.

CHAPTER 3

AFRICA AND SOUTH AFRICA

When Livingstone landed at the Cape in 1841, the geography of central Africa was still as much of a mystery to Europeans as it had been to the Greeks and Romans two thousand years before. It seems unlikely that so little was known of a continent which, over a thousand years before, had seen the establishment of Arab settlements along its eastern seaboard, but the Arabs had pursued a coastal

trade, leaving the native tribes to fetch to their settlements slaves, ivory, and gold dust from the interior. When the first European invaders tried to push inland six hundred years later their efforts were hampered by problems not to be overcome for four centuries.

These first European efforts had been made in the early sixteenth century by the Portuguese. By 1450 Portuguese ships had sailed south down the west coast of Africa past Sierra Leone, and just before 1500 Vasco da Gama had reached Mozambique and finally India via the Cape of Good Hope. During the first decade of the sixteenth century Portuguese forts were built along the east African coast from Mombasa to Sofala and the Arabs were crushed or overawed. Still confident, and driven on by rumors of inexhaustible silver and gold mines in the interior, the Portuguese thrust their way inland into east Africa up the Zambesi. By the middle of the century forts had been established at Tete and Sena, but the dreams of swift progress and easily accessible wealth had ended; the problems of tropical Africa were understood.

The Zambesi had been hard enough to sail into at all, and it was soon found that that river's surf-beaten sand bars and complete lack of natural harbors were defects to most African waterways. Then there were the cataracts, the intense heat, and the inexplicable and sudden deaths from malaria. The climate brought more than disease; periodic rains could turn flat, dry, easily traversable country into impassable swamp within a matter of weeks. Worst of all, the black inhabitants of the country clearly possessed neither wealth nor an easily exploitable terrain. All interest in Africa might have died away in the sixteenth century had not events elsewhere suggested a use for one African commodity: the African himself.

Six years before da Gama rounded the Cape, Christopher Columbus had landed in the West Indies. By the time the Portuguese were struggling up the Zambesi, their fellow countrymen were settling in Brazil, and the Spanish in the Caribbean, Mexico, and Peru. The European discoverers of the western New World soon found that its sparse population was insufficient for its development. More laborers would be needed for the mines, sugar plantations, and later for the cotton fields. At that very moment thousands of strong, hardy black men were known to be living lives of apparent idleness on the other side of the Atlantic. The transatlantic slave trade was the inevitable result. Taken up at first by the Portuguese and Spanish, the French, Dutch, English, and Danes were not slow to join in. The European

settlement of North America during the seventeenth century greatly increased the demand for slaves. The first English slaving fort was set up at the mouth of the Gambia river in 1618. Within a hundred years this commerce had become so essential a part of the British system of trade, and apparently so vital to the economy of the Caribbean and Americas, that it would take some fifty years to end British participation in 1833. For another thirty years after the triumphs of Wilberforce and Buxton, the British naval blockade on the west African coast would not be able to stop completely the flow of slaves.

The anti-slavery movement had implications for Africa that went beyond curbing the trade itself. In 1791 a British philanthropic association received a charter for the purpose of settling freed Negro slaves from the New World in their continent of origin. The result was the British colony of Sierra Leone. Liberia had similar beginnings. Running parallel with this humanitarian interest came a new fascination with African geographical problems. In 1788 the African Association was founded to promote exploration. Between 1795 and 1831, British explorers traced the Niger from source to sea, and in east Africa, Bruce had reached the source of the Blue Nile. These journeys were not followed up, largely because the problems known to the Portuguese for centuries now confronted the British.

Only in Africa south of the Zambesi had events been different; there, with a clement climate, no malaria and, in the Cape Colony at least, no tsetse fly, there was a real opening for a European colony to rival any in North America or Australia. But the British did not get there first; in 1652 the Dutch made their first small settlement at the Cape. The Directors of the Dutch East India Company had had no intention of founding a colony, let alone a nation; all they wanted was a victualing port for their vessels en route for the spice markets of the East. Although the settlement at Cape Town came to comprise over a thousand houses by the end of the eighteenth century, the decline of the Dutch East India Company through bad management and increasing French and British competition added to the colonists' miseries.

The 1750's and 1760's saw an intensification of Franco-British rivalry in India and this in turn led both powers to see the Cape as a useful strategic base for future acquisition. But neither nation was prepared to fight the Dutch for it. Only with the advent of the war waged by revolutionary France against Britain in the 1790's did the situation change, for the Netherlands were dragged in on the French

side. Britain, to protect her shipping routes to India and the Far East, occupied the Cape in 1795. This first occupation did not last long and the Dutch were handed back their colony when peace came. But when war again broke out between Britain and Napoleonic France, the British returned to the Cape in 1806 and this time they stayed.

Early in the colony's history, the entirely Dutch society had been a divided one: there were the townsmen at the Cape, predominantly European in dress, manners, and habits; and the farmers or Boers, who as early as the 1720's had started to trek east from the Cape beyond the Drakenstein Mountains into the plains of the Karoo. The further the Boers went, the more remote the Company's administration became for them, and the more these frontiersmen liked it.

In 1776 the Boers made their first contact with a new African people, the Xhosa, at the Great Fish river, five hundred miles east of Cape Town. Soon it was realized that while the Boers were moving east and northwest, a vast Bantu tribal migration was sweeping towards them from the north. Confrontation was inevitable. The Boers wanted the British to expand the borders of the colony and sweep back the Bantu, and the British administrators, seeing that this would create a wider and less accessible border, opted for a policy of containment. To implement the policy, troops had to be sent. To create a white buffer between the Cape Colony proper and the advancing Bantu, the administrators, acting with the British government, launched a state-aided immigration scheme for British settlers to come out and farm just west of the Great Fish river. The Boers viewed these new aliens as rivals and interlopers. The British got on well with the Dutch in and around Cape Town, but with the more distant Boers their relations steadily worsened. Additional cause for deterioration came with the arrival of foreign missionaries.

In the late 1730's a German missionary, George Schmidt, had enraged the Boers by baptizing slaves and was impelled to leave by the ensuing outcry. The missionaries, however, were men not easily intimidated, and in 1811 two London Missionary Society men, Vanderkemp and Read, informed the Governor of the Cape of crimes committed by various farmers against Hottentots and slaves. As a result a number of Boers were charged with brutal crimes and some were convicted. From that time the Boers considered the members of the London Missionary Society to be dangerous enemies.

With the abolition of slavery throughout the British Empire in 1833, some seven thousand Boers decided to trek northeast beyond

the borders of the colony. The Boers objected not so much to the emancipation but to the idea bred by the missionaries that natives should be considered the equals of white Christians. Their trek was also inspired by land hunger and the government's refusal to remove the Xhosa barrier to the east. The Boers, used to moving their cattle on when a given acreage was exhausted, were further incensed when the government informed them that in future land would not be granted freely but would be sold at auction. This combination of circumstances increased the numbers of those leaving the colony for the lands north of the Orange and Vaal rivers. The massive Boer exodus was welcome neither to the government nor to the missionaries. The government was now left with a depopulated eastern frontier at a time when Xhosa pressure was increasing, and the missionaries saw that, away from the powers of British officials, the Boers would be able to do what they wanted with the natives in the areas they had removed to. From now on, the same missionaries who had once been so strongly opposed to colonial expansion tried to persuade the government to extend the colony to include the new Boer republics. The missionaries would fail, for in 1852 the government was to recognize the independence of the Orange Free State and the Transvaal.

The government's new policy of *laissez-faire* towards the trekkers was to have serious repercussions for the missionaries long before the formal recognitions of the republics' independence. As early as 1805 the first London Missionary Society station had been established north of the Orange river in Namaqualand, outside the borders of the colony. Since then, Kuruman and Griqua Town had become not only the London Missionary Society's remotest missions but also their most cherished ones. With the arrival of the Boers just to the east in the adjacent Transvaal, the missionaries were convinced that they would attempt to stop the expansion of all missionary activity to the north and the east of their present situation. Trouble in Bechuanaland between missionary and Boer could not be far off.

Kuruman was used by the Directors of the London Missionary Society in all their propaganda at home to show what a mission station ought to be: neat, well laid out, well watered, houses made of stone with little gardens and orchards of fruit trees. There was an ideal missionary there too; Robert Moffat had started his work there in 1821 as a young man in his early twenties. Through his labors the

watercourses were dug, the houses built, and the orchards planted. Through his patient and inflexible persuasion the first converts had been made, not after weeks, nor even months, but after eight years of disappointment and frustration. The Directors of the London Missionary Society did not, however, dwell on the length of time that had passed before conversions had been made. Moffat had spent decades translating the Bible into Sichuana, the language of the Bechuanas. He had set up a printing press to disseminate the newly translated gospel and had run a school to teach the natives to read and write in their own language. His devotion to a single tribe and a single place for a lifetime exemplified the Directors' considered opinion of the best type of missionary life.

In the year that Livingstone came to Africa, the Directors of the London Missionary Society might have admitted privately that the speed and number of conversions had disappointed them, but they would have denied emphatically that any new missionary policy was needed.

CHAPTER 4

EARLY DISAPPOINTMENT: KURUMAN

The plan was that Livingstone should spend a short period at the Cape, recovering from his sea voyage, before going on to Bechuanaland and Kuruman to begin his life work. It had been arranged for Livingstone to stay with the veteran campaigner John Philip. The young missionary ought to have enjoyed his time in Cape Town staying with such a famous man as Dr. Philip, but from the beginning Livingstone felt uneasy.

When Livingstone had met Robert Moffat in London early the previous year, the venerable founder of Kuruman had launched into a scathing attack on Philip, claiming that Philip had started to use his position as the London Missionary Society's financial agent at the Cape to exercise authority over the missions north of the Orange river. Furthermore, Moffat went on, Philip had become senile, autocratic, and more interested in politics than in the conversion of the heathen. Livingstone had listened to all this and had believed it.

At Cape Town, however, Philip appeared to be a calm, reasonable, and unambitious man with no desire to exercise authority over Mof-

fat or anybody else. Livingstone wrote to a friend rather shamefacedly, acknowledging that he had come out expecting to find a monster and had instead discovered "an amiable man ... who claims no superiority over us." Philip evidently discovered from Livingstone that Moffat had been blackening his character in England, and decided to repay the compliment before Moffat could get back from his London fund-raising trip. The young missionary had soon sucked in Philip's stories about Moffat being a scandalmonger and troublemaker.

Livingstone might gasp with indignation at the squabbles and hatreds of his new colleagues, but before he had even reached Cape Town he had already taken a lasting dislike to William Ross, a London Missionary Society artisan traveling out to South Africa on the same ship. Ross's wife had been constantly seasick and Livingstone had tried his medical skills to bring relief; all he brought was a husband's fury and accusations that the young man had designs on Mrs. Ross. From then on Livingstone wrote off Ross as a man with "an exceedingly contracted mind," whose opinions should receive no more attention than an illiterate Hottentot child's. Ross repaid Livingstone by suggesting that he was unmarried because no girl would look at such a disagreeable young man.

On April 16, Livingstone and Ross boarded the *George*, this time bound for Algoa Bay, 450 miles to the east of the Cape. From there they were to collect their oxen and wagons for the five-hundred-mile journey north to Kuruman. From the very beginning of the journey Livingstone was delighted by African travel. The complete freedom of stopping where and when he wanted, lighting a fire and cooking when he was hungry, and looking across miles and miles of thinly populated country, seemed to mark a complete break with his cramped and regulated past existence.

Livingstone arrived at Kuruman on the last day of July; while he had not expected Kuruman to be an aesthetic paradise, he *had* expected the place where Moffat had labored for twenty years to be large, densely populated, entirely Christian and within reach of other heavily peopled areas. Moffat himself had spoken of the smoke rising from the fires of a thousand villages to the north. Livingstone was horrified to find that was a grossly distorted image. To start with, Kuruman was no more than a small village, with no native villages clustered around; most estimates of the population for twenty miles around did not exceed a thousand. Moffat's native congregation

amounted to about 350, an impressive figure, but of these just under forty were communicants. Forty Christians made in twenty years by the most famous missionary in southern Africa—Livingstone was staggered. He wrote telling the Directors that Kuruman could never become populous and would probably lose people in the future, since the Bechuanas were cattle-farmers and would inevitably choose better watered and more fertile places to graze their oxen and sheep. The Directors were not alarmed; nobody could seriously expect them to believe that their most publicized African mission station was an arid, under-peopled village that might soon be deserted. They put down Livingstone's complaint to youthful enthusiasm.

Livingstone concluded that the explanation for the tiny number of native converts was that the missionaries must have been going about things the wrong way. When he passed through Griqua Town and met the missionaries there he found that the reason why the Kuruman missionaries disliked their neighboring colleagues was the Griqua Town policy of using native teachers for effecting conversions. In Moffat's view no natives had been trained sufficiently to enable them to give a faithful and accurate version of the gospel. Livingstone nevertheless was certain that the Griqua Town Mission had found the answer. It seemed obvious to him that the natives would resist Christianity much less if it was offered to them by people with black skins like theirs. In theory he was absolutely right, but in practice he would soon find that suitable native teachers were very hard to find.

It was not long before he discovered that the tribes living roughly a hundred miles from Kuruman to the north had developed a dislike and scorn for the people of Christian-dominated Kuruman. The reason was that these more distant tribes had only been preached to a few times and their impression of Christianity was the usual distorted version: that the white man's religion was just a trick to get them to give up their wives. Livingstone became certain that this attitude would soon poison the minds of tribes living two and three hundred miles north of Kuruman. It therefore seemed imperative for a missionary to make contact with these untouched people before that happened. There was also a danger that if missionaries did not reach them soon, traders would get there first and give them quite the wrong impression of what white men wanted. Livingstone wrote telling the Directors this, but no satisfactory reply came. Resigned and by now thoroughly disgusted, all Livingstone could do was try to

cure minor native ailments and sit learning their language, Sichuana.

Had Livingstone been shown figures for conversions in other South African missions before he left England, he would have realized that Moffat had achieved as much at Kuruman as any other missionary elsewhere, inside or outside the colony. Had it been admitted that most missionaries labored for years before achieving anything at all, and that Africans only tolerated missionaries because they could mend guns and bring beads, the public would not have dipped their hands in their pockets. When missionaries returned to harangue the faithful, the heads of their Societies would not have thanked them if they had painted bleak pictures of failure.

Livingstone had been at Kuruman only a month when Rogers Edwards, the missionary with whom he was temporarily lodging, gained permission from the Directors to make a journey of several hundred miles to the northeast with a view to selecting a site for a new mission station. Edwards asked Livingstone if he would like to come too, and the younger man leapt at the offer. Livingstone had liked Edwards from the beginning, considering him "an excellent friend." Edwards was in his late forties and had been at Kuruman almost as long as Moffat. Unlike Moffat, however, Edwards had been an artisan missionary all those years and had never been promoted to the post of full missionary. He had disliked being what he called "Moffat's lackey" and saw the chance of forming a new mission as his last chance to gain promotion.

The journey that Edwards and Livingstone made between September and December 1841 led Livingstone to undertake two more trips on his own between April 1842 and June 1843. The three journeys together paved the way for the selection of a site for the new mission and its inauguration by Livingstone and Edwards in August 1843. During this two-year period Moffat remained in England and the Directors did not send Livingstone any further instructions; neither did they give their permission for him to join with Edwards in starting the new station till July 1843, when Livingstone had already made definite plans to do so.

The main tribes he was to meet were the Bakhatla, 250 miles northeast of Kuruman; the Bakwains, a tribe split under two rival chiefs, and situated 60 miles northwest of the Bakhatla; and the Bamangwato, 150 miles north of the Bakwains. The Bamangwato had already been visited by two ivory and skin traders, Wilson and Hume, in the early 1830's. So, while Livingstone met many natives

who had never seen a white face before, he was not breaking into totally unexplored country. The importance of the trips, apart from the ultimate foundation of the new mission, was the knowledge they gave him of the difficulties he would face when he began his own work as a missionary.

Livingstone realized that travel in Bechuanaland could be a lot less comfortable than his journey up to Kuruman. Any journey undertaken between November and January—the hottest time of the year—was an ordeal in a countryside with very little water. The wagon oxen might have to go two days without water in temperatures well over 100°, and the same would apply to human beings if a known water-hole turned out to be dry. On his first trip to the north, Livingstone described the heat as so great that "the very flies sought the shade and enormous centipedes coming out by mistake from their holes were roasted to death on the burning sand."

At first, native reactions to the arrival of so strange a visitor as a white man amused Livingstone. He noted how his straight hair was a source of fascination and incredulity, and laughed when a native woman touched his nose "to make herself sure that it really was so far elevated from the level of my face as it appeared to be and was not like her own little flat thing." But while European strangeness led the natives to show Livingstone respect, their automatic assumption that he was "a great wizard ... possessed of supernatural power ... capable of even raising the dead" did not please him. He realized that, while this kind of hold over the people was useful as a means for persuading them to dig watercourses and build small dams, it was a barrier to religious teaching. He was horrified to hear natives calling him by the Sichuana word for God, a title frequently given to chiefs.

When he tried to get across to natives the idea of praying to an unseen deity, and knelt down to show them the position in which Christians prayed, he was greeted with delighted laughter. Livingstone's head bowed to the earth convinced the watchers that he was talking to a god who lived under the ground. He did only a little better when talking to individual chiefs in private. Sekhomi, chief of the Bamangwato, when told that Christianity could change people's hearts, immediately expressed interest. Sekhomi explained to Livingstone that for a long time he had been afflicted by violent and quite unpredictable fits of rage. Christianity, he felt, might cure him. Livingstone did his best to point out that the gospel was not a

medicine, but Sekhomi brushed this explanation aside. If Christianity would stop his rages, he would accept it straightaway, if only his white visitor would give him the magic drink.

Reactions to Livingstone ranged from superstitious dread to skeptical indifference, and made him decide that a new approach to Africans was called for: a far less humble way of dealing with them. "I make my presence with any of them a favor, and when they show any impudence I threaten to leave them, and if they don't amend I put my threat into execution. By a bold free course among them, I have not had the least difficulty in managing even the most fierce."

All this did not however bring him any closer to explaining the Christian faith although he did manage, by pointing out the personal advantage, to persuade several tribes to dig small irrigation canals from distant streams to help their crops. At this early stage he began paying natives for work. Payment would be in tea, coffee, sugar or beads. By making himself useful as an agricultural adviser and general handyman, and by doling out rewards, Livingstone gained some popularity and standing, but this very popularity made him uncertain, when natives listened to his preaching, whether they were not simply doing so to encourage him to stay with them long enough to give more technical help.

Nevertheless there were small compensations, as when the Bakhatla allowed him to see their iron-smelting process: a sight never before witnessed by a European. The Bakhatla in fact showed Livingstone such friendliness that he felt safe to ask their chief, Moseealele, whether he would consent to have a missionary settle with him. Moseealele, recognizing that a missionary would possibly attract traders and would certainly bring a knowledge of gun-mending, agreed at once. Livingstone was not able to say when he and Edwards would come, but at least he had the chief's consent.

Back in Kuruman in July 1843, Livingstone heard from the Directors, who at last agreed to his joining in the formation of a new mission station but suggested that the move should not be made till Moffat came back. Feeling as he did about committees, Livingstone decided that unless he could get out of Kuruman before Moffat got back, he might have to spend years as Moffat's "lackey" just as Edwards had done. He confided his fears to Edwards and reminded him that both their futures were bound up in the new venture. Edwards was frightened of doing anything that might give the Directors offense but eventually he agreed. Once they arrived among the

Bakhatla, Livingstone and Edwards attended a meeting that Moseealele had called to inform his people of the missionaries' intended settlement and to gauge his subjects' feelings. After some discussion, Moseealele gave his formal consent.

The Bakhatla had independently made up their minds to move to the spot which Livingstone had selected for the new mission, and the missionaries bought the land they intended to live on and cultivate; they insisted that unless they paid they would be beholden to the chief. The area was a mile and a half in width and two in length; it was purchased with a gun, some powder, lead, and beads. The legal formalities over, the missionaries set to work to build a hut, fifty feet by eighteen. This would one day be the chapel, they hoped. Neither man, however, was under any illusions about why they were wanted. Livingstone's analysis was: "They wish the residence of white men, not from any desire to know the Gospel, but merely, as some of them in conversation afterwards expressed it, 'That by our presence and prayers they may get plenty of rain, beads, guns &c. &c.'"

So in August 1843, two years after his first arrival in Bechuanaland, Livingstone was about to embark on missionary work of his own.

CHAPTER 5

A FALSE START: MABOTSA

Before looking in detail at Livingstone's missionary work, it is necessary to have a picture of the people he was trying to convert. Livingstone's estimate for the population of Bechuanaland was thirty thousand, and he was probably not more than ten thousand out. He worked first with the Bakhatla and then with the Bakwains and they accounted respectively for 2,000 and 3,500 people. The primary activity of these tribes was cattle farming, with agriculture coming a poor second, maize and sorghum being the principal crops. A very low annual rainfall guaranteed disappointing results. The Bechuana tribes lived in towns or villages and these centers remained occupied for many years at a time. Shoshong, the capital of the Bamangwato, had over 3,000 people. Mabotsa was rather smaller with 400 huts and a population of about 1,500. The Bechuanas paid the price for keeping their established villages; as the cattle grazing

around them diminished, they had to move their cattle further away to distant cattle posts. Crops, too, were often grown many miles away. As a result people were often traveling backwards and forwards between their villages and the grazing pastures and gardens. These absences hindered consecutive missionary teaching sessions.

The heart of the missionaries' difficulties lay in the enormous differences between the social, moral, and economic requirements of nineteenth-century industrial Britain and those of a small African tribal community. Victorian virtues such as work, punctuality, thrift, monogamous marriage, and personal ambition were all vices which a good African tribesman wanted to avoid. In a tribal community men and women certainly worked, but they did not do so to grow rich or to build up a surplus of food. Work was limited to providing the necessaries of life and setting aside a small communal store of food to protect the tribe against drought and famine. In a society where there were no exchanges of goods made on a money basis, it was advisable to be generous if your own crops were fruitful, for the next year they might fail and you would be dependent on another's generosity.

On the subject of polygamy, the African was convinced that the white man was mad. It was as clear as day that to be satisfied with only one wife was to court social and economic disaster. While economic competition was alien to a tribal community, competition among the various headmen for influence within the tribe was quite legitimate. Such influence could only be acquired by a man with many dependants. One wife could only have a limited number of children; the implication was obvious: a man who wanted influence had to have many wives. These wives would also be able to grow more food than would be needed even by the enlarged family, and this would enable the head of the family to give feasts to gain prestige. With luck, if his feasts were impressive enough, he might be able to attract the dependants of other headmen. His position depended solely on the extent of his largesse. In their circumstances the tribesmen knew that monogamy would have brought disaster.

Grounds for misunderstandings between missionaries and their pupils were too numerous to be conveniently listed. Africans gained a reputation for lying and boasting that was partly due to the fact that a man who had inherited rights, from, say, his grandfather, would not find it odd to speak in the first person and use the present tense for things his grandfather did. Africans also got a reputation for impre-

cise thinking because of failure to give precise instructions to travelers. Sometimes the reason was that they had never traveled far from their home village, and anyway, they failed to see the point of geographical discovery. A pond was water and so was a large lake. Who but a fool would risk life and limb to gaze at gallons of water?

In this impossible situation it would have been strange if the missionaries had not worked out two main methods for comforting themselves. The first was to subscribe to an unquestioning faith in God's Providence. If failure came, it was obvious that God was holding things back for a good reason. The second source of comfort came from stressing and exaggerating the supposed depravity of the natives. Phrases such as "the poor African," "the untaught child of nature," and the "humble Negro," who might be "raised" with God's help, were all designed to bolster up the missionary's morale and persuade him that until the African grew from childhood to maturity he would not be able to appreciate the gift of true religion.

But by the middle of 1844, after only a year at Mabotsa, Livingstone was writing about Africans with a perception greater than that shown by any previous observer. First he realized, accurately, that Christianity was a direct threat to tribal society on every level. Christianity, he wrote, "appears to them as that which will reduce them & overturn their much loved 'domestic institutions.'" It was a crucial observation and, having made it, Livingstone came to other logical conclusions. He decided that missionaries had failed in the past by too readily condemning what they did not understand. The *boguera* or initiation rites had previously been treated as barbarous black magic and a perverted religious ceremony. "Those who have gone to the circumcision together," he wrote, "are bound into a cohort under one of the chief's sons or brothers for ever afterwards and have to render service, go wherever he is sent, do whatever he likes under pain of death." Livingstone saw that tribal unity and survival depended upon continuation of the rite.

Livingstone had no training or background reading to make him so responsive and it is truly remarkable that even when he made no impression on the Bakhatla he retained his liberal beliefs. It would be seven or eight years before he became convinced that every tribal custom, good or bad, would have to give way to British values if Christianity was to make any headway. Only a society in disintegration would prove responsive to any alien religion. The Bakhatla's indifference to his teaching did, nevertheless, drive him to the borders

of despair. While Edwards, his fellow-missionary, was married, he was not. He wrote to all his friends asking them to write as often as they could, but a letter could take from four to six months to reach England and as long again for the reply to come back.

At Kuruman, with his journeys and inflated hopes to take the edge off his isolation, it had been easy to sneer at the settled comforts of marriage as weak-minded escapism, but at Mabotsa, with the daily indifference of the natives and no diversions in prospect, he was left far more time to contemplate his personal loneliness. In the few letters he received from home, he was asked whether he intended to get married. But it was not easy to find a wife. Apart from missionary daughters, there were no white women in Bechuanaland, and few of them, knowing the privations of the missionary life, were prepared to spend their whole lives facing hardships.

Three miserable months passed at Mabotsa, during which Livingstone and Edwards finished the large hut they had begun on their first visit, completed a ditch and watercourse, and built one more hut besides. In late October news came from Kuruman that Moffat was at last on his way up from the coast. Livingstone and Edwards knew that they would have to go south to meet him and explain why they had not waited till his arrival before beginning their new mission. On his way to Kuruman, Livingstone felt apprehensive about the coming meeting; he remembered what Dr. Philip had said about Moffat and had not entirely got over his own feeling that the founder of Kuruman had deceived the Directors about the population of Bechuanaland. But just as he had been forced to admit that he was gullible to believe all he heard about Philip, Livingstone was soon admitting that he had been a credulous idiot to have misjudged Moffat too. The rapport between the two men was immediate and it marked the beginning of a long friendship.

It took a week or so to return to Kuruman. Livingstone, to his great relief, learned that Moffat was not so opposed to native teachers as he had been led to believe, nor, it appeared, was he in favor of a committee. But there were pleasures other than eager discussion to be had at the Kuruman home of Mr. and Mrs. Moffat. The Moffats had two daughters of marriageable age, Ann and Mary. Livingstone only stayed at Kuruman for two weeks, but during that time he managed to make some headway with Mary, who, although by no stretch of the imagination beautiful, was compliant and good-tempered. Livingstone knew that a man in his position could not afford to be

fussy. Although he had now made up his mind that Miss Moffat had better become Mrs. Livingstone, he decided that he ought to ask her formally on his next visit to Kuruman.

Shortly after Christmas, Livingstone was on his way back to Mabotsa, where he experienced far less pleasant embraces. As early as 1842 he had seen "a woman actually devoured in her garden" by a lion, and had noticed that there was a plague of these animals at Mabotsa. Nevertheless he had always remained unworried by the thought of personal danger. On February 16, 1844 some natives came screaming to him to help them kill a lion that had just dragged off some sheep. Livingstone fired both barrels at the lion but only wounded him. As he vainly tried to reload, the lion leapt on him, catching him by the arm. Livingstone was only saved by the sudden appearance of Mebalwe, an elderly native convert whom he had brought from Kuruman as a native teacher. Mebalwe snatched a gun from another native, loaded, and fired both barrels. The gun misfired but the lion bounded off to attack his new assailant. Mebalwe was badly bitten on the thigh and another native who tried to help him was in turn bitten on the shoulder. Then the lion suddenly dropped dead, killed at last by the wounds initially inflicted by Livingstone.

Livingstone was extremely ill for weeks, and his wounds suppurated for several months. The long-term effects were not as bad as might have been expected and he was subsequently able to shoot, lift heavy weights, and do everything that he had done before. In early July he left for Kuruman and a short period of convalescence. His stay was almost three weeks and during this time he proposed to Mary Moffat and was accepted.

Sophistication was never one of Mary's qualities, and if her manners were a little rough that was to be expected. She had lived all but four of her twenty-three years in Africa. But she was literate and had been taught by her mother all the household tasks a missionary's wife ought to be able to manage. She would never be homesick for England, since Africa had always been her home, and that was a considerable advantage. Livingstone was also convinced that having a wife would help his missionary work; she could run an infants' school and would diminish the suspicions which Africans unfortunately felt about a bachelor missionary questioning native women on fornication and adultery.

The marriage was one of convenience and both recognized this. Livingstone might know that he would be better looked after than

hitherto, but there were advantages for Mary too. Her mother was a domineering woman and it was a relief to her daughter to escape from the house at Kuruman to a home of her own. Like Livingstone she had also had very little choice of partners; added to that she was fat and plain and probably felt fortunate to be getting married at all.

Within weeks of his return to Mabotsa at the end of March 1845, with his new bride, Livingstone was to show himself capable not only of hypocrisy and self-righteousness in his dealings with colleagues but also of lies and double-dealing.

Between August 1843 and December 1844, in the months when Livingstone and Edwards were at Mabotsa together, their relationship had steadily deteriorated. Twice there had been rows over trivial incidents that led Edwards to claim that Livingstone was attempting to undermine his authority over the Bakhatla by taking the side of natives whom Edwards had censured for various reasons. It was unfortunate for Edwards that he chose minor incidents with which to challenge Livingstone; for it gave the younger man no difficulty at all in representing Edwards as a small-minded idiot who could work himself into a frenzy over trivial disagreements. This was the line Livingstone took when he wrote a 9,000-word letter to the Directors, telling them about Edwards's unstable temperament. In this letter of self-justification, Livingstone cannily relegated to a very secondary position the real cause for tension: Edwards's conviction that Livingstone was attempting to claim all the credit for the foundation of the new mission.

Edwards had good grounds too. A letter written by Livingstone in 1843, for publication in the *Missionary Chronicle*, had not included a single mention of Edwards as co-founder of Mabotsa. Livingstone cannot have failed to realize how important Mabotsa was to Edwards: it represented his last chance to establish himself as an independent missionary, his final opportunity to escape from a life dominated by Moffat. Nor, knowing Edwards's feelings about Moffat, could Livingstone have been surprised that Edwards was distressed to see Mary Moffat at Mabotsa. It was as though Moffat had established spies to report back to Kuruman.

The worst aspect of Livingstone's behavior was his failure to tell Edwards that he intended leaving Mabotsa anyway. Just after his wedding, before returning to the Bakhatla, he had written to some friends telling them that Mabotsa was too small to provide two mis-

sionaries with work. He went on to say that he did not fancy working with another man, for he wanted to be responsible for introducing the gospel to a tribe "wholly by my instrumentality."

Had Livingstone told Edwards that he meant to go, all Edwards's suspicions and worries would have melted away, yet it was months before he finally got round to telling him. When the older man then suggested that he would never have quarreled had he known, Livingstone used the admission as proof that Edwards had never had a leg to stand on.

After the row it was quite evident that the Livingstones and the Edwardses could no longer remain on the same mission station. Livingstone has been said to have left a well-established and thriving mission to his disagreeable fellow-missionary, simply out of the goodness of his heart; nothing could be further from the truth. Livingstone was relieved to be going because the Bakhatla had already shown definite signs that they cared not a damn for Christianity. Livingstone had met Sechele, chief of half the Bakwain tribe, on two of his early excursions from Kuruman. Sechele had impressed him by his intelligence and seemed a more likely candidate for conversion than the chief of the Bakhatla. Sechele had also recently moved to a place called Chonuane, only forty miles north of Mabotsa. Having asked Sechele if he would have him, and having received a positive invitation, Livingstone began making preparations for his move. He ought to have asked the Directors' permission first, but since their reply would almost certainly take a year to come back, Livingstone decided to move first and explain later.

CHAPTER 6

LIVINGSTONE AND THE BOERS: CHONUANE

The rapidity of Livingstone's move to Chonuane was understandable, but the choice of site could not have been worse. The water supply was dried up entirely for most of the year. 1845 had also seen a severe drought and most of the corn had been ruined. Sechele, compelled to plant crops forty miles away from his village, had recently heard that these new plantings had been wrecked by a herd of buffalo.

Food and water shortages were bad enough, but the Livingstones

also had to foot their moving bills and pay expenses connected with building a new house, a chapel, and a school. Mrs. Livingstone was by now expecting her first child and her husband was £30 in debt: an unhappy situation for a man earning only £100 a year. In spite of the hard labor that he had put in on the new buildings, Livingstone was determined. The Bakwains, he assured Robert Moffat, were altogether a superior tribe to the Bakhatla and the prospect for conversions was infinitely brighter. Sechele was in every way a most superior African, with hardly a barbarous habit to his name. Nonetheless Livingstone had to admit that Sechele had shown no interest in Christianity. Other signs were a little better and Livingstone clutched at any causes for optimism, however slight. Sechele's desire to possess various types of European goods sent Livingstone into rhapsodies. "That he is desirous of civilization I think we may conclude since he sent out goods with us [on a journey to Kuruman] to purchase a mattress—4 lanterns—6 candle boxes—a baking pot, a smoothing iron, a table, & soap."

But Livingstone soon had undeniable cause for rejoicing. Sechele had an astounding aptitude for learning, and incredibly made such progress in learning to read that he "acquired a perfect knowledge of the alphabet, large, small and mixed, in two days." Within a month he was spelling words of two syllables and asking questions about England. Soon he was compiling his own spelling books and persuading his five wives to read with him. In time three of them became Livingstone's best pupils.

Just when Sechele was making such excellent headway with his religious reading, Livingstone's hopes received a severe setback. For twenty years Sechele had ruled over only half the Bakwain tribe. The split had taken place during Sechele's childhood and had come about as a result of his father's murder. After a period of chaos Sechele found himself an exile, and two of the conspirators who had planned his father's murder divided the tribe and became chiefs of the two respective sections: Bubi took one and Molese the other. Eventually in 1829, at the age of nineteen, Sechele managed to oust Molese, but Bubi retained his hold over his part of the tribe. This was still the situation when Livingstone arrived at Chonuane in 1845. In August that year, Sechele sent Bubi a gift of gunpowder. Bubi, suspecting that this unexpected present was enchanted, set about dissolving the charm. The method he chose was to pass hot embers over the gunpowder. The result was an explosion that killed

him. After his death many of his subjects went over to Sechele but many stayed with Bubi's successor, Khake. Livingstone managed to dissuade Sechele from attacking Khake till very near the end of 1845. Out of respect for Livingstone, Sechele tried diplomacy. This merely led Khake to accuse him of cowardice. Then one day Livingstone saw Sechele's warriors arming for what he was told was an elephant hunt. Towards evening Livingstone emerged from his house to see "the wounded carried past the town" and this was "soon followed by the sounds of heathenish joy mingled with the loud wailing of those who had lost their friends." Probably not many more than fifty were killed but that was still a significant loss for a tribe numbering less than four thousand.

Livingstone's prestige suffered greatly, for it was widely known that the chief had ignored his missionary's advice. In the eyes of most of the Bakwains their chief had been right, for by fighting he had united his tribe. Although Sechele remained affable towards Livingstone and went on with his reading, the numbers attending public worship fell off dramatically. Since people had only come to hear Livingstone preach because Sechele had told them to, Livingstone was left to draw his own conclusions.

This repeated failure seemed to point more and more to the necessity for giving native teachers a proper trial. Livingstone brought two native teachers from Kuruman to Mabotsa and thence to Chonuane. Of the two, Mebalwe has already been mentioned; the other was called Paul. Both men had been among Moffat's early converts. Mebalwe had not only saved Livingstone's life but had since made himself quite invaluable as a general handyman. Livingstone therefore decided that Paul ought to begin independent missionary work first. With this end in view, Paul and Livingstone set out in July 1846, not without some trepidation, for a couple of months earlier the commandant of the Boers settled in the neighboring Transvaal had sent Livingstone a note informing him that any future missionary expansion should not take place without prior permission. Livingstone had sent a civil reply telling the commandant that his intentions were entirely innocent and could only meet with the approval of all good Christians. The Boers, with their allegiance to the Dutch Reformed Church, were, after all, nominal Christians. Their church did not however recognize the equality of black and white.

The Boers were not primarily worried about missionary expansion as such, but they saw Livingstone's plans to introduce native

teachers into the Transvaal as a political rather than a religious move. The native teachers would report back to Livingstone on the Boers' treatment of Africans, and Livingstone would then publish the reports and do his best to force the British governor at the Cape to end his policy of *laissez-faire* towards the Boers beyond the borders of the colony.

By early 1847 Livingstone knew that the Boers would never tolerate any native teachers in the Transvaal; he was therefore thrown back on Chonuane again with no better prospects of success than he had had in 1845. Livingstone now had to face the idea of spending the rest of his life with the Bakwains, making thirty or so converts, if he was lucky. It was not a pleasing prospect for an ambitious man in his early thirties, and he once more began to doubt whether he could endure the conventional static missionary life with its scant and ill-recognized rewards. Could a missionary, he asked himself, be reasonably expected to stay with a single tribe for more than ten years if that tribe showed no interest? Moffat would have pointed out that there would only be progress *after* ten years; but Livingstone preferred to ignore such inconvenient thoughts. He made up his mind that if a decade passed and the Bakwains were still resistant, he would "move on to the region beyond."

At any rate in 1847, after less than two years with the Bakwains, Livingstone knew that he would have to stay a little longer if he wished to avoid the derision of all his colleagues. Whether Livingstone or Sechele liked it, the Bakwains were to have one last chance; but the continued drought and the drying up of all springs within reach of Chonuane meant that that chance would have to be given somewhere else. Another move had to be made. This time it was to a place called Kolobeng, forty miles to the northwest.

CHAPTER 7

THE ONLY CONVERT: KOLOBENG

M oving had become almost second nature to the Livingstones, but it was no less exhausting for all that. In fact, for Mrs. Livingstone, now the mother of two children, it was far worse. Robert had been born early in 1846 and Agnes was just three months old when the Livingstones' wagon rumbled out of Chonuane for the

last time. Mary Livingstone's life had been hard even before the arrival of children, and she had needed all the skills her mother had taught her. In addition she had had to run an infants' school with numbers sometimes rising to eighty; she was hard put to keep order let alone teach anything. In less than a year after the arrival at Kolobeng, Mary was pregnant again and so the school had to be abandoned. Another son, Thomas, was born in March 1849; a daughter, Elizabeth, who survived only a month, in August 1850; and a further son, William, in September 1851.

The Livingstone children had few toys, and those they did have came from the Livingstone seniors in Scotland. A lack of toys was not all the children had to put up with. The Livingstone diet was at the best of times bizarre; often the whole family would sit down to a feast of locusts, which, Livingstone assured friends in England, were not unlike shrimps and excellent with wild honey. The children particularly relished a species of caterpillar and a large frog called *matlametlo*.

When the outer walls of the house had been built and the roof was at last in place, Livingstone started to think of possible improvements. He placed antlers on the walls and rather shamefacedly ordered a sofa from Cape Town. The last improvements Livingstone made were the doors and window frames. Strangely, he left the outside door to the very end. Before it was in place Mrs. Livingstone showed she was equal to any emergency, as her husband recorded: "A big wolf came. . . . Mary wanted me to go and see whether the room door were fastened, but . . . I advised her to take a fork in her hand and go herself, as I was too comfortably situated to go myself."

The Livingstones usually got up at dawn, had family prayers, breakfast, and then school for anybody prepared to come. The rest of the morning Livingstone devoted to manual work—sawing, ploughing, smithy work, and anything else that needed doing. Mary would spend her morning cooking, sewing, and looking after the children. Lunch would be followed by a short rest, and after that Mary went to her infants' school and Livingstone went on with his manual tasks till about five o'clock. After that he generally went into the town to talk to anybody who felt like it, milked the cows, and finally went to the chief's house to pray and give him special instruction. He would arrive home at 8:30, worn out.

The help given by a native couple made matters a little better, but not much. Livingstone's ten cows were quite inadequate to give

them milk all the year round—grazing was bad because of the drought. Worse still the Kolobeng river had "dwindled down to a dribbling rill" and was therefore useless for irrigation. A year later it had dried up altogether, and an increasing number of people believed that Livingstone's presence was responsible. Sechele kept the Livingstone family going by sending them what food he could spare. Livingstone got used to the drought, the fleas, the chirr of the crickets, the endless zebra meat that Sechele sent, and he even became hardened to his children's emaciated faces. But he could never get used to the Bakwains' indifference to the gospel. Every evening he wrote in his journal, and to keep his spirits up tried every form of self-deception. "It seems very unfair," he wrote, "to judge of the success of these [missions] by the number of conversions which have followed." That was how he had judged Moffat, but now it was another story. Livingstone concluded the passage almost in a pleading tone: "No mission which has His approbation is entirely unsuccessful. His purposes have been fulfilled if we have been faithful."

Yet strangely, at this very moment when almost the whole Bakwain tribe was showing complete indifference, Sechele requested that Livingstone should establish an evening prayer-meeting in Sechele's house for the chief's family. Livingstone could hardly believe it when Sechele told him that he "knew he was living in sin, but though he had not given up those with whom he sinned [his wives], he wished to pray in his family."

But a Bechuana chief who opposed his people's wishes ran a real danger of deposition, and Sechele knew that all his headmen and advisers hated the idea of Christianity. Under normal circumstances polygamy presented any chief wishing to be a Christian with impossible problems, but for Sechele they were worse than usual. Two of his five wives were the daughters of under-chiefs who had been directly responsible for reinstating him after his exile. Rejection of these wives would therefore make enemies of several of the leading families in the tribe.

In August 1848 Sechele came and asked for advice. Livingstone did not feel able to give it and pushed the responsibility back on to the chief by telling him to look in the Bible for guidance. When Livingstone learned that Sechele had decided on rejection, he told the chief to treat his wives gently "for they had sinned in ignorance." Sechele announced his intention to become a Christian and give up his wives on Monday, August 7, 1848.

Sechele's bravery must remove all doubts about the genuineness of his conversion. What had tilted the balance for him in favor of Christianity will never be known, but in view of the danger and inconvenience he caused himself, to say nothing of the suffering inflicted on his wives, it was little short of miraculous that he decided to take the plunge. On August 10 a large *picho* (meeting) was held to intimidate Sechele and it was proposed that he should at least allow his wives to remain in their old homes. He compromised and allowed them all the possessions from their former homes and gave them new clothing, but they were still to go to their parents or families. Mokokon stayed at Kolobeng because she had no parents to go to.

Three months after his baptism, Sechele was still standing up to his people's taunts and appeared to be making good progress. To Livingstone's delight he began learning English. It was not till five months after the baptism that Livingstone noticed that Mokokon, Sechele's rejected wife who had been allowed to remain, was showing symptoms that looked unpleasantly like pregnancy.

The blow to Livingstone was devastating, made more so because Sechele's fall was not the only one at this time. Livingstone had always looked on the families of Paul and Mebalwe as irreproachable; now he discovered that one of Paul's sons, Isak, had been regularly committing adultery and had got another man's wife pregnant. Livingstone sent Sechele a note: "My heart is broken. First Isak, then you. I can no longer be a teacher here."

Livingstone's attempt to make Sechele believe that the lapses were entirely responsible for his determination to leave the Bakwains was convenient rather than truthful. The first mention of plans not to stay with the tribe for longer than a given period had been made at Chonuane two years before, in March 1847. Later in that same year he had written to Robert Moffat suggesting that the two of them should attempt a journey to the unknown lake to the north. This plan had fallen through, partly through lack of funds and partly through Moffat's determination to press on with his translation of the Bible. Nevertheless Livingstone was not beaten; in June 1845, while still at Mabotsa, he had met an English hunter and traveler, William Cotton Oswell: a man with a bent for exploring and money to indulge it. So, late in 1847, Livingstone wrote to Oswell in an attempt to persuade him to come to the lake. Oswell wrote back saying that he and a companion, Mungo Murray, would arrive at Kolobeng

at the end of May, 1849, and that the three of them would then attempt to reach the lake.

Livingstone wrote to the Directors of the London Missionary Society in May 1849, on the eve of his departure for the lake—called Ngami by the natives. He explained the difficulties he had been having with the drought and argued that, since the Boers had prevented him settling native teachers to the east, the only direction for future expansion was the north. He briefly mentioned Sechele's lapse but gave it no weight. Instead he suggested that the real reason for a series of journeys to the north was the fact that the Bakwains would not be persuaded to believe "precipitously" and that in the meantime thousands of precious souls to the north were perishing.

CHAPTER 8

NORTH TO THE ZAMBESI

B etween 1849 and 1851 Livingstone twice traveled over three hundred miles northwest of Kolobeng to Lake Ngami in the extreme north of modern Botswana—formerly Bechuanaland. On the third crucial journey, he reached the upper Zambesi, almost exactly in the middle of south central Africa, in the area of the Barotse valley.

It is important, in view of Livingstone's reputation for being the first European to penetrate south central Africa, to record what was already known about the area. Lake Ngami had often been visited by natives from the south, but Livingstone's journey of 1849 is the first recorded by any European. Ngami however was a minor affair compared with Livingstone's arrival on the upper Zambesi in 1851, and there he had definitely been anticipated by other Europeans—the Portuguese.

The Portuguese colonies of Angola on the west African coast and Mozambique on the eastern side of the continent had been established during the sixteenth century and were well known to Livingstone and his contemporaries. Nevertheless the extent to which individual Portuguese explorers had penetrated the interior was far less widely appreciated. Silva Porto, a trader, had reached the upper Zambesi, between 1847 and 1848, at almost the very spot where Livingstone first saw that river. When Livingstone later met Porto

and other Portuguese traders on the upper Zambesi in 1853, he would inaccurately pronounce them Portuguese half-castes in order to defend his position as the only true European to reach the area.

Livingstone, on his £100 a year salary, would never have been able to make his three journeys between 1849 and 1851 had it not been for the generosity of William Cotton Oswell, who accompanied him on the first and third trips. Educated at Rugby and Haileybury, Oswell had entered the Indian Civil Service, but had retired after ten years for a life of leisure and the delights of African travel and big-game hunting. Oswell, however, was no mindless young man with a private fortune and little else. He was exceptionally generous, modest, and completely lacking in personal ambition. These last two qualities provide the key to the success of his relationship with Livingstone, who liked to get his full measure of praise, while Oswell conveniently never saw fit to press his own claims. Oswell's companion, Mungo Murray, who also came on the 1849 journey to Lake Ngami, was a man of similar character, who preferred doing things to talking about them afterwards.

The party that left Kolobeng for Ngami on June 1, 1849 was a large one, for it included not only Oswell, Livingstone, and Murray, with their dozen African drivers and attendants, but also thirty Bakwains sent by Sechele to bring back any ivory they might find near the lake. J.H. Wilson, a trader centered on Kuruman, had asked to come too and had been accepted as one of the party.

Five weeks after leaving Kolobeng, they reached the river Zouga and enthused about the large trees and thick vegetation on its banks. The Zouga was flowing from a west-northwesterly direction and the travelers had no doubt but that its source lay in Lake Ngami. Before they arrived at the lake, they discovered that another river flowed into the Zouga from the north. Livingstone was convinced that the area to the north of the Zouga would contain a major river network. In his view this completely eclipsed the impending discovery of the lake itself. So when Livingstone stood on the shores of Ngami he made no plans to walk around it or to ask the natives more than a few questions about its depth and extent. It was in fact shallow and, including the surrounding marshes, was about seventy miles long. While Oswell made detailed inquiries, Livingstone, still in a state of great excitement, thought about the river system to the north, sure that he was on the verge of proving that central Africa was a well-watered, fertile land instead of being a desert as large as the Sahara.

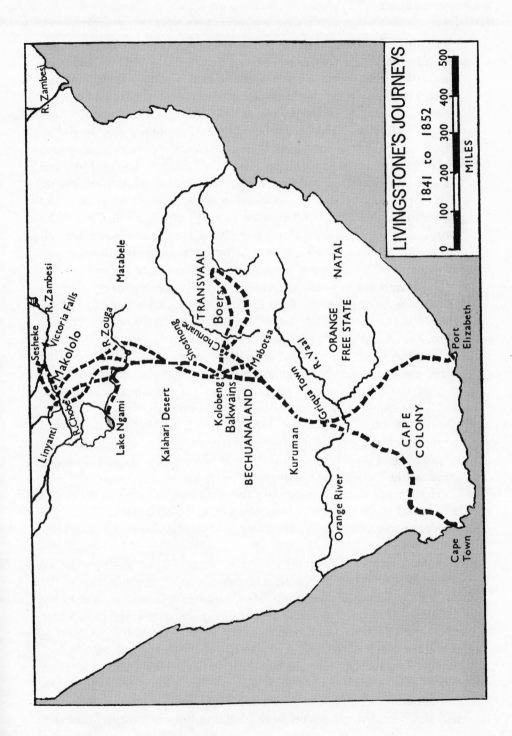

LIVINGSTONE'S JOURNEYS

1841 to 1852

MILES

0 100 200 300 400 500

R. Zambesi

R. Zambesi

Victoria Falls

Sesheke

Makololo

R. Chobe

Linyanti

R. Zouga

Matabele

Lake Ngami

Kalahari Desert

TRANSVAAL

Boers

Shoshong

Chonuane

Mabotsa

Kolobeng

Bakwains

BECHUANALAND

Kuruman

R. Vaal

Griqua Town

ORANGE
FREE STATE

NATAL

Orange River

CAPE
COLONY

Port
Elizabeth

Cape
Town

He therefore decided to set out for the area to the northeast. Unfortunately the Zouga had to be crossed first, and the chief of the principal tribe around Ngami gave orders that the white men should not cross. The chief knew that if the white men went about two hundred miles northeast, they would reach Sebitoane, chief of the far from peaceful Makololo. The chief of the Ngami people not only feared an attack by Sebitoane but also believed that the white men would make matters worse by selling guns to Makololo. Livingstone and Oswell tried to argue, but no canoes were forthcoming. Livingstone started to build a raft but the wood was too heavy and sank by its own weight. He then tried a lighter wood but this turned out to be wormeaten and absorbed the water like a sponge. So when Oswell offered to return to the Cape and bring up a collapsible boat on his next trip in slightly under a year's time, Livingstone agreed.

The return journey was uneventful and Kolobeng was reached on October 9. Livingstone lost no time in sitting down to write letters about his discovery. The people he really had to impress were the Directors of the London Missionary Society; he had not asked their permission to leave his post at Kolobeng and was uncertain what their reaction would be. Livingstone decided the best approach was to play down the purely exploratory goal of reaching Lake Ngami and concentrate on the river system to the north. This network of rivers he wrote: ". . . opens out the prospect of a highway capable of being quickly traversed by boats to a large section of well-peopled territory . . . I do not wish to convey hopes of speedily effecting any great works through my poor instrumentality. . . ."

What was new in Livingstone's thinking was the idea of using rivers as *highways* to open up the continent. It was a notion he would never get free of; rivers would bring him spectacular success and bitter failure.

In fact, Livingstone need not have worried greatly about the attitude of the Directors. Arthur Tidman, the Foreign Secretary of the Society, realized at once that if the discovery of Ngami was given publicity it would encourage public generosity. He published Livingstone's account of the discovery in the March 1850 edition of the *Missionary Magazine,* and the Royal Geographical Society decided to award Livingstone one half of the year's Royal Premium —the far from regal sum of £25. The prize would be good for quite a few donations to the missionary cause. The Royal Geographical Society had also seen the advantage of publicizing the discovery of the lake.

Founded in 1830, this body had been incompetently run for some years by a group of naval officers and was only just becoming what it had been intended to be: a society for the promotion of geographical discovery and for providing those interested in geography with published accounts of new discoveries. The Society's new president, the well-known geologist Sir Roderick Murchinson, knew, like Tidman, that subscriptions to any sort of society were the result of advantageous publicity. Tidman, for his own financial reasons, had no objection to Sir Roderick publicizing Dr. Livingstone's work, although the Directors of the London Missionary Society had no intention of starting new and costly ventures in central Africa. But if Livingstone wanted to go off traveling they were prepared to let him, especially since he had found a rich man to pay for most of it.

From the moment Livingstone had returned to Kolobeng from his first journey to Ngami, his only thoughts were to get back to examine the country further north. The results of this second journey were nil because Livingstone in the first place decided not to wait for Oswell to join him, and in the second decided to travel with his family.

The reason why he decided not to wait for Oswell is simple: he could not bear the thought of anybody else getting the credit for penetrating further north than Ngami. Livingstone later tried to excuse his behavior by saying that there had never been any prior arrangement between them. This was clearly a lie, since when Oswell did reach Kolobeng, shortly after the Livingstones had left, he brought the promised boat with him.

If Livingstone's behavior towards Oswell is confusing, his attitude to his family is many more times extraordinary. For a start, the children were very young: Robert was four, Agnes three, and Thomas only one when they left in April 1850. Mrs. Livingstone was five months pregnant. She would probably give birth on the journey home, possibly in the Kalahari Desert.

The Livingstones managed to get to the Zouga without mishap, but there for the first time Livingstone encountered the tsetse fly. As soon as the oxen had been bitten, they began to sicken and die. Livingstone had read about malaria in medical periodicals and therefore knew that quinine was then the only effective remedy. Mercifully he had had the foresight to bring some with him, for within days of their arrival at Ngami, his children had contracted fever. Added to that, the children had no vegetables for over four months. They soon became so weak that Livingstone knew that any thought

of going on north from Ngami would have to be abandoned. After re-crossing the Kalahari, the Livingstones arrived back at Kolobeng in mid-August. Mary's baby was already overdue. A week later she had a daughter. Already enfeebled, the Livingstone children soon caught a bronchial infection that was widespread among the Bakwains at the time. In turn the new baby succumbed to it and very soon died screaming. The final scream haunted Livingstone for a long time af-terwards but he still managed to clear his conscience with chilling ease. "It was the first death in our family," he wrote, "but just as likely to have happened if we had remained at home, and we now have one of our number in heaven."

At Mary's mother's insistence the whole family went down to Kuruman to convalesce from November 1850 to February 1851. The children enjoyed their first fresh fruit in months, but for the adults it was a tense and disagreeable time. The Moffats had discovered that Livingstone was planning yet another journey to the north, and once again intended taking his family. In early April Mrs. Moffat discov-ered that her daughter was pregnant yet again, and this time she wrote to Livingstone telling him precisely how she felt about his en-dangering Mary's life.

But, by April 1851, with his pregnant wife and his scarcely re-covered children, Livingstone was once more ready to set out on his third and, as it turned out, his most important journey made from Kolobeng. This time he had the sense to wait for the ever-forgiving Oswell. By mid-June the party had traveled 170 miles from the river Zouga and had now reached the river Chobe, which Livingstone would later learn was a major tributary of the Zambesi. Across the Chobe, Livingstone knew from the reports of the natives near Ngami, lived Sebitoane, the chief of the Makololo. Since the wagons were too large to transport across the river on native canoes, Mrs. Livingstone and the children were left while Livingstone and Os-well went some twenty miles upstream.

Sebitoane received his two white visitors with visible emotion, but his pleasure at their arrival had nothing to do with Livingstone's statement of the aims of his visit: "the preaching of the gospel" and the Makololo's "elevation in the scale of humanity." In fact the chief of the Makololo wanted guns; he had been fighting almost constantly for the last thirty years, so his desire was understandable.

A tribe of the southern Sotho group, the Makololo had been driven from their home, in what was to become the Orange Free State, dur-

ing the great Zulu emigration that took place in the first three decades of the nineteenth century. In the early 1820's the Makololo had been forced east into Bechuanaland but had then been driven north by the better armed Griquas after a battle near Kuruman in 1824. They had continued northwards and had finally reached the Chobe. During the next ten years they established themselves as overlords of the Barotse valley and the Batoka Plateau further along the Zambesi to the east. Their position was still not secure, for they were threatened by the Matabele, one of the Zulu tribes which had originally forced them out of their true home. To protect themselves the Makololo had withdrawn to the area between the Chobe and the Zambesi, for the two rivers afforded excellent protection. Unfortunately the surrounding swamps left the Makololo in the worst kind of country for malaria. They were in a death-trap and knew it. Apart from guns they saw another way of returning to the more healthy territory which they had been compelled to leave: diplomacy.

Sebitoane had heard about the extraordinary affection Mosilikatse, the Matabele chief, had developed for Robert Moffat, who had already twice made the 600-mile journey from Kuruman to Mosilikatse's kraal. The Makololo chief had also learned that Livingstone was Moffat's son-in-law. Sebitoane therefore reasoned that if Livingstone came to live with him, as his missionary, Moffat would use his influence on Mosilikatse to stop him attacking the Makololo.

Although he had been delighted by Sebitoane's extraordinary eagerness to keep him and Mary as his teachers and missionaries, Livingstone's principal aim was to get to the great river which he had heard lay a hundred miles to the north. His plans to get there were disrupted when Sebitoane unexpectedly died of pneumonia. It was not therefore till the end of July that Livingstone and Oswell were able to set out. Livingstone's arrival on the banks of the Zambesi near the town of Sesheke, on August 4, 1851, was to prove a turning-point in his life. Both he and Oswell were stunned by the size of the great river; neither had seen anything like it before. The river was between three and five hundred yards across and was flowing fast although it had been an unusually dry year. Livingstone, oblivious of Silva Porto's discoveries, was so moved by the thought that he and Oswell were the first white men ever to have seen this mighty river, that he was close to tears. The two men soon made the deduction that the Zambesi flowed into the sea in Mozambique. Although Livingstone had heard that there was a massive waterfall

eighty miles to the east, he resumed his reverie of a navigable *highway*. If this river did flow on for a thousand miles to the east coast of Africa, would it not be possible for traders and missionaries to come up it as far as the great falls? There might of course be other lesser falls, but Livingstone preferred not to think about them. His dream of the Zambesi as a God-given highway into the interior had already begun to take solid shape in his mind.

This idea could never have had such a momentous impact on Livingstone's thinking had he not made a further discovery on his return to the Makololo's town of Linyanti on the river Chobe. Livingstone's attention was drawn to the clothing made of European cloth worn by some of the Makololo. He lost no time in making inquiries about the suppliers of these items, and discovered that they were a tribe known to the Makololo as the Mambari, who came from the area around Bie in central Angola, six hundred miles northwest of Linyanti. Livingstone next made the disquieting discovery that the Mambari acted as middlemen and agents for Portuguese and half-caste traders living in Angola. His realization that the slave trade had reached the upper Zambesi made him still more determined that the region should be occupied by missionaries without delay.

In 1840, while studying in London, Livingstone had heard Thomas Fowell Buxton speak about the benefits "legitimate commerce" could bring to west Africa. The central idea had been that the African would no longer sell his fellow men to slave traders if he had an alternative means of acquiring European cloth, guns, and trinkets. If "legitimate" traders passed into the interior and offered to exchange cloth and guns for wax, palm oil, and ivory, chiefs would have this alternative and the slave trader would therefore be "cut out." The problem had always been how traders could be persuaded to penetrate hundreds of miles into an unknown continent where the tsetse fly ruled out carriage by wagon and oxen, and where malaria frequently killed those foolish enough to hack their way through tropical rain forests. Livingstone felt that his magnficent Zambesi would solve the problems that had bedevilled all the trading efforts in western Africa.

Unfortunately, Livingstone soon discovered that the Makololo themselves were eager slave traders too, and sold members of their subject tribes to the Mambari without any compunction. Livingstone's previous assumption that the Makololo were a simple and untouched people, without any of the vices of the already con-

taminated Bechuanas, now had to be dropped. To soften the blow, Livingstone tried to convince himself that the Portuguese and the Mambari had only arrived the year before and had therefore not had time completely to corrupt the Makololo. Livingstone's position was painfully ironic; he had come hoping to find an untouched people, and having found that they had already been corrupted by external influences, was now advocating far more contact with outsiders.

Ignoring the fact that tribalism served the present needs of the people and enabled them to survive famines and to operate in a country where trade with distant tribes was made impossible by the nature of the terrain, Livingstone found no difficulty contrasting African poverty with British industrial wealth. Thus he unthinkingly endorsed the common mid-Victorian equation of industrialism with progress and "civilization." There was no mention now of contact with Europeans making Africans worse; instead he wrote that Africans would only become civilized "by a long-continued discipline and contact with superior races by commerce."

Livingstone had abandoned much of his earlier thinking largely because of his passionate desire to make the area between the Chobe and the Zambesi a viable field for missionary work. He had felt that God had directed him north from Kolobeng to this region, and his discovery of the upper Zambesi had strengthened this belief. The fact that the Makololo spoke Sichuana was an added reason for his feeling that a mission with them could succeed. His conviction was so fixed that he would ignore or underestimate all the problems associated with his chosen field. Apart from the problems posed by the slave trade and the Makololo's involvement in it, there was malaria. Livingstone told the Directors of the London Missionary Society that traders, if they came up the Zambesi during June, July, and August, would not get fever. Livingstone's son, Thomas, had fever throughout June and July. In any case Livingstone's plans for the region depended on traders and missionaries being able to live there all the year. That would only be possible if a healthier and preferably higher adjacent area was found. Then the Makololo would have to be persuaded to move, and that of course would depend on the attitude of the Matabele. The greatest imponderable of all was whether the Zambesi would be navigable from the coast. If the river should prove impassable because of rapids or sand banks, then few traders would come to the area, for they would never be prepared, in sufficient numbers, to endure the long and perilous journey. Livingstone had

suggested that a brisk trade would be done in ivory, but indiscriminate slaughter of elephants would soon put an end to it. Apart from ostrich feathers and wax, he had few ideas for the establishment of longer-term trade. Instead, with typical optimism, he had suggested that since gold had recently been discovered in South Africa, it might be found further north. God, he claimed, would do for central Africa something "just as wonderful and unexpected as the discovery of gold." This prediction was mistaken.

Before Livingstone started south again in August 1851, he had nonetheless made two realistic decisions. He would return as soon as possible to the Zambesi, in the first place to see whether he could find a healthy spot for a mission and trading center, and in the second to reach the coast either to the east or west, to see whether the Zambesi was a realistic *highway*.

By September, Livingstone and his family had reached the river Zouga and there they had to wait a month, while Mrs. Livingstone gave birth to her long awaited child, William Oswell, named after their friend and benefactor. During this delay Livingstone wrote letters which would be ready for dispatch when he got further south. The most important was to the Directors. In it he outlined his new plan for sending his wife and family back to England while he took a closer look at central Africa and tried to open a direct way to the coast. Livingstone told the Directors flatly that if they would not support Mrs. Livingstone and the children in England, he would still go north. When Livingstone finally put his wife and family on a ship bound for England in April 1852, he had still had no reply from the Directors—but his failure to wait and hear what provision the Directors would make was typical of his attitude to wife and children. When they became a hindrance to his cherished plans, his family, and not the plans, had to be sacrificed.

Livingstone arrived at Kolobeng on November 27, 1851, and found that the Bakwains had moved on in search of a better-watered place. The sight of the deserted village pleased him. The Bakwains' move could be added to the list of excuses he had already worked out for leaving Sechele and Bechuanaland for good.

Although missionary failure had originally driven Livingstone north, his principal motive in 1851 for leaving Bechuanaland was his feeling that there was far more exciting work to be done among the Makololo. Bechuanaland could never offer the thrilling prospect of traders sailing hundreds of miles along a navigable river, nor could it

ever give scope to Livingstone's abiding ambition to "preach the Gospel beyond every other man's line of things." He sensed that his ideas on commerce and Christianity might have a revolutionary impact on Africa, far greater than anything that an individual missionary working with one tribe could ever hope to achieve. Missionary work in the conventional sense was often dull, usually disappointing, and never very successful. Livingstone had now chosen a far more attractive role, that of a man who opened the way for others, who would then follow and establish missionary and trading settlements. Then Livingstone would go on and open up more territory, and so on. The important thing was that he should lead and others follow. It was the ideal formula for the personally ambitious missionary.

CHAPTER 9

RETURN TO LINYANTI

From the moment he arrived at the Cape in March 1852, Livingstone's one thought was to get a passage for his wife and children as quickly as possible, so that he could head north again. When Mr. and Mrs. Moffat had asked Livingstone what plans had been made for their daughter and grandchildren in England, their son-in-law had to confess that he had no idea, but he added with more bravado than realism "that if they [the Directors] crimp my wife and family they will hear thunder." The Directors in fact heard nothing from Livingstone for several years and in the meantime Mrs. Livingstone spent a miserable four and a half years of poverty and homelessness.

She began by staying with her husband's parents and his two spinster sisters in Hamilton, Scotland. Mary was ill-suited for her new role and her strait-laced parents-in-law's constant meddling with the children soon drove her into rages. Within six months the situation had become unbearable. Mary left the house and told the Livingstone seniors that they were not to inquire after her and not to try to contact the children.

After leaving Hamilton, Mary and the children lived a wretched nomadic existence. Sometimes they stayed a few months in rented rooms, sometimes with friends her father had made during his last visit to England between 1839 and 1843. She was sustained by the

hope that her husband would return after two years, but as three and then four years passed she began to despair. She scandalized people by making bitter remarks about missionaries, and before long she began to drink. It was a habit she did not break till her death ten years later.

With his wife and children out of the way, Livingstone began getting his supplies together. The thought of leaving Bechuanaland filled him with joy. Finally, he left Cape Town on June 8 and arrived at Kuruman on August 29. He had been there only a few days when news came in that the Transvaal Boers had attacked Sechele near Kolobeng. The Boers claimed that Sechele had harbored the chief of the neighboring Bakhatla, who had refused the Boers free labor, and they also used Sechele's refusal to surrender his firearms as an excuse. The attack had really been a punishment for Sechele's rejection of a Boer demand to stop British hunters and ivory traders passing through his territory to the north. The Transvaal Boers believed that unless they stopped these men getting through, there was a real danger that the British might in the end encircle them and begin settlements to the north, in the area of modern Rhodesia.

In the attack Sechele lost three thousand cattle, eleven horses, forty-eight guns, and two hundred women and children as captives. Livingstone's house at Kolobeng was sacked. It might be thought that Livingstone's reaction would have been sympathy for Sechele; he had after all risked universal unpopularity by his acceptance of Christianity. But Livingstone was unmoved. The Boer attack, he wrote in his journal, was not in the least mysterious, it was simply the result of the Bakwains' refusal of the gospel. The other missionaries suggested that if Livingstone had still been with Sechele, he would have been able to negotiate with the Boers on the chief's behalf.

Livingstone saw matters differently. Had he been with Sechele, he argued, he would probably have been killed. God had clearly not intended him to die till he had achieved some more important work. It was this idea of the Providential role he had to play that kept Livingstone in Kuruman until he finally left on December 14.

Livingstone had not gone far when he met an angry Sechele heading south determined to take his complaint to the governor at the Cape. Livingstone told him he "might as well have remained at home." By the Sand River Convention of 1852, the governor of the

Cape had relinquished all pretense to any authority north of the river Vaal. Sechele however went on his way, but only as far as the borders of the colony, where he was compelled to turn back because his resources had been exhausted. Livingstone never saw Sechele or the Bakwains again after 1852. For the next seven years the Makololo would be the focal point of his hopes.

By April 23 the party was within striking distance of the Chobe, which they soon discovered had burst its banks, flooding most of the adjacent low-lying country. This forced them to travel for hours at a time through waist-deep water. Soon Livingstone's guides deserted, and his people refused to go any further. For the first time he proved his exceptional powers of endurance when he and one other man set off alone to try to find a way through the swamps. It took them two days to force their way through the bog to the river Chobe itself.

The Makololo were incredulous. They had assumed the swamps to be impenetrable at the point Livingstone had come through them. The Matabele had certainly never managed to get past them. The Makololo soon suggested a better way in which the wagons could be brought to the river without going through the swamps, and on May 3 the whole party crossed the river, wagons and all, on dozens of canoes lashed together into vast floating platforms. On May 23, 1853, Livingstone entered Linyanti in his wagon, watched by the entire population of the town: six thousand people. The first phase had ended and the real work was about to begin.

CHAPTER 10

FROM COAST TO COAST

In the spring of 1853 Livingstone found that the Makololo had a new chief, a young man of nineteen called Sekeletu. Sebitoane had been initially succeeded by the oldest daughter of his principal wife, but she had voluntarily abdicated in favor of Sekeletu, who was her brother. Livingstone found the new chief just as friendly as Sebitoane had been.

Sekeletu's main motive for being helpful to Livingstone was the Matabele problem, and like his father he wanted guns, cloth, and other European goods. So when Livingstone offered to take ivory to the coast and return with these items, Sekeletu eagerly accepted.

51

At the end of June, Livingstone, accompanied by Sekeletu and two hundred men, set out on the hundred-mile trip north from Linyanti to the Zambesi. There they all embarked in a fleet of thirty-three canoes and headed three hundred miles northwest up the river, bound for the Barotse valley. His aim on this journey, which lasted till mid-September, was to find a suitable site for a mission and trading post. He failed in this, but other factors contributed to the depression he felt on his return to Linyanti.

On his visit to Linyanti in 1851, Livingstone had been shocked to find that the Makololo sold members of their subject tribes to the Mambari, but he had considered this their solitary fault. His first shock on his journey up the Zambesi in 1853 was that they seemed much more bloodthirsty than any tribe in Bechuanaland. The Makololo, Livingstone soon confessed, "never visit anywhere but for the purpose of plunder and oppression. They never go anywhere without a club or spear in hand." "Nine weeks," he told a friend, "hearing their quarrelling, roaring, dancing, singing and murdering, have imparted a greater disgust at heathenism than I ever had."

In late August, Livingstone met two Arabs who had made an epic journey from the island of Zanzibar, fifteen hundred miles to the northeast. They were assessing the slave and ivory potential of Barotseland. These men later went on to Angola and then recrossed the continent to Mozambique, a journey even more formidable than the one Livingstone was about to undertake. Livingstone's depression deepened.

His last disappointment on his journey through Barotseland was due to his complete failure to find any place free of malaria. In 1851 he had confidently told the Directors that traders would be able to come to Barotseland between June and September in perfect safety. During these months he had had fever once every couple of weeks. He was extremely alarmed at the thought that if traders came they might die and "then others might esteem it a tempting of Providence to follow." Of course he could have made a clean breast of it by telling the Directors the real state of affairs, but that would certainly have prevented any future efforts being made in the area. Instead he decided to play down all the difficulties, including the firm foothold the Mambari and the Portuguese had established. So while Livingstone admitted to the Directors that he had not yet found a healthy locality for a mission, he informed them: "I have decided to try and fulfil the second part of my enterprise, viz. to open up a way to the

coast." Realizing that he would have to say a little more about fever, he assured the Directors that none of his party had died of it, and "if I had been able to regulate my diet, &c., I should not have been subjected to so many attacks." He concluded his letter by suggesting that he might well find a healthy spot east of Linyanti at a later stage. In his journal he told the truth: "We must submit to malaria and trust in God for the rest."

So when Livingstone returned from Barotseland and the Zambesi to Linyanti in September 1853, he faced an insoluble dilemma. Having failed to find a suitable place for missionaries or traders to settle in, even if he did then manage to open a suitable route from the sea, it would still not justify him in recommending widespread European penetration of the interior. This was a crucial setback, for all his plans had hinged on the establishment of European trade in south-central Africa. Missionary success, Livingstone was certain, depended on those two preconditions. With good reason Livingstone wrote miserably: "I am at a loss what to do."

Yet there was one thing he could not do, and that was to give up. If he backed down he would be accused of loss of faith and held up to universal ridicule. There was nothing else but to try to open a path to the coast, regardless of whether anybody would want to follow it once they knew the dangers they would face.

When Livingstone left Linyanti, on November 11, 1853, he took everything he possessed. An inventory included a rifle and double-barreled smooth-bore gun, a small collection of spare shirts and trousers, his Nautical Almanac, Thomson's Logarithm Tables, and his Bible. He had a tiny tent, a sheepskin blanket, and a rug. All this, including ammunition, beads, and a little sugar, coffee, and tea, fitted into four tin chests. His more precious possessions were carried separately: a sextant, a chronometer watch with a stop second hand, an artificial horizon, compasses, a thermometer, and a magic lantern.

From then on, while he was traveling by water, a routine was established. The party would rise at five in the morning and after coffee and the loading of the canoes, all would embark.

The next two hours are the most pleasant part of the day's sail. The men . . . often engage in loud scolding of each other, in order to relieve the tedium of their work. About eleven we land, and eat any meat which may have remained from the previous meal, or a biscuit with honey, and drink water. After an hour's rest we again embark and cower under an umbrella. The heat is oppressive.

Two hours before sunset they would stop for the night, have coffee again and, if no animal had been shot, eat a piece of coarse bread made of maize meal.

By late February 1854, Livingstone had traveled a hundred and thirty miles farther into the northwest than on his last journey. Most of the party were ill and thoroughly fed up with the dark rain forests. They had other difficulties too. Only by accepting guides from each village was Livingstone able to allay the suspicions of the people he was now passing, and these guides often took them to villages they did not want to visit, and deliberately detained them. Food was no longer given as gifts but had to be paid for. Since Livingstone's party had little to exchange, they often went hungry. Livingstone seemed unaware of the irony that the Africans' insistence on payment was one of the commercial habits he had hoped would break down the tribal structure.

On April 2 they were at last on the edge of the Portuguese settlement of Angola. Loanda was four hundred miles to the west. Ever since its foundation in the early sixteenth century, the prosperity of the Portuguese colony had depended on the continuance of the transatlantic slave trade. Most slaves leaving Angola were ferried straight across to another Portuguese colony: Brazil. In 1839 the British government decided to use force to stop all exportation of slaves from Africa, and Portuguese Angolans realized that the days of their prosperity were numbered. Nevertheless they still managed to smuggle out twenty thousand slaves a year—a quarter of their previous total. In 1850 the British government authorized the Royal Navy to seize and search suspected vessels within Brazilian territorial waters. This was the death-blow for the Angolan slave traders. By 1854, the year Livingstone arrived in Angola, the number of slaves exported numbered less than a couple of hundred. The effect on the Angolan economy was disastrous.

It is miraculous that Livingstone was welcomed so warmly at Cassange and at all the other Portuguese settlements where he stayed on the way from the Quango river to Loanda. The British Navy had wrecked the economy of the colony, and here was an Englishman, who called himself a missionary but probably was an agent of the British government, snooping around, taking longitudes and latitudes, and making numerous notes about everything he saw. The Portuguese never did really believe that Livingstone was a missionary but they still fed him and treated him as a friend.

Twenty miles outside Loanda, Livingstone began to wonder whether he was going to live. His fever was so bad that he could not summon enough strength to stay on his ox for more than ten minutes at a time. He was also suffering from chronic dysentery. When Livingstone was carried into Loanda on May 1, 1854, he seemed very close to death.

He had heard at the Cape that there were a number of Englishmen in Loanda but his men soon found that there was only one: a Mr. Edmund Gabriel, whose impressive official title was Her Majesty's Commissioner for the Suppression of the Slave Trade in Loanda. From Livingstone's later letters, nobody would have guessed how ill he had been on his arrival. Certainly none of his correspondents would have thought he had been all but given up for dead by Gabriel. As long after his arrival in Loanda as July 4, he was unable to write and had to dictate a letter to Edmund Gabriel so that the Directors would know that he was alive.

As usual, Livingstone's motives for playing down his sickness had little to do with a desire to save his friends and family unnecessary worry. It was his old device for making conditions appear less malignant than they were. Soon he was telling the Directors that had his party traveled in the dry season he would not have suffered nearly so much. Then if he had been able to take more food and changes of clothing, things might have been different. Livingstone told the Directors that he intended to retrace his steps to Linyanti and then attempt to reach the east coast. The reason for this new journey, he assured them, was not that the route he had "opened" was impossible but that a way to "the Eastern coast may be less difficult. . . . If I succeed," he went on, "we shall at least have a choice." He might try and fool others, but he could not fool himself; his journey, he knew very well, had established beyond doubt that commercial operations in the interior could never be begun on any scale from the west coast. There is no denying that Livingstone's success in reaching Loanda, under-provisioned and ill-equipped, had been a magnificent achievement. But since it had disproved almost everything Livingstone had wished to demonstrate, it was not simply self-effacing modesty that made him feel he would have to do better. The journey from Linyanti to Loanda had nearly killed him; now he was going to attempt not only to repeat that journey but also to go on another thousand miles east of Linyanti.

Livingstone left Loanda on September 20, 1854, and in mid-

December, still only two hundred miles from the coast, he heard that the ship carrying the letters he had written in Loanda had been wrecked. This detained him for a further two weeks, while he re-wrote everything, and he was not on his way again till New Year's Day, 1855. While he was doing this rewriting, letters from Gabriel reached Pungo Adongo, where he was staying. Enclosed was a cutting from *The Times*, dated August 8, 1854, describing Livingstone's journey as "one of the greatest geographical explorations of the age." Livingstone transcribed the cutting into his journal but made no comment.

The party reached Linyanti on September 13, 1855, having been away two months short of two years. The men who had come with Livingstone were soon boasting shamelessly about their experiences, talking about the large ships which had eaten "black stones"—there was no coal in Barotseland—and showing off their new clothes. Livingstone was immensely relieved that Sekeletu did not seem annoyed or surprised that he had not brought back more cloth and guns. In fact the chief was delighted that his white man had returned at all. When Livingstone explained to him that he intended to go down to the east coast, Sekeletu seemed as eager as ever to help him. This time, he said, he would lend Livingstone over a hundred men and would send much more ivory to be sold at the coast. In exchange Livingstone undertook to bring back the men and a long list of goods within two years. After that Sekeletu believed that Livingstone and his wife, the all-important daughter of Moffat, would come to live on the Zambesi. This would enable the Makololo to move away from the swamps without fear of the Matabele. Sadly for Sekeletu, time would show that Livingstone had used him. It would be five years before the two men met again and by that time Livingstone's interests would have shifted yet again. The Makololo were no longer God's chosen tribe. Livingstone gained fame and recognition for the journeys he made between 1853 and 1856, and without the help of the Makololo he could not have made them. But Sekeletu and his tribe gained nothing; in fact in the end they lost by their association with Livingstone. Already cut off behind the Chobe river, in an unhealthy place, and with little security, their reliance on Livingstone led them to reject the few traders who fought their way up to the Zambesi from the south. When no trade came up the Zambesi from the coast, as Livingstone had promised it would, they were more isolated than before. Unable to leave their swamps for fear of the

Matabele, the true Makololo were dying out through fever. When Livingstone left Linyanti in November 1855, the Makololo were eight years from extinction. Sekeletu would die in 1863 and the Makololo's Barotse vassals would seize the opportunity of a disputed succession to overthrow their overlords and butcher them all.

On November 3, Livingstone and his 114 porters set out for the Zambesi. His plan was to follow the river right down to its mouth on the east coast, just south of the Portuguese town of Quilimane. This intended journey was roughly a thousand miles, three or four hundred less than his journey to Loanda.

In late November, five years after he had first heard about the great falls east of Sesheke, Livingstone reached the falls of Mosioatunya or "the smoke that thunders." Livingstone was impressed, but a waterfall, even the most spectacular in the world, did not thrill him to the extent the Zambesi itself had done in 1851. Nevertheless he could see that although the falls would not help him in any practical way, they might still serve a purpose. He would call them the Victoria Falls, which might help interest the British public in the area where they were situated. For some time he had been thinking of calling some geographical feature after Her Majesty and this one was eminently suitable.

Immediately east of the falls the Zambesi loops to the south before flowing on east and then northeast. This arc was roughly 250 miles in length. Livingstone decided to travel on north of the river, cutting out the loop altogether. He had heard that the area north of the Zambesi and just east of the falls was high, fertile, and healthy. It might be the place he had so long hoped to find for missionary and trading settlements. As Livingstone pressed on eastwards across the Batoka Plateau, he became more and more convinced that he had made a crucial discovery. The plateau was relatively high and, although well watered by streams, it was not swampy. The area seemed suitable for cattle and supported sizeable trees. In a state of euphoria Livingstone tramped on, making detailed notes of all the favorable characteristics he could find. Of course he knew that the Matabele lived due south, across the Zambesi, but he was not going to let this worry him yet. Nor was his faith in the area shaken by the Batoka themselves, whom he considered even "more degraded than the Barotse."

It was late January 1856 when Livingstone passed Zumbo, the deserted Portuguese settlement about five hundred miles from the mouth of the Zambesi. Twenty miles beyond Zumbo at a place

called Pangura, Livingstone heard from a local chief called Mpende that the Zambesi flowed on due east for seventy miles and then turned sharply southeast. That being the case, if Livingstone headed southeast at once he would be able to cut off a corner and reach the Portuguese settlement of Tete much more quickly; Mpende's direct route was fifty miles shorter than the bending course of the Zambesi. Livingstone would not have been influenced by distance alone; for somebody who had traveled thousands of miles, 200 as opposed to 250 miles was not a significant difference, but Mpende also had told him that if he tried to follow the Zambesi he would have to cope with a hilly and rocky path. Livingstone, who was not feeling strong, decided to do as Mpende suggested.

By leaving the Zambesi at this point, Livingstone failed to discover the Kebrabasa Rapids, which were finally to wreck his hopes of the Zambesi becoming a navigable highway. Had he seen these cataracts in 1856, he would have been saved the ignominy of building up false hopes only later to have to admit to the public and the British government that he had been deceived.

When he did reach Tete, Livingstone made inquiries about the section of the Zambesi he had not seen.

> I was informed of the existence of a small rapid in the river near Chicova; had I known of this previously, I certainly would not have left the river without examining it. It is called Kebrabasa and is described as a number of rocks which jut out across the stream.

It is puzzling that Livingstone managed to leave Tete with the impression that Kebrabasa posed so slight a threat to future navigation of the river. A number of Portuguese living in the town had seen the devastating series of cataracts that extended along the river for thirty miles. Perhaps Livingstone never spoke to these men, or if he did, he heard what he wanted to hear rather than what he was told.

His own scientific calculations about the Zambesi certainly show a marked propensity for wishful thinking. He must have felt slightly uneasy at Tete, for he wrote down a list of figures in his journal designed to prove by the speed of the river's flow that there were no steep drops between the Victoria Falls and Tete. Unfortunately all his deductions were based on the false assumption that the speed of the river was the same for nearly a thousand miles. Livingstone had also made a crucial omission. Normally at significant points he estimated the height of a place by measuring the boiling point of water

with a special thermometer. At Pangura he had not done this. If he had, he would have discovered on his arrival at Tete that he was six hundred feet lower than he had been at Pangura. The only conclusion he could have drawn from such a figure would have been that the rapid could not be small. But he wrote to the Directors with his usual confidence, telling them that "the only impediment" to navigation of the Zambesi was "one or two rapids, not cataracts."

Livingstone's remarks about the Portuguese in Angola had been scathing; in Mozambique, they were to be openly hostile. The reason for his former tolerance had been his knowledge that penetration of the interior from Angola was impossible. On his arrival at Tete he was convinced that the Zambesi would be navigable, and thus he came to believe that British traders and missionaries would only be prevented from sailing up the river if the Portuguese government raised objections. Since the Portuguese were notorious protectionists, his doubts as to whether they would ever allow the Zambesi to become an international waterway were understandable. It was also unlikely that a Catholic nation would willingly bend over backwards to be helpful to Protestant missionaries. Livingstone must have realized at the outset that Portuguese recalcitrance might defeat all his plans, but, as with almost every other problem, he had refused to face it until he was forced to do so.

The condition of the inhabitants at Tete also posed an awkward question which some might ask Livingstone on his return to England. How was it, if the Zambesi was such an ideal commercial waterway, and if the potential of central Africa was really so attractive, that the Portuguese had not made anything of it in their three hundred years of residence? Livingstone gave the only answer he could give. The Portuguese were a decadent, lazy, spineless lot, who were rotting with venereal disease and drink.

Livingstone gave no credence to the possibility that the Portuguese might have been defeated by factors like the climate, malaria, and the nature of the terrain. Nor did he ask whether the Zambesi itself was everything that it appeared to be. The Portuguese could have told him that the sand bars at the mouth were a death-trap and that shifting sand and mudbanks in the river itself made navigation extremely difficult business for most of the year. But instead Livingstone concentrated on Portuguese shortcomings to explain every failure.

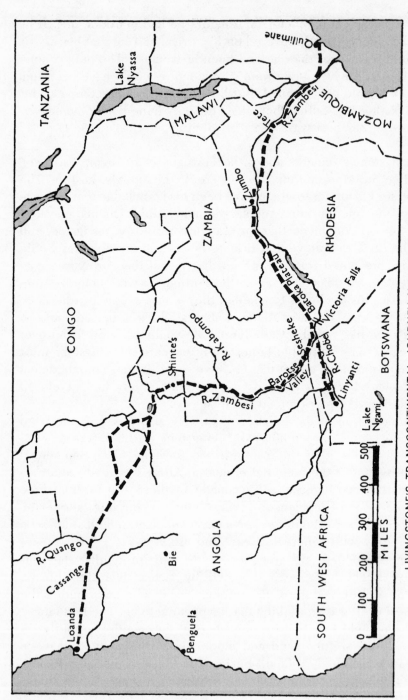

LIVINGSTONE'S TRANSCONTINENTAL JOURNEY November 1853 to May 1856

Modern State Borders - - - Livingstone's Routes ▬ ▬ ▬

(The Kebrabasa Rapids lie at the bend of the Zambesi east of Zumbo)

TANZANIA

Lake Nyassa

MALAWI

MOZAMBIQUE

Quillimane

R.Zambesi

Tete

Zumbo

ZAMBIA

RHODESIA

CONGO

R.Kabompo

Shinte's

Broken Plateau

Victoria Falls

Barotse Seshcke Valley

R.Chobe

Linyanti

R.Zambesi

BOTSWANA

Lake Ngami

ANGOLA

SOUTH WEST AFRICA

R.Quango

Cassange

Bie

Loanda

Benguela

MILES

0   100   200   300   400   500

Livingstone had arrived in Tete during the first week of March 1856, staying till the end of April. From Tete, Livingstone intended to go on down the Zambesi by canoe; this would clearly be impossible with all his Makololo attendants. Considering that he had characterized Tete as a moral sink, it may seem surprising that Livingstone made up his mind to leave his followers there. There was, however, very little else he could have done. The expense of bringing over a hundred Africans to London would obviously have been far too great, so the Makololo had to remain somewhere in Mozambique. Promising that he would return to take them home within a year, Livingstone set off downstream in a canoe with eight of his original followers. The remaining 270 miles to the sea were easier than any previous part of his journey. But for much of the way Livingstone was so ill with fever that when, on May 25, he arrived at Quilimane, within a few miles of the coast, he gave instructions for the sale of Sekeletu's ivory in the event of his death. Rather surprisingly he recovered within a few days and was contemplating the satisfying news that warships had been calling at the mouth of the Zambesi every few months to inquire about him. These calls had been made as a result of a letter written by Gabriel to the Foreign Secretary giving approximate dates between which Livingstone might be expected to arrive on the east African coast.

At Quilimane, Livingstone heard that H.M.S. *Frolic* had recently sent a brig over the bar at the mouth of the river to inquire about him. This vessel had capsized in the surf that always pounded the bar and eight crew members were drowned. This was distressing news. Livingstone did not however equate this tragedy with the unsuitability of the mouth of the Zambesi for shipping. He preferred to see it as a chance accident. Before Livingstone reached England the sea was to claim another victim. He had only intended to take one native home with him and had chosen for this honor his right-hand man and interpreter, Sekwebu. Unfortunately the same rough seas that had drowned the sailors were still raging when Livingstone and his companion were ferried out to the *Frolic* on July 12. Sekwebu, who had never seen the sea before and whose only experience of boats had been in canoes on the Zambesi, was terrified by the large waves. His next ordeal was being hoisted aboard the *Frolic* in a bo'sun's chair. It was not many days later that Sekwebu's mind broke under the strain of such novel circumstances. When *Frolic* anchored off Mauritius, Sekwebu leapt down into a boat that had been

launched. When Livingstone clambered down after him, Sekwebu backed towards the stern, screaming: "No, no! It is enough that I die alone." After a great deal of persuasion Livingstone managed to get him back on board. The officers annoyed Livingstone by saying that mad savages ought to be put in chains. He argued that Sekwebu would immediately assume he had been made a slave and that feeling would probably make him mad for life. The officers gave way. That evening Sekwebu tried to stab one of the sailors and then leapt overboard. The last Livingstone saw of his interpreter was his head and arms, as he gripped the anchor cable and "pulled himself down hand under hand."

More bad news was to come. At Cairo, Livingstone learned that his father had died. But this was nothing compared with a blow that he had already sustained at Quilimane. The Directors of the London Missionary Society had written a letter that seemed to negate everything he had been attempting to achieve.

The Directors, while yielding to none in their appreciation of the objects upon which, for some years past, your energies have been concentrated . . . are nevertheless restricted in their power of aiding plans connected only remotely with the spread of the Gospel. . . . Your reports make it sufficiently obvious that the nature of the country, the insalubrity of the climate, the prevalence of poisonous insects, and other adverse influences, constitute a very serious array of obstacles to missionary effort; and even were there a reasonable prospect of these being surmounted—and we by no means assume they are insurmountable—yet, in that event, the financial circumstances of the Society are not such as to afford any ground of hope that it would be in a position, within any definite period, to venture upon untried, remote, and difficult fields of labour.

Livingstone was bitterly angry. While his colleagues had accused him of being a traveler rather than a missionary, Livingstone had always derived comfort from his belief that at least the Directors understood his aims. But now it seemed that they had been as blind as everybody else. It must have been especially galling to Livingstone that although he had played down every difficulty, he had still not prevented the Directors taking alarm. The truth seemed to be that the London Missionary Society had encouraged his journeys as a fund-raising stunt and nothing else. They had made it appear that his work had been simple exploration with no practical application.

When Livingstone landed in England on December 9, 1856, he was famous, but he was also angry and sick at heart.

CHAPTER 11

NATIONAL HERO: THE FIRST VISIT HOME

During the time Livingstone spent in England, between December 1856 and March 1858, he received a measure of praise and adulation which, even in view of his impressive geographical achievement, strikes one today as excessive. The Royal Geographical Society gave him their gold medal, as did most similar organizations on the Continent, he became an honorary D.C.L. of Oxford University, and had a private audience with Queen Victoria. His book, *Missionary Travels and Researches in South Africa*, published in November 1857, sold seventy thousand copies, making him rich as well as famous. After a few months he was so well known in London that he had to be careful in case he was mobbed.

There is no one reason that accounts for Livingstone's sudden emergence as a national hero. Few people in Britain knew about previous Portuguese discoveries, largely because the Portuguese had never wished to interest other European nations in Africa. Livingstone's description of rivers and forests in central Africa therefore struck most readers as an incredible "discovery." As one journalist put it:

Europe had always heard that the central regions of southern Africa were burning solitudes, bleak, and barren, heated by poisonous winds, infested by snakes and only roamed over by a few scattered tribes of untameable barbarians . . . But Dr. Livingstone found himself in a high country, full of fruit trees, abounding in shade, watered by a perfect network of rivers.

But Livingstone was not simply praised as an explorer. The Livingstone myth was in the making. He became for many a great missionary too. One paper portrayed him as "this truly apostolic preacher of Christian truth." Most called him a "devoted" or "humble missionary," not for a moment trying to establish what form his missionary work had taken. It was an image of himself which Livingstone did not see fit to contradict; nor did the Directors of the London Missionary Society breathe a word about his solitary convert who had lapsed. The more it was assumed that he had converted thousands of savages, the more donations could be expected.

Much of Livingstone's initial publicity sprang from the determination of various interested parties to make him famous. Sir Roderick Murchison, the President of the Royal Geographical Society, had

hailed the discovery of Lake Ngami in 1849 as part of a conscious drive to interest the public in exploration and explorers. The London Missionary Society, with a current overdraft of £13,000, also had high hopes of what could be done by comprehensive publicity. Murchison, however, had beaten them with the first move, by arranging an official reception for Livingstone at the R.G.S. headquarters on December 15. The Directors of the London Missionary Society held a similar gathering the following day, with no less a figure than Lord Shaftesbury in the chair. Next a series of public lectures was arranged for Livingstone throughout the country. With his weathered face, and his strange, almost foreign, manner of speaking, he was sure to be a success.

Livingstone, as befitting his modesty and reticence—both virtues attributed to him by the press—acted his role well and wrote letters to friends telling them what a bore "this lionizing is." Be that as it may, he thoroughly enjoyed his new life, and his much vaunted claim that he disliked publicity comes strangely from a man who insisted on wearing a distinctive peaked cap wherever he went.

Without doubt, much can be learned about Livingstone's character at this time through a close examination of the manner in which he left the London Missionary Society and entered government employment. In the past it has always been assumed that Livingstone parted cordially with the Society, having magnanimously forgiven the Directors their thoughtless letter which he had received at Quilimane. The facts do not support this interpretation. Livingstone, it has previously been acknowledged, lied on occasions during the Zambesi expedition between 1858 and 1863, but the strain and the climate and dozens of other problems can be named as mitigating factors. It has not, however, been suggested that before that he was prepared to falsify and distort in order to get his own way.

Dr. Tidman, the Foreign Secretary of the London Missionary Society, had thought a great deal before sending the letter that had so much offended Livingstone. Having seen the way the press reacted to Livingstone's arrival in Loanda in 1854, he and his fellow Directors had realized that if Livingstone ever returned home alive, it would be as an extremely famous man. While this would be excellent from the point of view of fund raising there were other dangers. For a start Livingstone might try to put pressure on the Society to send missionaries to the areas he had traveled through. The public might support Livingstone in such rash expansionist ideas and the

whole thing might get out of control. It therefore seemed obvious to Tidman that he had to tell Livingstone that he should not think that forward moves in Africa would be made on any scale in the near future. But if Livingstone left the Society before his name could be used for fund raising, a unique opportunity would be lost. Unfortunately, none of the Directors supposed that Livingstone, prior to the offending letter, had any ill-feeling towards the Society. Had they known how wrong they were, Tidman would have played his cards very differently.

Tidman's real gamble had been that Livingstone would remain financially dependent on the Society for some time after his arrival in England. None of the Directors had had any idea that Livingstone had already opened correspondence with Sir Roderick Murchison. A letter from Sir Roderick had also reached Livingstone at Quilimane in the same batch as Tidman's. Murchison's praise was so rapturous that Livingstone had at once begun a long reply. Having gone over all his reasons for supposing that Africa would turn out to be a trader's paradise, he told him about his position with the London Missionary Society.

I suspect I am to be sent somewhere else, but will prefer dissolving my connection with the Society and follow out my own plans as a private Christian. This is rather trying, for, the salary being professedly only a bare subsistence (£100 per annum), we have in addition the certainty of education for our family and some provision for our widows ... Should I be unable to return I hope you will direct the attention of travellers to developing the rich resources of the country.

This was an open intimation that if Murchison found alternative employment, Livingstone would probably take it. From the moment he received this letter Murchison did everything in his power to see that Livingstone became financially independent. On January 5, 1857, Murchison had arranged a meeting, at the Mansion House, to inaugurate a testimonial fund for Livingstone. And that evening, deciding still more could be done, Murchison wrote to Lord Clarendon, the British Foreign Secretary, on his protégé's behalf.

The Directors of the London Missionary Society would not have got wind of these overtures to the government, but they must have known that with mounting public interest they could not remain inactive much longer. On January 12 the Directors held a special meeting with Livingstone as their honored guest. Tidman had already told Livingstone that, with the Society's funds in such a state of im-

balance, he could not contemplate new missions, but Livingstone was unmoved. At the meeting he told the Directors that they ought to send a mission to the Batoka Plateau and claimed that the Makololo would willingly move to that area as soon as such a mission was established. Livingstone went on to explain that a mission should also be started just to the south, with the Matabele, so that the Makololo Mission would not be threatened. Livingstone had evidently explained about the influence Moffat had with the Matabele, for the board minutes for the meeting stated: "That in his [Livingstone's] judgement the result would be promoted by the residence of himself and Mrs. Livingstone amongst the Makololo and with God's blessing almost certainly secured were Mr. Moffat to commence a Mission at the town of Mosilikatse, the chief of the Matabele."

So at this stage, a day after Murchison had written a second letter to Clarendon suggesting a meeting with Livingstone, the Directors of the London Missionary Society had been led to believe that if any mission to the Makololo went ahead, Livingstone would lead it. Yet Livingstone must have known about Murchison's efforts to interest Lord Clarendon in employing him. Oblivious of all this, the Directors, assuming Livingstone had meant what he said, submitted his proposals to the Southern Committee of the Society, which recommended the Society go ahead with the two missions, on condition that Moffat, or a member of his family, should head the Matabele Mission, and they went on to propose that "A missionary be appointed *to assist Dr. Livingstone in the organization of the intended mission* among the Makololo." (Author's italics.)

The words in italics have in the past been taken to mean that the committee understood that Livingstone's role was now to be one of organization and not participation. Yet it is inconceivable that this single weakly phrased sentence would have been the only mention of such a momentous alteration of plans. The minutes would certainly have included any refusal by Livingstone to fulfill his earlier promise. The obvious meaning of the wording is that Livingstone was to have a missionary helper to assist with organization of the mission prior to the actual departure. In view of Livingstone's other engagements there was nothing surprising in such an arrangement.

The Directors believed this was the position anyway. At the Society's General Meeting on May 14, they included a resolution adopted at a meeting of the Town and Country Directors on Feb-

ruary 10: "That two new Mission Stations should be opened—the one among the Makololo, north of the Zambesi, *under charge of Dr. Livingstone*, assisted by another missionary; and the other among the Matebele [sic] . . . . " (Author's italics.)

A mission over a thousand miles in the interior of Africa could hardly have been *under the charge* of anybody if he were not physically present. Livingstone attended the meeting on February 10 so he could well have objected to the form of words if he had chosen to. In fact he "expressed his entire concurrence." Nor at the General Meeting in May did he deny that his wife and he would be joining the Makololo Mission. His lack of objections taken with his previous assurances, written from Africa, that, should a mission ever be set up among the Makololo, he and his wife would go "whoever remains behind," must have left the Directors firmly convinced by May that even if the mission was risky, at least Livingstone would be there.

The fact is that by May, when Livingstone had given firm assurances to the Directors, Murchison's clandestine efforts with the British government had entered a crucial phase, and Livingstone knew very well that he would be offered employment of some sort. It might be argued that his double-dealing with the Directors served them right for having failed initially to see the long-term possibilities opened up by his journey. The matter cannot however be dismissed lightly, since the implications do more than touch on Livingstone's truthfulness.

From the moment Livingstone realized his popularity, he had encouraged Murchison's approaches to the government and had expressed wry amusement at the Directors' hasty moves to change the impression they had made before. Two weeks after his arrival in England he had written to Sir Roderick, stating magnanimously:

I have no wish to take any public advantage of their mistake, for such I now suppose they feel it to be . . . But you will perceive the reason why I said I should be willing to adopt the plan you suggested of a roving commission. . . . I have not the slightest wish or intention of giving up working for the amelioration of Africa. I have devoted my life to that and, if I could be put into a position where I could be more effective and at the same time benefit my children by giving them a good education, I should think it my duty to accept it.

So Livingstone had determined five months before the London Missionary Society General Meeting in May to leave them if a good

enough offer was made. In fact, on April 15, a month before the General Meeting, he wrote Murchison saying that he wanted to delay putting in a formal application for government employment till nearer the time of his departure, not because he intended to refuse it and not because the suggestions Clarendon had already made were unacceptable. "I fear if I got it [a government job] now, my friends of the Mission House will make use of the fact to damage my character in the public estimation by saying I have forsaken the Mission for higher pay. I have refused to take any more from them, and wish to do my future work in as unostentatious a way as possible."

Livingstone therefore appeared to be deceiving the Directors deliberately to safeguard his reputation. It might be claimed that his "consulship" would not conflict with his position on the Makololo Mission, but he would inevitably be away from the mission for long periods of time, charting the Zambesi and making commercial treaties with numerous tribes along it; and, secondly, he had already told Murchison in a letter, intended to be sent on to Clarendon, that roving government employment would enable him "to effect a much greater amount of good than I could do by settling down for the remaining portion of my life with any one of the small tribes which are dotted over the country." But, as his letter to Murchison of April 15 showed, he was sure about the government appointment and had, at his own wish, postponed an official announcement.

Meanwhile Tidman and his colleagues proceeded cautiously. Their appeal for funds for the two missions had only been started in March and the target of £5,000 would not be reached for some months. This, combined with Tidman's desire to make sure that Livingstone was going to stick to his word, accounts for his putting off writing to Robert Moffat till April 4. Moffat was sent a copy of the Board Minutes for the meetings attended by Livingstone on January 12 and 22, which set out the importance of Livingstone and Mrs. Livingstone being with the Makololo Mission and stressed the need for a simultaneous mission to the Matabele. Moffat was now to visit the chief of the Matabele and "devote about a twelvemonth" to preparing the ground for the mission, "No step to be actually taken." Tidman's motive for delaying everything was not just natural prudence. He had never been in favor of any mission to the Makololo, without the prior establishment of a chain of missions to connect it with the coast, and he probably hoped that, as time passed and the funds came in, Livingstone would grow impatient and go back alone,

either with or without the backing of the Society. If that happened, a lot of money would already have been raised, the missions could be shelved, and the Society would no longer be in danger of having to run its operations at the dictation of Dr. Livingstone or public pressure. Thus the Directors would be able to part with him without their reputation suffering. Much of this is hypothetical, but without such motivation it is very hard to explain Tidman's delay of over two months before writing to Moffat. Of course it is possible that Livingstone told Tidman about his government appointment in May and colluded with him to keep the matter secret so that Tidman's fundraising would not be impeded and his own reputation would not be damaged by remarks to the effect that he was leaving the Society hastily without giving the proposed missions a chance.

From May to October, Livingstone had no dealings with Tidman; in the meantime he worked on his book *Missionary Travels*, for John Murray. There is no evidence that Livingstone told the Society of his real intentions till October, five months after Clarendon had made his offer of government employment. But on October 27 there was a meeting at the Mission House and Dr. Tidman read to a stunned Board of Directors a letter from Livingstone, stating that "although he declined to receive pecuniary support from the Society, and would probably in future sustain some relation to the British Government, he would, there was every reason to believe, render the Directors his best assistance in the establishment of a Mission north of the Zambesi." Although many of the Directors were distressed, it now seemed to Tidman that after a decent pause he would be able to scrap the whole scheme. After all, acceptance of Livingstone's proposals had depended on his leadership, and clearly this could no longer be counted on. By this time Tidman obviously felt that since Livingstone had let the Society down, he would not have the gall to tell the Directors that it was their duty to proceed with the missions. But on February 22 an astonished Tidman read a letter from Livingstone, asking when the missionaries for the Makololo and Matabele were leaving Britain. Livingstone's tone was threatening. "Abundant funds having been furnished for all that is needed on the case . . . I should be glad to be assured that the intentions of the friends in subscribing so liberally are likely soon to be realised."

The implicit blackmail was clear; if the money was used to clear the Society's overdraft and not for the purpose for which it had been ostensibly raised, there might be some awkward questions asked in

public. Tidman was trapped and knew it. On February 27 he wrote to Livingstone claiming that a party would leave in May. On March 6 Livingstone wrote to Tidman, at last telling him what his true position was in relation to the Makololo Mission.

Should they [the missionaries] come through Mosilikatse's country to the Zambesi to a point below the Victoria Falls where our steam launch will be of any service to them, my companions will readily lend their aid in crossing the river . . . It might be better to go by Lake Ngami, as that is the only known opening Northwards.

It is not difficult to imagine Tidman's feelings on reading this. He had not wanted to embark on any mission to the Makololo and had been pushed into it against his will, on condition that Livingstone was leader. Now, a year after the mission had been approved, Livingstone had pressured the Society into going ahead, blandly informing them that the most they could expect him to do would be to help the missionaries cross the Zambesi, if by chance he happened to be at the right place at the right time. How much this "assistance" was worth could be seen at a glance. His suggested route would mean that they would cross the river above Victoria Falls and not below them. Thus Livingstone would not be able to help.

CHAPTER 12

THE PRICE OF OPTIMISM: THE MAKOLOLO MISSION

The Makololo Mission was dogged from the very beginning by false expectations. In *Missionary Travels* Livingstone had deliberately written about the Makololo in a much more favorable light than he had in his private correspondence. His predominant motive for appearing optimistic about the conditions in south central Africa had been the fear that if he did not, the area would be abandoned as hopeless.

The Directors however had plenty of evidence from his letters to show that any mission would be fraught with dangers. It is therefore all the more remarkable that they allowed a mission consisting of two missionaries, their wives, and four young children to go ahead. It is true that Livingstone had written: "I apprehend no great mortality among missionaries, men of education and prudence who can, if they will, adopt proper hygienic precautions."

But in the same letter he had talked of his own attacks of fever and the constant vomiting of blood. This was hardly the only reference to the severity of fever. The Directors had been told that the Makololo themselves were dying out because of it. The unhealthiness of Linyanti had led them to suggest that a move to the Batoka Plateau was indispensable. The Makololo would nevertheless have to be persuaded to move, and, as Livingstone himself told the Directors in 1853, this would be hard "Because the vicinity of Mosilikatse renders it impossible for Makololo or any other tribe to reside there. A change may yet be effected among the Matibele [sic] which would change the present aspect of affairs."

When Robert Moffat heard that Livingstone had left the Society and was to lead an expedition up the Zambesi his immediate thought, he told the Directors bluntly, was that it was madness for the missionaries to go overland, especially after what Livingstone had told them about fever, the tsetse, and the lack of water crossing the Kalahari. The obvious course was for them to go with Livingstone and to approach Linyanti via the Zambesi. Between April and July 1858, Moffat wrote repeatedly to the Directors, trying to get them to abandon the Makololo Mission for the time being, saying that unless he or Livingstone visited the Makololo in person the tribe could not be expected to move from the malarial area around Linyanti.

The Directors could hardly accede to this since the last letter they had had from Livingstone had given them no idea when Livingstone might be at Linyanti or anywhere near it. They had been given definite information in Livingstone's letter of March 6, 1858, that he would help the Makololo missionaries only if he happened to be at the Victoria Falls at the right time. It is therefore completely confounding that in 1859 all the Makololo party, and Moffat himself, still believed that Livingstone would meet them in Linyanti. It was this misapprehension, which at this stage was not Livingstone's fault, that contributed so much to the deaths of so many of the party.

One of the party, John Mackenzie, who did not go with the rest because his wife was due to have a child and was ill as well, was later to claim with absolute certainty that the leader of the party, Helmore, was sure Livingstone would meet them.

Above all his [Helmore's] great thought was to be at Linyanti in time to meet Dr. Livingstone there. He knew enough of the natives to be aware that a stranger would not be likely suddenly to acquire such influence with the chief and people as would be necessary to induce them to change their resi-

dence. Hence the importance of being introduced to the tribe by Dr. Livingstone as his friend. On no account must the Doctor reach Linyanti, and find that Helmore had not arrived.

So Helmore arrived at Linyanti in February, a month notorious for fever. This would never have happened had he not been terrified of missing Livingstone. Within two months of their arrival, Helmore and Mrs. Helmore were dead. So too was the other missionary wife, Mrs. Price, and five out of a total of seven children. Roger Price and two of Helmore's children were the sole survivors.

Although Price thought they had died through poison, he was almost certainly wrong. Fever accounted for all the symptoms mentioned. But the missionaries had some reason to suspect foul play. From the time of their arrival, the Makololo did not disguise their disappointment that neither Livingstone nor Moffat had come. From their point of view these strangers were no earthly use to them as protection against the Metabele. They had not even brought guns to trade with.

Sekeletu had expected his relationship with Livingstone to make him rich, and now it seemed all it had brought was a sickly group of people who only wanted to talk of God. As Price said later, Sekeletu was angry that Livingstone had not brought his men back; he had promised to do so within a year and now four had passed, and these missionaries could not even tell him when the Doctor was likely to come. Had Livingstone thought about Sekeletu's feelings earlier, he would have warned the missionaries that they might encounter hostility. But, shortly before leaving for Africa, he had told Tidman that there was no point in his meeting Helmore as he had nothing to tell him.

The Makololo Mission had already ended when Livingstone decided to take Sekeletu's men back to Barotseland in April 1860. He only took them back then because he could do no more on the lower Zambesi until a second steamer came from Britain, so it was chance that dictated the exact time he chose. To be fair, had he not encountered the horrifying obstacle of the Kebrabasa Rapids he might well have arrived very much earlier.

He did not hurry once he set out, and again he cannot be blamed. He felt that his last letter to Tidman, the one written on March 6, 1858, had made it clear that he could guarantee nothing. On August 9 he reached the Victoria Falls and stopped for several days to reassess

his previous measurements. Several weeks later he reached Sesheke, where he heard what had happened at Linyanti. When the initial shock had passed, Livingstone realized accurately that many people were going to accuse him of partial responsibility for the disaster. He set to work at once to try and forestall any such criticism. His letter to Tidman opened with conventional expressions of sorrow and then went on: "The poignancy of my unavailing regret is not diminished by remembering that the very time when our friends were helplessly perishing we were at a lower and much more unhealthy part of the river, and curing the complaint so quickly that in very severe cases the patient was able to resume his márch on foot a day or so after the operation of the remedy."

As though to rub in the irony of this, Livingstone went on to tell him that he had first tried quinine as a remedy as early as 1850 and that it "has been successful in every case of African fever met with since." Tidman might well have been wondering why Livingstone had not told him more about the remedy while he was in London. Livingstone's answer was that he had included a sentence about it in *Missionary Travels* "towards the end" and that he had kept quiet about it because it was bad medical etiquette to publicize anything till proper trial had been given it. Worse was to come. "From all I could learn the Makololo took most cordially to Mr. Helmore—they wished to become acquainted with him, a very natural desire, before removing to the Highlands, and hence the delay which ended so fatally. . . The Makololo are quite ready to remove, they are perishing themselves. . . . "

This claim that the Makololo had met the missionaries with friendship and had agreed to move once they got to know them was in direct conflict with all Price's evidence. He had claimed that the Makololo had absolutely refused to move, and had ordered the party to stay when they asked permission to leave for the healthier highlands to wait there for Dr. Livingstone.

Livingstone's praise of Helmore may have been due to genuine admiration, but Tidman would have had no doubt that Livingstone was commending him because he was dead and would therefore be unable to say anything unpleasant about the Makololo. Price, on the other hand, who had survived and was doing his utmost to discredit Livingstone's "faithful" tribe, was soon to be abused at every possible opportunity.

On July 5, Tidman replied to Livingstone's letter, pointing out that

the Makololo had not prepared to leave, and expressing anger that he had been told nothing of "an antidote of known efficacy" for fever. He also suggested that Sekeletu had misrepresented the case to avoid Livingstone's displeasure. This letter and its implications were, Livingstone thundered in his reply, "perfectly astonishing." The real trouble, he went on, was that Price had been unpopular. On one occasion he had kicked a man, on another tied a Makololo to the wheel of his wagon, and had threatened people with his revolver.

Price himself was horrified that Livingstone had accepted Sekeletu's story rather than his own and wrote to the Directors suggesting that the final proof of whether the Makololo had intended to move would be their actual removal. Livingstone however would have claimed that even if they did not move (and they did not) it would be because the missionaries had given them up.

Livingstone's vilification of the Makololo missionaries was not only due to his fear that, unless he could prove them responsible for their own deaths, he might be blamed. He was really trying to excuse his own failures by condemning Price and his colleagues. By 1860 Livingstone had discovered the impassable Kebrabasa Rapids and therefore knew that the Batoka Plateau and the Makololo could never be linked with the coast via the Zambesi. Now Livingstone took the deaths of the missionaries as an excuse. He claimed that the Makololo and the surrounding tribes would be abandoned, not because of Kebrabasa but because no traders or missionaries would dare go to them after a handful of stupid and culpably negligent men had allowed themselves to die. Furthermore, Price's *lies* about the Makololo being robbers would alone be enough to discourage potential traders. Livingstone had, he argued, labored for years to open the interior, and now a group of incompetents had wrecked it all.

When Livingstone wrote his own account of the disaster in his book *Narrative of an Expedition to the Zambesi* he took only two pages to do so. These pages are full of inaccuracies and false implications. Some of these slips may be thought to be due to faulty native information, but Livingstone's final criticism of the party leaves little doubt that the distortion was deliberate: "Had it been possible for one with the wisdom, experience and conciliating manners of Mr. Moffat to have visited the Makololo, he would have found them easily influenced to fairness, and not at all the unreasonable savages they were represented to be."

In a sense this statement was true, but not quite in the way that

Livingstone intended. The Makololo wanted a member of the Moffat family to live with them, so naturally they would have behaved better had Moffat himself come among them. Livingstone's real fault in the matter was not that he did not turn up in time to cure the missionaries but that he encouraged the Makololo Mission to go ahead when the original guarantee of success had been withdrawn. The success of the Matabele and Makololo Missions had always hinged on there being a member of the Moffat family in each party.

But it must be stressed that he was not directly responsible for the loss of life. He had told Tidman he would probably not be any help to the party, and yet this information was not passed on; both Price and Helmore believed that Livingstone would be at Linyanti to meet them. Tidman had also been warned several times by Moffat about the idiocy of sending the party before the tribe had moved, yet he had weakly yielded to possible public disapprobation and had let the thing go on.

So Livingstone, the Directors, and the Makololo were all to blame in various ways, but Livingstone comes out of the affair worst of all. He unleashed all the fury of his own already frustrated hopes onto men and women who had given their lives in an attempt to bring Christianity to an area he had now given up. He knew that no mission in Barotseland could survive without river communication with the coast, and by 1860 he knew such communication was impossible, but when Price said all this in Cape Town, Livingstone did his best to discredit him with accusations of lying and cowardice. It was the old story, Livingstone had been wrong and could not bring himself to say so.

CHAPTER 13

HER MAJESTY'S CONSUL

Livingstone's plans for south central Africa rested on a loosely thought-out voluntary scheme whereby European traders penetrated the area west of Portuguese Mozambique and began commercial operations there. By early 1856, while he was at Tete, Livingstone realized that the whole project depended on Portuguese willingness to allow the Zambesi to become an international waterway. The more he had thought about it, the more certain he became

that there was little chance of the Portuguese giving permission without some firm prodding. Since Portugal, a spent force though she might be, was still Britain's "oldest ally," there were clearly going to be some diplomatic problems. But Livingstone talked the matter over with Sir Roderick Murchison. Having persuaded Murchison that the Batoka Plateau could produce crops of cotton larger than the southern states of America, and having impressed upon him the enormous profits that English businessmen could make, if the government led the way, Sir Roderick's letter to Lord Clarendon, the Foreign Secretary, said everything depended on Britain's determination. "Either England and her ally Portugal may be made one for this great object, or the latter country might readily part with her Colony of Quilimane and Tete, etc., useless to her, but which in our hands might be rendered a paradise of wealth."

Lord Clarendon however doubted whether Portugal would "readily part" with her "useless" colony, and politely ignored the suggestion that he should try a little persuasion. Meanwhile rebuffs did not stop Livingstone developing his ideas.

That you may have a clear idea of my objects [he told a friend], I may state that they have something more in them than meets the eye. They are not merely exploratory, for I go with the intention of benefiting the African and my own countrymen . . . our ostensible object the development of African trade and the promotion of civilization, but I hope it may result in an English colony in the healthy highlands of central Africa.

Since Britain had plenty of overseas colonies by the middle of the nineteenth century, Livingstone's reticence about his colonial ambitions will seem theatrical and absurd unless more is said about the attitudes of politicians and public to the British Empire at that time. The empire certainly existed, but it had not come into being as the result of any unified or planned government policy. Britain's West Indian possessions owed their existence to the initial efforts of individual British planters and slave traders. Australia, until the 1840's, had meant no more to Britain than a suitably remote location for convict dumping. The North American colonies and Canada had been started by the arrival of English emigrants who had left their homes to escape religious discrimination and persecution in the seventeenth century. The Cape colony had been taken from the Dutch because of the tactical advantage it offered Britain during the Napoleonic Wars. India had become "British" because the London-based East India Company had started trading operations there in

the seventeenth century, and had later successfully defeated Dutch and French rivals. In short, there had never been a deliberate policy of annexation by superior might with the object of increasing Britain's power and influence.

The reasons for this were practical rather than moral. Mid-Victorian Britain did not need wider possessions to increase her wealth or power. Since she had a wider share of world shipping than any other nation and could out-manufacture and out-export all potential rivals, free trade and a policy of colonial *laissez-faire* suited her interests better than any more overtly assertive policies. Livingstone had seen this in South Africa. In 1852 the British government had given independence to the Boers north of the Vaal and Orange rivers, rather than embark on expensive and probably unremunerative advances.

But one other crucial consideration militated against Livingstone's hopes for a British colony, or colonies, in central Africa. His contemporaries, when they heard the words "The British Empire," did not think of multi-racial subject nations bowing to a central imperial power. Their pride in empire was not the late-Victorian love of prestige and power, but a pride in the idea that British men and women had settled in distant and previously thinly populated parts of the world, and were there reproducing all that was best in the British way of life—a free press, trial by jury, and government by representative institutions. Most of Livingstone's fellow countrymen during the 1850's saw empire as the link of common nationality that bound together, more by voluntary union than by power, a mother country and her white-settled, and soon to be self-governing, colonies overseas. In this *family*, the West Indies and, above all, India were seen as strange anomalies simply because they, unlike for example Canada, Australia, and New Zealand, had large "native" populations and were not predominantly "British" and white. The problems encountered in India, where a handful of whites were vastly outnumbered by the indigenous "colored" population, had taught British governments to think twice before contemplating committing themselves to any new colonies where the whites could only ever be a minority. So in 1857 the prospects for new colonies were bad everywhere, but in a *black* continent like Africa they seemed hopeless.

Livingstone was not oblivious to the public mood or the government's attitude on these matters; for that reason he had not risked writing to Clarendon himself about ousting the Portuguese,

but had got Murchison to do it for him. Livingstone knew that if he was to gain a Foreign Office appointment and Treasury money to support any new African venture, he would have to tread gingerly.

Convinced as he now was that individual traders could not, unassisted, undermine tribal society, he wanted organized colonization to do this work, which he saw as an essential prelude to Christian success. Livingstone would therefore have to prove that the area was commercially viable and that steamers could sail up the Zambesi without hindrance. When all this had been established, the British government might then exert pressure on the Portuguese to make the Zambesi international, and they might eventually oust the Portuguese altogether.

Commercial prospects could only be assessed by expert judgments on the Batoka Plateau's real potential for growing sugar, wheat, coffee, and cotton. The quality and quantity of the coal and iron ore in western Mozambique would also have to be estimated. Livingstone would not be able to perform this work alone, so he would need an expedition, and that could not be mounted without government aid.

In May 1857, Sir Roderick had managed to persuade the Foreign Secretary to offer Livingstone employment as a British consul with a roving commission, at a salary of £500 per annum. No detailed plans had been made and Livingstone's demands to date had been cautious to the point of cowardice. He had not made any mention of an expedition with a steamer and other European members, but had confined his requests to two simple cotton gins, two or three iron ploughs, and two small rollers for extracting the juice from sugar cane. Livingstone clearly had wanted to secure a definite offer of employment before stepping up his demands. Even later he preferred to gain concessions from Clarendon by the representation of third parties. For example, when he lectured before the British Association at Dublin that August, he gave his listeners such an alluring description of the commercial prospects of the Batoka Plateau that General Sabine, soon to be the President of the Royal Society, asked him whether he would object to an official petition from the British Association to the Foreign Secretary on the subject of providing a steamer for his next venture. Livingstone did not decline.

After the offer of employment, in May 1857, no more official moves were made till the following October. This gap can be explained partly by Clarendon's preoccupation with the Indian Mutiny and by Livingstone's commitment to the writing of his book *Missionary*

Travels, which was not finished till October. In that month Clarendon began a correspondence with Livingstone and the British Ambassador in Lisbon over the role of the Portuguese in any future expedition. In December 1857, Livingstone was told by the Prime Minister, Lord Palmerston, that preparations for a full-scale expedition would be set in motion at once.

Clarendon's first move towards the creation of the Zambesi Expedition was a letter of instructions to Captain Washington, an influential Admiralty official, asking him to draw up a few alternative plans; by the end of December there were two suggested schemes on the Foreign Secretary's desk. Both of these were for ambitious projects, not unlike the 1841 Niger Expedition that had involved a number of ships and two hundred men. This was not at all what Livingstone had in mind and he immediately rejected both plans on the grounds that such large parties would prove unwieldy and unmanageable. A week later, on January 7, he put forward his own much more modest scheme, which Clarendon at once accepted.

The expedition Livingstone outlined was to consist of seven Europeans, including himself, ten natives, a paddle-steamer of shallow draught, and an iron house in sections. Livingstone indicated that the six other Europeans were to include an economic botanist, a geologist, and a naval officer. Livingstone's itinerary was to be accomplished, he hoped, within two years.

He intended to reach Tete and then to proceed to the Kebrabasa Rapids "to discover whether the launch would be able to steam up there when the river is high." Having proved the Zambesi to be navigable, the next step would be to steam on upstream to the Batoka Plateau, erect the iron house as a center for stores, and begin agricultural experiments. Meanwhile some expedition members would go on to explore the upper reaches of the Zambesi.

There was however one imponderable: Livingstone had never seen the rapids he hoped so confidently to ascend "when the river is high." Since the area below the rapids was notorious for malaria, the success of the expedition depended on getting beyond them to his much vaunted Batoka Plateau. The steamer could clearly not be taken to pieces and carried without wheeled transport, pulleys, and a large number of mules or oxen. When he had first visited Tete, Livingstone made some inquiries about the rapids, but they had not been exhaustive. It was well known in Mozambique that the cataracts were impassable, for the Portuguese Minister of Marine and

Colonies told the British Ambassador in Lisbon, towards the end of 1858, that native canoes always had to be carried overland at Kebrabasa. But if Livingstone worried about the crucial gamble he was taking he did not show it. In any case the matter was now in Captain Washington's hands and not his. In fact Washington had approved plans for a steamer before Livingstone had told him how many men he wanted. In spite of this the steamer was no liner: 75 feet in length and 8 feet in beam.

.Once stores and equipment had been dealt with, there were only a few loose ends left. These included the attitude of the Portuguese. Ministers in Lisbon had read transcripts of Livingstone's English speeches with less amusement than anger. It was obviously unpleasant for them to have to read thousands of words about all the marvelous economic possibilities of their African colonies, which they had failed to realize because of addiction to the slave trade and official corruption and ineptness. The Portuguese government was not unnaturally suspicious of a British government-sponsored expedition that claimed only to be seeking new geographical and scientific information. Nevertheless it would be unwise to forbid the expedition altogether. Britain was an extremely powerful nation.

But, while promising Livingstone all the help they could give him, the government in Lisbon took steps to try to preclude the making of any later territorial claims. On February 4 a royal decree came from Lisbon, stating that: "The name of Zambesia shall be given in all official documents to all the territories to which the Crown of Portugal has a right in the valley of the Zambesi from the mouth of that river to beyond the fortress of Zumbo." Livingstone wrote angrily to Clarendon telling him that this must be challenged since it implied that the Portuguese had authority over the independent tribes along the river and the right to exclude international trade from the Zambesi. Clarendon remonstrated but was not prepared to make an issue of the Portuguese attitude.

But the real problem Livingstone faced centered on his own exaggerated accounts of what might be expected from the regions he was going to. Sir Roderick Murchison, normally a calculating and sober individual, had spoken of the Batoka Plateau becoming "a paradise of wealth." Similar assurances had been made by Livingstone to businessmen up and down the country. Now he was saddled with enormous public expectations. He had promised miracles and he would have to perform them, if he wished to remain a national hero.

CHAPTER 14

THE ZAMBESI EXPEDITION SETS SAIL

The Zambesi Expedition set sail from Liverpool in the steamship *Pearl* on March 10, 1858. Flurries of snow stung the faces of the more intrepid members of the party who had stayed on deck to see the coast of England out of sight. Within an hour or so the ship was pitching violently and most of them were below, very sick. Among those afflicted in this way were Mrs. Livingstone and her youngest son, six-year-old Oswell. The other children had been left with their grandparents and a succession of guardians.

By the time the ship was off west Africa and heading south for the Cape, everybody had recovered expect Mrs. Livingstone. Livingstone soon knew why. Mary was pregnant again. This news stunned her husband, but not because of her grief that she would now have to be left at the Cape to have the baby at Kuruman. Livingstone was more concerned with the inconvenience to himself. "This is a great trial to me," he confided to his journal, "for had she come with us, she might have proved of essential service to the expedition in cases of sickness and otherwise." Another consideration worried Livingstone, too: people would think him a fool for having got her pregnant at such an awkward time. So in most of his letters he referred to her condition as an "illness."

Several of Livingstone's colleagues guessed what was the matter with Mary and were not sorry that she would have to stay behind. Africa, they felt, was no place for a woman. One of these was Livingstone's second-in-command, Commander Norman Bedingfeld, R.N. Bedingfeld had impressed Livingstone when he had met him briefly in Loanda in 1854. Later Livingstone discovered that he had been twice court-martialed and once dismissed from his ship for "contempt and quarrelsome conduct towards a superior officer." When Captain Washington warned Livingstone about Bedingfeld's record and advised him not to take him, Livingstone brushed this well-meant warning aside. He would regret it later.

Dr. John Kirk, who at twenty-five was ten years younger than Bedingfeld and twenty years Livingstone's junior, had done medical work in the Crimea and was an experienced botanist and a doctor of medicine. Unlike his colleagues, Kirk would prove consistently reliable and hardworking. He also had the good sense to confine his complaints to his journal.

Richard Thornton, the geologist, was not yet twenty when the expedition sailed. Sir Roderick Murchison had described him as one of the most brilliant students ever to pass through the Royal College of Mines, but Livingstone would make little use of him. Thornton, like Bedingfeld and Thomas Baines, the artist and storekeeper, would be dismissed. Baines, with the exception of Livingstone, was the oldest member of the party. At thirty-eight he was an experienced man too. He had left England for South Africa as a young man and, after working in Cape Town for a while as an ornamental sign-painter, he had been employed by the army as an official war artist. He was an easy-going, modest man, eager to work hard when the occasion demanded it. But, although all the others liked him, he would fall foul of Livingstone.

George Rae, the engineer, like Kirk managed to stay the course. Perhaps it helped that he had been born at Blantyre like Livingstone. He was to prove competent at his job, and the dourness which most of his colleagues disliked did not distress Livingstone, who hated idle social chatter.

Livingstone's most startling appointment had been his choice of his younger brother Charles. Livingstone had not seen him since 1840, when Charles had sailed for America to get an education there. Quite by chance, Charles had returned for a brief trip to England in 1857 and had been offered a job as the Zambesi Expedition's "moral agent." This post had been created for him by Livingstone, who wanted him mainly as a personal assistant to support him in any troubles that might erupt with other members of the party. Charles's qualification was his theological education at Oberlin College, Ohio, and his subsequent ordination as a nonconformist minister. Nothing in their past relationship gave any hint of the ascendancy which Charles was soon to establish over his brother with such distressing consequences. Livingstone ought, however, to have known that since Charles had married only a few years before and had three small children, he might have personal problems to face which would make him a very difficult companion.

Livingstone himself would in many ways prove to be the weakest link in the party. Needless to say, his weakness would not be physical. He would simply prove a disastrous leader. Had the British government thought about it, a man who had just passed four years entirely without European company was hardly an ideal person to lead, live, and work with six other men in claustrophobic proximity. With

the exception of his wife and family, whom he had seen little enough of, Livingstone had done his best to avoid Europeans.

His years alone had made him self-sufficient and disinclined to talk unless he had something specific to say. He could not make jokes when things went wrong nor encourage his party by showing that he appreciated what they did, nor could he laugh at himself. The same attributes that had made him successful as a lone traveller were often those that made him a failure when journeying with others. He had always hated any kind of restriction and had never been constrained on his epic journey; he had rested when he decreed and set out when he was ready. Now there would be countless checks and delays: the steamer had to get steam up; the others had to pack up their gear and finish what they were doing; and for any smoothness of operation each member had to know what the others were up to. Perhaps his most crucial mistake was not to realize that since the leader would get most of the credit if the expedition was a success, he could not expect his men to push themselves to the same limits of endurance as he pressed himself. Instead he was aware only that if the expedition failed he would be blamed and get no credit for having exerted himself more than everybody else.

While it was gratifying to Livingstone to find many of those who had once laughed at him for his uncouthness and poverty falling over themselves to be agreeable, his meeting with Robert Moffat, then in Cape Town waiting for the Makololo missionaries, was far from happy. Moffat was angry that Livingstone was not going with the new missionaries and felt that he had deceived the London Missionary Society. Then there was the general sadness about Mary Livingstone. When she watched the *Pearl* sail from Cape Town, it would be four more years before she saw her husband again. Ahead of her lay a year in Kuruman and nearly three in Scotland with her disagreeable in-laws.

CHAPTER 15

THE ROCKS IN GOD'S HIGHWAY

On May 14 the *Pearl* anchored off the maze of sandbanks and mudflats that formed the mouth of the Zambesi. During the next two weeks two separate attempts were made to enter the Zambesi

proper, and both failed. Tempers became frayed and the Kongone mouth, discovered at the end of the first week of June, was found only just in time to prevent serious quarreling.

Livingstone's plan was to get everybody up to Tete in one trip in the *Pearl*. From Tete, Livingstone proposed to sail on in the smaller vessel, past the Kebrabasa Rapids to the Batoka Plateau, where the agricultural experiments were to begin. The metal parts of the steamer were soon taken off the *Pearl* and bolted together by George Rae, the engineer. Livingstone called the vessel the *Ma-Robert*, because that had been the Makololo's name for Mrs. Livingstone, and meant "mother of Robert." Robert was the name of Mary's eldest son.

Within a week, navigation had become slow and hazardous and by June 16 it was clear to everybody that the *Pearl*, a steamer 160 feet long, was not going to be able to go further. Livingstone's much-vaunted river was shallow and had channels that shifted from month to month. The river was falling; if *Pearl* went further she might be stuck for six months or more. The blow was stunning to Livingstone's hopes of getting the party through the malarial lower reaches of the river quickly. Now the iron house for stores would have to be set up barely fifty miles from the sea and all the stores brought up to Tete in the small *Ma-Robert;* the job could take months, during which time no scientific work could be done. In the meantime morale and health would suffer.

The conditions faced by the party during the first few months of the expedition were entirely new to most of them and far worse than anything they had expected. All had read *Missionary Travels,* and because Livingstone had omitted almost every unpleasant feature of African travel, they had come out expecting adventure, even danger, but certainly not the continual debilitating hardships they were soon enduring. The *Ma-Robert* was always overcrowded due to the greatly increased quantity of stores she had to carry. Consequently everybody was squeezed into close proximity, at a time when many were experiencing fever for the first time. The temperature was usually more than 100°F and the only place to escape the sun was the tiny cabin of the steamer, which, although shaded, still heated up like an oven. Because the river itself was much shallower than expected, and the steamer considerably overloaded, the vessel was perpetually grounding on sandbanks. Hours of almost every day were spent dragging the boat along with ropes and winches; mos-

quitoes, ticks, tropical ulcers, and an unfamiliar diet were other causes for irritation and distress.

Barely two months after entering the Zambesi, Livingstone faced the first real test of his leadership. Arguments broke out between Commander Bedingfeld and the master of the *Pearl*, Captain Duncan, over navigational command. Livingstone publicly sided with Duncan, a mere officer in the Merchant Navy, thereby insulting the commander. After another row over the *Ma-Robert*, Livingstone obliged Bedingfeld to return to Quilimane to await passage on the next ship that called.

To make matters worse, the *Ma-Robert* was a disaster. Fuel was sometimes consumed at such a rate that a day and a half's wood cutting would not be enough to keep the boilers going for one day's steaming. Mr. Laird, the builder, had of course had no idea that his steamer would have to carry loads in excess of ten tons several hundred miles up a shallow river against the current, but that did not stop Livingstone from accusing him of greed, deceit, and incompetence. Laird had used a new kind of steel in thin sheets to build the hull of the steamship, and here all Livingstone's criticisms were sound, for this steel sheeting had not been properly tested and soon started to rust through in a honeycomb of holes that had to be plugged with clay.

Throughout July, August, and September the *Ma-Robert* chugged up and down the Zambesi in a painfully slow series of five separate trips to drop off supplies upstream at Shupanga, Sena, and Tete. Only in November had all the supplies been removed from the temporary base near the river mouth. By then morale was low and early eagerness had gone for good. Most members of the expedition felt that Livingstone had deliberately deceived the government about the Zambesi. Sometimes the river had been less than two feet in depth at its deepest point. The *Ma-Robert* drew three feet. Three days aground was not uncommon, nor was it unusual for the vessel to have to be dragged two hundred yards across mud and sand.

All Livingstone's plans, both immediate and distant, depended on the steamer being able to sail past the Kebrabasa Rapids on to the Batoka Plateau. In short, if the *Ma-Robert* failed to get through, the basic aim of the expedition to examine the agricultural and mineral potential of the plateau would be vitiated; all plans for traders to reach the Makololo and the new missions from the coast would have to be abandoned. The effect on Livingstone's reputation if the rapids

proved impassable would be dramatic. During their first few days at Tete, Kirk was worried to hear Livingstone talking about blasting a way through if need be. Kirk found it strange that, although Livingstone had made light of the rapids in England, he now spoke about the possibility of getting army sappers sent out.

In spite of his troubles, Livingstone could at least enjoy his reunion with the Makololo whom he had left at Tete in 1856. Yet even this reunion brought Livingstone some worries. The Makololo seemed to enjoy living with the decadent Portuguese, and some of them even suggested that they did not want to go back to Sekeletu.

On November 8 Livingstone, Kirk, and Rae set out for Kebrabasa in the *Ma-Robert*, leaving Charles, Thornton, and Baines in Tete recuperating from fever. After a day and a half's steaming, the Zambesi narrowed to only thirty yards across. The current had soon become much faster and the *Ma-Robert's* progress against it was reduced to a crawl. On each side of the stream, sheer black rocks rose up to form cliffs several hundred feet high. The steamer managed to pass the first small rapid she came to, but at the second, the force of the current swung her onto a rock, holing her above the waterline.

The next day Livingstone and Kirk set off on foot over rough, rocky country; by mid-afternoon they came to a point where the river split into several channels and the two men separated to examine a channel each. A little later Kirk was looking down at the water pouring over a ledge "at a considerable angle and becoming a mass of broken water at the bottom." Livingstone's cataract was as bad, with a fall of eight feet within twenty yards. Towards evening they came to two more rapids which were worse. Kirk's view was that when the river was in flood, the speed of the current would be so great and the pull of the eddies so strong, that no steamer could hope to pass up or down in any safety. Livingstone disagreed. "I believe," he wrote in his journal, "when the water rises about six feet, the cascades may be safely passed. If not, then at flood, when the water is spread over all the dell." Livingstone's optimism rested on the assumption that the river would rise enough after the rains to burst its rocky banks and thus reduce the speed of the current. Kirk's opinion, which would prove correct, was that the banks were quite steep and high enough to contain an enormous amount of water; enough perhaps to rule out flooding altogether. Livingstone would not admit defeat. Already he began thinking up excuses to use at a later date, one being the limited power of the *Ma-Robert*. Since local natives said that there

were other rapids many miles further on, Livingstone decided to return to Tete again to collect the other members of the party before coming back to Kebrabasa for a thorough survey.

No sooner was he back than Livingstone began making feverish inquiries about Kebrabasa. One Portuguese trader, José St. Anna, confirmed Kirk's view. Natives, he said, tried to get down from time to time, in canoes, and never lived to tell the tale. Livingstone began looking for ways to justify his earlier optimism. The thought that he had gained such popularity because of exaggerated claims tortured him, and he now tried to delude himself and others into believing that he had written his book and given his lectures against his will. "The honours heaped upon me were not of my own seeking," he wrote hopelessly. "They came unbidden."

Before the end of November the whole party had left Tete for a thorough survey of the rapids, although Thornton and Baines were still ill. Soon the sick men were holding up the party. Charles Livingstone however was the main offender. According to Kirk, "more than half the time is occupied allowing Mr. L. to have a little snooze every half hour." While Livingstone criticized Baines and Thornton, he ignored the constant delays caused by his brother. It was the beginning of a favoritism that was to break up the last remnants of the expedition's unity.

They had now traveled for four days without seeing any worse rapids than Livingstone and Kirk had encountered on their first visit, and Livingstone decided that the worst rapids had already been passed and that they might as well return to the steamer. His spirits were much higher than they had been for weeks.

They had been clambering homewards for a couple of hours when one of the Makololo casually mentioned that he had heard something from some local natives near the place where they turned back. Livingstone said that any detail was interesting, and so the man told them that some miles further upstream there was supposed to be a fearful waterfall as high as a tree and so dangerous that anybody, even a man "perishing with thirst . . . would retire in fear from it."

Livingstone listened in stunned silence, furious that, at the very time when his spirits were rising, this man had known something that would destroy all his hopes with a few words. After yelling at the offending Makololo for having kept such crucial information to themselves, he rounded on the rest of the party. They could all stay where they were, he would go on alone to finish the job. Now that

defeat seemed a foregone conclusion, Livingstone found the sight and company of his companions unendurable. After a pause Kirk said that he was able to go on, and Livingstone agreed to accept him.

On December 2, after clambering up an almost perpendicular cliff, the two men were rewarded with a sight that made Livingstone's blood run cold. Below them was a waterfall thirty feet with the water thundering over it at less than 30°. For a while Livingstone was unable to say anything, but then to Kirk's amazement he suggested that if the water rose eighty feet after the rains, even this waterfall might not prove an insuperable barrier. Livingstone wrote to the new Foreign Secretary, Lord Malmesbury, on December 17, telling him: "We are all of the opinion that a steamer of light draught would pass the rapids without difficulty when the river is in full flood." Since Livingstone knew that within a year or so the already rusting *Ma-Robert* would be finished, he decided that it would be an ideal time to ask the Foreign Office for a replacement. Thus he would be able to persuade them that only the *Ma-Robert* had prevented the party reaching the Batoka Plateau as planned. Of course he did not tell Lord Malmesbury that when the new steamer came, whatever else he used it for, it would not be to get past Kebrabasa. Now Livingstone knew he would have to play for time in the hope of making face-saving and prestigious new discoveries before eventually being forced to admit to a crushing initial failure. The Zambesi and the Batoka Plateau were to be deserted for another river.

The Shire flowed into the Zambesi from the north at a point roughly one hundred miles from the coast. Livingstone was not sure that it was navigable, but he knew that if it was not, he might as well cancel the order for the new steamer and disband the expedition. The Shire offered the only possible alternative open to him. The whole venture was a gamble but Livingstone was comforted by the memory of what he had been told in 1856 by a Tete trader, Candido José da Costa Cardosa. Candido claimed that the Shire was fed by a vast lake which could be reached directly from Tete in forty-five days' march. At the time Livingstone had been sufficiently impressed to draw a map based on Candido's information. Livingstone now decided that he would not take the overland route but would try to reach the lake via the river Shire. If the lake really was a large one he would be able to keep quiet about Candido's previous discovery and claim it for the expedition and himself. A major geographical find would do a lot to make up for Kebrabasa.

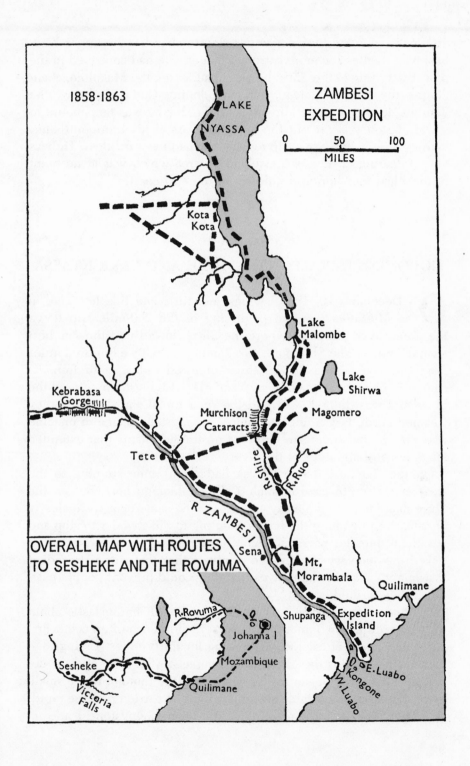

1858-1863

ZAMBESI
EXPEDITION

0   50   100
MILES

LAKE
NYASSA

Kota
Kota

Lake
Malombe

Lake
Shirwa

Kebrabasa
Gorge

Murchison
Cataracts

Magomero

Tete

R. Shire

R. Ruo

R ZAMBESI

OVERALL MAP WITH ROUTES
TO SESHEKE AND THE ROVUMA

Sena

Mt.
Morambala

Quilimane

R. Rovuma

Johanna I

Shupanga

Expedition
Island

Seseke

Mozambique

Quilimane

E. Luabo

Kongone
W. Luabo

Victoria
Falls

Of course Livingstone's new decision to abandon the upper Zambesi was a volte-face more extreme than any he had contrived in the past. By turning to the Shire he was abandoning the Makololo, abandoning the Batoka Plateau, and abandoning God's Highway: the Zambesi itself. The new direction he was taking was tantamount to an admission that all but the very last part of his transcontinental journey and his previous trip to Linyanti had been fruitless. He was now preparing to devote himself to an area which was at no point further than four hundred miles from the east coast.

CHAPTER 16

COLONIAL DREAMS: THE SHIRE AND LAKE NYASSA

On December 20, 1858 Livingstone, Kirk, and Rae left Tete in the *Ma-Robert* on the beginning of the 200-mile trip down the Zambesi to the point where the Shire flowed into the Zambesi from the north. The Shire joins the Zambesi roughly a hundred miles from the sea, having flowed three hundred miles south from its source in Lake Nyassa. On New Year's Day Livingstone entered the Shire and was delighted to find the river broad and deep. As they steamed north, it was not long before Livingstone began to imagine rice, cotton, and sugarcane growing on the flat plains that extended for miles on both sides of the river.

On the Zambesi itself, natives had often come running to the steamer simply to gaze at such a strange-looking boat, but on the Shire many natives ran away and those who came near were clearly hostile, running along the banks shouting to the steamer to stop and pay them dues for passage. Livingstone refused these requests and risked the showers of poisoned arrows rather than set a precedent that might convince the natives that they could prevent people passing if they wished.

In spite of the hostility, Livingstone was still enthusiastic about the river Shire. On January 9, however, they encountered the first rapid in a chain of cataracts extending for thirty miles. Livingstone named these rapids the Murchison Cataracts. After several days' depression his sprits began to rise again with the thought that a smaller vessel, made in portable sections, might be carried past the rapids at a later date. Before steaming south again Livingstone made in-

quiries about the area to the north and heard that it was a high, fertile country with hills and a great lake. He convinced himself that he had found a substitute for the Batoka Plateau.

Livingstone returned to the Shire in August with Kirk. They had heard that before reaching the great lake, they would discover a smaller one, Lake Shirwa, forty miles north of the cataracts. Since Livingstone reckoned that the "discovery" of this lake would be a major achievement for the expedition, he decided that he ought to try to map the lake and stay there for some time. This would mean a return to Tete for the other members of the party and for more supplies. It was therefore late August when he once more set out north from the Murchison Cataracts.

The first hundred miles of the 200-mile journey to Lake Nyassa took three weeks, and by the time the expedition members started to climb into the highlands they were exhausted and irritable. Livingstone was in a terrible mood, largely because it was dawning on him that the slave trade was already firmly established in the area, the local Ajawa tribe acting as middlemen for Arab slave traders operating further north.

In fact, when Livingstone gazed out over the waters of the vast lake, he felt no elation or sense of triumph, for he was not the first European to have reached Nyassa. The Tete trader, Candido José da Costa Cardosa, had told Livingstone in 1856 that he had reached a very large lake about three hundred miles from Tete, the source of the Shire; Livingstone had written this information into his journal, with a map. After his arrival at Nyassa, Livingstone did his best to make it appear, from certain inconsistencies in Candido's descriptions, that the trader had been to a different lake altogether. But try as he could, Livingstone could not suggest what other lake he could possibly have seen. But Livingstone was successful in getting himself accepted as the "discoverer" of Nyassa and not one of his previous biographers has refuted it.

That Livingstone had been beaten to Lake Nyassa was not his major worry. Ever since he had first heard about the Shire Highlands and the region around Nyassa, he had been determined that this would be the new area for traders, settlers, and missionaries. But the problems in this region were immense.

In 1840 the Sultan of Muscat had moved his court to Zanzibar, the administrative center of his east African coastal possessions. By the end of the decade his Arab subjects, in eager pursuit of slaves and

ivory, had penetrated inland beyond Lake Nyassa as far west as Katanga. Nyassa itself soon lay directly on the slave route from Katanga to the coastal town of Kilwa. But Livingstone was alive to another problem: he had heard on arrival at Nyassa in September 1859 that the area to the north was being devastated by an exceptionally aggressive tribe called the Mazitu, a part of the Ngoni people.

As if these problems were not enough, there was one further serious threat to any future exploitation of the Shire Highlands: the area could only be reached via the river Shire, which could only be entered from the Zambesi. The future of the Shire Highlands therefore rested on Portuguese goodwill, since the Zambesi could be closed to foreigners by orders from Lisbon at any time. By the middle of 1859 there was very little goodwill left. Officials in Lisbon and Mozambique could not see how encouragement of British trade in Africa could work without British territorial claims being made.

The Portuguese, to forestall any future British advances, decided to make their position plain by building a customs post at the junction of the Shire and the Zambesi and a fort at the Zambesi's Kongone mouth. The best policy Livingstone could have adopted would have been one of diplomatic conciliation, but instead he made no secret of his now bitter feelings towards Portugal, and his letters and journals gave constant proof of this.

There was another significant cause for friction: the Portuguese in Mozambique were beginning to expand rather than contract their external slave trade, for demands for slaves by the plantation owners of the French islands in the Indian Ocean once more stimulated the Portuguese in Mozambique to renew their old pursuit. Livingstone was not slow to realize that since he had just pioneered a new route up the Shire, the Portuguese might soon start slaving operations on the lower reaches of that river. When that happened, the Shire Highlands would suffer from Portuguese raids from the south, Arab raids from the north, and general Ajawa disruption in the middle.

By the end of 1859 Livingstone saw that, whatever the agricultural and climatic advantages of the Shire Highlands, no future occupants, whether traders, colonists, or missionaries, were going to have an easy time. Aware of all these problems, he played them down because he felt that if the Shire Highlands had no future, all the work he had so far done from 1858 onwards in south central Africa would have been wasted.

So, having made up his mind that the Shire Highlands were the

only place for future exploitation, both Christian and colonial, Livingstone had to think of ways in which action could be taken quickly enough to anticipate further deterioration. He decided that, in these circumstances, he could no longer keep his colonial plans a secret and in March 1859 he had started a correspondence with the Foreign Secretary, in which he proposed a scheme for government-sponsored emigration and the creation of a new colony.

The area was represented as ideal and peaceful at present, but menaced by certain threats which would bring disaster unless colonists arrived soon. This was all right as far as it went, but Livingstone wanted the Foreign Office to grant an additional request, which would involve him in admitting that the Arab slave trade was already a serious menace. Livingstone could see that until the Arab slave routes across Lake Nyassa, and just to the south of it, were blocked, there could be no real stability in the Shire Highlands. The only way to sever these routes was to employ an armed steamer on the upper Shire and Lake Nyassa itself. Since Livingstone did not wish to pay for such a vessel out of the profits of his book, he could only ask the Foreign Office to ask the Treasury to vote the necessary funds. But the matter did not stop there, for this steamer would have to be built in portable sections which could be carried thirty miles overland, past the Murchison Cataracts. But in any case Livingstone's arguments fell between two stools. The extent and severity of the east African slave trade, in one sense, offered Livingstone his only realistic weapon for enlisting government assistance. But if he used it too much, and admitted how bad conditions were already, he would have no hope of trying to persuade potential colonists to risk their lives.

Livingstone did not receive Prime Minister Lord Palmerston's rejection of his proposals until early 1861. But during this time of waiting he set in motion a definite chain of events which he would later bitterly regret having started. During 1857 he had made speeches at Oxford and Cambridge, appealing for young men to dedicate themselves to a life of service in Africa. During the first months of 1859 he heard that, due to his appeal, a combined Oxford and Cambridge Universities Mission had been formed, with Durham and Dublin also joining the venture. In March 1859 Robert Gray, the Bishop of Cape Town, had written to Livingstone telling him about the determination of the Universities Mission to begin work in central Africa. Gray went on to ask what area Dr. Livingstone would recommend as

a suitable field for these men. The decision was a difficult one. In Livingstone's view the Shire Highlands needed colonists and not just an isolated group of missionaries, who would be able to do little about the serious problems which would face them there. On the other hand if he told the Bishop of Cape Town that the Shire Highlands was not a suitable area for missionaries, this news would get back to London and the Foreign Office, and would probably end any plans for a colony. So on October 31, 1859, Livingstone wrote to the Bishop telling him that the Shire Highlands were an ideal location.

The arrival of the Universities Mission in early 1861 would mark the beginning of a new and crucial phase in the history of the Zambesi Expedition; meanwhile, there was taking place the complete disintegration of the morale of the expedition itself. Baines and Thornton were dismissed by July 1859, at Charles Livingstone's urging; George Rae was sent back to England to supervise the building of the new boat. This left Livingstone and his brother Charles, and Kirk. Finally a feud between the two brothers broke out, according to Kirk, over "an old pillow which had rotted in the ship, like many other things." The triviality of this is a good indication of the state of mind the two men were in.

For several weeks Charles sulked and occasionally muttered about his brother being "no Christian gentleman" and being employed "in the service of the Devil." Then one day Charles, who had recently fallen six feet into an elephant pitfall, lost his temper with the headman of the Makololo and kicked him with all his strength. Since they were now within days of reaching Sekeletu's town, bringing home the Makololo, this was not a sensible thing to do. Livingstone flew into an uncontrollable rage and Kirk confessed that he listened to "the most abusive filthy language ever heard in that class of society." From July 1860 till the middle of 1863, when Charles returned to England, Livingstone saw him and talked to him only when he could not avoid doing so. From now on Livingstone felt entirely alone.

The three men were back at Tete by the end of November, and there Livingstone read the Foreign Secretary's answer to his suggestions for the development of the Shire Highlands. While dismayed that his colonial plans had been rejected out of hand, he could comfort himself with the news that Lord Russell had agreed to prolong the expedition for a further period up to three years. The steamer to replace the *Ma-Robert*, he was told, had started from England earlier the same year, which meant that she should already be at the mouth

of the Zambesi. The Foreign Secretary had refused an additional vessel for Lake Nyassa, and so Livingstone realized that the ship Rae had gone to order would have to be paid for with the remains of his book money.

The most important news Livingstone received was from the organizers of the Universities Mission, who wrote telling Livingstone that the first members of the mission could be expected at the Zambesi mouth during January of the new year. Livingstone could not help being alarmed about the prospects of the new mission; none of its members had been prepared in any way for the problems they would shortly have to face. If a disaster like that at Linyanti happened to these members of the established church, it was going to be a lot harder to explain away than the deaths of several nonconformists and their children.

With the Portuguese and Arab slave raids, and the intertribal conflict between the Ajawa and the Manganja very much in mind, Livingstone decided at once to try to qualify some of his earlier unrestrained enthusiasm, just in case anything went wrong at a later date. He wrote to the Secretaries of the Mission telling them that, while the country was healthy and fertile, the missionaries should expect some hostility and suspicion from the natives on account of the slave trade. He wrote in similar terms to the Bishop of Oxford, informing him that, although the area held out "glorious prospects," "there were difficulties . . . an unreduced language, and people quite ignorant of the motives of missionaries, with all the evils of its being in the slave market. But your university men are believed to possess genuine English pluck, and will, no doubt rejoice to preach Christ's Gospel beyond other men's line of things." Livingstone went on to assure the Bishop of Oxford that the missionaries would have nothing to fear from malaria, which, if treated correctly, was no worse than a common cold.

Livingstone had heard that the Universities Mission was to be headed by a bishop, and he realized that the creation of a bishopric in an area that was not a British possession was equivalent to a quasi-claim over that territory. For this reason the British government had been against the consecration of a bishop as leader of the new mission. Livingstone was delighted for the very reason that distressed Lord Russell so much: namely that, if the bishop was hindered by Portuguese or Arab slave traders, there might be a massive upsurge of public feeling in favor of annexing the area. Yet Living-

stone could see that if harm came to the bishop, public anger might turn on the man who had sent him to so difficult a region. As Livingstone left Tete in early December and headed downriver towards the mouth of the Zambesi, to meet the newcomers, he knew that a great deal hung on the success or failure of the new bishop and his colleagues: not just the fate of the Zambesi Expedition and the Shire Highlands, but the kind of attitudes the British government and public would entertain towards colonial expansion in Africa for perhaps the next twenty or thirty years.

CHAPTER 17

DEATH OF A FIGHTING BISHOP

The first members of the Universities Mission arrived at the Kongone mouth of the Zambesi at the end of January 1861. Livingstone, Charles, and Kirk had spent a wet and gloomy month in a group of damp, mosquito-infested huts, waiting for the new arrivals. A few days before reaching the mouth, the *Ma-Robert* had done what she had promised to do for some months: she had gone to the bottom. Fortunately the crew had enough warning to get out most of the supplies and goods. Before leaving Tete, Livingstone had selected a fresh crew to man the new steamer that was expected to arrive at the same time as the missionaries.

Bishop Mackenzie was an energetic and hearty man in the best traditions of muscular Christianity. He had had a brilliant career at Cambridge, and had then gone to work among the Zulus as a missionary in Natal, soon rising to the rank of Archdeacon of Natal. He had recently been consecrated Bishop in Cape Town. Kirk dubbed him "a trump of a fellow" and Livingstone, with rare generosity, pronounced him "A-1." Livingstone was also delighted with the other members of the party. At this stage Livingstone had not become acquainted with the extremely High Church views of the bishop and his deacon, Henry Rowley. But he had genuinely taken to an Anglican priest, H. C. Scudamore, and to a young man designated as "lay superintendent," Horace Waller. In addition to these men, the mission included a carpenter and a cockney laborer whose official title was "agriculturalist." A doctor, John Dickinson, and another young clergyman, Henry Burrup, were expected to come out shortly.

In spite of all the initial goodwill, discords were not long in coming. Mackenzie had expected to be taken to his new mission field without delay. Livingstone told him that he would have to wait three months. Livingstone wanted to explore an alternative route into the Shire Highlands before taking the missionaries anywhere. The Doctor had never been entirely satisfied with the river Shire, partly because the upper reaches became very shallow in the dry season, but mainly because the Portuguese could prevent entrance via the Zambesi. Recently Livingstone had made up his mind that the river Rovuma, which flowed into the Indian Ocean some six hundred miles north of Quilimane, had its source in Lake Nyassa and would therefore prove an ideal *highway* into the Shire Highlands. The Rovuma was also situated ideally outside the northern limits of Portuguese Mozambique.

Eventually Mackenzie reluctantly agreed to wait three months. He knew very well that if any misfortune did befall his men, and it was subsequently discovered that he had rejected Dr. Livingstone's advice, there would be some unpleasant recrimination in Britain. This did not stop him from telling Livingstone that in his view the delay would mean a loss of morale and possibly the cooling of public enthusiasm for the venture at home.

The missionaries had been surprised in the first place that Livingstone was putting so much faith in the Rovuma's potential. They had heard that the river had been surveyed by a naval officer and found to be navigable by steamer for only forty-five miles. Captain Crauford of the *H.M.S. Sidon* told Mackenzie that when the river was low, and it was in the first quarter of the year, Livingstone could not expect to get more than thirty miles upstream. Crauford was right. When Livingstone met the missionaries again in April, they had ceased to think of him as quite the man of judgement they had been led to believe he was.

The party steamed into the Zambesi on the *Pioneer, Ma-Robert's* replacement and the bonhomie of January became a thing of the past. Livingstone had offered to do all he could for the missionaries, and now he had been landed with the job of transporting them around with all their gear. He had been quite firm with their organizers when he had suggested that they bring their own vessel, but, although the appeal for the venture had reached £20,000, no steamer had been ordered. The *Pioneer* had arrived with a master, Mr. May, who thought that he was to succeed Bedingfeld. Living-

stone assured him that he was mistaken, whereupon May resigned. So now Livingstone was in charge of the *Pioneer*, plus his own expedition, plus, for the time being, the missionaries. Kirk was particularly depressed by a typical piece of his leader's thoughtlessness. Livingstone had not told him that he had asked for another medical officer and botanist to come out with the *Pioneer*, but now, without any warning, a Dr. Meller had arrived. Kirk immediately liked Meller but still felt that his appointment was a slap in the face. Meanwhile Charles was doing his best to try to set the Low Church section (Waller and Scudamore) against the High Church section. Worse, all the missionaries, except Rowley, had now suffered from fever and had discovered it to be a far worse affliction than a "common cold."

On May 8 Mackenzie wrote telling his sister that they would all be at the Murchison Cataracts within seventeen days. The estimate was sadly optimistic. A week later the *Pioneer* went aground, and for the next two months it was rare when she was not being dragged along by anchors and ropes. Livingstone had asked the Foreign Office to see that his new vessel should draw no more than three feet, but overloaded way beyond any limit that had been envisaged, she drew over five feet.

It says a lot for the characters of these missionaries that, after their disappointment over the initial delay due to the Rovuma, they did not criticize Livingstone for misinforming them about the navigability of the Shire, nor for suggesting that the Shire valley was well populated, when in fact it was not. And despite Rowley's misgivings about the state of the river Shire and the possibility of trade through the sea, Waller and the Bishop, a born mixer and all-around good sport who was liked by all, still trusted Livingstone, if not as a miracle worker, at least as a man who would guide them to a safe and peaceful place from which to begin missionary operations.

On July 15 the whole party, led by Livingstone, set off on foot from a village just below the Murchison Cataracts. However, after a few hours of the seventy-mile march towards Magomero—the village chosen by Livingstone as the new mission site—any good spirits started to decline. The porters were soon slacking, and Mackenzie, who was unused to this normal hazard of African travel, made matters worse by prodding dawdlers with his crozier. But real trouble was not far off.

Livingstone and the Bishop had already argued about whether missionaries should carry arms, and although Livingstone had managed to win over all the other members of the University party to the view that arms were the best means of deterring attack, Mackenzie had only reluctantly given in. Thus, as he marched, he was painfully aware of the incongruity of carrying a double-barrelled gun in one hand, and his bishop's crozier in the other. But the events of July 16 were to banish his pacifist leanings for good; on that day he and his companions saw their first slaving party.

There were eighty-four slaves, many of them women and children, with their hands tied and their necks secured to forked wooden taming-sticks. The missionaries were euphoric as they watched most of the slave drivers run away at the appearance of the combined Christian party. Clearly the hand of God was behind it. Livingstone remained less rapturous. Portuguese slave operations had already reached the heart of the Shire Highlands. The implications were not pleasant for the future of the Mission.

While Livingstone had told Mackenzie about the Portuguese slavers, he had not warned him about the role the Ajawa played as Arab middlemen. Nor had he admitted that the Ajawa were fighting a tribal war against the Manganja.

Mackenzie was at first inclined to move to a more peaceful region further south, but Livingstone was against this for two reasons: Magomero was in an ideal defensive position, being on a peninsula formed by a stream, and the Ajawa would soon take their revenge on the local Manganja, who would be without a place of refuge if the missionaries moved away. There were disadvantages at Magomero too. It lay in a hollow, and water drained into rather than out of it. This would pose health problems since the excrement of 150 people would not be carried away by the stream. But Livingstone dismissed this difficulty and prepared to leave. He wanted to make a thorough survey of Lake Nyassa to see whether the Rovuma really did flow out of it.

Before Livingstone left Magomero he warned Mackenzie that Manganja chiefs would ask for help. "You will be oppressed with requests," Livingstone told him, "but don't go." This advice was good but hardly much use. The missionaries had already been committed to the Mangaja cause by the events of July 22 when they'd come face to face with Ajawa aggression and had been forced to fire upon them. If they gave refuge to the Manganja, the Ajawa would automatically

view the missionaries as their enemies. And they would lose even the slender hold they now had over the Manganja if they sat back while the Ajawa destroyed village after village.

Livingstone was away at Lake Nyassa till mid-November, and during that time he achieved little that he wanted to. When he reached the *Pioneer* below the Murchison Cataracts in early November, he wanted good news. Instead he heard that Bishop Mackenzie had made two separate attacks on the Ajawa. Livingstone's immediate thought was not for the welfare of the Bishop and his men but for his own reputation at home. His journal makes this very plain. "People," he wrote, "will not approve of men coming out to convert people shooting them. I am sorry that I am mixed up with it, as they will not care what view of my character is given at home."

Livingstone had further reasons to be uneasy. Before he had realized quite how gruesome conditions in the Shire Highlands were, he had agreed to the idea of Mackenzie's elderly spinster sister coming out to help at Magomero. At the same time Livingstone had sent word to his own wife in Britain telling her that she could come too. Mrs. Livingstone, forced by her pregnancy in 1858 to stay in South Africa for a year, had then returned to Scotland to stay with her husband's parents for a further three years. Also, Livingstone had approved Mackenzie's permission for the young bride of Henry Burrup to come out at the same time. All these females were expected within a month or two.

Livingstone knew that he was going to have to cooperate with Mackenzie to get these new arrivals to Magomero; in fact he did not expect the exercise to inconvenience him a great deal, since his next plan was to take the portable steamer he was expecting up past the Murchison Cataracts to Lake Nyassa. But, since the ladies would probably arrive early in the following month, when the Shire was low, the *Pioneer* would not be able to get up very far. With this in mind Livingstone told Mackenzie that he would have to meet the steamer on New Year's Day 1862 at the point where the river Ruo flowed into the Shire, 130 miles southeast of Magomero. Livingstone also suggested to Mackenzie that he would have to open up a route overland from Magomero to this point so that the ladies and several tons of supplies expected by the missionaries could be safely conveyed to the mission.

As soon as the *Pioneer* left, the Bishop hurried back to Magomero, where he immediately gave instructions to two of his colleagues,

Procter and Scudamore, to go south to open a suitable path to the Ruo. The two men had only been travelling for a couple of days when they were attacked by hostile villagers and narrowly escaped with their lives. Most of their African attendants were taken captive. Mackenzie had little choice: within a couple of days he was setting out south at the head of a hastily assembled punitive expedition. There was no fighting when they reached the village, for the inhabitants fled at the appearance of the Christians, but Mackenzie's followers still plundered the place and set fire to all the huts. Nevertheless an hour or so later the villagers rallied and counterattacked; one of the Bishop's native followers was killed in the fighting that ensued. The attack had solved nothing, for now all the surrounding people would be hostile. The Bishop was therefore obliged to return to Magomero to try to reach the mouth of the Ruo via the Shire. By now Mackenzie was hopelessly behind in his plans to reach the agreed meeting place by New Year's Day. In fact it was already January 2 when he got back to Magomero. There he decided that he and Burrup should leave at once for the Shire and then go downstream in a canoe.

Unfortunately neither man was in good health, and both were suffering from diarrhea when they began their journey in teeming rain. The other missionaries had begged the Bishop to wait before starting, but he had been badly shaken by Livingstone's attitude in November and he was scared that if he failed to reach the Ruo within a few days, he might forfeit forever any further assistance from the unpredictable explorer. By January 9, after a week's traveling through non-stop rain, the two men procured canoes for their journey downstream. As the days passed, Mackenzie became totally obsessed with the idea that Livingstone might not wait for him.

By the merest of coincidences Livingstone had actually been at the place where he had arranged to meet Mackenzie on the appointed day. But he had not had Miss Mackenzie with him, nor Burrup's young bride. In fact the Doctor had not been down to the sea at all. He had spent the month and a half since he had said goodbye to the Bishop dragging the *Pioneer* through mud and sand. While he had cursed the Shire and the *Pioneer* and his crew, he had had little time to think of the Bishop. Livingstone's worry was that the ship bringing Mrs. Livingstone and the other women might arrive at the Kongone mouth and leave before he could get there—taking with them his precious portable steamer.

When he finally arrived at the Kongone mouth on January 10, a month later than planned, it was to hear that the brig *Hetty Ellen* with the steamer and his wife on board had called three weeks earlier and had been forced by heavy seas to sail again. In a state of abject depression the party prepared to wait till the ship returned.

On January 11, the day after Livingstone had arrived at the mouth, Bishop Mackenzie and Henry Burrup came to the point where the clear waters of the Ruo joined the muddy currents of the Shire. The two missionaries had endured the most appalling journey. Several days before, their canoe had filled with water and they had lost all their medicines. They had also suffered terribly from dense clouds of mosquitoes; but both men were elated to have arrived at the rendezvous alive. At once they started making inquiries about Dr. Livingstone. To their horror they discovered that the *Pioneer* had last been seen steaming *downstream*. Further questions however seemed to prove that the steamer had not come up from the Shire but had only gone down. The two men knew about the sandbanks and came to the right conclusion. In one way this was comforting: at least they had not been too late and could not be blamed on that account. In another respect the situation was potentially calamitous; they would have to wait in a notoriously unhealthy low-lying area for as long as it took Livingstone to return. Nevertheless they were certain that Livingstone would by now have met the ladies and would be back within the next ten days.

By January 18, Burrup's diarrhea had worsened and the Bishop was also suffering from the same complaint. Soon fever came too. After this neither man could communicate with the other. By the 31st the Bishop was close to death but Burrup had not quite given up.

On this same day, Dr. Livingstone sighted two ships off the East Luabo; the vessels had not gone off for two months but only for three weeks. Through a telescope he could see that the largest of the two vessels was a man-of-war and that she was running up a signal: " 'I have—steamboat—in the brig—' to which we replied, 'Welcome news." Then 'Wife—aboard.' With 'accept my best thanks' concluded this conversation." On board too was Burrup's bride of less than a year and Miss Mackenzie, both very eager to get to Magomero.

At roughly the time Livingstone was exchanging signals with H.M.S. *Gorgon*, Bishop Mackenzie's labored breathing stopped. Burrup was soon surrounded by the local natives, who implored him to bury the body at once to avoid enchantment. Hardly able to stand, he

and his African followers wrapped the body in cloth and took it to the mainland; there among the tall reeds they cleared the ground beneath a mimosa tree and dug a grave.

Burrup's supply of cloth was now all but exhausted and the sick man realized that soon he would not be able to buy food. There was therefore no question of remaining to wait for Livingstone. He would leave a letter and return to the mission. He died in Magomero on February 22, of a combination of dysentery and fever.

Ever since the *Hetty Ellen* had anchored off the mouth of the Zambesi on January 31, 1862, Livingstone's life had become a nightmare. His object was to transport his new portable steamer as quickly as possible to the Murchison Cataracts and thence to Lake Nyassa. First the steamer would have to be assembled for the trip up the Shire; then she would have to be dismantled for the overland journey past the Cataracts, and finally she would have to be reassembled again on the other side. Unless he could get his steamer into the Shire within a couple of months, the river would be low again and the attempt would have to be abandoned till early the following year, and that in turn would mean that the steamer would not be floating on Lake Nyassa till the end of 1863. By then the extended time limit which the Foreign Office had granted the Zambesi Expedition would have been exhausted. What he now needed above all else was a calm atmosphere and a united, well-organized band of helpers. At this crucial time he was in fact surrounded by disunity, chaos, and confusion.

For a start Mrs. Livingstone was no longer the placid and tranquil lady he remembered. In the intervening decade little had happened to Mary to make her sweet-tempered and optimistic. She had had to shoulder the responsibility for bringing up a large family completely without her husband's assistance and had suffered a great deal from the behavior of Robert, her eldest son, who had become quite unmanageable. Mary felt that her husband's conception of his divine duty had destroyed any happiness which she and the children might ever have had. Now in 1862 she had few kind words to say for missionaries or mission work. In Livingstone's eyes this was a terrible state of affairs, but worst of all was his growing feeling that Mary had lost her faith. It was not long too before Livingstone heard some unsavory rumors about his wife.

Expedition gossip had it that James Stewart, the good-looking

young representative of the Free Church of Scotland, sent out to plan another mission for the Shire Highlands, had had an affair with Mrs. Livingstone. The idea, on the face of it, was preposterous, for Stewart was a sensitive and handsome man of thirty, while Mary, at forty, was, in Kirk's eyes at least, "a coarse vulgar woman" and extremely fat as well. Nevertheless Rae's stories that Stewart had visited Mrs. Livingstone's cabin at night on the boat coming out were true. Mary in fact was a heavy drinker, who, Stewart later acknowledged, often drank enough "so as to be utterly besotted at times." During these bouts of excessive drinking Stewart had been summoned by Mary's maid to calm her mistress down. Stewart usually administered some laudanum and then went back to bed. He certainly never enjoyed these nocturnal visits and normally returned to his cabin "with feelings," as he put it, "which I am not disposed to chronicle." Mary had distressed Stewart in other ways too. Her need to drink led her to borrow money from him; and when Stewart finally refused any more, she treated him to a stream of angry abuse.

While Livingstone never believed that anything improper had taken place with Stewart, his wife's drinking was a fact that he could not deny even to himself. His peace of mind was further disturbed by the internal bickerings and hatreds in his now greatly enlarged party.

Shupanga was reached at the end of February; two weeks before that, Captain Wilson and Kirk had volunteered to take Miss Mackenzie and Mrs. Burrup on ahead in an open boat to meet their men-folk at the mouth of the Ruo. When they reached the Ruo there was no sign of anybody, and the natives denied ever having seen Burrup or the Bishop. On March 3, just below the Murchison Cataracts, Kirk and Wilson heard that the Bishop was dead; poor Mrs. Burrup had to wait another week before hearing that her husband too had perished. There was no question of the two women going to Magomero.

When Livingstone heard that the Bishop was dead, he murmured, "This will hurt us all." After Mackenzie's attack on the Ajawa, Livingstone's first reaction had been to work out how he might dissociate himself from any blame. The present situation seemed to him to call for similar tactics. A great many people were going to say that Dr. Livingstone had lured a group of godly men to their deaths by duping them into believing that central Africa was a healthy and idyllic area. That the two men had died in notorious low-lying marshy country, and not in the Shire Highlands, was likely to be over-

looked, and if that happened all chances of trade or colonization would disappear for good. With this in mind, as well as his reputation, Livingstone set out to blame the dead men for what had happened to them. Early the following day he was writing a dispatch to the Foreign Secretary telling him that "coarse living and rash exposure have ended in the sad loss of life."

Only when Livingstone heard, early in 1863, of a packed meeting that had taken place during the previous summer in Oxford did he begin belatedly to defend the missionaries. At that meeting, Dr. Pusey had attacked Dr. Livingstone and the missionaries for using firearms, even in self-defense, for by doing so they had denied themselves that most prestigious of Christ's rewards: a martyr's death. This inanity at last forced Livingstone to admit to Horace Waller, one of the missionaries who by now had become a personal friend: "I thought you wrong in attacking the Ajawa . . . because I thought you had shut yourselves up to one tribe, but I think differently now and only wish they would send out Dr. Pusey here." Livingstone also paid glowing tribute to "the good and noble Bishop Mackenzie," but his change of heart came over a year too late. Already, influential men like Murchison and Admiral Washington had resigned from the Universities Mission Committee. When Livingstone saw that there was a danger of the Mission being withdrawn, he fought against it, for at last he had grasped the fact that such a move would destroy all his hopes, whether for traders, colonists, or missionaries, to come to the Shire Highlands.

CHAPTER 18

DISASTER AND COLLAPSE:
THE END OF THE ZAMBESI EXPEDITION

When Livingstone knew that the Bishop was dead he decided to take the bereaved women down to the mouth of the river himself, to put them on to the *Gorgon* for the return voyage to England. But when the *Pioneer* reached the Kongone mouth it was discovered that the *Gorgon* had been forced by dwindling stocks of coal to sail for the port of Mozambique. This meant that for the next two and a half weeks Livingstone's party was forced to remain in the notoriously malarial Zambesi delta, awaiting the *Gorgon*'s return.

Mrs. Livingstone had been worried and out of sorts ever since James Stewart had foolishly told her what people were saying about them both. On April 21, less than a week after her return from the Zambesi delta to Shupanga, she fell ill with fever. By the 25th there was no doubt that her condition was serious; soon she was tormented by terrible spasms of nausea every quarter of an hour. The following day there was still no improvement and she was moved from the *Pioneer* to the one stone house in Shupanga. Kirk and Livingstone used every method they had learned to try to reduce the fever, but even the most massive doses of quinine seemed to have no effect.

Livingstone stayed by her bed day and night, vainly trying to feed her. Early on the morning of the 27th she started moaning uncontrollably and could hardly drink water from a spoon. Livingstone had remained hopeful until she lost the power to swallow. After that his self-control cracked and he started to weep. At 6 P.M., scandal or no scandal, he summoned James Stewart from the *Pioneer*. The man had been his wife's friend and she had been fond of him. Livingstone asked him to say a prayer, while he and Kirk knelt. Afterwards her breathing became labored and irregular. Livingstone once more broke down and, taking his wife in his arms, choked: "My dearie, my dearie you are going to leave me . . . Are you resting on Jesus?" He was uncertain whether she had heard what he said because the quinine had deafened her. But she had looked upwards when he had spoken and he took this to mean that she had understood. Just after seven he kissed her and she did not respond: "lying with her mouth a little open she gently shut it and breathed her last."

In the depths of his grief Livingstone at last seemed to understand what his children had lived through. His wife's death left him a more understanding father, and from then on the tone of his letters to the children became more personal and less homiletic. He told each one of their mother's death and in none of these letters did he attempt to cloak his grief with conventional phrases of religious consolation.

The day after her death Mary Livingstone, age 41, was buried at noon under the shadow of a massive baobab tree. Livingstone asked Stewart to conduct the service and he was proud to do so. Four sailors carried the coffin to the grave and afterwards mounted guard over it to protect the body from wild animals till a stone cairn could be built.

After his wife's death, Livingstone was eager to get away from Shupanga, but the *Lady Nyassa* was not ready for launching until

June 23. The operation was a shambles and the steamer nearly sank stern first during it, but after twelve hours of constant heaving and shoving, she was forced down into the water over rollers made from the trunks of palm trees. Most of the party doubted whether the new steamer would ever reach the Murchison Cataracts, let alone the lake.

There was so little water in the Rovuma that, from the beginning, it was obvious that Livingstone and his companions would have to go up in two open boats. They got off to a bad start when Rae flatly refused to travel in the same whaler as Charles Livingstone. After a reorganization, Livingstone and Charles were put in one boat and Rae and Kirk in the other.

After five days the river was a maze of shoals, and the main channels never more than a foot deep. But Livingstone seemed oblivious to this. When the water dwindled to a few inches he was quite undeterred and began hiring natives to carry the boats over distances of anything up to half a mile. Kirk was soon writing in his journal: "I can come to no other conclusion than that Dr. L. is out of his mind."

During the evening of September 26 they at last came to a cataract, and there, to the amazement of Livingstone's companions, he began making arrangements for the boats to be carried up over the rocks. The following day he changed his mind and gave the order to turn back. His reason for returning was his fear that if they got stuck, he might miss the next flood season in the Shire and Zambesi and thus fail to get the Lady Nyassa up to the Murchison Cataracts.

Before they reached Shupanga again, in mid-December, George Rae had told his leader that he would resign as soon as the Lady Nyassa's engines were installed. If he did so, Livingstone knew that there would be no hope of getting the steamer past the Murchison Cataracts. He had no choice but to swallow his pride and allow Rae to be as abusive and insubordinate as he wished. Discipline had reached a new nadir. The next few months were to be the worst any member of the party had ever known.

The previous year there had been a terrible drought in the Shire Highlands and on the lower Shire, and the low rainfall, besides ensuring that there was much less water in the river than usual for the time of year, had also caused all the native crops to fail.

As February dragged on, Livingstone and his unwilling companions soon saw very real evidence of the severity of the famine. Bodies began to float past them downstream, crocodiles tearing at

bloated stomachs and fighting each other to get more of an arm or leg. Soon fever added to their misery. Within a month Scudamore died in agony from ulcers on the neck and chest.

On April 10 the two steamers at last lay at anchor below the Murchison Cataracts. The last sixty miles had taken them ten weeks. Before Livingstone could make any preparations for the next stage of the work, the dismantling of the *Lady Nyassa,* another death occurred. In the summer of the year before, Richard Thornton had agreed to rejoin the expedition on condition that he be allowed to continue working independently. Livingstone, who had wanted to add Thornton's geological notes to the expedition's scientific data, had agreed to this. He had been working near the mission in early 1863 and, on discovering how little food they had there, offered to travel overland to Tete to bring back goats and sheep. He returned to the mission on April 13, but the journey had overtaxed his strength and he died five days later of fever and dysentery. Livingstone once again showed little sorrow, just a puzzled contempt for human weakness. *He* had not died, *he* had not stopped working nor asked to go home. Why should others be pitied when they succumbed to a disease that he had lived through and fought off so often? Only the weight of so many failures and disasters can explain Livingstone's contempt for those who died. The disappointment at Kebrabasa, the disaster of Linyanti, the chaos in the Shire Highlands, the death of the Bishop, and the loss of his own wife had numbed Livingstone to all normal human emotions except one: the dull anger of despair.

When Charles and Kirk asked permission to leave, a week after Thornton's death, Livingstone did not withhold consent. "It would be well to get rid of them all and have no more," he wrote, and added that all his white colleagues had never been more than "a complete nuisance." When Kirk left, after six years of loyal service in hellish conditions, Livingstone did not even thank him.

Now George Rae was the only original member of the party left with Livingstone. There was one other officer, Lieutenant E. D. Young, who had been in charge of gunnery on the *Gorgon,* and had stayed on with the expedition after the other sailors had left in April the previous year. In Young's opinion the thirty-mile road, which would have to be built before the pieces of the *Lady Nyassa* could be transported past the Cataracts, would take a year to construct and would need the constant work of a hundred natives during that time. There were barely twenty natives who could be relied upon to work

for a week, let alone a year. The famine had left all the people too weak to devote any of their time to anything other than the search for food. Cloth could not buy the services of starving men. Livingstone by now realized that his own food supplies would not last more than two months, at the end of which he would be forced to go to Tete or the coast for more supplies. Once down the Shire he would never get up again. Failure he could see was certain.

But Livingstone would not publicly admit that he had given up. He wanted it to appear that when the order of recall came, it alone had stopped him achieving the successful launching of the steamer on the lake. So to the amazement of Rae and Young, Livingstone gave orders for the *Lady Nyassa* to be taken apart for the land journey past the Cataracts. Livingstone himself, with the handful of natives he could persuade to work for him, started on the road, felling trees and rolling large rocks out of the way. At the same time he wrote a dispatch to the Foreign Secretary claiming that he was still determined to get the steamer up to Nyassa, but painting such a bleak picture that Lord John Russell would have no alternative but to recall the expedition.

In fact Lord Russell did not need Livingstone's dispatches; the deaths and dismissals had already persuaded him that nothing more would be achieved, and on February 2 he had issued the order of recall. The dispatch did not reach Livingstone at the Murchison Cataracts till July 2, when Adams, the cockney laborer from the mission, appeared on the shore and yelled: "Hallo you *Pioneer* chaps—no more pay for you after December. I brings the letter as says it."

The reason Adams had known the contents of the dispatch was simple. It had been brought up from the coast by the new Bishop who had been sent to replace Mackenzie. Bishop Tozer had felt little compunction in reading Livingstone's official papers, since the future of the expedition would crucially affect the future of the Mission. For a start, once the expedition left, the Mission would have no link with the coast, and the naval warships that had called regularly at the Kongone mouth to collect official dispatches would no longer come. Tozer was convinced that the Mission would have to be withdrawn. To avoid accusations of cowardice he decided to give the Mission a final trial further south, on a mountain near the junction of the Shire and the Zambesi.

It was unfortunate that Livingstone so quickly got wind of Tozer's

intentions, for with the collapse of the expedition the Doctor had decided that the Mission offered the "one ray of hope" in an otherwise hopeless area. The truth was that he wanted the missionaries to stay on, not because he thought they could achieve anything, but because he felt that their continued presence in Africa would help him to claim, on his return to England, that he had left behind a stable and flourishing Christian community in the Shire Highlands.

Livingstone in 1859 had described Mount Morambala, where Tozer reestablished the Mission, as an ideal "sanatorium," which the Portuguese had been mad not to utilize. As soon as the new Bishop went there, the mountain changed its character and became "a mountain 4000 feet high, where clouds rest perpetually at some seasons and the condensed vapour drops constantly through the roofs of huts." It was a terrible choice.

Tozer was soon writing angrily to the Bishop of Cape Town, telling him what he thought of Dr. Livingstone. "The idea of making a Portuguese sanatorium here, is a good specimen of the way in which Livingstone leaps to any conclusion he may wish to see adopted." But, as Baines, Thornton, or Bedingfeld could have told Tozer, to criticize Dr. Livingstone was a hazardous undertaking. When Livingstone knew Tozer had set a date for leaving Africa, he wrote to the new Bishop telling him that he, Livingstone, would make him regret this decision "till his dying day." The Zambesi Expedition ended as it had begun, with bitterness and recrimination.

At the mouth of the Zambesi, in early February 1864, Livingstone handed over the *Pioneer* to Lieutenant Young to sail her to the Cape. He himself wanted to sell the *Lady Nyassa* at the nearest port where buyers might be found. Zanzibar, nearly a thousand miles to the north, was the closest possible market. A long sea voyage would be a dangerous undertaking in a small steamer that had been designed for lake and river use rather than as a sea-going vessel. When he arrived at Zanzibar in April and found no buyer, he made an even more remarkable decision; he would sail his tiny forty-foot ship two and half thousand miles across the Indian Ocean to Bombay, where he was told he would have a better chance of selling her. Not even the desertion of his long-suffering engineer, George Rae, could change his mind. Nor was he daunted by the information that the monsoons would break in roughly three weeks. But although he had only been able to carry enough coal for five days' steaming, Livingstone made it to Bombay, mainly under sail, in forty-five days. As his insignificant

vessel entered the harbor, the first monsoon rains started to fall and the gales broke the following day. Livingstone embarked for England on June 24 and was back in London by the end of July.

On January 20, 1863, the editor of *The Times* had assessed the results of the Zambesi Expedition as follows: "We were promised cotton, sugar and indigo . . . and of course we got none. We were promised trade; and there is no trade . . . We were promised converts and not one has been made. In a word, the thousands subscribed by the Universities and contributed by the Government have been productive only of the most fatal results."

Given the vast distances traveled and the enormous amount of energy expended, this judgment inevitably seems harsh, especially since the Zambesi Expedition had made important discoveries. For a start it had proved beyond doubt that the Zambesi was useless for navigation beyond Tete. The Shire Highlands had been found to be accessible only via the river Shire, which was shallow and treacherous for six months of the year above the junction with the Ruo. Important new facts about the Arab slave routes across Nyassa had also been brought to light. And although the lake itself had previously been reached by Candido, the Tete trader, Livingstone had fixed its position accurately for the first time and had produced a reliable map of its southern and western shores. In fact, had Livingstone set out with the limited but still significant aim of finding out with scientific objectivity about the geographical problems of south central and southeastern Africa, with related facts on the number and disposition of tribes and their relations with the Arabs and the Portuguese, he would have returned home disappointed but satisfied that he had brought back the information he had set out to provide. Yet by promising too much too soon, he was left with the feeble and untrue excuse that the malice of the Portuguese and the cowardice of the missionaries had robbed him of success. Nor would this be enough to convince many people that the expenditure of £50,000 of government money and the loss of a dozen lives had been satisfactorily justified or explained by Dr. Livingstone.

And yet the disconcerting fact remains that without his overoptimism, and without the determination that his work should have more far-reaching effects than the increase of geographical knowledge, Livingstone would never have crossed Africa and would certainly never have been able to summon up the superhuman tenacity and endurance which had alone kept his deeply divided and disil-

lusioned expedition in being. And there is a still more important consideration regarding Livingstone's false expectations: unless he had formulated plans for the colonial occupation of Africa, at a time when the prospects for such moves were negligible, his later influence on the course of African history would have been no greater than that of any other explorer. But in 1863, when he had been bluntly told that it was out of the question for him to take possession of discoveries in the Queen's name, he predicted that there would one day be British colonies in central and eastern Africa. Then he proceeded to describe the colonial system which would become the pattern for the British African Empire fifteen years after his death.

Less than a decade after his death, Nyasaland became a British Protectorate, and this would be the result of Livingstone's posthumous influence. But it would be misleading to believe that Livingstone was entirely confident in his predictions in 1864. At the time that he was writing optimistic letters about his certainty that the future would prove him right, his journal tells a different story: "I shall have nothing to do at home," he wrote miserably on the crossing to Bombay. "By the failure of the Universities Mission my work seems vain. Am I to be cut off before I can do anything to affect permanent improvement in Africa? I have been unprofitable enough."

Livingstone had to face the fact that, unless he thought up a brand new justification, if ever he went back to Africa it would be as an explorer, no more, no less. The Portuguese, after what he had said about them, were most unlikely to let him in again. If he returned to Africa, he was going to have to start in a new area and abandon any idea of utilizing any of the work he had done in the last ten years.

CHAPTER 19

THE LAST VISIT HOME

When Livingstone reached London in July 1864, there were no banquets and official receptions as there had been in 1856. Lord John Russell, the Foreign Secretary, had not merely been annoyed by criticisms of the Zambesi Expedition in the press and by the complaints of High Churchmen blaming Dr. Livingstone for the failure of the Universities Mission; the Foreign Secretary had been far more acutely embarrassed by Livingstone's constant outbursts

against the Portuguese. Not only was Russell opposed to unnecessary diplomatic entanglements, but he resented Livingstone's attitude to the nation which had, after all, given permission for the expedition to enter the Zambesi.

Nevertheless Russell did not wish to turn away with nothing a man who had suffered a great deal of personal hardship. He told Livingstone that if he intended to return to Africa, the government would pay £500 towards the cost of his supplies, provided he did not go near any territory where the Portuguese claimed direct or indirect authority. Livingstone left Russell's office trembling with anger and wounded pride. No expedition lasting two years could possibly be mounted on less than £2,000 and the government was only going to provide a quarter.

In early August, Livingstone left for Scotland where he was relieved to discover that popular support had not diminished so much as in the south. The main purpose of his journey north was not the pursuit of cheering crowds, but to spend some time with his neglected family. He had seen none of his children for nearly seven years and the youngest, five-year-old Anna Mary, who had been born in Kuruman in 1859, he had never seen. Agnes, the eldest daughter, had only been with her father for six of her eighteen years. Livingstone's time in his parents' small house in Hamilton was not happy. His mother was evidently dying and her mind was deranged. She did not recognize her son but talked to him as though he was one of his own children. Often she would ask him what had happened to his brother, meaning his eldest son Robert, who had gone to America to fight against the Confederates. He was wounded in a skirmish at Laurel Hill, Virginia, and taken prisoner. He died in a prison camp in Salisbury, North Carolina, on December 5, 1864; a few days later he would have been nineteen.

Now Livingstone's real efforts to make up for his past failures as a parent were directed at his eldest daughter, Agnes. Agnes was to have everything which had been denied the others. She could go to Paris to improve her piano-playing and her French. There she could also take lessons in riding and drawing if she wished. Only "injurious" French novels were to be forbidden her. His real affection for Agnes cannot be denied. The large number of letters he wrote to her until his death are proof of that.

From September 1864 to April 1865, Livingstone and Agnes stayed at Newstead Abbey, the Nottinghamshire country home of William

Webb, a former big game enthusiast, whom Livingstone had met in Bechuanaland through William Cotton Oswell, his first traveling companion. Livingstone's days at Newstead were among the happiest in his life and, while there, he was affectionate, unassertive, and kind. It was at this time that he confided more regrets to his friends over his inattention to his children. "Oh why did I not play more with my children in the Kolobeng days? Why was I so busy that I had so little time for my bairns?"

At Newstead Livingstone set about his second book, *A Narrative of an Expedition to the Zambezi and its Tributaries*. The *Narrative* was entirely for public consumption and glossed over all the problems and troubles which Livingstone had faced.

In September 1864 Livingstone broke off his writing to go to Bath for the annual meeting of the British Association. The main attraction was to be a debate between Richard Burton and John Speke on the probable location of the source of the Nile. Although Livingstone never acknowledged it, the Speke vs. Burton Nile controversy marked the beginning of his own passionate interest in that river and consequently changed the course of his life.

In 1856, Speke and Burton had set out into the interior from Zanzibar in an attempt to reach a large inland lake which numerous Arab and native traders had visited. The two men stood on the shores of Lake Tanganyika in February 1858, over a year before Livingstone reached the more southerly Lake Nyassa. On the way back to Zanzibar Speke had made a detour north on his own and had arrived at the southern shore of a vast lake which he named Victoria Nyanza. From the great height (3,700 feet above sea level) and apparently gigantic size of this lake, Speke at once decided that he had found the source of the Nile. Burton, who was irritated beyond measure not to have accompanied Speke, dismissed contemptuously his companion's excited claims. Speke had returned to the northern side of his lake in the summer of 1862 and had found an outlet, which he called the Ripon Falls. This discovery he was certain clinched the matter. It did not. In March 1864, Samuel White Baker, who had met Speke and his new traveling companion, James Grant, in 1863, north of the Victoria Nyanza, discovered another large lake, 150 miles northwest of Speke's. Baker now claimed that his lake, which he called Lake Albert, was the *true* source. He had also found a spectacular waterfall on the eastern side of the lake, which he was to name the Murchison Falls. Whether this waterfall was fed by the

same river that began at Speke's Ripon Falls, Baker did not know, nor could he claim with any certainty that the large body of water that flowed out of Lake Albert at its northern end was the Nile. That claim could only be substantiated by tracing that river north and seeing where it went. It was also impossible for Speke to make absolute claims for his lake until he had traveled north from the Ripon Falls far enough to be able to prove the Victoria Nyanza's connection with the lower Nile.

Thirteen years later it would be discovered that Speke had been right and that the waters leaving the Victoria Nyanza at the Ripon Falls were the most southerly source of the Nile. In fact the Nile begins in the Victoria Nyanza and, after joining Lake Albert at the Murchison Falls, flows on out of the northern end of Albert as the Nile proper. Lake Albert is therefore at best a secondary source.

In September 1864, the extent of Baker's discovery was not yet known and, in any case, when it was the following year, there was still no certainty that Baker's Albert or Speke's Victoria were individually or jointly responsible for the lower Nile. Even before Lake Albert was found there were other very plausible alternatives to Speke's lake being the source, and Burton was prepared to put forward all of them in September 1864 at Bath.

Livingstone was briefed by Sir Roderick Murchison on all the arguments likely to be employed during the great debate, and his interest was keenly aroused, and not simply because it was common knowledge that the two men hated each other. The day set for the eagerly anticipated geographical slanging match was September 16. But at 4 P.M. on the day before, John Speke, out shooting on his uncle's estate just outside Bath, clambered over a low wall. Before he reached the other side his gun went off, blasting a gaping wound in his chest, and he died shortly afterwards. Although there was a lot of talk about suicide, the evidence was far from conclusive. This tragedy increased rather than diminished public speculation about the Nile's source.

When Livingstone heard about Baker's Lake Albert in 1865, he decided that the Nile source probably lay southwest of Lake Tanganyika. His theory was that these sources drained into Tanganyika and that a river, issuing from the northern end of Lake Tanganyika, joined the southern end of Lake Albert and flowed on north as the Nile proper. If this was so, Speke, Burton, and Baker had all been working several hundred miles too far north; with all the available

knowledge of 1864 and 1865, Livingstone's theory seemed rather more likely than Speke's.

Before 1865, Livingstone had concentrated most of his vitriol on the Portuguese trade, but after his first extensive survey of Lake Nyassa, he had realized that the Arab trade was a far more serious problem. The reason Livingstone had not given it more attention was because Arab slave raids had been concentrated in the area north and west of Nyassa—they could not be used as an excuse to explain the chaos in the Shire Highlands. The Portuguese were far better scapegoats. But now Livingstone realized that if he went to the area just south of Lake Tanganyika to search for the source of the Nile, he would find himself in the heart of Arab slave trading activities. This then provided him with the ideal justification. He would not only be looking for a river but would be reporting back on the slave trade too. Perhaps his information might persuade the government to intervene directly in central Africa.

When Sir Roderick wrote to Livingstone on January 5, 1865, formally inviting him on behalf of the Royal Geographical Society to return to Africa to clear up the mystery of the source of the Nile, he had felt able to accept, though they offered £500. If he took the money Russell had offered, he would have to raise an extra £1,000 to have enough to last him two years in Africa.

He therefore wrote to the Foreign Secretary and on March 11 was invited to meet Austen Layard, the Permanent Under-Secretary at the Foreign Office, who confirmed that Livingstone could have his £500 and would be given the honorary rank of consul with certain exemptions from normal duties. It was a shock, when he received his consul's commission and instructions dated March 28, 1865, to read a separate enclosure signed by Russell:

Whilst I have been willing to obtain the grant of £500 from the public funds . . . I wish you distinctly to understand that you are not to receive additional consular salary for the service in which you are now engaged, and that your consular appointment gives you no future claim on Her Majesty's Government for a consular pension.

Livingstone had not expected either a salary or a pension, but he was mortally offended that the refusal had been put in writing and in such dismissive terms. Quite apart from this, Livingstone felt that if his appointment was renewed beyond the two years, a situation might arise in which he ought to get a pension.

Whenever Livingstone felt depressed or ill on his last journeys, he remembered this communication and it cut him to the heart. Over and over again he referred to it in his letters.

In mid-August of 1865, just after Livingstone had left for Africa, the Foreign Secretary belatedly sent the deeply wounded man a letter which made matters worse rather than better. Livingstone described the contents of the Foreign Secretary's letter to a friend: "Lord Russell says that he intended to give me £500 a year if I settled anywhere. My position he said was somewhat anomalous in not being stationary." This seemed to Livingstone to be nothing more than a macabre joke on Russell's part. The Foreign Secretary knew that Livingstone had agreed to search for the source of the Nile for the R.G.S. and had received £500 for that purpose. Russell must therefore also have realized that Livingstone could not settle down without abandoning the work he had gone out to do.

One person who treated Livingstone well in 1865 was James Young, the inventor of paraffin, whom Livingstone had first met as a student in Glasgow. Young gave Livingstone the extra £1,000 which enabled him to set out. During March, April, and May 1865, when Livingstone was obsessed with money and his relations with the government, it is hardly surprising that he neglected other important matters. He was not with his mother when she died in May, nor did he find the time to have an operation for the severe hemorrhoids that had plagued him on the Zambesi, causing loss of blood and constant diarrhea. It was to prove a fatal mistake.

CHAPTER 20

NYASSA TO TANGANYIKA

Livingstone planned to return to Africa via Bombay, since the *Lady Nyassa* had still not been sold and he hoped finally to dispose of her. He also wanted to re-employ the Africans he had taken over to India at the end of the Zambesi Expedition. It was a wise decision. Four of these Africans would be with Livingstone eight years later when he died. Two, Chuma and Wikatani, had been among the slaves freed by the missionaries back in 1861. The other two, Susi and Amoda, had first been employed by Livingstone at Shupanga to fit together the pieces of the *Lady Nyassa*.

In Bombay, Livingstone stayed with Sir Bartle Frere, the governor, who suggested Livingstone choose eight of his party from the government-run school for freed slaves at Nassick, where the pupils were given an elementary education, a dozen sepoys from the Bombay Marine Battalion, and ten men from the island of Johanna.

Livingstone intended to travel with a small party of sixty men—he already had thirty-five and intended to hire twenty-five more either at Zanzibar or on landing in Africa—a party of less than half the strength usually employed by African explorers.

Before Livingstone left Zanzibar in March 1866, he heard that the British Consul and Political Agent at Zanzibar was resigning. Since Livingstone knew that Zanzibar was going to be his only lifeline with the outside world, he was keen to get somebody he knew appointed for the job. He had resumed reasonably friendly relations with John Kirk in England, and tried to use his influence to get Kirk appointed. He finally succeeded in getting Kirk the job of Surgeon to the British Agency in Zanzibar, a stepping-stone to the consulship.

Livingstone sailed from Zanzibar for the mainland on March 19. He began his last journey with a disastrous tactical mistake, which he could have avoided had he taken Sir Roderick Murchison's advice. Both Livingstone and Murchison believed, mistakenly, that a river flowed out of the northern end of Lake Tanganyika and ultimately joined Baker's newly discovered Lake Albert. According to this theory, Lake Tanganyika, or more probably a river flowing into the lake from the south, would provide the key to the Nile's source. Since this theory cut out Speke, Burton, and Baker, Livingstone was determined to believe it. Sir Roderick however sensibly suggested that it was imperative for Livingstone to check the connection of lakes Tanganyika and Albert before searching for sources south of Tanganyika. But Livingstone had other ideas:

Supposing that [he told Murchison], as I almost fully believe Tanganyika goes into Baker's lake, the discovery of this would leave the matter very much as it was before. The source would have to be sought for still . . . and I should be obliged to come away back to it in order to give a feasible account of the ultimate origin of the Nile. Much more time would be required for this than by my plan of going at once to the headwaters.

This decision would account for many of Livingstone's future geographical misconceptions. Livingstone had landed just north of the Rovuma at the small port called Mikidani with his party of thirty-five

men and a bizarre assortment of baggage animals: three buffaloes and a calf, six camels, four donkeys, and two mules. Livingstone's reason for bringing so many different kinds of animal was to find out if any one should prove immune to the tsetse fly.

As in the past, initial false optimism accounted for much of Livingstone's misery once things started to go wrong. He had hoped to add another twenty or thirty porters to his party at the coast, but no local tribesmen would come with him for fear of being captured in the interior and sold into slavery. This meant that he had to leave behind stores that he could ill afford to lose. The first few weeks of travel were fraught with difficulties. He had landed, it appeared, at one of the few points on the coast where there was thick jungle. This had to be hacked through with axes, and the size of the camels meant that a much wider path had to be cut.

Ten days after leaving the coast he noticed that his sepoys were maltreating the baggage animals, a matter far more serious than simple cruelty. If the animals died from maltreatment, the experiment to judge their resistance to tsetse would be vitiated; worse still, since the party was short of porters, if the animals were lost more stores might have to be abandoned. Overloading the camels and mules was therefore sabotage, but Livingstone reacted with a mild rebuke.

On July 14 Livingstone came upon the first slave caravan that had not deliberately avoided his path. The leader was an Arab called Seph Rubea, who, on hearing that Livingstone was short of food, made a detour to meet him and, as Livingstone put it, "came forward like a man and brother with an ox and big bag of flour." After seeing the corpses of so many murdered slaves, it might be thought that Livingstone would have refused the gift, but the hungry traveler squared his conscience; if he starved, he would not be able to report on the slave trade and these reports were his only hope of getting the system stopped. Besides, if he offended the Arabs by rejecting their hospitality, he would never be able to elicit information from them. Even so, Livingstone realized the ambiguity of his position, and later, when he actually traveled with Arabs, he would find it necessary to make a distinction between the southern slave traders on the Nyassa-Kilwa route and the northern traders operating directly from Zanzibar in the Lake Tanganyika region. "If one wanted to see the slave trade in its best phases," he wrote the following year, "he would accompany the gentlemen subjects of the Sultan of Zanzibar... to describe its worse form he would go with the Kilwa traders."

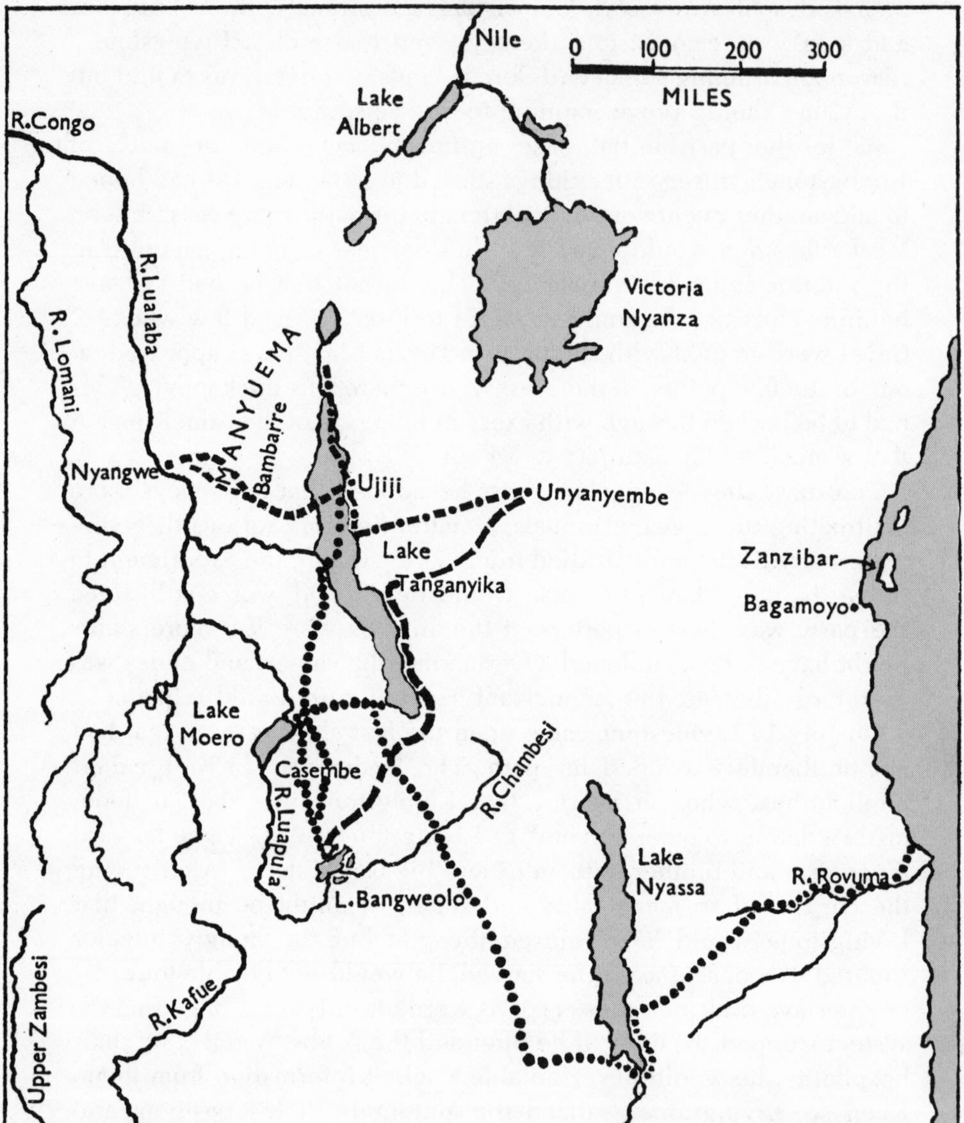

Nile
0
100
200
300
MILES
Lake
Albert
R.Congo
Victoria
Nyanza
R.Lualaba
R. Lomani
MANYUEMA
Bambarre
Nyangwe
Ujiji
Unyanyembe
Lake
Tanganyika
Zanzibar
Bagamoyo
Lake
Moero
Casembe
R.Luapula
R.Chambesi
Lake
Nyassa
R.Rovuma
L.Bangweolo
R.Kafue
Upper Zambesi

LIVINGSTONE'S LAST JOURNEYS Routes: March 1866–March 1869 ••••• July 1869–October 1871 ---- November 1871–February 1872 -•-•- August 1872–April 1873 ▬ ▬ ▬

(Livingstone's death occurred some distance S.S.E. of Lake Bangweolo)

Yet, for a Kilwa trader, Livingstone thought Seph Rubea to be an excellent man, and managed to learn a great deal from him: namely that most of the slaves taken across Nyassa came from the area southwest of Lake Tanganyika where Livingstone hoped to find the Nile source. Seph also told Livingstone something that impressed him greatly: one hundred Arabs had died on the Kilwa route during the past year. Maybe, Livingstone reflected, similar European sacrifices might be necessary before philanthropists managed to get the trade stopped. Since Seph seemed friendly, Livingstone handed him the letters he had recently written, asking him to see that they reached Zanzibar.

A few days later, the sepoys, in line with their previous behavior, killed and ate the buffalo calf and then concocted a story about it being eaten by a tiger. Livingstone asked whether they had seen the tiger's stripes. They eagerly assented. Since there are no striped tigers in Africa, Livingstone was unimpressed. At last Livingstone had come to the end of his patience, and he discharged them. They were given eighteen yards of cloth and left at a village to wait for the next caravan to the coast.

At the beginning of August, Livingstone's party—now reduced to twenty-three—started to climb into the tall mountains that flank Nyassa. On August 6 he could see the blue water of the lake, ten or so miles away. Two days later he was on the shore itself. "The roar of the waves and a dash in the breakers was quite exhilarating."

Unable to get a dhow to cross the lake, Livingstone rejected the shorter route around it to the north because it was rumored that the Mazitu or Ngoni were ravaging the area. Instead he chose to go south and cross at the most southern point of the lake, where the Shire ran out from it.

At this time, one of the boys who had been with Livingstone since 1863 decided to rejoin his family in the Shire Highlands. A few days later the Johanna men deserted, leaving his party eleven men in all. It was now dangerously small.

Incredibly, although Livingstone faced a host of terrible problems, due to the loss of so many porters, he was still able to write serene passages of natural description.

The morning was lovely, the whole country bathed in bright sunlight, and not a breath of air disturbed the smoke as it slowly curled up from the burning weeds . . . The people were generally busy hoeing in the cool of the day.

One old man was carefully paring a stick for stirring the porridge, and others were enjoying the cool shade of the wild fig trees . . . . I like to see the men weaving or spinning, or reclining under these glorious canopies, as much as I love to see our more civilised people lolling on their sofas. . .

This passage evokes all the pleasure he had felt in his early travels and is the more poignant since the same day a series of thunder storms shattered the rural calm and turned paradise into a muddy hell, where paths disappeared under water and small streams became rivers. The rains would last for two months. Soon the old problem of food shortage was added to the "excessively adhesive mud" and the waterlogged paths. Because of the Mazitu raids, people were frightened of Livingstone and his small party and were therefore even less willing to part with any precious food.

On December 6 the only entry in Livingstone's journal was: "Too ill to march." The night before, the whole party had been badly wetted by a storm and had slept in soaking clothes. Bad health was now to be a recurrent problem. December passed miserably. On January 6 the first serious mishap of 1867 occurred. They were clambering down the steep slopes of a ravine and the path was so slippery that two of the porters fell; one of these men was carrying the precious chronometers, without which no accurate longitudes could be taken. Unfortunately, for the next eighteen months they would be some twenty miles to the eastward in error, undoubtedly due to the damage to the chronometers. These mistakes did not have any immediate effect, but errors of this nature could, over a long period of time, dangerously mislead the traveler who relied on his observations being accurate. Two weeks after this incident, the man carrying the party's medicine chest deserted. Livingstone thought this a far worse disaster; in fact he called it "the sentence of death." He was wrong; the real death sentence was to come when he returned to this same general area six years later, and relied on his previous observations.

At the end of January, Livingstone crossed the Chambesi river, but did not realize that it flowed southwest into Lake Bangweolo. He had not been able to establish the precise position of the lake, and now, pressing on north, he had passed fifty miles to the east of it. By the time Livingstone realized his mistake a few weeks later, the lake lay one hundred miles to the southwest. Instead of retracing his steps, Livingstone made up his mind to continue his northward march, in the hope of finding the point where the river, which he as-

sumed flowed north from Bangweolo, entered Lake Tanganyika. Apart from the flooded state of the country, there was another reason why Livingstone decided not to retrace his steps to Bangweolo: by now he was seriously ill with what he suspected was rheumatic fever. "Every step I take jars in the chest, and I am very weak; I can scarcely keep up the march, though formerly I was always first. . . . I have a constant singing in my ears, and can scarely hear the loud tick of the chronometer."

February 3 brought the first gleam of hope he had known for months. He met a party of Arabs who were going to Bagamoyo on the mainland opposite Zanzibar. At last here was a chance to get letters to the outside world. One letter was to the consul, Mr. Seward. Livingstone asked for goods to be sent to Ujiji on Lake Tanganyika, where he hoped to be within a couple of months. He described his almost constantly gnawing hunger and ended: "Don't think, please, that I make a moan over nothing but a little sharpness of appetite. I am a mere ruckle of bones . . . wet, hunger, and fatigue took away the flesh." Livingstone could of course have painted a far grimmer picture. He could hardly travel at all at this time, and although in early February he was only 150 miles from the southern end of Lake Tanganyika, he did not reach it till April 1.

Once at Tanganyika, Livingstone was eager to head north when he heard that war had broken out, north and west of his position, between local tribes and several large parties of Arab traders. There was nothing he could do but head south again, in the hope that he would be able to make a looping detour around the trouble spot. But he did not get far, for soon he was laid out for a month by the worst attack of fever he could ever remember.

Just before he fell ill, Livingstone had heard of a large lake, a hundred miles to the west, called Lake Moero, which he felt certain must be linked in some way with Lake Bangweolo. Now that he could no longer entertain the idea of finding an inlet on the western side of Tanganyika, Livingstone's new plan was to reach Lake Moero as soon as possible. But he did not feel able, with his tiny following, to risk traveling far to the west. Instead, as soon as he was strong enough, he set out south for the nearest Arab settlement, where he hoped to discover how serious the war was.

Livingstone joined the Arabs on May 20 and remained with them till August, waiting for the war to end; his well-supplied hosts raised no objection to his presence. During July there was an earth tremor,

which played further havoc with Livingstone's chronometers. Now a further error crept in, and from this time his longitudes erred in the opposite direction, being fifty miles out to the west. Now Livingstone would have seventy miles more of space on his map than was in fact there.

When peace came in mid-September Livingstone set out for Lake Moero; since a party of Arabs was going in that direction, he decided to take advantage of their supplies by traveling with them. He stood on the banks of the lake on November 8.

Within a few days, with the help of native reports, Livingstone had made some important and entirely accurate deductions about the lake. He was convinced that a large river, the Lualaba, flowed out from the northwestern corner of Lake Moero in a northerly direction. He also concluded that, to the south, Moero was linked with Lake Bangweolo by another river, the Luapula. Thus the ultimate source of the Lualaba, which was a colossal river, lay 150 miles south in Lake Bangweolo. From the moment Livingstone first heard about the Lualaba, he knew that his major task would be to find out where it went. Believing secretly, as he did, even in November 1867, that it was the Nile, he would now have to sort out whether the Lualaba continued its northern journey from Moero into Tanganyika, and then, through that lake and via a river at its northern end, to Lake Albert, or whether instead it joined Albert directly without touching Lake Tanganyika.

In December 1867 Livingstone could certainly not risk setting out on a long journey northwards down the Lualaba, until he had first picked up his stores from Ujiji, 250 miles northeast of Lake Moero. It still remained for Livingstone to make up his mind whether he should travel the 150 miles south to Bangweolo and "discover" the Lualaba's source, before making his long detour to Ujiji. In the end he decided to abandon Bangweolo for the time being and head north with an Arab called Muhammad bin Salim, who intended to go straight to Ujiji. Unfortunately, by the time Salim and Livingstone left the trading center of Chief Casembe the winter rains had set in, and by the end of March 1868, after three months' traveling, the two men and their followers had only progressed fifty miles north of Casembe. Ahead of them the rains had turned the entire region between the point they had reached and Lake Tanganyika into an impassable swamp. Now it appeared that his only course was to find a village and sit out the rains with Salim for another two months.

Livingstone estimated that, as things were, he would not reach Ujiji before June and would therefore be unable to get back to the Lualaba until October or November; since he had only counted on being away from England for two years in all, and had already been in Africa a year and eleven months, this was an extremely depressing time. He suddenly cast aside all previous indecision and told the astonished Salim that he would not wait for the rains to stop but would head south at once for Lake Bangweolo and return north to Ujiji only when he had made sure of the Lualaba's source.

On April 13 Livingstone told his nine followers to prepare to march. Salim argued with Livingstone and told him that to attempt the 200-mile journey south before the end of the rains would kill him and all his men. Livingstone was unmoved by this warning and did not change his mind when five of his followers refused to come with him. The party of thirty-five was now finally reduced to four.

In the month that it took Livingstone and his four men to retrace their steps to Casembe's, *en route* for Bangweolo, they were often up to their waists in water for stretches up to four hours at a time. Unexpected areas of soft mud could unexpectedly plunge them up to their armpits in slime. Apart from midges and mosquitoes, they had to contend with leeches; with hands and fingers numbed by the water, these parasites were extremely hard to pull off.

But in spite of such dreadful conditions, Livingstone and his followers reached Casembe's after twenty-seven days' traveling. Livingstone left Casembe's and headed south on June 11. This time he went with Muhammad Bogharib, an Arab trader going to the Bangweolo district in search of ivory and copper. In spite of the fact that Bogharib also dealt in slaves, Livingstone soon grew to like him. Bogharib proved more than a friend, for he shared his own food with Livingstone and personally nursed him when he was sick.

By the beginning of July, Livingstone and Bogharib were within thirty miles of Lake Bangweolo, and native reports absolutely confirmed Livingstone's opinion that Bangweolo was the source of the Lualaba. Now that he knew that he would be at the Lualaba's source within a few days, Livingstone decided that, before that historic moment, he should abandon his secrecy and tell the world that the Lualaba was the Nile. His confidence would have surprised no geographer possessed of the same information, at the same date.

On July 8, still a few miles short of Bangweolo, Livingstone began a dispatch, which he was certain would be the most important he had

ever written. It was addressed to the then Foreign Secretary, Lord Clarendon.

I may safely assert that the chief sources of the Nile, arise between 10° and 12° south latitude, or nearly in the position assigned to them by Ptolemy . . . If your Lordship will read the following short sketch of my discoveries, you will perceive that the springs of the Nile have hitherto been searched for very much too far in the north. They rise some 400 miles south of the most southerly portion of the Victoria Nyanza, and, indeed south of all the lakes except Bangweolo.

In a letter to Kirk, written the same day, Livingstone gave him the same information about the Lualaba being the Nile and then added, almost as an afterthought: "I have still to follow down the Lualaba, and see whether, as the natives assert, it passes Tanganyika to the west, or enters it and finds an exit into Baker's lake [Lake Albert]."

On July 18, Livingstone at last arrived at Lake Bangweolo and after a couple of days persuaded some local natives to take him out onto the lake in a canoe. The vessel, however, had been stolen and to his anger Livingstone had to be content with two days instead of four on the lake as agreed. It meant that he mapped the lake wrongly. Livingstone had been taken out from the northern shore of the lake to one of four islands. Gazing south and east from this low island, he had looked across what appeared to be an uninterrupted stretch of water as far as the eye could see. Unfortunately his line of vision was restricted by the fact that the highest point on the island was only forty feet. He thus failed to see the beginning of a line of swamps just over the horizon. Had the natives been prepared to paddle on southeast for two hours more, he would have discovered that Bangweolo was only twenty-five miles long, and most of the area Livingstone thought was water was, in fact, marsh and swamp.

The fact that he saw Bangweolo at the end of the rainy season was not his only reason for exaggerating its size. For his estimate, he had also relied on the longitudes he had taken in 1867 and in the summer of 1868. One set, it will be remembered, had been twenty miles out to the east, the other fifty to the west. He thus added seventy miles more to the lake's length than he would otherwise have done. These errors did not affect his most important deductions about Bangweolo: that it was fed by the Chambesi, which he had crossed on his way to Lake Tanganyika in 1867, and that the Luapula left it for Lake Moero, after which it became the Lualaba. The only trouble would come if Livingstone should ever choose to return to the lake from a

different direction and at a different time of year. Then he would not recognize any of the landmarks he had seen on his first visit, and his incorrect longitudes would lead him hopelessly astray into the swamps.

Two days later, on August 1, Livingstone rejoined Bogharib at his encampment ten miles north of the lake; when Bogharib told him that he was planning to visit Manyuema, the area west and northwest of Lake Tanganyika, the very region through which, according to native reports, the Lualaba flowed on its journey north, Livingstone made up his mind to join him.

Almost two months later, the party arrived at the point, a few miles west of Lake Moero, where Livingstone had left Muhammed Salim five months earlier. A large caravan of both parties was formed but when Arab friction broke out with local African tribes over runaway slaves, the group was forced to detour first to Ujiji on Lake Tanganyika to dispose of their slaves and ivory before continuing to Manyuema. Livingstone was disappointed as the caravan altered course from north to northeast but without supplies of his own he was dependent upon the Arabs.

In early January 1869, the caravan was still sixty miles southwest of the point where the Arabs intended to cross Lake Tanganyika for Ujiji. Now the first of the rains began and, after his exploits of the year before, Livingstone's resistance to cold and damp was very low. Soon he was seriously ill. The entry in his journal for January 7 reads:

Cannot walk; Pneumonia of right lung, and I cough all day and all night: sputa rust of iron and bloody: distressing weakness. Ideas flow through my mind with great rapidity and vividness, in groups of twos and threes: if I look at any piece of wood, the bark seems covered with figures and faces of men, and they remain, though I look away and turn to the same place again. I saw myself lying dead in the way to Ujiji, and all the letters I expected there useless. When I think of my children and friends, the lines ring through my head perpetually:

I shall look into your faces,
And listen to what you say,
And be often very near you
When you think I'm far away.

Soon he was too ill to write and to think coherently. When he was conscious, one thought above all others gave him heart: at Ujiji there would be letters for him. During the long periods of delirium which

he suffered throughout January and February, only Bogharib's devoted care and nursing kept Livingstone alive. At last in mid-February the caravan arrived at the western shore of Lake Tanganyika, but it was another month before the crossing had been made and Livingstone was carried ashore on the other side at Ujiji. Here at last Livingstone believed he would find stores, food, and, most important of all, medicines and letters. An hour later he knew that three-quarters of his supplies had been pillaged. The only provisions waiting for him could have been packed into one chest: a little sugar, tea, and coffee, some low-quality beads, and a quarter of the cloth he had ordered in Zanzibar.

CHAPTER 21

FANTASY IN MANYUEMA

Ujiji, situated seven hundred miles due west of Zanzibar, had been since the early 1840's a thriving Arab trading center. From Ujiji's small harbor a procession of dhows crossed Lake Tanganyika, transporting caravans to the slave and ivory fields, west and southwest of the lake. In Ujiji itself the streets were rarely empty and, as a rule, groups of Arabs in white flowing robes, strings of slaves laden with grain and ivory, and flocks of sheep and goats on their way to market, all gave the place an air of activity and bustle.

As soon as Livingstone was well enough to be up and about, he sent a letter to the coast asking Kirk, who was at present standing in for the Consul of Zanzibar, to send stores with the next caravan.

While Livingstone convalesced at Ujiji during the spring and early summer of 1869 he came to the conclusion that there were three main interconnecting "lines of drainage" in central Africa, running roughly parallel with each other from south to north. The western line originated, according to the theory, due west of Bangweolo and joined the central line of drainage somewhere north of Lake Moero. The central line itself ran from Lake Bangweolo, through Moero, and then on north as the Lualaba. The eastern line, Livingstone believed, began at a point just north of Lake Moero, where the Lualaba split in two, sending the main body of its water due north, to continue as the central line, and the rest of its water northeast into the western side of Lake Tanganyika. Thus Lake Tanganyika and Lake

Albert—Livingstone thought that the two lakes were connected by a river flowing from the northern end of Tanganyika to the southern end of Albert—formed the eastern line of drainage.

Although fundamentally mistaken, in some respects Livingstone's theories were correct. A modern map of Africa shows that lakes Albert and Tanganyika do lie at opposite ends of a chain of lakes, but this chain is not connected. The Lualaba does flow northwards from Lake Moero for six hundred miles between the chain of lakes to the east and the river Lomani—a major tributary of the Lualaba—to the west. The major flaw in Livingstone's thinking was his conviction that the Lualaba was the Nile. It is in fact the upper Congo. Yet Livingstone's claims for Lake Bangweolo being the Nile's source did not depend solely on the ultimate destination of the Lualaba; he still had the eastern line of drainage up his sleeve. It was most unfortunate that he had not done what Sir Roderick Murchison told him to do in 1866 and gone straightway to the northern end of Lake Tanganyika to check whether the river there flowed into or out of the lake. If it flowed in, the eastern line of drainage could have no possible connection with the Nile, since it would have been proved that lakes Albert and Tanganyika were not linked.

Before leaving England in 1865 Livingstone had read all the classical allusions to the Nile's source, and one important reference was in Book Two of Herodotus' *History*. When Herodotus visited Egypt in the fifth century B.C. he made inquiries about the source of the Nile, and on his return home he wrote: "Not one writer of the Egyptians or of the Libyans or of the Hellenes, who came to speech with me, professed to know anything, except the scribe of the sacred treasury of Athene at the city of Sais in Egypt." But the scribe made up for all the others: he said most specifically that at a point midway between two hills with conical tops "are the fountains of the Nile, fountains which it is impossible to fathom: half the water runs northward into Egypt; half to the south." This detail, about half of the water flowing south and half north, immediately led Livingstone to the conclusion that the scribe of the sacred treasury had been right. The Arabs had spoken about a hill between the four sources, and one hill was not so very different from two hills with conical tops. Herodotus had only quoted the story because it was all he could discover about the source of the Nile, not because he had believed it. Livingstone was convinced that the scribe had had access to definite information which had since been lost.

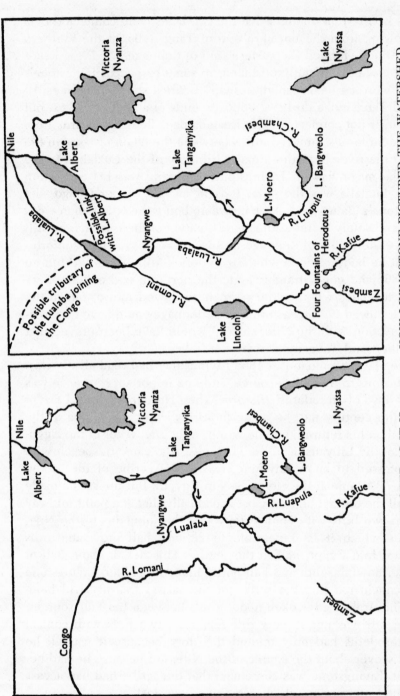

THE CENTRAL AFRICAN WATERSHED AS IT IS
Where Livingstone was mistaken over the direction of flow of rivers he had heard about, but not seen, is indicated by arrows.

HOW LIVINGSTONE PICTURED THE WATERSHED
From deductions made between May 1869 and April 1871. His discovery in December 1872 that lakes Albert and Tanganyika were not linked did not change his view of the Lualaba.

He also had read Ptolemy's *Geography* and had carefully scrutinized his map of Africa. Ptolemy suggested that the source of the Nile consisted of two springs situated in a range of hills which he called the Mountains of the Moon; the mention of twin sources left Livingstone still more convinced. Ptolemy, who lived in Alexandria during the second century A.D., had been a remarkable man, and his astronomical theories were accepted till the time of Copernicus and Kepler; but to take his maps of Africa seriously was madness. In fact by the end of 1870 the whole patchwork of Livingstone's thinking had become an impossibly intertwined web of fantasy and reality. Livingstone had allowed his determination that his Lualaba should not be the Congo to make him clutch at every thread of information that made it seem probable that it was the Nile.

Toward the end of March 1871, after six weeks' traveling, Livingstone reached the Lualaba at a town called Nyangwe and gazed across its two miles of slowly moving water. Soon after his arrival he started hearing unpleasant stories that the Lualaba soon bent westwards, and not eastwards as he hoped. At Nyangwe itself the river's flow was due north. Livingstone would obviously have to follow the river north to make certain of its course. The natives and Arabs at Nyangwe generally believed that the Lualaba did ultimately flow westwards, but Livingstone never listened. He might have had he not heard about a river called the Lomani a week after his arrival in Nyangwe. The natives told him that six days north of Nyangwe the Lomani ran into the western sides of the Lualaba, having flowed parallel with the Lualaba for several hundred miles. No native had any idea where the Lomani's source was. Unfortunately Livingstone thought he did: obviously the Lomani was the river that flowed from the twin sources northwards into the unvisited lake and then joined the Lualaba several hundred miles north of Lake Moero. Considering it a foregone conclusion that the Lualaba was the Nile, Livingstone thought only of tracing the Lomani south to reach the twin sources. When natives refused to let him have canoes to cross the Lualaba—and he would have to get to the western bank before being able to reach Lomani—he offered Dugumbe, the leading Arab in the town, £400 and all his supplies at Ujiji if he would get him and his men across the river. Dugumbe was still considering this proposition on July 15: the day a terrible disaster occurred in Nyangwe.

On July 15, as on every other market day, Livingstone wandered among the two or three thousand buyers and sellers and tried to

forget his problems, but the day was hot and sultry and he did not stay more than an hour. As he was leaving, an argument over the price of a chicken broke out between a native and three armed Arabs. Livingstone heard shouting but thought nothing of it; haggling was often spirited. He had walked another thirty yards when suddenly two shots rang out behind him; a moment later screaming men and women were rushing past him. The three Arabs were now firing wildly into the backs of the fleeing crowd. Hundreds of people swarmed down into the creek and pandemonium broke out. Many canoes were swamped without leaving the shore, and others cast off without paddles. Only three canoes got away and all these were capsized by the frenzied efforts of those in the water to pull themselves aboard. Soon Livingstone could see a long line of heads drifting away downstream. The Arab estimate of four hundred dead was probably a couple of hundred too few.

When the shooting stopped, it was discovered that in the turmoil several hundred slaves had broken loose and had looted the market. On the other side of the river similar massacres were taking place and before long Livingstone could see plumes of smoke rising from burning villages. Dugumbe and his partners had launched a deliberate campaign of arson and murder to frighten the Manyuema into abject obedience to all Arab demands. After what he had witnessed, Livingstone knew that he could never accept help from Dugumbe, even if the Arab offered a fleet of canoes for nothing. Only one course remained to him, and on October 23, after three grueling months traveling, Livingstone returned to Ujiji.

Within a couple of hours of landing Livingstone realized with a sinking heart that the supplies Kirk had sent from the coast had been stolen and sold off by the man who had brought them to Ujiji and by other Arab traders in the town. There was virtually nothing left out of £600 worth of goods. To the east of Ujiji the war still went on, and there could be no immediate hope of getting goods from the coast to replace those stolen. All that Livingstone could do was to write to Kirk explaining what had happened and asking for a further lot of stores. The prospect ahead of him was at least ten months of waiting at Ujiji with no certainty that Kirk would manage to get a caravan through. During all that time, Livingstone knew, he would have to exist on Arab credit.

Two days after his arrival at Ujiji, Livingstone was amazed to hear that a white man had recently left Unyanyembe, two hundred miles

east of Ujiji. Who this white man was or where he was going, nobody had any idea. His nationality was as much a mystery as his name. Livingstone, in spite of himself, could not help hoping, praying that this stranger, if he existed, would come to Ujiji.

Livingstone only had to endure three more days' suspense, and then at noon on what he reckoned to be October 28, but was in fact a day in early or mid-November, shots were heard outside the town announcing the approach of a caravan. The rumor spread rapidly that the newcomer was an Englishman and soon crowds started to form outside Livingstone's house. In a few minutes the column of men had reached the center of Ujiji and Livingstone could see that they were all dressed in long white robes and turbans, and they were carrying enough to sustain a traveler for years: tin baths, tents, saddles, a folding boat, an impressive array of gigantic kettles. Then out of the advancing crowd stepped the white man himself; a huge native preceded him carrying the stars and stripes. The stranger was immaculately dressed in a freshly pressed flannel suit; his boots glistened and his helmet was a dazzling white. The crowd parted and Livingstone now moved towards the newcomer, who lifted his hat and said, as formally as he could, in a voice that nonetheless trembled with excitement:

"Dr. Livingstone, I presume?"

CHAPTER 22

STANLEY AND THE LIVINGSTONE MYTH

On October 28, 1869, Henry Morton Stanley, a young journalist on the staff of the *New York Herald*, had been summoned to an important meeting by the owner and editor of that paper, James Gordon Bennett Jr., who was currently staying at the Grand Hotel, Paris. Stanley's account of the interview shows he did not waste time in coming to the point:

"Where do you think Livingstone is?"
"I really do not know, sir!"
"Do you think he is alive?"
"He may be, and he may not be!" I answered.
"What!" said I, "do you really think I can find Dr. Livingstone?"

And the answer of course was an emphatic *yes* from Bennett.

When Stanley gasped that the venture would prove extremely expensive, his employer contemptuously brushed the objection aside:

Draw a thousand pounds now; and when you have gone through that, draw another thousand, and when that is spent draw another thousand, and when you have finished that draw another thousand, and so on; but FIND LIVINGSTONE.

It is no mean tribute to Bennett's journalistic sense that, at the time he was preparing his paper's greatest scoop, Livingstone, for the British public at least, was a forgotten figure. In December 1866 the Johanna men, who had deserted Livingstone near Lake Nyassa, had arrived in Zanzibar with a story that their master had been killed by natives in the interior. When obituaries appeared in the British press in early March 1867 they were short and unemotionally factual. Only the Council of the Royal Geographical Society had reacted positively. Murchison had pressured a reluctant British government into an expedition to prove or disprove the story of Livingstone's death. E.D. Young, who had served with Livingstone on the *Lady Nyassa*, had been appointed as leader of this search party. During the autumn of 1867 Young had reached the southern end of Lake Nyassa and had collected evidence that Livingstone had passed through that area without meeting his death. The same month letters from Livingstone reached the British Consulate in Zanzibar. By the end of 1868 no further news had been heard of Livingstone and again rumors that he had died began to circulate. Bennett however believed that a face-to-face interview by one of his journalists with this British explorer, who had not seen a white man for five or six years, would prove a story with such emotional and dramatic impact that the previous lack of interest in Livingstone would become entirely irrelevant.

When Stanley left Bennett he realized that if he found Livingstone he would be made for life, both financially and professionally. Socially, he knew, there would also be rewards, and for a man who had experienced an even harsher childhood than Livingstone's, this was an added spur. Stanley had been born in Wales, the illegitimate son of a Denbighshire cottager. Deserted by his mother in infancy, he had been looked after by two uncles for a few years until, at the age of five, he had been consigned to the St. Asaph workhouse. For the next nine years, according to his own later accounts, Stanley suffered the constant brutalities and humiliations perpetrated on all the

young inmates by James Francis, the master, who was later found to be insane and put in an asylum. At the age of fifteen, Stanley was driven by an unusually savage punishment to attack Francis and beat him unconscious. The only course then open to him was to run away.

Stanley went to Liverpool and signed on as cabin boy on an American ship bound for New Orleans. In New Orleans he met and was later adopted by a prosperous wholesale merchant, who took him into his home and gave him his own name: Henry Morton Stanley. For two happy years Stanley traveled with his new father in the Mississippi valley, preparing himself for a business career, but in 1861 old Stanley heard that his brother in Cuba was seriously ill, and decided to go to him; shortly after his arrival in Havana, he died of fever. In the meantime the American Civil War had broken out, and Stanley enlisted in the Confederate Army. After a year's service he was captured and imprisoned in shockingly unsanitary conditions. A few months later his health failed and he was released.

In the autumn of 1864, he enlisted as a ship's writer in the Federal Navy and his official accounts of the war impressed a number of newspaper editors and encouraged Stanley to leave the navy and take up journalism as a career. By 1868 Stanley had attracted enough notice to get an offer of employment from James Gordon Bennett of the *New York Herald*. The *Herald*'s reputation was founded on its ability to print sensational and scandalous stories, more with a view to the number of papers sold than to the truth. But the *Herald* also on occasion produced genuine scoops which astounded all rival editors. In his first year on the paper Stanley contrived just such a scoop.

At this time the British government was planning a punitive expedition into Ethiopia, where King Theodore had imprisoned the British Consul and a number of British citizens. Stanley reported Sir Robert Napier's campaign and managed to send home news of the British victory before any other reporter. Because of this success Bennett had decided to send Stanley on the far more challenging search for Livingstone.

Perhaps because a letter from Livingstone unexpectedly arrived in Zanzibar in the autumn of 1869—the one he had written to Kirk from Ujiji in May that year—Bennett decided against sending Stanley to Africa straightaway. Instead he told Stanley that he should first send reports on other matters from Egypt, Turkey, Persia, and Bombay. This Bennett knew would occupy Stanley for a year, by which time Livingstone would with luck be thoroughly *lost* again. In fact when

Stanley eventually arrived at Zanzibar in January 1871, no further news had been heard from Livingstone. Bennett's instinct had proved correct.

From the time he met John Kirk, who had been the Acting British Consul in Zanzibar since June 1870, Stanley decided that Kirk was standoffish, arrogant, and unhelpful. Stanley's wretched childhood had made him almost as sensitive to possible insults as was Livingstone. Since Stanley's relations with Kirk would later prove a crucial factor in Livingstone's refusal to come home with Stanley, it is important to see how the trouble started.

Although Stanley had told Kirk that his sole purpose in coming to Africa was to examine the Rufiji—an insignificant river which flowed into the Indian Ocean a hundred miles south of Zanzibar—he felt that Kirk had seen through this ruse and realized that he had really come to look for Livingstone. When Stanley asked Kirk what Livingstone's reactions might be if by coincidence "I might stumble across him?" Kirk's reaction was to tell the journalist that Livingstone would probably be extremely angry to be "found." "I know," Kirk had continued, "if Burton, or Grant, or Baker, or any of those fellows were going after him, and he heard of their coming, Livingstone would put a hundred miles of swamp in a very short time between himself and them." Kirk might have lent a more sympathetic ear to Stanley had he believed that Livingstone was short of supplies; but between the end of 1869 and November 1870, Kirk himself had dispatched three separate caravans with stores for the Doctor. The chances were that if Stanley did "stumble across" Livingstone, the young journalist might well arrive having exhausted his own supplies and in bad health. Thus he could easily be a drag on Livingstone. The very idea of Livingstone being "found" seemed idiotic to Kirk. In May 1869 Livingstone had written saying that he was about to set out for Manyuema; and Kirk was sure that, in due course, the Doctor would return to Ujiji, where he would write further letters explaining his future plans.

Unaware of any of Kirk's thoughts, Stanley assumed that the Acting British Consul had been dismissive as the result of a purely personal antipathy to him. But Stanley did not let his grudge against Kirk interfere with the preparation of what was to be an exceptionally lavishly equipped expedition. Before leaving Zanzibar a month after his arrival there, Stanley had spent £4,000. His purchases included nearly twenty miles of cloth, a million beads, and 350 pounds of

brass wire. Determined to be ready for anything, he also bought a couple of collapsible boats and took seventy-one cases of ammunition and forty guns. Stanley's stores eventually weighed roughly six tons. In contrast with the thirty-five porters Livingstone had led into the interior in 1866, Stanley set out with 192. His abilities as an organizer were outstanding. The speed with which he traveled was proof of this. Whereas Speke and Burton had taken five months in the dry season to reach Unyanyembe, Stanley covered the same five hundred miles in just over three months, and in the rainy season too. Stanley's methods were not Livingstone's; he used the whip a great deal. On November 3, with a much reduced party of fifty-four, Stanley triumphantly entered Ujiji.

Stanley was not a naturally religious man, and yet he began to see his journey as a pilgrimage: a divinely appointed task, and not merely as a journalistic assignment which would make him both rich and famous. He could not admit, even to himself, that there was any chance at all that Dr. Livingstone might be anything other than a unique and saintly man. In fact, by the time Stanley met him, the sufferings of the past five years had substantially softened Livingstone's personality. But even so, when Stanley noted unpleasing aspects in Livingstone's character, he tried first of all to persuade himself that they did not exist, and, when that failed, made up his mind that nobody else should know.

Stanley knew that whatever he first said to Livingstone would be likely to go down in history. After all, his words would be the first a white man had spoken to the Doctor in six years. He tried to imagine what an upper-class Englishman would have said and done in the same situation. Poise and understatement were great Anglo-Saxon attributes and he would emulate them. And so Stanley walked up to Livingstone at a steady pace, doffed his hat, and said the four words which he was to regret for the rest of his life. The words Stanley had hoped would lend dignity to a solemn occasion were later hailed with explosions of laughter and disbelief. They were used in music hall burlesques; friends or strangers greeted each other substituting their own names for Livingstone's. Stanley himself was often met with "Mr. Stanley, I presume." But he could never see the joke. The greatest irony of all was to be the fact that later generations would forget almost everything about the main achievements of the two men but would remember the phrase.

But in November 1871 Livingstone did not laugh, for as he took

Stanley's hand he felt tears coming into his eyes. There can be no doubt that Livingstone had never been so pleased to see a white face as he was to see Stanley's. He was not exaggerating when he told Stanley: "You have brought me new life." Stanley, who could not immediately have appreciated the absolute despair Livingstone had been in before his arrival, considered the Doctor's genuine and outspoken gratitude to be the first indication of a saintly character. Of course Livingstone would have been outrageously inhuman had he not responded emotionally to Stanley's arrival; for the journalist had not only brought food, medicines, supplies, and a package of letters; he had brought Livingstone the first proper accounts of what had been happening in the outside world that he had heard for five years. Livingstone was soon listening open mouthed as Stanley told him about the Franco-Prussian War and the fall of Paris. Stanley filled him in on the inauguration of the transatlantic telegraph, the opening of the Suez Canal, and the death of British Foreign Secretary, Lord Clarendon. But the information Livingstone listened to with most attention was that, due to Sir Roderick Murchison's efforts, the Treasury had at last agreed to let him have more money for supplies. The sum voted had been £1,000. The knowledge that he had not been entirely forgotten in England did not make him any the less grateful for what he called the "disinterested kindness of Mr. Bennett, so nobly carried into effect by Mr. Stanley."

Livingstone's belief that Mr. Bennett had acted only out of affection for him was of course a ludicrous overstatement of his debt to the newspaper owner, but from the beginning, Stanley behaved with a kindness and consideration which gave the lie to almost all his previous behavior. He divided everything he had brought into two piles and gave Livingstone one of them. He prepared food for the old man with his own hands and saw that he had four meals a day. In every way that he could think of he made life easier for the Doctor, whose health soon seemed to improve. In letter after letter Livingstone lavished praise on the newcomer. He told Agnes: "He came with the true American characteristic generosity—the tears often started into my eyes on every fresh proof of kindness." But there was more to it than that. Livingstone had always disliked all forms of pretentiousness and cant. Stanley was awkward, shy, defensive, and given to bluster, but he was rarely pretentious or hypocritical. Both men shared the same shyness and as a result were often thought brusque and rude. This could have led to violent misunderstanding

but it did not, for they seemed to recognize the same traits in each other and to make allowances accordingly. Livingstone was not in any way offended when he heard that Kirk had been saying that Stanley would make his fortune out of him. Livingstone's reply was characteristic: "He is heartily welcome, for it is a great deal more than I could ever make out of myself."

Livingstone wrote two letters to Mr. Bennett within ten days of Stanley's arrival and both were of course for publication. If Stanley and Bennett stood to gain, so he felt did he. He was able to put his views on the slave trade before a vast audience and to give enormous publicity to the massacre he had witnessed at Nyangwe. In fact the publicity given to these and other letters written by him, and the general furor caused by Stanley's feat, were of crucial importance in the revival of public indignation in Britain and America at the continuation of slavery in east Africa.

Kirk had suggested to Stanley that Livingstone would dash off as soon as possible after being "found," and had added that the old veteran hated publicity. When Stanley realized that Livingstone had no desire to get rid of him and was eager to cooperate in giving information about his travels to date and his plans for the future, the young journalist was so overwhelmed with gratitude and relief that he at once assumed that all the stories he had heard from Kirk and others about Livingstone's perverse antisocial behavior had been malicious fabrications. Stanley made up his mind to remedy the situation; he knew that the dispatches he would send back to the *New York Herald* would be published in other papers throughout the world. So he set about canonizing Dr. Livingstone: a figure "without spleen or misanthropy," a man as near an angel "as the nature of living man will allow." Nor was Livingstone gloomy or inward-looking, for he had a "fund of quiet humour." "His gentleness never forsakes him; his hopefulness never deserts him. No harassing anxieties, distractions of mind, long separation from home and kindred, can make him complain. . . . His is the Spartan heroism, the inflexibility of the Roman, the enduring resolution of the Anglo-Saxon—never to relinquish his work though his heart yearns for home." This was the picture of Livingstone which Stanley gave the world. He repeated it in speeches, articles, letters, and finally gave it more permanent form in his worldwide best seller, *How I Found Livingstone,* published in England and America in 1872. But the lasting effect of Stanley's character study was its acceptance by almost all those who read it.

Stanley cannot be accused of deliberate insincerity; the great personal meaning with which he had invested his meeting with Livingstone influenced him, to some extent unconsciously, and Livingstone's unfeigned gratitude and genuine liking for Stanley did the rest. Livingstone's infinite patience with all Africans, even those who had deserted him, also justifiably impressed Stanley. But after a couple of months with Livingstone, Stanley wrote in his diary: "I have had some intrusive suspicions, thoughts that he [Livingstone] was not of such an angelic temper as I believed him to be during my first month with him; but I have been driving them steadily from my mind. . . . "

A little later, however, Stanley was certain that his suspicions were well founded and that Livingstone by "reiterated complaints against this man and the other" had proved that "his strong nature was opposed to forgiveness." Livingstone had in fact been going over all his old quarrels that had taken place during the Zambesi Expedition. But in subsequent dispatches and articles Stanley made no qualification of his earlier rhapsodic praise.

Stanley became even more aware of the weaknesses in Livingstone's character when he came to talk to the Doctor about John Kirk. Stanley had become convinced that Kirk had neither taken sufficient care in the selection of members of the caravans dispatched with goods for Livingstone, nor taken routine precautions to see that these caravans had set off from the coast at once. Before Stanley's arrival, Livingstone had not found fault with Kirk; the Doctor had realized that, due to the war outside Unyanyembe and also as a result of successive outbreaks of cholera in Zanzibar and along the coast, assembling caravans at all could have been no easy matter during 1869 and 1870. Livingstone, usually inclined to believe that former friends had let him down, accepted Stanley's charges, and was soon writing letters to most of his correspondents, telling them no longer to refer to Kirk, as Sir Roderick Murchison did, as "companion of Livingstone." One friend was told that Kirk was "too lazy and indifferent to serve David Livingstone."

Stanley, who had merely intended to discredit Kirk, had had no idea that Livingstone might begin to see the whole matter as a monstrous conspiracy against him, in which Kirk, the British government, and the Council of the Royal Geographical Society were all in league. Livingstone soon suspected that Kirk had been acting on instructions from the Foreign Office to force him home. The extra

£1,000 grant had merely been a blind to deceive him into believing that the government still supported him. The Foreign Office was ganging up with the members of the R.G.S. who wanted him home to get their hands on his precious notes. So when Stanley attempted to persuade the old man to come home to recuperate, get some artificial teeth, and build up his strength in England before returning to Africa for a final effort on the Lualaba, he was surpised and wounded that Livingstone refused even to consider the suggestion. Ironically Stanley remained unaware that his attack on Kirk had made Livingstone's refusal a foregone conclusion.

Stanley and Livingstone spent five months together in all. During November and December 1871 the two men did their only piece of mutual exploring—they traveled to the northern end of Lake Tanganyika and discovered that the river there—the Lusize—flowed into the lake and not out of it. This finally proved that lakes Tanganyika and Albert had no connection.

On December 13 the two men returned to Ujiji and two weeks later set off for Unyanyembe, Stanley on his way home, Livingstone to collect any supplies from Kirk's caravans that had not got through to Ujiji. The two of them drew up a list of supplies which Livingstone would need for the long journey ahead, and Stanley promised to send everything with fifty porters as soon as he could after reaching the coast. These fifty men he swore would be free men and reliable too. As the time grew closer for parting, Livingstone tried to detain Stanley a little longer, till the rains ended, but Stanley, although in many ways reluctant to leave, was in others eager to get away: he had yet to telegraph his news to the world, and he knew that the longer he stayed with the Doctor, the longer Livingstone would have to wait for his fifty porters and the supplies.

On the evening of March 13 all Stanley's preparations for departure had been completed. Livingstone handed over to him the letters he had written while they had been together and, as a sign of his complete trust in Stanley, his journal. This was sealed with five seals and marked not to be opened until his own return to England or his death. In England it was to be entrusted to Agnes. Livingstone did not waste words on the parting. "Mr. Stanley leaves," was all he wrote. But there was no doubt at all that he felt considerably more. In letters to most of his friends he instructed them to treat Stanley with friendship and kindness "just as you would do to me." As a great privilege Livingstone had confided to Stanley all his thoughts

about the central African river system. "He has a clear idea of the geography," Livingstone told H.W. Bates, the Assistant Secretary of the Royal Geographical Society. Stanley did not doubt Livingstone's conclusions, because Livingstone had visited the Lualaba and he had not. Also, being a self-educated man, and never having read any Ptolemy or Herodotus, Stanley did not see anything strange in relying on their information.

Within a week of Stanley's landing in England on August 1, 1872, the story of his meeting with Livingstone had swept all other items off the main news pages of all the major papers in Britain. His arrival brought information about the slave trade, in the form of Livingstone's dispatches, at a crucial time. During 1871 a House of Commons Select Committee had been set up to review the problem of the east African slave trade. By the end of September 1872, Gladstone's government had decided on the abolition of the sale of all slaves, whether for domestic use or for export. Sir Bartle Frere, the governor of Bombay, was appointed to sign a treaty with the Sultan of Zanzibar to that effect. On June 5, 1873, after being threatened with a British naval blockade, the Sultan signed, and that day the slave market in Zanzibar was closed forever. It was tragic that Livingstone himself never lived to hear about Frere's treaty.

CHAPTER 23

THE LAST JOURNEY

As Livingstone waited at Unyanyembe, throughout the spring and summer of 1872, he knew nothing about the fame Stanley had brought him, nor did he have any idea of the impact his anti-slavery dispatches had had. All that came his way was news that a Relief Expedition had been sent and had broken up after Stanley's arrival at Zanzibar. Livingstone's son, Oswell, had been a member of the expedition, and like the others had decided not to press on. His father was shocked by this, and, even when he knew that, since the others had resigned first, Oswell would have had to have gone on alone, Livingstone did not forgive him. And when, several weeks later, Livingstone received two letters from Oswell, telling him that his prime purpose in coming to Africa had been to persuade his father to come home, an enraged Livingstone not only accused Os-

well of cowardice and duplicity but also described his letters as "the most snobbish and impertinent I ever received or read." Oswell, he continued, was "as poor a specimen of a son as Africa ever produced": a young man who "does not think of supporting himself by his own labour" but prefers "to run away home calling loudly for more money." Livingstone felt that at the moment when he stood poised to begin the most important and arduous of all his journeys, his family—Agnes excepted—far from encouraging him, were doing everything in their power to discourage him so that he would consent to come home and write another best seller for them to live off. That they might have been genuinely worried that unless he returned home, Africa would kill him, did not occur to him.

At last, on August 9, an advance party of Stanley's men marched into Unyanyembe, fifty-six men in all. Stanley had equipped each man with a musket and had provided ten kegs of powder and three thousand bullets. Flour, sugar, coffee, tea, numerous varieties of tinned food, a new journal, a chronometer, and a pile of Nautical Almanacs made up a part of the stores the men came with.

The first weeks of Livingstone's final journey were smooth in comparison with his experiences in 1866 and 1869. Nevertheless a series of minor misfortunes would together prove significant. First of all a case of dried milk was left behind at Unyanyembe. Then his ten cows were allowed to stray into a belt of tsetse and died as a result. Milk was the only food which restored Livingstone's health when he had dysentery, so these two misfortunes coming together did not augur well for the future.

The heat was so intense that the porters' bare feet were blistered and burned by the soil. In these conditions it was a mistake to hug the shores of Tanganyika, since this meant constant clambering up hills and out of valleys. But Livingstone was determined to map the southern part of the lake.

By the beginning of October they were nearing the southern end of Lake Tanganyika, and the hardships of climbing were over. The rains however were not far off and, although the going was easier, the country was thinly populated and food was hard to come by. On November 9, Livingstone's old problem of anal bleeding stopped them all for a few days.

As they pressed on south the food shortage increased, and a native guide warned that if they continued southwest the food situation would get worse. Reluctantly Livingstone allowed the guide to take

him to the western shore of Bangweolo. This journey of 170 miles was to take over a month, for day after day the rain fell. Streams burst their banks, flat land became swamp, and the party was held up for days on end trying to get canoes to cross the larger rivers.

Ironically when he did arrive near the western shore of the lake and when the guide told him where he was, he refused to believe him. He was convinced he was on the northeastern side of Bangweolo, this conviction due to the faulty longitudes he had taken on his first visit to the lake in 1868. Those observations had been forty miles too much to the west and so now he reckoned he was far east of the position the guide claimed to have brought him to. He wanted to get to the southern shore of the lake to make sure there were no sources south of it, before heading for Katanga as planned. Local natives told him the best way around the lake was to head southwest. To Livingstone, who imagined himself northeast of the lake, a southwesterly course seemed madness. Instead he would head east and get around that way. It was to prove a disastrous decision.

The longer he went on, the more confused he became. He expected water but found only endless reeds and mud. There was no high ground from which he might see any distance. By mid-January 1873 he had arrived at the northeastern side of Bangweolo, the point which he had thought himself at weeks before. Now he believed himself safe to head south and thus skirt the lake. If he had then been as far east as he believed himself to be, this decision would have been all right. But south from the northeastern shore of the lake led straight into the swamps, which stretched away almost a hundred miles to the southeast.

No landmarks that he had picked out on his previous journey were any use to him, for in the rains everything looked completely different. In early February the sky cleared enough for him to make new observations for latitude. Had he believed his new observations, all might have been well, but these new figures proved that he had been mistaken all along. This Livingstone would not accept. In his view the observations he had made in 1868, in far better conditions, were more likely to have been right. From that time on he was doomed. For the next two months he would never again be sure where he was.

By January 1873 Livingstone's strength had reached a very low ebb. He was losing blood daily and with the constant cold and wet and the lack of milk and decent food there was no hope of his condi-

tion improving. The party rarely covered more than a mile and a half a day and even that was taxing their leader's powers to their limit.

Miraculously stoical though he was, the steady loss of blood and increasing weakness soon affected his thinking again. From now on he became more and more obsessive about the Nile and Herodotus' four fountains. Hopelessly lost, and by now bleeding slowly to death, Livingstone began writing dispatches to the Foreign Secretary —dispatches that would never be sent. Livingstone wrote as though he had already made his discovery.

But a week more in the constant rain, with no proper food and no warmth, weakened him still further, and by April 10 he had to admit the seriousness of his position. "I am pale, bloodless and weak from bleeding profusely ever since the 31st. of March last: an artery gives off a copious stream and takes away my strength. Oh! how I long to be permitted by the Over Power to finish my work."

At this time the canoes were abandoned and the party went on again on foot, moving southwest, away from the worst swamps, in a broad arc around the south of Bangweolo. Even in the face of his rapidly increasing weakness Livingstone was inclined to make light of the agonizing pain he was suffering: "Very ill all night, but remembered that the bleeding and most other ailments in this land are forms of fever. Took two scruple doses of quinine and stopped it quite." The next day, April 19, he wrote the greatest of all his many understatements: "It is not all pleasure this exploration."

On April 21 he knew that he was too weak to walk unassisted even a few steps, but he still tried to ride the surviving donkey. It was no use, as he soon discovered. After a few yards he fell to the ground exhausted and faint. His men then carried him back to his hut. Death was near now, but Livingstone still refused to recognize it. Seeing that he would not walk again, but knowing that he would not rest in one place, Chuma and Susi constructed a litter of *kitanda* for the remaining miles. For the next three days they carried the dying man on through the same flooded, treeless waste. On the 25th, when they reached a village, Livingstone summoned a number of local men and with great difficulty asked them whether they knew about a hill and four adjacent fountains. All shook their heads. Unable to conceal his grief, Livingstone dismissed them, explaining that he was too ill to continue talking. If the fountains existed, surely they would have known. To have come so far and to have suffered so much for yet another disappointment seemed intolerable.

By the next day no goats had been found and so no milk could be procured. Even so, Livingstone still wished to press on while life was left. Since by now he could not walk even to the door of his hut to reach his *kitanda* outside, he instructed the men to break down the wall of the hut and bring the litter up to his bed. After several hours a substantial river had to be crossed, and, since none of the canoes were wide enough to take the *kitanda,* he had to be lifted.

Once on the western bank they approached the village of Chitambo, a local chief; they were seventy miles S.S.E. of the southern shore of Lake Bangweolo. His followers did what they could to make his final resting place comfortable. The bed was raised from the floor by sticks and grass and his medicine chest was placed by his side. It was agreed that somebody should keep constant watch with him night and day.

On April 30 Chief Chitambo came to pay a courtesy visit but Livingstone sent him away. He was too ill to speak. He dozed through the day, only occasionally troubling his people. Then, in the evening, he asked Susi suddenly: "How many days is it to the Luapula?" Susi told him three. A little later, as if in great pain, he half sighed "Oh dear, dear!" and then fell asleep. Shortly after this, Majwara, the boy left to watch, fell asleep. He did not wake for three or four hours.

At 4 A.M. he burst into Susi's hut, in terrible distress, begging him to come at once. Susi roused Chuma and three others, and the six of them went to their master's hut. The sky was faintly tinged with the first light of dawn. A dim glow came from the entrance of the hut; a candle stuck with its own wax on to the top of a box was still burning. To their amazement Livingstone was no longer in his bed. As he had felt death coming, with a final superhuman effort, he had somehow managed to crawl from his bed into a kneeling position. For a moment Susi thought he was praying. The men did not go in at once but waited for some movement. When they saw none, one went in and touched the kneeling man's cheek. It was almost cold. David Livingstone had been dead for several hours.

For the sixty Africans, who had followed Livingstone's instructions without question since leaving Unyanyembe the previous August, the sudden loss of their leader, so far from their homes, could have proved catastrophic. But Chuma and Susi acted with a calm decisiveness that no European could have bettered.

Susi knew that the easiest and safest course would have been to

bury the body and return to the coast. He was well aware of the powerful superstitions held by many tribes about corpses. At best, if they were discovered carrying a body through some villages, they would be fined heavily; at worst they might be attacked as witches. But Susi, who had been chosen to lead the party by common consent, needed no time to make up his mind what he wanted to do. Whatever the risks involved, Livingstone's body should be carried to the coast and shipped to England for burial.

The day after Livingstone's death, Chuma went to see the local chief, Chitambo, and, hiding the fact that his master was dead, told him that the white man's followers wanted permission to build a place outside the village, since they did not like living among the huts; work began the same day. A group of huts was built within a palisade. Slightly apart from the domestic buildings, a separate hut was constructed. This structure was open to the sky at the top and had specially strong walls to keep out wild animals. Inside, the corpse was prepared for the journey. An incision was made in the abdomen, and the intestines and internal organs were removed, placed in a tin box, and buried. Jacob Wainwright, one of the Nassick boys, sent out with Stanley's men, read the burial service as the box was lowered into the ground. When taking out the intestines Chuma and Susi noticed a clot of blood several inches in diameter obstructing Livingstone's lower intestine. Such a large obstruction must have caused him horrifying pain.

To preserve the body, the Africans first placed salt in the open trunk and next allowed the corpse to dry for fourteen days in the sun—the dry season was beginning. When this was completed, the face was bathed in brandy, as an extra preservative, and when the body had been wrapped in calico and encased in a cylinder of bark, it was sewn into a large piece of sailcloth. Susi tarred the bundle to make doubly sure that it was watertight.

Susi's abilities as a leader were confirmed by the speed with which he led his party to Unyanyembe—five months. During that time ten men died. They suffered all the usual ravages of disease and on one occasion had to fight their way out of a hostile village.

Chuma was sent on to Zanzibar and there he discovered that Kirk was in England on leave and that Captain W.F. Prideaux was acting for him. Prideaux, on hearing that Livingstone's body was at Bagamoyo, dispatched a warship, H.M.S. *Vulture,* to collect the corpse. Although Prideaux was aware that these sixty Africans had

performed an amazing feat, he was completely at a loss as to what should be done. He was only standing in for Kirk, and was too timid to risk sending any of Livingstone's men back to England with the body without first getting the consent of the Foreign Office. So Prideaux decided that, rather than be blamed later for causing the Foreign Office unnecessary expense, he would pay the men—he had to do so out of his own pocket since Livingstone's last £1,000 had been spent—and send them to their homes. Prideaux in fact did not recover his money from the government until 1877. But the sixty Africans who had risked so much were not in a position to understand the acting consul's financial dilemmas. At great personal risk they had brought the body of a man, whom they supposed to be famous in his own country, to the coast, and they were being sent away with their wages. For Chuma, Susi, and Gardner it seemed a ludicrous ending to eight years' service. By the time the Royal Geographical Society struck commemorative medals for the sixty men the following year, they had all dispersed and very few ever received this reward, which they would never have understood anyway; cloth, beads, rifles, cattle would have been fine—but a medal! Chuma and Susi in the end did gain by their association with Livingstone. A year later, James "Paraffin" Young, who had given Livingstone such important financial aid, paid for his two most faithful followers to come to England to help edit the explorer's *Last Journals,* and fill in verbally any gaps in the narrative. After that they both returned to Zanzibar and became much sought-after caravan leaders.

One African attended Livingstone's funeral in Westminster Abbey and he ironically had only been with Livingstone since August 1872; Chuma and Susi arrived too late to see Livingstone buried.

CHAPTER 24

LIVINGSTONE AND THE BRITISH EMPIRE

The morning of April 15, 1874 was wet and windy, but shortly after dawn crowds started forming around the docks and quays of Southampton. By eight o'clock the mayor and aldermen of the town, dressed in their fur-trimmed robes, stood assembled on the quay. Behind them a military band was waiting, and not far away a company of the Royal Horse Artillery prepared to fire off 21-gun sa-

lutes at one minute intervals. The crowd all stood looking out to sea.

A few minutes before nine, the silhouette of a battered and insignificant-looking steamer was sighted at the mouth of Southampton water. The first of the salutes boomed out across the silent town, and the telegraph operators started eagerly tapping out the news. Through binoculars it was soon possible to see on the deck a coffin draped with a Union Jack. Beside the mayor and aldermen a small black boy had now taken his place and lifted up a placard decorated with sable rosettes and streamers, bearing the inscription: "TO THE MEMORY OF DR. LIVINGSTONE, FRIEND OF THE AFRICAN."

The body was conveyed from Southampton to London by special train, and that evening was examined at the headquarters of the Royal Geographical Society so that a positive identification could be made. After eleven months the features were unrecognizable, but the lump in the bone of the left humerus, which had been shattered by a lion nearly thirty years before, was perfect proof.

For the next two days the body lay in state at the R.G.S. building in Savile Row, and crowds filed past the coffin constantly. On April 18 burial took place in Westminster Abbey. The press acclaimed the hero and announced his virtues. Westminster Abbey has opened her doors to men who have played larger and greater parts in the history of mankind; but the feeling that afternoon was that seldom has been admitted one more worthy than the brave, modest, self-sacrificing, African explorer.

Livingstone's bravery, endurance, and self-sacrifice during his last years deserved tributes like this one. His dogged refusal to give up in the face of hopeless odds, his uncomplaining acceptance of agonizing pain, and finally his lonely death, conjure up images so powerful that his contemporaries' adulation seems, in retrospect, the only possible response. That any man could voluntarily have undergone such hardship seemed, and still seems, so remarkable that to ask whether he achieved his aims or deceived himself appears in the end almost churlish. The fact that Livingstone in his last years had allowed himself to accept as true what he had wanted to believe, rather than what his scientific observations suggested, seems to call for sympathy rather than criticism. Those who wept in the streets on the day of his funeral did not know that the Lualaba was not the Nile—had they, it is doubtful they would have cared. Knowledge of Livingstone's mistake would only have deepened for them the pathos of his death.

DAVID E. SCHERMAN

A DIFFERENT WOMAN

A condensation of the book by

JANE HOWARD

CHAPTER 1

PUT YOUR FEET UNDER MY TABLE

My mother and I had a sure instinct for riling each other, like stalking beasts in a forest. Once, in my adolescence, I can't remember why, I made her so mad she threw a hairbrush at me. Often, in those days, I would sigh heavily and say things in an annoyingly well-modulated voice like, "That's precisely what I *intended* to do, Mother," and although I was nearly thirty-six when she suddenly died of a stroke in 1971, there was still something of that tone between us.

There were other things about her, though. Once, endearingly I thought, she had a laughing fit in a Quaker meeting. She was an inspired maker of turkey stuffing, steamer-off of old wallpaper, refinisher of furniture, dressmaker for her granddaughter's toy bunnies, and arranger of dried weeds and pussy willows. She cared about the trees my father planted, and noticed owl's nests and the songs of bobwhites.

"It's a most gorgeous day," she wrote in the last letter I ever got from her. "You'd go out of your mind. The redbud and dogwood should be in bloom when you come here. If I hurry I can burn some leaves (pollute) before the church circle meeting at Corinne's." The sociable aspects of church meant more to her than the theological. She felt most herself, I think, in a roomful of approving others.

She had a litany she would repeat every night when my younger sister, Ann, and I were small: "I love you up to the sky and down again and around the world and back again." As unlovable as we sometimes were, I think she always did. When I would arrive home for a visit, there would always be a multicolored Crayola sign she had made, taped to the kitchen door. It said WELCOME HOME! YEA, JANIE!, as if I were a basketball team. And when my visit was

153

over, she would stand there at the airport gate waving until not only I but my airplane had vanished entirely from sight. Not everybody is a waver, but my mother definitely was. And before I left the house she would always repack my suitcase, a gesture I found at once thoughtful and inquisitive. Into it she would tuck a dishcloth she had just crocheted, or a box of Auntie Pearl's ranger cookies, or both.

Often, as we drove around the prairie, she would observe that pin oaks were her favorite trees, because they didn't know which way they wanted to go. Neither, a lot of the time, did we. Indecision seemed to be in our genes, like big feet and high foreheads. Okay, we had decided we would definitely go out for dinner, but where? A lot of what we decided would depend on how our hair looked that day, and how many comps we were likely to get. Comps—compliments—were at all times welcome.

"That's a pretty sunset," I might say as we drove along.

"Thank you," she would reply. The Blithe Spirit, she said her kinfolk used to call her, not only for such flashes of zaniness but because as a teenager and young woman she had gallantly, without much complaint, endured a long series of maladies. She had diphtheria, a tracheotomy, recurrent sinus trouble, and surgery which robbed her of her sense of smell.

With Ann and me, our mother was not often blithe, nor were we with her. It's odd. We were thought in our circles to be amusing, and so was she in hers, but regrettably seldom did we laugh together. We never developed enough rapport. Sometimes mothers and daughters do have strong rapport; I have seen it. But in those cases, the daughters seem less close to each other or to their brothers. Is it somewhere written that you can have real, ready access to your parents or else to your siblings, but not to both?

Although my mother was vain about her Davidow suit and her elegant engraved informals from Black, Starr & Gorham, and hardly ever could bring herself to throw out invitations to parties, she had a snakeboot side, too. "Snakeboot" has become family slang meaning unpretentious and practical, because snakeboots, with anklets under them, are often worn by my unpretentious, practical Aunt Millie in the Catoctin Mountains. It was snakeboot of my mother, for example, to stuff wadded-up toilet paper into the locks of the booths of ladies' rooms, so the next customer could get in free.

Friendship was her vocation. "Your mother," one of the neighbors once told me, "always thinks everybody is just darling." She wanted

to think so, anyway. She had, undeniably, a heart rather easily made glad. Another little litany she liked to recite went: "There's so much good in the worst of us/ And so much bad in the best of us/ That it hardly behooves a one of us/ To talk about the rest of us." She kept confidences; she did not gossip. Instead, she was always doing people, who in turn did her, preferably when her feet were under their tables, or theirs under hers.

Let me explain. "Do" means to take under one's wing, to shelter, succor, nurture, concentrate on, listen to, cause to feel central. "Hey, go do Dr. Covington, she's standing all alone over there," Ann or I might whisper to each other at a party. We all do and in turn are done by our friends, who are all, from time to time, our caseloads, just as we are theirs. We become caseloads when we are Worse. Worse is one of the three possible human conditions, applicable alike to men and nations. The others, as you might expect, are Better and The Same. This method of explaining things may lack refinement, but it offers a convenient shorthand.

"How's Julian?" I might ask Peggy.

"He's The Same," she might reply. "We're not going to have to do him just yet. But Liz is Better." (Julian's wife Liz, annoyingly enough, is always Better.)

These people constitute part of what if I were Jewish, which I sometimes wish I were, I could call my *mishpocha*. If I were a social scientist, which I almost never wish I were, I would call it my extended, as opposed to nuclear, family. By this is meant not just a string of unconnected wellwishers but a network of persons who have some kinship, by blood or spirit, not only with me but with each other as well.

New links must be forged as old ones rust. Only children should be brought up close to other only children, so they will not someday have to reminisce alone. We who are unmarried, only children of another sort, must deepen and cultivate our friendships until water acquires the consistency of blood, until we develop new networks as sustaining as orthodox families.

I have spent weekends and sometimes entire weeks with nuclear families, but I rely more on the *mishpocha*. It supplies me with the feeling of connectedness my mother got through her sixty-six years from her seven aunts, the Hoard sisters, four of whom still live together in Pomona, California, in the house their parents bought before 1920. Although Auntie Grace, the senior member of that household, is at this writing a regal ninety-seven, she still chainsmokes happily, does

paintings, and joins her three sisters in frequent games of Canasta.

One thing that sustains those women, I think, is their fierce sense of clan. Since the clan in question is a fertile and mobile one, keeping track of it can be a full-time job. On my father's side, too, there is a strong tradition of family reunions. Some sheep have strayed far from the fold, but everyone knows where they are and how to reach them.

"You girls," our mother would sometimes marvel, "have a precious thing going." It gratified her to see us laugh even when our humor was, shame on us, at her own expense. I guess I like to laugh about as much as I like anything, and I wish that my sister and certain others who can readily make me do so lived closer at hand, but mine is not, alas, a geographically feasible *mishpocha*. It is damnably inconvenient, in fact, to have its members scattered so widely. I'm not talking about people who say, "Lunch, *soon!*" Plenty of them are well within reach, as are a few whom I really do love. I'm talking about the remote others whose proximity would be such a delight that we tease each other by asking long distance questions like, "What are you wearing?" and "We'll be having the lamb tonight; why don't you come over?" as if "over" didn't mean a couple of thousand miles.

On Sunday, April 25, 1971, Suzanne Szasz and I were too busy running around Milwaukee in our rented yellow Mercury to think of calling the Ramada Inn for messages. Suzanne was taking pictures and I was getting quotes for the story *Life* had assigned us to do on feminism in the heartland. A couple more days ought to wrap it up, we agreed over a leisurely German dinner. Then we drove to a 7 P.M. meeting at the Non-Violent Feminist Center. That was where I heard the news.

My thoughts and heart pounded as I drove the 250 miles toward Springfield, asking myself: What's a stroke, anyway? Did people recover from massive cerebral hemorrhages? Dying? Dead? Me, a motherless child? How had I lived this long without losing anyone close? If it has to happen, isn't this a good way? Is there ever a good way? Why hadn't I looked more attentively at the old magazines she had brought up from the basement, just to show me, the last time I saw her?

I arrived at the hospital, the same one where Ann and I were born, at about 2 A.M. "Her toe just twitched," said the nurse in the intensive care room. "That might be a good sign." But Ann and I could

tell that there wouldn't be any good signs. Dad and Ann's husband David had gone home, as I did after a couple of hours, but Ann refused to. When I did arrive home, just a while before dawn, my father came downstairs in his pajamas and said, "Well, she sure raised a couple of fancy daughters, anyway."

It was over. Neighbors arrived with casseroles and pies. "We thought a lot of your mom," they assured us. Relatives came. We made decisions. King James, not Revised. Bach, don't you think? That Friday I witnessed the burial of my mother's ashes in the Bangor, Iowa, cemetery, which is a secluded and pretty place, if you like cemeteries.

The death of my own mother made me feel like a deck of cards being shuffled by giant, unseen hands. Parents, however old they and we may grow to be, serve among other things to shield us from a sense of our doom. As long as they are around, we can avoid the fact of our mortality; we can still be innocent children. When a parent goes, half of that innocence goes, too. Something, someday will replace that innocence, maybe something more useful, but we cannot know what, or how soon, and while we wait, it hurts.

Since this was the spring of 1971, I saw my own hurt, or something akin to it, multiplied wherever I looked, not by private grief but by a public and resolute assault on a whole matrix of attitudes about the female sex. It was not only personally, I began to realize, that I would have to do some overdue growing up. I was a thirty-six-year-old motherless child and that was too bad, that was something I would have to get used to, but I was also going to have to try to figure out what it meant to be a woman.

One afternoon I sat in a bar in Greenwich Village, talking of such matters with the wife of a colleague. "I used to think I was happy," she told me, "but suddenly I started wondering: was I really? All of a sudden we're being put down. Maybe they're right, the people who say we're jerks. Maybe I really *am* stupid. After all, all I went to was high school. This past year I decided that's it, no more, I'm going to be me; it always worked before, it better work now. Then I thought, 'Oh, Christ, I really *am* becoming neurotic.' This is ridiculous, this Women's Lib. It's really screwing me up."

Needless to say there are those who find it anything but ridiculous. Another woman I chanced to talk to, whose job is to travel around the country recruiting nurses, could not say enough for the new exhilaration she found wherever she went. "In middle America," she

said (using the term sociologically), "women are a lot more ready than they used to be to try new things. They're listening more and seeing more and feeling a lot more impatient with what they used to think were their limits. They'll never be the same."

She was right, I think. Women won't ever be the same. I have hardly found a one of late who has not to some degree been affected by the new, inescapable tidal wave of feminism. Even those who loathe it, and they are many, can hardly deny it. Nor can men. One of this movement's male champions, a forty-four-year-old musician I know, delivered some impromptu thoughts on this subject.

"Women's Liberation," he said, "is much bigger than the black revolution or the proletarian revolution or, so far as I'm concerned, anything in my time. It's changed my whole life, my whole way of looking at people and at myself. I wish I had learned sooner that I didn't have to measure up to the image of Don Juan or Gary Cooper, that it wasn't sissified or girlish of me to love and need someone. But there are still a lot of men my age who have to bluster along."

Aren't there just. "Oh, kiddo, look," I heard a junior high school principal say, "Women have it easy. There's a lot less pressure on women. They don't know how to take orders, follow a chain of command, be obedient. I've got a wife and I bought her a car—now *that's* what I call liberation. She can go wherever she wants. I'm the one who has to worry about gas and insurance. A man's got to get out of the sack every morning whether he feels like it or not, but a wife can just lay there and dawdle with magazines for an hour or two. Women can just sit and chew the rag, while a man's got to *produce*. Women of today have lost what the older generation had: love and respect for their husbands. . . .in the old days, the man was boss. . ."

My own thoughts on this omnipresent subject often involved my mother. Quite often I wish that we had talked to her, and she to us, less guardedly. What, I wonder, were we all afraid of? Why was there so much pretense on both sides?

Maybe it is to atone for my own pretense, my own evasions, that I have been preoccupied since my mother's death with what I hope has been honest talk with surviving women. Maybe that is why I have been traveling around this country with a dogeared *Rand Mc-Nally Road Atlas* and an uncommonly thick address book. I go around calling up people whose names are in that book, visiting with them, listening.

Sometimes I wonder if there is any place I truly belong.

Springfield, where I was born, to which my parents returned only after I left home? Chicago, where I sold Kool-Aid and bought war stamps? Winnetka, where I went to dancing school and baby-sat? Ann Arbor, where I was talked out of depledging the sorority after all, but spent most of my time at *The Daily*? New York, the only city in which I have ever voted? Surely not those distant other places which I have passed through just long enough to say phrasebook things, all in the present tense.

But given a choice, and I guess I have been given a choice, I have so far preferred brief bivouacs to being trapped. It is hard for me to resist going anywhere, but the places I like best to visit are those with the thinnest phone books. Perhaps because I am not very rooted myself, I am most charmed where roots are deep, and the smaller the town, it seems, the deeper they grow. I mourn, incidentally, the loss of postmarks. On two occasions I have driven miles out of my way just so I could send postcards from Bumble Bee, Arizona. The last time I was in Bumble Bee I visited for a bit with the postmistress.

"Many people stop by here?" I asked.

"Not too many," she admitted. "Day like this, I wouldn't be surprised if you'd be the only customer I had."

"Don't you get lonesome?"

"Oh, no. I bring my ironing."

I wish I had talked more with that lady (I am sure she would wish to be thought of as a lady), but one of the lessons I am slowly coming to accept is that it is in fact not possible to go everywhere, meet everyone, and do everything. One must choose from the options, however painful the act of choice may be.

I wish I had talked more with my Aunt Martha the last time I saw her, too. Aunt Martha takes a folding chair with her to the forty-yard line of high school football games in Cambridge, Minnesota. I think she could tell me a lot I would like to hear. So could the very young woman who was leaning, crying, against a frail new tree for a long time at my street's block association fair last spring. So could most of the American women. There are 105 million of us.

My quest, if I had talked at any length with these women, would have been to try to find out more about the texture of their lives, whom and what they loved, what was on their minds, and in what ways they were like and unlike each other and the rest of us: what it is, if anything, that is unifyingly "American" about us.

These are among the things I have had on my mind in the course

of talks I have had in the past two years, with women and ladies and girls and gals and broads and chicks and matrons in zip codes all over the country. Few whom I talked to were especially famous or especially militant or especially anything. Certainly none of them was on any list of Most Admired Women, except maybe now, in some cases, my own.

This book is, by design or deliberate lack thereof, more a patchwork quilt than a balanced, definitive survey. My experiments along these lines never led to any foolproof formula, so what I did was play it by ear. Sometimes I would just walk up to a strange woman in a public place, gulp, and ask if I might visit with her for a while. Other times elaborate advance arrangements had been made. Some talks lasted less than an hour, and other times I would hang around for a week. Usually I had a crumpled list of questions somewhere in my purse, questions like, "What's the most you've ever spent on a dress?" But as time went on I referred to these less and less.

Question-and-answer interviews seem to me a stultifying approach to colloquy. If you want to find out what is on someone's mind, you don't sit there staring at her and asking what she thinks are the central issues facing her community today. Take a drive around the mountain together, or have her teach you how to make popovers, or at least go with her while she picks up the dry-cleaning. Try, if you can, to see for yourself where she lives and with whom and to get some sense of how she and they seem to feel about each other. And never dare to suppose, however much rapport may develop, that you are getting anywhere near to the core of her soul. Because the more a woman talks, however candidly and trustingly, the more mysterious and complex she proves to be. "What would happen," Muriel Rukeyser asks in a book of poems called *Speed of Darkness*, "if one woman told the truth about herself? The world would split open." Perhaps it would at that.

CHAPTER 2

NO CHOCOLATE EGGS THIS EASTER

B ut you're not from here *originally*," fellow New Yorkers sometimes say, almost accusingly, when they learn that I have been in their city since the fall of 1956. They are quite right. It's a good

thing I have no yen or cause to conceal my midwestern origins, because to do so would be exhausting, involving at the very least a lot
of elocution lessons, and maybe impossible. If I should live to be
ninety-six without ever again beholding a cornfield or eating a sweet
roll (as opposed to a Danish) over a copy of the *Chicago Tribune,* I
would still look and sound midwestern. I do not, it is true, say things
like "real fancy" and "prit-near" and "extry." But I am marked for
life with the amply nourished lantern-jawed look, the tell-tale broad
"a," and the resonant "r" of the prairies. And if you ask me if I'd like
some more turkey stuffing, I'll answer "shirr."

Anyone given to crossing state lines these days knows how deplor-
ably similar American cities are getting to look. Their downtowns are
reached by streets clotted with franchised tacos, donut shops, karate
parlors, and intersections with plastic-pennanted gasoline stations on
all four corners. The more I see of this sort of thing, the luckier I feel
that in my own past there figured a town so tiny and proud that a sign
on its outskirts could boast "CLEMONS, IOWA. POP 200. SIZE OF A
DIME, HEART OF A DOLLAR."

Now I did not technically grow up in Clemons, but I put in a lot of
impressionable weeks on a farm near there. The farm, called Home-
lands, consists of the same 640 acres my father's grandfather home-
steaded and is presided over to this day by my Aunt Janet. My
mother's childhood was more nomadic since her father worked for
the Milwaukee Railroad, but she was indisputably midwestern too,
and with such a heritage I ought to be much abler than I feel to
define what distinguishes us from people who came of age in other
regions. It pretty well goes without saying that we are not as charming, and need not be as defensive, as those from the South, that we
are not as breezy and effusive as westerners, nor as reticent as eastern Yankees. Landlocked, we were raised to wariness of things and
people and ideas from afar. But we were also brought up equidistant
from two oceans and nothing seems inaccessible to us.

Nor is the Mother Midwest inaccessible to us, her exiled children,
at least not to those of us in whom was stamped early an instinctive
family loyalty. One way or another, you go home a lot if you are such
a midwesterner. If you fly, you can tell the minute you step off your
plane at O'Hare in Chicago that you aren't in the East anymore.
Trousers are baggier, neckties are narrower, men's hair is cut shorter,
waitresses and cabdrivers are friendlier. Strangers, quick to offer
thumbnail autobiographical sketches, expect the same of you.

161

Genealogy is an honored calling in my Midwest. Ann and our cousins and I would be drilled as if for a surprise quiz with the names of our antecedents. William D. governed a state, Patrick H. superintended a railroad, James R. was once seriously considered for Secretary of Agriculture. We learned of these and of any number of humbler men who threshed grain, milked cows, kept books, preached, taught school, and once in a while were wards not, God forbid, of the state but of each other. And we would learn the names of their stalwart womenfolk, who kept (and still do keep) track of family pregnancies, graduations, weddings, illnesses, and plans for the summer.

It was often implied that if we couldn't think of anything nice to say we had better keep still, and that controversy was somehow in poor taste. Why, my mother would ask us, did we always have to *analyze* everything? Why were we so critical? During my high school years the parents of a couple of my friends were divorced, but those friends never, ever talked about it, and nobody else did, either. Monogamy, in our sheltered world, was the overwhelming norm. Not until years later did I hear the rumor that Mr. Baldwin, down the street, might not have died in his office, as we had been told, but in the arms of his paramour.

Books were held in high esteem. I developed a precocious taste for them, perhaps in part to vex my mother, who often said, "Shirr, shirr, shirr, I'd like to read more, too, if I had time." Before she married my journalist father, when they both were twenty-eight, she had worked for a while as a newspaper reporter herself. But for one reason or another, by the time she and I got at all acquainted, she was more preoccupied with things like cleaning up the house really well because tomorrow Julia, the cleaning woman, was coming.

When my father could take time off from covering the state legislature and other political matters, the whole family would take trips south or east or west by car. "All roads," my mother used to observe, "lead to the farm." "Hello-grandmother-and-granddaddy," we were trained like seals to chant on arrival at the farm, "it's wonderful to be here." It was also quite restful. On many hot afternoons it was an event of some note when a car drove past. "Well," someone would comment, "I wonder who *that* could have been? It looked like Delbert's car, but he just went to town this morning to get the separator. Why would he be going again?"

World War II seemed less important than, say, thank-you notes.

162

"No chocolate eggs this Easter," my mother wrote in her diary in 1942. "The country is just going crazy," she had written on Pearl Harbor Day. "Nothing counts now except our families. Wonder what is in store for us and our little girls and what kind of world they will live in. God bless them. All I hope is that all my dearest ones will be well and safe in this crazy world of ours, and that we can always keep our little group safe and intact."

We sang lines like, "Hi-hi-hee for the field artiller-ee," and drew caricatures of Hitler, Mussolini, and Tojo, and seemed to be sick a lot. "Drove to Glencoe," my mother noted one day. "Ann *didn't* get carsick. Bob's new boss may take us to the Pump Room Saturday. Hope it will work, I'm crazy to go."

Tratty, as we called our distant cousin Edna Tratt, would drive out to Winnetka from Chicago on Sunday afternoons to keep my mother company. Tratty was long divorced and had twin sons, one of whom had died. She went to a lot of movies and played bridge with socialites and colonels. To Ann and me she seemed the very height of urbane sophistication, living as she did in a sunless apartment on the Near North Side all done in dusky French rose and smoked mirrors.

Tratty would sit there at our piano, on those long Sunday afternoons, and play "I'll See You Again" and "Alice Blue Gown," with considerable feeling. Later we might go for a drive in Tratty's car past the houses of the Old Money and eat out at the Indian Trail, waiting until ten or so for our father to come back from work.

If anyone ever said anything unkind about the *Tribune,* our mother told Ann and me, "just tell them it's your bread and butter," which, since for most of his career our father worked there, it was. Mother was not much given to philosophical discourse as to why elephants were so much better than donkeys; they just were. In 1970, when my father retired, his associates planned an enormous testimonial dinner. They gave him a good selection of plaques and a check which he turned over to a college scholarship fund. When the speeches were over someone came up to me and said, "Well! I saw you sitting with a *Democrat!,*" as if I had taken up with a Maoist pygmy.

Midwesterners who come to New York have as much in common, are as much *landsmen,* as people who have come from County Mayo or the Ukraine. When we get together, we talk of old folkways. With my friend Russell Oberlin, who comes from Ohio, I have often discussed midwestern attitudes toward matters of taste. Russell remembers how, when he was a boy in Akron, certain of his neighbors

thought that aluminum storm doors with an initial on the front were "just a little nicer" than plain ones. "We didn't fall for that *ourselves*," Russell says in quick defense of his own family. "After all, we were Episcopalians. But the phrase 'just a little nicer' is one I can remember having heard all my life." I can too. My own first such memories concern snapshots; I remember being told that those with a dull finish were just a little nicer than glossy ones. My mother probably told me this as she sat pasting the products of her cherished Brownie box camera, which really *was* brown and which later was replaced by an Instamatic, into Ann's and my separate but equal Kodak books.

Those books grew chubby, as did we, with the passage of time. There we still are, The Girls, gazing up in a snapshot at the Rockefeller Center fountain, in stunning homemade twin denim costumes. The Girls: at the seashore or the skating rink with friends, on the farm with cousins, secured forever in albums with those black Nu-Ace corners. And if ever anyone in any group snapshot did not look his or, much more likely, her best, do you know what Eleanor Howard would do? Why, she would go get her manicure scissors and deftly trim off a fat hip here or a double chin there and paste the picture in with Elmer's glue instead of Nu-Ace corners. She would write who it was in white ink. She was quite fond of monograms, name tapes, and all forms of identification.

Once, when someone asked what she would save if the house were burning down—what possession, in other words, she cherished most—she said she would run for her husband. No, whomever she was talking to said, what *thing?* Easy: Ann's and my baby books, as opposed to Kodak books, mine with a blue cover and Ann's with a white, full of tiny footprints and first Valentines and cute sayings. Could any two children of our station and period have had a more extensively documented childhood?

Winnetka is a handsome town. Noble trees arch over roads and lanes well tended by people most of whom moved there specifically to give their children the proverbial advantages. Autumn Saturdays we would sit on the bleachers outside New Trier High School and sing the school song. At Christmas there would be mother-daughter teas and maybe tasteful little dances. Our vices, those of which I was aware anyway, were laughable. Some of us experimented on the sly with nail polish, but it was considered "cheap" to smoke, much less drink even beer, before college.

We had crushes on unattainably older boys—"But of course it's hopeless, he's a *senior*"—and passed more evenings than it is comfortable to recall either baby sitting or else having giggly slumber parties. At these we would shriek when boys tapped playfully on the windows, talk soulfully about Keats and Edna St. Vincent Millay, and bewail the frizziness of our godawful home permanents. It was little comfort that these permanents, as their name did not imply, lasted about a semester. We'd always have another and would sit there feeling doomed, passing curlers shaped like chicken thighbones to our beautician mother.

Summers, while our classmates sent us postcards from Banff and Wianno, Dad got jobs for Ann and me in offices in Chicago, so we could help pay for tuition. One summer, loath to use my father's pull in job hunting, I decided to find something myself in "publishing" and was hired to write form letters to people who had not paid their installments for F.E. Compton's Pictured Encyclopedia. A month or so later I was fired for making up my own form letters.

Some of my friends had been dispatched in glory to Mount Holyoke and Smith. I, with lower grades and leaner funds, made it as far east as Ann Arbor, which even in the apathetic fifties was a vast and rich cafeteria of a place, where midwesternism was diluted. I met not only rural Michigan Elementary Ed majors who made light of lesson plans but New York Jews who seemed far more exotic than turbaned foreigners, with their talk of *yentas* and *tsurus*.

I got a bachelor of arts degree in a singularly anticlimactic rainy day ritual and not long afterward took an all-night, sit-up train to New York City to seek, as they say, my fortune. Dad was out of town the evening I left, covering the convention in San Francisco, but Mom determined that I should have a proper send-off. Before I got on the sit-up train she took Ann and me to dinner at the Pump Room.

CHAPTER 3

MARK VAN DOREN, THE DALAI LAMA,
AND JIMMY STEWART

L ord Baden-Powell, founder of the International Scouting movement, is said to have decided whom to marry on the basis of her tracks. His heart stood still, apparently, the moment he first be-

held the future Lady Baden-Powell's footprints in the dirt. On behalf of the unattached women in late twentieth-century America, I both salute him and envy him his moment of epiphany. I wish our search were anywhere nearly as simple. But in these complex times, with so many of our streets being paved, it is not easy to locate the partners of our dreams. Our dreams themselves, to make matters worse, are mystifying and confused. I once heard a woman, more sure of herself than many, declare that she personally was on the lookout for "a good dresser who knows how to order." But most of us ask more. Once some friends and I made a list of the Forty Most Important Qualities in the Opposite Sex. The Quality that sticks most in my mind, after quite a few years, is Affinity for Wood.

Two or three times a year, at about four-thirty in the morning, my phone rings and I groggily pick it up to hear the voice of my sentimental old roommate, Bonnie. Having had several drinks in Redondo Beach, California, where it is three hours earlier, Bonnie wants to know whether I have met Mr. Right yet and to reflect with nostalgia on the good old days when we first came to New York and lived together. In those years she and I and most of our friends were programmed to prosper in our chosen professions and to find men, not necessarily in that order.

Our programming had been subtle and happenstance, for the most part, but every now and then my mother, who was by default the source of most of my instructions along these lines, would let slip some specific hint. My sister and I were not only to empty-the-garbage-and-sweep-the-floor, leave the kitchen spotless, try if possible to be dainty and have tiny waists but, "settle down someday with a big, handsome, wonderful hunk of an Ivy Leaguer."

In the early part of my quest I therefore looked with concupiscent awe upon that species, not yet aware that Ivy Leaguers could have clenched fists and clenched minds just like the boys back home. I certainly rejoice for my late mother's sake that, totally though I failed to make this dream of hers come true, Ann at least bestirred herself to locate a handsome hunk of, if not an Ivy Leaguer, a Big Ten man.

My mother more fundamentally hoped, she said, that we would find men who loved us as much as our father did her, and vice versa. Apparently they really did love each other. At least after she died, when Ann and I went through all her stuff (a more painful ritual, by the way, than any of the formal ceremonies), we kept finding Valentines they had sent each other and notes he had left her saying things

like, "Good morning, it's a real nice day and I love you and hope you sleep late."

Had the occasion arisen, Mother would have given me three further lessons she vouchsafed to Ann: always have placemats on the table when he comes home, never go to bed mad, and always be home when the kids come home from school. Well, fine, although the latter point may be arguable, but where were we supposed to look for the senders of such Valentines? How would we know if we met one? Would the earth move? Once, when she quizzed me about some man whose name I had mentioned, she asked me what his background was.

"Well," I began, "he went to Yale Law School. ... "

"He sounds *wonderful*," declared my mother.

My guarded letters home did not go into great detail about my efforts to find any sort of big, wonderful hunk, but I did once allude in my mother's presence to having spent a weekend off somewhere with a man. Correctly intuiting that there had been no chaperone at hand, she winced and said, "Well, that sure wasn't the way we did it in *my* day."

"How *did* you do it in your day?" I somehow never asked. "Please," I never could quite bring myself to implore, "tell me how you're supposed to do it. Not how to be an English major, not how to work up a good case of guilt, not how to be career-oriented, but how to live!"

I suppose if she had known she would have told me, or the word would have got around somehow. I guess none of my friends at Katharine House on West Thirteenth Street knew either. Katharine House was a residence for genteel, allegedly young persons, run by something called the Ladies' Christian Union. That was where Bonnie and I and two other recent college graduates gravitated together in the fall of 1956 to plot our escape.

The West Ninth Street apartment we moved into was like a stage set for some comedy about ingenues in the big city, a drama which we proceeded to enact. The place had two tiny bedrooms and an air of claustrophobia when we were all home at once, so we tried not to be. With easily acquired new friends we went to Rienzi's coffee shop and to bars like the White Horse and Romero's and Julius's and, on special occasions, to Marie's Crisis and the Five Spot. We also kept up on lectures at the New School and woodwind quintet concerts around town.

I craved, and finally could afford, more space. I moved into a third-floor floor-through on Perry Street, with two other roommates instead of three, and a room of my own. My room had an enchanting view of other people's back gardens and its own fireplace, which was astonishing luck, but there was a catch: there was no other way for anyone to get to the bathroom. Nobody minded much, though.

One morning I woke up and decided I was sick of having any roommates at all. I went out with *The Times* real estate section and signed a lease for the first apartment I looked at, a fifth-floor walkup at Fourteenth Street and Seventh Avenue. Moving meant I had to acquire furniture of my own, among other things a bed.

"*Double*, huh?" Bonnie observed when she saw it.

"Same price as single at Gimbel's," I said defensively.

"Yeah, right, sure." Only very privately, say among ex-roommates, was it conceded that a hale unmarried woman in the second half of her twenties might succumb to an occasional craving not to sleep alone.

In those years I was starting to write bylined articles for *Life*, because it was clear that I was supposed to, and a number of Dear John letters, because it was not at all clear that I was ready at that point to marry. The very idea of going steady seemed alarming enough. I announced an odd triumvirate of heroes: Mark Van Doren, the Dalai Lama, and Jimmy Stewart. These, I said, were my ideal men. It figured. Homage to the cinematic idol of my youth, along with wistfulness at having been born too late for the grand old days at Columbia's English Department, and too soon for Hare Krishna. Totally unrealistic expectations, and therefore totally safe.

I felt scared whenever things got complicated with the actual men—boys as I believe they were often still called—who did enter my life. Hence the Dear John letters. Dear Lloyd, You deserve someone better, and besides our metabolisms are different. Dear Louis, You're too old. Dear Jerry, You're too married. No, Al, I said NO. "Wise?" Al once asked rhetorically. "This girl knows *all* the answers." In fact I knew damned few. I did not, as they say, know even the questions.

"Pardon my male tendencies," an Ivy Leaguer named Tim once memorably said at the end of an evening, as he began a tentative assault on my person. "Why, Tim," another friend reported having once said to him under similar circumstances. "What are you *doing*?" In God's name what did she think he was doing? What did any of us

think we were doing? Why were we not born in time of coeducational dormitories and reality?

Some chord in me responded when my friend Grace once said she always felt she was supposed to be Daddy's boy. As the older daughters we were both certainly, though never intentionally, given the idea that our mission in life was to achieve. Just as unconsciously, our younger sisters were exhorted to be popular and pretty.

But slowly, a decade before consciousness-raising came along, we began to realize that even we, in our late-blooming way, could at times secrete a certain emanation we referred to as Musk. Musk was an ephemeral fragrance which could drive men mad with desire.

"If only," my friend Grace once mused, "I could turn my Musk on at will!" She had been enduring a long dry spell.

"The trouble with you," our other friend Andrea told Grace, "is that you don't get around enough."

"Andrea's right, Grace," I said. "You ought to get out of the rut you've been in."

"Why don't you let *us* plan some weekends for you?" Andrea said. "If you do what we tell you to, you'll find happiness."

"Happiness," I promised, "and romance. You won't feel like Daddy's boy any more, either." Andrea and I shared a strong managerial streak, a confidence that in small ways, if not large ones, we could make order from chaos. We set to work changing Grace's life.

The Modern Art Museum, we ruled, was a cliché. We dispatched Grace instead to the Museum of the American Indian, preposterously far uptown, where she might be found by some footloose ethnologist. Concerts at the Cloisters and the Frick were recommended, and on Sunday mornings she could have her choice of the hearty Unitarians, the pensive Quakers, or other houses of worship where services were conducted entirely in French, Greek, or sign language. You never knew. On Saturday we suggested she go on an Appalachian Mountain Club hike over some trail in the Berkshires. She did, and met a cardiologist whose effect on her own heart was salutary.

On a slip of paper stuck into an old journal I recently found this note, in my own hand: "Guilt about Ron. Guilt guilt guilt guilt guilt. Oh shit." I could not recall whether this particular attack of guilt pertained to restraint or to excess, but I did suddenly feel that those of us who were born in the middle 1930's would have grown up faster

and clearer-headed had we been given a less distorted, less idealistic picture of the opposite sex.

It turned out that not all the boys in our class were enchanted with this state of affairs either. At least Peter Yorkus had not been. Peter Yorkus was my classmate in high school, and I had not seen him in nearly twenty years when we suddenly were both asked to the same dinner party. I confessed to him, freed by the passage of time, that I had always secretly thought he was rather nice. He told me he had secretly thought I was too.

"Then why," I asked in exasperation, "didn't you invite me to the prom or anything? Do you know I never went to one of those damned proms?"

"Me neither," he said. "Come to think of it, I wish I had asked you. But I guess I was afraid."

I am much pleased to report that the general feeling these days is considerably less hectic and desperate. Anyway, it isn't pathetic anymore to be single. As a friend of mine had the wit to reply when someone asked if she were married, "Good God, no, are *you?*" As much as anything, an unmarried person nowadays is the object of envy. I have not felt for some time that I had to apologize for my state, to myself or to anyone else, nor that I must fill my unplanned hours with nonsensical encounters designed to prove (to whom?) that even I, though a firstborn, can be popular.

Not to say that I rule out the prospect of matrimony. That state is becoming so unfashionable, and I have all my life been so consistently out of step, that my time may well be drawing nigh. The subjunctive mood grows wearisome; commitment sometimes beckons. It's not that I want someone to watch over me; I want continuity. It is sobering, of course, to note how disillusioning how many other people have found such things, but I still might have to try it, someday, for myself.

CHAPTER 4

WHAT'S SO GREAT ABOUT SOFAS?

If I had an acre for every hour I have spent in rap sessions, I would own the equivalent of, at least, Connecticut. No issue was so complex that someone somewhere did not propose to unravel it in the

course of a simple five- or six-hour rap session, in which it did not go without saying (nothing went without saying) that everyone would let everything all hang out. I longed for silence, but it was my lot to heed and record and sometimes even organize rap sessions. At the very hour my mother lost consciousness, I was rapping about feminism in Milwaukee, with a new recruit to a group called the Non-Violent Feminist Co-Operative.

The women's movement had come to Milwaukee in 1968, when the small and self-described "hard core bunch of nuts" who founded the original chapter of the National Organization of Women decided to stage a sit-in at an all-male restaurant. The restaurant manager obligingly called them something like "Communist, Fascist trash," so silly a claim as to catch the eye of numerous housewives who had been reading Betty Friedan and wondering.

Before long women's consciousnesses were stirring in every neighborhood of Milwaukee. Over on Wells Street, across from a pornographic movie house, the West Side Women's Center painted giant flowers on its pink walls and threw open its doors. Everybody was invited in for coffee, to read magazines, to rap, and for lessons in driving, macramé, and nutrition. In one corner was a free clothing and toy exchange, with a sign that said TAKE WHAT YOU NEED, BRING WHAT YOU'RE THROUGH WITH.

What the West Side women were through with themselves was the coeducational Left. Most of them had come from the civil rights and peace movements, in which they had felt demeaned by their male colleagues. Their political aims had not changed, but they weren't going to be subordinate to men any more. They held no special brief for the nuclear family—"Ultimately," one said, "our goal is to smash it."—or for such established conventions as heterosexuality. The Non-Violent Feminist Co-Operative wasn't like that. Most of its members were middle-class housewives who had, or had had, or expected to have, tricycles cluttering their not very spacious front hallways. On their kitchen bulletin boards hung signs that read SHALOM and ANOTHER MOTHER FOR PEACE.

I first met Bede Yaffe over lunch and told her that I had been hearing so much talk about feminism that it was time for me to take a break and go someplace like the Milwaukee Zoo. At once she gave me the keys to her car and urged me to be off. I had a good time wandering around the zoo. On returning I reported to Bede the lyrics

of a song I had heard on the car radio: "Hey, little woman, please make up your mind/Come on into my world and leave your world behind."

"So," she said to me, "it's getting to you, too, is it?"

"Sort of," I said, "but I have an aversion to movements."

"Then how come you write about them so much?"

"Fair question," I said.

People never believed Bede at first when she told them that her oldest son was twenty-eight. She looked more like a Cub Scout den mother. When I first met her she had a part-time job at an art gallery, where the following fall there would be a one-woman show of her paintings.

Painting was coming to matter to her more and more. "When people say, 'Oh, painting, that's a nice hobby,' I'm just now starting to be able to reply, 'It's not a hobby, it's my *guts!*'"

For different reasons, latter-day sisterhood in Milwaukee seemed puzzling to friends of Bede Yaffe. They could not see why she had taken up what struck them as so unseemly a crusade. "You have everything you want," they told her. "Why this?"

She did "have" a lot. She dressed impressively, went to encounter groups, and talked of Jung and Krishnamurti. By her first husband she had three grown sons. Her second was a kind and prosperous businessman, with whom she lived in a comfortable house with a studio in which she could paint, sculpture, and make rugs.

"I felt like a misfit and a freak at first," Bede said, "because it seemed very radical and strange for me, who used to be afraid of my own shadow, to go around wearing buttons with equality signs and clenched fists. But I've always been a late bloomer. It's taken me a long time to realize a lot of things. Let me tell you how stupid I was when I was divorced after twenty-three years of marriage— which is one of the ghastliest experiences anyone can go through.

"I was so crushed and broken that when I went to the attorney all I could do was bawl and say, 'I don't want a penny of *his* money; I just want out.' It took that poor lawyer three or four months to make me see that I was *entitled* to some of that money—that I had put in twenty-three years of my life and raised three sons and been a good wife—and that he, as a lawyer, could not in good conscience let me go out without any money. Was I stupid! What if I'd been paid by the week for twenty-three years?

"Now people ask me, 'Does Frank give you *permission* to go to all

those meetings?' Well, he isn't exactly jumping for joy, but he's come to realize that if he can go away all the time on business trips, which he does, and play poker with the boys one night a month, and spend whole weekends in the fall watching football on TV, then I should be able to get away and do things that are important to me, too. It can be such a spiritual awakening. When you open yourself up, a whole world opens up to you. But maybe you have to suffer before you can know this. There's great suffering and loneliness in the upper middle class.

"I keep trying to tell people it's as important for men to be liberated as for women. I'm sure a lot of women of my age and station in life agree with our principles, but the connotations and the image scare them off."

By "connotations," Bede of course meant homosexuality, a word about as popular in Milwaukee as carcinoma. The subject was rarely discussed, but it did come up in the course of an impromptu rap session held in my room at the Pfister Hotel.

" 'Lesbian' is a potent, damaging label that scares a lot of women away," observed one of the women who came to this *salon*.

"But it's one of the most important steps toward liberation," argued another of my guests. "For most women at least a try at a partially sexual relation is a step toward liberation. It's silly to talk about trust if you don't go all the way. Just being able to touch, hold hands, hug a woman is a huge step."

"But," broke in a woman from the Non-Violent Feminist Cooperative who sounded a little nervous, "you have to be able to go that far without going farther."

"Nonsense," said a West Side woman who was holding a friend's hand. "The only answer when someone asks if there are a lot of Lesbians in the movement is 'Yes, and right on.' "

"But since this is the *key* taboo," said her friend, "we'd better quit emphasizing it, or we'll never get power."

"You don't really think *all* men are oppressors, do you?" I asked one of the women from the West Side.

"Some of them may be coming out of it," she answered, "but how long is it going to take? What would have happened to the black race if they'd waited for the whites to come around?"

"But if you're involved with a man," said an NVFC member, "you can recondition him."

"Or else leave him."

"It's like the difference between reupholstering an old sofa and buying a new one."

"Or maybe having none at all. What's so great about sofas?"

"Come on, how can a straight woman get along without a man?"

"I have, for over a year."

"Aren't you—well, horny?"

"No. I'd rather have no sex at all than sex without love. Sometimes I think celibacy may be an even bigger taboo than lesbianism."

"But a whole *year*?"

"It takes practice. You have to learn to love yourself."

Until quite recently, Linda Majchszak had no use for the movement. "I was totally against Women's Liberation," she said, "because I felt I already *was* liberated and all the organizations were a waste of time. But then I went through some terrible changes, and I'd wake up crying and thinking, 'My God, it's true, I really *am* oppressed.'

"Oh, I could tell you so many times I've been angry, since I've been into Women's Lib. This one male I knew wouldn't bring back the facial sauna I lent him. 'I thought I'd be doing you a favor,' he said, 'taking away one of your supposedly feminine articles, now that you're liberated.' Now isn't that ridiculous?"

The movement, Linda said, had helped her realize the error of her previous assumption "that all other women were giddy, stupid, fluttering butterflies, or competitors, or both." She also realized that a lot of men she had thought were her friends really only wanted to seduce her. Lately she had been trying some experiments. "I notice that men don't like it when I turn the tables and put *my* arm around *them*, or give *them* a pat on the rear end, or suggest to *them* that we go out for dinner." At her own expense, because "my father wants me to *marry* an attorney, not be one," she was putting herself through pre-law courses.

Other changes the NVFC had brought were spectacular only cumulatively, not in themselves. Carolyn Mueller wasn't sorting her husband's and children's socks any more—"They can just all find their own or go barefoot." Patti Novak had quit plucking her eyebrows. Sue Williams, who looked, and for most of her life had acted, like a madonna, had told a man at a party to go fuck himself when he made disparaging remarks about his wife who "had it easy," staying home with their three children while he went off to conventions in the Caribbean.

174

Steve Kutner lost four buttons off his sport jacket, and his NVFC wife Jan had said, "Look, I hardly know any more about buttons than you do, and what I do know I am now about to teach you. I'll sew on three and then you do the fourth, okay?" It was okay, except with Jan's cousin, "the one I gave *Sisterhood is Powerful* to for Hanukkah. You know what she said? She said 'How emasculating! How castrating!' "

"Oh, that word 'castrating,' " said another feminist. "I used to play Ping-Pong with some guys in an office where I worked, and if I won, they'd talk about castration. If their balls are that fragile, who needs them? Who wants to spend a whole life with someone like that?"

"Marriage brings sex and social approval: a lot of women only get married to have the stigma of old-maidiness removed. But who needs it, if it means playing games, stopping your growth and whining?"

"Who even needs dates? Dates are just one miserable big play-act. If you could really be comfortable and yourself, okay, but that game-playing business I can't stand. When you act like yourself men are threatened."

"Hey, *girls!*" said a regressing NVFC member.

"Not girls, women."

"Well, hey *women*, do you know how we're *sounding*?"

"How? Like manhaters?"

"Manhating is a stage," said a seasoned feminist. "You get over it. Anyway, when men get used to the idea of liberation, they're relieved. It takes a load off everybody's shoulders. Sometimes I wish I were meeting my husband now for the first time, instead of thirteen years ago, when I did."

"Would you still marry him?"

"I think I would, but I'd like to have grown up first."

CHAPTER 5

WHEN SHALL I WASH MY HAIR?

Why, that darling girl," my mother once said of someone we knew, "why should *she* have to go to a psychiatrist?" Because the darling girl was having trouble putting one foot in front of the other, that was why, but such unsettling ambiguities were not something my mother wished to confront. Neither, for a long time,

did I. I brought with me to New York the firm midwestern prejudice that only gibbering looneys went to shrinks: that if you were reasonably bright, and had friends who would listen to you, you ought to be able to figure out your troubles for yourself.

But time chipped away at this notion. The tussles and minuets and fencing matches of which my life seemed to consist became awfully repetitious. Maybe there were patterns I wasn't seeing, or was afraid to recognize. I don't think I've ever had what could be called even a marginal nervous breakdown, but I did burst into sentimental tears once over the lyrics of "My Grandfather's Clock Was Too Large for the Shelf"—surely a danger signal, I thought—and I did keep having these two recurring dreams. In one, upon discovering a whole room in my house (sometimes it was an apartment) which I had never noticed before, I would wonder with urgent panic how that room should be furnished. In the other dream, I had just boarded some train or plane or ship bound for a remote destination I suddenly realized I had no wish whatever to visit, but it was too late to turn back and go home.

I figured it might not be a bad idea to hire some wise navigator to point out the shoals where my craft was prone to get stuck. Walter G. Dyer M.D. proved a providential choice, if hardly a showy one. His thinning gray hair is not combed forward to give an illusion of youth: it is obviously tended by a neighborhood barber, not a stylist. His eyes, blue and kind, are what one notices about him. So is his perspective, which soon came to seem as exalted as his office, eighteen floors above the park.

One day I wore a wig I had just bought to his office. Even Dr. Dyer, not ordinarily one for *ad feminam* small talk, observed that I seemed to have changed my hair style. My friends were more direct about that wig. They hated it. If I continued to wear it, they made clear, they would not be seen with me.

"But," I told them, "it cost forty dollars at Bergdorf Goodman."

"Tough," they said, as one. "Deduct it and throw it out, or hide it away and wait for Halloween."

"But I'm not going to have time to be getting my hair done," I explained, or tried to, "I have to make all these *appearances*."

That was my most surreal summer. Because my first book, on the topical subject of encounter groups, had just come out, it was my lot to rush around the country to publicize it. I made speeches and went on a good many television programs; when the emcee of *To Tell*

the Truth said "Will the real Jane Howard stand up?" it occurred to me to keep sitting. I wasn't sure who the real Jane Howard was.

Dr. Dyer helped keep me sane that summer, and so did a house whose rent I shared on Springy Banks Road in East Hampton, Long Island, a tiresome drive from the city at best. Few sensations I know of can match the abandoned, whelming surrender of leaping into the surf out there. The afterglow of that feeling can sometimes linger for hours or even days, but that summer it never did. That summer I always had to be thinking about promoting the book in Washington tomorrow or Chicago next week, and when, I always wondered, can I wash my hair?

Loath to face the clotted traffic of the Long Island Expressway on Sunday evenings, my friends and I would tarry late on Springy Banks Road to eat leftovers and watch the sun go down behind the trees. Not until midnight or so, when we were sure the roads would be clear, would we head back west, keeping the radio on loud so as not to be lulled to sleep by the sameness of the exit turnoff signs.

"Well, at least driving by night means postponing the visual shock of returning to ugliness," we would yawn and tell each other. (We were all quite sensitive.)

"Yes, but if we didn't live here who would we talk to? We could live without movies and delis and bookstores, but if we lived in Baton Rouge or Sioux Falls, who would comprehend us on a sullen Thursday evening?"

"Maybe we'd be surprised; maybe we'd find people who would. Maybe we're too provincial. Maybe if we lived somewhere else—*anywhere* else—we'd have more of a sense of community."

"We'd also probably get more sleep." But sleep is not the only thing one sacrifices if one returns from the Hamptons at three in the morning and has to get up early the next day. One also loses the margins, the white space in one's life, and this is a loss that comes to seem more grave with the passage of time.

It strikes me what a paradigm of an American I am, with my domestic glut, confused foreign relations, and implicit credo that if something is possible, or somewhere accessible, I'd better get busy and do it or go there, and make it snappy. I talk such matters over with Dr. Dyer, who agrees that mobility is a useful thing, "but why, with you, does it have to be such a *principle*?" He suggests that for me a saner course might be to try slowing down and staying in one place, just to see how "dailiness," as he puts it, might feel. He does

not say so in so many words, but he hints that the marginless, seemingly adventurous surface of my life may represent a clever trick to evade the fact that real risk scares the hell out of me. He succeeds where friends have failed: he makes selectivity seem alluring.

But Dr. Dyer notwithstanding, I still make mistakes. An engaging, literate letter arrives from a man who, having read my book, wants to take me to dinner. I accept. He helps me into my side of his fancy, low-slung sports car. I reach over to unlock his door, to save him the trouble. "I always know," he says as he slides into the driver's seat, "that when a girl does that, I'm going to score."

"One of the hardest things in a person's life," another letter-writer tells me when I finally meet her, "is to learn to shut certain doors. You don't just shut them; you barricade them."

I have just left *Life*'s masthead, a volunteer refugee in what comes to be called the Great Purge. The staff must be shrunk by many salaries, so I decide after fifteen years to go off the payroll and take a contract. I am to do four stories in the coming year for only a little less money than I had been earning. How nice and free it will be, with all the new time to myself, right? Wrong. The bond to that place and its people proves as absorbing as ever it was. I won't really leave *Life*, as it turns out, until *Life* leaves me and everyone else.

But the profit-sharing money I get, combined with some royalties, enables me to buy an apartment overlooking the Hudson, and the cherry trees of Riverside Park, and the sunsets. At last, a room of one's own to work in, and daylight enough to sustain plants.

The vistas from my square footage slow me down. Dailiness doesn't seem so dull any more. My father comes, soon after I move in, to wallpaper the bathroom. His visit touches me. Shower curtains, and like matters, obsess me for months. A superb procrastinatory device for a writer: how can I work until I have the ideal environment?

I see Dr. Dyer less frequently, busy as I am with shelf paper and all, but I don't quit. Something has happened between us: I suppose it is that phenomenon known to some in his trade as transference. His approval can make me feel in a state of grace. Not that he always approves; far from it. Once, when I recount to him how I have stalked back and forth in front of the brownstone of a man I crave to talk to, instead of calling up that man on the phone, Dr. Dyer looks at me and says, "You know what, Jane? You're crazy."

"I guess that's why I'm here," I say. We both laugh. We often do. If we didn't, I'd have drifted off long ago. But at times, with Dr.

Dyer, I also stammer and swear, and weep. On two occasions I stay up there in that room for much longer than the allotted fifty minutes. He does not look at his watch and say, "Well, we'll stop here." Instead he offers me instant coffee, which seems almost a sacrament. One of these extended visits comes just after I return from the burial of my mother's ashes. The other is on an autumn Saturday afternoon when the cause of my gloom is a good deal less specific. It is so vexingly untraceable, in fact, that I spent the morning trying to figure it out, typing a list of twenty-two reasons why I am depressed. Dr. Dyer listens, as he always does, with his whole being. He convinces me, in the course of a long and gentle talk, that the fundamental reason is a twenty-third which had not crossed my mind.

Among doctrinaire feminists the party line is that women should see women analysts: keep it all in the family because They, the enemy men, will only scheme to get us married off. I did see a woman once for a while, some years back, but no special rapport arose between us. Several years later, socially, I met a female Jungian analyst in California. She had a fascinating office. In it there was a sandbox with a bunch of tiny different toys. She said she sometimes could tell a lot more about her patients by which little toys and figures they picked up to fool around with than by what they actually said.

"Some of the stuff in that sandbox is junky," she said. "Most of it is pretty. There's one terrible pink plastic woman whose posture suggests, 'I'm waiting for it to happen to me,' but I keep it there because it's plastic, terrible, nonfeeling, which is the way a lot of people are. There are hundreds of figurines, a mermaid with great bazooms and terrible little hands. She's a terrible sex object, romping around mindlessly."

Gee, I think, it would be fun if Dr. Dyer had a sandbox full of toys, but he would no more do that than take up with the Primal Scream crowd, or give his practice over to consciousness-raising sessions. The female Jungian has doubts about these groups too.

"Sometimes they raise false bravado," she said. "They can lead some women to go home and make confrontations they can't back up with their own strength, because the strength is vicariously borrowed from the group. The poor guys they confront at home are slumped over and confused."

The Jungian and I had a quick Mexican supper together. "Very different things happen with a male analyst than with a female," she

said. "I can't prove it, but I strongly suspect that totally different stuff comes out of the unconscious. A woman analyst activates the psyche in different ways. Outer reality is where the female analyst might have a little more to offer. A female has her whole psyche there when a patient chatters on, whereas a man may go to sleep on it and think, 'Well, we'll get to the real stuff later.'

"I have several patients who are afraid that if they ever saw a man analyst, they would be too flirtatious, because they'd always had success charming men. But there are very successful analyses when a doctor uses the female, nurturing side of his nature."

Food for thought, all this. Had I been unconsciously flirting with Dr. Dyer, trying to con him? Hope not. Does he come on like a motherly male nurse? Maybe, some. (Come to think of it I did once dream he was a woman.) Is there anything I've held back from telling him? Probably. But would I have been any more open with a female confessor? I doubt it. One thing I have never lacked for is confidantes of my own sex.

My sister phones from Illinois to ask whether I think she should keep or cancel an appointment with her psychiatrist, a Dr. Hahn. She has seen him four or five times, sporadically, since our mother died. It touches me that Ann should seek my help; it used to seem that I was the only vulnerable one. But I don't know how to solve her present problem which, so far as she can pin it down, is that she has just turned thirty-five.

"Look at it this way," I suggested. "Two years ago I was thirty-five myself. David used to be thirty-five. Dad used to be thirty-five."

"But thirty-five is half my life, if I'm lucky," said Ann, "and what have I got to show for it? What can anyone say of me other than, 'Oh look, she got her car started all by herself.' I have the feeling that I'm on hold, that nothing promising is happening."

"You can always come here, you know."

"I know, thanks; David urges me to go see you, but I don't need New York now. I need solitude."

"How *is* David?"

"Resilient. He's not like me. He doesn't brood, pout, sulk, mope. If he's mad he blows up and gets it out of his system. Right now he's just terribly busy, and he doesn't need all this flack from me just because he forgot to remind the kids that it was my birthday. How were they supposed to know? They don't have little date-bookettes at their

age—what would they be if they had? And what's such a big deal if he and they *don't* remember?"

"I know, though. I always carry on about birthdays too. I always secretly think alternate-side-of-the-street parking regulations should be suspended on mine."

In Fort Lauderdale, where our paths once crossed for a day or so, she and I had a binge with Reese's Peanut Butter Cups. Endlessly, we discuss the domestic heroes of our shared youth, trying to puzzle them out, feeling sorry for only children who must solve such matters for themselves. We agree that in most of the households to which we have been privy, the moms, as Ann puts it, seem to exert more influence than the dads. The women shield and protect and manipulate the men, and secretly, if not openly, run the show. We further agree that this is not necessarily a laudable state of affairs but that we can't think of any solutions.

"I'd like to intensify my relationships with everybody and everything," she says on the phone. "I could use more sophisticated communication than I get, I need somebody I can hash it all out with."

"David?"

"He's not bad at it, but I don't think very many men are good at it. They aren't bred to be."

"The quality of talk does usually change, doesn't it, when a man walks into a room where two women are deep in conversation? Certain nuances are lost. There are a lot more signals and subtleties between women and women than there are between women and men."

"You know, I used to criticize Her [our mother] because all she seemed to specialize in was circulating her recipes. . . . "

"Remember all the things we found in the freezer after she died? Those frozen casseroles she'd made, and pies with perfectly fluted crusts?"

"Sure I remember. That's part of what I'm talking about. That's what I don't put down any more, and I'm ashamed I ever did. Now that I'm older, and realize I probably won't be coming across a Salk vaccine in my own basement, I think what she did—keeping everybody fed and together—was a lot."

"You know what I ran across this morning?" I asked. "That speech I made right after she died, at the Springfield Mental Health Association. Remember?"

"Have you got that speech handy?"

"It's right here."

"Read me the part you left out, the sympathy note you got from John Dunne."

"Okay," I said. " 'Theirs was a generation'—he's talking about his father's and our mother's—'sadly perhaps the last, with a definite sense of place, a definite idea of who they were, and that survives in us, no matter what the buffeting. It's not a bad legacy, and I hope that in some deracinated way we can pass it on.' "

"I guess that's what I hope, too," said Ann. "You know what I've decided?"

"What?"

"I think I *will* cancel the appointment with Dr. Hahn. There must be somebody who needs him more. I think maybe I can make it on my own."

CHAPTER 6

POMP AND CIRCUMSTANCE IN GROUNDHOG HOLLOW

Every morning Matilda Titus Hastings fixes her husband, Wayne, a panful of biscuits and gravy to go with his specially fried eggs. Perhaps as a subtle consequence of this repeated alchemy, in the same way that dogs come to resemble their masters, Matilda looks something like a biscuit herself, wholesomely puffy.

But Tildy, as she is usually known except to the twelve who call her Mama and the three dozen or so to whom she is Granny, is not really all that fat. What she is is comfortable looking. Her hair, which never in her life has been cut, is pinned up in braids. "Before it got so thin," she says, "the braids were about as wide as my wrist."

She wears glasses for sewing, the only work for which she has ever been paid, and for reading, which is her furtive pleasure. (She reads on the sly, the way some people gamble.) Outside, on bright days, she puts on a homemade sunbonnet. Most of her dresses she makes herself, for about a dollar each, but once she spend sixteen dollars on a three-piece lace outfit. She owns two costume-jewelry pins. One, crown-shaped, is composed of the birthstones of her ten daughters and two sons. The other, made of coal, is shaped like West Virginia.

I met Tildy through my friend Sally Wells. Sally, for nearly three years, was the director of a West Virginia cooperative named Moun-

tain Artisans. All over the state groups of rural women like Tildy were organized to work from Mountain Artisans designs. They filled orders for patchwork quilts, pillows, and quite a lot of such improbable high-fashion items as evening skirts. Painstakingly marketed by Sally and her staff, these products were sold in stores like Nieman Marcus and Bergdorf Goodman, for prices which allowed seamstresses to earn more money than they ever had.

The Hastingses' two-story house is modest by many standards, but in West Virginia it is thought to be imposing. To get to that house you have to take a rough ride up Groundhog Hollow Road. The car bounces and jounces and rattles and shakes and so, if you are a passenger, do you. "I tell people that's how come I had so many girl babies," Tildy jokes during one such ride. "Going up and down this road all the time, I shook the balls off them."

Groundhog Hollow Road leads down a steep hill to Atkins where the Hastingses shop. Turn right there and drive four miles and you will come to Rollo, where they get their mail. All around that region you will see cars with Kentucky and Virginia license plates, because both state borders are nearby. Medical facilities, however, are not. If something is wrong with the Hastingses' teeth, for example, they have to drive thirty-five miles to Welch.

McDowell County, in which the Hastingses live, has been called the Coal Bin of America. Slag heaps in the wake of strip mines desecrate the lyrically lovely hillsides. Abandoned car hulks rot in stream beds. The best of the roads are poor. Incest is not unheard of—"They try to hush it up, but word gets around."—nor is illiteracy.

Movie theaters and libraries are scarce, but churches abound. Just down the road from Groundhog Hollow, in Atkins, is a church whose members believe that the command given in Mark 16:18, "They shall take up serpents," must be followed literally. On Saturday evenings they really do handle real snakes. I wanted to visit this church the weekend I spent with the Hastingses; to me it sounded as exotic as a mosque. Wayne said we could, but first we would go to the Church of Christ, where he sometimes preaches. The service there lasted so long that by the time we got out the snake-handlers had gone home.

Tildy does not share her husband's enthusiasm for the Church of Christ, by which he is in fact ordained and to which he converted dramatically in 1953. Nothing can lure her away from the Jacob's Ladder Branch Church of the Old Hosanna Regular Primitive Baptist

Association. She and Wayne can argue for hours about theology.

"Wayne is interested in death and the hereafter," she says. "He believes in hell and damnation, everlasting fires. I'm interested in Christ and salvation. I believe we get our punishments and our blessings right here on earth. You should come here sometime the first Sunday in August, when we have, in my church, our old-time foot-washing. Ladies wait on female members, men on men, and it doesn't matter whose feet we wash, because we all just love each other so much we want to be at each other's feet in humility."

If you were setting Tildy's life to a musical score, you could draw from three sources: "Earnestly, Tenderly, Jesus Is Calling," "Turkey in the Straw," and "Pomp and Circumstance." Nothing in all the Hastings house is more arresting than the array in the living room of twelve high-school graduation pictures. Six graduates on top, six below, born between 1928 and 1947, each one dressed in cap and gown, some with diplomas clutched close to their cheeks.

The youngest of these children did not technically get a diploma but a certificate of attendance. "She had to fight to finish high school; she wanted so bad to have that picture up there with the others. Her I.Q. is 85, and she doesn't retain information. Wayne thought it was the teachers' fault; he thought they didn't try hard enough to pound the learning into her. In his own childhood, you see, people weren't retarded. They were crazy."

Tildy herself, the second of nine children, only went as far as the eighth grade, because her father didn't believe in sending girls to high school. Sometimes she would contemplate stealing something from the country store so that she might be sent to reform school, "because at least it was a school."

From the moment she first saw Wayne Hastings, "I thought he was about the handsomest guy in the world. I was at a spring, dipping water, and he passed by and said, 'How do you do?' There was never another man in my life before and there hasn't been one since.

"One night Wayne walked me home from a tent meeting and we started keeping company. He never proposed and I didn't, either. One day he said, 'I'm not going to walk this ridge so much.' I said, 'Oh? Why not?' He said, 'I'm going to make *them* come to *us*.' He was twenty-two and I was seventeen when we got married on September nineteenth, nineteen and twenty-eight. We never knew what a honeymoon was, except that somebody caught us a catfish so long it wouldn't lay flat in a three-dollar washtub.

"My mamma warned me that Wayne was from a family that drank right much, and for a long time he did. I left him once, over drinking, but I couldn't abandon the babies, so I came back. He never missed a day's work over it, and he was always a good provider. In October of nineteen and fifty-three he joined the church and never had a drop since, not even after the accident."

A rock "as big as a mattress on a bed" fell onto Wayne's spine inside the Island Creek Coal Company mine in 1959. "He was hunkered on his heels—they were blasting to get the coal out and he was shot fireman. They weren't sure he would be able to walk at all, or have any use whatsoever of his sexual organs." A two-year period of rehabilitation at a United Mine Workers hospital restored partial use of the lower half of Wayne's body, but life has been difficult ever since then both for him and his wife.

"My one prayer is that I'll outlive him, so I can care for him as long as he lives. I don't think the children could cope with him. When I'm gone he never eats the right food, and he won't go visit his sisters. They offer to do for him, but he won't have it."

Before they moved into their present house, in 1949, the Hastingses lived in a four-room log cabin half a mile or so down Groundhog Hollow. Before Wayne's illness there was no telephone; only since 1962 have they had indoor plumbing. Tildy can remember the first car she ever saw: "In nineteen and eighteen it sounded like a helicopter sounds now. When I heard it coming up the hill, I hid."

Her babies were delivered in the old log cabin, with the help of a midwife. "Her fee was five dollars, and if she had to she'd stay around for a week at a time. She was a wonderful woman, and I was blessed to sit by her bed and hold her hand when she left this world.

"If I had it to do over I'd have fewer children, because there isn't room enough in the world for everyone to have as many as I did, but I sure can't tell you which of them I'd give up. Once I had six under the age of five, and when my youngest daughter was three months old my system wasn't too strong, and I almost had a nervous breakdown. If the company doctor hadn't got my tubes tied, I might have had more still. Wayne would divorce me if he heard me say so, but I feel more strongly about sterilization than abortions, though I think there are times when abortions should be permitted too."

Tildy tells of a doctor's visit to an equally fecund friend of hers. The doctor, calling on the woman in another old log cabin, suggested that properly timed cold baths might help to reduce chances of preg-

nancy. "Doctor," the woman asked him, "do you see that creek down there?" He saw it, a good 150 yards away. "Doctor, do you think I'm going to go down there four or five times a night to take a cold bath? Because, Doctor, if you do, you'd better think again."

Wayne and Tildy, like many American couples, have their failures in communication. "A lot of times I find out from other people what's going on with him," says Tildy. They have chronic disagreements, too. Wayne, for example, is still not persuaded that reading anything other than the Holy Scripture is a worthwhile activity. "Wayne says that reading costs money and that time spent reading could be better spent doing something different. But I've always read, all my life, and I'm not about to stop. I used to read to the kids, one on either knee, whether they wanted me to or not. Once, when I was missing my copies of *Life* magazine, I went to ask the postmistress how come they hadn't been coming, and she hinted that Wayne had them sent back. I said to him that if my magazine didn't come that next week, I'd go to the drugstore and buy a copy, so that was the end of that.

"I watch television some, but not as much as a lot of people do. Television's changed things a lot. Before television people used to be more friendlier, pay more attention, be more relaxed and settle-minded. Used to be whole families would come for a visit and stay overnight. Now sometimes weeks pass and nobody stops by here."

Not one of the Hastings children has settled in West Virginia: "They all went other places to find work, and they all found it too." Most of the children live close enough, in neighboring states, to make occasional visits. Once in a while, in a masterful triumph of choreography, the whole family is reunited. July, when many of the dozen came home, they chipped in to buy their parents a new dinette set. "A couple of them took us down to the store in their car," Tildy remembers, "and when we drove back, they'd keep saying, 'Wonder if Santy Claus has been here?' When we got home, we saw the old chairs we'd been using out on the porch and the new set inside. Both our reclining chairs were gifts from the children too. Oh, we couldn't be more proud of them all."

Had she not had so many children, Tildy thinks she might have been a nurse or a writer. "I love to take care of people and I love to tell about people. You don't raise twelve children and help with a lot of grandchildren without doing a lot of nursing.

"But there's lots of things I want to do. I'd like right much to look into genealogy. They tell me my people go back to 1066, and that

we're descended from a queen of England. I'd like to travel too, right much more than Wayne ever wanted to. It's hard for the kids to entertain their daddy when he and I come to visit. One thing he did like, when we went to Washington to see Louella, [their eighth child] he liked the Wax Museum."

In West Virginia, as in other stops during my journey, I was struck by evidence that American women seem to be more venturesome than their husbands. I thought of the Hammills, a couple my parents' age who lived in Indiana. All her life Laura Hammill had wanted to go to Europe, but her husband, Arthur, had always found a reason why they shouldn't. Not money; they had plenty. Not sickness; both were robust. Not time; they weren't all that busy. Finally, after a year in which her friends and relatives had joined her in a campaign to persuade Arthur, he relented. They ordered plane tickets, round-trip to Paris, and flew first to New York. After two days they had gone back to Indianapolis. What had happened? The answer was simple: "Arthur got scared." Poor Arthur. No, poor Laura: doomed, as long as she was his wife, not to see the other side of the Atlantic.

"I don't think I can stay on the Mountain Artisans board," Tildy said, "because of my health. But being *paid* to do the kind of work I've always done anyway since I was seven has given me a self-confidence I never had before.

"One year I earned $841, and some have made plenty more than that. For some, including me, it's the first money we ever made in our lives, and for others it's the only source of income at all. Not that I expect to be paid for all I do. I like working in the community too, trying to get school buses to go up into the hollers to get to the children, organizing a buyers' club, helping with Head Start, and helping with the old people too. Seems to me whatever more pleasure they can get, they sure do deserve it.

"Old women seem to me more lonely than old men, because old men can get together more, on street corners and in barber shops. Women are more sure of themselves than men, in this area anyway, but to me women'll always be women, and they shouldn't try not to." Tildy put on a checkered sunbonnet and walked out her back door to look up over the hill. "But I don't think any person, male or female, should be a doormat," she went on. "I've heard married couples to say they've never had an argument in their lives. All I can say to that is they must be mighty meek and mild. I'm sure glad *I'm* not married to a man like that, and I'll bet the men wouldn't like it much either. I

guess it works out about equal most of the time, but you could put it this way, if you understand what I mean: we make men *think* they run the show."

CHAPTER 7

I'M IN LOVE WITH A HANDSOME MOMMY

W*hat?*" Marcus was saying. "I can't *hear* you."
    "I guess I should have called you from someplace else," I yelled into the phone. Almost any phone booth in the city would have been quieter than this one, just east of the Empire State Building on Thirty-fourth Street. Toward me, that April Saturday afternoon, were marching a couple of thousand women, my sisters, all chanting "WOMEN UNITE! ABORTION IS OUR RIGHT!"

"Listen," I said to Marcus, "I'll meet you and the Regans at around four by the playground." The Regans and their daughter Hannah had weekly picnics in the park, and Marcus and I liked to join them. But I wanted to see more of the abortion parade because, having just returned from West Virginia, where Matilda had had her twelve pregnancies, I was much concerned with the business of the unborn and the born. Wombs, and what use we women might or might not make of them, were on my own and, it seemed, everybody else's mind. We are the first generation to choose whether or not to reproduce ourselves. The question now was whether I wished to, or could, breed myself.

Abby Heyman and I had come to the parade together from her apartment in the Village. I had gone there earlier for coffee and to look at the prints from two rolls of film she had shot, a couple of months before, of her own abortion.

"I've come to feel very involved with the whole women's movement," Abby had said over coffee. She was a short, earnest, redhaired twenty-nine-year-old, and I admired the photographs she had been taking of other women as well as those of her abortion. "The movement has affected me just the opposite of a lot of women. It's given a lot of women the courage not to get pregnant."

"You mean they feel they can be defined other than as mothers?"

"Right, but what it's made *me* feel is that *I* can be defined other than by my work. I used to be afraid that if I had a child, I would

stop working—that I had to make a clear choice between children and work. The movement made me see I might do *both* things."

"Then why. . . ."

"Why did I have the abortion? Because I feel the need to be established in terms of work before I become a mother. When I say 'established' I don't mean in terms of public reputation, I mean in terms of my own self-image."

"I didn't think you meant publicly."

"The operation was kind of weird," she said as she showed me her pictures. "I went in the hospital at one and came out at five. The operation took ten minutes.

"I can actually say that it was fun in a way. The doctor clued me in to each new procedure. It put the nurses in a very good humor, to see me wheeled in there with a camera and two rolls of film under the sheets. The doctor got special permission for me to take the pictures, because he wanted them published."

"I want people to see how simple, available, and safe abortions can be," Dr. Richard Hausknecht told me when I went to see him later in his office. He had been part of the abortion reform movement, he said, since 1964. "It was sensible and calm of Abby," he said, "to use her own unwanted pregnancy to try to help other women."

"But isn't she, or won't she be, depressed?"

"Unwanted pregnancy," he said, "is the only psychiatric disease curable by a surgical procedure. Most women who've had abortions experience a colossal sense of relief. The whole abortion thing has helped women to learn about their bodies. Women are just now feeling free to talk in detail about their sex lives, which is a healthy side feature of all this."

"It was strange when I heard I was pregnant," Abby Heyman told me. "In spite of everything, even though I wasn't sure I wanted to have the baby, I was actually happy, because at least I knew that it was possible for me to conceive."

"I'd be reassured if I knew that for a fact too," I told her.

"A lot of people ask how an educated person like me could have been careless about contraception," she said, "but I guess in a way I doubted whether I really could get pregnant, so I figured it wouldn't matter."

"What about the baby's father? How did he feel about the whole business?"

"Guilty, a little," she said. "He and I had been involved for a long time. My lover volunteered to go to the hospital with me, but I said, 'Oh no, I can go by myself.' Maybe I shouldn't have; I felt the aloneness very acutely."

"Would he have helped you bring up the baby?"

"No, we agreed that if I'd had the baby he wouldn't have been a father to it, financially or in any other way. I could have supported the child. The first doctor I went to, when I told him I wasn't married, said I should get an abortion because he didn't see how I could support the child myself."

"Pretty presumptuous."

"I thought so. I was annoyed at his automatic assumption that a woman would have no economic ability."

"What name would the baby have had?" I asked.

"My own of course," said Abby. "I guess I'd have had to make a lot of changes in whom I associated with, though. I guess a lot of people would have dropped me and not let their children play with mine. I guess I'd have had to look for some communal arrangement with other single parents."

"You don't quite feel like doing all that?"

"Not yet. For now it's important for me to keep on the way I am," said Abby. "Now my whole life is geared to being flexible and free—not just free to travel, but free to *grow*, whenever and in whatever ways may seem necessary."

That's how my life has been, too, and the price I have paid for freedom is childlessness. On bad days I brood over children I might have had. On good days I think about her or him or them whom I might someday still bear. On all days I reflect with gratitude on the existence of a certain few, borne by others, whose company matters as much to me as anything in the world. I need kids in my life as much as I need men. To hold a snuggling, trusting child on one's lap is to feel a deep and peaceful intimacy as necessary, to me at least, as any feeling I know.

No more any old kid than any old man. Some children, like some men and for that matter some women, leave me neutral or downright hostile. Jane Howard Jacobs is not among these. At three, she amuses herself by making up songs when her parents go driving in the Land Rover. Once, when her mother was at the wheel, Jane, in the back seat, was heard to sing, "I'm in love with a handsome mommy."

190

"What'd you do?" I asked Kathy, her mother.

"I probably stopped the car," said Kathy, "and got out to give her a great big hug."

Kathy and Ann and their husbands are all inspired parents, with a genius for sanctifying the mundane and making a special occasion of the most lackluster day. One summer Ann and David and their children were to pay a week's visit to the house I helped rent on Springy Banks Road in East Hampton. It would be our first reunion in a good while. The thought of leaping with the children into huge waves filled me with impatience. Driving eastward from the city, I couldn't get there soon enough. When I arrived in my Volkswagen they were already there. Sarah heard me pulling in and rushed out to the balcony of that house to shriek, "SHE'S HERE!" I don't think I have ever felt more purely welcome in my life.

In a workshop at an all-day sex clinic in Fairfield, a woman was talking about when she Came Out, and she did not mean at a debutante cotillion. "When you're Out," she said, "you put yourself in the reject bin, but before you're Out, it's worse. It's like you're constantly waiting for a shoe to drop. 'If they *knew*,' you think, 'I couldn't be here. If my boss knew, he'd fire me. If my friends knew, they'd reject me, and I'd reject me too.' "

One of the women in that classroom, during the Lesbian workshop, was a black minister of the gospel. "It's going to be very fashionable to be gay in another year," the minister predicted. "It'll be a fad. It'll be, 'If you're not gay, you're not with it.' What I mean is not necessarily in terms of sex, but an alternate life-style."

"What a lot of straights don't understand," the reverend went on, "is that gay women aren't looking to other women for what men do. Women look to each other for something more, something far removed from face and figure and all that. Gay people can have long-term relationships without having to go through all the hassle of divorce, the whole heavy bit of role-playing."

I suppose people must wonder whether I am gay. Why should I be exempt from such universal speculation about all single people and in fact some married ones too? My voice, after all, falls in the alto register; I hail cabs and catch waiters' eyes better than many men. But nobody ever said I ran like a boy or threw a ball like one. As a matter of fact I don't feel like one. I wish women in the gay liberation movement Godspeed, although I take issue with their premise

that all men, without exception, are intruding vandals bent only on the oppression of womankind. I submit that some of them can be welcome guests.

CHAPTER 8

WHEN I GROW UP

Alison Busch had moved only recently to an apartment in Austin, Texas, but the place had a settled snug air about it. Alison had the look of a gentle, alert rabbit. At fifty-two, she wore size eights and looked as if she got a lot of exercise. There was one thing missing: a husband. A couple of years before, after nearly three decades of marriage, "a man from the court came up to me and handed me divorce papers. I wouldn't file, because I had no grounds whatsoever. Bob said, 'I'm not good for you,' but I wondered, if that were true, why he hadn't told me so years before.

"I had to find out from the children, not from him, that the real reason was he wanted to remarry. He finally said to me, 'We have nothing in common.'

" 'No, nothing at all,' I said to him, 'just four kids, twenty-seven years, and a lot of shared interests—can you call that nothing?' " He could. Alison became the first woman in her social circle, "and Lord only *knows* the first in my family, ever, to have a divorce.

"In my sane moments," Alison said, "I wonder how I could have put up with Bob for as long as I did. When I can be objective, I realize that I'm well rid of a lot of things about him. Boats, for one thing. We were forever making payments we couldn't afford."

"Why'd you marry him?"

"Oh, there was a war on, brave boys were going off to the front, everybody else was getting married, why shouldn't I? It looked like security, and it would get me out from under my parents' thumbs."

"Was Bob attractive?"

"I guess so. He's always been terribly concerned about his appearance. He has quite a thing about not getting old. His birthday is five days after mine, and we always used to have parties together. On our fiftieth birthday, he hired a caterer and invited friends to *his* party, without telling people it was my birthday, too. I guess that should have been a clue that I didn't matter to him any more."

"What's his new wife like?"

"She's a lot younger, with four kids and a richer father than I had. A friend of mine, who knows her, says they deserve each other. She likes sailing and parties and I hear she's just as demanding as Bob is. One reason she got rid of her first husband, I hear, was his financial irresponsibility. Wait until she finds out what she's in for now! If she's also the type that has to get all the time without giving, they can't last long.

"Even though I'm a grandmother," said Alison, "I still feel like a kid. I still wonder what I'm going to do when I grow up."

To judge by what Alison and other divorcees told me, the solo postmarital trip to Europe is an effective *rite de passage* for newly abandoned women of a certain age and certain income level.

"You think about architecture," one said, "You take delight in the curved pats of butter, the patterns of cement on the sidewalks. Your exhilaration mounts as you discover you can get on the right train at the right time all by yourself and that you can go whenever you want wherever you want, without having to argue with anyone. With luck you might meet congenial soulmates to eat dinner with or maybe do more than that with, but even if you don't, you feel buoyed as you write your postcards home."

"Tell me something, Alison. Have you ever given any thought to polygamy?"

"I have, in fact," she said. "Maybe if a man had *four* women to mother him, it might almost be enough. But the ideal thing would be polyandry."

"You mean us having four men to father us?"

"Does it sound so bad?"

"It could be quite a nice stopgap solution," I said. "More privacy, less possessiveness, less jealousy. I've heard worse formulas. It would mean a lot of logistics. I wouldn't like all that furtiveness."

"Are you ready for it on a non-furtive basis?"

"I suppose not. I guess the real adventure, for me, would be old-fashioned, hard-core monogamy."

"That's because you didn't jump into it automatically when you were twenty-two," Alison said. "In a way, I envy you. You already know how to live alone: you must know how to, because you've always done it. I'm having to learn now what you already know, because before Bob left me, the bastard, I'd never lived alone in my whole life! What a thought! But it's true."

CHAPTER 9

SOMEBODY'S GOT TO GET A LOSER, RIGHT?

Listen," Arlene Zermiak asked me as we drove in my Volks-wagen down a parkway in Brooklyn toward the tavern where her husband tends bar, "would you mind if I introduced you as my girlfriend Sharon from New Jersey? See, I've never lied to Dom in my life before, but I don't think he'd like it—in fact I know he wouldn't like it—if he knew I let some strange lady writer come into our house."

"Well, okay, I guess," I said, "but what if he asks me something about what I do or how things are in New Jersey?"

"Never mind," she said. "He won't ask. He don't know my girl-friends and I don't know many of his man friends. Oh, we have peo-ple over sometimes, but not too often. Home to him is a very special place."

Home to them is the second floor of a house with an asbestos-siding façade and a backyard vegetable garden, across from a play-ground in the Bensonhurst section of Brooklyn. All the rooms are spacious. The bedroom, facing the street, has a collage of snapshots of both their families. In the living room is a phonograph. (Arlene likes music, "especially ballads I can relate to.") The kitchen has the television, flower decals on the refrigerator door, plastic flowers here and there, and three pairs of plaques on the wall: a pot pouring into a cup, a couple of masks, and a couple of cats. A couple of real cats, Tiny and Jinx, referred to as "the kids," slink around.

I had a hard time finding her place. Although we live only about twelve miles apart, I knew as little of her borough as she did of mine. Manhattan, to her, is a place the catering service sometimes sends her on jobs. Brooklyn, to me, is a place I pass through sometimes on the way to the airport. The odds against our ever meeting, we agreed over rye whiskey mixed with Seven-Up and crackers covered with cheese spread, were great, but we are both uncommonly curious.

"I don't have too many friends," she said. "Friends need a lot of time, and if you don't have the time, why bother? I can't see picking one person out of a crowd and saying, 'You! You're going to be my friend!' I'd rather have fifty thousand acquaintances, because they don't ask much, and I don't feel like committing myself. Besides, I can't see letting friends interfere with my own life."

There wasn't much she didn't tell me about her own life in the

194

three hours we sat in her kitchen, and I began to suffer from wrist cramp.

"I love subway trains," she was saying. "I like to ride them back and forth. When I was in my teens I'd get up at three, four, five in the morning, get on the train, get off at Coney Island, look at the water for a while. It really worried my mother but I loved to do it. I'd stay twenty minutes or so, walk along the water, then get back on the train and come home."

"I've got this idea," I interrupted. "My car's outside. Why don't we drive and go look at the water now?" So we took rather a long drive, to see the boats lined up at Cross Bay Boulevard, near where Arlene lived as a child. "The change in this neighborhood is really something," she said. "Like when I was little there was nothing here but the Bow Wow and the pizza palace, and look at it now. Hey, want to get a hamburger?"

Sure. And then, since Dom wouldn't be home until very late, how would I like to drop by his bar? Why ever not? Inebriation, it was clear, was a strong motif of our acquaintance, whose beginning she recalled more clearly than I did.

"I wanted to get a glass off you," she said, "and you didn't want to let go of it. It was toward the end of that wedding—no, it wasn't a wedding, was it? We usually work weddings, but this was some other affair." It had in fact been the annual extravaganza of the American Academy of Arts and Letters, at which painters and writers get awards and feel silly and are engulfed by hangers-on like me, who feign jaded cynicism, deplore the lack of eye contact but keep assenting to maybe just one more daiquiri. If I'd had one less I probably would not have confided in a waitress what book I was trying to write. It's a good thing I did, though, because Arlene had said, "You ought to talk to *me*: I'm only twenty-five and I've had three marriages and a nervous breakdown and *I* know a thing or two about how it is to be an American woman."

Arlene took pains with her appearance. No dark showed at the roots of her pale blond hair, tied back with a coral-colored scarf which just matched her bell-bottom slacks. She had plucked and arched her eyebrows carefully, and gone to the trouble of putting on green eye shadow and mascara. Her blouse was black nylon, her cardigan embroidered with flowers, her shoes white wedgie sandals, and on her face was a look of nervous native wit.

For a twenty-five-year-old she had indeed known her share of an-

guish. Her present husband, the bartender, had terminal cancer. "We were married last September and found out in October.

"Before I married Dom," she said, "I was always in such a hurry to get no place. My first husband, I knew him since I was thirteen, I married when I was seventeen, earlier than the other girls in my crowd. (As a kid I was always wild, a leader, I'd take chances, and I'd think of my girlfriends, even the ones who were older than me, as little children.) I was two months pregnant when we got married; we eloped.

"He was a very smart, intelligent man, more educated than me, but we never discussed anything, never went out. I always figured he'd loosen up when we were together more, but that didn't happen. He worked for a beer company and we had a pretty house out in New Jersey. I didn't know I was missing anything. I had a part-time job as a floor girl in a dress factory, and I'd come home to watch Jack LaLanne and do housework.

"Well, one day I came home too early and found him with a man. When that happened I just turned away, seeing I wasn't needed, and tripped down the stairs. When I came back he was gone, and he never did come home that night; we never did discuss it. He went to Mexico and got a divorce. I can't even read the divorce papers; they're in Spanish, but a lawyer told me it was okay. I had a miscarriage. I was six months along; that marriage lasted four months.

"A year and a half later I married again, this time a big deal with the white dress bit and 250 guests, because my second husband's idea was he didn't want anyone to know I was divorced, because you don't take in someone else's laundry. The whole image of divorced women is garbage, but that's how he felt.

"He was a bookbinder, and we'd go to this yacht club. His father belonged, so we got to go. Listen, if you ever want to meet a bunch of phonies, just go to a yacht club someday. All they do is lounge around and feel like hotshots because they're there. My husband liked it, and he liked photography and fishing, and he got a second job as a painter. He was also fooling around. We had sex problems.

"He was a supersexy man, and I couldn't reach a climax. I didn't know how to fake it. Now I'm better at faking it. You learn. Hell, I like the emotion part of it, but it's not the end of the world if I don't click. I didn't worry about it for a while, but then I'd read those books and think, Jesus, everyone else is having them but me.

"But even if I would have clicked with him, he still would have

gone after others. He started on narcotics after we were married too. He said pot made him see visions clearer. I've never wanted to try drugs myself, my own worst vice is drinking.

"So that marriage didn't work either, and then I had another boy-friend, and that didn't work, and that's when I had my breakdown, when I needed some assistance psychological-wise. I just retreated, I didn't even eat or wash, I'd sit on my bed or else I'd sleep. I tried to kill myself by taking a bottle of rye and a bottle of aspirin, and I got deathly ill, all right, but not the way I wanted to. They brought a stomach pump and all that.

"The psychiatrist I had at the hospital was a woman, and she did me good. She'd never answer anything, she'd bounce my questions back at me. She'd say, 'Your own brain has all the answers, so if you have a problem you take a sheet of paper and write down all the pros and cons.' So that's what I do now, that's how I keep sane. I haven't seen her in three and a half or four years, but I'd go back again, sure, because I'd rather get a little help than flip out and hurt somebody.

"My health's okay otherwise, except I have a bad heart. There's some valve supposed to open and close that when I get nervous it stays open. That's why I flunked the physical to get on the police force. I'd like to have been a detective, but they'd probably just have made me a meter maid even if I got in. Or some kind of social worker, maybe, but that would have been bad because I'm the kind, I take my problems home with me. My husband laughs at the way I do that, but somebody's got to, right? I figure there's less problems in the world if people listen to each other, so I take it upon myself to be one of the ones that listen.

"I've traveled some to different places and I always expect people to be different, but they never are when you actually talk to them. Basically they're the same as you, they just want to survive. I've been to Virginia and North Carolina and Florida and Canada, mainly around Niagara Falls. I don't like traveling alone, if I don't have somebody to say, 'Hey, look at that mountain.'

"I'd like to go back to the South; I liked the people and the climate there. I like New York, but I'd get away if I could, it's too fast here, and down there it's so much more relaxed, you have more of a chance to unwind, and maybe it's easier to talk to people.

"Who do I talk to here? My mother, and one married woman lives near her. I save all my mending for my mother when she comes over, because it makes her feel like I need her. She pretends to complain,

197

but you can see she really loves it. She's a pretty religious person, she goes where I used to go as a kid, the Lutheran Church. I only went because I sang in the choir and in school choruses, but I blew my career when I took up smoking. I can't hold the high notes no more. I'm not too keen on Jesus Christ, but I do believe in God; I think there must be somebody or something in charge. I'd go to church now if I didn't have to get up so early. With Dom not coming home sometimes until four in the morning, we like to sleep late.

"My parents are Austrian descent. They were separated for ten years and they just got back together again. My mother cried her heart out while he was gone, but now they're getting along good. My dad's an alcoholic, but he's cured. He works as a quality-control tester for a real benevolent paint company, they give you your birthday off along with all the usual holidays.

"He's a handyman too; he taught me how to do electricity and plumbing and all that stuff. I'm as good at that stuff as Dom is. He'll wash my floors and he'll vacuum; he feels he wouldn't ask me to do anything he wouldn't do himself, and vice versa.

"I've got two older brothers. I miss the one who's in the navy, who lives in Florida, because we used to be very close. The other one's in the police force. Even though his precinct is right across the street, he never stops or waves or anything. He went into the police full of the milk of human kindness—he was going to help people and all that—but now he just looks the other way a lot of time. He ain't even going to give a ticket, with all that red tape. So much of it's ridiculous with the postponing and court calendars and all that.

"The idea of stronger gun laws makes me laugh. To be truthful, I have a gun in there in the bedroom. It's not registered; it's illegal. I wouldn't know how to shoot it. Sometimes I think the old West, like in the movies, was better: shoot first, ask questions later. They didn't kill innocent bystanders in those days.

"I think if I wanted to vote—I don't, because I don't follow it that closely—I'd join the Conservative party. Dom doesn't vote either. We both figure whoever you get in there can't be any better than the one before, or any worse. I guess we shouldn't have got into the Vietnam war, but once we did it was too bad they never sent enough men over there to do a job.

"Dom was in the army for about eight years, in the time of Cuba and all that. He went to a couple grades in high school but he didn't finish. I quit after the third year, not so much because of finances (my

mother's a financial wizard, in fact) but because I wanted to. If I'm smart it's from talking to people, not writing or reading or math. I've read books like *Oliver Twist* and *A Tale of Two Cities,* though. I don't read the newspapers, it's all the same stuff all the time. I'll watch TV. In fact my programs are on tonight, *Adam 12* and *Perry Mason* and *Cannon.* I like mysteries and musicals and anything to do with the police. I have a great respect for law. Even though I jaywalk and stuff like that I'm basically a very law-abiding person.

"My first job was as an operator in the telephone company, and it bored me to death, not being able to see the people I was talking to. Now I work for this catering service that gives me waitress jobs at weddings and big parties. I don't bartend, because barmaids have to know how to handle six-foot drunks.

"If there's a fight in Dom's bar, though, I'm right in the middle, trying to calm it down, instead of in the corner where he wishes I'd be. He's protective, and he thinks I'm very gullible because I have a lot of faith in people. He's Italian and Polish, he's still got relatives in Poland. He was brought up in Ozone Park, and he has an adopted brother married to a Jew and a sister married to a Filipino who has multiple sclerosis. His parents burned to death in a fire.

"The guy Dom works with is a hypochondriac, and Dom's always covering for him. He worries more about the bar than the boss does. He's there at that bar until two-thirty, three-thirty, sometimes four in the morning. He drinks a lot himself, but he holds it well.

"You know what he looks like? He looks like a kewpie doll, you'll see. He's a supergreat man; you should hear how he listens to the troubles of everyone in that bar. He's a bank, he's a carry-home taxi service, he's a shrink, he's an everything. He's thirty-two, which is late for a man to marry, but I'm his first wife. He used to be a machinist for twelve years, but his temper got the better of him one day and he slugged his foreman, so that was the end of that job.

"When he gets mad he has a muscle that twitches in his cheek. Somebody else might not notice it, but I always do. I think knowing a person that well is really a part of loving. I never knew anyone so well before, and I only knew him six months when I married him. If nothing else it proves that there is such a thing as a good marriage and that if you be patient you *can* find someone who cares.

"I have a great need to be needed, it's been a fault of mine all my life. I truthfully don't think I could make it on my own, without a man. I don't mean financially, but emotionally.

"As far as Women's Liberation, I think it's dumb. Those women seem not to need men. What those women say they want and what they really want is two different things. A man's ego is really super, it's something you shouldn't play around with. These dumdums who want every single right a man has, to tell you the truth they look to me like dykes. They seem to be striving for a world without men, and if they get it, they're going to be sorry. What's so great about China and Russia, where everybody wears the same thing?

"I think a woman has much more chance of individuality than a man. You take twenty men, they all work at the same job and do the same thing all day, but twenty women—why, you can go into all their homes and every one of them will be differently decorated. Women can wear whatever they want and look different every day. I never felt I was missing any freedoms; lack of education hasn't stopped me from getting jobs, and I don't think the men I worked with were paid any more, either, but maybe they *should* be, like in the catering men have to set up tables and do more work than we do.

"After all, a man don't ask much. He wants his dinner, he wants clean socks, what's wrong with that? And Dom, he likes me to look nice. I like nothing better than running around in dungarees and pajamas, but if we go out, I'll wear a dress.

"He wears dark glasses all the time, because he has ulcerated eyes. Nothing aggravates me more than when someone says to him, 'take off your glasses, I can't see your eyes.' People put too much emphasis on stuff like that. What's important about Dom is the way he treats me, and other people too. Generous? You ought to see: I ask him for potatoes and he brings me a fifty-pound sack. Ask him for a slice of watermelon, you get the whole thing.

"He's a very good-natured man most of the time. He's one for helping people, and he's very protective of me. When we're in public, he's in charge completely. He'll listen to my logic, if I make logic. If I think he's wrong, I'll wait until we get home before I tell him, because I don't want to embarrass him. If we're out and I do a booboo, I get a *look* from him that if looks could kill, forget it.

"Yeah, Dom's got cancer in the lungs and stomach. Oh, yeah, it's terminal; he's got about a year yet, but I figure you can store up a lot of memories in a year. He's not much for painkillers; he likes to keep active. He eats a good meal, even though he's not supposed to. He figures if he follows all the doctor's orders he may live another six months, but it would be very boring, so who needs it? He's a very

heavy drinker; he can kill a bottle of Scotch in a day, easy. Not me, I get looped on less than a bottle.

"I'd like to have his child, because I've never found a man who deserves one more, but even though it would be nice not to be alone when he's gone, I don't want to stand by a grave with a baby in my arms. And he'd worry thinking how he wouldn't be here to see it raised. There's lots of things a father can do that a mother can't, like give the child strength and extra affection when the mother has to do the discipline. Besides, with a child where am I going to find another husband? And even if I had one I wouldn't want to go back to work and leave the child with a baby-sitter and have him wonder who's Mom. I've got to face facts: each week Dom gets sicker—and if I had a miscarriage, I think that would cut my heart out.

"Abortion? I believe in it, but not at six months, maybe because I lost one of mine at six months. (I had two other miscarriages, too, at four months.) I'll give a woman three months not to notice—maybe she's busy—and one month to make arrangements, but no more.

"But first of all you shouldn't get pregnant in the first place, there's no excuse with fifty thousand contraceptives on the market. If you use two at a time like I do—I use pills and foam—you have no excuse. I've been told to get off pills, but I won't, because when your husband gets romantic there's nothing worse than ruining the whole mood by running for a diaphragm.

"Our honeymoon was our only vacation. All we did was watch my brother's house while he took his vacation. Don't come here the second and third week in July, though, because we'll be together here then, and I'm hoping it'll be romantic. We like to stay home. We play cards, chess, checkers, and right now I'm working on a hooked rug, too, to put at the bottom of our bed.

"How do I feel about what's happening to Dom? Well, I figure somebody's got to get a loser, right? If I get a loser, somebody else won't. I really don't know how I'll react when the time comes, but I'm getting used to picking up my marbles and going home."

On the way to the bar we noticed a spider on the inside windshield of my car. Arlene asked if we could please stop and get it out. "I wouldn't want you to kill it, but if there's one thing I really don't like, it's bugs. Dom says I have a special voice I use to scream for him to come and kill bugs or get them out."

The spider wasn't hard to get rid of, and then we went into the bar. It was dimly lit and convivial. Dom really did wear dark glasses and

he really did look sort of like a kewpie doll; I could see what Arlene meant. When she told him I was Sharon from New Jersey, all he said was, "Oh, yeah, hi."

"I'm not coming home tonight," he said to Arlene.

"You're not?"

"Not until two-thirty."

"Good," she smiled. "I'm making you steak with wine sauce."

CHAPTER 10

I DIDN'T BRING ENOUGH BURNT SIENNA

You wanted to fly in the daytime to Tucson, fifteen hundred miles farther west than you ever had been before, so that you could see the terrain from above. As our plane descends, you look down onto the desert and sigh.

"I didn't bring enough burnt sienna," you say.

Our trip is fraught with possibility. We have come this far to find out whether we can stand each other. We are here because, okay, you're right, in all these off-and-on years of our entanglement, I never have given you my whole attention. Always there has been somebody else around the corner, or waiting in the wings, maybe because I was afraid for there not to be. Maybe we've both been afraid it might work. At heart, perhaps, we don't want to trade our familiar, comfortable sighs of resignation for the strange new oxygen of hope.

But of late I have been having what some call fantasies, starring you. Having no idea whether you were still available, I counted to ten and took deep breaths and called you. After some nervous parrying about the *New Yorker*'s two movie critics it turned out you still were interested. We talked anew of a possible joint future. Might it work? Our temperaments are flagrantly different, sure, but maybe that's good. Maybe with the new me around, you would be inspired to do more of your magnificent, tender landscapes. Maybe with the new you around I would uncoil and stop being so flippant. Might we after all forsake all others, cleave together, merge? On the chance that we might, we have made what, for two such wary people, is a serious emotional commitment. We have agreed that as soon as the semester is over and you stop teaching, we shall journey together to

202

the West, where in all your five decades you never have been. A native New Yorker, your travels have been to Sussex and Tuscany and the valley of the Rhone, except for that one time in Iowa City. Now, since you have the whole summer off, you will accompany me to the West, where I have to go anyway in the course of my work.

We pore over the atlas and imagine: home fries and a twist of orange automatically served with breakfast, gas station attendants who are not sullen all day, vistas that ought to make a painter's heart, such as your own, leap. And while your heart is leaping, while you perhaps are making sketches, I shall be gathering material for the book I am doing on our countrywomen. The constricting impasses of New York we shall trade for the fresh new realities of the road, thereby discovering our true selves and, with luck, each other.

Oh, and you'll finish learning to drive. Since from Tucson onward we shall travel by rent-a-car, and since you say it isn't fair for me to have to drive all that way, you have actually hired the AAA Academy to teach you enough to get a learner's permit. In so doing you have begun to overcome a lifetime phobia, to a standing ovation from all our friends, who join me in urging you to get a license.

The fact that you don't drive obsesses me unprettily. I am not mollified to know that Vladimir Nabokov doesn't drive either, or that Edmund Wilson couldn't. I forgive them, but not you; I have too mean a spirit. I am a willful, limited, grownup brat from Sangamon County, Illinois, and any man who aspires to be a man of mine had better be able to do a mean U-turn. Oh, I make a real metaphor of it. Driving means going where you want when you want—get it?—not having to rely on bus schedules or friends. What driving really mostly means, in the matter of you and me, is that I have an outsized fear of being, or even seeming to be, the one who is in charge.

The road between Tucson and Phoenix is straight, uncomplicated, and not very interesting. Marcus drives, and ably, too. I switch the car radio on, hoping to hear a bit of country western; Marcus writhes and winces for a while and reaches down to switch the dial off, giving a discourse on the cultural poverty of the American interior. A while later, since it is high noon and we are in the desert, I switch on the air-conditioner. He writhes again.

"Would you mind not turning that thing on?" he asks. "It seems unnatural."

"Fine," I say. "We'll just sweat. It's probably not quite in the hundreds yet." Oh dear. Some of the best conversations of my life have

been in cars, on long trips like this one. There is something freeing about being encapsulated and uninterrupted, something conducive to the heights of humor and depths of gravity that separate good talk from blather about logistics. I guess I had hoped that Marcus and I would have such conversations on the open roads of America. I guess we aren't going to.

I am at the wheel at dusk, when we get to the Grand Canyon. I drive past several outlook points, trying to find the most spectacular view of the setting sun. Marcus seethes: he is afraid it will be dark before I stop. I finally do. We get out and stare down the south rim. I know exactly what he is going to say, and he does not disappoint me.

"That," he announces, "is a *big* mother." He cannot see enough of it. The next day we are both happy. He makes sketches of the canyon. It pleases me immoderately to see him engaged in a pursuit of his own.

Something about Prescott, Arizona, through which we pass on our way to Los Angeles, enchants me at first sight. I am smitten with the courthouse square and the men sitting around on park benches. I love the lady who waits on us in the coffee shop and am tempted when a man in cowboy boots whom we talk to there suggests we stay on that night for a street dance. Marcus says he will if I really want to, but that we ought to get going. Prescott seems just another town to him.

As we head relentlessly westward on U.S. 60, I grow more fidgety about the juxtaposition of Marcus and Los Angeles. That place can unsettle me enough when I go there alone; how am I going to handle it with the most discerning companion in the Western world at my side?

CHAPTER 11

THE ONLY MAN IN THE POLO
LOUNGE WITH A LEARNER'S PERMIT

The Beverly Hills Hotel is a sumptuous pink monument set off Sunset Boulevard by an imposing horseshoe drive. You don't park your own car there, attendants do it for you. The desk is good about messages and whenever you pick up the phone in your room the switchboard operator greets you by name. All over the premises

you see lithe, bronzed, gilded people with unlikely teeth, standing around oozing importance, paging each other at poolside and having phones plugged in at their tables in the Polo Lounge so they can call New York. When I would go to Los Angeles for *Life,* to do stories on people like Jacqueline Susann, a room would always be booked for me at the Beverly Hills.

I had not planned on staying there with Marcus. Intuition told me that with him I should stay in some modest place right on the ocean, so that he could swim or sunbathe, if he wanted to, while I was off working. Besides two magazine assignments, I hoped to gather some material for my book on women. While I was doing all this, Marcus and I had agreed, he would discover the city for himself. Since I would need our rent-a-car he would get around by public transportation. It was more or less true that nobody we knew had ever known anyone, socially, who ever had taken a bus in Los Angeles, but so much the better: his forays would be the stuff of anecdotes.

Maybe, if he gave Los Angeles a chance, he would even like it. A lifetime movie addict, he could steep himself in the mystique of Hollywood. A painter, he could assess the museums and galleries. Meanwhile, we had to hurry up and find a place to stay. The Santa Monica motel where we had made reservations turned out to be seedy, which was why I was telling Marcus about the Beverly Hills.

"You know I'm a bed and breakfast man at heart," he said. "But if you say so, okay, let's go there."

"Hey," I said when I returned to our hotel room a couple of nights later, after an interview in Pasadena, "have you been watching the election returns? McGovern won the primary."

"Rlmph," said Marcus, who had fallen asleep with the light on. "Good for him."

"Sorry to wake you up."

"That's all right."

"I tried to call you this afternoon. What'd you do today?"

"The County Art Museum. Not a bad collection. You've seen it, haven't you?"

"I've always meant to go there, but. . ."

"In all the trips you've made to this city you've never once been to the County Art Museum?" Now Marcus was fully awake.

"As I say," I called from the bathroom, "I've meant to."

"But these sociological trends you write your stories about keep you pretty busy, huh?"

"You put it so graciously."

"Sorry," he said. "How was the woman you just talked to?"

"She was a sixteen."

"A what?"

"That's how the Bank of America categorizes its employes, by numbers. It's so personal and nice. The president of the bank is a thirty, and the file clerks are ones, and Betty is a sixteen."

"I assume she doesn't *like* being a sixteen?"

"She's got a law degree and a *summa cum laude* in math, and she's forty-four years old with a lot of experience, and in the five years she's been there, they haven't given her one promotion."

"How come she doesn't split and find some other job?"

"Because she has this uncanny loyalty to the bank. She wants to help change it from within."

"Will she fit into the article you're doing?"

"I hope so," I said.

"I don't see how you'll ever get it done," he said.

"Thanks."

Betty, the sixteen, was suing the bank she worked for. When she told her midwestern father that she had joined in a lawsuit against her employers he was as worried as he had once been years earlier, when she broke an engagement.

"The way I was raised, you always remembered to be thankful for what you had, no matter what you didn't have," Betty said the evening she and I talked. "That's why I haven't been militant in the women's movement up until now. But now I go to work every morning with a sense of dread. Somebody at the office advised me, 'Look, for the sake of your friends here, don't be too friendly, because friendship with you could be a handicap.'

"All my working life," she sighed, "I've been told, 'You're doing great, but we can't give that promotion to a woman.' What am I supposed to do, go to Sweden and get a sex change operation?"

"Far out," said our friend Luther. "Think of it, Marcus, the only man in the Polo Lounge with a learner's permit." We were having dinner with Luther and his wife Gwen in an Italian place on Sunset, and Marcus was telling of his adventures with public transportation. Never, he said, had he met more courteous bus drivers. His only regret, he told us, was having allowed a Zionist, pro-Nixon barber on Fairfax Avenue to cut off rather too much of his hair.

"You should have seen the way Marcus's hair was starting to look," I said to Luther and Gwen. "It was thick and luscious."

"A bit too Ben-Gurion, though," said Marcus. "But it'll grow back. It'll be *perfect*, you know what I mean?" He was making a determined effort, it was clear, not to be negative. "Hey, guess what else I did? I paid homage to the footprints at Grauman's Chinese Theatre! Quite a thrill, for a kid from Eighty-ninth and First."

"If you'd like to have a tour of one of the studios," said Luther, who was writing a screen treatment, "we could lay that on for you."

"Thanks," Marcus said, "but the only thing of that nature I'd really like would be to meet Jimmy Cagney."

"So would I," said Gwen, "but who knows how to do that?"

"These zinnias are magnificent," I said to Gwen and Luther. "It was great of you to bring them to us."

"It *was* thoughtful of them," Marcus said later as we drove homeward along Sunset Strip, "but how come they didn't invite us to see their house?"

"Maybe their house was a mess," I said. "After all, they just got back from Mexico. Maybe they just didn't want to. There are times when I don't feel like having people over, either."

"Still," he said, "it gave me an odd feeling."

"Look over there," I told him. "See those sort of gable roofs? That's the Chateau Marmont, where I once lived for three months."

"Maybe we should have stayed there instead of the Beverly Hills."

"Maybe so, but I didn't think you'd like being on the Strip."

"It's a weird phenomenon, all right," said Marcus. "To tell you the truth, I don't know what you see in it."

"I don't recall ever saying it was pretty," I told him. "But as American thoroughfares go, it's about as vital and revealing a one as any I can think of. Look at the energy of it."

"I suppose so," he said, "if what you're interested in is history, or sociology, or the future."

"And you're *not* interested in those things?" I asked. "I guess you're really not, are you? Wow: you're ruling out a lot." I couldn't help myself: since we weren't far from home, I reached down to turn on the car radio. After half a minute he switched it off. The ensuing spat did honor to neither of us.

"Silence is intolerable to you, isn't it?" asked Marcus.

"Yeah, right," I said. "That's why I once spent two months doing a piece on it. I like an occasional cantata and madrigal too, you know,"

I reminded him pompously, "but it also nourishes my soul to keep abreast of the Top Forty once in a while."

"Your soul," he said, "is so wonderfully protean."

"I can't wait until Brandace gets old enough to give me some really good advice," Karol Hope was telling me in the hotel restaurant, the next morning, as Marcus slept late. "At eight and a half she's doing pretty well already. She wishes a man would come along that we both liked at the same time, and I guess that's what I wish, too."

But Karol, who is six feet tall, has a number of other wishes. "The new culture we're trying to create," she said, "seems drastic to those who guard the traditions we're trying to get away from. Even the women's movement is only slowly becoming aware of single mothers. What we're essentially trying to do is to make our lives more than just a foggy limbo between one heavy relationship with a man and another."

When Karol Hope says "we," she is talking about 250,000 other single mothers—one doesn't say "unwed mothers because some of them have been wed"—in Los Angeles, and more than seven million others in the rest of the country. *Momma,* a magazine Karol conceived and edits, was founded to meet the needs of these mothers, most of whom are divorced and a few of whom are widowed. These needs concern welfare, jobs, housing, child care, and a lot more sociability than is readily to be found in cities like Los Angeles.

"In other cultures," Karol said, "single moms aren't isolated, but in ours they are. I think fewer and fewer people are going to have kids, as they find out all that being a parent involves. It's really hard to be a single mom in a city like this. There's so little sense of community. The ideal way would be to go to a bar or coffee house on Monday night where you could meet somebody you could be sure you'd see there again on Wednesday."

"How come you live here, then?"

"Because of the innovations, the imagination, the openness. It's such a change from the authoritarian way I was raised. Sometimes I wonder if I'll end up in a mental institution, for having stepped so far from the mainstream."

"Were you ever really *in* the mainstream?"

"I had a church wedding," said Karol, "and I wore all the things my mother wanted me to wear. I was afraid that if I didn't marry this man, he would split or pull away. I really married him because I was

into getting out of the house, and I was afraid to hurt his feelings."

"What attracted you to him?" I asked her.

"He represented adventure, excitement, do-it-a-different-way-ness. He'd been married before, he was ten years older, six inches taller—for the first time in my life I could wear heels—and he was very powerful in my life. I listened to him a great deal, and I guess he liked me because I was young and enthusiastic. At that point—I was nineteen—I was incredible, tragically unaware of relationships, love, and how marriage really could be. What scared me was confronting him with how I really felt. We were married for four years, and like so many of us, I walked into that life-style without knowing what I was doing."

"What do you think the answer is?" I asked Karol. "Communes?"

"Not exactly. I studied communes in anthropology, and there are two things that make or break them: enough space so that everyone can be alone, and honesty, so that people really can say where they're at and how they really do feel, instead of how they ought to.

"Single mothers," she said, "are forever being told how they *ought* to feel about things. We always live under the burden of someone else's expertise. Still we feel total responsibility for the care and well-being of kids. It's amazing what effect it can have on your energy to know you can't possibly say to someone else, 'Here, *you* take over for ten minutes.'

"It's scary, but single mothers have an overwhelming necessity to survive. There's a lot of consciousness-raising going on, and a lot of single mothers are starting to reject the pressure they've always had, to be linked up with a man—any old man will do."

"What'd you talk about at breakfast?" Marcus asked later.

"Oh," I said, "the problems of mothers who don't have husbands."

"What about men whose women are never on the scene?"

I looked at him and said nothing.

CHAPTER 12

I WANTED JUST WHAT I GOT

Why, officer," I said as I pulled over to the side of the road. "I had no idea I was going over the speed limit. I guess we were so busy trying to find a motel to stay in that I just wasn't noticing."

"Let's see your driver's license, lady." For the next twenty minutes, it seemed, the patrolman laboriously copied the data from the document onto a ticket, which led to a twenty-five-dollar fine. The moral of this vignette is that you don't mess around while driving through Eureka, California. That cop did us a favor, though. He said we might find a place to sleep in the fishing village of Trinidad.

Even in the dark I could tell I was going to like this small town on a harbor. The Ocean Grove Lodge seemed a promisingly unfranchised, individual place to stay. The manager showed us to a cabin around which there seemed to be redwoods, and when we said we were hungry he said that even though the cafe part of the place was about to close he would let us go on in. Our vegetable beef soup and apple pie, all flawlessly homemade, were served by a stalwart tall waitress named Doris Van Velkinburgh.

"If I didn't work," Doris told us as we ate, "I'd get fat as a pig and weigh 200, but as it is I keep down to 170." In addition to being a waitress in this cafe, she was also, like her husband and her father before her, a fisherman. She did not say fisherperson.

Doris wiped off the counter and said she believed she would go into the bar and have a beer, to unwind a bit.

"Hey, Marcus," I whispered. "Remember, I told you I've been hoping to find some terrific western woman who does a man's work? That was why I was thinking of going on to Utah or Idaho after this?"

"You'd like to go in there and talk to her."

"And you'd like not to, I know. Would you mind if I did?"

"Do what you have to do," he said, and retired to Cabin Nine. I asked Doris if she would mind if I joined her, just to visit a little. Mind? Doris?

"Oh yeah," she said as we sat on adjoining stools in the bar, "you go out there fishing and I'll tell you something, you forget your troubles, especially when it gets a little nippy. Our boat don't have railings, and I tell you, you've got to have nimble feet. Sure I wear rubber stuff and outdoor gear. Last winter we lost a big boat, three hours after I'd been in it. If I'd still been in it, I would have saved it. That boat was worth $22,000, and you can't get no insurance out of Trinidad because it's an open harbor.

"Fishing's good out of Trinidad. We fish for crab and salmon. Crabs are the hardest and most temperamental; they might bite fine here but not at all one fathom away." Not having a notebook with me, I was writing down what Doris said on the back of cardboard

bills the bartender kept giving me, bills that said "THANK YOU! Your Patronage Is Appreciated."

"Darn right I get paid the same as men," Doris said. "I get the same percentage of the day's haul as they do: fifteen percent for crab, twenty percent for salmon. I'm called a puller. I unload the pots and do rebaiting. There's two sizes of pots: big heavy eighty-five pound ones for the deep sea and lighter ones for in close.

"On the big boats the men pee off the side and treat you like a man. They say if you want to work like a man, you'd better expect us to treat you like one, so when they cuss like the devil I just cuss back. My favorite expression is 'bull-shitty.' At the dock, if I said, 'will you please move?' they'd look at me like I was crazy. The thing they understand is, 'Get your ass over here.' I'm like one of the boys; you don't find them fooling with me.

"I have to wash my hair every day with oil shampoo, because it gets all fishy, scaly, and crabby. I don't care much for fancy clothes, but once when I had a pilot's license and ran a yacht out of San Pedro, a man gave me a $120 tip and I spent it on a dress.

"Oh, I've had some times. I've been all over almost all the U.S., drove to Alaska once, been to Honolulu several times, and been fishing all the way up and down the coast from the Bering Sea down to Chile. I was seventeen when my dad took me to the Bering Sea. Up there we fished for salmon. It was fun, but a lot of work, and when we got in storms my dad would treat me like a boy.

"Chile was dirty. Down there we fished for shark liver and got eighty, ninety cents a pound for it, because they used it for medicine and perfume, but the next year synthetics came along, and the price went down to seven or eight cents." The bartender looked wonderingly at all my notes. "If I knew you were going to write down that much," he said, "I'd have given you some big sheets of paper." Don't worry, I told him.

"Where I used to live in Oakland is all black now, not that I'm against black, don't get me wrong. If any came up here we'd be nice to them, but none do. See, Trinidad's the oldest incorporated city in California, and it's kinda cliquey here. There's just 650 or 700 people, and you're not family unless you've been here ten years. That's why I try to be extra nice to new people. Most people move here because it's a good place to bring up kids.

"We've got a Catholic church—I'm Catholic—and a Protestant, and a beauty parlor, a grocery store, a gas station, and a grammar school

up to the eighth grade. Then there's Mom's fishhouse. It's called Katy's Smoke House. She's been at it twenty-six, twenty-seven years, selling crab and smoked and fresh salmon. You might want to go talk to her too, if you're here in the morning."

I was, and I did, while Marcus prowled delightedly around a beach where there were astonishing small driftwood formations, a bit farther up the coast. They entranced him, and so did the sample I brought him of Katy's smoked wares. Katy didn't have much time to talk, but she told me how for eight years she had cooked all the crab for the famous Trinidad Chamber of Commerce crab feed, held every year around May twenty-first, "I did it," she said, "up to when it was 10,000 pounds and didn't charge them because I was a member of the Chamber of Commerce myself, but now it's up to 14,000 pounds. I married for the first time at the age of fourteen. I guess you'd say I was a child bride, but I knew more than some of these do now at twenty-four or thirty. I've been lucky to have the kind of husband who'd understand me, otherwise my marriage wouldn't have lasted two minutes. I don't need no man to tell me how to run my life."

"I met my husband in Southern California," Doris went on, "when we were fishing for albacore. We got married in Las Vegas, when I was twenty-two, against my father's wishes. My dad didn't want me to marry a fisherman, or if I did he wanted him to be at least a captain. My husband was a game warden for seven years, but the state don't pay that much. Now he's gone back to fishing. He gets up at five A.M. Our younger boy goes out there too. He does water-taxiing in a sixteen-foot skiff with an outboard. The fishermen blow their horns when they want him, and tip him.

"I've worked here in this cafe for four-and-a-half years. I'm used to working. I've just always worked, and when I'm not working here I work at my mom's. I've got two in college now and three next year, and you know what they cost. My oldest is twenty, she's stationed with the navy in Washington State, doing security bomb disbursements. Another girl's at Humboldt College. She wants to be an ombudsman. The boy who's seventeen, he'll graduate this June. The girl who's fifteen, she don't think about nothing but boys.

"They're a whole bunch too free with their sex, kids of that age, or maybe it's just that that's what we hear. My Sue, she's eighteen, she's a good girl, she told me she had intercourse with a boy. Shoot, I guess I did it at eighteen too, but I wouldn't have dared to tell my mother. I always tell them, if you get into trouble, tell Mama first. I

told my girls, if you're going to do it, we'll get you some pills, because I want you to finish college and I want to make sure you'll stay clean. If you ever suspect you're not, we'll go to see the family doctor. He's a swell man, he knows us like books and it would never go past his lips.

"Shoot, they teach sex education here in the sixth grade, and I think it's real good that they do. They showed a VD movie at a PTA meeting I went to. Pretty raw stuff; it made me cringe. Drugs worries me quite a bit, too. It'd just about kill me if our kids got on them. If that happened, the first thing I'd do would be find me a mental clinic and drag their fannies down there.

"I've been in the PTA for years but I don't have much time to help except to send them pies. I used to have the girls' drill team in high school. We took fifth place in the whole West. We went to Sacramento and Oregon and all over. We'd do stars, blocks, oblique rights and lefts, circles, and unwind. We'd practice two nights a week. The girls wanted to do it, so I figured, shoot, it'd keep them out of trouble. Oh, I was rough, though. Like I told them, no goofing. Any girl who misses over two practices without a medical reason, you're out.

"I went to college myself, two years in Skagit Valley, Washington, where my dad was fishing at the time. I studied sociology, of all things. Ain't that something? No, I didn't want to stay longer. I wanted just what I got: to get married and raise my family.

"The worst thing that ever happened to us was one Christmas Eve morning when our house burned down. We've got just one volunteer fire engine but it came, and I'll tell you what a small community will do for you: they brought us clothes and furniture and everything. Lisa was in the hospital for eleven months. She's been grafted twelve times. Ninety percent of her body was burned. She can't have no kids, because there's so much scar tissue her tummy won't stretch. For a while she thought she wanted to be a nun, but now she's had an operation so she can't get pregnant.

"There's lots of poverty up here in the winter. Our two industries, woods and fishing, are both bad in the winter. I took a lady friend who was down on her luck to Eureka to get food stamps, and there were big, strapping, healthy, hulking men there getting food stamps too, and I couldn't help but wonder why they didn't wash windows or mow lawns. The ones who feel down on the world aren't doing anything about it, they just protest and cry and bitch. Those filthy

hippies with their beards, what are they doing to help? They're trashy, that's what they are. My husband says he'd like to take them down to the ocean and dump them in.

"I like organ music and the music of my own time: calypso, Glenn Miller, Tommy Dorsey. In the winter I like to go skiing, not here, where we just get a sprinkle, but nineteen miles away. We don't have to go far to go hunting for deer, either. We smoke it and make venison jerky. Movies? I haven't been to one in four, five years. Seems to me they don't make good ones any more. I used to love John Wayne. I'd tease my husband and say, 'John Wayne can put his shoes under my bed any time.' "

With that, since my wrist was cramped from note-taking, I thought it might be time to take my own shoes off in Cabin Nine. Before I left, the bartender, to whom I had mentioned that I liked wine, insisted, "Here, you try some of this, it's Gallo cream sherry, and don't it taste good?" Another big seller, he said, was tomato beer: beer with fresh tomato juice. Would I like to try it?

"Another time," I said.

I really wouldn't mind going back there again.

CHAPTER 13
A CITIZEN OF THE REALM

I could be wrong about travel being a metaphor for life, but I figure that if we cannot survive a single day on the road without squabbling and seething, then Marcus and I wouldn't be able to at home, either, and we'd better stop kidding ourselves. It isn't that he drove the car off the highway into a ditch along the Oregon coast; that was a minor error any novice driver might have made. It caused no harm except to his psyche. I knew that I had been foolish to place such an emphasis on his becoming a motorist: in doing so I had been revealing nothing so much as my own shallow insecurity.

What matters is that our moments of tenderness and humor have been far too infrequent to outweigh the acrimony. When we get to Eugene, Oregon, where I am to talk to the writer Ken Kesey, it has become clear to Marcus and me both that our travels together are over. Both our teeth, or rather all our teeth, have been gritted most of the majestic way up the coastline.

214

Still, although there have been times during our trip when I have physically longed for our moment of parting, it does not delight or even much relieve me to take Marcus to the Eugene airport. He has worked his way into some of the innermore labyrinths of my head, from which I could not banish his influence even if I wanted to. In spite of everything he has understood me, and I him, in a way neither of us can easily duplicate. He is rare and fine, and someone of calmer temperament, beset by fewer, or at least other, demons, will if she is lucky discover and deserve him, as I do not. He is flying now to New York, by way of Portland, and after a few days he will proceed to London. London gives him something I cannot.

Faye, you might have thought, would be the obvious one for me to talk to. Faye the beatific, Faye the Ur mother, Faye the keel who had kept the craft afloat through the sixteen years of her often stormy marriage to Ken Kesey, Faye who had not even minded when another woman bore a child Kesey had sired, "because," Kesey put it, "all that sort of happened under other auspices, and we all get along real good."

Faye, heedless of auspices, sewed and made applesauce bread and fed Rumiyako, the pet macaw, and imperturbably ministered to the needs of her husband, their three children, and all other sentient beings in sight. She had slightly tilted, Finnish-looking blue eyes, and the calm air of a madonna. It was said of Faye that once, warned of the possible imminence of earthquakes, she responded by going out to prune the fruit trees. I recognized her worth. But somehow even though she and I were of an age I could not seem to strike up an unstilted conversation with her. I felt shy. Maybe we both did. I doubt very much that she meant to, but she, and in fact the whole lot of them at Kesey's place, made me feel just a bit like a comparison shopping, super-straight Junior Leaguer from someplace like Grosse Pointe. Maybe it's just that after five weeks on the road I was tired.

Kesey and Faye and their kids live in a huge barn outside Pleasant Hill, which in turn is outside the state university town of Eugene. That same barn used to be a commune, before Kesey ejected the several dozen other residents. "What it boiled down to," he said, "was we realized we can't live in the same kitchen. We're too human; we bicker and brood and gossip." But a lot of those same people have settled close by. Their lives still revolve around Kesey's. He is still, as he puts it, the honcho.

Rumor had it, in June of 1972, that Kesey was nearly finished working on a third book, his first in nearly ten years, to be called *Garage Sale*. It was supposed to incorporate a screenplay called *Over The Border*, which would tell of the months Kesey had spent in Mexico as a fugitive from justice when he was wanted for possession of drugs. Those same adventures had inspired Tom Wolfe's *The Electric Kool Aid Acid Test*, which had done as much to make Kesey famous as had Kesey's own novels, *One Flew Over the Cuckoo's Nest* and *Sometimes a Great Notion*. Wolfe told of all this and of Kesey's ebullient followers, called the Merry Pranksters, who shared his feeling of evangelism about LSD and speed.

With so many of the Merry Prankster alumni living nearby, all the ingredients of a topical magazine piece seemed on hand. Whither, such a piece could ask, the drug generation? Is acid really obsolete? If communes don't work, why don't they? Is there any truth in all the talk about permanent brain damage? What made Kesey change his mind, after he told Wolfe he planned to write no more "because I'd rather be a lightning rod than a seismograph?" How come he was suddenly into, as some might put it, seismography?

But since *Garage Sale* was farther from completion than anybody wanted it to be, my interest shifted. I paid more attention to the place of women in the counterculture. I didn't use the word "counterculture" much. I used it, in fact, only once, on a hot afternoon when a dozen or so of us were sunbathing next to Kesey's yard by a pond which we shared with ducks, geese, and trout.

"We don't talk that way," Gretchen Babbs told me evenly and pleasantly, after I had used the word. Gretchen had clean dark blonde hair and wore a long Indian print skirt. She always had at least one child on her lap. "Counterculture," she said, "isn't in our vocabulary. We're not into bagging people here."

"How would you describe yourself?" I asked.

"I consider myself a citizen of the realm," she said. That was what made me decide to focus on Gretchen, who seemed circumspect and kind. I hoped she would tell me more of how it felt to be a citizen of that particular part of the realm.

Technically her name is not Gretchen Babbs. Not being technically married, she is legally still Paula Sundsten, the name she was given in Hood River, Oregon in 1943. But having lived with Kesey's close partner Ken Babbs since 1964, and borne him four children, Gretchen does not "feel I have to go through somebody else's ritual

to prove I'm married." She has been know as Gretchen—more properly Gretchen Fetchin—only since the momentous transcontinental bus trip of which Wolfe wrote in his book on Kesey.

During that trip she met Babbs. "Babbs was still married then, so it was two years before we were together permanently, but he and another guy and I shot a movie and put it together in Santa Cruz. Babbs's wife lived around there too. She and I became good friends. I'd take care of her kids when she went to classes. In Santa Cruz we started doing the acid tests. After she met another guy and got remarried, Babbs and I got started with our own family."

They have since been evicted and bought land of their own, but when I met the Babbs family in late June 1972 they rented a sprawling, friendly farmhouse for $70 a month. Chickens ran around the backyard, which had giant trees and a beanfield adjoining. Babbs drove me there one evening on his way home from the office in the loft above Kesey's barn. Three other people, counting Kesey, worked with him at the headquarters of the Intrepid Travelers Information Service, to produce, among other publications, a magazine called *Spit in the Ocean*. These ventures were not at the time visibly profitable, and so the Babbs family subsisted on a $125 monthly check Babbs's mother in Ohio sent them from his late father's insurance. For $8 they could then buy $180 worth of food stamps, and it pleased them that "you can use the stamps to buy anything you like, including marinated artichokes."

"I'm the oldest of four kids," Gretchen told me as I helped her hang her wash on the line, envying her the fragrance the clothes would have. "My mother wanted me to be a college graduate and have a professional job. I lasted one term in business administration. Then I tried art, which proved too unstable, and art education, which I liked all right because it dealt with people. I was expected to get married in a lovely ceremony at age twenty-two, but I think my mother must have figured out by my sophomore year in college that it wouldn't quite work out that way.

"Even in high school, when kids that age were just beginning to be radicalized, I did some political stuff as well as the typical rebellious stuff and was scolded for having a negative attitude. They told me if I didn't cool it in two weeks, I wouldn't graduate. I did graduate. At the University of Oregon I was the first freshman ever to live off campus. I started the whole movement and battle about that, and it was a good thing I did. Living in dorms and dealing only with

a certain age group doesn't teach you anything about how to deal with real life situations.

"Although everyone told us not to, a girlfriend and I went to New York the summer between sophomore and junior year. We got jobs as waitresses at Jack Dempsey's restaurant and had a fantastic time. The next year I decided to go back. That year I'd met Kesey, who'd been hanging around the campus, and I thought he seemed to have pretty straight vision. He had this bus he was driving East, so I went along for the ride." So did Babbs.

"Eli," said Gretchen, "is the only one of our children to have been conceived and born in the same bed. I highly recommend having kids at home with your old man right there. I was the first one in our county health nurse's experience to do it that way.

"Dope interferes with motherhood. Women seem to do less dope than men do, partly because dope breaks down your resistance, and women need strength to deal with more interruptions, like runny noses. If you don't pay attention to your kids, they'll really be screwed up. So the way it works out, men have a much better chance of finishing what they start than women do. To do dope with kids around is a waste anyway; the two things don't mix.

"Dope has done a lot to change women. It's turned them on more to *being* women. It brings out their spirit. The vibrations I get from Women's Liberation make me shy away from it completely. All the women I've met who are into it seem very unhappy. They're searching so hard that they're turning off the very thing they're really searching for, which is a good relationship with a man. By trying to force him into a certain position, and dealing with him as 'a man' instead of as a human being, they blow it."

I wondered what Marcus was doing right then. Maybe he was still in New York, where it was three hours later. Maybe he was already heading toward London, crossing the Atlantic, going farther away.

"Dope's changed my feelings about religion, too," said Gretchen. "We say grace every night here, because we think it's a good idea to give up your ego once a day to somebody else. My religion now is a daily, secular thing, rather than being a matter of Sundays.

"We've talked about renting a hall on Sundays and singing hymns and whooping it up. I hope we do it, because I like to play the piano, and I think we should keep that stuff going. Hymns and spirituals are good for the kids. We do other rituals too: jack-o-lanterns, Thanksgiving, Easter egg coloring.

"What would I do if I didn't have kids? Well, I'd definitely have something going, go back to working in movies, maybe. There's a lot of things I'd like to do, when the kids don't need so much attention. Babbs says he has to laugh at birth control, at man's arrogant attempt to take over for what God does, because he says, to him, kids are like blessings. Well, they are, but I think I'd like to take a break from blessings for a while."

One afternoon Kesey drove me into Eugene to visit his mother. She had invited him and his brother Chuck and their families for Sunday dinner. Mrs. Kesey looked like everybody's mother, and reminded me of a lot of my aunts. Her house, painted pink, was immaculate and cheerful. Her husband, she told me, had died at age fifty-six of an incurable disease of the central nervous system.

"When my husband was alive, I never took a job or even thought of it. He was of the old school. If I'd left home when the kids were little, there'd have been a divorce. He was in business, you see, and he expected me to be on call at home. If he phoned to say, 'I'll be home in half an hour with four guests,' then I knew I'd better be ready, and I always was, too.

"Since he died, though, I've been working. I sell dresses in a department store, and I like it. Ken wasn't so sure I should, but Chuck, my younger son, liked the idea. I got bored playing cards, drinking coffee with the girls, doing volunteer work, bowling, golfing, all that crap. You have to change your own pattern, because nobody else is going to feel sorry for you if you feel sorry for yourself."

Mrs. Kesey got up and went into her kitchen to fetch the coffeepot.

"Want another cup of mud?" she asked.

CHAPTER 14

ACHIEVE, ACHIEVE

Thick tan humid smog shrouds the whole Eastern seaboard the day I land at JFK Airport. My cab driver curses the clotted traffic. His radio says the air is unacceptable. It is, but somehow I don't care, because pretty soon I can unpack. Unpacking, after so long on the road, is an almost erotic pleasure.

"What happened with Marcus?" my friend Alice calls to ask. She and her husband Dean are spending the summer at their farm.

"He's gone to Europe," I tell her. "It didn't work out."

"Oh, dear. How're you feeling?"

"Numb, really. Numb and of course guilty—as you know I have a *vocation* for guilt—because I'm two months behind in my work. I've got to do a lot of work, and I've also got to unwind."

"If you really mean it about unwinding," she said, "come on up-state this weekend. There won't be a thing going on. The only excitement we can offer is homemade ice cream: we just got a freezer for our anniversary."

Alice, as it turns out, was wrong about the quiet weekend. We are all asked to an impromptu pot luck supper by the couple up the hill, to celebrate the wife's big book advance. The neighbors not only ask five or six other families but they have a houseguest. The houseguest's name is Charles Lawrence Nicholson, and he and I are asked to take charge of making the ice cream. Our product, peach with rum in it, is inspired.

The next day Charles Lawrence Nicholson, not known as Charlie or Chuck, gives me a ride back to the city. Two years my senior, he is a divorced geneticist at Rockefeller University, the father of three daughters, and as classic a specimen of an Ivy Leaguer as ever my mother could have envisioned. Seven inches taller than I am, with abundant blond hair just starting to gray, he is a breakfast-eating, Brooks Brothers type with steel rims. He and I seem to be ready for each other, at least momentarily. Entertaining the possibility that we may in fact have been born for each other, I make a private vow: this time I won't be aloof or coy or evasive. Maybe that's what went wrong with Marcus. I like this man, I like him a lot, and I'm not going to pretend I don't.

One bond we discover early on is that Charles and I are both compulsive achievers. In this respect we differ from Marcus, from Charles's former wife, who resented all the time he spent at his laboratory, and in fact from nine-tenths of humanity. "Listen to this," Charles reads me from a paper: " 'Only ten percent of the population is achievement-motivated, and women in that category are likely to experience intense conflicts, especially in regard to a possible loss of femininity.' Are you experiencing such an intense conflict, my dear?"

"Not with you around I'm not," I told him, "but don't you ever secretly wonder whether it might not be nice to be just a *little* more contemplative?" I asked him. "Maybe we're too much caught up in

accomplishing—too much defined by bylines and discoveries at the lab?"

"Not really," said Charles, "I honestly love what I do at the lab. I love the idea that I have a good chance to be named the next full professor. I love being good at what I do. And come on, Howard, you know you love it, too."

"You know something I don't love?" I asked him. "Being called Howard."

"Fair enough," he said. From then on that evening our communication was nonverbal.

"I'm supposed to go up to New Hampshire next week," I told him the next morning over strawberries. "I wish I didn't have to."

"Why?"

"I'd rather hang around here and see more of you." With a guarded, reticent past like mine this was quite an admission, I thought.

"That's sweet," he said, "but next week I'm really clobbered. I'm going to have to be late at the lab just about every night. I don't even know if I'll get to see the girls." His daughters lived with their mother in Manhasset.

"Then maybe it's as good a time as any for me to be gone?"

"I suppose it is," said Charles as he poured himself more coffee. "What have you got to do up there, anyway?"

"Well, New England's a part of the country I really haven't been to in years. I figure at some point I ought to go up there and just drive around, talk to different women for this project I've got."

"Are you just going to drive around by yourself?"

"I thought I'd told you. This friend of mine, Peggy, is taking her vacation next week, and that's why I ought to go then, because she's agreed to go with me."

"Is she the one you said was to you as Bebe Rebozo is to what's-his-name?"

"We've been each *other's* Bebe Rebozos," I corrected him. "Rebozohood is, or should be, a two-way street." Rebozohood, Charles and I had earlier agreed, was a rare, distilled form of friendship beyond pretense.

"I used to have friends like that in the navy," he said, "and one or two in school, but not many since. I guess it's less common for men than for women."

"Of course you were married for so long."

"That is a factor. Friends are more important when you're single. I was just twenty when we married—I did it to stop having dates."

"An excellent thing to stop having." (Should I tell him in so many words how ready I am to stop having them?)

"What's Peggy like?" Charles abruptly asked. (Maybe I've gone too far already.)

"Game, sympathetic, curious. Comes on strong. Men sometimes find her overpowering. Sometimes you wish there were a volume control dial, so you could tune her down."

"Better that than a mumbler."

"Do you hate mumblers too? I can't stand them. Mumbling seems to me an inverted form of arrogance. Anyway, Peggy is also capable of total silence. So, as long as I can't go up there with you, her company will do nicely. And she likes New England."

"Any sensible person would," said Charles. "Have you spent a lot of time up there?"

"Not recently, but over the years, yes, a lot." And almost always, I thought, with pleasure. Maybe it takes a midwesterner to revere and savor New England. Images flash to mind. A yellow cottage on the Pamet River in Truro. Dislodging mussels from rocks in ponds.

"I do wish we could go up there together," I told Charles when this reverie of mine was over. He had been reading the paper.

"Maybe we will, sometime," he said. "Maybe later this summer I'll drive around up there with the girls. It sort of clears the head."

"So do you," I heard myself saying, "and that's not all you do."

"Enough, woman," he said. He gave me a playful slap. "Begone. Or rather I'd better be gone. I've got work to do."

"Of course you have," I said. "Achieve, achieve."

"What is it you women say? 'Right on'?"

"Some women do," I said.

CHAPTER 15

HONOR YOUR CORNER PARTNER

How are the Jensens?" I asked Peggy. "I'm sorry I didn't get to see them before they left for Quebec."

"They were sorry too, but they had to get going." Sally and Lars Jensen were old friends of ours, especially of Peggy's. Just before my

arrival they and their five children had left for a month's camping in the Gaspé Peninsula and urged us to stay in their huge farmhouse as long as we liked. The house was vacant except for Lucy, a twenty-three-year-old biologist whom the Jensens had hired to stay and look after the horses and dogs. Lucy, who was trying to decide whether or not she wanted to go to medical school, had a single dark brown pigtail and an imperturbable manner.

"How long ago did the Jensens get married?" she asked Peggy and me as the three of us sat having breakfast.

"Must have been ten years ago," I said.

"That was some wedding, wasn't it?" asked Peggy.

"Sure was," I said. "You caught the bouquet, didn't you, Peggy?"

"They still threw *bouquets* in those days?" asked Lucy as she put honey in her tea.

"I caught a lot of them in my time," said Peggy. "I'm sure everybody figured I'd have paired off with somebody or other long before this."

"Me too," I said.

"Are you sure you *want* to get married?" Lucy asked us.

"I don't know of any better ideas," said Peggy. "Devotion and commitment—that's a pretty hard combination to beat."

"I'm not so sure I want to," said Lucy. "Three years ago I'd have jumped at the chance, but now I'm not so sure at all. I've been living with Zach for a year now—we went together two years before that —and it's been a real eye-opener. I'm not sure I wouldn't prefer to have him live about a block away so that we could see each other when we really both felt like it, when we wanted to share space and time."

"Where's Zach now?"

"He's gone home, to see his family. He hasn't been back there for six years."

"Back where?"

"Nigeria."

"Wow."

"The funny thing is, he's the one who urged *me* to get into feminism in the first place. He told me about this eight-week course called Women and Their Bodies. Out of idle curiosity, I went. What an experience. I didn't stop bubbling for the whole eight weeks."

"You spent eight weeks just talking about Fallopian tubes and such?" asked Peggy.

"Not just that. The great impact of the course was the idea that women really are just as important as men and should be respected as professionals. Since I took the course, Zach and I have had some heavy, involved discussions as to whether it's more important for him to become a big international doctor than it is for me to become whatever I might become."

"You've been with him three years? That's a long time."

"Maybe too long," said Lucy. "But I do miss him. We'll see. This fall I'm going to live in a house with other people, instead of just alone with him. That way I'll get more support when he's gone, and be with him when his eyes aren't closed, when he's in the mood."

"I envy Lucy her options," Peggy said that evening, "don't you?"

"I envy that whole generation," I said.

Orpha Smith was twenty-three in 1935, the year I was born. Peggy and I spent an afternoon talking to Orpha, in her kitchen near the Canadian border of Vermont, two days later. Orpha, known locally as the Maple Sugar Lady, was another specimen of that staunch breed of country women, liberally scattered around the United States, who might never give lip service to the feminist movement—might even, if pressed, speak against it—but who exemplify it whether they mean to or not.

We were sitting in her kitchen, where she was taking a break from making maple candy, in the shape of maple leaves and little maple women and men, and little tinfoil boxes of maple fudge, and maple syrup, and bewitching stuff called maple butter. The furniture and floors in her house were, of course, maple. She must have waxed and polished it all a lot, because it smelled immaculate. It looked cheerful with African violets here and there, but it felt a bit lonely.

"We built this house twenty-five years ago," Orpha told us with what could have been a catch in her voice, "and it's never been as empty as it is now. Now that the kids are gone, we don't have such big Thanksgivings and Christmases as we used to. Maybe this year they'll come home—who knows?"

Orpha had thick, wiry silver hair and tilted harlequin glasses. When we first met, her voice sounded high and tight, as if she hadn't been using it as much as she might have liked to. She wore a plaid housedress, which, like most of her clothes, she had made herself, and tennis shoes without socks. "I usually just go around in dungarees," she said, "though I had quite a lot of fun this past spring: I went out and bought me a new dress."

Her husband, Hue, she told us, was off in Maine, working on a family construction project. "He comes home with the crows in the spring to help with the sugaring," she said, "but the other nine months of the year, he's gone."

"Don't you and he miss each other?"

"I guess, but I don't want to go to Maine. I'd rather stay here and keep the business going, and he doesn't want to stay here—so there you are. But we've been married thirty-nine years, which is more than what happens with some of your big hoo-rah church weddings.

"I can't say I thoroughly approve of divorce, though. Nobody's ever happy with anybody all the time, and these days too many of 'em just seem to quit without giving it a fair try."

"Is Hue fun?"

"Oh, he can be, when he wants to be, but he usually says 'No' automatically, before he even knows what I'm going to ask him. He and his brothers just live to work."

"You're not exactly a sluggard yourself."

"I guess I'm not. I've been baking sugar cakes ever since I came back here from New Hampshire, four year after I was out of high school."

"What were you doing there?"

"Oh, domestic work. I went there originally because I was all het up to save money to go to the YWCA School of Cooking, but then my mother got sick, so I came home. I never did go. I married Hue instead. It seemed like the thing to do; we'd both been brought up here on this same hill."

But motherhood and work, more than marriage, were what had defined Orpha. "I guess what I'm probably proudest of," she said, "are the kids and the grandchildren. Our three kids are all doing okay. If I hadn't had my own, I think I'd have adopted some. It makes me mad to see my sister living over there on the home farm just the way it was when we were kids, just there with her husband and cows and horses and dogs. Without children, what's she got to live for?"

"Will any of your kids take over the sugaring business?"

"It doesn't look that way, but when they're married their life is their own. Seems too bad: we've tapped every maple tree around this part of the country. I've been making syrup all my life, ever since I could go in the woods. It's a good quick income for your small farmer."

"Do you have much competition?" asked Peggy.

"Your competition's not like it used to be. You've got your big sugar companies in Newport and St. Johnsbury, but they're more like factories."

"It must be nice to work outdoors so much."

"It is. I wouldn't want any part of living in a city. I lived in a city of 10,000 once, and I could hardly wait to get back to the grass. The grass and snow. Snow usually starts up here around November, and sometimes it gets to thirty below. Then in the spring we go tap. You tap as low down on the tree as you can. Some of these trees up there probably been tapped for seventy years. We had fifty-four barrels this year, thirty gallons a barrel. We get around one gallon of syrup to every thirty-five or forty gallons of sap."

If there is a kitchen somewhere in rural or small-town America in which there does not hang a framed motto expressing some sentiment of its owner, I haven't been there yet. In Orpha's kitchen the sign says TO A FRIEND'S HOUSE THE ROAD IS NEVER LONG, and the friend in question would appear to be her neighbor Lila, who lives just down the road.

"Lila's the one I call up when I want somebody to visit with," said Orpha. Lila, who came over while Peggy and I were there, would appear to be Orpha's Bebe Rebozo. "Oh, we've had some good times, driving around," said Orpha. "I think I'd hate to lose my driving license more than anything I've got.

"I'd hate to lose that feeling of independence. I've traveled some, I've been to Vancouver twice to visit some of Hue's folks, and as far south as North Carolina, but I'd like to do it a lot more. I'd like to go see Alaska sometime; I've heard they have twenty-two hours of sunlight and that the fruits there get to be just huge."

"Why *don't* you go there sometime?"

"All that keeps me here is lack of money. If somebody came along and said let's go somewhere, anywhere, it wouldn't take me long to pack my bag. And I'd take Lila along. Lila and I, we just like to poke along the back roads."

So do Peggy and I. Right then, in fact, we said we had better get going, because we hoped to go to a square dance that night at the centennial celebration in a town we passed through.

"Wouldn't you girls like to have just a little spin around the mounting before you go?" asked Orpha. Well, since she put it that way, of course we would like to. We all got in the Volkswagen and had a

spin, driving past the house where Orpha's barren sister lived, going to see the mill where the sap was piped in by plastic tubes, and at one point crossing the line so that we were technically in Canada. We were not too late for the square dance, but it was disappointing: they had it in a parking lot, and the music was recorded.

The next day, back at the Jensens', there was a message for me to call my sister. "Urgent," the message said.

"You'll never guess," Ann correctly predicted, "what Bob-bob is going to do." Bob-bob is what her children call their grandfather.

"What's he going to do?"

"Are you sitting down?"

"Yes."

"Bob-bob is going to get *married!*"

"*Madre de Dios,*" I said not very audibly.

"Hello?"

"I'm here; I'm just a tiny bit surprised. Have you met the lady? Is she the one he said was nice, from Philadelphia?"

"I have, and she is. That should have been a clue enough, shouldn't it, his even mentioning he'd met a lady. You know what she said to me?"

"What'd she say?"

"She said, 'Your father isn't a very good Frisbee player, is he?' "

"Oh, my goodness. Imagine it. Well, good for him. Good for her, too. How did he meet her?"

"She was in Springfield visiting her widowed sister, and someone had a dinner party, and I guess they figured there were too many women and they needed an extra man, and let's see—I know! What about Bob Howard?"

"What's she like?"

"Svelte and stunning. Salt-and-pepper hair cut short. Six children, all married, and twenty-two grandchildren. Cheerful, bright, and straightforward. She admitted she was nervous when he brought her over to meet us, and that was refreshing. She was wearing pants. She was nice with the kids. They liked her. I think we will too. It'll just take some getting used to, is all."

"How long have they known each other?"

"Since March, I think. She went back to Philadelphia in April, but came back to see her sister again—so important for them to keep in touch, don't you know—in June. The June visit still isn't over." This was the middle of July.

"When are they going to do it?"
"I guess it depends on when you can come out."
"I guess I'd better call him."
"You mean *them*."
"Okay, them."

CHAPTER 16

TEARS OF JOY

I *hope* those are tears of joy," our new stepmother, Beth, said soon
after the Presbyterian minister had pronounced her and
my father wife and man. Ann and I had wept audibly during the garden ceremony.

In a way, our tears were joyful. Why should we not be glad that
this slim, energetic widow had given up all her boards and committees in Philadelphia to make a new life in central Illinois? Why
should we not rejoice in our father's release from stoical homemade
Granola and long-playing opera records turned up loud, mostly to
have some sound in the house? Did we want his involuntary
bachelorhood to last any longer than it had to? Of course not. Had we
not said we hoped he would find some nice woman? Of course we
had. But did we think he really would? Of course we didn't. Here
the two of them were, though, looking and acting entranced.

Our faces might not have shown it, but we did welcome Beth even
as she said "I *certainly* do!" to the minister's rhetorical questions
(among them, at her request, a promise to "obey" her new husband).
I guess we were not crying for any immediate, rational reason, but
because this occasion, more than any other, seemed to mark the real
end of our protracted childhoods.

Beth's kin and friends outnumbered us for the weekend festivities,
which began with a picnic outside our house on the eve of the wedding. The next day, at a prenuptial lunch, we sat on a lawn with
some of our new step-siblings to draw a family tree so we could see
whom they had married and borne. Two of Beth's daughters had
come with their husbands, from Washington, D.C., and Palo Alto,
and one of her sons flew in from Seattle. It wouldn't have mattered if
they and we had cordially disliked each other, because it was hardly
as if we were going to all live under the same roof, but, as a bonus,

we all got on fine. We had been to a lot of the same places and knew the same songs. We were almost late to the wedding, because just before it began we had all swum out to a raft in the middle of Lake Springfield and passed a bottle of wine around to toast the bride and groom. Much later that night we had another swim, and then a song-fest around the kitchen table. We all traded addresses and promised to send prints of the 35-millimeter film we had been shooting. Like most Howard occasions, it was a thoroughly documented affair.

Halloween is my stepmother Beth's birthday. I rather envy her that. I went back in 1972 to help celebrate and to congratulate my father on the publication of his history of the state. The next afternoon I put my feet under Beth's kitchen table and we had a talk. She told me how skittish she had felt, when she returned East just after meeting my father for the first time. Would he remember her? Would she ever hear from him? Once, miraculously, there came from him a postcard signed "yours." She had been enraptured. Once Beth decided to phone my father, from Philadelphia, and dialed the ten digits five different times, hanging up after each dialing, before she could summon the nerve to wait for his voice. I found all this quite human and familiar. It was nice to know that other grownups had such feelings. Moreover, hers was a story with a happy ending.

We talked about having children. "When I was a child," she recalled, "I disliked the world of adults so much I never wanted to grow up myself. For me, having children was a way to continue being a child and make sure I'd have friends who were children.

"Coming here," Beth said, "has been a kind of inner homecoming for me. Your father is the best thing that's ever happened to me. I think he's the reason I was born. I found it a wonderment not only that I could do it—come and make a new life here, I mean—but was strongly impelled to do it. Your father is not at all like my own, or my late husband, but I feel that he's on his own base, and it's a sound base. He isn't static. Don't you think he'll like having his study moved to the old sunroom?"

"It is a lot sunnier down there," I said.

"There are so many things we want to do, places we want to go, but I'm just so happy staying right here that I don't feel any urgency about it. When your father quits working at the State House [upon his retirement three years earlier he had of course begun another job the very next day] he has such a world of things he'd like to write about, study about.

"The fact that I can be with someone as different as he is is the greatest growing experience I could have at this age. He wouldn't have been foolish enough to marry me, either, if he planned to stay stuck in one place. And I've found him a really good listener too. If there's one thing I know for sure, it's that marrying him was a really healthy decision."

I told Beth she appeared to be one of the most positive women of any age I had ever encountered. "Oh, I've made mistakes in my life," she said, "but they're over with. I can't keep harking back to all that. How can I be sixty-three and make the same mistakes? The needle has to move on to another groove in the record."

To many new grooves, I thought. I also thought of something I had recently underlined in Margaret Mead's autobiography: "Watching a parent grow is one of the most reassuring experiences anyone can have, a privilege that comes only to those whose parents live beyond their children's early adulthood." She was right.

CHAPTER 17

A TUNNEL'S NO PLACE FOR A WOMAN

The two hundred people who live year-round in Georgetown, Colorado, tend not to know their exact street addresses. They walk to the post office to get their mail. Sixty miles west of Denver, Georgetown is a renovated nineteenth-century mining center whose chief civic aim now is to attract tourists, especially those who ski. In all directions rise humbling Rockies, covered with evergreens and quaking aspen which in the fall turn a stabbing yellow. The houses of Georgetown, painted in fanciful colors, have steeply gabled roofs.

The air is fresh and sweet and fragrant around Georgetown, but thin. In the Pretzel Kaffeehaus there hangs a sign that says WATCH YOUR STEP: 8,513.76 FEET ABOVE SEA LEVEL. Leonard McCombe, newly arrived with his cameras from sea level, said he felt funny from lack of oxygen. Our breakfast conversation shifted between two topics: the altitude and Janet Bonnema.

Our rendezvous in Georgetown was to do a story for *Life* (my last, as it turned out) on Janet, a thirty-four-year-old engineering technician who was suing her employers, the Colorado Department of Highways. She was suing them for $100,000, because they forbade

her and all other women to work inside or even set foot inside the Straight Creek Tunnel, an awesome engineering project under construction fifteen miles away and another 3,000 feet up. It would be bad luck, they said, for women to go in.

Janet and her class action lawsuit were a tidy metaphor for the widespread struggle of women to find work in places where men did not welcome them. Besides, Janet's goal was so nice and unambiguous. All we had to do was drive up past timberline to the Loveland Pass, near the Continental Divide, to see it: the mighty, four-lane Straight Creek Tunnel. Designed to carve for 8,900 feet through the Rockies, the largest high-altitude tunnel ever built, it had presented all manner of tricky engineering problems in the five years of its construction. Seven hundred men had worked on it. It would cost something like $90 million. I could not join Leonard on his guided tour, but I was given a lot of facts while I waited.

Janet worked in one of several trailers parked a few hundred yards from the eastern mouth of the tunnel. She worked ably, too; nobody denied that. "She's got a real good sense of the third dimension," her supervisor told me. "I've had her do a lot of special drafting." Her job, in the Rock Mechanics Section, was, as she put it, "knowing what they do in the tunnel, so I can make graphic presentations. I would be a lot more useful if I could get this knowledge firsthand, the way all the other technicians do." Her male counterparts had been issued hard hats and wet boots, so that they could enter the tunnel at will. Janet stayed behind and did paperwork and wished she could go in too. As her $100,000 lawsuit said, she was being denied "irreplaceable experience at a unique and highly important engineering project." It would have looked pretty good, in short, on the old resume. But as things stood, Janet said, "I'm not advancing; I'm treading water."

Personally, tunnels make me feel claustrophobic, so at first I was relieved not to enter Straight Creek. But the more I heard about the superstition against females, I almost felt like sneaking in. This superstition, apparently the legacy of Welsh miners who came to work in Colorado in the 1850's, held that there was no telling what dangers might ensue if a woman went into a tunnel or mine.

"Some years ago I took my wife into a tunnel," one of Janet's bosses said, "and the next day we had a man get killed. So you never really know."

"You never do," said another official. "A tunnel's no place for a

woman anyway. You know how men are. They might relieve themselves right where they're standing and not wait to get to a toilet. You wouldn't want a woman hearing the kind of language we use down there, either. Besides, women couldn't take it physically. They don't have the stamina."

"That's what *he* thinks," Leonard said later as we, in our sedate rent-a-car, followed Janet back to Georgetown on her Honda CL-350. Nearly five feet ten, zooming along in her day-glow orange flight suit she was an imposing figure indeed.

"When I wake up in the morning," she had told us, "I like to ask myself not 'What shall I wear today?' but 'Who shall I *be* today?' " She had already been a lot of things—a cab driver, a pilot, a teacher, a global hitch-hiker, the captain of Colorado University's ski team, and the dutiful daughter of people who taught her to believe, as she still did, in the Republican party and in a life hereafter. The one thing Janet never dreamed she might become, but had, was a symbol of the women's movement. Unlike many feminists who are clannish and doctrinaire in their solidarity, Janet had never been to a consciousness-raising session in her life, much less allied herself with any sect or group. She preferred to stay home crocheting hot-pads, fixing her motorcycle, or playing with her cat.

You never could tell about Janet. Sometimes she would wear her waist-length hair in a single businesslike pigtail, but on other mornings she arranged it in an eleborate eighteenth-century cascade of ringlets. At lunch you'd see her batting her eyelashes at a table full of elderly miners, and that afternoon, on a climbing expedition, she would be scrambling out of sight over a nearly vertical cliff.

She lived in the east half of a duplex on Rose Street. In the other half lived her landlady, Olive Barnes. Janet went to watch television at Olive's sometimes, especially when she was on it herself. Olive worried about Janet. She wasn't sure it was wise for her to walk along the highway picking up beer cans. Janet did this not to beautify the landscape but so she could crush them and sell them for scrap aluminum. She was saving to go to Africa.

Janet's tiny living room also served as a garage for her Honda, which she kept under a giant paper parasol. She had brought the parasol home from the Orient, after three and a half years of hitch-hiking around the world. On the living room wall hung a signed color portrait of a beribboned Air Force general who had become her special friend in Saigon, and next to it a framed studio portrait of

Janet herself. Across the room were framed twin pictures of her parents. Upstairs was a chess set she had carved herself, and in the icebox was split pea soup made from scratch, as was her daily oatmeal.

If people found Janet a puzzlement, as many did, then that was their problem, not hers. Once, by writing to a male friend on stationery decorated with roses, she showed him a new aspect of herself. "When he wrote back he told me I wasn't just schizophrenic but *polyphrenic*," said Janet, "which I guess meant a personality not split just in two ways but many ways. Well, maybe he's right."

"Of course I'm in favor of equal pay," say people who are tired of talking and even hearing about the goals of the women's movement, "but hasn't that been pretty well taken care of?" In point of fact it has not. The average female college graduate earns $7,930 per year, only a little more than the average male graduate of eighth grade, who earns $7,140. The average male college graduate's salary is $13,320. Of the forty-three percent of American women who have jobs, making up thirty-eight percent of the total labor force, seven percent earn five-figure salaries or hold managerial positions. The wage differential was worse in 1972 than it had been seventeen years earlier. In 1955, women earned not quite sixty-four percent of what men did. In 1972, the figure had dropped by four and a half percent. Women felt lucky and even proud to have jobs at all.

"The worst thing about women," I heard sociologist Dr. Jessie Bernard say, "is the low opinion they have of themselves." If pay was low and advancement slow, a good many women would rationalize, "Oh, well, it must be just me—I'm not really working as hard as I might anyway, and besides men have families to support." Moreover, among people who had been brought up, as Janet Bonnema put it, to be "conservative and blendy," it wasn't considered ladylike or nice to make trouble.

It used to be that employers could get by paying lip service to the principle and the laws of equality. "Nothing really gets done," said Todd Jagerson, one of an emerging new species of consultants to companies perplexed by new discrimination rulings, "until somebody breathes down their necks—until the cost of responding to the law becomes less than the cost of ignoring it."

That is what has happened. Ignoring the laws has become costly indeed. Companies which do business with the federal government,

of which there are some 250,000, are now obliged not only to quit discriminating on grounds of sex but to file affirmative action programs for the hiring and the advancement of women. These programs must redress both present and past effects of discrimination. Until March 1972, there was no federal statutory law that applied to state agencies like the one Janet worked for. About ninety-five percent of all employers had in fact been exempt, because the minimum number of employes—now lowered to fifteen—had been twenty-five. Religious and academic organizations had been exempt too, but were no more. Equal pay, it was ruled, was due not only for the same work as men did but for comparable work, and to executive, administrative, and professional employes, as well as to sales personnel.

"The trouble with suing state agencies," said Janet's lawyer Sandra Rothenberg, "is that they usually stall for a long time and say they're negotiating, but who can tell whether they really are? Janet's suit, though, could be embarrassing. It could stop the tunnel."

The biggest legal advance was the new ability granted the Equal Employment Opportunities Commission to take errant employers to court, in class action suits like the one in which Janet, on behalf of a "class" including all women, sued to get into the tunnel. The cost of settling these charges, in or out of court, was coming to threaten employers. "Some of these suits could get into the hundreds of thousands, maybe millions of dollars," Jagerson said. "Some could wipe out three years of profits." By late 1972, women had filed something like 6,000 discrimination complaints. An exponential rise in this figure seemed possible, as employers were made to face such stringent demands as reinstatement of dismissed workers, forced promotions, punitive damages, and back pay. Back pay made employers especially nervous. Since 1965, more than $43 million had been awarded to 104,604 workers, nearly all of them female.

One evening Janet took us to a high-rise apartment building in Denver to meet her widowed mother, who had spent the afternoon on a birdwatching expedition. Mrs. Bonnema, who had a doctorate in education, was more taken with birding and with a movement to reform spelling than with feminism. But it was clear that she supported her daughter's struggle, and she thought her late husband would have too, for all his conservatism. She told us he used to confide to her a private worry he had about his three daughters. "They're all the first ones in their class," he would say, "but what good, since they're girls, will that do?"

When Janet applied to work at Straight Creek, in the fall of 1970, she scored eighty-seven on a written exam and was notified in a letter misaddressed to "Mr. Jamet" P. Bonnema that an opening as an engineering technician was available, at $492 per month. The work sounded interesting, but the salary was not what she had in mind. She called to see whether there had been some mistake. Imagine the surprise at the other end of the line when "Mr. Jamet" spoke.

"You don't want that job," said the voice at the other end.

"I think I do," replied Janet.

"Well, you can't have it," the voice said. "No women are allowed in the tunnel." But Janet, encouraged by her mother, protested. Two months later a special technician's job, limited to office work, was invented for her. She was awarded back pay for the time she had had to wait, but the money mollified her no more than did manful efforts to explain why she could not go underground.

"Economics was the basic issue, for all the talk about superstitions and sanitation," said Janet's lawyer Sandra. "The Civil Service Commission just wasn't in the habit of hiring women for jobs like that. Her case was the strongest of its kind in the state, and it was fun too." Economic insecurity is probably at the root of most such grievances, and the cause least discussed. Men politely evade talking about their historic tendency to replace themselves with women only in emergencies. In Victorian England, in fact, women and even children worked in mines, and the ancient law that "woman's place is in the home" is said to have begun as a battle cry to get women, for their own sakes, out of the mines.

Like her fellow plaintiffs elsewhere, Janet gradually became aware of a complex of interwoven issues hostile to her cause. Much more to the point than the Welsh superstition, it seemed to Janet, was the fact that men simply like to get away from women. Lionel Tiger's book *Men in Groups* calls this phenomenon "male bonding." Although aggrieved feminists have been known to do a good bit of bonding themselves, they don't forgive the tendency in men.

Even less popular with women is the tendency of their male adversaries to suggest, as one executive did of a plaintiff, "All she needs is a man—if I'd known about her before all this started, I could have taken care of her myself, if you know what I mean." I knew what he meant. There were also those who thought that all Janet Bonnema needed was to locate that elusive fellow Mr. Right, but fortunately they had the sense not to say this to her face.

"There's a lot more to life than having a husband," Janet told Leonard and me one evening as she served us lasagna in her kitchen. "It might be nice to get married someday, sure—to have a regular audience when I fix a good dinner and someone to share things with. But what business is it of anybody's if I have a boyfriend?

"A lot of my girlfriends find the social stigma of being single unbearable. Not me. I don't want to have children at this point, either. I'm too old to commit my life to a twenty-year program of any kind, which is what having a child would mean. Rather than breed new children, I like the idea of taking care of existing ones. I do have a stepdaughter in South Africa, through the Christian Children's Fund, and if I go through a spell of feeling motherly, I can write her letters of advice.

"I have a lot of very good male friends too, who are very understanding through thick and thin year after year, but it all goes on year after year and nothing happens. I'd have a hard time choosing between them now, because what one has, another lacks. And when none of them is around, if it's a question of going alone or not going someplace at all, I'll go alone. I'll land on my feet too."

True to form, Janet did land on her feet. In July 1972, after a year-long investigation, the United States Department of Transportation ruled that to bar women from Straight Creek Tunnel was to practice sex discrimination. When her bosses chose not to heed this ruling, Janet filed the suit that came to a triumphant end on a snowy morning in November.

Suddenly Janet was surrounded by television crews and inevitable banter about light at the end of the tunnel. She put on a hard hat and goggles and was ushered all the muddy way through to the other end of Straight Creek. Her case had been settled out of court for $6,750. From then on, the tunnel was open to women.

Observers noted that the tunnel did not cave in. Sixty-some workers threatened to quit, but in fact only one did. Janet felt philosophical. Her small step into Straight Creek, she hoped, might help speed that giant leap for womankind in which, before long, all females might find work wherever they liked. Meanwhile, Janet thought she would use some of her winnings to go to Africa. Later she might look for a job having to do with mass transit or the rebuilding of Southeast Asia. She also had another idea.

"I hear they aren't hiring women as highway patrolmen," she said. "Maybe I'll send my application over there."

CHAPTER 18

CREAM CAN CURDLE

N ow they'll have to invent a new superstition," said Sandra Rothenberg when her client Janet Bonnema won her lawsuit to get inside Straight Creek. "Now they'll have to say it's good luck for women to go inside tunnels."

One evening several months before I met Sandra and Janet, I was dining in a San Francisco restaurant with Barbara Phillips and one of her clients. Her client was a plaintiff in the class action suit against the Bank of America. What I found more interesting even than the suit against the bank was Barbara's account of how her own thinking had evolved in the ten years she had been practicing law.

"I've changed a lot just recently," she said, "but basically I'm so conservative that even the green stationery we're using for the bake sale seems a bit bizarre to me."

"Bake sale?"

"For the Women's Defense Fund. Very few women, you know, can afford to pay the costs of their litigation. We need to raise money, and we thought this might be a good tactic. It's funny: none of us has ever been involved with a bake sale before."

"A bake sale is just what those gray-suited men on Montgomery Street need. It's quite a departure for you, you say?"

"I was programmed to be conventional," Barbara said. "I started out as a tax lawyer, after all. I worked very hard at first for one of the most prominent tax firms in San Francisco, earning much less money than the going rate for men. When I suggested that I needed more pay, even after they'd given me a raise, they said, 'But after all, we started you out above the secretaries, didn't we?'

"I'd worked hard there. They'd said I was one of the best associates they ever had. I was brought up, as we all were, to believe that cream rises to the top, and virtue is its own reward. But when I had the temerity to ask for a better office, they said, 'Look, apparently something hasn't been made clear to you. You're never going to be a partner in this firm, because you're a woman.' Not only that, but I was fired."

"You learned that cream can curdle, and virtue go unnoticed?" Barbara nodded.

"I found out for myself," she said, "how it feels to get to the gate with all my marbles in my hand and be told, 'Oh, sorry, you're in the

wrong race.' I don't think anybody who hasn't experienced discrimination personally can know how totally demoralizing it is or how much stamina and determination it takes to fight these battles."

"A lot of women are afraid to sue," Sandra Rothenberg said when I visited her Denver apartment, "because jobs are scarce. Sometimes it's a matter of bullying companies. One woman client of mine hadn't had a raise in six years, so I wrote her boss a letter implying that this might be a discrimination case. Guess what? Quick like a bunny, she got a raise. I'm involved in suing the State Board of Education too. They discriminate blatantly. There's not one female superintendent of schools in this whole state. Some factories start women off at $1.60, and give men a minimum wage of $2.50."

"Have you been specializing in class action suits all along?"

"I was too busy to know much at all about sex discrimination until last year," Sandra said, "when I brought suit against the FBI for not hiring me as a special agent."

"Did you *want* to be a special agent?"

"Not really, but I wanted the training. I wanted to know what it would be like, and it made me mad that I couldn't find out. Since Hoover's death they've changed that policy and started hiring women, only you have to be five feet seven and weigh 140. It occurred to me to make an issue about that, because what woman voluntarily weighs 140?

"Now I do criminal work, and I think and hope I do it very well. This is a dingbat trade, though. I get a lot of dingbats in my office. Some of them need my ex-husband more than they need me."

"The psychiatrist, you mean?"

"Right. That's how I came out here to Denver in the first place. We both wanted to. We got married in a classic ceremony; I wore a beautiful white dress. It was all just right, but one morning we woke up and realized, 'We're not happy, we're not making it,' and that was pretty much that.

"I was married to a hell of a nice guy, too, but I work as hard as I can, and I'm often not home until late, and that didn't make me any dutiful wife. Besides, law and psychiatry don't mix. A lot of psychiatrists are caught up in strict, Freudian, anatomy-is-destiny theories, and they're not equipped to deal with women. I'm beginning to feel that all psychiatrists try to get women to adjust to their concept of what we should be. They tend to dismiss all problems as unresolved

Oedipus. A lot of women today just aren't into patterns like having children in order to fulfill themselves."

"Do you want to have children yourself?"

"I'd love to," said Sandra, "and I intend to, but I think they'll have to be illegitimate. Legitimacy, after all, is only a matter of property rights, and that's not too important. Not that I have anything against men. I like my father and brothers a lot, and I like my ex-husband too. But marriage? It just seems too confining. I can't imagine ever not being preoccupied with my work."

"Early in life I realized I'd have to work," Barbara Phillips said in the San Francisco restaurant, "or I'd live everyone else's life instead of my own. It's my temperament, my energy level, and that's all there is to it. My husband's a lawyer too, and we're both competitive, but I don't compete with him. I compete with myself. He and I have an amazing balance worked out between us.

"Before I got into discrimination cases I always had a lot of projects—I was president of the San Francisco Barristers Club, for one thing—but I was never a cause person. Now legal specialists in sex discrimination are a rare new breed of experts.

"I took on women's cases because they're not only interesting but socially worthwhile and constructive. Not all law work is. A few lawyers are socially destructive. Essentially, we lawyers are information brokers. There are those who call us the witch doctors of society. Our work gets more burdensome and complex all the time, the more complex society becomes.

"But with these women's cases, we're not trying to screw anybody. All we're asking is that the skills and talents and loyalty of employees be taken into account. Is that so much? When we win, everybody wins."

CHAPTER 19

DIDN'T YOU ALMOST DROWN WHILE INTERVIEWING SAUL BELLOW?

And of course you love your job," a fond uncle of mine told me when he came to New York and took me out to dinner, not long after I had arrived there. He didn't ask me; he told me. At that point,

in fact, I did not love it at all, since my task was to wear a smock and sort photographic negatives, then file them in translucent sleeves. Still, according to the ethic by which I had been raised, one unquestioningly loved one's work. Was it not what defined one? Certainly it was, until some more biological definition came along. Meanwhile until that happened, one got oneself hired if possible by a large, generous daddyish corporation, of which there may never anywhere be a more classic example than Time Inc.

I was on the payroll there for fifteen years, mostly with *Life*. *Life*'s last year, I was on a contract. The contract took up more time than I had thought it would, and in the fall of 1972 I often announced to people that I had decided I wouldn't take such a demanding one the next year, or that I might even let it drop altogether.

If anyone had asked me, as a neophyte employe, to guess what I might be doing on December 8, 1972, the day *Life*'s death was announced, I would have envisioned being a faculty wife somewhere, with a Cub pack or maybe a Brownie troop, and a lovably disarrayed chignon. I would have guessed that before my marriage to this nice Mr. Chips I would have studied or worked abroad for a couple of years, on one pretext or other. We would have season tickets to lecture and concert series and I might have learned to say things like, "Of course we left before the Dvorák." We would take most of our vacations in a Volkswagen camper, and make our own Christmas cards out of linoleum blocks. That's what we'd have been doing in early December: getting those cards done.

Instead, *Life* had become my arena, my stage, the channel for most of my energies. Its masthead was such a nice coherent hierarchy, and the bylines it gave were such a nice outward and visible sign of merit, like A's in English, sure to invite approval. *Life*'s assignments, much if not all of the time, involved travel and invited us to stretch our minds. I was obliged to be, or at least to seem, conversant with the argots of pianists, hairdressers, diplomats, soothsayers, poets, sculptors, evangelists, a professional atheist, politicians—maybe not all sorts and conditions of men, but a good many.

Life's rituals and traditions, moreover, gave my own life an order and a structure I would otherwise have been obliged to seek elsewhere, and the notion of "elsewhere" became less and less inviting as time went by. The office gave me a semblance of a family; a *mishpocha*. It made me feel connected and important.

My employee number was 3274 and my office was 3022, next to

Dick Meryman's and well within earshot of Dita Camacho's and Tommy Thompson's. I had to walk half a block to the ladies' room, but only a few short steps to the Xerox machine, that now most lamented of lost amenities. One afternoon in early 1971 an affable writer named John Thorne stopped by my office, looking affably desperate. He had to find someone whose recent adventure in the line of duty might inspire copy for a slow week's Editor's Note. "Come on," he implored me, "are you *sure* you didn't almost drown while interviewing Saul Bellow?"

Alas for his purpose, I had not. There was a myth of glamour and danger about the place, all right, but near-drownings were the lot chiefly of war correspondents and superstar photographers, with whom I associated only peripherally. But my own timing was lucky. If I had turned up there five years earlier, I might have resigned myself to the anonymity that was then the norm and never had shed my cocoon—more an armor, really—of timidity. I might, for example, have been persuaded to stay on answering letters to *Time,* which I did for a while in my trainee period. I was good with those letters, and it was hinted that I could have a future there.

But I turned up just at the time when kindly mentors began to encourage some of us to try to write, or rather Write, and some of us did. The old joke that to be a writer for *Life* was like being a photographer for the *Reader's Digest* gradually stopped seeming funny. What I did, for quite a while, was to follow around persons who had written bestsellers or won elections or choreographed hit shows or otherwise distinguished themselves and take down what they said. The resulting quotes would appear in articles called Close-Ups, overseen by my friend Dave Scherman. Later, promoted to staff writer, I did longer stories and once or twice, to my chagrin, was billed as *"Life's* Jane Howard."

The hell you say, I thought, but the extent to which the magazine did encroach on our lives could worry both us who worked there and those on the outside who cared for us. "You'd better get out of there," more than one friend advised me, "because you're in a rut, a nice, elegant rut." Right, I would answer. Sure. I'll do that. But even after I took a year's leave of absence to write a book, I came back, back to where it was warm and where projects were finite and where if you were so disposed you could make off with the odd roll of typewriter ribbon here and toilet paper there. (I always forgot to buy my own.) The out-of-town bureaus, always chicly located near

Saks or the American Express, whichever might apply, were cordial
places. Our colleagues there tended to be helpful and funny when
we showed up, pulling bottles of Jack Daniels from their desk drawers for impromptu "pours," at which they would roll their eyes sky-
ward as they confided what indignities "New York" made them suffer. Still, they and we all felt part of something imposing.

If we thought we were hot stuff, the outer world could either dis-
abuse us at once of that notion or else unctuously concur. Sometimes
we had to defend our connection with what was seen as the enemy
pig imperialist homogenizer, but more often we were the objects of
blatant and shameless fawning. A Mr. Heep was often on the other
line, waiting to talk to us. (One of the pleasures of no longer working
there is the appreciable drop in the number of calls from
flacks—whom we did not often call Public Relations Representatives—who fawned over us and said "I'll have that *on* your
desk *in* the morning." Of course we had to get in there and fawn ourselves from time to time, convincing our story subjects or their lack-
eys that nothing could suit them better than coverage in *Life*. And although I don't like to remember it, there was such a thing as
interoffice fawning, too. We were never fawned over, naturally, by
people whom we esteemed. If they were nice to us, it only
confirmed what we had known all along: that they had superior
judgment.

A few among us had been rich kids, but most of us were raised by
Depression-minded parents who had taught us to scrimp, a habit we
gradually lost at *Life*. Not only were our paychecks quite handsome
by general standards, but there were a number of other blandish-
ments: taxis instead of subways, picking up the check at costly
lunches ("to discuss possible future story" we would explain on expense accounts), and the assurance that if it were really a desperate
emergency, we could go ahead and charter a plane. Such extrav-
agance seeped its sinister way through the thin membrane that
separated our professional and personal lives.

To work at *Life* was to possess to dizzying degree what Marianne
Moore said was the charm of New York City: accessibility to experience. The magazine was such a vast and diverse organism that every
set of memories of working there is unique. My own include the
time I chartered a seaplane with Bob Peterson, a photographer who
early on had resolved to become a living legend in his own time. In
the wilderness of British Columbia we descended, literally out of the

blue, onto an armed camp of right-wing extremists from Indiana. There had been no way of letting them know we were coming or imagining what their scene would really be like. Our story never did run, because it turned out there were only two families of extremists, and they did not seem as menacing as we had imagined they might. But the trip was a glorious way to see Wakeman Sound and to learn something about abandoned lumber camps and paranoia.

In Tangier one day (where else could I have got license to begin a sentence that way?) the photographer Terry Spencer was lecturing a hotel maid who scolded us for cluttering up our rooms with real flowers from the marketplace instead of plastic ones. "But, Madame," Terry told her in courtly French, "you too will grow old, and you too will die like these flowers, and you too must be appreciated while you are in bloom." The story we had been sent to Morocco to do, on the expatriate authors Paul and Jane Bowles, never did run. Too bad. We both did a good job. But those things could happen, especially back in the days before economy waves. The Bowleses weren't as manifestly commercial as our next subjects, the travel author Temple Fielding and his wife, whom he usually called My Nancy, who lived in Mallorca. It wasn't bad being in Mallorca, either.

Once, on less than a day's notice, I was assigned to rush from Lansing, Michigan, where I had been working on a story about a child mathematical genius, to Jamaica in the West Indies, to ghostwrite a piece by Wiley T. Buchanan, who had been chief of protocol in the Eisenhower administration. It was Mr. Buchanan's opinion that the guest artists at White House functions of late had lacked a wholesome common touch. "Mind you," he said, "I've got nothing *against* Pablo Casals—after all, he's tops in his field."

There are any number of really tops people I probably would never have encountered had it not been for *Life*, and tops places I would not have seen. I think that as a result of these undeniable prerequisites some people thought of me as they would have thought of a totally irresponsible, carefree go-go dancer, unbound by anything but whim, at liberty at all times to jump from one exciting, cushy world nerve center to another. Need I say that this notion was mistaken? In retrospect I resent very much the fact that in my early years there my only tested quality was endurance. The fourteen months or so which Charlotte Smith and Tira Faherty and I spent on the Clipdesk (a year after Charlotte and I had been hired, with max-

imum fanfare, and told how promising we were) felt like a decade. We consoled ourselves by keeping a file called "Ugly Brides," on the unliberated late-fifties theory that if they could find husbands we could, too. We further trusted that one day Marian MacPhail would phone, in her constantly imitated baritone, to ask "Got a minute?" which would signal that we could become bona fide Reporters.

I resent that long wait, to be sure, and I resent the hackneyed notion that the average reader's mental age is twelve, and I resent the emphasis on brevity and alliteration, which subtly caused me, for one, to think of my own life in terms of snappy 800- or 2,500-word episodes, instead of as a more seamless whole. I could name a good many more things I also resent, but that would sound vindictive now that the big beached whale has expired. That would be to overlook the fact that every once in a while, after painful retreats with armloads of notes, I learned more about myself than I had about any celebrity subject of a Close-up. *Life* not only gave me experiences, and friends, but it taught me my craft.

I didn't think I would cry on December 8, when we all trooped into the Ponti Auditorium to learn that the magazine really was going to fold, but I did. I cried even though I had heard the rumors, known the magazine was ailing, expected this news to come one day. But I no more thought it would come that particular morning or even that season than I had been prepared for the sudden death of my mother. It makes me uncomfortable to think how similarly these two passings hit me. Maybe it shouldn't. My mother, after all, was more or less in charge of the first seventeen years of my existence, and *Life* of the sixteen that began four years later.

Wakes for the magazine went on for a week or so, until even the most compulsive wits among us, who were many, had been wrung dry of gallows humor. After so many weepy hugs and farewell speeches and post-mortems, it finally became a relief to pack up our stuff, or start to anyway, and get busy Christmas shopping. Now that some months have passed, I have "adjusted," you might say, more "bravely" than the bereaved sometimes do. I have spent most of the intervening days in the room where I sit at this moment, all alone to be sure, but not quite so piteously cut off from the mainstream of society as I had thought I might feel. My phone works. I still see or hope to see, most of the people I cared about at *Life*. It gives me pleasure to write "Self-Employed" when I have to fill out forms. The only thing I really miss, as I said, is the Xerox.

CHAPTER 20

FRAGMENTS OF COMFORT AND JOY

S teady girl, I told myself. Easy. Think of the space-time continuum. So what if there isn't so much as a sprig of holly in this whole house? Aren't the birds outside as vivid as ornaments and the flowers as gay as packages? Is not the tropical sun a deal more warming than a hearth in the north? And so what if the custom here does seem to be nonstop firecrackers, sounding like cannons and machine guns, instead of medieval carols? And anyway, when you wake up tomorrow it will be the twenty-sixth, and then all this won't matter anymore.

It wasn't as if anyone had forced me to spend Christmas in El Salvador. I had come quite of my own choice because my friend Miguel had invited me. Miguel is a designer who speaks five languages, plays chess, knows the constellations, draws masterly sketches of unsuspecting people on buses, and can make me laugh. When he lived in New York he had often asked me to visit his country. What better time than now, with no more paychecks in sight? Funiculi funicula, right? And I encountered, surprisingly, a houseful of norteamericanos who seemed to be having an impromptu seminar on a topic close to my heart: the decline of families.

"Maybe ten years from now, when I'm in my late thirties, I'll be sick of all this moving around," said Diane from her hammock on Tony's porch, "but for now I just can't see staying put. After Argentina I think we'll try Africa, and then maybe the Middle East." By "we" Diane meant herself and her pigtailed, ten-year-old daughter, Denise. Denise, whose ears were pierced, was fussing restively with a coloring book. Tony, their host, was an acquaintance of Miguel's we met on the beach, who asked us to stop by when we had had enough sun.

Diane and Denise had with them two sleeping bags, two hammocks, a backpack, a daypack for Denise, three airline flight bags, and two large suitcases, one filled with clothing and the other with toys. "You might think that's a lot," said Diane, "but remember: we have to think about the high Andes as well as the tropics, and we'll be gone for a year. We have to get to Argentina by March, because that's when the school year starts. Every now and then I like to have Denise spend a whole school year in one place. I think it's good for her.

"We're going to live in a ski resort. There are these two guys I met in Paris who live down there. They'll help us find a place to stay, and I'm sure they'll help me find a job too."

"Do they know when you're coming?"

"No, they don't know we're coming at all. But even if they aren't there I won't have trouble finding work. I've worked as a book-keeper, receptionist, chambermaid, waitress—I've done a lot of things. All I care about is being where there's skiing, where there are exciting panoramas you can get to without a motor.

"A resort town would be the only place I could stand to stop for a whole year. At least there's a steady flow of new people in a resort town, and they're not the kind of people who care whether you have a nice car or apartment. That's why I keep traveling; the people you meet on the road don't care about stuff like that."

"Do you ever wonder if you're running *from* or *toward?*" asked Tony.

"I don't feel into heavy questions," said Diane. She was wearing an embroidered Guatemalan blouse over her bikini. You would have guessed that she was from California by her luminous skin.

"We left San Diego in October," said Diane, "and we planned to be a lot farther south than this by now, only we got hung up in Belize. The people in British Honduras were so nice! And the Guatemalans—the Guatemalans were dynamite. People here seem nice too. I could see staying on this beach for a long time, only I can't wait to get to Costa Rica, because in Costa Rica we'll have our first mail in two months. I'm sort of worried. For all I know, everybody could be dead."

Everybody, to Diane, meant her thrice-married mother, her alcoholic father, her suburban sister, her ex-husband, and assorted other relatives. "I don't speak to about ninety percent of my family," she said, "or rather they don't speak to me, but I really do care about my mother. She's a good lady, and she's all for what I'm doing. She wouldn't leave my dad until I talked her into it, even though she said the last fifteen of her twenty-five years with him were hell. It's funny, my mom's more like a daughter to me than Denise is. Lots of times I feel like Denise is my mother and I'm her daughter."

"I know what you mean," I said. "I often feel that my niece Sarah is in fact my aunt. Sarah's seven now, but her true spiritual age, my sister says, is and always has been forty-two. She's forever lecturing us to quit smoking."

"Hey, Mom," asked Denise, "how many packs of cigarettes have you smoked today?"

"Not even half, so far, but it'll be a full pack by night. Hey, Denise, why don't you go get a Sno-Kone at that restaurant across the way? Here's some money.

"She doesn't like my life-style," Diane said when her daughter had gone. "She misses cold milk and television, but she wasn't into staying with her father or my sister, either. Her father is remarried to a bitch, and my sister has two boys who tease the daylights out of Denise, so I figure she's better off on the road with me. She's been around a lot, for a ten-year-old: she's lived in Seattle, L.A., the French Alps, Spain, Germany, Paris, back in the States a while, and now here."

Had Denise not been conceived, Diane would never have married Mike, a salesman who referred to her as "the wife" even when she was in the same room. "But he made one mistake," said Diane. "He bought a second car for me to use, and the minute I laid eyes on it I knew that this would be the way I'd escape, and one day it was. One day, before Denise could even walk, I packed us both up and drove off."

By the time Denise was three she and her mother were settled in the French Alps. Diane worked as a chambermaid and fell in love, "for the first and only time in my whole life," with a French skier. "It was really dumb of me to leave there and go to Spain, but I did." In Torremelinos and Marbella she worked for an artist who did flattering twenty-minute portraits of tourists. In Garmisch, Germany she put Denise in a Montessori school and worked as a governess.

In Paris Diane found "a so-so job at a snobbish club for very rich American women whose idea of a really big deal was to be invited to a luncheon by Eunice Shriver." Diane got free rent in exchange for baby-sitting for another American couple, and discovered a night club "where they had this really neat, fantastic South American music, which was what turned me on to coming down this way in the first place. That was where I met the guys we're going to look for. In that club they had every kind of instrument you can think of, including a harp. Have you ever heard a harp played with rhythm and life? You can't imagine what it sounds like. Before we leave here, I'd like to get a couple of cane flutes for Denise and me."

Diane's mother, whose second husband had been killed in a motorcycle crash, came over to France to job-hunt, but nobody

wanted to hire a fifty-year-old American widow. Before long she took her daughter and granddaughter home to California, where Diane stayed put a couple of months before she hitchhiked, by air, to see an old flame who had moved to Philadelphia.

"My sister's friends in California were all really nervous about their husbands. If they didn't get home before their husbands did, or if they hadn't waxed the floor or watered the lawn or whatever they'd promised they were going to have done by that night, they would be literally scared. It was like their daddy, instead of their husband, would punish them, by not letting them go to the prom next week."

Diane's mother, who is "always into Zen or astrology or something," went to a singles dance where she met a man who also had a Gemini daughter. On the strength of that coincidence they were married. "He's a nice guy," says Diane, "but you know where they live? In a mobile home moored in concrete. It's got bigger rooms than a lot of mobile homes, but still. His idea of a vacation is the Disneyland Hotel, which is around five miles away. He never wants to go anyplace."

My own father likes traveling just fine. He studies guide books in advance, gets out of the car to examine historical markers, and always knows what railroad goes over an underpass. He and my mother went to Europe twice, on charter flights, and they were forever driving around the States. The last Christmas of her life they went to California. Ann and I urged them to, promising we would have our annual reunion later. When they finally agreed, we felt as Kenya must have on the day of Uhuru: free but nervous. But then Christmas always made us nervous. It obliged us to declare who we were and to whom we belonged, questions I never felt ready to answer.

The Christmas of Uhuru, Ann and David and their children went to the Caribbean. I joined them later, after devoting the twenty-fifth to a lame-duck reconciliation with a man about whom my feelings had long been mixed. He and I went to the farmhouse of some friends in the Berkshires. The farmhouse was idyllic, and the friends were stouthearted and true, but I cannot recommend lame-duck Christmases. This one was confusingly bittersweet, to say the least. Late that afternoon I bade the man in question another in a series of farewells, dropped him off with other friends in Dutchess County, and drove back to New York.

Santa and I, before then, had always returned to Illinois, for a pagan amalgam of tributes more to him than to Jesus. We would go

either to Springfield or Decatur, my parents' or my sister's house.

What a jumble of memories. The primal smell of the greens, for one, and the chance that in some day's mail there might come a half-inch stack of cards with a handwritten message on each, and my favorite rite of all, the wrapping of presents. All the fuss about paper and Scotch tape and tags, and the way they all look under the tree, makes me feel actually merry, the way you're supposed to.

Nobody was ever too old, or too canine or too feline, to hang up a stocking, nor could anyone ever lollygag abed after daybreak. Down we would file in our bathrobes, to say, "You *should,* if you know what I mean," when others said they liked our Serious presents. Serious presents, which cost in the two-figure range, were supplemented with cheerful unserious stuff, edible and otherwise, and all manner of nontoxic notions and knicknacks. One year my mother gave me a Baggie, tied with a red ribbon, of stones she had collected the previous summer in Michigan, and polished by hand.

After we had opened the "gifts" we had "received" we would "display" them for a while, each taking over a chair surface for the purpose and then, with carols on the phonograph, go eat sausage and eggs and coffeecake. Later would come dutiful phone calls, if the circuits were free, to or from distant loved ones and thank-you notes. One record year we had all our acknowledgments posted by the twenty-sixth. Sometimes we would rate all the cards, on a one-to-ten scale.

Different parts of the world offer different comforts. Down here there wasn't a phonograph, but up home nobody in my immediate ken had much in the way of servants. Even at Tony's beach shack there was a deferential caretaker called Segundo, who had just carved a hole in another coconut; Neal, the surfer who had met Diane at the bus station, had forsaken his hammock to go find some more of a local fluid called Tik-Tak.

"Neal's an odd one," she said. "He looks like a hippie, but you know what he told me? He told me he's saving money to get married, as soon as he finds the right girl. It's funny, but in the last seven years, since women have been into not marrying, men have been *dying* to find wives. Being married simplifies their lives so much. If they have wives, they don't have to go to the laundromat."

"Well, a contract of property is part of it, too," said Tony. "Marriage is essentially a matter of finding someone you can stand who

can stand you too. Don't knock it; it's a lot. Only dreamers like both my wives think there's more to it than that."

"If there's no more to it than that, forget it," said Diane. "It would be different if I wanted another child, or if I had faith that any marriage would last, but who needs divorce and the hassle of *suing* somebody? I could only see it if I fell in love, and I don't think I know what love is any more. I've met so many guys I like, I can't imagine settling for just one."

"We're spoiled," I said.

"You are," said Tony, "and you're too impatient. You split from your marriage as soon as it wasn't groovy, right, Diane? That's the trouble with a lot of women. Marriages take around five years to mellow. This friend of my wife's, she drove off in her husband's car with a sleeping bag, so she could see the sunrise. She left her kids behind and now all she wants to do is screw everyone in sight, probably because she never had any fun before she got married."

"Hey, Tony," I said, "doesn't your wife mind that you're gone for Christmas?"

"I guess so," he said, "but she's going to Europe in the spring, so it all evens out."

"But how come you married her, if you don't even want to be with her on Christmas?"

"You're really Miss Yule Log, aren't you? Christmas doesn't have to be that big a deal. I married her because I couldn't get rid of her. She hung around my house all the time and her parents were after me too. So was my own mother. You know what my mother said when I asked her to give me one good reason why I should get married again? She said, 'Christ, who're you going to *yell* at, if you don't have a wife? You don't want to be all alone when you're pissed *off*, do you?' And maybe that's as good a reason as any."

"Hey, Mom," said Denise, who had come back from climbing some trees and rocks by the beach, "how long did you say we're going to stay here?"

"*You* know," said her mother, "until the buses start running south. It might be soon."

"Do you ever miss having roots?" I asked Diane.

"Not much," she said. "Everyplace I go to there's something worth seeing. I don't figure that any experience is wasted."

Suddenly I thought of one reason why Mark Van Doren had been a part of my triumvirate of heroes. There is a sentence in his

Autobiography which strikes me now as much as it did when I first read it: "I tend to approve of any place I am in, simply because I am there." Or, as I once heard a Yoga teacher tell his class, "Wherever you are is where you should be." Oh, to believe that more often.

Usually hammocks make me feel so blissfully weightless that I never willingly get up from them, but gravity suddenly seemed an inviting idea. Miguel rose from his hammock too, and we walked together down to the shore, to watch the tide come in and the sun go down. We stood there in stillness and watched it for quite a while.

"Tomorow will be the twenty-sixth, won't it?" I finally asked.

"Indeed," he said. In the dark I could barely see his smile.

CHAPTER 21

YOU'VE GOT TO BE BURIED BY OLIVER

She-crab soup, more succulent presumably than he-crab, is the perfect thing to have for lunch if you happen to be stuck between planes in Charleston, South Carolina, just after the South's first big blizzard in fifteen years. She-crab soup is fortifying, and at such a time a transient needs all the fortification she can get.

I was more than an hour late arriving at the airport in Norfolk, Virginia, but there waiting for me, God love them, were Mr. and Mrs. H. M.P. Tunstall, all bundled up in unaccustomed extra scarves and full of the solicitude for which their region is famous. Apart from a few phone calls I was a total stranger to them, but they welcomed me as effusively as if I were a foreign student newly arrived on a nonstop flight from Pakistan which, come to think of it, is more or less how I felt. Not only had they driven over perilous roads to fetch me to their house for dinner, but they wouldn't hear of my spending the night in a motel.

A friend in New York had suggested that I might find Cro Tunstall to be one of the champion talkers of the entire South. Our friend had met Cro while he was stationed in Norfolk during World War II. "She's got as deep a sense of roots and her own identity as anyone I can think of," he said. "If you ever get around to it, you might want to look her up, and give her my love." That's one thing I'm good at, running around giving people other people's love, and so I did.

Cro, her old friend had added, was the first person who ever made

him want to—no, feel he had to—read Proust. "It was in self-defense," he remembered. "She and her sister would gossip about Madame de Guermante's party as if it had happened next door, last week. Someone else told me that when her sister was dying Cro sat there in the hospital reading Trollope to her. They were real autodidacts, both of them."

"Harriet was truly beautiful," Cro said of that sister. "See this picture?" I saw; it was true. "Of the five of us, she and I were the closest two, and I was desolate of course when she died. The only consolation was that she didn't have to grow old and lose that beauty. It's not much, but it's something, to think of it that way." Cro herself was more arresting than beautiful, with prominent brown eyes and a chignon which kept coming undone. I had not often met a woman as energetic as Cro, or couples as content with each other as she and her husband seemed to be.

"Hugo never finished college until later, when he was forty," Cro told me. "When he fell in love with me he couldn't see any percentage in having a diploma, so he went into real estate. We got married on $100 a month and had a child on $125. Hugh hated the real estate business, so he got the hell out of it and worked for a while at a plant up in Bristol, Virginia, until he and several other people got axed. Then he got the idea of being an accountant, so we went on up to Charlottesville for a year to study, and then we came home here to Masters Corner at last."

Their cheerful small house in the Masters Corner section of Norfolk is, in fact, only eight blocks from the one in which Cro had been born sixty-one years before. "Essentially a lot of the people we know best have been here for most of their lives," she said. "They aren't the people we're necessarily most in sympathy with, but there's something to be said, isn't there, for all that shared history?"

It was not usual, I gather, for young ladies of Masters Corner, members of certified First Families of Virginia, to grow up and teach Black Literature to college students. That isn't all Cro teaches at Old Dominion University, where she was one of the first students ever to get a master's degree and where she is now an assistant professor. She also teaches freshman and sophomore English, and Latin when there is enough demand for it. But she is especially animated when she talks of Black Literature.

"This black renaissance," she said, "is really something. There are so damned many extremely gifted young blacks writing now that it's

like Periclean Athens. I've got all my friends alerted to send me anything they find on the subject, and I'm reading constantly to keep up. The course has been made required, and there are usually two or three quite shockable lower middle-class students in it, but I can usually win them over by showing them injustices.

"I've always gulped books. I read every waking hour like a boa constrictor. I pay a price for it, though. The price is I can't listen to music any more. When Hugo and Alec (their thirty-five-year-old son and only child) are in the other room listening attentively to a record, they don't talk, they don't read. They truly listen. Then Hugo might come in and ask me, 'What would you like to hear now?' and I'll say, 'Oh, play the Brahms Violin Concerto,' and he'll smile and say 'But we just played it.' I think it's been ten or fifteen years since I really heard music.

"There's been a diminution of our involvement in civic affairs as the years have gone by," Cro said. "We've dropped the chamber quartet, and before Hugh retired—he's semi-retired, actually, from working as a CPA—we also dropped the little theater. There's no denying that live music has a lot to offer, but it's a hell of a strain to go out on a school night. Oh, it's *possible* to give an evening quiz and then make it to the concert, but only just.

"Hugh was on the symphony board for a while, and we had to go to these God-awful crummy parties. Parties down here aren't to everyone's taste, there's sort of a rule that you never let people talk more than three minutes together, so as to keep moving. To be candid, it's sometimes rather tacky ladies who get involved with the symphony sort of thing. Is tacky a word in your vocabulary? It is? It's a good word, isn't it? It says so much.

"Class angles just fascinate me, don't they you? If you lived in the South, you'd know the special way in which people ask 'who is she?' Why, you might answer, she's Jane Smith; but you'd be missing the point. 'Who is she?' means whose wife, whose daughter, whose descendant, where her grandparents lived, all sorts of other things.

"One thing you have to know, if you live in Norfolk, is that you've got to be buried by Oliver. If you're buried by anyone other than Oliver, you're disgraced, or your survivors are. When my sister's husband died she had him buried by one of his friends, who owned another firm, and she had to explain and apologize for weeks.

"Most of the people I've known all my life are untouched by Women's Liberation. They all have their stories about how they

253

worked hard, were brilliant, had it made, but ran into opposition because they were women, but *Ms.* and all that sort of thing leaves them absolutely cold. If they ever ran into Steinem and all that masturbation talk, they'd have none of it. Language, that's what really shocks them most. Generally speaking, anyone over fifty is simply not going to whip out those four-letter words. In their forties they will, a few, and from there down to age seven, they will any time.

"Students in my classes think I'll be more shocked than I am when they use such language. One of them said, 'As far as I'm concerned that book was bullshit—Oh, excuse me, Mrs. Tunstall.' What really shocks me more than that is that some of them don't even know who Martin Luther King was."

I told Cro that in the South Carolina town where I had awakened that morning, the Presbyterians appeared to have the most prosperous and established church. "They're not the top of the heap around here," Cro said. "They're allowed, of course, but Episcopalians are it. It was the shame of my mama's life that she had an aunt who got converted and became a Baptist.

"When my sister Harriet moved to the little town of Urbana, Virginia, all the neighbors brought her over rolls or a cake or something and asked her what church she belonged to. She didn't belong to any, but from habit she said Episcopalian. Well, from then on the others were cordial to her, but only the Episcopalians, it was clear, were expected to keep in touch with her socially.

"Daddy had four of us daughters and presumed we'd all marry. It never occurred to me to find a way to make a living for the rest of my life. It seems to me that's the big difference. Any girl now automatically thinks of how she'll earn a living. All I wanted to do was learn a lot of languages and read a lot.

"Our father was a lawyer, and although he knew it was wicked he was a compulsive book-buyer. We had these bills every month from the publisher, and my mother would have to sneak antiques out to the market to get some extra money. She never knew how much he earned. Money, I sometimes think, is a much more personal subject than sex. Asking how much money Daddy makes is, in many families, as unheard of a question as any you can imagine. I've had friends who've said, 'I don't know what Jim makes and I don't want to know; he pays all the bills and gives me an allowance.' That's not the way Hugo and I've done it. We've had a joint checking account, and before I worked, I paid the bills and we discussed it all."

Cro is an alumna of Sweet Briar. "I wanted to go to Vassar," she said, "but we didn't have the railroad fare. The only reason I went at all was because my sister did, and she only went because her friends went. I finished in '31 and the main aim we all talked about then was to get married or to go to New York and get a job at Macy's, because it was fun in New York. Daddy'd never have let me go there, though. When I got out of college I made my debut, and that took up a year. Then I decided I'd like to be a teacher, but I had no education courses. I went to study law, but my father didn't like the idea of women lawyers.

"I finally got a job as a school librarian. I'd never heard of the Dewey Decimal System, so I made up my own. It wasn't much, but it was mine. The man who got me the job was the first Jew on the Norfolk school board. He said us minorities (meaning Jews and Episcopalians) have got to stick together.

"The sad thing about girls nowadays, I think, is that the bulk of them set their sights so low. Every now and then I get a class of whom sixteen will *all* be nurses. They all say, 'I want to be a nurse and when I get married I'll quit and then later I can go back and help my husband.' They have no background in reading, but they can tell you that the drapes of their house will be Provençal and that they'll have two cars and two TVs and that their children's names will be Steven and Brenda. It's real pitiful; they're nice little girls with real wit, some of them. I guess it's purely economic. I guess they're the first ones in their families to make it.

"Of course the real hope for the whole women's thing, don't you think, is when women's jobs start to attract men."

"That's begun to happen, I think," I told her. "Haven't you read about men becoming stewardesses—stewards, rather? And I believe there are a lot more male nurses around these days."

"I have my freshmen write papers on What They Want To Be, and I ask them, 'Whatever it is, what's it going to cost you? Have a pot belly when you're forty?' My son has one at thirty-five; he's a systems analyst in the very rarefied upper reaches. I took a course at ODU to see what the theory of it was. One of the great things about being on the faculty is that you can take advantage of all the courses.

"As I said, I try to call my students' attention to what they're giving up when they make their choices. Whatever it is, they're giving up a hell of a lot. You know that Frost poem 'The Road Not Taken?' I call their attention to that."

Cro did not say, nor did I think to ask her, what sacrifices her own life had entailed, other than not really listening to music. Whatever they were, they had not visibly diminished her.

"From '35 to '38," she told me, "Hugh and I were very hung up on radical politics. We were Mr. and Mrs. Spanish Civil War. For our generation that was it. Czechoslavakia was sad; Hitler was expected, but the Spanish Civil War really got us all. Then in '38 we had Alec, and I put in three years nursing. I wrote a detective story but quit after I got two rejections. I wrote some book reviews, for the *New York Herald Tribune* and for the local papers, and I wrote a short story that took third place in a local contest for which I'd been a judge before. Mortifying, that third place.

"When Alec was in kindergarten I got a job teaching, and that's what I've wanted to do ever since. That and keep learning. When I retire I'll go down there to the university and take geology and the whole works. Who knows, maybe I'll end up taking Pre-Stressed Concrete 101.

"Oh look at the time! It's nearly midnight, and I've an eight o'clock class." My wrist was tired, and so was the rest of me, so I did not object, except to wonder what would happen to the dishes.

At about 7:30, earlier than she usually left for class, Hugh drove her off. Bundled against the freak cold she looked like a nine-year-old on her way to fourth grade.

"I'd better take a book along," she said. "The maddening thing is I might get there twenty minutes early after all, in spite of the icy roads. Must go, give me a kiss. If you sit in this room here while you have your coffee, you can watch the sun come up over the house next door and see the birds at the feeding station. The dishes? Oh, Hugh's done them."

When I grow up, I thought as I watched the bluejays fighting over suet, I could do a lot worse than to live this way.

CHAPTER 22

CHICANOS DON'T SAY *OLÉ*

W hen I was a child in Winnetka, Illinois, I used to wish we had a car. Until we finally did get one, when I was in high school, we'd have to borrow other people's or make do without. It was em-

barrassing. Everyone else had a car. Once in a while I would imply that we had one too, only it was away somewhere, maybe being fixed, maybe off at camp. I also used to wish my cardigans were cashmere instead of lamb's wool and that we had a shower as well as a tub and that I wouldn't have to share the closet in Ann's room.

Nelba Chavez grew up in Pascua Village east of Miracle Mile in Tucson, where families of ten commonly live in two-room houses. She was born there in 1941, and her childhood was about as filled with conveniences as that of Abraham Lincoln. Her house had kerosene lamps and dirt floors and a wood stove. Nelba's grandmother took in large bundles of ironing for twenty-five cents each, and the only way she had to heat the irons was on the stove. Flour to make tortillas came in sacks from which her grandmother made Nelba's underwear.

Nelba was raised by her grandmother because her mother (one of fifteen children of whom seven survived infancy) was an alcoholic. She married an alcoholic too. Nelba's parents lived right across the unpaved street, so she saw and heard them fight. Nelba had many relatives. Some of them were in and out of jail.

When Nelba first went to school it amazed her to learn that not all children had parents who drank and that there were people who had hair the color of a yellow Crayola. At school she was hit if she spoke Spanish on the playground and tied with a jump rope and put in the closet if she spoke it in the classroom. Nelba decided, she still is not sure why, that she would be different from the people around her. She did not, for example, join her friends who all had crosses tattooed on their hands when they were seven. She took part in gang fights only when she had to, for survival's sake. By the time she got to fifth grade, she had a teacher she liked. As a junior in high school, she decided she would apply for a scholarship at the state university. Her guidance counselor laughed at the very thought. How could Nelba, whose annual family income it said right here was $1,600, expect to afford college even if she did win a scholarship?

"Besides," the guidance counselor added, "people of your kind never make it."

Nelba did, though. When we met, she was dividing her energy in three directions. She taught at Pima Community College, she led groups of pre-delinquent children, and she was a psychiatric social worker at La Frontera, which treats the highest percentage of Mexican-Americans of any mental health clinic in Arizona. When I

met her, Nelba was one of two Spanish-speaking masters of social work in the state. The other was her friend Grace Burruel. They both got their advanced degrees in 1971, from UCLA, and they were both nationally regarded as experts, which seemed to them both funny and sad.

This expertise made them special, but what made them truly freakish by the standards of their culture was their marital status. Nelba was thirty-two and Grace twenty-eight, and both were uncommonly attractive, but they did not have husbands.

"My mother went into a severe depression when I went to graduate school," Grace said the evening I met her and Nelba in her office at La Frontera. "The more educated I am, the less men want to have to do with me. I've been ostracized by my brothers and brothers-in-law, because I'm threatening to them. My family nag me constantly because they know of no definition of happiness outside marriage."

I had to wait until their workday was over to meet Nelba and Grace, because they were booked all day long with nonstop therapy sessions, some with individuals and some with couples and families. "We deal with Mexicans and Chicanos of all age levels," they said, "and every conceivable problem."

"Let's get this straight," I said. "Who's a Chicano and who isn't?"

"Any Mexican-American who feels like one is a Chicano," Grace said. "Chicanismo—awareness of the roots of Mexican-American culture and concern about injustice—is a state of mind. But to some 'Chicano' is a dirty, derogatory word. Elderly people think it's too radical and militant. People who've just arrived from Mexico don't consider themselves Chicanos, either."

"It used to be hard to get help from the community when I was working my ass off over in the village where I grew up," said Nelba, "until suddenly the word 'Chicano' became fashionable. Do-gooders would all of a sudden rush over to help, and I'd feel like saying, 'Where the hell were you when we needed you?' "

Grace, having spent most of her childhood in Mexico, did not speak English when she arrived in Tucson and enrolled in high school. "They gave me an IQ test and I came out a moron," she said. "My counselor suggested I might be a beautician, and she meant it as a compliment.

"You know why the statistics show that Mexican-Americans don't have many mental health problems? Because ours is one of the few

clinics where Mexican-American needs are met in the whole Southwest. We are, you will find, quite well represented in penal institutions, alcoholism, drug abuse. Oh, is it really seven-thirty? I'm going to have to go. The group will be waiting."

"Who's in the group?" I asked.

"Mostly Mexican-American women concerned about emancipation," said Grace. "We have a lot of groups devoted to that subject. Sometimes we get women as old as forty-five who still live at home with their parents and still feel guilty about wanting to get out."

"Sometimes men come in here and want to get us," said Nelba. "They threaten to kill their wives, kill us, put a bomb in the place. The idea of emancipated women totally undermines their authority. It's very traumatic what happens to a man when his wife sees herself as emancipated. My reaction to the women's movement is you Anglos don't know how lucky you are. If you only knew *our* problems!"

"A lot of what we try to do," said Nelba, "is have women come out and do something with their lives. Unless Mexican women emancipate, we're lost. In our culture the double standard is far worse. Latin men can do anything they like, but women are sheltered, protected, chaperoned, and raised from birth to be slaves to men."

"But what about your extended families?" I asked. "Isn't there supposed to be something special about having all those *compadres* and *tíos* and *sobrinas* and *primas* and *cuñadas*? Doesn't it give you a warmth and security we could use some of to have them around?"

"My own family," said Grace, "is so close it's suffocating." She and Nelba had been to a conference in Washington, D.C., where, much to their wonderment, Anglo psychiatrists had presented different proposals for the rediscovery of roots of extended families. To them this made about as much sense as bringing back polio.

"You Anglos," said Nelba, shaking her head. "Hell, we've been living in extended families for years. Some of what you say about closeness and security is true, of course, but those ties can be too close. What you're trying to bring back is what we're trying to get away from."

Grace went off to lead her group of women concerned with emancipation, and Nelba and I decided to go to La Fuentes, a fancy Mexican restaurant on the Miracle Mile, to talk some more. Glittering in their sequins, the mariachi band wandered around the restaurant's several rooms, playing whatever songs people asked for. It was understood that everyone would have a favorite song to request. I felt

unnerved; the only song I could think of was "South of the Border," a shameful choice for a Muzak-hater like myself. But I asked for it anyway, and the musicians obliged with gusto. When they were through, some tourists at the next table shouted, "*Olé!*"

"Chicanos don't say *Olé!*, do they?" I asked Nelba.

"No," she said, smiling. "Just you guys."

CHAPTER 23

VODKA GIMLET TO GO

I'm too tired to stay awake any longer. Even though it's only eleven o'clock here, it's midnight in Tucson, where I've just flown from, and tomorrow in Europe, where I was last week. Besides, I'm still taking pills called V-Cillin-K for the flu I caught last week. Everyone understands. I am shown to a room with a king-size bed. Tomorrow, if the fog lifts, I can look out at the Pacific. I am in California again, La Jolla this time, in the bedroom of a nineteen-year-old named Robin.

"Oh, poor Robin, I'm putting you out."

"No, that's fine," she says. "It means *I* get to sleep on one of the waterbeds."

It is a measure of my fatigue and general churlishness that my first, barely suppressed reaction to this news is annoyance: why didn't they assign *me* to the waterbed? Don't they know I've always wanted to sleep on one? But how, my voice of reason retorts, could they possibly know that? "They," this time, are my hosts Audrey and Bill McGaw. I have come to talk to Audrey because Bill has told me "she *really* knows what it is to be an American woman."

I suppose there is not an adult female between Samoa and the Bay of Fundy who could not lay some claim to expertise on the subject, but something in Bill's voice has lured me. He met me at the San Diego airport in the famous glittering black hearse he bought last summer in London, the very one which once belonged to the Beatles and which appeared in *A Hard Day's Night*.

When Bill bought the hearse the previous summer it had taken four days of his total attention. That made Audrey mad. "He got *obsessed,*" she said. "It smelled of such selfishness. While the kids and I waited for him to do all that paperwork, we had to change all

our plans. I was tempted to just take the kids and leave, instead of hanging around. I don't like losing control of my life, being at the whim of somebody else. In those three or four days I didn't feel loved by him. We had it out, though."

"We always do," said Bill. "We fight big and love big. We don't let anything slide anymore. We both know what it's like to have a bad thing, because we had bad things before." Between them the McGaws have six children. Robin and three boys now live in La Jolla. A son of Audrey's is in Hawaii, and a daughter of Bill's lives most of the year with her remarried mother in the East.

I first met the McGaws five years earlier, when they were leading an encounter group. They had co-led seventy or eighty such groups, mostly for married couples and families and many under the auspices of the Center for the Studies of the Person. The Center, in La Jolla, was established by a group including the psychologist Dr. Carl Rogers. I had last seen Audrey in Pittsburgh four months earlier, when she and Dr. Rogers both helped lead a filmed encounter group of nine Irishmen imported for the occasion from Belfast.

I thought that after having led so many groups for troubled marriages, Audrey might have some sage things to say about how women were changing. "The big difference I notice," she said, "is that women are realizing now that they're responsible for themselves, instead of feeling like society's victims. We're getting to see that we shouldn't blame our troubles on men, God, the president, or our mothers, but on ourselves. It's ridiculous to say you can't change yourself, because you can."

"I've always thought it was pointless for people over the age of twenty-five to blame their parents for anything," I said. "I just made that up, but don't you think it makes sense?"

"I think it does," said Audrey. "But a lot of women like to stay in the past. As long as they stay in the past, instead of right now, they're very secure, because they can always avoid responsibility, always say, 'What can you expect, with a mother like I had?' "

"Why," I asked her, "do you think women come to encounter groups?"

"Mostly from a gnawing hunger for some sort of recognition. In the groups we've done I'd bet that eighty percent of the women bring their men along, instead of vice versa. Men are bewildered when they get there, they say, 'Well, of course I love her; I wouldn't live with her if I didn't,' but they don't understand. They think it's just a

matter of sex. Women don't mean just that. They mean being touched, as opposed to being fucked. What women have to learn is that if they want to accept freedom, a responsibility comes with it. It's safer to avoid the responsibility and choose enslavement.

"And a lot of people are screwed up by images. Bill and I used to have big scenes because he didn't like gardening and woodwork. I might have got some joy out of the yard if I'd worked in it myself, but I didn't because it was his job. Some women often say, 'How do you expect me to make love when I've been up till two in the morning doing your job?' Withholding sex is often a punishment for not living up to images."

"Do you think women run the show most of the time?"

"They do, in a peculiar way—not hypocritically or even consciously, but because they don't accept responsibility for the position they're in, from resentment."

Two years earlier, Audrey had been so full of resentment herself that she wrote Bill a letter. He wasn't off on a trip, he was right there in the house with her, but somehow she felt like writing down what was on her mind instead of saying it aloud. "There've been four or five times in our marriage," she says, "when I haven't been able to find words. I brood about it for a while, whatever it is, then write everything down and give it to Bill when I'm quiet."

The letter she wrote him then said, among many other things, that "I'm dull & uninteresting most of the time. I'm unkempt & dishonest. Nothing I do is lasting. . . . I'm not comfortable with myself. I'm getting older & gray & wrinkled & I smoke & eat too much & I don't do anything worthwhile for anyone or myself. I feel taken for granted, overworked, misunderstood, underappreciated, ugly, wronged, helpless, lost, ashamed, pitiful. I feel disgust for myself. . . . I find I am easily irritated by you, the kids, our friends, the yard, the house, the laundry, the kitchen, the refrigerator, doghair, dogshit, trash & dirt & mess & clutter & lunch & dinner & endless dishes & ashtrays & chairs out of place & telephones & crumbs & cats & meals & food & marketing & cars & bills & bathroom mirrors & the patio & the windows & the walls & making the bed & picking up clothes & being fat & not having clothes look right & cooking & marketing & spots & etc etc etc."

Could this be the Audrey I saw before me? This stately, radiant, expressive woman?

"How did things change afterward?" I asked.

"Well," said Audrey, "before that letter, I used to take pleasure in housework. My house shone better than anybody's. There was no dust, no clutter, because I had no other way of proving my value. My children were well-behaved, whatever that means."

"What about the groups you led with Bill?" I asked. "Didn't that give you value?"

"Not enough," she said. "Besides, by then I'd tapered off from doing them."

"So you felt that housework was what defined you?"

"Sure. When Bill would say, 'Come meet me for a drink after work,' and I'd say, 'I can't, I have to do the floor,' and he'd say, 'Oh, the floor isn't important,' I'd explode: if the floor wasn't important, since the floor was my work, what did that make *me*?"

Just then Robin and her cousin Cindy came in from church. Robin, her mother later told me, "believes in God and Christ and a lot of things I've always been negative about, but that's fine, because the kids she hangs around with are really alive, neat, marvelous people."

Robin, I later learned, had recently reconciled with her boyfriend after a dismaying split. "It bothered me," Audrey said, "that she should have been *grateful* to him for liking her. That meant she thought he was the king, just as I used to think Bill was. Bill never asked for that throne in the first place, but as long as it was there he didn't want to abdicate.

"I was on the way into making Robin into a matriarch, a hideous role which would have made her brothers resent and dislike her. It used to be that they never did dishes because the kitchen was her place. No more. Since then I've tried to make her see that the path she picks for herself needn't be any narrower than anybody else's, just because she's a female.

"She's starting to think a lot of things out now, things which in the depth of her pain she didn't acknowledge, because all she wanted was for the boy to come back. She says she's in a very different place with him, that if he starts treating her carelessly again, she won't take it."

"Good for her," I said. "Do you think these changes came from the women's movement?"

"I think it's more a natural evolvement," said Audrey. "Since we had our showdown a couple of years ago, we all care more about each other and listen more to each other. Before, the male-female thing kept the kids from being as close as they are now. We've had so

many little changes. Like the boys cooking. Sandy makes the best *quesedillas* now, no matter how hard the rest of us may try. Par even said he'd like to learn to cook. Bill, too. He used to just do steak and lobster, now he's into tempura."

Bill McGaw first laid eyes on Audrey in a bar after a Christmas party in the office where they both worked, eleven years earlier. "I pointed to her and told a fellow girlwatcher that someday she'd be my number one. 'Impossible,' the friend said, 'I happen to know she's married.' 'Even so,' I said, 'Just wait.' "

In time, when Bill heard that Audrey was divorced, which he had been himself for a couple of years, he began his pursuit. Learning that she was in the habit of driving to a certain beach where her children could let off steam while she watched the sunset, he drove there, parked his car next to hers, stayed in his, and talked to her.

"If you weren't so stubborn," he said, "you'd have let me bring you a drink."

"You couldn't have brought the only kind of drink I like."

"What's that?"

"Vodka gimlet."

"Excuse me," said Bill. He drove to a bar, ordered a double vodka gimlet, poured it into a glass he happened to have in his pocket, returned to the beach, and said, "Now can I sit in your car, if I keep way over to the other side?"

"Still," said Audrey, "I was wary. I didn't want to get into another relationship that didn't work. I wasn't any better for my first husband, an artist who did technical illustrations for a living, than he was for me. He never finished things because he didn't want to be judged, but I kept urging him to. In his case, if I'd been a devoted wife I'd have just let it go.

"I was twenty-one but I might as well have been twelve. I married him mostly to get away from my mother." In 1961 that marriage ended, and on the day after Christmas in 1964 Audrey married Bill.

"It was the kids who got him to move in, bit by bit, shirt by shirt. They'd say, 'Gee, Bill, you spend so much time here, why don't you bring your favorite painting over so it'll be more homelike for you?' They loved finding him on the couch in the morning. After a while they said, 'Why do you sleep on the couch when Mom's got such a nice big bed?' At first I was concerned what the neighbors would think, but as long as the kids were happy, the neighbors didn't give us any static. But it bugged me when Bill's parents came to visit and

he moved back to his own house. All my friends and family knew; I didn't see why his shouldn't. I guess he was just reluctant to talk about marriage. But then once, when he was off on a trip, I sat and looked at my reflection in the window and had a conversation with it."

"With your reflection?"

"Yes. A textbook case of taking a look at myself. I asked my reflection what it was I wanted. 'You know,' the reflection said, 'you want children and a dog and a house and to love and be loved.' And I said, 'Jackass, that's what you've got right now!' The reflection said, 'I'll be goddamned, it's true—if you have what you've always wanted what difference does it make if you're married?' I said, 'None—who says a piece of paper will make things any better?'

"Then when Bill came home I totally gave myself to him for the first time. All the pressure was gone. Two weeks later, he wanted to get married, because there was no reason not to have a binding piece of paper. A few days after that he bought a washing machine and dryer to replace the clunky old thing I had, and that meant he was really going to settle in."

Settle in he did, and with him, off and on, his three children, who got along astonishingly well with Audrey's. When any friction developed, there were always the Tuesday night meetings. "We'd eliminate potential disaster at those meetings," Bill said, "by talking about and sharing our real feelings, with I-messages instead of U-messages—the idea was not to say 'You're a bastard and a bully' but 'I feel like a worm when you treat me that way.' "

Now the McGaws have a new idea: each child will design a ten-day vacation within a 1,200-mile air range for Bill and Audrey and him or herself. Bill belongs to a flying club and has access to planes. "We're all excited about the idea of being with one child for a whole week in a setting away from home. They're getting older, and we'll lose them soon enough."

It pleased Audrey, she wrote in her letter to Bill, that he had "broken tradition and chosen not to work eight hours a day five days a week to pay the bills. You may work much less than that, in spurts, and often don't even earn enough to support the family. Everyone, including me, thinks that's marvelous. No one expects or wants you to change. I'm ready to buck tradition too, in choosing not to work seven days a week at slave work in the house. I don't care who doesn't approve. Except you, of course. I do need you."

"I'm not a first-class crusader," Bill said later. "I'm a third- or fourth-class crusader. I'm selfish, hedonistic, need time to be with my family. I don't respect myself, nor do they, if I sit on my ass for six weeks, but it is important for me to spend much more time with them than conventional fathers do. Of course if I had a shitty wife I might feel different about it.

"Why the hell be married, why have a family, unless you create a place where you can go to recharge your batteries, maintain mental health? We all have a strong need to support each other in the family. If home isn't the one place in the world where you can get a support system for role relief, you're lost. I can come home and be feminine, she masculine, kids can be mother or baby. Churches should do this for us, but they don't."

"Maybe the nuclear family isn't in such bad shape after all," I said.

"Oh, it's going to take a hell of a beating," said Bill. "Marriage has been going on a hell of a long time and it's only now being challenged. It's good to rip it open and see how goddamn ugly it's gotten to be, and try to change it."

"Hey," said Audrey, "I'd better go to the supermarket."

"Can I go with you?" I asked. I love California supermarkets. This one even had an elevator, and it made the ones I go to on Broadway seem like miserable company stores in a coal town.

After we shopped Audrey and I drove around La Jolla. We stopped and looked at the ocean. "I look at it more often now," she said. "For a while I just took it for granted. I wouldn't go for months on end. I enjoy cooking more now too. I've been here twenty-two years now, half my life. I grew up really right here on Wind & Sea beach, and it's like my mother. I've done a lot of crying, screaming, walking on this beach, I used to bring David down here every day. He's in Hawaii now. He had some minor brain damage and dyslexia, can't read well. Not retarded, but slow. He needs to be by water, he went to live in Hawaii where he could build his own house, grow vegetables. He wanted to find out if the land was friendly to him, if he could make it. Now he says, 'I am in a part of the world that cares for me, and when I go into the ocean it is my friend. I have enormous peace with this land and this world.'

" 'I think patience is what love is,' he said, 'because how could you love somebody without it?' "

"He doesn't sound retarded at all," I said.

"When he was about fifteen I, like a lot of mother hens, wanted

David and Bill to love each other as if they were a father and son. I didn't realize that they already did, in a different but no less real way than my image of how it should be. With all the problems, failures, and doubts I was constantly explaining David to Bill and Bill to David, and I kept interfering, until David finally said, 'Would you please butt out of my life and let me have something with my father that's mine, even if he hates me?'

"My mother came out here to visit from Detroit after I had all three kids, which was a thrill because she'd never been able to afford to go anywhere. She didn't like my house, kids, style of life. I was thirty-two then, and during her visit she said, 'You know, Audrey, I've never really loved you and don't now, and I don't think I can, because I don't understand you, but I respect you.'

"I heard a roaring in my ears. I realized she was trying to do something nice but I couldn't stand it, and went into the bathroom to vomit. I think that was the moment I started to grow up. I went into a slump for a while thinking if my own mother doesn't love me then why should anyone else? But then I realized I'm not the child I was. The past can't comfort me; there's nothing for me in the past.

"All our friends thought she was the neatest person in the world. She could give to them, but not to us. Nor would she take from us. She wouldn't let any of us do anything for her—get her coffee, rub her shoulder, help her in any way. When we went to clean out the house after she died, we found boxes labeled for each one of us, filled with all the gifts we'd ever sent her over five or ten years. All the Christmas, birthday, Mother's Day presents—warm sweaters, all the things we thought she might like or need. It was as if she was reaching from her grave to say 'screw you.'"

"How has this affected you?"

"I guess mine is the only good marriage of the lot. I'm the only one who has a good thing going, which makes me feel both lucky and sad. Bill's dad, when he died it was just the opposite. He went hideously, of cancer, but Bill gave up his job and family and everything a month before the end and was there. He didn't want to be anywhere else in the entire world, so he went. He stayed there in that hospital room in Cleveland and he'd say, 'I'm here, Daddy, I love you,' and hold his hand. Let your parents need you. Let your kids need you."

"Let people in general need you," I said.

"Right," said Audrey.

CHAPTER 24

IS THAT MISS OR MRS.?

M y friend George is not an ornithologist, but he has a Life List all the same. His is a list of things he wants to see and do before he dies. He would no more miss a chance to stand on that Southwestern spot where four state lines intersect than he would turn down an invitation to a royal wedding. He might be called what someone once called me, an Experience Freak. Now and then he telephones to suggest that we have an Experience together. Our most recent Experience, at the Radio City Music Hall, was a midnight concert called "Colossus of the Keyboard." Colossal it was, too. First E. Power Biggs, that most aptly named of modern artists, played his heart out at the mighty Wurlitzer. Then no fewer than ten pianos rose in grandeur, as from Iolanthe's dark exile, into our range of vision. The stage revolved not only up and down but all around, like the setting for a Busby Berkeley musical. It was truly an evening, or rather a morning, to remember, and I always shall, among other reasons because George observed, as I don't think he or most men would have a couple of years before, that it wasn't fair: all the ten pianists were men, and their page-turners all were female.

Feminism has come to tinge all my thoughts, particularly those which concern my late mother. My sister recalls an evening in Winnetka, when we were both probably in high school, when we sat at the dining room table with our mother (our father didn't get home until ten most nights), and Mother's eyes nearly brimmed over as she said, "People *used* to think I was fun."

I don't remember that particular supper hour myself, but those were not years in which my mother would often say, "We just *howled!*"—a favorite accolade from the Blithe Spirit whose strong suit, it will be recalled, had been mirth. Corinne Stocker, the last in a sixty-six-year series of the Blithe Spirit's best friends, said what her predecessors in their different ways said, too: "What I miss most about Eleanor is her humor. I can't expect to find humor like that again." The last time they ever talked on the phone, just before Corinne left on a week's vacation, my mother told her: "Hurry home, I miss you already."

Toward the end, apparently, the Blithe Spirit had regained blitheness and a sort of peaceful balance. I'm glad of that. "She was starting," Ann said, "to get to the bottom of her trunk." All her things

were in order, as if she sensed how soon Ann and I would be throwing out her lipsticks, going through her drawers.

I guess it undid her to be faced suddenly with two galumphing
daughters of her own, no longer darling little things, before whom
suddenly stretched the fearsome options of adulthood. What, for instance, was she to make of me, her firstborn, a non-sewing, non-
tennis-playing recluse not much sought by swains, whose social
calendar bore so little resemblance to those of the soda-guzzling, hot
rod-riding keen teens of popular lore? How could she tell me what I
would need to grow up? It was all she could do to give me my first
box of Modess. Almost never did we talk of the long-range implications of womanhood, or of anything controversial or ambiguous or
abstract. If Ann or I would say, "Come on, what's really so terrible
about socialized medicine?" Mother would call, "Bob! You handle
this one!" The more we acted like docile children, the more we were
praised. "She's a good kid," we noted, was a compliment paid as approvingly to octogenarians as to our own classmates. We must have
deduced that the thing to do was to keep on being kids, good ones if
possible.

To be a kid constantly, though, became a strain. Occasional relief
was needed. Early on I figured out how to escape. I fell into the
habit of retreating to whatever handy place smelled the most like
Daddy's office. I went wherever I could find the urgent, pungent
scent of newsprint, the heady excitement of fast-breaking news, free
passes to conventions, free tickets to concerts, the shrugging martyr-
dom of last-minute plan cancellations. I never consciously planned
to be like Daddy, but offices that smelled of newsprint, from
grade school on, were a good place to find congenial people whose
talk was not evasive. Anyway, writing had seemed a glamorous thing
to do since the time I was around seven, when I spilled ink all over
the dining room rug. I well remember my punishment: "You can't
use a pen until Thanksgiving." The pen, and later the typewriter,
were symbols of privilege. Using them made me feel less a child.

The Blithe Spirit was proud of my bylines and clippings. She
pasted them all in scrapbooks, and showed them to her friends, and
that was nice, but it didn't make her relax. Nothing seemed to, for
long. Yet compared with some women of her generation, a sad and
confused one by and large, the Blithe Spirit was a model of serene
poise. I know of one mother who wept to see her daughter marry,
because there would be no more intrigue over girlish romances.

269

"Since I got my first valentine from a boy in third grade," that daughter said, "those intrigues were all that kept my mother going." My own mother at least had a few other things to think about.

Once in a great while the Blithe Spirit would even let slip that perhaps Mrs. X was not quite as darling as Mrs. Y after all, and that there were unresolved questions of relativity and degree even under the protectively arching elms of Winnetka. Almost in spite of herself she passed on to me a preference for tributaries over mainstreams, a curiosity about the peripheries of things, a capacity for certain intuitive leaps.

Sisterhood, as introduced by the women's movement, did not fall on my parched soul like rain on a desert. Whatever solace it has brought to others—a good deal, apparently—it only makes me think back to my nearly manless childhood in Winnetka, when nobody's daddies were around very much and ours, owing to the demands made on him by Colonel Robert R. McCormick, was hardly there at all. Perhaps because we saw so little of men other than our classmates and some teachers, we were not told we had to simper and be fluffy when we grew up. I wasn't, anyway. My attention was called to Mrs. Van Der Vries, who was in the legislature, and Mrs. Hahn down the street, who was a sculptor, and Aunt Janet, who had a distinct flair for management. I cannot say that anyone ever programmed me not to "succeed" in "work," or to be afraid of success. President Matina L. Horner of Radcliffe College recently said that women avoid success because they fear its consequences. If this is true of me, it is so in a roundabout way; I am reasonably comfortable with professional success, and take pleasure in what I have done. What would frighten me, by its very novelty, would be success in affairs of the heart.

I think sometimes of the Aldine paper dolls. They weren't paper, really, they were bright red oilcloth, cut out by Eleanor and Bob in an endless chain of alternating boy and girl figures, holding hands, glued to the walls of a room called the Nursery in our apartment on Aldine Avenue in Chicago. It was assumed that one day we, the occupants of the Nursery, would grow up and find partners to dance with too, just as symmetrically. Symmetry, perhaps as a consequence, means more to me than it might. I have sense enough to go to parties alone at times when I'm not involved with anyone, but doing so makes me feel conspicuous. What am I supposed to do, I asked my sister, pick up one of those darling nineteen-year-old

French sailors with red pompoms on their caps like I saw at the Central Park Zoo? (Why not? she asked. Why don't you take up with the garbageman? I asked her.)

Shirley Chisholm said if she could choose anybody in the world to take with her to a desert island, she would take herself. Maybe if I were a politician I would too, because in that line of work people don't have many opportunities to encounter themselves. But creaking along as I do in reactionary old Consciousness II circles, I would elect to go to a desert island, or just about anywhere, with a mature specimen of the opposite sex. I guess that friend was right who told me once, "Of course you shouldn't get married until you feel like it, but hurry up and feel like it." I guess John Berryman was right, too, when he said, "It's terrible to give half your life over to someone else, but it's even worse not to. It's too bad that when you get married they won't let you say 'I hope so' instead of 'I will,' but it's still important to try. You've got to try." Okay, I'll hurry up and try, as soon as I find someone who is so busy doing what he does that he'll not mind my doing what I do, with whom I need not play games, and who knows that I'm a Ten on a One-to-Ten scale. Not everybody recognizes that fact at a glance. Some people can't even tell, the dummies.

I would not like to live like the ladies who sat in Jack and Millie's living room the sunny April afternoon of Jack's sixty-fifth birthday party at their farm in the mountains of Maryland. Women all sat inside in the living room, visiting about their children and grandchildren, saying how proud they were of them, while the men were outside in the sun.

"Aren't you proud of *yourself,* too?" I could not help asking a woman who had been talking of her grandson's stamp collection.

"That sounds like a Women's Lib question to me," she said.

Sometimes I go to Jack and Millie's with my friends in Washington. We went this past year, the day after Thanksgiving. Julian had to work, but Molly and Liz and I went. We hiked up a long series of ascending meadows, squeezing under barbed wire fences when we had to, until we got far enough up to look all around us and see the diffuse glow of red sunset all over the stands of cedar and birch, everywhere wheat and lavender and gold. And in the distance came the cracks of guns, because it was hunting season. Liz, who knows about such things, said the guns were probably farther away than they sounded, but still the shots were unsettling.

271

"Don't shoot us," I called, half in jest, as if the hunters could hear.

"Quiet," said Liz, "or they might get ideas."

They might have, too. The human race, as you have noticed, is not entirely rational. It is *meshuga,* as some of my best friends say, and its lunacies certainly affect women. "There's something crazy about our society," I heard one woman say, "if half the women in it are going nuts because of child care and the other half because nobody needs them any more."

Some women object to getting mail addressed "Ms." I don't mind at all; I like it. I like being snippy to airlines personnel, too.

"Is that Miss or Mrs.?" they ask when I make a reservation.

"Are you Mister or Master?" I answered once, when the voice on the telephone was male.

"It's Reverend," I said another time.

"Fine," said the voice. "Tell the Reverend he can pick up his tickets half an hour before flight time."

"But *I'm* the Reverend," I said.

"You *are?*" Well, I guess I could be. I guess I could aspire to be just about anything, and I don't doubt that I owe this profusion of options to legislation which surely would not exist without the feminist movement. For the energy which has transmuted yearnings into laws, I and all women must be grateful. We owe whatever support we can give to continuing efforts to remove archaic barriers. Many such barriers remain. Not all can be legislated away. Some will last until attitudes are softened. To soften such attitudes, we have to be persuasive. That's where some of us make mistakes. Nothing is less persuasive than a tirade from a rigidly orthodox heretic.

I'm a sympathizer, a femsymp if you will, but some feminists come on so abrasive they alarm even me. I can only lament the impression they must make on the undecided. Some of these zealots remind me of Pentecostal Christians who grab your elbow and stare you down and demand, "Do you know the Lord?" But Pentecostal fervor happens not to be my style, nor does evangelical feminism. There are ways and ways of being saved. I have heard the message, *sorores.* I agree. But I'd rather be in the woodwind section than the percussion, and I don't think you can afford to alienate the piccolos, or to forget that there are other contexts in which to view life. Is not your cause more important than that?

I think your cause—okay, our cause—is important. Do not, for all

my reservations, misunderstand me. I think that if women felt they had access to more realistic power our homes would be less damagingly matriarchal. Yes, I think our homes are damagingly matriarchal. I think we run the show at home, to too great a degree, in part because we have sensed we cannot run it elsewhere. And something about the way we run the show at home scares men away. They have abdicated. They and we have drifted apart. To fill the vacuum their absence creates, most of us have become more vital and imaginative and resourceful than most of them. We are also funnier. When I dial the phone numbers of most households I am close to, by no means all but most, I catch myself hoping the woman will answer instead of the man, because I have more to say to most women than to most men, and I am more curious about what they will have to say to me. We understand each other better. Men, as one man I know neatly put it, are more wary and mooselike.

I do not applaud this state of affairs. It alarms me. Intuition and humor and alert peripheral vision are qualities I deeply esteem and would like to find everywhere. I don't want us to have any monopoly on them. But have we robbed men of these strengths? Does our being strong mean they must be weak? If the only way I can make you feel strong is to feign coy frailty, then we're both in trouble, because in this one respect I have changed irreversibly: I can no longer pretend to be submissive and helpless.

I think we need each other. Much as I love certain women, I am not signing up for any separatist Amazon commune, to get away from those men who are dolts and beasts. I should sorely miss those who are not. I think men need us as much as we need them, and that it is urgent for us to figure out how to talk to each other, not always with words, until we have stopped scaring each other or boring each other or whatever it is we have done that has made things go so sour.

Wholesomeness is exotic to me. I pretended to like the era of strobe lights and deafening acid rock in discotheques, but a lot of that sixties frenzy really just made me nervous. More and more I am drawn toward stillness. So it is with the women's movement: its theorists interest me less than those Closet Feminists, as I have come to think of them, who wrest sap from the trees, fish from the seas, or fashion quilts from scraps of cloth. Yoked to their menfolk, to whom they are faithful and whom they survive, they flourish on a fraction of the options granted most of us. Without being ideological about it or even articulating it at all, these women embody the

movement's best principles. They don't confuse strength with gender, nor do they use their sex as an excuse to avoid responsibility. There are still a lot of these American noblewomen around. Maybe before their breed dies out, which as society grows more complex and labor more abstract it surely and sadly will, the rest of us can learn something from them.

This is the watershed time in my own life. Motherless, I have nobody to paste my clippings into scrapbooks, so I shall achieve, or try to achieve, what I want to and because I want to. Maybe some of my achievements won't even involve the printed word. Jobless, I have no office to go to, no boss to tell me where to be next Thursday, and so I shall move at my own pace away from the conventions that structured my past. Perhaps in so doing I shall seem at the same time appallingly brassy to those I leave behind, and hopelessly timid to those on the farther shore. Tough.

I am not making any resolutions. Anyway, there are certain things about myself I like; I'm not in the market for a total metamorphosis. I don't plan to stop getting out of cars to pick wildflowers along highways (although I would prefer to pick them elsewhere). I'm not such an Experience Freak any more; the Life List doesn't matter so much. I am not so indiscriminately receptive. Some things human *are* alien to me. I still grope, but the spectrum of my mistakes narrows. Most of my worries are over how to mix honesty with charity. The poles to avoid, for me, are glibness at one extreme and self-pity at the other.

I hope to make fewer and longer trips. I hope to go only where I can either learn something worth knowing, or else be fussed over by people who don't need to be reminded that I am a Ten (they will be Ten too, of course), or both. I wish to hold and be held, laugh and be made to laugh, commune in every way I can, but solitude doesn't scare me. I can always stay home and alphabetize my phonograph records, learn languages, maybe figure out how to read music.

It might be nice to stop being a kid, too. My sister and I, according to the actuarial tables, are at the midpoints of our lives. We are older than some astronauts, older than some Watergate defendants. She is, after all, the mother of a person five feet two inches tall. I have, after all, been on the Johnny Carson show. We are both taxpayers, voters, concerned citizens. Just because our mother defined us as children doesn't mean we have to accept that definition. We can transcend it. We can try to be what we hope to be in spite of her, as well as because of her.

Her death, we thought, was surely, at last, the long-delayed end of our childhood. We were wrong about that, though, because our father's remarriage inspired an even more final feeling; we could all but hear that great door ceremoniously shutting. But the door must not have been locked, because I had the same terminal sensation still another time, on the occasion of the death of *Life*. Such reflections force me to consider the possibility that maybe that door is not meant to be shut. Maybe we should leave it a bit ajar, and try to be good kids.

New York St

Friday's Volume, 10,900,000 Shares

Volume since Jan. 1: 1969   1968   1967
Total sales   1,127,162,071   1,163,885,453   1,006,288,782

MOST ACTIVE STOCKS

	Open	High	Low	Close	Chg.	Volume
Ill Cent	60½	61¼	60	60	−¾	253,900
US Plyw Ch	73	73	70½	70⅞	−2½	223,800
Elect Music	8	8	7⅞	7⅞		205,000
Roan Sel Tr	9½	9½	9	9	−⅜	202,200
Brunswk	24⅜	24½	23¾	23⅞	−⅛	155,400
Cont Oil	38	38⅜	38	38⅜	+⅜	151,600
Natomas	104½	113½	102⅜	110¼	+5½	147,600
Atlas Cp	6⅛	7½	6½	7	+⅜	126,300
Perfect Film	31⅝	31¼	27¼	28¼	−3¼	113,200
Rdg Bates	28¼	29¾	28	29½	+3⅝	94,700

Average closing price of most active stocks: 38.52.

A-B-C

	−1969− High	Low	Stocks Div.	Sales in 100s	Open	High	Low	Close	Net Chg.
	38½	28½	Abacus .49f	171	37	38¼	37	38	+⅛
	76	45½	AbbtLab 1.40	57	74¼	74¾	73½	73½	+½
	66¼	47¼	ACF Ind 2.40	x221	51⅛	51⅜	50⅛	51½	+⅛
	30⅝	24	AcmeCl 1.40a	57	24¾	25¼	24½	24½	−¼
	51	41¼	Acme Mkt 2b	52	48½	48½	48⅛	48⅛	+¼
	20¼	17	Adamfl 1.51g	21	18¾	18¾	18¼	18¼	−¼
	22¾	17	Ad Millis .20	17	18½	18¾	18¾	18¾	−¼
	82¼	65¼	Address 1.40	115	78	80½	78	78	−¾
	21⅜	15	Admiral	29	19½	19¾	19½	19½	−¾
	65¼	46½	AetnaLif 1.40	142	52	52½	51½	52½	+1
	32½	15¾	Aguirre Co	208	29½	30¾	28½	30½	+½
	46⅛	40¼	Air Prod .20b	76	43¾	43¾	43¼	43½	+½
	34¹	27¾	AirRedtn 1.80	188	27¾	28	27¾	27½	−½
	18¼	12½	AJ Industries	113	15½	15½	14½	14½	−½
	20½	18	Ala Gas 1	20	18½	18¾	18¼	18¼	+¼
	48	35¾	AlbertoC .32	23	45½	45¼	45	45½	+1¾
	32⅝	26⅛	AlcanAlu 1.10	101	31⅞	32	31½	31½	+⅜
	28¾	18¼	Alleg Cp .10g	52	32	33½	32½	32½	+½
	62¼	58½	AllegLud pf 3	3	60	60½	60	60½	+¼
	66	58½	AllegLud 1.28	74	23¼	23½	23¼	23½	+½
	25¾	22	AllegPw 1.28	148	33¼	33¾	33¼	33⅜	
	37¼	29½	AlliedCh 1.20	148	33½	33½	32½	33¼	
	33	25	Alld Main .40	29	30	31½	30	30⅞	+⅛
	51¾	40	AlliedMill .75	9	29½	29¼	29½	29½	
	53¾	40½	Allied Pd .68	5	42¼	42¼	41½	41½	+⅛
	41⅝	34¼	AlliedStr 1.40	298	41½	41½	41¼	41½	+¼
	21	14¾	AlliedSup .60	109	15¼	16½	15¾	16	+¼
	32¾	25	Allis Chalm	112	32	32	32	32	
	25¼	17¼	AlphaPC .20g	49	25	25	25½	25	
	84	69½	Alcoa 1.80	69	81	81½	80½	80½	+½
	38¼	31½	AmalSug 1.60	40	32	32½	32	32¼	+¼
	30¼	23¾	AMBAC .50	72	27	27	28½	28	+¼
	29¼	21	AmerEs 1.20	4	28	28½	28	28½	+½
	64	50	AmerEs pf2.60	9	50½	50½	50½	50½	+½
	129½	99¾	Amerada	103	127½	127¼	127¾	126	126	−1½
	37¾	28	AAirFiltr .80	25	32½	33½	32½	33¼	+½
	34½	31½	Am Airlin .80	230	33½	33½	32½	33¾	
	22¼	19½	Am Baker 1	75	21	21	20	20½	
	31½	26½	AmBk Note 1	2	27½	28¼	27½	27½	
	76½	56½	AmBdcst 1.60	42	71½	71½	70½	71	−⅛
	58½	46	Am Can 2.20	54	57	57	56¼	56½	+¼
	30½	27¾	ACan pf 1.75	4	28¼	28¼	28¼	28¼	+¼
	20¼	16¾	Am .Cem .60	43	17¾	17¾	17¼	17¾	
	43	35½	A Chain 1.40	8	36½	36½	36	36	
	29¼	22	AmCredit .90	9	23	23	32	23½	+¼
	33½	28¾	ACrySug 1.40	7	30½	30½	30	30½	
	28½	27¼	Am Distill 1	172	32¾	34	32	32	−½
	19½	13½	ADualVt .20j	1	14½	14½	14½	14½	+¼
	14½	13¼	ADuel pf.84a	18	14	14	14	14	
	40¼	34½	AmEIPw 1.58	133	37½	37½	37¼	37	+½
	32	25¾	Am Enka	15	31½	31½	31½	31½	−½
	50½	30	Am Exp Ind	51	40	40½	40	40	+½
	25¼	17½	AmHoist .70	52	18	18¾	17¾	17¾	+⅛
	61	52½	A Home 1.40	132	60¼	60¾	60	60	
	91	77½	A Home pf 2	1	90¼	90¼	90¼	90¼	−¼
	37¾	19¾	Am Hosp .22	x61	35¾	35	35	35	−⅜
	21½	19¾	Aminvst .20		20½	20¾	20	20¼	
	27½	22¼	AmMFdy .90	38	22¼	22½	22¼	22¾	+¼
	55	44¾	AMet Cl 1.90	38	52½	52½	51½	51½	+½
	14	10½	Am Motors	3,27	10¾	10¾	10½	10½	−⅛
	37½	37½	AmNatGas 2	40	38¾	39¼	38½	39¼	+1¼
	17½	12½	AmPhot .20g	104	13¾	13¾	13¾	13½	+½
	194½	154½	AResrch .20g	47	189	195	189	195	+5
	32	25½	Am Seat 1	12	29	29	27	27¾	+½
	32½	23¾	Am Ship .60	29	23¾	23¾	23	23½	+½
	61	49¼	A Smelt 1.90	375	37¾	38	37	37⅞	+¾
	69½	56	AmSoAfr .70	57	56¼	56½	55½	56	
	47	39½	Am Std 1	86	41½	41¼	41½	41⅞	−¾
	126	109½	AmStd pf4.75	25	116½	116½	115½	116	−¼
	32½	26¼	Am Steril .48	10	33	33	32½	32½	−½
	32⅞	28⅛	A Sugar 1.60	22	29¾	29¾	29¼	29½	−¼
	11	10½	AmSug pf .68	5	10¾	10¾	10½	10½	−½
	58½	51¼	Am T&T 2.40	571	57	57	56¼	56¾	−⅜
	41¾	34½	Am Tobac .56	2	37½	37½	35½	35⅝	−⅝
	14½	13¾	AmWWks .56	21	13½	13½	13	13	
	20	18¼	AWWSpf 1.20	x260	19¼	19¾	19	19¾	+¼
	19¼	17¾	AW pref 1.25	200	17½	17½	17½	17½	−¼
	26¾	23¾	AW 4.1pf 1.43	x390	24¾	25¼	24¾	25¾	+¾
	27¾	21¼	Am Zinc	14	30½	30½	30	30½	+½
	32¼	29¼	Ametek	14	30½	30½	30¾	30½	+¼
	44¾	34	Amfac .80	37	40½	41	40½	40½	+¼
	55¼	39½	AMK Cp .30	134	43	43½	42½	43	−½
	45¾	32¾	AMP Inc .48	47	44¼	45¼	44½	45½	+½
	44¼	32½	Ampex Corp	103	42¼	42¼	41¼	41¼	−¼
	53¾	44	Amsted 2.40	10	44¾	44¾	44½	44½	+¼
	27½	18¼	Amtel .32	x46	23¼	23½	23	23¼	+¼
	66	43½	Anacond 1.50	669	43½	43¾	43½	43¼	−½
	45¾	42⅛	Anch Hock n	52	45¼	45¼	45½	45¼	+¼
	41¾	28¾	And Clay 1.30	4	39¼	39¼	39¼	39¼	−¼
	48½	39¾	ApcoOil 1.42f	90	42¼	42½	42	42	−¼
	48⅛	39¾	Aqua Chem	125	40	40¼	38½	38½	−2
	117½	100½	ARA Svc .84	11	106½	106½	105½	105½	−¼
	68	55	ArchDan 1.60	57	57	57	55½	55½	−¾
	27¼	23½	ArizPubSvc 1	33	25¾	25¾	25½	25⅝	+¼
	43⅛	33½	Arlans DS .20	25	36½	36¾	36	36	−¼
	37½	31½	ArmcoSt 3.20	63	65½	65½	64⅞	65½	+⅛
	35¾	27½	Armco Stl wi	2	33	33	33	33	
	44¼	37½	Armour 1.60						−¼

	−1969− High	Low	Stocks Div.	Sales in 100s	Open	High	Low	Close	Net Chg.
	54½	42¾	CaterTr 1.20	278	53½	54½	53½	54½	+¼
	13½	11½	CCI Margdt		13	13¼	13½	13½	+⅛
	50½	32½	CCI MA pf1.25	3	41½	41½	41¼	41¼	−½
	34¾	25¾	Ceco Cp .80	5	29¼	29	29	29	+½
	72¾	62½	CelaneseCp 2	55	69½	69½	68¾	68⅞	−½
	69½	64½	Celar pfA4.50	2	65	65	65	65	+½
	64½	55½	Cenco Ins .30	56	59½	60½	59½	60	
	30	19¼	CentFdy .20d	16	19	19	19	19	−¼
	27½	24½	Cen Hud 1.48	3	27½	27½	27½	27½	−¼
	77	60	C IllIPS 1.32	35	71¼	71¼	71	71¼	+⅛
	25	21½	CenIIIPS 1.12	83	23¾	23½	23¼	23½	+⅛
	26¼	22	CentLaEl .88	7	23½	23½	23½	23½	
	51	44	CenMPw 1.12	44	50¾	50¼	50	50½	+½
	29¾	22	Cent SW 1.80	26	24	24	23½	23½	
	29½	23¾	Cent Soya .80	27	25½	25½	25	25½	+½
	28¾	23½	CenTelUt .80	73	25½	25½	25	25½	
	32½	24½	Cerro 1.60b	26	34	34	33½	33½	−¼
	36	24¼	Cert-feed .80	35	34	35½	34	35½	+½
	36	27¾	Cert-ted pf.90	1	35½	35½	34½	34½	+½
	30¼	25½	CessnaAir .80	24	29½	29½	29½	29¾	
	17½	11½	CFI Stl .80	187	27¾	28	27½	27½	−½
	32½	27½	Chadbrn Inc	159	15½	15½	15	15½	−¼
	32½	27½	Champ5 1.20	20	51¾	51¾	51½	51½	+½
	60	49¾	CharterNY 2	20	53¼	53¾	53	53	−½
	36	26½	ChaseBk 1.80	167	52½	52½	52	52	
	38½	30½	Checker Mot	1	38	38	38	38	−½
	68½	62	Chemetn 1.80	17	38½	38¾	38½	38½	+⅛
	48¼	39¼	Chemetr 2.60	38	64½	64½	63½	65½	+¾
	18½	14	Chemway .20	24	15	15	14½	14¾	
	48	39¼	Ches Va 1.40	3	43½	43½	43½	43½	
	75¼	47	Ches Ohio 4	17	68½	69	68½	68½	−¼
	48	38½	Chesebro .82	17	46½	46½	46½	46½	−¼
	18½	15½	ChicEast Ill	7	16½	16½	16¼	16½	−⅛
	58½	44	ChiMll StP P	2	55½	56½	55½	55½	+⅛
	33¾	24¾	ChiMStPP ct	x6	29½	29½	26½	26½	+½
	51	40½	Chi Music.1	1	23	41½	41½	41½	+½
	32½	24¾	Chi PneuT 2	23	41½	41½	40½	40½	+½
	31⅛	24	ChRIP ct UP	5	26	28	26	28	+½
	30	23¾	ChRIP ctNW	10	27½	27½	27½	27½	+¼
	71½	15¾	ChockFull .60	17	16½	16½	16½	16¼	−¼
	21¾	15½	Chris Cft n.60	85	20½	21½	20½	20½	+¼
	28¾	20¼	ChrP cref 1	4	21¾	21¾	21¾	21¾	
	57½	47½	Chroma1 .44	20	39	39	39	39	
	57¾	47½	Chrysler 2	297	50¾	50¾	49¾	50½	+¼
	32	26¾	CinnGE 1.40	62	29½	29½	29	29	
	77½	71	CinGe pf4.75	240	72¾	72¾	72	72¾	+1
	69¾	63½	Cin GE pf 4	x210	64	64	63	63½	+½
	65½	56	CinMill 1.40a	13	49½	49½	48½	48½	−¼
	52¾	46½	CinSuTel 2.40	8	48½	48½	48½	48½	+½
	48¼	37¼	CITFin 1.80	65	38½	38½	38½	38½	
	80	57	Cities Svc 2	385	68½	69	67¾	67½	−¼
	35½	24¾	City Inv .30b	x49	34	34	32½	33¾	−¼
	58½	42½	CityInv pf2.52	5	53½	53½	52½	52½	−¾
	73¾	49	CityIn pf1.31	3	67	67	66	67	−3
	24½	16½	City Strs .40	12	19½	19½	19½	19¾	−¼
	40¼	33	ClarkEg 1.40	45	38¼	38¾	38	38½	
	58¼	39	Clark Oil .40	x65	51½	51½	51	51½	+¼
	60¼	41	ClevCliff 1.60	x6	51	51	51	51	
	43	37½	CleveEllll 2.04	39	39½	39½	39	39½	
	33½	52½	Clev Plt 3.50	x100	34	34	54	54	+1½
	93	72	Clevite 2.8	14	88½	89	88	88¾	+¾
	27¾	18	Clorox .90	50	25½	25½	25½	25½	+⅛
	36¼	29½	CluettPea .90	5	37	37½	36	33½	+⅛
	25¾	22¾	CluettP pf 1	27	23¾	23¾	23	23¾	+½
	28½	26½	CNA Fin wi	1	26¾	26¾	26	26¼	+⅛
	63½	47½	CNA Fin 1	45	53½	53½	52½	53½	+½
	39½	31½	CNA pfA1.10	91	34¼	34¼	34	34	+⅛
	42½	38	Coast St Gas	209	36¾	37½	35½	37½	+⅛
	42½	39	Cst5Gs pf1.19	x2	41¾	41¾	41½	41¼	+⅛
	75	63½	CocaCol 1.32	212	75	76	75	75½	+½
	38¼	30½	CocaBtlg 1.20	40	37¾	38½	37	38½	+⅛
	52¾	46¼	Colg Pal 1.20	15	51½	51½	51¼	51¼	+⅛
	61½	45½	Colg P pf3.50	x210	57¾	57¾	57½	57¾	+¼
	52½	42½	CollinAlk 1.50	24	43½	43½	43	45	+¼
	69¾	42	CollinRad .80	297	54	54	53	53½	−½
	56¾	54¼	Coloinst 1.60	207	63	63¼	62¼	63½	
	56¾	54¼	Colt Ind .90a	5	86½	86½	86	86½	−¼
	41	30½	Colt In pf4.25	1	41½	41½	41½	41½	+⅛
	59½	44¾	CBS 1.40b	x249	55	55	54	56	+½
	31½	28½	CBS pf 1	x103	33	33	33	33½	+⅛
	31½	28½	ColuGas 1.60	44	28	28½	28	28½	+⅛
	42	37½	ColuPict .30g	22	34½	34½	34	34½	+½
	55½	37¼	Col SoOh 1.68	24	39	39	38½	39	−½
	72¾	63¼	CombEn 2.40	31	56½	66½	65½	65½	−½
	38½	30½	ComE pf1.70	4	38	38	37½	37¾	−½
	48¾	42¼	ComlSolv .40	40	47¾	47¾	47	47¾	+¼
	34½	29½	ComwEd 2.90	40	47¼	47¼	47	47¼	−½
	29½	21½	Com E pf1.42	5	29½	29½	29	29½	+⅛
	75½	49	Comw Oil .60	123	23	23½	22½	23½	+½
	41¼	38¼	CompScl .02g	27	72	72	72	72	
	24½	18½	Comsat	28	49½	49½	48½	49¾	+¼
	24½	18½	Cone .Mills 1	9	19	19	18½	19	+⅛
	33½	23	ConracCp .60	x31	48½	48¾	48	48½	−¼
	20½	16¾	Con Edis 1.80	53	17¾	18	17¾	17¾	−⅛
	104¼	99¾	ConEdis pf 6	4	100¾	100¾	100½	100½	−¼
	78¾	74	ConEdis pf 5	20	74½	74¾	74¼	74½	−⅛
	48½	40	Con Foods 1	20	46½	46½	46	46	−¼
	116½	105	ConFd pf4.50	4	110¾	110¾	110¼	110¼	−¼
	43½	33½	ConFreight 1	54	33½	33½	33¾	33¼	−¼
	43½	31	ConNatG 1.76	122	29½	29	29	29¾	
	45	40	ConsPwr 1.90	48	43½	43½	43½	43½	−¼
	74½	69¼	ConPw pf4.52	x20	70	70	70	70	−¼
	74½	69½	ConPw pf4.50	1	71	71	71	71	+½
	24½	16¼	ContAirL .50	199	17	17	17	17	
	71½	52	Cont Can 2.20	27	70	70	70	70½	−½
	70½	69	Cont Copp .30	x2	71	71	71	71	+½
	21½	16¾	Cont Tel .68	143	25½	25½	25½	25¾	
	21¾	17¾	Cnt Cop pf1.25	3	18½	18½	18¼	18¼	−⅛
	66	50	Cont Cp .40	126	49	50	48½	48½	−½
	56½	53½	Ct Cp pfA2.50	30	55	55	55	55	+¼
	56½	53½	Ct Cp pfB2.50	1	55	55	55	55	+1
	50½	27¼	CtMtge 1.12e	6	48	48	48	48	−½
	27½	19	ContMot .0p	2	19	19	19	19	−¼
	56	48½	Cont Oil 1.50	1516	38	38½	38	38½	+½
	53½	50¼	Cont Oil pf 2	1	54½	54½	54½	54½	−¼
	47½	21½	Cont Stl 1	5	35½	35½	34½	35½	+½
	159¼	127½	Control Data	154	154	151	151½	151¼	−1¼
	69½	54½	CnDat pf4.50	x90	65½	65½	65½	65½	+½
	73¼	50½	Cor.wood 1.80	24	35½	35¾	35	35½	+½
	44½	28¾	Cook Unit .50	x29	35½	35½	34½	35½	+¾

(Right column — G-H-I)

	−1969− High	Low	Stocks Div.	Sales in 100s	Open
	58¼	50½	FactorA .87	12	56½
	91¼	63½	FairchC .50e	111	65
	24¼	16½	Fairch Hiller	35	17½
	27¼	21½	Fairmont 1	2	25¾
	17¾	12½	Falstaff .40	48	13
	33½	17	Fam Fin 1.20	18	24¼
	33½	20½	Fansteel Inc	28	20½
	24	14	Far West Fin	21	20½
	87½	58	FaranMt .60b	21	70¾
	62½	44½	Fedders .60	44	56
	37½	27½	Fedders wi	4	33¾
	37½	32½	FedMog 1.80	68	32¾
	43½	29½	FedPac Elec	120	38¼
	29½	22¾	F Pac pf1.26	21	25
	43½	28½	FedPapBd 1	9	33
	51	30½	FedDStr .95	157	37¾
	19¾	14	Fed Mfg inv	15	16
	42½	32	Ferro Cp 1.20	32	40½
	54½	40	Fibrebrd .70		32
	23½	18	FieldctM 1.40	1	31¼
	54½	40	Filitrol	1	
	66½	57½	Fin Federatn	13	60¾
	60½	57½	Firestne 1.60	335	45½
	51¾	35¾	FstCrt 1.68t	335	45¾
	57½	45½	FstNCy 1.70g	178	69¾
	57½	41½	FstNStr .90g	22	39¾
	32½	28	Fischbch 1.60	4	32½
	23½	16	FisherScl .16	32	23¾
	43½	31½	Fleming .90	9	40½
	32½	24¾	Flintkote 1		32½
	38½	28½	Flint pfA4.50	z20	91
	33½	28	Fla E Coast	186	34½
	44	28½	Fla Gas .40	41	21
	51½	42	Fla Pow 1.52	2	47
	76½	60½	FlaPwLt 1.88	x50	73½
	79½	60	Fla Steel .90	69	79
	33¾	23½	Fly Tiger .10	51	24½
	57½	50	FMC Cp .85	256	51½
	23½	16½	FMC pf2.25	4	50½
	52½	40	FoodFair .90	192	25½
	18	15	Foote CB .80	7	18
	16½	14	Foote Min	16	15½
	38	32	Foote pf2.20	2	36
	47½	40½	FordMot 2.40	402	51½
	33¾	27¾	ForMcK .75	x93	29¾
	5½	3¾	FMcK pf1.80	x2	5¾
	31½	22½	FostWhl .60b	27	25½
	25	17	Fost Wh pf 1	2	18
	28½	18	Foxboro .60	15	28
	46½	32	Frank Sfr .32	36	38¼
	34½	31½	FreepSul 1.60	149	32¼
	47	34	FruehCp 1.70	95	36½
			Fuqua Ind	12	
			G-H-I		
	66¾	41	GAC Cp 1.50	264	64½
	31¼	25½	GAF Corp .40	165	27¾
	28½	24½	GAF pf1.20	21	25½
	38½	32½	Gam Sko 1.30	23	33¾
	38½	30¾	Gam5 pf1.75	3	33¾
	38½	30¾	Gam5 pf1.60	7	41½
	39½	30½	Gannett .65	7	41½
	11	7½	Gar Wood	8	7¾
	38½	30½	GardDen 1.30	26	36½
	26¼	22	Garlock .80	3	23½
	16¼	14½	Gemini Cap	10	17¼
	12	11	Geminln .56a	5	11½
	33½	27½	GnAInv 2.20g	13	28½
	80½	55	GAmOil .60b	49	77
	36½	36½	GATran 1.80	41	32½
	17½	14	Gen Banc .15	5	15½
	36½	23½	Gn Cable 1.20	121	23½
	38½	30	Gen Cig 1.20	23	30½
	40½	29½	GnDevel .74f	x73	36¼
	30½	26½	GenDynam 1	92	28¾
	98½	85½	Gen Elec 2.60	183	98½
	36½	29¾	Gn Flrpf .10g	7	18½
	88½	74½	Gen Fds 2.60	101	85½
	37	26½	Gen Host .40	29	36½
	24½	20½	Gen Inst .54f	164	31½
	51½	44½	Geninstr pf 2		51½
	61½	53	Gen Mills .80	63	54½
	65½	57½	GenMot pf3.75	9	62½
	83¾	75¾	GenMot 3.40a	367	82
	61½	55½	G Mot 5pf 5	3	82½
	65½	57½	G Mot pf3.75	9	61
	25	19	GenPCem .80	33	22½
	62½	44½	GPubUt 1.60	62	17¾
	17¼	13½	Gen Refract 1	17	13½
	26½	22	Gen Sig 1.20	22	56
	106	97	Gen Sig pf 4	2	101
	40½	30½	GenStlInd .80	90	34½
	40½	37½	G TelEl 1.48	204	39½
	51½	45½	G TelEl pf2.50	11	48½
	65½	57½	GTell pf1.25	290	50½
	20½	19½	GTel pfB1.30	z2160	20¾
	34	24½	GenTime .80	31	37
	24½	19	Gen Tire 1b	90	24½
	55	37	G Tire pf 2	z220	72
	51	37	Genesco 1.60	106	40½
	24½	17½	GenuinePts 1	15	19½
	46½	31	Ga Pacific 1b	31	100½
	71¼	61	GaPac pf1.64	3	70½
	36½	20½	GaPac pf1.40	6	35½
	36¾	24½	Gerber 1.10	35	36
	41½	28	GettyOil .38g	119	79½
	21½	15	Giant PC .30	77	17½
	29	22	Gibralt Fin .1	6	22½
	57½	46	Gldd Lew .80	38	48½
			Gillette ..		

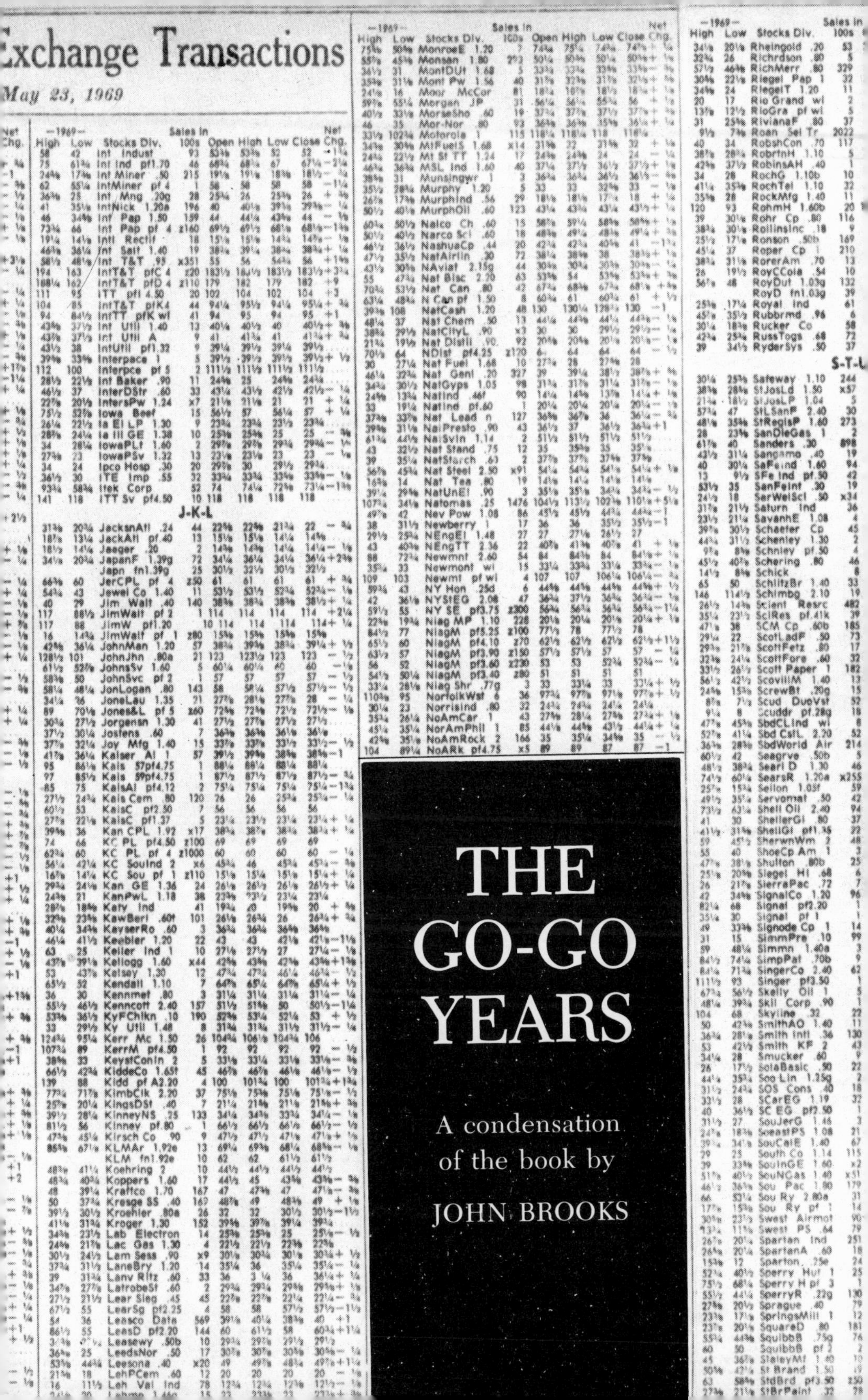

Exchange Transactions

May 23, 1969

(New York Stock Exchange daily transaction table — columns: 1969 High, Low, Stocks Div., Sales in 100s, Open, High, Low, Close, Net Chg.)

THE GO-GO YEARS

A condensation
of the book by

JOHN BROOKS

CHAPTER 1

CLIMAX

O n April 22, 1970, Henry Ross Perot of Dallas, Texas, one of the half-dozen richest men in the United States, was so new to wealth, at forty, that he was not listed in *Poor's Register* and had just appeared for the first time in *Who's Who in America*. Only a small fraction of his countrymen had ever heard of him.

Yet that day Perot made a landmark in the financial history of the United States and perhaps of the Western world. It was hardly a landmark to be envied, but it was certainly one to be remembered. That day, he suffered a paper stock-market loss of about $450 million. He still had, on paper, almost a billion dollars left afterward, but that wasn't the point. The point was that his one-day loss was quite possibly more in actual purchasing power than any man had ever lost in a single day since the Industrial Revolution brought large private accumulations of money into being.

It was Earth Day; the environment had recently become a national mania, especially among the young, and a group of conservationist leaders headed by Senator Gaylord Nelson of Wisconsin had picked April 22 as a day of national dedication to the cause of eliminating pollution in all its forms. (Were preposterously large paper stock-market profits such as Ross Perot had made to be considered a form of pollution? Quite possibly.) In Washington, in front of the Department of the Interior building, twelve hundred young people milled around shouting "Off the oil!" and "Stop the muck!" to protest government leases to oil producers whose operations were thought to cause pollution. There were antipollution rallies of twenty-five thousand or more (watched by the F.B.I., it became known later) in New York, Chicago, and Philadelphia. In New York City, children rode bicycles to school; huge, lighthearted crowds gamboled on an

automobile-free Fifth Avenue; at Seventeenth Street people were offered the opportunity to breath "pure air" from the nozzle of a block-long polyethylene bubble; and so on, as all the artillery of promotion and public relations was turned, momentarily, in an unfamiliar and uncharacteristic direction.

All this resolution and high spirits fought upstream against one of the deepest moods of gloom to darken any American April since the Civil War. The first My Lai revelations were five months old; the dangerous and disturbing New Haven strike in support of the Black Panthers, which would spread quickly to campuses all over the northeast, was to begin that same day, April 22; the stunningly unpopular invasion of Cambodia was eight days off, the Kent State University killings of students by National Guardsmen twelve days off. The gloom, compounded by signs of an approaching national economic recession, had caused a stock-market panic that, though far from over, was already comparable in a remarkable number of ways to that of October 1929. The Dow-Jones industrial average of common stocks had sunk relentlessly through almost all of 1969; then, after holding fairly firm through the first three months of the new year, it had gone into a sickening collapse that had carried it, by April 22, to a level some 235 points below where it had been at its peak sixteen months earlier. Much worse, the Dow did not begin to tell the whole story. Interest rates were at near-record highs, strangling new housing construction and making most industrial expansion impractical. The dollar was in bad trouble in the international markets, with foreigners holding American currency worth many billions more than the national gold hoard. One hundred or more Wall Street brokerage firms were near failure. As for the Dow, made up as it was of the old blue chips that had long since been deposed as sensitive and accurate market leaders, it was a pale, watered-down reflection of the real stock-market situation. A better indication is to be found in the fact that in May 1970, a portfolio consisting of one share of every stock listed on the Big Board was worth just about half of what it would have been worth at the start of 1969. The high flyers that had led the market of 1967 and 1968—conglomerates, computer leasers, far-out electronics companies, franchisers—were precipitously down from their peaks. Nor were they down 25 percent, like the Dow, but 80, 90, or 95 percent. This was vintage 1929 stuff, and the prospect of another great depression, this one induced as much by despair as by economic factors as such, was a very real one.

The visible parallels to 1929, in the business and financial spheres, were enough to make a man agree not merely with Santayana, who said that those who forget history are condemned to repeat it, but with Proust, whose whole great book, read one way, seems to say that man's apparent capacity to learn from experience is an illusion.

Of course, there were tremendous differences, too—not just the fact that the more recent crash did not lead to a catastrophic national depression (though it did lead to a severe one), but differences in style and nuance and social implication that will be the main subject of this chronicle. One might, in comparing 1929 with 1969-70, even find a certain appositeness in Karl Marx's observation that history repeats itself the first time as tragedy, the second time as farce.

Wall Street, in the geographical sense, was to become an actual battleground that spring, less than three weeks after Earth Day and Ross Perot's Down-to-Earth Day. By Wednesday, May 6, 1970, a week after the Cambodia announcement and two days after the Kent State incident, eighty colleges across the country were closed entirely as a result of student and faculty strikes, and students were boycotting classes at over three hundred more. Most New York City schools and colleges were scheduled to be closed that Friday, May 8, in a gesture of protest, and among the student antiwar demonstrations being planned was one to be held in Wall Street.

That Friday morning—a damp, drizzly, bone-chilling morning, such as New York can often produce in early May—beginning at about seven-thirty, boys and girls by the hundreds began debouching from Wall Street's two principal subway stations, the Seventh Avenue-Broadway stop at Chase Manhattan Plaza and the Lexington Avenue at Broadway and Wall. Most of them were from New York University, Hunter College, and the city's public high schools. Eventually, something like a thousand strong, they jammed into the financial district's central plaza, the intersection of Broad and Wall, where they milled around under the apprehensive scrutiny of a good-sized cadre of city policemen who had been dispatched there in anticipation of their arrival. But the students seemed to be in no mood to cause the police any trouble. In light rain, under the columns of Federal Hall, where George Washington had once taken the oath of office as the United States' first President, and facing the intimidating entrance to the great marble building from which imperial Morgan had once more or less ruled the nation, they spent the morn-

ing rallying their spirits and formulating their demands. The demands, not too surprisingly, turned out to be the same as those agreed upon a few days earlier by a secret convention of radical youth leaders in New Haven, and now being put forth on dozens of northeastern campuses. One: immediate United States withdrawal from Vietnam and Cambodia. Two: release of all "political prisoners" in the nation—a pointed, not to say loaded, reference to the Black Panthers imprisoned on charges of participating in the torture and murder of Alex Rackley, a Panther accused of being a police informer. Three: cessation of all military-oriented research work under the auspices of American universities. Unlike many student demonstrations in the spring of 1970, this one was wholly nonviolent.

Eleven fifty-five: suddenly, simultaneously from all four approaches to the intersection, like a well-trained raiding force, the hardhats came. They were construction workers, many employed in the huge nearby World Trade Center project, and their brown overalls and orange-and-yellow helmets seemed to be a sort of uniform. Many of them carried American flags; others, it soon became clear, carried construction tools and wore heavy boots that were intended as weapons. Later it was said that their movements appeared to be directed, by means of hand signals, by two unidentified men in gray hats and gray suits. There were perhaps two hundred of them.

As they pushed through the mob of seated students, it became manifest that their two objectives were to place flags at the base of the Washington statue in front of Federal Hall, otherwise known as the Subtreasury Building, and to break up the demonstration, if necessary by violence. As to the first objective: they marched toward the statue shouting "All the way, U.S.A.!" and "Love it or leave it!"; their way was barred on the steps by a thin line of policemen; the policemen, overwhelmed by greater numbers, were brushed aside; and the flags were triumphantly planted under the statue. As to the second objective: construction workers repeatedly struck students with sticks, fists, boots, screwdrivers, and pliers, as they chased the screaming students of both sexes down the canyons of the financial district. For more than a week afterward, Wall Street bristled daily with police as if it were in a fascist state.

To the extent that it had any part in this dispiriting affair—this small but fierce and rancorous struggle that came so close to being a crystallization of the whole nation's tragedy at that moment —professional Wall Street, the Wall Street of finance and law, of

power and elegance, seemed to be on the side of the students. Perhaps out of common humanity, or perhaps out of class feeling, the bulls and bears felt more kinship with the doves than with the hawks. At Exchange Place, Robert A. Bernhard, a partner in the aristocratic firm of Lehman Brothers, was himself assaulted and severely cut in the head by a construction worker's heavy pliers, after he had tried to protect a youth who was being beaten. A few blocks north, a young Wall Street lawyer was knocked down, kicked, and beaten when he protested against hardhats who were yelling "Kill the Commie bastards!" But most of the mighty of the Street—Communist bastards or not—had no part in the struggle. They were not on the street. Like the famous, allegedly anarchist bombing on Wall Street in 1920, when thirty persons were killed and hundreds wounded, the riot of 1970 occurred just before noon: not quite lunch time. There was a racket in the street, and everyone above (or everyone privileged to have a window) looked out. The market was unaffected. Most of Wall Street's elite working population watched the carnage from high, safe windows.

Indeed, there was little else they could sensibly have done; no purpose would have been served by their rushing down and joining the fray. Nevertheless, there is an all too symbolic aspect to professional Wall Street's role that day as a bystander, sympathizing, unmistakably, with the underdogs, the unarmed, the peace-lovers, but keeping its hands clean—watching with fascination and horror from its windows that looked out over the lovely (at that perspective) Upper Bay with its still-green islands and its proud passing liners, and down into the canyon from which there now rose, inconveniently, the cries of hurt or frightened children.

The event (like the unreal gyrations in the fortunes of Perot) called attention to the relationship, or the lack of one, between Wall Street and the nation in the new times.

All through the stormy course of 1967 and 1968, when things had been coming apart and it had seemed that the center really couldn't hold—the rising national economic crisis culminating in a day when the dollar was unredeemable in Paris, the Martin Luther King and Robert Kennedy assassinations, the shame of the Chicago Democratic convention, the rising tempo of student riots—the silly market had gone its merry way, heedlessly soaring upward as if everything were O.K. or would surely come out O.K., as mindlessly, maniacally euphoric as a Japanese beetle in July. Or as a doomed man enjoying

his last meal. One could only ask: Did Wall Street, for all its gutter shrewdness, have the slightest idea what was *really* going on?

Beyond that, wasn't Wall Street the very living symbol and embodiment of everything—the Protestant work ethic, Social Darwinism, market orientation, money-madness—that America was only now learning, if not to reject, at least to get into a new and lesser perspective? Wasn't Wall Street backward-looking, a kind of simplified, idealized version of the older and now largely discredited America, unrelated or even antipathetic to the new America that was struggling now to come into being?

Wall Street was not only a place sorely in need of physical and spiritual "greening," but had been almost the first place in the nation to be literally ungreened. A print made in 1847, long before the coming of large-scale industrialization, the age of asphalt, hangs in the famous old restaurant Sweets in Fulton Street. It shows almost the whole six-hundred-yard stretch of Wall Street looking toward Trinity Church, and the scene contains exactly one tree. With the physical ungreening went—and goes—the spiritual concomitant, a certain dehumanization. For generations, Wall Street as a social ambiance has tended to represent what is hardest, coldest, and meanest in America.

One gets off the subway at Broadway and Wall and begins to feel depressed. Men's faces seem pinched and preoccupied. Pretty women seem flesh without magic. In winter a savage wind curls around the corners of those canyons; in summer the air lies heavy, dank, and sunless. The debaters of theology who cluster outside the Bankers Trust seem disturbingly psychotic, not engagingly zany. Not greed nor avarice, but bad temper, is too often the prevailing mood.

In a revolutionary time like 1970, could it be that Wall Street, that summary of so much that is least engaging about our national tradition, was coming to be—in the cliché of the moment—irrelevant?

Not to Ross Perot. To him, Wall Street was a Puritan's Hell, dangerous and fascinating, and also, as he well knew, the source of his almost incredible riches. He had entered Hell, conquered it, and remained pure. By environment and temperament he was a perfect Western populist, feeling toward "city slickers," including those in Wall Street, a fear and suspicion not unmixed with envy and contempt. His boyhood in East Texas, as the son of a depression-ridden small-town cotton broker and horsetrader, had set the pattern of his

life: he had broken horses for pay before he was ten (and repeatedly broken his nose in the process), become an Eagle Scout, learned the cult of self-reliance, and learned to make a holy Calvinist doctrine of the pursuit of the honest dollar by honest effort. In some senses he was an anachronism. He had grown up, before and during World War II, believing that the frontier not only existed but still dominated American life.

He was of pioneer stock; his grandfather Perot, son of an immigrant from France to Louisiana before the Civil War, in the true frontier days, had made his way upriver and overland to New Boston, Texas, where he had hacked out a clearing, hewed timber, and built a trading post and general store. Ross Perot, after high school and two years of junior college in nearby Texarkana, had wangled an appointment to the Naval Academy, where he had graduated in 1953 with an average academic record but had been recognized for leadership through election as class president. Already he showed promise as a supersalesman. After four years of active Navy duty he had taken a job as a computer drummer, on commission, for I.B.M. in Dallas. He had soon turned out to be such an overachiever that any promotion to a salaried job would have involved a cut in pay, so the company had taken drastic steps to control his income. It had cut his commission on sales by four-fifths and assigned him an annual sales quota beyond which he would get no commission. For the year 1962, he had made his annual quota by January 19, thus putting himself effectively out of business for the next eleven months and twelve days. After brooding on his dilemma, he quit I.B.M. that June and incorporated his own company—Electronic Data Systems Corp., designers, installers, and operators of computer systems—taking with him a couple of brilliant young I.B.M. colleagues, Milledge A. Hart, III, and Thomas Marquez. He had no investors or backers; his initial investment was $1,000, the minimum required for incorporation under Texas law; his directors, apart from himself, were his wife, his mother, and his sister. Hard times followed for a while. But persistence and salesmanship paid off. In 1965, opportunity knocked for E.D.S. when federal Medicare legislation was passed and E.D.S. quickly got in on the ground floor.

Perot actually spent a spell working part-time for Texas Blue Shield, which had a contract with the Social Security Administration to develop a computerized system for paying Medicare bills. Out of this association came a subcontract from Texas Blue Shield to E.D.S.

That was only the beginning. Eventually, E.D.S. had subcontracts to administer Medicare or Medicaid in eleven states, including Texas, California, and Indiana; the firm derived the major portion of its revenue from these contracts, and was, as *Ramparts* remarked scathingly in 1971, "America's first welfare billionaire." All told, by 1968 E.D.S. had twenty-three contracts for computer systems, 323 full-time employees, about $10 million in assets, annual net profits of over $1.5 million, and a growth curve so fantastic as to make investment bankers' mouths water.

Of such cloth was cut the man who, by early 1970—and by methods that we shall soon see—had beaten every one of the city slickers on their home ground, and become the single biggest winner in what the writer "Adam Smith" called "the money game," emerging with paper assets to his name of almost $1.5 billion. His personal relations with Wall Street and its slickers began early in 1968, when the market was going through the roof and the hungry investment bankers had suddenly realized that Perot's little clutch of refugees from the fur-lined trap of I.B.M. was now ripe for a public sale that might be a bonanza all around. Seventeen investment bankers visited Perot in rapid succession and urged him to put his stock on the market. At first he said, as he had always said previously, that he never would. He didn't want outside interference in his company's affairs, he just wanted to be left alone to do a job. But the seventeenth banker got to Perot. He was Kenneth Langone of R.W. Pressprich and Company, a respectable enough Wall Street firm. Other investment bankers had offered to sell Perot's stock at thirty times current annual earnings, then at fifty times, then at seventy times. Langone, however, offered one hundred times, possibly somewhat more. Perot said yes to Langone.

Then began Perot's education in the ways of the slickers, and he proved to be an astute pupil indeed. First of all, Langone wanted to know, who were the company's directors? His wife, his mother, and his sister, Perot reported. Langone said that wouldn't do. So Perot wrote himself a more acceptable board, consisting of Hart, Marquez, and other principal employees. Next, the company would have to be recapitalized: say, 11.5 million shares. A preposterous capitalization for a company that earned only $1.5 million a year? Necessary, Langone explained, if you wanted that high earnings multiple and also a reasonable stock price. E.D.S., then, would be the seller of 325,000 shares of stock; Perot himself would be the seller of another 325,000.

The rest would be kept by Perot and the E.D.S. employees—around 1.5 million shares for the employees (he had issued it to them by way of bonuses), and not quite 9.5 million for Perot himself. Wasn't 650,000 shares for public trading a dangerously small float, likely to make for a highly volatile market in which small investors might possibly get hurt? Langone told Perot it was plenty. After all, he pointed out, R.W. Pressprich itself would make the market, and could be counted on to maintain a fair and orderly one. The offering price finally agreed upon was $16.50 a share—118 times current E.D.S. earnings, and an infinite number times current dividends, since there were none.

Through all the negotiations Perot played barefoot boy to the hilt, pretending to be baffled by Wall Street's baroque rituals, while actually learning to turn them to his own advantage. But when, on September 12, 1968, the E.D.S. stock was publicly offered and was quickly subscribed for in one of the most sensationally successful new-issue promotions of the whole headlong era, the bumpkin came out overnight with $5 million in personal cash and more than $200 million in stock equity at market value. All the tolerant Wall Street smiles faded abruptly.

The stock took off. Institutions began buying it. Strange orders came in from places like Geneva and Lebanon, and this made the xenophobic Perot uneasy. Sometimes he would protest: "Don't sell my stock to him! I don't want him for a stockholder!" But the traders would laugh and sell the stock at ever-rising prices. At last, early in 1970, E.D.S sold at 160. Perot, with his 9-million-plus shares, was now worth on paper almost $1.5 billion—which, it happens, is about 40 percent of the whole United States federal budget for 1930, the year he was born.

The new billionaire saw himself, characteristically, not as a grandee, but as an example to the nation's youth. He set about being a moral billionaire. He decided to will only modest sums to his five children, "so they'll have the same opportunities I've had." Substantially all of his fortune would go, sooner or later, to "the improvement of American life." For a starter, he gave a million dollars to the Boy Scouts in the Dallas area. He gave over two million to the Dallas public school system to finance a pilot elementary school in a black ghetto area. He refused to avail himself of his legal right to take personal income-tax deductions on his charitable contributions on the ground that morally he owed the tax money to a country that had

done so well by him. In 1969, he became obsessed with the plight of United States prisoners of war in North Vietnam, and that December he attempted personally to intervene with the North Vietnamese authorities in their behalf. (His efforts, which included two excursions to Indochina in chartered airliners, failed, but they seem to have been not without rewards in personal satisfaction—in serving to convince people, perhaps including himself, that one man alone is *not* powerless in the modern world, and that Americans, particularly capitalist Americans, are a force for good no matter what anyone says.)

He made what he did a virtue, and a virtue of what he did. But was Perot a hypocrite? Hypocrisy in common morals, like fraud in common law, is an offense that requires an element of "scienter" — knowledge of the offender that he is committing the offense. Viewed in that light, Perot, without scienter, was innocent.

The way Perot received the news of his monumental setback on April 22 was casual to the point of comedy. All that morning he was closeted in his Dallas office with executives of a potential client company to which E.D.S. was making its sales pitch. On emerging around one o'clock, he picked up a phone and called down the hall to Tom Marquez.

"What's new?" Perot asked.

"Well," Marquez said, "the stock is down fifty or sixty points."

Exactly what happened to the market in E.D.S. on the morning of April 22 is not known and may never be known in detail. What is certain, however, is the fact that its collapse was not based on any bad news about the company's operations. To the contrary, the news was all spectacularly good. Quite evidently, there had to be some other cause.

E.D.S. was traded in the over-the-counter market. Less than a year later the operation of that long-notorious thicket of rumor, confusion, and secrecy would be revolutionized by the introduction of an electronic marvel called NASDAQ—a computer system that makes it possible for an over-the-counter trader, by merely punching some buttons and looking at a screen on his desk, to see precisely which firm is making the best current bid and the best current offer in any of several thousand stocks not listed on the stock exchanges. In effect, NASDAQ would bring the over-the-counter market up from *under* the counter, a nether region it still inhabited to a marked ex-

tent in April 1970. At that time, there was no such screen on the trader's desk; to get the best price on a thinly traded stock like E.D.S., he might have to telephone a dozen other firms to get their quotes, engage in shouted conversations with other traders in his own firm to find out what kind of bids and offers they were getting, and finally agree to a price that would never be reported to the public at all. In such a market, the opportunities for manipulation were endless. Conducted in windowless back rooms by excitable hagglers, many with a full measure of larceny in their blood, and policed only negligently by the overworked and understaffed S.E.C., the over-the-counter market in the nineteen sixties was the perfect arena for the feeding of lions and the ingestion of Christians.

What was "wrong" with E.D.S. was that the price of its stock had not dropped at all while the rest of the market had been going through a panic. By way of comparison, University Computing, a leading company in E.D.S.'s very industry, was selling on April 22 at a price 80 percent below its peak of the previous year; meanwhile, E.D.S. was selling almost *at* its peak. Good earnings record or not, E.D.S. stock at around 150 was, from a technical standpoint, in an almost freakishly exposed position. At the same time, much of the available supply of stock was in the hands of fast-performance mutual funds that, at any sign of decline, would quickly unload. This is a condition known to market players as "weakly held." Such facts do not go unnoticed, nor did they on April 22. Presumably some big punter or a group of them—perhaps in Geneva, perhaps in Lebanon, perhaps right in New York—saw a golden opportunity to recoup the drastic losses they had suffered over the previous days in other stocks. So they mounted a bear raid on E.D.S., probing its strength with testing short sales. As it gave way under the pressure and dropped a few points (it may be presumed), they increased the sales. The suddenly lower price then came to the attention of the itchy-fingered portfolio managers of the fast-performance funds that held E.D.S. With their celebrated speed and dexterity, the portfolio managers began unloading. Down and down the bid went—to 145, 135, 120—and the panic was on. The men in the back rooms decide fast and move instantly, and in their market a selling panic can blacken the sky as quickly as an August afternoon's thunderstorm.

Toward noon, with E.D.S. down in the 80-90 range, it firmed; presumably the bears who had started the slide felt that their killing was made and were beginning, leisurely, to consume their prey. That is

the scenario that may be reasonably deduced from events known.

Thus the greatest one-day fall of a titan ever. But what of the investing public? The tens of thousands who, either directly or through the investments of their mutual funds, had put some of their savings into E.D.S., were far more than bemused spectators at a landmark event in financial history. In a word, they were losers, perhaps of a college fund or a vacation fund or part of a retirement nest egg. Few of them were so fortunate as to have bought their E.D.S. stock at or near its original offering price of $16.50. As is usual with hot new issues, particularly in such manic markets as that of 1968, most of the original issue had soon found its way into the hands of professional traders. Many small investors had come in later, buying from the professionals after the stock had been talked about in brokerage offices and mentioned in the market letters and pushed by the eager commission producers—and, of course, after its price had shot up almost out of sight. In the familiar pattern, the investing public, with its thousands rather than billions, had suddenly become interested in hot stocks at the very height of the boom, and had bought E.D.S. near its top. For an investor who had bought it at 150, the $15,000 he had risked had in a single day become $10,000, or the $1,500 he had risked became $1,000. To him, whatever had gone on in Lebanon or Geneva or in Wall Street on Perot's Down-to-Earth Day was emphatically not abstract. In human terms, the real and necessary hundreds or thousands that he lost were more important than the abstract millions that Perot lost.

The E.D.S. crash and Perot's dizzying personal loss were symbolic, in magnitude and unreality, of the 1970 panic. They are its single event that stands out in memory, like Richard Whitney's appearance on the Exchange floor to bid 205 for Steel on behalf of the bankers' pool, at the height of the panic on October 24, 1929—Black Thursday. Nor is it without symbolic importance that the larger market calamity of which the E.D.S. crash was a part resembled in so many respects what had happened forty years before—what wise men had said, for more than a generation, over and over again as if by way of incantation, could never happen again. It *had* happened again, as history will; but (as history will) it had happened differently. The nineteen sixties in Wall Street were the nineteen twenties replayed in a new and different key—different because the nineteen sixties were more complex, more sophisticated, more democratic, perhaps, at bottom, more interesting.

CHAPTER 2

THE LAST GATSBY

The stock-market collapse of 1962—which broke the 1961 bucket shops and their eager patrons, sent the Dow industrials down more than 25 percent, and taught a whole new generation of investors and gamblers alike that it is possible to lose—looked back to the past rather than forward to the future. It was a thing not of firsts, but of lasts: the last crisis in which little brokerage offices in distant towns and villages, and the amateur plungers who frequented them, were a significant factor; the last time in Wall Street that the tune was called not by the computer-assisted decisions of institutions like mutual funds and pension trusts, but by the emotions—fear and greed, chiefly—of individual men and women acting for themselves.

Diabetic coma, the preventable catastrophic crisis of a human disease, comes on slowly; the sinister lassitude it induces neutralizes the rational alarm that would otherwise lead the patient to take measures to head it off. So it is with stock-market crashes. That of 1929 had actually been going on, in important ways, for a year or so before it reached its climax, and that of 1962—a smaller model in all respects—for some five months. What a falling market needs to become a diving market is not a reason but an excuse, and in April it found one when President Kennedy chose to engage in a to-the-death confrontation with the steel industry and its bellwether, U.S. Steel, on the matter of a price increase. In the Kennedy grand manner, the clash became a thing of high melodrama, like the Cuban missile crisis six months later; there were closed-door White House meetings between Kennedy and Chairman Roger M. Blough of U.S. Steel, there were F.B.I. men ringing doorbells at dawn, and at last there was a clean, soul-satisfying ending—the steel industry's capitulation and price rollback.

But at what a cost! Investors, who had profited so handsomely from the "Kennedy market" of the previous year, suddenly decided that the energetic young man in the White House was an enemy of business, after all. Whether or not Kennedy, in the heat of confrontation, had actually said in private, "My father always told me that businessmen were sons of bitches," was not the point; the point was that a good proportion of the 17 million American owners of corporate shares believed he had said it. For several weeks in succession, the market slumped ominously, until the week of May 21-25 saw the

worst decline for any week in more than ten years. And then, on May 28, the day that has gone down in Wall Street annals as Blue Monday, the Dow average dropped 34.95 points, a one-day collapse second in history only to that of October 28, 1929, when the loss had been 38.33. Moreover, the decline took place on the then-fantastic volume of 9,350,000 shares. Twenty billion dollars in paper values that had existed in the morning had evaporated by evening.

But it was on Tuesday that confusion was compounded. Sell orders in dozens of leading stocks, including blue chips like I.B.M., so overwhelmed buy orders that trading simply couldn't be opened; the stocks that did open were down so drastically that at the end of the first hour the Dow had fallen another 11 points. Around noon, without warning, a strong rally started, and the ticker, fifty-six minutes late, was caught telling the ultimate Wall Street lie—it was solemnly recording the prior down market rather than the current up market. When the carnage ended that afternoon, the Street, with its vaunted pretensions to being an efficient market place, was clearly in disgrace. The rally continued, and by Thursday night all of the losses of Monday and early Tuesday were recouped. But soon the decline resumed at a more leisurely pace; by mid-June the Dow had sunk to 535 and the Kennedy boom—a sort of prologue in miniature to what was to come later in the decade—was something of the past.

Who lost, or lost the most, in the 1962 "little crash"? Most obviously, the hot-issue boys, the penny-stock plungers, the bucket-shop two-week millionaires of 1961, who, operating on the thinnest of margins in the most volatile of stocks, were wiped out either before May 28 or during the first hours of that disastrous day. But what about those who dealt more conservatively, on wider margins in more respectable issues? The Stock Exchange, rueful about its technical collapse, made a study later in the year to determine who had done what in the events of late May. The results were instructive. The great rising giant of American finance, the mutual fund industry, had come out with honors. Cash-heavy, still conservatively managed in the prudent fiduciary tradition, the funds had bought on balance in the falling market of Monday, and had sold on balance in the rising market of Thursday; thus, besides protecting their shareholders from excessive risk, they had perhaps actually done something to stabilize the market. The panic had been among individuals —especially people in rural areas, especially foreigners, and especially the nouveau riche of whatever sex or nationality. It was a per-

sonal crash, the effect of a mass mood that swept suddenly over Broadway and Little Falls, Zurich and Grand Junction; and if May 1962 was the last great stock-market event controlled by people rather than institutions, it is fitting that its most conspicuous victim, its symbolic loser, should have been such a past-haunted romantic as Edward M. Gilbert.

Gilbert was born in December 1922 into the curious half-world of smalltime New York City millionaires and soon-to-be millionaires. His father and his uncle were substantial owners and principal operators of Empire Millwork Company, a solid little lumber business that their father had founded, and that had first flourished on contracts generated by the mysterious and lethal bombing of Wall Street in September 1920. Long afterward, Eddie Gilbert's father, Harry, said of him, "As a kid he ran everywhere he went." But Budd Schulberg's Sammy Glick was only a part of Eddie Gilbert; he grew up dreaming more complex and grandiose dreams than that of becoming a ruler of Hollywood. From the first, he was a bright but lazy student with a particular aptitude for mathematics, a talented and fanatical athlete, and something of a spoiled darling.

Matriculating at Cornell in the early stages of World War II, he made a name for himself in tennis and boxing, won the chess championship of his dormitory, and earned a reputation as a prankster, but went on neglecting his studies. In his first or second year he left to enlist in the Army Air Force. Shipped to North Africa and later Italy, he worked there for Army newspapers, and showed a marked interest in and aptitude for acquiring foreign languages.

Back home at the end of the war, he returned to Cornell for a spell, but did not stay long; soon he joined his father's company. During the period of his business apprenticeship he embarked on a series of personal ventures that were uniformly unsuccessful. He backed a prizefighter who turned out to be a dud. He was co-producer of a Broadway play, *How Long Till Summer?* that starred the black folksinger Josh White's son and that, as a pioneer in the equal-rights-for-all genre of entertainment, won the public approval of Mrs. Eleanor Roosevelt. But *How Long Till Summer?* was either ahead of its time or wrong for all seasons; it opened at the Playhouse Theatre on December 27, 1949, got disastrous notices, and closed a week later. Gilbert also dabbled in the stock market without any notable success. While thus conforming to the old tradition that the prince-

ling sons of successful businessmen show scant aptitude for business, he was acquiring a deep and genuine love of music and, in particular, of opera. He seemed to be assuming the familiar shape of that ineffectual, esthetic second generation—an impression that could scarcely have been more wrong.

His career at Empire Millwork came to an early crisis. The firm, flourishing in the postwar building boom, sold stock to the public, and the sale left Harry Gilbert with a liquid and bankable fortune of around $8 million. He was ever ready to use his money to indulge his son, and over the years he would do so again and again. Harry Gilbert had never been the brains of Empire Millwork; he was an amiable man who had inherited a tidy concern. His son's deals were made possible by the father's money.

As early as 1948, Eddie Gilbert had decided that the family company was too small to hold him, and he began to dream of using it as a vehicle to construct, through mergers with other companies, an enterprise that would live up to its grandiose name—a true Empire. In 1951, when he was twenty-eight, he demanded of his father that he be given greater responsibility in the form of a directorship. When Harry Gilbert turned him down, Eddie Gilbert quit to enter the hardwood-floor business on his own.

It turned out to be a case of *reculer pour mieux sauter*. There are two versions of what happened to the younger Gilbert's independent business venture. In one—the one published in 1962—the venture was a success, and four years later Harry Gilbert bought it out, and thus brought his son back to Empire, in exchange for 20,000 shares of Empire stock. In another, Eddie, through his own company, made a bumbling attempt to corner the lumber market, failed, lost considerable money, and was rescued by his father, who bailed him out to bury the costly mistake. At any rate, in 1955 Eddie returned to Empire with new power and freedom to act. Ever since 1948, when he had done a stint at an Empire plant in Tennessee and had there become acquainted with E.L. Bruce and Company, the nation's leading hardwood-floor company, he had dreamed of acquiring Bruce as a gem for Empire's crown. With net sales of around $25 million a year, Bruce was considerably larger than Empire, but it was a staid firm, conservatively managed and in languid family control, of the sort that is the classic prey for an ambitious raider. In 1955, Eddie Gilbert persuaded his father to commit much of his own and the company's resources in an attempt to take over Bruce.

294

Now Eddie came into his own at last. He began to make important friends in Wall Street—brokers impressed with his dash and daring, and delighted to have the considerable commissions he generated. Some of the friends came from the highest and most rarefied levels of finance. He apparently won over John Loeb, Sr., of Loeb, Rhoades, by pledging $100,000 to Loeb's beloved Harvard; later he could claim to be an important client of André Meyer, the shy eminence of Lazard Frères and close friend of Mrs. Jacqueline Kennedy Onassis. At the same time, Gilbert began gathering unto himself a coterie of rich social allies, people who might tap him for his stock-market tips and whom he could use in turn for the aura of social acceptance their propinquity implied.

The key word for these new friends is "social." Like almost all of the great American financiers of the nineteenth century, Gilbert believed that a special quality of human possibility attached to the rich. In his case the quest took the form of striving to become a part of the uneasy American version of court life that we have always called Society. It is interesting that he apparently made little distinction between Real Society, based on inherited money and Anglo-Saxon lineage, and the newer, less exclusive, more flamboyant version associated with the entertainment world called Café Society. He sought them both impartially, although he kept them separate.

If Gilbert believed that Society no longer existed in turn-of-the-century form, he gave no clue. On the contrary, it seems clear he believed in its vitality, and sought to fulfill himself through it. In fact, he had much to offer his new friends. In his early thirties, a short, compact man with pale blue eyes and a sort of ferret face under thinning hair, Gilbert had a direct, personal charm that compensated for his vanity and extreme competitiveness. Sometimes his newfound friends patronized him behind his back, laughing at his social pretensions and his love of ostentation, but they continued going to his parties and, above all, following his market tips. Some accused him of being a habitual liar; they forgave him because he seemed genuinely to believe his lies, especially those about himself and his past. He was a compulsive gambler—but, endearingly, a very bad one; on lucky streaks he would double bets until he lost all his winnings, or draw to inside straights for huge sums at poker, or go for broke on losing streaks; yet at all times he seemed to take large losses in the best of humor. It was almost as if he lost just so that he

could show what a sport he was, and how little money as such meant to him. He was spoken of as interesting—a natural, a source of conversation to those who followed the gossip columns and who in turn spread the gossip even wider.

At his constant urging, his newfound friends bought Bruce stock—and so did his parents, his sister, his cousins, his aunts, and anyone else susceptible to his persuasion. The buying began to approach its climactic phase in March 1958, when Bruce was selling on the American Stock Exchange at around $25 a share. All that spring, the Gilberts and their relatives and Eddie's friends accumulated the stock, until in June it had reached the seventies and was bouncing up and·down from day to day and hour to hour in an alarming way. What was in the process of developing in Bruce stock was the classically dangerous, sometimes disastrous market situation called a corner. As the price had risen, the Bruce family management had come, belatedly, to realize that a raid was in progress; their defensive countermeasure was to begin buying the stock themselves, thereby redoubling the upward pressure. Meanwhile, a third group, consisting of speculators, had been watching the wild and apparently illogical rise, and had seen a chance for a profit in short sales—sales of borrowed stock that could presumably be bought back and delivered at a lower price later, after the bubble had burst. Thus it came about that in May and early June, much of the stock bought by the Bruce side and the Gilbert side alike was bought from persons who did not own it at all. Borrowed from a "floating supply" that was more theoretical than actual, it was stock that really did not exist; and in June when the price reached 77, the two antagonist factions together owned, or had documents to show that they owned, more shares than were actually outstanding. The short sellers were squeezed; if called upon to deliver the stock they had borrowed and then sold, they could not do so, and those who owned it were in a position to force them to buy back what they owed at a highly inflated price.

Corners have a long and infamous history in Wall Street. In the Bruce case, probably neither Gilbert nor the Bruce management had wanted a corner—it was an accidental by-product of the fight for control—and, because of the insignificance of Bruce in the larger economy, there was no danger of a national panic. There was, however, a danger that Bruce stockholders not involved in the fight would become accidental casualties, and, moreover, in Wall Street

the very word "corner" was frighteningly evocative of a disreputable past. So in mid-June the Amex acted, suspending trading in Bruce to protect the innocent bystanders. Immediately the stock began to be traded over the counter, and the short sellers, wildly buying what few shares were available in a scramble to fulfill their commitments, sent the price rocketing insanely up to 188. (The available shares came from the innocent bystanders, and perhaps a few from the faithless among Gilbert's friends, who sold their loyalty for quick profit.) The S.E.C. stepped in, there were negotiations and recriminations, moves and countermoves, and at last a compromise was reached between Gilbert and the Bruce family; when the dust settled in September, Gilbert had 50 percent of Bruce stock and was made chairman of the Bruce board. Empire took notice of its new enhanced status by changing its name to Empire National; later, in 1961, when Empire National and Bruce were formally merged, the surviving company took the name of E.L. Bruce and Company.

Eddie Gilbert, coming out of the fray in the fall of 1958, seemed to have arrived at last—apparently paper-rich from his huge holdings of high-priced Bruce stock, rich in the esteem of his society backers, nationally famous from the publicity attendant on the corner he had brought about. Now, as the winner, he began to spread himself. He kept a regular Monday box at the Metropolitan Opera—a lover of music, as not all of his fellow box-holders were, but one who loved appearing among them, too. He cultivated the two leading arbiters of Café Society, Elsa Maxwell and Igor Cassini; sometimes he would self-indulgently ask Cassini if he knew anyone Gilbert's age who was richer and more important than he, and Cassini, with a smooth smile, would shake his head. He hired Cassini's firm, Martial and Company, as public-relations counsel for Bruce; it does not seem to have bothered either man that the items about Gilbert's doings that appeared in Cassini's newspaper column had been supplied by Cassini himself as Bruce's press agent, meaning that in effect Gilbert was simply buying, and Cassini selling, space in the column. He sent his wife, a beautiful Brooklyn girl named Rhoda, to a speech therapist and a posture school. Eventually his market transactions came to be handled by Francis Farr, clubman and broker, brother of a member of the aristocratic law firm of White and Case and a vestryman of St. James Episcopal Church. He installed flooring in Le Club, a raffishly élite New York membership-by-invitation discothèque, in exchange for a charter membership. He acquired a

huge Fifth Avenue apartment and filled it with French antiques, a fortune in almost-first-rate paintings, and a staff of six. Sometimes he lived in a mansion at Palm Beach, epitome of Real Society in faded turn-of-the-century photographs. He took an immense villa at Cap Martin on the French Riviera, where he mingled when he could with Maria Callas and Aristotle Onassis and their like, and gave huge outdoor parties with an orchestra playing beside an Olympic-size swimming pool. At his parties, Eddie was always the maestro, directing, giving whimsical instructions, trading hospitality for the right to command. "Let's all go bowling!" he might shout to his assembled guests after lunch, so ingenuously that forty or fifty of the rich and chic or almost-rich and almost-chic of the world would dutifully jump into their cars, or into one of his waiting limousines, and be off to Monaco's elegant four-lane bowling alley to indulge him. He was living a dream, filling out its details as he went along, and waiting, like Gatsby, for the sound of the tuning fork struck against a star.

And he was not really rich, in any genuine sense. Probably he spent beyond his income every year except 1961. It was believed that at his peak he had a paper net worth of around $10 million, but in retrospect this seems unlikely. His paper profits were built on borrowing, and he was always mortgaged right up to the hilt; to be thus mortgaged, and to remain so, was all but an article of faith with him. He was habitually so pressed for cash that on each January first he would draw his entire $50,000 Empire salary for the coming year in a lump sum in advance. By the summer of 1960 he was in bad financial trouble. Empire National stock was down, Gilbert's brokers were calling for additional margin, and Gilbert was already in debt all over New York. He owed large sums to dozens of art dealers. Some sources maintain that, counting his personal debts to his father, he was by then insolvent by at least $1 million. But he hung on gamely; when friends advised him at least to liquidate the art collection, he refused. To sell it, he explained, would be to lose face.

What saved him at that particular moment was the bull market of 1961, and a timely psychological boost that came about in an odd way. On the advice of a friend, he sought out as a consultant Jerry Finkelstein, the powerful business and political figure (later New York City Democratic chairman) who was then generally considered the top financial public-relations man in the country. Depressed as he was, Gilbert made an offer to Finkelstein, expecting rejection. But to his joy and amazement Finkelstein bought a big block of Bruce

stock and took stock options, but not for services. And then came the curious part: his self-confidence restored by the mere fact of Finkelstein's acceptance, Gilbert was transformed into a demon and proceeded to do on his own the job that he had wanted the leading expert to do. Association with a champion released the champion in himself, and Finkelstein had little to do but collect his profits when Bruce stock rose sharply. Gilbert's buying power in the market had also been vastly increased, not only by the rise in value of his own holdings but by a swift and apparently miraculous increase in the number of "friends" who would gladly put their money where he told them to. It all induced a dangerous new euphoria. By May 1961, Gilbert was feeling so flush that the urge for expansion overtook him again, and he embarked on the venture that would destroy him.

What he wanted for his empire, called Bruce but truly an empire now, was Celotex Corporation, a large and important manufacturer of building-insulation materials with headquarters in Chicago and a listing on the New York Stock Exchange. He began by buying its stock at around 30, stepped up the pace when it conveniently fell back to 24 later in 1961, and then chased it all the way up to 42 early in 1962. His acquisition work was cut out for him this time, since Celotex was bigger game than Bruce; half-again as big in sales, Celotex had more than three times as many shares outstanding. But Gilbert, convinced now of his infallibility, was confident. He held perhaps half a million Bruce shares, some in Memphis, some in Switzerland with moneylenders, some in other places; it gave him several million dollars' buying power. He began using this to buy Celotex; he put his friends (and cousins and aunts) into Celotex up to the last dollar they would allow; he borrowed still more cash from his father, and put *that* into Celotex too. Even the Bruce family became so mesmerized by the man who had wrested control from them that early in 1962 they authorized his use of $400,000 of the company's money to buy Celotex shares, and later they raised the ante by a round million more. In March, Gilbert showed his cards. He held 10 percent of Celotex stock, he announced, and he wanted a place on the board of directors. Henry Collins, Celotex's president, at first refused, but did so in such a tentative way that it was clear he felt he was simply postponing the inevitable. Gilbert seemed on the verge of a stunning success.

And then two events in quick succession, one public and one private, hastened the course of his destiny. The market started to go

sour with the Kennedy-steel encounter, and Gilbert, whose marriage had gone sour the November before, flew to Las Vegas to serve the six-week residency that was a prerequisite to getting a Nevada divorce. Gilbert took elaborate security precautions, apparently to forestall any panic in the market for Bruce and Celotex stock that his flight might cause.

His personal predilections, and the turning of the earth, imposed a strange and exhausting schedule on Gilbert in Las Vegas. The three-hour time differential meant that the New York markets opened at 7:00 A.M. Nevada time. Every morning, therefore, Gilbert would be up.at the desert dawn and on the phone getting early New York quotations from brokers. Then at the market opening the pace of his telephoning would be stepped up, and he would keep the wires humming until lunch time in Las Vegas, when the day's trading ended in the East. In the afternoon he would wander into the casinos, where he would gamble on into the evening.

Sometimes, like a wary spider, he would make a quick foray out into the real world, and then hasten back into hiding. Twice, early in May, he made trips to New York in search of additional cash. But the stock market had begun its descent in earnest now, and with it Gilbert's claim to solvency, and the moneylenders were unwilling to accommodate him. Indeed, his Nevada-based trips were not only worthless but probably counterproductive; the word spread swiftly among lenders that Eddie Gilbert was in trouble and running hard. At the middle of the month he went to Chicago to see Collins of Celotex. In Chicago, Collins now offered Gilbert a seat on the Celotex board and the right to choose one other director. But Gilbert, for the sake of his crumbling credit status, needed the board seat immediately, and Collins insisted on holding up the announcement until after the next Celotex board meeting on June 20, so the victory Gilbert brought back to his desert hideaway was a hollow one.

Gilbert's Celotex holdings now amounted to over 150,000 shares, and for each further point that the stock dropped, he had to find and deliver $150,000 in additional margin or risk being sold out by his brokers. Those of his friends holding Celotex on his advice now numbered around fifty, and they, too, since most of them held it on margin, were being squeezed as the price continued to fall. Many of them also had positions in Bruce. Their alternatives were three: to sell Celotex; to sell Bruce to cover Celotex, which would depress the price of Bruce and thus be equally disastrous for Gilbert; or to find

more cash margin. Gilbert himself had all but exhausted his borrow-ing power. His debts to brokers, to friends, to Swiss bankers, to New York loan sharks on the fringes of the underworld, all loomed over him, and the market betrayed him daily by dropping even more.

The third week of May became for Gilbert a nightmare of thwarted pleas by telephone—pleas to lenders for new loans, pleas to brokers to be patient and not sell him out, pleas to friends to stick with him just a little longer. But it was all in vain, and in desperation that same week Gilbert took the old, familiar, bad-gambler's last bad gamble —to avoid the certainty of bankruptcy he risked the possibility of criminal charges. Gilbert ordered an official of Bruce to make out checks drawn on the Bruce treasury to a couple of companies called Rhodes Enterprises and Empire Hardwood Flooring, which were ac-tually dummies for Gilbert himself, and he used the proceeds to shore up his personal margin calls. The checks amounted to not quite $2 million; the act amounted to grand larceny.

It was a bold stroke, based, of course, on the faint hope that the prices of Bruce and Celotex would suddenly rise enough to reduce Gilbert's need for margin and enable him to redeem the improper checks and repay Bruce. By his own calculations—which no doubt excluded his huge debts to his father—he was solvent were Celotex above 31 and Bruce above 32. On Friday, May 25, Celotex closed at 31 and Bruce at 32⅜, actually up a fraction for the day. Thus he still had a fingerhold on survival. But for the first time Gilbert was not op-timistic. That Friday he told a part-time secretary, "The way this is going, Monday will be murder." Later he told M.J. Rossant of *The New York Times*, "I suddenly knew that I couldn't get through this without getting hurt and getting innocent people hurt." It is ironic that Gilbert's market prescience, such as it was, should have worked so well at a time when, through pyramiding of debt and then through misappropriation of funds, he had trapped himself in a net so confining that it prevented him from taking advantage of what he knew. As the reader will recall, the Monday he said would be "mur-der" turned out to be Blue Monday, the Stock Exchange's second worst day of the century up to then.

That fateful Monday morning Gilbert was closeted in his motel room, his telephones in constant use, learning minute by minute of the progress of the Wall Street collapse almost three thousand miles away. All morning long, Bruce held teeteringly at 30. The blow fell at around noon, New York time, when a broker told Gilbert that

Bruce was now quoted at 23. Stunned into disbelief, he hung up and called another broker, who confirmed the devastating news. Hardly a moment later, the phones began jangling with incoming calls from his frightened creditors in New York and Switzerland.

Gilbert now admitted to himself that he was beaten. He said later that he spent the rest of Monday "like a punch-drunk fighter going through the motions." Bruce closed for the day at 23, down 9⅜, and Celotex closed at 25, down 6. Gilbert's personal losses for that Monday came to $5 million. In addition to the creditors, he had to deal all afternoon with the friends he had tipped to buy Bruce and Celotex, who now had disastrous losses of their own. In the big turnaround on Tuesday, Bruce gained 5⅜ points, but the recovery was too moderate and too momentary to save him; Celotex did not recover at all, and his other, unredeemable debts, including the $2 million he had taken from the unsuspecting Bruce company, remained outstanding.

Late on Tuesday, Gilbert assessed his position as coolly as he could. Clearly, the dream of capturing Celotex was ended. It was a question now not of building an empire or even protecting one, but of avoiding bankruptcy and, if possible, the penitentiary. His hope, as he saw it, lay in finding a block buyer for all or most of his Celotex holding, and using the proceeds to pay back what he had "borrowed" from Bruce. He remembered that a company in the building-materials business called Ruberoid had expressed interest in taking a position in Celotex. Whatever the chances of swinging such a deal, they depended on his availability in New York for more than one-day flying trips. So, with only a couple of weeks remaining in his Nevada residency term, he abandoned another dream, that of getting his divorce, and on Wednesday, the Memorial Day holiday, he flew to New York and moved back into his suite at the Waldorf.

Thursday the storm around him gathered new force. Gilbert found that the earliest appointment he could get with the officials of Ruberoid was the following Monday, June 4. Yet all day Thursday his Waldorf suite was besieged by creditors, some of whom had come from Switzerland for the purpose. He could give them no satisfaction, only vague hopes of a possible sale of Celotex. On Friday, friends to whom he confided his position, and the criminal action it had led him into, urged him to declare bankruptcy at once. Rueful and contrite, but still stubborn, he refused.

In fact, Gilbert still had a little time—to be precise, six business days. Tuesday, June 12 was the scheduled date of the next Bruce

board of directors meeting, at which the matter of $2 million loans to Rhodes Enterprises and Empire Hardwood Flooring was almost certain to come up; so he would have to have some solution ready by then or stand exposed. The six borrowed days were the last loan he could negotiate—a loan of time rather than money. On Monday the fourth—Day One—he met with Ruberoid officials as planned, freely admitted to them that he was in a squeeze, and suggested that, since they wanted to purchase a block of Celotex shares anyway, they might take profitable advantage of his distress by assuming his Celotex holdings. The Ruberoid men seemed interested, but stopped short of giving him a firm and binding commitment. On Day Two, still desperate, he told the whole story to his lawyers at the firm of Shearman and Sterling. Understandably, they were horrified, and set about taking such defensive steps as were available. To prevent Gilbert from compounding his felony in panic, they instructed Bruce officials not under any conditions to sign any more checks on his instructions. As a first step toward redeeming the felony he admitted to having committed, they ordered him to give the company personal notes backed by his personal property.

Day Three passed without any promising developments, but on Day Four—Thursday the seventh—there suddenly appeared a ray of hope when the executive vice president of Ruberoid gave Gilbert the almost incredibly good news that he believed his firm was ready to buy 300,000 shares of Celotex at a fair price. The sale, when and as consummated, would not save him from bankruptcy, but it would enable him to save his friends and followers, and to bail himself out of his improper borrowing from Bruce.

Gilbert spent the rest of Thursday and then Friday frantically rounding up the Celotex shares from his friends, to have them ready for delivery; and on Monday the eleventh, the last day before the Bruce meeting, with the shares safely in hand, he savored for a few hours the feeling that he might still end the affair with some sort of honor, and perhaps without losing everything—his villas, his followers, his place in the great world. The Bruce meeting convened at 10:30 Tuesday morning; Gilbert was there smoking a cigar, dapper in a gray suit and black loafers. For two hours he told the other directors—some of whom already knew, or knew enough—the story of his frantic, reticulated dealings and of how they had led at last to an unauthorized withdrawal from the funds with which the men in the room were jointed entrusted. There followed a heated debate;

some wanted Gilbert's immediate resignation, while others coun-
seled caution, or at least a delay until after the day's market closing
to forestall a further panic in Bruce stock. It was in the midst of this
tense and gloomy discussion that word came to Gilbert from
Ruberoid that the company had withdrawn its offer to buy his block
of Celotex shares.

It was the coup de grace for Gilbert. The meeting broke for lunch,
but he did not join his fellow directors in the meal. Instead, he went
home and packed a suitcase, visited his bank vault and picked up
$8,000 in cash, and made a reservation on a plane leaving that eve-
ning at 7:30 for Brazil. His last legitimate escape hatch sealed off, he
had decided on literal and figurative flight. Brazil at the time had become a secular sanctuary for erring American financiers; down there
already, wasting time, boasting about old triumphs, playing poker,
and putting together such penny-ante local deals as they could manage, were Lowell Birrell, the well-brought-up eviscerator of companies; the giant Texan embezzler BenJack Cage; and Earle Belle, a
youthful jobber of watered bank stocks. Gilbert must have hated the
prospect of geographical association with these grimly comic rogues;
later he would maintain with indignation that he had nothing in
common with any of them. But the fact was that on June 12, 1962, he
had one thing in common with them all—the pressing need for a distant jurisdiction like Brazil that had no effective extradition treaty
with the United States.

Gilbert appeared back at the Bruce meeting, cool and confident,
when it reconvened that afternoon at 2:30. His need now was to persuade the Bruce board to postpone public announcment of his resignation and its disgraceful cause until he was out of the country. Just
until 7:30! he pleaded. Why that particular hour? He explained that
he needed just five hours to approach one final potential lender.
After another long and heated argument, the board acceded, and
Gilbert breathed again. Of course, the potential lender was mythical.
He departed his Bruce office around 5:30, ostensibly to see the last-
hope lender, saying he would be back around 7:00 with news of the
results. While the other directors waited tensely, Gilbert hired a
limousine and picked up his parents, who then accompanied him to
Idlewild Airport. In the car, Harry Gilbert said later, Eddie was
"frantic and hysterical." But at the airport he was calm enough to pay
cash for his ticket and board his Rio-bound flight without attracting
attention.

At the Bruce offices, the directors became progressively more apprehensive. At 8:15 they called the S.E.C. and reported all that they knew. It was too late. At 8:30, as Eddie Gilbert's jet reached altitude and sped southward, Harry Gilbert called the Bruce directors to say, ruefully, that his son would not be back.

In Brazil he lived in relative quiet, taking an only moderately plush apartment in the Copacabana section of Rio, often going unshaven, avoiding nightclubs and casinos, writing letters, dabbling a bit in local business, exercising his language skill by studying Portuguese. (He did allow himself a chauffeur-driven Cadillac.) From time to time his ever-loyal parents sent him money. "I just can't face people," he told *The Times'* Rossant, who visited him there; but he also said more resolutely, "I will pay back everything if it takes the rest of my life." Meanwhile, he was sometimes heard to put the blame for his debacle on anybody and everybody but himself: on Lazard, on Loeb, Rhoades, on Collins of Celotex, on faithless friends, on President Kennedy. To one visitor from home he complained, "I'm just an ordinary guy. They called me a genius, but I'm not. If they hadn't blown the whistle on me, it could all have been avoided."

At home, meanwhile, there were the predictable recriminations and unseemly squabbles, lending a sort of false dignity by contrast to the lonely exile pouring over Portuguese grammar. At the end of June, the Bruce company sought and got a court injunction to prevent Mrs. Gilbert from disposing of the couple's furniture and art collection for her own benefit: particular reference was made to Boucher's *La Toilette de Venus* and *Psyche and Cupid,* asserted in the injunction plea to be worth $95,000; Monet's *Flowers,* $75,000; and Fragonard's *Portrait of a Young Woman,* $92,000. At about the same time, the Justice Department got an indictment against Gilbert on fifteen counts of securities fraud, and the Internal Revenue Service added a touch of comedy by filing tax liens against him dating back to 1958 and amounting to over $3 million. In mid-July, he was further indicted in New York for grand larceny in connection with the Bruce misappropriation. As for his friends, a few of them loyally insisted that he was a misunderstood man who had never meant to do wrong; others, however, would no longer acknowledge that they knew him. His old pal and business associate Igor Cassini, who had lost money on Bruce and Celotex, now found it appropriate to pro-

nounce Gilbert "a crook." And then, in November, by which time there were federal and state charges outstanding against him the penalties for which added up to 194 years in prison, Gilbert suddenly came home. He got off the plane in New York flanked by federal marshals. He was arrested, and then promptly released on bail.

He said he had returned because he was bored with inaction and the Latin American spirit of mañana, and surely this was true. (Some of his friends joked that five months is as long as a Jewish boy can stay away from home.) But it also seems clear that Arnold Bauman, the New York criminal lawyer whom Gilbert's father had hired in his absence to defend him, had told him that the coast was now as clear as it would ever be. And that, it turned out, was pretty clear. Gilbert remained free on bail for no less than four and a half years, while he and his lawyer dangled before the various prosecutors the promise that he would implicate other wrongdoers. He could implicate various people, he said; he had something on Lazard and Loeb, Rhoades. These promises were never fulfilled. In May 1963, he and Rhoda Gilbert were finally divorced, and a week later he married a Norwegian airline stewardess named Turid. The villas, the art collection, and the poolside parties were now in the past, but Gilbert and his new bride did well enough for a time. They dressed well; they lived in a Park Avenue apartment, they had two children, and they went to Puerto Rico on vacation. With help, as usual, from his father, Gilbert set himself up in a new business, the Northerlin Company, flooring brokers. He was still a good salesman. Northerlin made over $200,000 its first year, and Gilbert, besides beginning to fulfill his promise by paying off some of the smaller of his old debts—$2,300 to a painter of his old Fifth Avenue apartment, $138 to F.A.O. Schwartz—began trying to live in his old way on $100,000 a year. He began again to wheel and deal in the market—in his wife's name. Very tentatively, a few of the not-so-beau monde began to take notice of him again.

There are second acts in some American lives, but not Eddie Gilbert's. Given his temperament, his comeback attempt could not succeed, but even so, it was quite a feat. Still under multiple indictments, free on bail, bankrupt for over $10 million all the while, between 1963 and 1967 he twice "got rich," twice "went broke," once even managed to get himself investigated by the S.E.C. He cut too many corners in his operations at Northerlin; the promising young company began to lose money, and finally had to be sold for a tax

loss. And time ran out on his unfulfilled bargain with the civil authorities. In 1964 he pleaded guilty to twelve counts of grand larceny and three of securities fraud; in each case a sentencing date was set, and in each case, when the date arrived, sentencing was postponed. It almost seemed as if he might escape imprisonment indefinitely. But in 1967 the authorities finally lost patience with his failure to come up with usable state's evidence. That April—with only a trivial fraction of his 1962 debts repaid, and with a flock of new ones accumulated—the federal penitentiary doors finally closed on him. He would be paroled a little over two years later, but by that time his career as Gatsby was gone for good.

CHAPTER 3

PALMY DAYS AND LOW RUMBLINGS

U sually after general disaster in Wall Street or elsewhere, one man takes charge of cleaning up and putting things back together, of dragging the bodies offstage and rearranging the set for the next performance—rearranging it neatly and primly, as if in hopes that subsequent action will turn toward drawing-room comedy rather than more bloody melodrama.

After the shambles of 1962, the man Wall Street turned to was the chairman of the S.E.C., William Lucius Cary. In 1962 Cary was a lawyer of fifty-one with the gentlemanly manner and the pixyish countenance of a New England professor. He had graduated from Yale and then from Yale Law, practiced law a couple of years in Cleveland, then done a long stretch in federal government—first as a young S.E.C. assistant counsel, later as an assistant attorney general in the tax division of the Justice Department, then as an Office of Strategic Services cloak-and-dagger functionary in wartime Romania and Yugoslavia. In 1947 he had entered academic life, teaching law first at Northwestern and later at Columbia. He was in the latter post, taking one day a week off to go downtown to the "real world" of Wall Street and practice law with the firm of Patterson, Belknap and Webb, when John F. Kennedy appointed him S.E.C. chairman soon after assuming the Presidency in January 1961.

Cary never knew how he came to be tapped. He had made friends in the upper echelons of the Kennedy ranks, and one or another of

them must have suggested his name to the President-elect. At all events, the appointment proved to have been a brilliant one —perhaps the most brilliant to that post since Franklin D. Roosevelt, to the dismay of all good liberals, had chosen the ex-stock manipulator Joseph P. Kennedy to be the S.E.C.'s first head back in 1934. Cary brought to the organization a vigor and a drive that it had lacked for years.

"Regulatory bodies, like the people who comprise them, have a marked life cycle," John Kenneth Galbraith has written. "In youth they are vigorous, aggressive, evangelistic, and even intolerant. Later they mellow, and in old age—after a matter of ten or fifteen years —they become, with some exceptions, either an arm of the industry they are regulating or senile." In June 1941, the S.E.C. had a roster of 1,683 employees; in 1955, by which time the industry it was supposed to regulate had expanded vastly, the number was down to 666, and when Cary assumed office some six years later the total was around 900. The S.E.C.'s premature onslaught of senility, then, was compounded by starvation. While the Birrells and the Gutermas were weaving their schemes and the Amex was all but falling to pieces, the sparse staff at S.E.C. headquarters—restored to Washington now, but assigned there to an unimpressive temporary building on Second Street called the "tarpaper shack"—generally contented themselves with routine; they were never seen on the trading floors of the exchanges, they enjoyed all too amiable social relations with the authorities of those exchanges, and one S.E.C. chairman developed the comfortable habit of falling asleep during the Commission's deliberations. "Literally and figuratively, the S.E.C. slept for most of the decade," Louis M. Kohlmeier, Jr., a historian of regulatory agencies, wrote of the nineteen fifties.

A strong *Report on Regulatory Agencies to the President Elect*, commissioned by the President-elect himself and written late in 1960 by James M. Landis, who had been an S.E.C. chairman in New Deal days, showed that Kennedy was bent on bringing the S.E.C. back to life, and it set the stage for the Cary regime. Cary concentrated on recruiting talented and enthusiastic lawyers, devoting perhaps a third of his time to the task. His base supply naturally enough consisted of his former students and their friends; the atmosphere at the tarpaper shack soon changed from one of bureaucratic somnolence to one of academic liberal activism.

Cary treated the securities industry warily, and generally, as he

liked to put it, "with deference," but hardly with friendship Two actions during his first year in office gave the financial district an inkling of Cary's mettle and the S.E.C.'s new mood. One was a case called *In the Matter of Cady, Roberts and Co.*, which concerned events that had taken place two years before. In November 1959, Robert M. Gintel, a young member of the brokerage firm of Cady, Roberts and Company, had been informed one morning by one of his associates, J. Cheever Cowdin, that Curtiss-Wright Corporation was about to announce a drastic cut in its quarterly dividend. Gintel had the very best of reasons to believe that Cowdin knew what he was talking about, since Cowdin was a director of Curtiss-Wright and had presumably participated in the very decision he was reporting on. Possessing this classic piece of inside information, Gintel immediately ordered the sale of 7,000 shares of Curtiss-Wright stock on behalf of his firm's customers. The order was executed at above 40; one-half hour later the dividend cut was publicly announced, and the first trade in Curtiss-Wright thereafter was at 36½—not quite 10 percent lower.

Such profitable use of privileged information was apparently illegal under Rule 10B-5 of the S.E.C., promulgated in 1942 under authority of the 1934 Securities Exchange Act, and intended to prohibit precisely this sort of thing. But so firmly entrenched was the Wall Street tradition of taking unfair advantage of the larger investing public, and so lax the S.E.C.'s administration of that particular part of the law between 1942 and 1961, that not a single stockbroker had ever been prosecuted for improper use of privileged information during those two decades. In the tarpaper shack, 10B-5 was the law in name only, and thus prior to Cary's time the S.E.C. had taken no action in the matter of Cady, Roberts. But now, in an opinion written by the new chairman himself, the S.E.C. decided that in not waiting until the public announcement of the dividend reduction before selling Curtiss-Wright stock, Gintel had violated the antifraud provisions of the law, and accordingly it suspended him from trading in securities for twenty days.

The sentence was light, but the implication was far-reaching: at last the S.E.C. had affirmed that the easygoing days were over and that Rule 10B-5 now meant precisely what it said. Presumably the agency would pursue the new policy in the future—as, in fact, it did in 1966, when it brought, and for the most part eventually won, a civil complaint against Texas Gulf Sulphur and thirteen of its directors

and employees charging that they had made improper use of inside information of a Canadian ore strike, in a case that shook Wall Street to its foundations. The Stock Exchange turned around and issued a strong set of new directives to its members against the use of inside information by brokers. Thus the stock market had moved in the direction of fairness for the outsider, and no pillars of finance had fallen; that is to say, regulation had worked as it is supposed to work.

When a market panic is in progress, the S.E.C. is as helpless as a meteorologist in a storm. No power vested in it enables it to turn markets around. When a panic does occur, as one did in May 1962, the regulators can only watch ruefully, and prepare to get back to their regulatory drawing board as soon as possible.

So it was with Cary and his S.E.C. in 1962. What comfort they could find came from the fact that the previous year they, with help from Congress, had recognized the unhealthy state of the markets and had attempted to do something about it in advance—but not far enough in advance, as things turned out. In June 1961, when Cary had been in office three months and the speculative market was near the peak of its unhealthy flowering, he told a subcommittee of the House Committee on Interstate and Foreign Commerce that he strongly favored the immediate undertaking by the S.E.C. of a comprehensive study and investigation of the adequacy of protection to investors provided by the rules of all the major stock exchanges and the over-the-counter market. Recognizing the need for action, in August 1961 the House and Senate passed a measure authorizing $750,000 to the S.E.C. for a two-year Special Study of the Securities Markets—such a study as had not been undertaken for a generation—and on September 5, President Kennedy signed it into law.

Work began almost at once; a blue-ribbon staff of sixty-five was assembled, headed by Milton H. Cohen, a Chicago lawyer whom Cary imported, with the S.E.C.'s own Ralph Saul as second in command. But when the bottom fell out of the market in the spring of 1962 the Special Study could be of no immediate use because it was less than half finished.

Through that summer and fall work went on, and late in November Cary gave an indication of what was to come. The occasion he chose was a speech he gave at the annual meeting of the Investment Bankers Association, at Hollywood, Florida. Into this sun-warmed outing of fat cats only slightly thinned and chastened by the events of the

past May, Cary injected a shaft of criticism like a sharp New England icicle. He singled out the New York Stock Exchange, the National Association of Securities Dealers, and the Investment Company Institute as specific organizations that had been consistently recalcitrant about regulating themselves and correcting abuses. Then Cary made the most telling jab of the icicle. "Every member of the New York Stock Exchange will concede," he said, that the Exchange, for all of its ever-more-important public function, "still seems to have certain characteristics of a private club—a very good club, I might say."

It was a deliberate reference to Wall Street history. On November 23, 1937, at a time when the S.E.C. was heading into its greatest confrontation with the Stock Exchange up to then on the matter of the Exchange's internal organization, William O. Douglas, then S.E.C. chairman and later a Supreme Court justice, had inflamed the Whitney Old Guard and its allies by speaking of the leading stock exchanges as "private clubs" that in the context of public marketplaces were "archaic." Their rage at the criticism had goaded that particular regiment of Old Guardsmen into excesses of intransigence that, a few months later, would be their final undoing. Cary in 1962 was a Douglas admirer of some thirty years' standing—ever since he had been a law student of the eminent jurist at Yale. His quotation from his old master was conscious and intentional and surely intended to achieve the same effect Douglas had achieved in 1937. For its part, Wall Street knew that it was not to be let off with a slap on the wrist. Serious reform was in the offing.

As the work drew toward a close early in 1963, Wall Street braced itself. The S.E.C. announced that the study would be released in three sections—the first on April 3, the second and third in July and August, respectively. As the date for the first installment drew near, there was such tension as had never before attended the impending release of any document from the S.E.C., or perhaps from any regulatory agency. A sharp, reactive drop in the market was feared, and elaborate precautions were taken against premature leaks of the contents of the study. At length, just after noon on the appointed day, the first part of the Special Study was released simultaneously to Congress and to the press.

The document's tone was reasonable but stern. "Grave abuses" had been found in Wall Street's operations, Cary wrote in his letter of transmittal to Congress, but the picture was "not one of pervasive

fraudulent activity." Specifically, the first installment said that insider-trading rules should be tightened; standards of character and competence for stockbrokers should be raised; further curbs should be put on the new-issues market; and S.E.C. surveillance should be extended to the thousands of small-company stocks traded over the counter that had previously been free of federal regulation. In sum, it was a fair and moderate report that Wall Street could take more or less in stride; the expected sell-off of stocks did not materialize. But, of course, there was another shoe still to drop—or rather, two more shoes.

The second part of the study, duly issued in July, concentrated on stock-exchange operations, recommending that brokers' commissions on trades be lowered; that the freedom of action of specialists be drastically curtailed; and that floor traders—those exchange members who play the market with their own money on the floor itself, deriving from their membership the unique advantages over nonmembers of being at the scene of action and of paying no commissions to brokers—be legislated right out of existence through the interdiction of their activities. The third and final part, out in August, was probably the harshest of the three—and in view of political realities the most quixotic. Turning its attention to the wildly growing mutual-fund business, the S.E.C. now recommended outlawing the kind of contract, called "front-end load," under which mutual-fund buyers agreed (and still agree) to pay large sales commissions off the top of their investment. It also accused the New York Stock Exchange of leaning toward "tenderness rather than severity" in disciplining those of its members who have broken its rules.

All in all, the Special Study was a blueprint for a fair and orderly securities market, certainly the most comprehensive such blueprint ever drawn up, and if all of its recommendations had been promptly put into effect, what follows in this chronicle's later chapters would be a different tale. But, of course, they were not. Once the study had been published, there began a long, tedious, and often frustrating process of fashioning the recommendations into a bill and of getting the bill passed by Congress. The law that was finally passed—the Securities Acts Amendments of 1964—had two main sections, one extending S.E.C. jurisdiction to include some twenty-five hundred over-the-counter stocks (about as many as were traded on the New York and American exchanges combined), and the other giving the

government the authority to set standards and qualifications for securities firms and their employees.

As far as it went, it was a good law, a landmark law, a signal achievement for Cary and his egghead crew. But it fell far short of what the Special Study had asked for. For Cary the greatest disappointment must surely have been that the Act left the club about as private as it had been before. The New York Stock Exchange continued to have thirty-three governors, only three of them nonmember representatives of the public; and of those three, two continued customarily to be corporation heads hardly likely to be passionate proponents of the small-investor point of view. The Exchange continued to have rules and qualifications for election to its board that stacked the deck strongly in favor of "floor" members—those who never dealt with the public and often felt little concern for its welfare —over "upstairs" members, the commission brokers who were more inclined to consider the public because their livelihood depended on it. And—bitterest pill of all—there continued to be floor traders, those specially favored Exchange members who, to Cary, were the very crux of the private-club issue.

When Cary had come to the S.E.C. there had been more than three hundred Exchange members who sometimes availed themselves of their privilege of trading for their own accounts on the floor. The Special Study asked that their privilege be revoked out of hand. A fierce outcry—probably the fiercest against any of the study's recommendations—arose first from the Stock Exchange and later from business in general. The sacred freedom of the marketplace was invoked, and so, at the other extreme, was the welfare of the investing public. The Exchange commissioned the management firm of Cresap, McCormick and Paget to study the problem and come up with a conclusion as to whether floor trading served the public weal.

Cresap, McCormick and Paget labored mightily. One may imagine the Exchange's gratification when the report, finished at last, concluded that abolition of floor trading would decrease liquidity and thereby introduce a dangerous new volatility into Stock Exchange trading, doing "irreparable harm" to the free and fair operation of the auction market. But perhaps the Exchange's gratification was less than complete. The magisterial authority of the report was somewhat sullied when James Dowd, head of the Cresap team that had compiled it, stated publicly that his actual finding had been that floor trading was far from an unmixed blessing for the public, and accused

the Stock Exchange of having tampered with the report before publishing it. It seemed that the schoolmaster had not entirely liked the student's report on him, and so had exercised his prerogative to improve upon it. Cary wanted to hold S.E.C. hearings on the matter, but was voted down by his fellow commissioners. At all events, enough of the people's tribunes in Washington accepted the Stock Exchange's point of view to keep abolition of floor trading out of the 1964 Act.

Thus frustrated, Cary's S.E.C. came to achieve through administration much of what it had failed to achieve through legislation. In August 1964, just before the bill became law, it issued stringent new rules under its pre-existing authority requiring Stock Exchange members to pass a qualifying examination before being allowed to operate as floor traders, and once qualified, to hand in after each day's trading a form detailing each of their transactions. Whether through the threat of exposure, or the extra work, or just the insult to dignity implied in the test and the daily reports, the new rules had the desired discouraging effect on floor trading. "They sat us down with a pencil and a glass of water and handed us this test, right in the Board of Governors room," a floor trader cried in outrage. "Our seats were even spaced far apart, so we couldn't crib!" Shortly after imposition of the new rules, the number of floor traders on the Stock Exchange dropped from three hundred to thirty. As an important factor in the market, floor trading was finished. Cary had won through indirection.

On November 22, 1963, Wall Street did itself little credit. During the twenty-seven minutes between the moment when the first garbled rumors of the President's assassination in Dallas reached the Stock Exchange floor and the emergency closing of the market at 2:07 P.M., stocks declined at their fastest rate in the Exchange's 170-year history to erase $13 billion in values. For an ordinary citizen to react to news of a President's death by thinking first of protecting, if not enlarging, his personal treasure, is perhaps defensible behavior in a materialistic civilization, though it can hardly be called attractive behavior. But for investment professionals, whose jobs have a fiduciary aspect, to react similarly is not defensible.

Did the pathetic, rootless Lee Harvey Oswald really kill for once and all the spirit of a proud nation? Or had the nation, having citizens who could act as some did in Wall Street, lost all unnoticed the spirit at some earlier time? Those are questions still unanswered a

decade later. For the short term, the nation and its barometer, Wall Street, chose—quite humanly—to pretend that nothing irreparable had happened, that no national wound had been opened, that everything was somehow going to be all right. On November 26, the first day of business after the assassination, the market performed its symbolic function of eliminating—literally wiping out—the damage that had been done Friday, by producing the greatest one-day rise in its history. And the new President, wanting to thank someone for this timely miracle, grabbed his telephone and congratulated Keith Funston, president of the New York Stock Exchange. The rise continued through December; 1963 ended with the Dow at an all-time high.

Then came 1964, a market year for bulls to dream about, as everyone's taxes were cut and an American space craft took the first close-up pictures of the moon; as northern children went to Mississippi to spread the gospel of equal rights (three not to return) and the United States asserted itself at Tonkin Gulf ("Don't tread on me!"); as people talked about what was "In" and what was "Out" and Johnson was elected President in his own right along with the most liberal Congress ever. No one could know, of course, that 1964 would be the last year of the decade in which the market would rise in an almost straight line.

Meanwhile, Cary's day as Wall Street's conscience came to an end. He found himself less happy under Lyndon Johnson as President than he had been under Kennedy; Johnson had a habit of telephoning him from time to time about political matters, something Kennedy had never done. Moreover, in December 1963, Johnson called the heads of all the various regulatory agencies into the Cabinet Room of the White House and said to them, in connection with the role of regulation, "we are challenged . . . to concern ourselves with new areas of cooperation before we concern ourselves with new areas of control." It was a clear enough warning to slow down and not rock the boat; and Cary, over the following months, gradually made up his mind that he had been at the S.E.C. long enough. He resigned on August 20, 1964, the day the Securities Acts Amendments became law, and was succeeded by Manuel F. Cohen, who, Johnson's warning notwithstanding, would run a reasonably tough S.E.C. regime over the next five years. As for Bill Cary, gentle strongman or strong gentleman, he went back to his favorite parlay, teaching law at Columbia and practicing it one day a week in Wall Street.

CHAPTER 4

THE BIRTH OF GO-GO

S ometime in the middle nineteen sixties, probably in late 1965 or early 1966, the expression "go-go" as used in the United States came to have a connotation that the dictionaries would not catch up with until after the phenomenon that it described was already over. The term "go-go" came to designate a method of operating in the stock market—a method that was, to be sure, free, fast, and lively, and certainly in some cases attended by joy, merriment, and hubbub. The method was characterized by rapid in-and-out trading of huge blocks of stock, with an eye to large profits taken very quickly, and the term was used specifically to apply to the operation of certain mutual funds, none of which had previously operated in anything like such a free, fast, or lively manner.

The mood and the method seem to have started, of all places, in Boston, the home of the Yankee trustee. The handling of other people's money in the United States began in Boston, the nation's financial center until after the Civil War. Trusteeship is by its nature conservative—its primary purpose being to conserve capital—and so indeed was the type of man it attracted to Boston. And yet, the Boston trustee was not unimaginative; he was an outward-looking Athenian, not the ingrowing Spartan he was often accused of being. As early as 1830, Justice Samuel Putnam of the Supreme Judicial Court of Massachusetts wrote in a famous opinion:

All that can be required of a Trustee to invest is that he conduct himself faithfully and exercise a sound discretion. He is to observe how men of prudence, discretion, and intelligence manage their own affairs, not in regard to speculation, but in regard to permanent disposition of their funds, considering the probable income, as well as the probable safety of the capital to be invested.

The Boston-born "prudent man rule," as it came to be called, represented a crucial liberalization of the law governing trustees, and such a durable one that it is still their basic guide almost a century and a half later. In 1924, Boston was the site of another epoch-making innovation in American money management, the founding of the first two mutual funds, Massachusetts Investors Trust and State Street Investing Company. And then, in the years after World War II, the go-go cult quietly originated hard by Beacon Hill under the un-

likely sponsorship of a Boston Yankee named Edward Crosby Johnson II.

Johnson was born in a Boston suburb in 1898, the son of a partner in the old Boston dry-goods firm of C. F. Hovey, and a descendant of John Johnson, a Puritan freeman in seventeenth-century Massachusetts. He was named for another ancestor who had been a Union officer in the Civil War. He went to Milton Academy and then, all but inevitably, to Harvard; he married another Brahmin, his second cousin Elsie Livingston. In deference to his father's wish that he become a lawyer, he went on to Harvard Law and then joined the proper Boston law firm of Ropes and Gray. He stayed there for fourteen years, from 1925 to 1939, specializing in corporate reorganizations and mergers. But all the while his heart belonged to the stock market.

The market bug first bit him in 1924 when he read a serialization in the old *Saturday Evening Post* of Edwin Lefèvre's "Reminiscences of a Stock Market Operator," the story of the career of the famous speculator Jesse Livermore. "I'll never forget the thrill," he told a friend almost a half century later. "Everything was there, or else implied. Here was the picture of a world in which it was every man for himself, no favors asked or given." Under the influence of Lefèvre's book, this young romantic of commerce began playing the market in his spare time between legal chores; his colleagues teased him for keeping stock-market charts on the walls of his law office. He lost along with everyone else in the 1929 crash, but, unlike many, survived the setback and, in the following years, as the market sank into the abyss, he scored his first coup. "I'd noticed a certain group of signs that, when they came together, meant a big bust was ahead," Johnson recounted long afterward. "I saw the signs, and I anticipated the 1931-1932 drop. I sat on my little poop-deck potting away, and kept my capital intact. God, it was glorious!"

In 1935, Johnson became counsel for Incorporated Investors, a small, old-line Boston mutual-fund firm. Gradually, he was drawn by his predilection deeper into finance and further from the law. In 1939 he left Ropes and Gray to become full-time vice-president and treasurer of Incorporated Investors. Four years later, he was offered the opportunity to take over Fidelity Fund, another Boston mutual-fund operation that then managed only the unimpressive total of $3 million—and Johnson had an investment company of his very own.

Right from the start, Johnson's approach to investing Fidelity

funds was an unorthodox one that he would later describe in the following characteristically picturesque terms: "We didn't want to feel that we were married to a stock when we bought it. You might say that we preferred to think of our relationship to it as 'companionate marriage.' But that doesn't go quite far enough, either. Possibly now and again we liked to have a 'liaison'—or even, very occasionally, 'a couple of nights together.'"

His maverick operations as head of Fidelity, while they fell far short of creating a scandal on State Street, nevertheless caused a certain amount of talk there during the nineteen forties. But what he was doing then was only the beginning, and the next stage in Fidelity's evolution began with Johnson's first encounter with Gerald Tsai, Jr.

This encounter occurred in 1952, when Johnson received a telephone call from a friend of his at the investment counseling firm of Scudder, Stevens and Clark. "I've got a young Chinese here, a clever fellow, but we don't seem to have a place for him at the moment," the friend said. "Anything you can do for him?" Johnson asked his friend to send the young man around. When Tsai appeared, Johnson liked his looks and hired him on the spot as a junior stock analyst.

The young man, then twenty-four, had been born in Shanghai in 1928 to Westernized Chinese parents; his father had been educated at the University of Michigan and later become Shanghai district manager for the Ford Motor Company. In 1947, with the war over at last, the younger Tsai was sent to America to college. He went first to Wesleyan University; finding Middletown, Connecticut, too much of a hick community for his liking after the bright lights of Shanghai, he transferred to Boston University, where he felt right at home, and applied himself so diligently that he finished his undergraduate courses in economics six months ahead of schedule, and devoted the last term of his senior year to writing a master's thesis on "Economic Development in Shanghai." Thus, in the summer of 1949, he was able to take his B.A. and M.A. in quick succession. He worked for a year with a textile company in Providence, then for another year or so with the securities giant Bache and Company in New York, getting married along the way to a Chinese-American girl. Then he went back to Boston and, having decided once and for all that stock investment was his métier, met Johnson and Fidelity. "I liked the market," he would explain years later. "I felt that being a foreigner I didn't have a competitive disadvantage there, when I might some-

where else. If you buy GM at forty and it goes to fifty, whether you are an Oriental, a Korean, or a Buddhist doesn't make any difference." The reader's attention need hardly be called to the similarity between Tsai's reason for liking the market and that of Edward Crosby Johnson II.

At Fidelity, Tsai was not long in making his mark. Always impeccably groomed, his moon face as impassive as a Buddha, he showed himself to be a shrewd and decisive picker of stocks for short-term appreciation, and so swift and nimble in getting into and out of specific stocks that his relations with them, far from resembling a marriage or even a companionate marriage, were often more like those of a roué with a chorus line. Sometimes, to continue the analogy, the sheets were hardly cool when he was through with one and on to another. Johnson—"Mister" Johnson to Tsai, as he was to almost everyone else in his own organization and the mutual-fund business in general—was fascinated and ever so slightly scandalized.

By 1957 Tsai felt confident enough of his position at Fidelity to write Johnson a memo asking—indeed, very nearly demanding —permission to start his own growth fund. "It took him only half an hour to decide," Tsai recalled long afterward. "He called me into his office, handed my memo back to me, and said, 'Go ahead.' "

Tsai's fund was called Fidelity Capital Fund, and it was the company's first frankly speculative public growth fund. Right from the start, he operated it in a way that was at the time considered almost out-and-out gambling. He concentrated Fidelity Capital's money in a few stocks that were then thought to be outrageously speculative and unseasoned for a mutual fund (Polariod, Xerox, and Litton Industries among them). He bought in huge blocks of ten thousand shares or more at a time, coolly notifying his brokers that if they couldn't assemble the block without pushing the price up substantially—say, more than a point or two—the deal was off. The brokers grumbled, but usually assembled the large positions; with huge commissions at stake, if one broker wouldn't deal with Tsai according to Tsai's specifications another assuredly would. His annual portfolio turnover generally exceeded 100 percent, or a share traded for every one held—a rate of trading unheard of in institutional circles at the time. He got a well-deserved reputation for catlike quickness in calling a market turn. "It was a beautiful thing to watch his reactions," Johnson says. "What grace, what timing—glorious! Why, if he had been on the Stock Exchange floor, he'd have become its

number one trader in no time." As Fidelity Capital's net asset value rose and new money poured into it, Tsai came to be close to key men in corporate management: Harold Geneen of International Telephone, Nathan Cummings of Consolidated Foods, Laurence Tisch of Loews. And, gradually—although his name was still unknown to the general public—he came to be known and feared in corporate circles. The sudden dumping of ten thousand shares of one's stock was not to be taken lightly, and the man capable of doing it on a moment's whim was worth cultivating.

All rising artists suffer setbacks, and this young Picasso of the portfolio suffered one in the bad market of 1962. But Tsai was quick to recover. After the Cuban missile crisis that October he suddenly turned decisively bullish. In six weeks, he put $26 million into stocks for Fidelity Capital; the market leaped upward, and by the end of the year the fund's asset value had risen nothing less than 68 percent within three months.

Tsai had now perfected his method, and over the following three years he had the ideal market in which to project it. At the same time he began to rise within his own organization. By 1963 Tsai owned 20 percent of the Johnson management vehicle, Fidelity Management and Research—half as much as Edward Johnson—and was beginning to think of himself as Johnson's successor. Up and up went Fidelity Capital's asset value, and finally, for the vintage market year of 1965, the fund achieved a rise of not quite 50 percent on a turnover of 120 percent.

The go-go years had begun, and Gerry Tsai, more than any other one man, had brought them into being. Suddenly, he was nationally famous. As once "Jesse Livermore is buying it!" had been the signal for a general stampede into any stock, so now it was "Gerry Tsai is buying it!" As the first big-name star of the new era, he created fresh problems of regulation that the regulators in Washington did not at first recognize.

In 1965, Tsai's career with the Fidelity organization came to a fork in the road. The elder Johnson was over sixty-five now and likely to retire soon. Who was to be his successor—Tsai, or Johnson's own son Ned? Self-confident with fame and success now, a national force in the market, Tsai could no longer be expected to sit quietly in the counsels of Fidelity. Finally he put the question of succession directly to Johnson. It must have been a hard moment for both, but

Johnson faced it forthrightly and without evasion: he said simply that Ned was his son and that he intended that Ned should eventually succeed him. Tsai understood; he knew that Fidelity was basically a family business. But he also knew that he could not and need not endure a future of being permanently number two man. Later that year he resigned, sold his Fidelity stock back to the company for $2.2 million, and set out to New York to organize a new mutual fund of his own.

The movement he had had such a major role in starting toward a new, exciting, and dangerous conception of how to manage other people's money was by now a national groundswell. As mutual-fund asset values went up, new money poured in. Tsai and others like him seemed to have invented a money-making machine for anyone with a few hundred or several thousand dollars to invest. There were around three million holders of shares in standard mutual funds, and at the end of 1965 their holdings in those funds amounted to $33.5 billion. True enough, the holders were paying through the nose for the privilege of having their money managed by Tsai or the likes of Tsai; half of their first year's investment often went for the original sales commission, and in late 1966 the S.E.C. would indignantly declare these charges to be excessive. But that was after the market had dropped; as we have seen, reform is a frail flower that languishes in the hot glare of prosperity, and at the end of 1965 the S.E.C. remained silent. So, for that matter, did the customers themselves, and no wonder. Wiesenberger Reports announced that for the year, twenty-nine leading "performance" funds had averaged a net-asset-value rise of just over 40 percent, while the laggard Dow industrial average, made up not of swingers like Polaroid and Xerox but of old-line blue chips like AT&T, General Electric, General Motors, and Texaco, had risen only 15 percent. Here, then, was a new form of investment in which it appeared that by picking your fund at random you could still make 40 percent on your money in a year's time. The trick seemed to be to pay your front-end load, relax, and be happy. You got what you paid for—assuming, of course, what just about everybody did assume, that the Dow would appreciate annually around 15 percent and the performance funds 40 or 50 percent. It was the sort of assumption that is widely made only in times when people have taken leave of their senses.

A constellation of money-management stars rose swiftly around Tsai; some of the stars in that constellation will have roles, lightly or

not so lightly shaded, in the rest of our chronicle. There was Fred Alger, a mere thirty years old, of Security Equity Fund in New York: a man with one foot in the Establishment and one out, his stance perfectly symbolized in the career of his father, who was on the one hand a former U.S. ambassador to Belgium and on the other a former Detroit pol; himself a graduate of Yale, yet a favorite of the scapegrace international mutual-fund operator Bernard Cornfeld; a man with tousled hair and broad suspenders and quick reflexes whose widely publized fund set an industry performance record for 1965 by shooting up 77.8 percent. There was Fred Carr, not yet thirty-five, a veteran of the Ira Haupt-salad oil fiasco of November 1963, who had then done a stint in the Hollywood-style brokerage house of Kleiner, Bell, and who now sat in his Los Angeles office surrounded by antique furniture and op art, swinging his Enterprise Fund in and out of emerging (and, one might add, frequently merging) growth companies that nobody had previously heard of. "The Enterprise Fund," Carr professed in a pronunciamento aimed at his conservative competition, "will no longer trade an imposing building or pinstriped suit for capital gains." In Wall Street itself, there was Howard Stein, one-time violinist, eminence of the Dreyfus Fund, following in the footsteps of Jack Dreyfus, who in a decade had brought the fund's assets from $1 million to over $300 million, and showing, as Dreyfus had done, that people who stood at the dead center of the financial world—the imposing-building and pinstriped-suit set—could be light on their feet, too. These men, along with Tsai, were the early stars of the go-go years; and, at a time in the world's financial history when stock investment had become a milieu for the millions, they were becoming something like a new kind of national hero.

Moving half-consciously toward apotheosis, Tsai in late 1965 cleared his desk at Fidelity, said a deeply regretful good-bye to Edward Johnson and a more coolly casual one to Ned, and moved himself to New York to establish his own Manhattan Fund. He set about selling shares, at $10 each, to establish initial participation in his new enterprise and give him some assets upon which to work his presumed investment magic.

How many shares of Manhattan Fund would be sold before the official opening date, February 15, 1966? Tsai set himself on an original conservative goal of $25 million worth. But he far underestimated the extent to which he had captured the public imagination. It is possible to believe that more was at work than rational appraisal

based on Tsai's record. There was in the middle sixties an underground current of thought in the country that said the West had failed, that its rational liberalism was only a hypocritical cover for privilege and violence; that salvation, if possible at all, lay in the more intuitive approach of the East. Such ideas, to be sure, did not seem to have taken firm root among the kind of people who invest in mutual funds. But perhaps many of the original investors in Manhattan Fund, contemptuously as they might reject such ideas in their conscious thought, were reacting to them unconsciously when they decided to entrust their savings and thus a part of their future to Tsai. At all events, checks poured in to Manhattan Fund in a torrent. What would the opening total finally be, then? Not twenty-five but one hundred million? Or, unbelievable as it sounded, one hundred and fifty?

Not at all. On February 15, at the staid Pine Street offices of Manhattan Fund's staid bankers, the Chemical Bank, there took place the chief event of that season in American finance. Harold L. Bache, head of the firm that managed the Manhattan Fund offering, handed Tsai a check representing the proceeds of the sale and the original assets of his mutual fund. The sum inscribed on the check was $247 million. At the standard management fee of one-half of 1 percent per year, Tsai's new organization, called Tsai Management and Research, was starting life with an annual gross income of a million and a quarter dollars.

He was off and running on his own. As the magazine *The Institutional Investor* reported later, he

set up Manhattan Fund just like Fidelity Capital. He loaded it with all his big glamour favorites. To facilitate his chartist maneuverings, he built an elaborate trading room with a Trans-Jets tape, a Quotron electronic board with the prices of relevant securities and three-foot-square, giant loose leaf notebooks filled with point-and-figure charts and other technical indicators of all his holdings. Adjoining the trading room was erected "Information Central," so aswarm with visual displays and panels that slid and rotated about that it resembled some Pentagon war room. Three men were hired to work full time maintaining literally hundreds of averages, ratios, oscillators, and indices, ranging from a "ten-day oscillator of differences in advances and declines" to charts of several Treasury issues, to 25-, 65- and 150-day moving averages for the Dow. "We keep everything," [said] Walter Deemer, a former Merrill Lynch analyst and boss of Information Central who regards his charts the way an expert horticulturalist might regard a bed of prize geraniums. . ."

All the time there were ironies abounding. The social impartiality of the stock market, and the fact that the performance record of a mutual fund was as reducible to exact figures as a ballplayer's batting average—the factors that had worked in Tsai's favor when he had been an unknown Chinese boy knocking at panelled doors in a land far from home—had now turned into factors against him. He was on the spot, watched by a nation of investors and *expected* to make 50 percent profit a year on his customers' money. Less would be failure, and the fickle public would convert its hero overnight into a bum. And the timing of the situation was inexorably bad. The market was too high. The leather idol in Tsai's office was not a bull by accident. Temperamentally he was a bull himself, and therefore he needed an up market to keep winning. But by the greatest irony of all, he happened to start his own fund only a few weeks after the bull market of the nineteen sixties, as measured by the Dow industrials, had reached a peak that it would not reach again. So Tsai in 1966 rode unawares toward his fall.

Through its first two years, the Manhattan Fund, as well as the other smaller funds Tsai managed from his new independent stronghold, stayed popular with investors though they were generally undeserving of popularity. Away from Johnson's benign paternal surveillance, Tsai seemed to lose his stock-picking flair. After performing creditably in 1967, his funds took a beating in the tricky market of 1968; for the first seven months of that year, Manhattan Fund's asset value per share declined 6.6 percent, leaving it 299th among the 305 leading funds whose performances were regularly analyzed and compared by the brokerage firm of Arthur Lipper. But if Tsai no longer seemed to know when to cash in the investments he made for others, he knew when to cash in his own. In August 1968, he sold Tsai Management and Research to C.N.A. Financial Corporation, an insurance holding company, in exchange for a high executive post with C.N.A. and C.N.A. stock worth around $30 million.

Thus Tsai, just in time and in one stroke, joined the nearly big rich of America. As executive vice president and the largest individual stockholder of C.N.A., he turned over the running of Tsai Management and Research to others and devoted himself to heading C.N.A.'s acquisition program. As a fund manager, he was retired.

By a strange irony, he got rich in a way that would shortly be called illegal. In June 1971, Judge Henry J. Friendly of the U.S. Court of Appeals for the Second Circuit held that any profits from

sale of a mutual-fund management company belong not to the sellers of the managment company but the shareholders of the fund. The decision was a return to the traditional doctrine—from which, as we saw, Edward Johnson had benefited in acquiring Fidelity back in 1943—that a trustee may not traffic in his trust. Had the decision been in effect in 1968, Tsai wouldn't have been able to sell out.

CHAPTER 5

THE CONGLOMERATEURS

Nobody seems to know who first applied the term "conglomerate" to corporations given to diversifying their activities through mergers with other corporations in other lines of business. At any rate, the new usage made its popular appearance in 1964 or 1965, shortly before conglomerates became the darlings of investors. Derived from the Latin word *glomus*, meaning wax, the word suggests a sort of apotheosis of the old Madison Avenue cliché "a big ball of wax," and is no doubt apt enough; but right from the start, the heads of conglomerate companies objected to it. Each of them felt that *his* company was a mesh of corporate and managerial genius in which diverse lines of endeavor—producing, say, ice cream, cement, and flagpoles—were subtly welded together by some abstruse metaphysical principle so refined as to be invisible to the vulgar eye. Roy Ash of Litton Industries thought "conglomerate" implied "a mess" and pleaded for the term "multi-company industry" to describe Litton; Rupert Thompson hoped wistfully that people would speak of his Textron as engaging in "non-related diversification." In vain. Wide-based or narrow, stuck together by synergism or chewing gum, they were called conglomerates, and for a time, almost everybody made money on them.

The aversion of the *conglomerateurs* (as *The New York Times* social page called their leading lights) to the term is understandable. Conglomerates, like prostitutes, had from the first a sufficiently shaky moral reputation to call for the use of euphemism. During their most flourishing years (roughly 1966-69), they were said to represent, variously, a forward-looking form of enterprise characterized by freedom from all that is hidebound in conventional corporate practice; the latest of a long series of means by which "ruthless capitalists

practice the black arts of finance to their ends"; and "a kind of business that services industry the way Bonnie and Clyde serviced banks." Their increasing prevalence, for better or worse, is indicated by the simple fact that in 1968 about forty-five hundred mergers of U.S. corporations were effected—far more than in any previous year, and three times as many as in any given year early in the decade. Also in 1968, twenty-six of the nation's five hundred biggest companies disappeared, permanently, into the bellies of other corporate whales through conglomerate merger, twelve of the victims being monsters with assets in excess of $250 million, and several of these same leviathans being swallowed by predators far smaller than themselves.

The movement was new and yet old. In the nineteenth century, few companies diversified their activities very widely by acquiring other companies or by any other means. In the Puritan and craft ethic that for the most part ruled nineteenth-century America, one of the cardinal precepts was that the shoemaker should stick to his last. American companies were as specialized in their product lines as the vendors of dog collars and nutmeg graters in Victorian London; diversification was considered irresponsible if not a form of outright immorality, and when it occurred it usually did so inadvertently, as when the Western railroads found that the land they had acquired for settlement and track right of way made them proprietors of mines, oil wells, and forests.

Early in this century, some of the biggest companies took to diversifying from within—adding new products not closely related to their old ones simply because they had the resources and the machinery to do so. General Electric and General Motors were notable examples. Between 1925 and 1930 du Pont, which had previously pretty well confined itself to making explosives, ate such indigestible-sounding corporate morsels as the Viscoloid Company, National Ammonia, Krebs Pigment and Chemical, and Capes-Viscose. In a limited way, it was a pioneer conglomerate. It was during a new spell of general affluence in the nineteen fifties that the phenomenon of really uninhibited diversification first appeared. The results were the first genuine late-model conglomerates—but nobody had yet wrapped up the new packages in a catchy name. Among the first companies to be called conglomerates were Litton, which in 1958 began to augment its established electronics business with office calculators and computers and later branched out into typewriters, cash

registers, packaged foods, conveyor belts, oceangoing ships, solder, teaching aids, aircraft guidance systems, and Textron, once a placid and single-minded New England textile company, and eventually a purveyor of zippers, pens, snowmobiles, eyeglass frames, silverware, golf carts, metalwork machinery, helicopters, rocket engines, ball bearings, and gas meters.

Corporate affluence was only one element in the complex chemistry of the conglomerate explosion. Another was a decline of the stick-to-your-last philosophy among businessmen, parallel to a decline of the stick-to-anything philosophy among almost everyone else. Another was the rise in influence of the graduate business schools, led by imperial Harvard, which in the nineteen sixties were trying to enshrine business as a profession, and often taught that management ability was an absolute quality, not limited by the type of business being managed. Still another was the federal antitrust laws, which, as traditionally interpreted over the years, forbade most mergers between large companies in the *same* line of business and thus forced companies that wanted to merge at all to be, so to speak, exogamous.

But there was one more factor, less reputable and in economic terms more ominous, behind the trend. It was the fact that merging enabled a company to capitalize on its current stock-market value. The crux of the matter was that never before had a company's reported earnings per share meant so much in terms of its stock-market price. As we have seen, the average investor of the sixties was a comparative novice, interested in just three figures concerning a company whose stock he owned or was considering buying. One was the market price of the stock. The second was the net profit per share—the famous "bottom line" of the quarterly earnings report's financial summary (which, curiously, seldom actually appears at the bottom). Let the average nineteen-sixties investor be handed the latest annual report of his favorite company; his gaze would slide rapidly over the shiny four-color cover, over the glowing (but perhaps a bit glutinous) prose of the chairman's report, over the pictures of happy employees and earnest, manly executives, and would fix raptly on that bottom line. (It may come as a surprise to some modern investors to learn that this was not always so. During the boom of the nineteen twenties, the big news for both brokers and investors was more commonly dividends than earnings. High taxes on ordinary income, and favored tax treatment of capital gains, were the principal factors in bringing about an historic postwar shift in public attention from dividends to earnings.)

The third figure that engaged our investor's interest was, of course, the relationship between the other two. Called the price-to-earnings multiple, or ratio, its function was to give the investor a yardstick with which to judge whether the stock was a bargain or not. A multiple of ten was usually considered a bargain, while a multiple of forty might be (but often wasn't) thought to be too much. In the absence of his friendly broker, the average investor had to calculate the multiple for himself, a feat he could easily accomplish provided he had the two other figures and a command of short division. Making this calculation marked the outer limit of his investment sophistication.

Unfortunately, in the case of conglomerates this degree of sophistication was inadequate. Where a series of corporate mergers is concerned, the current earnings per share of the surviving company lose much of the yardstick quality that the novice investor so trustingly assumes. The simple mathematical fact is that any time a company with a high multiple buys one with a lower multiple, a kind of magic comes into play. Earnings per share of the new, merged company in the first year of its life come out higher than those of the acquiring company in the previous year, even though neither company does any more business than before. There is an apparent growth in earnings that is entirely an optical illusion. Moreover, under accounting procedures of the late nineteen sixties, a merger could generally be recorded in either of two ways—as a purchase of one company by another, or as a simple pooling of the combined resources. In many cases, the current earnings of the combined company came out quite differently under the two methods, and it was understandable that the company's accountants were inclined to choose arbitrarily the method that gave the more cheerful result. Indeed, the accountant, through this choice and others at his disposal, was often able to write for the surviving company practically any current earnings figure he chose—a situation that impelled one leading investment-advisory service to issue a derisive bulletin entitled, "Accounting as a Creative Art." All of which is to say that, without breaking the law or the rules of his profession, the accountant could mislead the naïve investor practically at will.

The conglomerate game tended to become a form of pyramiding, comparable to the public-utility holding company game that flourished in 1928, crashed in 1929, and was belatedly outlawed in the dark hangover days of 1935. The accountant evaluating the results of a conglomerate merger would apply his creative resources by writing an earnings figure that looked good to investors; they, reacting to the

artistry, would buy the company's stock, thereby forcing its market price up to a high multiple again; the company would then make a new merger, write new higher earnings, and so on. The conglomerate need neither toil nor spin—only keep buying companies and writing up earnings. It was magic, until the pyramid became top-heavy and fell.

James Joseph Ling, born in 1922 in Hugo, Oklahoma, of South German ancestry, had a rootless, drifting, poverty-ridden childhood during which he showed no special talent for anything much. At nineteen he arrived in Dallas and went to work as an electrician. In 1944 he joined the Navy and became an electrician's mate, stringing power lines and recovering equipment from sunken ships in the Philippines. Released from service in 1946, he went back to Dallas and, with $2,000 savings, set himself up in business as an electrical contractor.

Later he would say, in nineteen-sixties jargon, "I don't know what turned me on"—but assuredly something did. After several ups and downs, his little company grew to have an annual gross of $1.5 million. In 1955 he decided to sell stock in it to the public; when Wall Street underwriters just laughed at him, he and some associates sold the stock themselves, handing out prospectuses from a booth at the Texas State Fair. They peddled 450,000 shares at $2.25 each. The astonishing success of the venture was the turning point of Ling's life; he learned from it that pieces of paper can be exchanged for cash. Armed with the cash, he made his first corporate acquisition—LM Electronics, a West Coast firm on which his down payment was $27,500—and changed his own company's name to Ling Electronics. Thus the once and future king of conglomerators was on his way.

His deals over the succeeding decade were so complex, innovative, and ultimately bewildering that to describe them comprehensibly at book length would be a literary tour de force, and to describe them in a few words impossible. In essence, though, they were all geared to the crucial discovery that Ling had made at the Texas fair—that people like to buy stocks and that their overpayments for stock can be capitalized by the issuer to his advantage. His basic tool was leverage —capitalizing with long-term debt to increase current earnings. In 1958 he gained entry to Wall Street when White, Weld and Company undertook a private placement of Ling Electronics convertible bonds. Then the deals came faster and more bewilderingly. In 1959 he took over Altec, University Loudspeakers, and Continental Electronics; in 1960, Temco Electronics and Missiles (government contracts, the big

time now); in 1961, Chance Vought Corporation, an aviation pioneer. So overextended personally that at one point he had to sell all but eleven shares of his own company's stock, Ling nevertheless bulled ahead. By the end of 1962, he controlled an aerospace and electronics complex (by then called Ling-Temco-Vought) capable of competing for contracts with any other in the country. Then, in 1964, he suddenly launched what he whimsically called Project Redeployment, in which he began selling to the public shares in the companies he had acquired. It looked like a stunning reversal of policy but in fact it was more of the same—all part of Ling's basic scheme to take advantage of the public's and the financial institutions' insatiable appetite for common stocks. He would sell off, say, a quarter of the shares of a Ling-Temco-Vought subsidiary; the magic of Ling's name would propel the price of the shares well up in the market, and the three quarters that Ling had retained would be temporarily worth far more than it had been worth a few days or weeks before. A Wall Street man called Project Redeployment "getting something for nothing."

But it worked. In 1965, Ling-Temco-Vought ranked number 204 on the *Fortune* directory of the largest U.S. industrial companies; in 1967, 38; finally in 1969, 14. Net income per share—before allowing for dilution by all those convertible shares—nearly tripled in 1966 and then went up some 75 percent more in 1967. As a result, the market price of the company's stock, from the beginning of 1965 to the peak in 1967, multiplied more than ten times. Could there be any wonder that the huge new investing public loved it?

Ling at his peak was a mogul in the nineteenth-century manner, as lordly as a Vanderbilt or a Yerkes. At a reputed cost of over $3 million, he built himself an imperial mansion in Dallas, with a façade of Roman columns, a portico lined with classic statuary, bathrooms with gold faucets (an Italian marble bathtub worth $14,000 in one of them), and its own golf course. (His address, as listed in *Who's Who*—10,300 Gaywood Road—astonishingly conveyed the democratic suggestion that his pleasure dome was merely one of many). Inside the mansion was a collection of seventeenth-century books that their owner genuinely cherished without, in many cases, having the vaguest notion what was inside them. He was not above deceiving his guests. Once he met Oskar Morgenstern, the famous Princeton econometrician, and invited him to "a small dinner—five or six people." The dinner was for thirty, and after coffee Morgenstern, unwarned, found himself asked by his host to "say a few words." One did not refuse Ling in his house—nor

did one quibble about the terms under which one was inside it. Morgenstern complied.

In 1968 Ling embarked on his most ambitious venture and the one that, along with other factors, would eventually bring about his downfall. It was nothing less than the acquisition of Jones and Laughlin Steel, an old and solid member of American big business' traditional pantheon, for a cash tender offer of $425 million, the largest ever made by one company for another. But in 1967 the high school dropout and onetime dustbowl roustabout was a Caesar not only in his own eyes but in those of a majority of his corporate peers as well.

Meshulam Riklis, born in Odessa the same year Ling was born in Hugo, Oklahoma, grew up in pre-Israel Tel Aviv in comfortable circumstances, making such frequent and intricate deals with his playmates that they took to calling him derisively the Minister of Finance. He was no ordinary Jewish boy, but, it was sometimes maintained, an eighth-generation descendant of Baal-Shem-Tov, founder in eighteenth-century Poland of the celebrated ultra-orthodox Jewish sect called Hasidism. Nonreligious like his father—a Palestine businessman who had once been an officer in the Turkish army —Meshulam Riklis showed an early bent toward scholarship, leading his mother to hope fervently that he would get a Ph.D. and become a teacher. He did, for a time, become a teacher. Having served in the British army in wartime and later having lived for a while with his bride in a kibbutz, he came to the United States in 1947, graduated from Ohio State University in 1950, and then moved to Minneapolis, where he taught Hebrew at night and spent his days as a novice stock salesman for a local brokerage firm.

At the daytime occupation he made a quick success. Soon the rich Jews of Minneapolis were willing to finance him in independent ventures, and he began buying and combining small companies on a shoestring. He would line up backers to help him get control of Company A; then he would use the assets of Company A to take over Company B; and so on. In 1955 he took over a firm called Rapid Electrotype; in 1957 he merged it into another called American Colortype; and the combination, which was to be Riklis's key corporate vehicle thereafter, he named Rapid-American Corporation.

Naturalized in 1955 and a millionaire before the end of that decade, Riklis *was* Rapid-American in the flesh. In 1970 he told a reporter, "I am a conglomerate. Me, personally." He had built one and seen it

nearly fall before the term "conglomerate" had come into use. By 1962 his Rapid-American controlled McCrory Corporation, a combine of retail stores, and Glen Alden, a consumer-products company. After the market crash that year the empire found itself in a bad bind, and creditor banks demanded Riklis's resignation; he refused, the market recovered, the banks relented, and the crisis was weathered. And Rapid-American went on to new heights, adding companies to its holdings at a fast pace through the following years. Eventually Riklis came to control a complex with sales of $1.7 billion, including such well-known companies as International Playtex, B.V.D., Schenley Industries, Lerner Shops, and RKO-Stanley Warner Theatres. In 1966, at the height of this headlong expansion, Riklis did a characteristically unexpected thing—he went back to Ohio State for the summer and took a master's degree in Business Administration, writing his thesis on his own business career and methods.

Perhaps the most striking thing about Riklis as a conglomerator is the way he exploited his Jewishness rather than suppressing or ignoring it as so many Jewish businessmen in an alien culture had done before him. Once he began a pitch to a prospective lender with the taunt, "I understand you guys are anti-Semitic"—and got the loan. He was always ready with a dialect story, and his most famous saying—that Rapid-American owed its success to "the effective non-use of cash"—is perfectly in the tradition of rueful and realistic Jewish wit. Once, after a luncheon at the Bankers Club in Wall Street with an ex-partner of White, Weld, he described the occasion to a friend by saying, "I've never seen so many *goyim* in my life," and then went on to tell with what distaste he had eaten his first raw oyster. In making corporate acquisitions, he went almost exclusively for firms that were Jewish-controlled. Other Jews he felt he could deal with; what he prudently avoided was any confrontation with the Protestants. A man making his way, Riklis believed, had enough trouble without *that* complication. Yet the Jewish-American business world had by Riklis's time become a commodious one, and his self-imposed limitation scarcely cramped his style. "I will not go into the steel business," he once pronounced. "Jimmy Ling, he's entitled. He's got the right religion."

Charles Bluhdorn, also foreign-born, lacked Riklis's subtlety, wit, and streak of intellectuality; he was more nearly the traditional brash gambler who will bet with anybody on anything, and yet—like so many brash gamblers—he was a secret conservative, more cautious and cal-

culating than he wanted to seem. Several years younger than Ling and Riklis, he was born in Vienna, the son of a Czech-born importer, and came to the United States at sixteen, a refugee from Nazi anti-Semitism, in 1942. In his middle twenties he made his first million with a series of breathtaking deals in the commodities market. Of this period in his business life he would say twenty years later, when he was the head of a vast empire, "Today I wouldn't have the nerve." But he retained plenty of nerve in the sense of *chutzpah*. In 1957, just past thirty, he bought control of an automobile parts manufacturing company called Michigan Bumper. Bumpers moved slowly, and Bluhdorn's firm attracted no special attention; it entered the nineteen sixties with sales of $8.4 million and a small annual deficit. Eight years and more than eighty corporate deals later, his enterprise—by then famous to everyone who follows the stock market as Gulf and Western Industries—would have sales of $1.3 billion and net annual income of $70 million; over the same period its stock price multiplied twenty times, and Bluhdorn became known as the *enfant terrible* of the conglomerate scene—a distinction, from the business-Establishment point of view, somewhat comparable to being called the wickedest man in Hell.

Bluhdorn and Gulf and Western came late to conglomeration. In the first part of 1965 his was still essentially a small car-parts firm; but that year he managed to borrow $84 million from the Chase Manhattan Bank with which to buy control of New Jersey Zinc Company, the largest zinc producer in the country. After that, acquisitions followed at a dizzying rate: E.W. Bliss, Desilu Productions, South Puerto Rican Sugar, Consolidated Cigar, a mixed bag of others. Bluhdorn's rationale for diversifying so widely and so wildly was simple; he wanted, he explained, to be in a lot of different lines of business so that when hard times fell on one of them the others would serve as a counterbalance and pull the entire enterprise through. He was at less pains to point out that nearly all of Gulf and Western's acquisitions were made with debt and convertibles, meaning that this year's net profit was being inflated at the possible cost of next year's; or that Gulf and Western, until belatedly prodded by the S.E.C., neglected to point out to its stockholders and the public the potential dilution of their holdings that was inherent in the issuance of all that paper.

Undoubtedly Bluhdorn's acquisition masterpiece was Paramount Pictures in 1966. The company was in trouble, losing money on feature films, wary of plunging too deeply into large-scale television produc-

tion, propping up its earnings by selling off its assets. With no prior experience in motion-picture production, Bluhdorn personally took over as president and appointed a new management team charged with instituting new, bolder policies. For the short term, it was a case study of the conglomerate theory triumphant. In less than three years, Paramount became the hottest studio in Hollywood.

Bluhdorn at his most flamboyant was almost a parody of the hyper-thyroid business genius—fast-talking, with just enough Viennese accent to make him type-cast for his role: emotional, visionary, impatient, an artist at the work of business. Essentially a haggler on a grand scale, Bluhdorn gloried in his reputation as such. He was surely aware that in conservative circles such a reputation was deemed a business liability; indeed, a sympathetic investment banker once told him that his chief weakness was his inability to conduct himself according to accepted canons—his tendency to sputter, fume, and shout when only dispassionate facts were required. Another banker has since made the curious and suggestive criticism that in his corporate acquisitions for Gulf and Western, Bluhdorn frequently showed a lack of taste—not in the way he corralled them, but in his choice of companies to acquire. The concept of taste, as applied to a chief executive's choice of corporate acquisitions, may well merit some study by business students of the future.

In one important respect, Bluhdorn was constantly maligned. Almost universally considered to be among the wildest and most suspect of the conglomerators, and certainly in truth among the least restrained users of debt and convertible securities, he was guiltless of the principal offense usually alleged against his sand-castle breed, that of "buying" spurious earnings by taking over companies with price-to-earnings ratios lower than his own. The record shows that, on the contrary, Gulf and Western usually bought companies with ratios higher than its own, and thereby temporarily *reduced* its own earnings through its acquisitions. Even in the Paramount deal, Bluhdorn paid seventy times the movie company's current earnings; the multiple of Gulf and Western at the time was less than eight. As Arthur M. Louis pointed out in *Fortune*, during the decade of the sixties Gulf and Western bought high-multiple companies so often that the transactions, in themselves, actually reduced net earnings by almost $1.50 a share. Bluhdorn floated far too much corporate underwear, he often let his accountants play fast and loose, and probably he shouted too much on the telephone; but he bought companies because he believed in them, and through most of the decade Gulf and Western's "internal" growth—the old kind of

growth based on doing more business—averaged almost 20 percent a year.

Whether immigrants like Riklis and Bluhdorn, self-made natives like Ling and Eugene Klein, or Harvard Business School products like Roy Ash and Charles (Tex) Thornton, the conglomerators were all uninhibited free enterprisers, anti-organization men, throwbacks to the nineteenth-century age of individualism in American business. Like the old trusts that Theodore Roosevelt set out to bust, the conglomerates were essentially one-man or two-man companies. Like the robber barons, the conglomerators tended to collect art and otherwise flaunt their wealth (in contrast to the organization men of the previous decade, whose goal was not to excel or exceed but to fit in). James Ling's Dallas palazzo was far from the only conglomerator's marble showplace. Klein, a onetime used-car salesman who built the great West Coast conglomerate, National General Corporation, bought an old Beverly Hills mansion, spent a million and a half decking it out with Picassos, Modiglianis, and choice European antiques (a Marie Antoinette foot bath, two Lord Nelson mirrors, a desk set once owned by a czarina of Russia), and rode around in a $3-million corporate jet and a Rolls-Royce formerly owned by Queen Elizabeth II. In naming their enterprises, as in decorating their houses, the conglomerators showed a penchant for instant grandeur usually at the risk of bombast (Rapid-American, National General), but sometimes the names went in another direction, and suggested down-home folksiness, which investors also seemed to love. There was Minnie Pearl's Chicken System, Inc., later more austerely called Performance Systems; its stock rose wildly under the first name and dropped disastrously under the second. Sometimes it seemed as if the company namers deliberately injected just a hint of comic larceny, calculating, perhaps correctly, that the investing public and the money managers had a taste for such things.

An era of showoffs and shenanigans, then, of American enterprise parodying itself on a grand scale. But the conglomerate movement also had serious and dangerous consequences within the world of corporations. With Litton openly aiming at acquiring fifty companies a year and with dozens of lesser conglomerates eager for entry into the great world of conglomerate colossi, hardly any company anywhere in the country that had its stock on the market could feel safe from a takeover attempt at any time. As a result, executives who should have been devoting themselves to running their businesses

found it prudent and often necessary to neglect such duties and spend much thought and energy on the financial maneuvers and the information-gathering necessary to anticipate or repel raids by voracious conglomerates.

What with the arithmetic of stock multiples making it possible on occasion for smaller companies to take over much larger ones, size alone offered no protection. Every now and again, in the conglomerate era, a company minnow would successfully ingest a corporate whale, and the other monsters would tremble. Not until virtually the whole business community had been aroused in 1969 by the attempts of raffish Resorts International (formerly Mary Carter Paints) to take over Olympian Pan American World Airways, and of brash Leasco Data Processing to forceably marry matronly Chemical Bank, would the temporarily chastened conglomerates lose some of their appetite for prey bigger and more prestigious than themselves.

The defender against a hostile takeover was not without resources, however. On the contrary, a whole array of chesslike countermoves was available to him, and whole subdivisions of law and public relations sprang up overnight to devote themselves entirely to planning and executing such strategy. What came to be regarded as the classic defense was mounted in 1969 by B.F. Goodrich, the celebrated old-line rubber company, to foil a takeover attempt by Northwest Industries (clothing, pesticides, steel, and for a time the nation's only profitable commuter railroad, the Chicago and North Western). Goodrich changed its accounting methods so that its 1968 earnings appeared to have increased by $1.28 over 1967's, whereas under the old methods the increase would have been only forty-three cents. It achieved not one quickly planned merger of its own, but two. It bought newspaper ads to revile Northwest and its tactics. It changed its charter to provide for staggering the terms of its directors, so that regardless of who might own the stock, no aggressor could control the board for several years. Goodrich vigorously—or, in another view, ruthlessly—used its influence to get government intervention in both its home state, Ohio, and in Washington, and it did this so successfully that the Ohio attorney general issued an injunction against the merger, while the Department of Justice brought an antitrust suit to block it. The defense won; B.F. Goodrich, an unexpectedly formidable old monster when aroused, survived unconsumed.

And all the while individual people, as well as corporations, were being profoundly affected. The executives, particularly the top ex-

ecutives, of the captured companies were subject at worst to summary dismissal and at best to reshuffling and serious loss of morale. The economy and amour propre of whole communities became disrupted. Conglomerates' headquarters were mostly on the two coasts, and often enough their corporate victims resided in the cities in between. The result was the repeated reduction of mid-American cities' oldest established industries from independent ventures to subsidiaries of conglomerate spiderwebs based in New York or Los Angeles.

Finally, there is the profound question of the vast social and political power that conglomerates might derive, if they so wished, from their huge concentrations of wealth—and of how they might choose to exercise such power. For the most part, to all appearances, they chose not to try to exercise it at all. Or so it appeared until the largest of them all, International Telephone and Telegraph, began to emerge as a monstrous exception.

Founded in 1920 as a communications service company operating outside the United States, I.T.T. in 1960 was still essentially that, its business overwhelmingly overseas, its assets just under the $1-billion mark and its net annual income around $30 million. That year its new president—Harold S. Geneen, flinty, British-born but naturalized an American in childhood, then just fifty and already spoken of as one of the most brilliant executives in the nation —began remolding it into a conglomerate giant. Nine years and more than one hundred mergers later, I.T.T. had amassed assets of $4 billion; its net income, running at an annual rate of $180 million, had gone up for forty-one consecutive quarters; and it had become the eleventh largest American corporation. Because of the breadth and importance of its acquisitions, its hand seemed to be everywhere in the American marketplace. As *Time* pointed out in 1972, a consumer who became annoyed with I.T.T. would have a hard time boycotting it: "He could not rent an Avis car, buy a Levitt house, sleep in a Sheraton hotel, park in an APCOA garage, use Scott's fertilizer or seed, eat Wonder Bread or Morton's frozen foods. . . . He could not have watched any televised reports of President Nixon's visit to China. . . . [He] would have had to refuse listing in *Who's Who:* I.T.T. owns that, too."

Through the years of its growth under Geneen, I.T.T. had been generally thought of in the conservative business community as an atypical "good" conglomerate, its emphasis on real growth, its

337

takeovers nonhostile, its resorts to accounting tricks few. Even its stock-market performance was moderate by conglomerate standards; between the 1962 low and the 1968 high, its price hardly more than tripled. Even the style of its managers appealed to business conservatives. Taking their cue from the hard-driving and colorless Geneen, they refrained from building mansions or amassing art collections and devoted themselves with fierce dedication to unmitigated work. I.T.T. embodied the old Protestant ethic clad in new conglomerate clothes. It was the Establishment's conglomerate.

Not surprisingly, in view of these attitudes, I.T.T. was also the most Republican-oriented of conglomerates. And when, in 1969, after years of coexisting with Democratic regimes, it found itself with friends in power in Washington, I.T.T.—like so many earlier business enterprises that had found themselves in similar circumstances—seems to have lost its head and its Protestant ethic. Whether or not in 1971 it offered a contribution to the Republicans in exchange for a favorable settlement of a government antitrust suit remains in dispute (although the company's use of its now-famous paper shredder to destroy documents scarcely suggests a clear conscience). Most persuasive, however, is the clear evidence that in 1970 the company maneuvered—and offered to contribute $1 million—to block the election as president of Chile, where I.T.T. controlled the Chilean Telephone Company, of the Socialist Salvador Allende; or the evidence that, having failed to prevent Allende's election, I.T.T.'s self-designated proconsuls negotiated with the United States government at the White House level with a detailed plan, involving economic sabotage and the use of the Central Intelligence Agency, to bring about the overthrow of the Allende government.

The plan was turned down, but the damage was done. Here were shades of Manifest Destiny and gunboat diplomacy; here, naked and unashamed, was immense power without a sense of place, proportion, or responsibility, a planned attempt to enlist public officials to tamper with another nation's affairs in the cause of private profit. With the revelations, made in 1972 and 1973, I.T.T. came, with one stroke, to win the gold from General Motors as the ordinary man's prize symbol of consummate corporate arrogance and insensitivity. The sinister possibilities of conglomerates, including the multinational ones, for the first time exposed themselves to the public in a manner to cause not-soon-to-be-forgotten comment and concern.

Revitalizers of the moribund and modernizers of the obsolescent, or wreckers of lives, plunderers of cities, and meddlers in the affairs of nations, the conglomerates for a time made American boardrooms and executive suites into a takeover jungle where there were only the hunter and the hunted, and where fear and aggression dominated the world's greatest marketplace. But only for a time. It could not last, because—perhaps happily—the aggressors, sleek beasts of prey during the years of plenty, would soon be revealed as toothless tigers.

The start of the decline of conglomerates can be dated. By 1967 Litton Industries had become a gray eminence among conglomerates, its reputation impeccable, its stock soaring, its earnings rising steadily as they had been doing for a decade, its self-image so assured that it could decorate its annual report for that year with pictures of medieval stained glass "so that we may signify our respect and responsibility toward the achievements of the past." No market expert on Litton, whether in Wall Street or in the company itself, seems to have dared dream that profits might not continue to rise in 1968. But that January, when Litton's top officers met at the company's Beverly Hills headquarters, a totally unanticipated state of affairs was revealed. Several of the divisions were discovered, apparently for the first time, to be in serious trouble; as a result, profits for the quarter ending January 31 would, it now became clear, fail to rise at all, and in fact were headed substantially down. In simple words, business was decidedly off, and top management hadn't seen it coming.

When the public earnings announcement was made—21 cents profit a share against 63 cents for the same quarter the previous year—in the stock market it was, as a Wall Street pundit put it, the day the cake of Ivory soap sank. Litton stock dropped 18 points in a week, and within a month or so it had lost almost half of its peak 1967 value. Gulf and Western and Ling-Temco-Vought slumped in apparent sympathy, and the first tremors of panic shook the whole conglomerate world.

It wasn't all over by any means; there would be some wild conglomerate maneuvers and some soaring conglomerate shares in the two years ahead. But the era was on its way to its end when, in January 1968, it was shown for the first time that conglomerate management—even the best of it—could lose track entirely of the progress or regress of the far-flung enterprises it ostensibly controlled and thus fail utterly of its function. In short, the root theory of conglomeration might simply be wrong, its temporary success founded chiefly on the gullibility of the stock-buying public and its professional advisers.

CHAPTER 6

THE ENORMOUS BACK ROOM

It has become a commonplace for social commentators to say that 1968 was the year when the fabric of American life unravelled—when the moral ground shifted and quaked under American feet; when the political far left turned violent and took on ominous fieldmarks of the far right; when the democratic idealism and optimism of the mass of Americans seemed to become a delusion. In January, the U.S.S. *Pueblo*, on a mission of espionage, was seized in the Sea of Japan with its eighty-three-man crew by North Koreans, and so the mightiest nation in the world was humiliated both morally and physically by one of the smallest and weakest. In February, the Kerner commission on civil disorders, a formally constituted government body, affirmed what many Americans had uneasily come to suspect—that the black violence and riots of the previous year had been caused chiefly by a profound racism on the part of the white majority. In March—although it was not known until much later —American soldiers murdered hundreds of unarmed women and children at My Lai. At the end of that month, the then President made a personal confession of failure by withdrawing from candidacy for re-election. In April, Martin Luther King, Jr., was murdered; in June, Senator Robert Kennedy. In May at Columbia University, students made a public mockery of parental and educational authority while parents and teachers stood by and let them. In August, there was disheartening police violence attending the national convention of the Democratic Party in Chicago. In December, when the United States astronauts Borman, Lovell, and Anders became the first men to see the far side of the moon, there were many of their countrymen too stunned by the year's events to feel properly proud.

And while this systemic eruption of sores covered the body politic, Wall Street, an organ of barometric sensitivity, had its own convulsions and its own loss of grip and tone. The loss amounted, indeed, to perhaps the single most dramatic technical failure of the free-enterprise system on record anywhere.

It was the year Wall Street nearly committed suicide by swallowing too much business, and by compounding its own near-fatal folly by simultaneously encouraging more of the same. The pace of trading had been picking up in the latter months of 1967 as a new speculative binge—the second in the decade—began to take shape.

The average daily trading volume for 1967 on the New York Stock Exchange came to 10,080,000 shares, an all-time record by a wide margin—but not one destined to stand. Nineteen sixty-eight was to be the year when speculation spread like a prairie fire—when the nation, sick and disgusted with itself, seemed to try to drown its guilt in a frenetic quest for quick and easy money.

Trading volume was such as had never figured in any broker's wildest dream of avarice. During the week after the Johnson withdrawal, which the market considered highly bullish, the Stock Exchange set new volume records almost every day. April 10, 1968, was the first day in history when Exchange trading exceeded 20 million shares; before the year was out there had been five more 20-million share days, with a peak of 21.35 million on June 13. New investors and new money were coming into the market in torrents. During the first five months of the year, Merrill Lynch opened up over 200,000 new accounts; in other words, that winter and spring one American in every thousand—counting men, women, and children—opened a new brokerage account *with a single firm*. Brokers, of course, were reaping the harvest in commissions. Some of them had personal commission incomes for the year running to more than $1 million.

One million dollars income in a year, with no capital at risk —merely for writing orders for stock! It was enough to convince anyone that the Stock Exchange had indeed become Golconda revisited, that ancient city within whose portals all, according to legend, became rich, and so desirable was membership in the Exchange that the price of a seat rose from $450,000 in January to an all-time record in December of $515,000, topping even the peak prices of 1929.

As early as January, there began to be high cirrus cloud warnings that the back offices, the paper-handling departments of the brokerage firms, were in for a storm of trouble—that, as constituted, they were simply unable to process the new business, and that therefore, as Hurd Baruch of the S.E.C. would put it later, the best of times for Wall Street were in danger of becoming the worst of times. The main barometric measuring-device for the seriousness of back-office trouble was the amount of what Wall Street calls "fails." A fail, which might more bluntly be called a default, occurs when on the normal settlement date for any stock trade—five days after the transaction itself—the seller's broker for some reason does not physically deliver the actual sold stock certificates to the buyer's broker, or the buyer's broker for some reason fails to receive it. The reasons for fails in

most cases are exactly what one might expect: either the selling broker in his confusion can't find the certificates being sold on the designated date, or the buying broker receives them but in *his* confusion immediately misplaces them, or someone on one side or the other fouls up the record-keeping so that the certificates appear not to have been delivered when in fact they have been.

The rule of thumb in Wall Street in 1968 held that an acceptable level of fails on New York Stock Exchange transactions at any given time ("acceptable," the bemused observer must conclude, in relative terms) amounted to one billion dollars' worth. Let a mere billion dollars of the customers' money be more or less missing in Wall Street, the conventional wisdom went, and things were still within the ball park. Late in January, the fails level rose well above the figure, and the exchanges took action. Starting January 22, they and the over-the-counter market cut back daily trading hours by an hour and a half; closing time for an indefinite period became 2 P.M. instead of 3:30. The move—in retrospect an extremely timid one—was nevertheless made over loud opposition from a minority of the exchanges' governors. (The governors were brokers, and brokers, to say it right out, make money on heavy trading.)

In April, N.Y.S.E. fails were up to a level of $2.67 billion; in May, to $3.47 billion. All over Wall Street, committees were formed and recommendations made on the back-office problem, but nothing substantive was done. At last, when the fails level was up to $3.7 billion, the exchanges finally took a measure of drastic action themselves. Beginning on June 12, the securities markets were closed tight every Wednesday—a measure not used since 1929—in order to give the back offices a regular mid-week breather in which to make a stab at catching up. But the order for Wednesday closings was unaccompanied by such logical, if painful, further measures as a prohibition on advertising and promotion designed to bring in still more business, or on the hiring of still more salesmen and the opening of still more branch offices. The lure of new money and additional commissions was irresistible. Brokerage ads continued to fill the financial pages and the airwaves; new salesmen were hired, new offices opened. Wall Street had become a mindless glutton methodically eating itself to paralysis and death.

In December—when the bull market proceeded majestically to its climax, oblivious of all the cautious efforts of the wise men of Wall Street and the marginally stronger efforts of the scarcely wiser, but

certainly more detached, wise men of Washington—the fails levels climbed to a record high of over $4 billion. As never before, not in the fabled panics of 1873 or 1907 or even 1929, the American securities industry was in a state of total disarray.

It is time that we looked closely at the source of the trouble, the 1968 back office. Known informally, and suggestively, as "the cage," the back office was an unlovely and constricting place to work. In its role as the dirty and clanking machinery of Wall Street, unseen and taken for granted by stock salesmen and customers alike, it had no need, from a sales point of view, to be impressive or even humanly gracious in its physical appointments. It was often sparsely and frugally furnished with dilapidated tables in need of paint, chipped desks with drawer handles loose or missing, malfunctioning typewriters, and creaking swivel chairs with missing casters. In fulfillment of its sole purpose—to keep records and to move physically money and stock certificates in conformity with transactions made in the front office—it was subdivided into a bewildering variety of departments with such discouraging names as "receive and deliver section," "box and vault section," "box tickets," and "update stock record." Operating this complex machinery required the performance of a wide variety of small jobs, all routine. Pay was low —much below that for unskilled blue-collar work; the back-office worker's hope for a decent year's pay lay in the possibility (never a certainty) that the firm would have a good year and hand out big bonuses in December. Opportunity for advancement was slight. Annual back-office turnover ran around 50 or 60 percent.

Enter a 1968 Wall Street back office and what kind of atmosphere did a visitor find? A workaday, time-serving atmosphere, as might have been expected, the tedium of routine chores performed under close supervision relieved by a good deal of horseplay, grudgingly tolerated by the supervisors. The jokes revolved around a single theme: "Any idiot could do this job without straining himself." On a busy day the atmosphere was friendly, but on a slow one it was apt to turn mean—needling, veiled insults, not-so-veiled racial slurs. (By this time, a good number of back-office employees were black.) As a social unit, the back office was much like an army platoon, its morale high when there is a job to do and low when there is time to waste. And the supervision of the back office was often patterned closely on military command. At Merrill Lynch, in the interest of keeping good

order, back-office employees were told when to take their lunch breaks, and sometimes even marched to the rest rooms under supervision. Small wonder that they complained about being treated like children.

It is fair to say, then, that Wall Street in 1968, like the sweatshop owners of an earlier time, had cut its own throat through its complacency, greed, and lack of foresight. And yet the solution was easy only in theory. Two clear-cut steps might have prevented the whole mess: automation of back-office operations and elimination of stock certificates. As to the first, it would have required a degree of planning, and an amount of capital outlay, that Wall Street in 1966 and 1967 clearly had not been able to muster. The second step, elimination of stock certificates, called for something more than planning or expense, and something that perhaps no amount of wisdom could have accomplished—finding a way of persuading the cautious and possession-proud American stockholder that a monthly statement from his broker showing his holdings was an adequate substitute for the embossed stock certificates that he kept locked so lovingly in his bank safe-deposit box.

Immediate elimination of certificates was, for all practical purposes, a mirage. And, of course, once the back-office crisis had fairly begun it was not even that. Who would suddenly begin to trust in a broker's records as evidence of ownership at a time when those records were in such a state that the broker could not trust them himself?

In mid-1968, the Stock Exchange made a good, but far too late, effort to ease the situation through automation. Eventually, the Central Certificate Service would get its bearings and become a useful service. But in the time it was needed most, its first months of operation in early 1969, the facility intended to eliminate brokerage back-office problems became, instead, one more monstrous back-office problem itself.

The key Wall Streeters of the 1968 crisis were the back-office employees themselves. They were young—seventeen to twenty-five in most cases; they were high-school graduates or dropouts. Few had attended college even for a year. They were quite thoroughly mixed as to sex and race; white male supremacy in Wall Street, at the clerk level, had yielded to social change and practical necessity. A solid majority, nevertheless, were white, coming from the near suburbs or the city boroughs other than Manhattan.

A brilliant and dedicated observer—John W. Faison of the Wall Street Ministry, formerly a sales executive of Allied Chemical —adopted in the latter part of 1968 a classic investigative technique to the study of the goals, problems, and aspirations of back-office people. He, and four students working with him, took clerical jobs in back offices themselves.

Faison's first conclusion, based on his firsthand back-office experience, was that "we are all playing in a new ball game: this goes for Wall Street as for the universities, the political conventions, the cities, the unions. People in all their associations are calling for new rules and the umpires cannot call 'safe' and 'out' the way they could a few years ago." For example, those familiar old forces so long so helpful to business management in getting the most possible work out of low-level employees—company loyalty and personal competitiveness—scarcely seemed to operate on the new breed of back-office employees at all. Faison found that their loyalty was chiefly to themselves, and that it consisted almost entirely in a desire to do the job decently and to appear knowing in their own eyes and in those of their colleagues. There it stopped. Generally, Faison found, the back-office employee "does give a day's work and that's as far as loyalty does or should go in his eyes."

Faison found a pervasive mood of disappointment. The clerks would put up with unlovely and overcrowded working quarters, and even with overwork; such things they could understand and accept. What they could not understand or accept was the sense of not, after all, being where the important things were happening—the sense of being segregated out of sight, brushed under the rug.

Meanwhile the back-office supervisors seem to have had no idea that it was a new ball game, and went on calling "safe" and "out" in the old way. They could not understand why their charges did not feel company loyalty or want to compete for advancement. Nor could they understand why the clerks felt an absolute right to joke and talk while working, or why measured praise for work well done was received with cynicism. Faison told later of a teletype man who was praised by his supervisor for his fast and efficent work on the previous day. "That and a token will get me home on the subway," the teletypist retorted and turned back to his work. When the supervisor had left, the teletypist turned to Faison, who was working next to him, and said, "Some day I'm going to give him an honest answer. The reason my figures were good was that we were talking the whole

day. If you do nothing but this dum-dum job all day you make mistakes out of . . . out of . . . well, I don't know out of what, but you make mistakes."

In their frustration and boredom, back-office employees found satisfaction in asserting their individuality through constantly discussed outside hobbies and eccentricities, through acquiring nicknames like Damon Runyon's Broadway characters: Surfin' Sally, Harry the Handicapper, Poolroom Marty. "I have borrowed a word from the hippies, and call these interests 'things,'" Faison wrote. "When the subject came up for discussion, the final word belonged to the clerk who had this or that as his 'thing.' The 'thing' was more important than the job, the office, the company. It got the possessor status. . . . The clerk who attacked a 'thing' made an instant enemy. If he wanted to stay inside the gang, he made amends and recognized his colleague's 'thing' at the earliest possible opportunity. But what does this tell us of his job, if his major commitment is to some 'thing'?"

The back office was an old story, then, told before by Dickens and Charles Chaplin, among others; a story of "young people risking what are to them the golden years," as Faison put it, and getting their return chiefly in frustration. But the old story now had an entirely new twist. Its characters were different. The young people this time were the new breed of human beings born since World War II: born, that is, as no one had ever been born before, not knowing a world without television, or jet travel, or automation, or nuclear weaponry; and knowing only by hearsay, if at all, of a world with the shared standards, conventions, and assumptions that had been undermined and finally destroyed by too-rapid technological change. Their belief in having an understanding of the climate of the modern world that their elders could never share was characteristic of the back-office people. As well expect them to feel loyalty to the company or be sincerely pious about small errors in accounts, as ask a modern scientist to devote his life to alchemy.

When at length the back-office crisis passed, it did so without benefit of the wisdom of either Wall Street or Washington. During a wild December, the fails level peaked out at the all-time high—$4.12 billion. Nevertheless, beginning on January 2, 1969, the exchanges resumed a five-day trading week with 2 P.M. closings. Wall Street at the turn of the year had tried all such remedial measures as it was willing and able to make, and they had all failed.

It was saved, not for the first time, by a *deus ex machina*. The end of the crisis was coming, and coming in its own way in its own time. In January, prices and volume both dropped sharply on the Stock Exchange, average daily trading from 15 million shares to 12 million, the Dow industrials from the December peak of 985 to the 920-930 range. The fails level responded by dropping 20 percent to $3.3 billion. In February, volume dropped to 11 million shares a day, the Dow to below 900, fails to below $3 billion. By the end of March, fails were down below $2.5 billion; in June the Dow sank to 870, in July almost to 800. Starting early in July, the exchanges began lengthening their daily trading hours, in thirty-minute stages, until closing time was back to 3:30.

The back-office crisis was over, ended less by reason and intelligence than by the advent of a bear market destined to bring new and unforeseen crises.

CHAPTER 7

CONFRONTATION

Spring of 1969 in the business world was a time of Davids and Goliaths: of threatened takeovers of venerable Pan American World Airways by upstart Resorts International, for example, and of venerable Goodrich Tire and Rubber by upstart Northwest Industries. As we have seen, such brazen challenges to the long-established and mighty by the newly arrived and aggressive were made possible by a vast, if temporary, popularity in the stock market of the shares of young and fast-growing companies; whether the threatened takeovers represented, on the one hand, constructive efforts to bring legitimacy to vested power, or, on the other, irresponsible acts of unprovoked assault by ravenous treasury raiders, is still being debated. Undoubtedly, though, the David-and-Goliath act of early 1969 that most caught the popular imagination was an attempt upon the century-and-a-half-old Chemical Bank New York Trust Company (assets a grand $9 billion) by the eight-year-old Leasco Data Processing Equipment Corporation of Great Neck, Long Island (assets a mere $400 million), a company entirely unknown to almost everyone in the larger business community without a special interest in either computer leasing, Leasco's principal business until 1968, or

in the securities market, in which its stock was a star performer. In that takeover contest, the roles of Goliath and David were played, with exceptional spirit, by William Shryock Renchard of Chemical and Saul Phillip Steinberg of Leasco.

William Renchard, the leader of Chemical, grew up in Trenton, New Jersey, where his father served as an agency manager for the New York Life Insurance Company. Trenton in the nineteen twenties, when Renchard was in his teens, was a characteristic old city of the Eastern Seaboard, already dominated in numbers by recent immigrants and light industry, yet in power and influence still controlled by an American squirearchy looking backward with nostalgia and pride to a historic past.

After graduating from Trenton High School, Bill Renchard, like most reasonably well-off Trenton boys, aspired to go to Princeton; unlike many high-school boys in the days when Princeton still leaned strongly toward preparatory-school graduates, he made it. At Princeton he shared a room on campus with his brother John, quietly did his academic work, joined one of the many eating clubs, and took no part in the extracurricular activities that were the recognized pathways to standing on campus.

However self-contained, Renchard was a tall, alert young man with an emergent air of command, and he was among those late bloomers who in adult life humble the social winnowers and sorters of their undergraduate classes. After graduation in 1928, he went to New York City and landed a job as clerk with the National Bank of Commerce. In 1930, he moved to the Chemical Bank and Trust Company, as it was then called, where he served successively as a clerk, an assistant secretary, and an assistant vice president. By 1946, when he was thirty-eight, he was a full-fledged vice president; in 1955 he became executive vice president; in 1960 he was made president, and in 1966 chairman of the board of the same institution, which was by this time called the Chemical Bank New York Trust Company. When Renchard became Chemical's chairman, the bank had $9 billion in assets—one of the nation's largest capital pools—and was the nation's sixth largest commercial bank.

Renchard's rise to this pinnacle of American banking had been accompanied by marriage to a pretty and sociable woman; a move to New York banking's favorite living quarters, the north shore of Long Island; directorships in half a dozen large corporations; trusteeships of various hospitals and civic groups; and membership in a substan-

tial list of metropolitan and country clubs, including the famous Creek Club in Locust Valley, of which he became president. In 1969, at sixty-one, Renchard seemed to have become the prototypical old-style Princetonian, radiating the essence of gentlemanly aggressiveness, of polite personal and professional leverage.

Saul Phillip Steinberg came from a background similar to Renchard's in only one respect—the families of both were firmly entrenched members of the American petit bourgeoisie. To begin with, Steinberg was a full generation Renchard's junior. Born in Brooklyn in August 1939, the son of Julius Steinberg, proprietor of Ideal Rubber Products, a small-scale manufacturer of such objects as kitchen dishracks, Steinberg, at high school in Lawrence, Long Island, was an unexceptional boy—an average student, an enthusiastic dater of girls, a competent but less than dedicated athlete—who was set apart from his classmates chiefly by the fact that he was a precocious subscriber to and regular reader of the *Wall Street Journal*. After high school, he went to the Wharton School of Finance and Commerce at the University of Pennsylvania. At Wharton—a senior at nineteen, precocious, brash, with a round babyface—Steinberg experienced a species of commercial epiphany. One of his instructors suggested that he write his senior thesis on "The Decline and Fall of I.B.M."

"My instructor was sure I.B.M. was some kind of fandangle," Steinberg told the writer Chris Welles a decade and many millions of dollars later. "And he wanted me to go out and prove it. I was the kind of student who was prepared to believe anything was bad, so I accepted the assignment. After I had gotten into it and done a lot of research, I discovered that . . . I.B.M. was an incredible, fantastic, brilliantly conceived company with a very rosy future. But when I told him this, he wouldn't believe me. He wouldn't even look at my research. So I ended up having to write on another subject."

Steinberg's scorned and discarded research left him with the conviction that I.B.M.'s method of doing business allowed a shining opportunity for a bright, ambitious young man to make a lot of money, and that he was the young man. The basic question involved was the effective life of industrial computers before they became obsolete, and the opportunity lay somewhere in the fact that nobody precisely knew the answer. I.B.M., which dominated the computer-making business, took the sort of conservative view that is characteristic of giant corporations riding the crest of a wave. Assuming that any given computer would become obsolete sooner rather than later, it

offered its customers short-term leases, usually cancellable on short notice, for high rental rates. Steinberg proposed to offer computer-using corporations the opportunity to save money by gambling that I.B.M.'s equipment would have a longer useful life than I.B.M. itself appeared to assume. He would borrow money and buy I.B.M.'s immensely expensive computers outright; he would then lease them out—long-term and uncancellable—at rates that would be substantially below I.B.M.'s own rental charges, but still high enough so that he would recover most or all of the cost of the computer during the longer, uncancellable term of its initial lease. Thus, in the simplest terms, Steinberg would have got his purchase money back and still have the purchased computer itself left over to sell or lease again.

In 1961, with $25,000 supplied by his father, he started his computer-leasing business in a Brooklyn loft with his father and his uncle as nominal partners, and his company name—Ideal Leasing Company—cribbed from his father's rubber-goods business. Banks, however wary of his extreme youth and his too-bright-schoolboy manner, liked his scheme and were willing to advance him money to buy computers provided he had leasing customers for them. It took him three months to get his first lease; he interrupted his honeymoon to come home and sign it. Ideal Leasing was incorporated in 1962; at the end of its first corporate year it had net income of $55,000 on revenues of $1.8 million. In 1964, when earnings were up to $255,000 and revenues to $8 million, Steinberg decided to go public. In June 1965, the company's name was changed to Leasco Data Processing Equipment Corporation and a public sale of Leasco stock brought in $750,000.

The computer business was booming, I.B.M. continued charging high rates for cancellable leases, and Leasco's assets leaped from $8 million in 1965 to $21 million in 1966, while profits in 1967 were more than eight times those for 1966. Meanwhile, the stock, traded first over the counter and later on the Amex, soared upward. Leasco began to be talked about in Wall Street as one of those interesting little situations. As might be expected of a young company with ambition, a voracious need for cash, and a high price-to-earnings multiple, Leasco became acquisition-minded. In 1966, Steinberg hired Michael A. Gibbs, a young whiz from the management-consulting firm of Booz, Allen and Hamilton, as vice president for corporate planning, and gave him the specific assignment of hunting up candidates for merger. In 1966 and 1967, Leasco increased its corporate

muscle by buying several small companies in fields more or less related to computers or to leasing: Carter Auto Transport and Service Corporation, Documentation, Inc., and Fox Computer Services. These acquisitions left the company with $74 million in assets, more than eight hundred employees, larger new headquarters in Great Neck, Long Island, and a vast appetite for further growth through mergers.

The events leading to the merger that put Leasco firmly on the national corporate map began in August 1967, when Edward Netter, of the deal-making brokerage firm of Cater, Berlind and Weill, came out with a report entitled "Financial Services Holding Company," in which he set forth the rosy possibilities available to both sides in mergers between companies engaged in financial services, such as Leasco, and fire-and-casualty insurance companies. The nub of Netter's argument was that the ultraconservative financial policies of the fire-and-casualty companies had in many cases resulted in cash-heavy reserves far in excess of those required by law to cover policy risks. Netter was pointing out—in the hope of earning finder's fees and brokerage commissions for his own firm—that ambitious diversified companies were missing a chance to better their circumstances by not marrying fire-and-casualty companies for their redundant capital—or, more bluntly, for their money. Many diversified companies were to acquire insurance companies over the following years, the greatest such merger (and indeed, the greatest merger in corporate history) being the celebrated and controversial wedding between International Telephone and Telegraph and Hartford Fire in 1970.

One of the numerous desks the Netter report crossed, not by chance, was in the offices of Leasco, and near the end of 1967, Netter met with Gibbs to discuss the views expressed in it. Netter evidently got an enthusiastic reception, because, early in January 1968, Gibbs sent a memo to Steinberg setting forth in detail the considerable advantages to Leasco of acquiring a fire-and-casualty company—no specific company was mentioned—and the same day Arthur Carter of Carter, Berlind and Weill wrote to Leasco setting forth the brokerage firm's terms for handling the acquisition of such a company (still not named) through a tender offer to the insurance company's stockholders. The terms stated included a finder's fee to Carter, Berlind of $750,000, making abundantly clear why Carter, Berlind was going to so much trouble to serve as marriage broker.

351

It subsequently became equally clear that the unnamed firm Carter, Berlind had in mind was Reliance Insurance Company, a staid old Philadelphia-based fire-and-casualty underwriter with more than five thousand employees, almost $350 million in annual revenues, and a fund of more than $100 million in redundant capital.

In March 1968, preserving security by trading through a numbered bank account at the First National Bank of Jersey City, Leasco began buying Reliance stock on the open market in daily quantities of anywhere from one hundred to more than seven thousand shares. By early April, Leasco held 132,600 Reliance shares or about 3 percent of all shares outstanding, and had completed Phase One of the takeover. Phase Two consisted of preparing a tender offer to Reliance shareholders, and contriving to overcome any resistance that the Reliance management might mount. In May, Leasco prepared a registration statement for its tender offer—a move that brought matters out into the open. Since the statement was necessarily a public document, the public, and Reliance management, now knew at last what Leasco had in mind. On June 13, Steinberg and A. Addison Roberts, president of Reliance, met for the first time, and Roberts stated in the clearest possible terms that Reliance would be unreceptive to a Leasco takeover attempt. Nevertheless, on June 21 Leasco went ahead with its tender offer, writing Reliance stockholders and offering them Leasco convertible debentures and warrants—a classic bundle of those often dubious securities that we have heard derogated as "corporate underwear," but still a bundle that, because of the high price of all Leasco securities, had a current market value well above the current price per share of unswinging Reliance—in exchange for their Reliance stock. Three days later, Roberts, still defiant, wrote to Reliance stockholders strongly urging them "to take no hasty action with respect to your stock," and the following day he capped that action by filing a lawsuit (later withdrawn) against Leasco and its brokers, charging them with violations of the securities laws.

On the surface, it looked to be total corporate war. In retrospect, however, it appears that Roberts, for all his crustiness toward Leasco, was never entirely adverse to a merger, and that what passed for furious self-defense was really something more akin to canny negotiation. On August 1, Roberts declared himself. Leasco, he wrote the stockholders, had sweetened the terms of its offer somewhat, and Reliance management had "agreed to discontinue taking any action to

impede." By mid-September Leasco had over 80 percent of Reliance; by mid-November it had over 96 percent. The takeover was complete.

Truly—to change the metaphor—it was a case of the minnow swallowing the whale. Reliance was nearly ten times Leasco's size, and Leasco, as the surviving company, found itself suddenly more than 80 percent in the insurance business and less than 20 percent in the computer-leasing business. Nor did the whale seem to have been hurt by the ingestion; indeed, at first glance everyone concerned seemed to be decidedly better off. Roberts, still boss of Reliance although now under Leasco's control, came out with a fresh five-year employment contract at his old salary of $80,000 for the first four years and a raise to $100,000 in the fifth, plus a generous portion of potentially lucrative Leasco stock options. Saul Steinberg came out a multimillionaire at twenty-nine, said by *Forbes* magazine to have made more money on his own—over $50 million, on paper—than any other U.S. citizen under thirty. As for Leasco, as a result of its extraordinary feat it suddenly had assets of $400 million instead of $74 million, net annual income of $27 million instead of $1.4 million, and 8,500 employees doing business in fifty countries instead of 800 doing business in only one. In stock-market terms, as of December 31, 1968, the price of Leasco stock had, over the five years preceding, appreciated by 5,410 percent, making it the greatest percentage gainer of all the five hundred largest publicly owned companies during that period: in sum, the undisputed king of all the go-go stocks. But our tale of financial derring-do is not yet ended; rather, it is only begun. Adventurous Leasco was now poised for the decade's greatest, and to defenders of the status quo most disturbing, venture in corporate conquest.

As early as December 1967, Leasco began looking into the possibility of acquiring a large bank. The stocks of banks, like those of insurance companies, often sold at low price-to-earnings multiples, giving a stock-market high-flyer like Leasco the leverage it needed to take over companies larger than itself. Moreover, Steinberg felt, as a business principle, that it would be advantageous to anchor Leasco's diversified financial services to a New York money-center bank with international connections. It appears that during 1968, at the very time when the Reliance takeover was in process, Gibbs's corporate planning department at Leasco was picking out a banking target as

carefully as a bomber command draws a bead on an enemy ammunition dump.

By the fall, when the Reliance acquisition was all but wrapped up, the gaze at Great Neck had come to light on Renchard's $9-billion Chemical Bank. A code name was assigned for inter-office use—in this case, "Faye," as in Faye Dunaway. As a first step in Leasco's campaign, an elaborate dossier on the history and operations of the prospective target was prepared: "Faye was originally the banking arm of New York Faye Manufacturing Company," and so on. *Who's Who* entries of "Faye" directors were reproduced for ready reference, along with annotations. It was convenient for Leasco—and it tells something about the two firms—that practically all of Faye's directors had long entries in *Who's Who*, while no directors of Leasco at the time were listed there at all.

The scenario that had been so effective in the case of Reliance was followed as closely as possible. In November, Leasco began buying Chemical stock. Within a few days, 50,000 shares were quietly bought at a cost of more than $3.5 million, without giving rise to untoward rumors or market disruptions. Meanwhile, Reliance, now a Leasco subsidiary, held more than 100,000 additional shares, giving Leasco control of well over 1 percent of all Chemical shares outstanding. In January 1969—still maintaining strict security, and still, of course, with no contact established between the executives of Leasco and those at Chemical—Leasco proceeded to prepare a hypothetical tender offer to Chemical stockholders. Still, Leasco had not yet decided to go ahead with the offer when, on the last day of January, Chemical through its regular intelligence channels finally got firm word that Leasco was preparing a takeover attempt.

The news did not catch Renchard completely by surprise. As early as December 1967, Chemical had begun following Leasco's acquisition activities in a wary, if desultory, way, and the following autumn Renchard had begun to hear rumors that "a leasing company" was interested in acquiring the bank. Rather astonishingly, the November purchases of Chemical stock went entirely unnoticed, no one at Chemical caught so much as a whisper of the code name "Faye," and the rumors seem to have died down. However, on getting the first firm information on January 31, Renchard was in no doubt as to Chemical's response. He and his bank were going to fight Leasco with all their strength.

Renchard went into vigorous if belated action. He set up an

eleven-man task force to devise strategy for fighting off any such takeover attempt, under the direction of Chemical's chief loan officer, J. A. McFadden—"a bright fellow, good at figures," as Renchard described him later, "not exactly a tough guy, but no pushover, either." He assigned another bank officer, Robert I. Lipp, to prepare a memo outlining all of the possible defensive strategies available to Chemical, and on February 3 Lipp came through with a list of seven different courses of action. (Out in Great Neck, almost at the same moment, Leasco was putting the finishing touches on its proposed tender offer, and was making further extensive purchases of Chemical stock—to be precise, 19,700 more shares at a cost of $1,422,207.) Renchard said long afterward, "At that time we didn't know how much of our stock they had, or what kind of a package of wallpaper they were going to throw at our stockholders in their tender offer. We were guessing that they would offer stuff with a market value of around $110 for each share of our stock, which was then selling at 72. So we knew well enough it would be tough going persuading our stockholders not to accept."

On February 5, Renchard made his move, and a drastic and risky one it was. He decided to force Leasco out into the open by giving a story to the press. That afternoon, H. Erich Heinemann, banking specialist on *The New York Times'* financial reporting staff, telephoned him to say that he had heard rumors of an impending takeover attempt and to inquire whether there was anything in them. Rather than make the routine denial that he would have made under ordinary circumstances, Renchard replied that there was, indeed, something in the rumors. He went on to give a few details and some pointed comments, and the following morning *The Times* carried a piece, under the by-line of Heinemann's colleague, Robert Metz, who had developed his story independently:

Can a Johnny-come-lately on the business scene move in on the Establishment and knock off one of the biggest prizes in sight?

That, it appears, is what the Leasco Data Processing Equipment Corporation hopes to do next in its dynamic acquisition program. The rumored target is one of the nation's most prestigious banks, the Chemical Bank New York Trust Company, founded in 1824. . . .

Try and get confirmation that something is going on . . . and you get nothing. In fact, Leasco's public relations people called to get a statement from the reporter.

Is Chemical in the bag? Hardly. William S. Renchard, chairman of the

Chemical Bank, sounded like a Marine Corps colonel in presenting his battle plan for what he believes may well develop. . . . He said, "We intend to resist this with all the means at our command, and these might turn out to be considerable."

Understandably, the article was the talk of the banking world that day. Renchard went on with his planning, holding new strategy sessions at which one of the possibilities discussed, as phrased in a memo prepared for one of the meetings by McFadden, was the following: "There is some question about the breadth of the market on the Leasco stock and it might be possible to attack its value if need be."

Such an "attack"—carried out by making sales or short sales of Leasco stock over an extended period—would hit Leasco where it lived, since its high stock price was the source of its power and, above all, of the possibility of its taking over a firm like Chemical that was many times Leasco's size. The difficulty lay in the fact that such an attack—a bear raid—would constitute stock manipulation and would be a violation of the securities laws punishable by fines and imprisonment. For obvious reasons, no one has ever been willing to say that at Chemical's February 6 strategy meeting that particular recommendation was adopted for action. The striking and undeniable fact is, however, that on that very day, Leasco stock, which had been hovering in the stratosphere at around 140, abruptly began to fall in price on large trading volume. By the close of the next day Leasco was down almost seven points, and over the following three weeks it would drop inexorably below 100. Rumors of impending mergers, particularly between titans, customarily drive a company's stock price *up*, not down. Long afterward, Steinberg said of the curious coincidence in timing as to the proposed Chemical takeover and the beginning of the Leasco slide, "It *is* odd—so odd that Congressman Wright Patman asked me the same question. But we've never been able to pin anything down." As for Renchard, he later told a Congressional committee that he thought the stock drop was simply the result of institutional holders beginning to lose confidence in Leasco; but still later than that, he pointed out, without elaboration, that one of the defensive techniques discussed in the Chemical strategy meetings had been drawn from a *Harvard Business Review* article called "multiple flogging." "Multiple flogging," in the context, was a fancy new name for an old-fashioned bear raid. By using various concealment devices, it is theoretically

possible to carry out a bear raid without detection by the authorities. The evidence suggests, at least, that on February 6 somebody, identity unknown, started lowering a very heavy boom on Leasco.

On Friday, February 7, the day after the *Times* article, Steinberg had lunch with Heinemann. By Steinberg's account the timing was pure coincidence, since the lunch had been arranged weeks before; it was, however, an obvious windfall for Heinemann as a reporter to be seeing Steinberg at the very moment when the meteorically successful boy wonder was at the center of the biggest financial story in the nation. At the lunch, Steinberg insists that he first made certain it was understood that everything was off the record; then he proceeded to discuss Leasco's plans freely, not to say indiscreetly. When he had finished, he asked Heinemann, as a man knowledgeable about banking, for his impressions. According to Steinberg, Heinemann replied that in believing for a moment that he could get away with taking over Chemical Steinberg showed himself to be "an innocent." At any rate, Steinberg later decided that he had been an innocent about Heinemann. That afternoon, Heinemann called up the Chemical Bank and talked to a public-relations officer there, to whom he reported in detail what he had heard from Steinberg. That afternoon, the public-relations officer sent Renchard a memo that read, in part:

Heinemann just came back from lunch with Steinberg, and passed on the following results.

They said they are beginning to feel the pressure. They knew there would be absolute opposition, and they fully believe that when they come in with their proposal it will be rejected. . . .

Erich was told that it is a better than 50-50 chance that Leasco will announce their intentions and plan at the annual meeting next week. Steinberg took the position that their offer will be most beneficial for us. . . . Steinberg said flatly that the way we handle international business . . . is wrong and will be changed.

(Heinemann's version of the episode differs from Steinberg's in several crucial respects. In the first place, he said later that his luncheon with Steinberg had not been arranged weeks previously but only four days before—at the urgent request of Steinberg's public-relations counselor. Moreover—and more crucially— Heinemann avows that at the luncheon he was not asked for and did not give any assurance that what was said be held confidential,

and that he subsequently called Chemical, as a conscientious reporter, in an attempt to elicit additional information for a possible new
story.)

Steinberg said later that the memo gave a generally accurate account of what he had said at the lunch, with the notable exception
that he had said nothing about pressure—that, indeed, he had felt no
pressure from banks at that time, although he was to feel plenty of it
later on. The nearest thing to pressure on Leasco as of February 7
was a conversation Steinberg had that day with Donald M. Graham,
chairman of Continental Illinois Bank and Trust Company, a leading
Leasco creditor, in which Graham expressed the view that a Leasco
attempt to take over Chemical would not be a good thing for
banking—and added, most unthreateningly, that his bank highly val-
ued its association with Leasco and expected it to continue. (Renchard, in fact, had talked to Graham and urged him to discourage
Steinberg.) The memo seemed to give Chemical a momentary edge;
and, seizing the initiative, the bank took the comparatively drastic
step of planning a full-scale strategy meeting at 20 Pine Street the
following morning, even though the day would be Saturday.

It turned out to be a wild weekend of feints and counterfeints.
Steinberg was busy with a semi-annual conference of Leasco district
managers, and on that account, he stayed in town at the Regency
Hotel. By another coincidence, that same weekend was the occasion
of the American Bankers Association's annual trust conference, and
consequently New York City was swarming with hundreds of important bankers from all over the country.

On Sunday, New York City was hit by a fifteen-inch snowstorm,
the worst in seven years, and as a result, airports were closed, roads
were clogged, rail service was disrupted, and the bankers in town
were trapped. There was nothing for them to do but stay and talk
—largely about Leasco and Chemical. The bankers, and the subject,
were caught in a kind of pressure cooker. That evening, Chemical
held a large reception for the visiting bankers at the Plaza. There
Renchard took considerable kidding; the prevailing attitude among
the bankers he talked to seemed to be that the whole thing was
ridiculous, an attitude that Renchard felt he had little reason to
share. "Don't joke," he would say. "If this is successful, the next
target may be you."

On Monday, with the city still snowbound, Renchard and Steinberg, who had previously never so much as talked on the telephone,

met at last. That morning Steinberg, carrying out his plan, called Renchard at his office and asked if they could get together. Renchard said, "Sure. I'll buy you lunch, but I have to go to a meeting right afterward. Do you have transportation?" Steinberg said he hadn't. "I'll send my car to get you," Renchard replied.

The lunch that Renchard "bought" Steinberg took place in the Chemical Bank's private dining room. One may imagine the first reactions of the antagonists to each other. One was lean, iron-gray, of distinctly military bearing, very conscious of the entrenched power of the nation standing behind him, very much a man of few and incisive words. The other was round-faced, easy-smiling, a man of many words who looked preposterously younger than his already preposterous twenty-nine years, and given, as he talked, to making windmill gestures with his arms and suddenly jumping galvanically up from his chair; a *South* Shore estate owner (twenty-nine rooms, tennis court, two saunas, Picassos and Kandinskys).

The two men's accounts of the ensuing meeting, as told to me several years later, differ to some extent as to content, but to a greater and perhaps more interesting extent as to style and emphasis.

Renchard: "Steinberg, at some length, gave his ideas on how commercial banking was going to be revolutionized over the next few years. Mostly I just listened, and so did my colleagues [President Howard] McCall and [Vice Chairman Hulbert] Aldrich, who joined us toward the end of the session. The whole industry was to benefit greatly, Steinberg said. I asked him why he had singled out Chemical. He said he liked our philosophy, that is, we were in the process of forming a one-bank holding company that would enable us to diversify, thereby showing that we believed in the principle of bank diversification.

"I said I wasn't sure he appreciated what might happen to our business when someone with no banking experience moved in on a takeover basis. Directors and officers might leave. I made it clear that I didn't think *I'd* be around. In the trust area, for people to leave their estates with a bank you need confidence built up over many years. Will appointments would leave in droves, I said, not because of anything about him but because it was a takeover. Then there was the worry about somebody acquisition-minded having access to our stockholder lists. The confidential relationship of banker to client might be endangered.

"I think it impressed him a little bit. Steinberg said he had no in-

tention of making an unfriendly takeover—that is, that he didn't want to, but might. There was a hint of a threat. I said, 'If you want to get into a fight, I'm a pretty good gutter fighter.' He said, 'I've already found that out.' He said he wanted to make a full presentation of Leasco's plans the next afternoon, after his company's annual meeting, in the hope that Chemical would change its mind and want to cooperate, after all. I enjoyed the luncheon. There was some kidding around, too."

Steinberg: "When I got to 20 Pine Street that morning, I got out of Renchard's car and walked into the bank. It was a day when not many people were there, because of the snowstorm. Renchard's secretary was very friendly—'Oh, hello, Mr. Steinberg, I'm so glad to see you.' Renchard came out and shook my hand and said, 'Hello, Saul. Call me Bill. Can I take you around and show you the place?' Well, I wasn't terribly interested in looking at the real estate right then. So we went and talked, first in his office and later in the bank's dining room.

"We did some kidding at first. He asked me why I wanted to become a banker and I said, 'God looks after drunks and bankers, and I don't want to be a drunk.' Then I started in giving the facts. I told him how many Chemical shares Leasco had—more than three hundred thousand. I said we weren't going to accumulate much more because it was getting too expensive. I told him frankly that the *Times* piece had disrupted Leasco's plans; we had wanted to wait until the forthcoming new law regulating bank holding companies was passed, and that might be six months or a year. Now our hand was forced, and I volunteered that for us it was premature.

"I went into my philosophy of how Chemical's management, and all commercial-bank managements, should be more responsive to stockholders and customers, and how I thought we could make it that way. I said I thought that adding a broad range of services to a bank's regular functions would add to the intrinsic value of its money, and on that he expressed absolute agreement in principle. He began to talk about the possible detriments to the bank's business from a hostile takeover. He said top management would probably resign. He mentioned losing customers, and I said they would hardly leave in a hurry at a tight-money time like that. He talked about damage to the trust business. I asked, 'Does it make money?' He laughed, and said he wasn't sure. He said if I wanted a fight he was a pretty good gutter fighter, and I said my record as a gutter fighter was considered to be

pretty good, too, at least for my age. But then I said I wasn't planning a hostile takeover, although I wasn't ruling one out. I told him that in four days I was going to Puerto Rico on vacation with my wife and kids—it was the kids' winter semester break—and that I was professional enough not to be planning such a thing as that if I were thinking of attempting a hostile takeover. He looked surprised and asked, 'Are you really going to Puerto Rico?' I said yes. He was obviously relieved. Everything became very relaxed. I thought it was a rather constructive meeting. Everything was friendly and affable. The atmosphere was dampened at the end though, when McCall and Aldrich came in—McCall for lunch with us, and Aldrich at the end of lunch. McCall just didn't seem to want to have anything to do with me one way or the other, and Aldrich seemed downright hostile. But Renchard interrupted them to say, 'Look, Saul has stated that he has no intention of a hostile takeover.' McCall's face lit up, and he said, 'Well, when can we meet again?' I suggested after my trip to Puerto Rico, and he and Renchard said, 'Oh, let's do it before that,' and we arranged for the following afternoon, after our stockholders' meeting. I came out in a positive frame of mind. The only thing was that Aldrich was still cold. But wait—come to think of it, he wasn't any too cordial to Renchard, either."

So the first meeting of the rival chieftains was a standoff. That afternoon, Renchard heard from Roberts of Reliance Insurance. The apparently satisfied subject of Leasco's previous conquest said he thought a merger of Leasco and Chemical would be a fine thing for the bank. "I told him he was off his rocker," Renchard said later. "I said computer leasing has nothing to do with banking. He said the Leasco-Reliance merger hadn't hurt Reliance. I was disappointed in him." Also that afternoon, McCall had someone at Chemical prepare for him a list of Leasco's creditor banks, and when the list later came to the attention of a Congressional committee, it was found that checkmarks had been made beside the names of certain of the banks; the purpose of the list, and the meaning of the checkmarks, is not known, but the fact is that on that very afternoon Steinberg began to feel "pressure" from the banking business in the form of calls from Leasco's two investment bankers, White, Weld and Lehman Brothers, informing him that they would refuse to participate in any Leasco tender offer for Chemical.

At Leasco's annual stockholders' meeting, held the following afternoon in the auditorium of the Chase Manhattan Building, matters

proceeded smoothly enough, with no mention of the subject that was in everyone's mind, until Steinberg observed that Leasco's commitment to becoming a comprehensive financial-services organization included the objective of entering the field of banking. "The realization of so large a plan," he went on, "requires the exercise of careful and deliberate judgment. At the present time, we have not made a decision as to a particular bank."

A hush filled the room; Steinberg broke it by asking for questions. A stockholder asked flatly whether Leasco was planning to acquire the Chemical Bank. Steinberg replied that Leasco had made no statement regarding that bank or any other. Then, a bit later, another stockholder asked whether Leasco had already had merger discussions with Chemical.

Steinberg was on the spot; over the weekend he had planned to announce his tender offer on this occasion, but now, with the door still open to possible agreement with Chemical officers at the meeting to be held in only a couple of hours, he had decided to hold off. For diplomatic reasons, it would be best to evade the question, but he rejected that course. "I said to myself, 'Heck, I'm not going to lie,'" he recounted later. He answered, "Yes, we have met with the Chemical."

But later that afternoon, at the private meeting between Leasco and Chemical officers, the crack in the door that Steinberg had discerned at the previous day's luncheon seems to have narrowed perceptibly. Both sides later characterized the meeting as cordial, although Steinberg felt that it had been "not overly friendly." It concluded with Renchard saying, in effect, "We have lots to consider. Will do so. They will hear from us—maybe end of week, maybe middle of next week."

In fact, Steinberg would hear from Renchard again that Friday, February 14, but in the meantime the Chemical defense battalion was far from idle; on the contrary, it was now trundling up its big guns, those "resources" that Renchard had described at the outset as "considerable." Chemical held another full-scale battle meeting at which the discussion centered on the possibility of changing Chemical's charter in such a way as to make a Leasco takeover legally difficult if not impossible. There was also talk about perhaps buying a fire-and-casualty company to create an antitrust conflict with Leasco's ownership of Reliance, or even, as a last resort, of ar-

ranging to have some giant insurance company take over *Chemical*—suggesting a positively Oriental preference for suicide rather than surrender.

As it happened, none of these schemes was carried out; certainly, though, the last one reflects the bankers' mood of grim intransigence. Probably the most effective of Chemical's various salvos was on the legislative front. Beginning on February 14, Richard Simmons of the Cravath law firm, on retainer from Chemical, began devoting full time to the Leasco affair, concentrating his attention on the drafting of laws specifically designed to prevent or make difficult the takeover of banks similar to Chemical by companies that resembled Leasco, and to getting these drafts introduced as bills in the State Legislature in Albany and the Congress in Washington. Does it seem odd that a proposed new law, hand-tailored by a chief party at interest, should be accepted without question by tribunes of the people in a state or federal legislative body? Whatever the answer, Governor Rockefeller chose that very week to urge the New York Legislature to enact a law enabling the state to stop any takeover of a bank by a non-bank, within its boundaries, in a case where "the exercise of control might impair the safe and sound conduct of the bank." By Friday, precisely such a proposed law (not from Simmons's desk) had been dispatched to Albany, and a national one of similar intent to Senator John J. Sparkman, chairman of the Senate Banking and Currency Committee in Washington.

By the following Monday and Tuesday, the would-be attackers were plainly on the defensive. A *Wall Street Journal* article published on Monday raised questions as to the future earnings prospects for Leasco. Leasco stock dropped eight points that day, to 115, and two and a half points more the following day. The anti-bank-takeover bill was duly introduced in Albany on Tuesday. (It was subsequently passed, and became law in mid-May.) Leasco suffered a further setback when the company got a letter from the Department of Justice saying it had heard of Leasco's plans to merge with Chemical and commenting, "Although we do not suggest that such a transaction would violate the antitrust laws, questions under these laws are raised thereby, particularly under Section 7 of the Clayton Act." (Just how the Justice Department came to send such a letter at that particular moment has never been explained.) While these things were happening, Steinberg was with his family at the Dorado Beach in Puerto Rico, playing tennis, swimming, and, he insisted later, talk-

ing on the phone to his office in Great Neck only twice. It is hard, though, to imagine that he did not learn one way or another about the *Journal* article, the continuing Leasco stock drop, the bill introduced in Albany, and the ominous letter from Justice.

Steinberg's day in Washington—Wednesday the nineteenth—was a depressing one. All occasions now seemed to inform against him. For one thing, the mysterious decline in Leasco's stock price was reducing the company's takeover power day by day. But the situation was not yet hopeless on that front. The other pressing concern was the national legislative situation—the matter that had brought Steinberg to Washington—and here he found a bleak picture indeed. The nation's legislators were in a grimly anticonglomerate, antitakeover mood. During the day Steinberg talked to half the members of the Senate Banking and Currency Committee and to several members of the Federal Reserve Board; without exception, he found his interviewees adamantly opposed to a Leasco takeover of Chemical on grounds that seemed to him to be entirely unreasonable. Time and again, he explained that his object was not the destruction of the bank but its revitalization, and he argued that takeovers of one company by another, far from being automatically bad, are a valuable and necessary part of the free-enterprise system, and in some cases the only way by which backward and outmoded management methods can be replaced by aggressive, forward-looking ones. Time and again, he found his arguments going unanswered, and himself being treated as a sort of business pirate bent on seizing and looting property that did not belong to him. The climax of these brief and sketchy dialogues was one with the key man, Senator Sparkman, part of which went, according to Steinberg's account, as follows:

SPARKMAN: A couple of weeks ago I had a fellow in here complaining that somebody moved in and took over his bank and then fired him. Now, we can't have things like that.

STEINBERG: But, Senator, the whole economy runs on profit. If a bank president isn't delivering, he should be replaced just like anyone else. Unless you want to change the whole system—

SPARKMAN: No, no, I don't want to do that. By the way, have you seen the bill I'm going to introduce against bank takeovers? (Calling to his secretary) Miss ——, where's that bill the lawyer for Chemical Bank sent in? I want to show it to Mr. Steinberg.

It was thus that Steinberg learned for the first time of the bill Simmons had drafted at Chemical's behest and, as Senator Sparkman

so candidly put it, "sent in." As it happened, Sparkman introduced the bill in late March; unlike the New York State legislation, it was never passed; but on March 19, the knowledge that a lawyer on Chemical retainer was apparently functioning as a sort of unofficial legislative assistant to the chairman of the Senate Banking and Currency Committee served to deepen Steinberg's gathering despair. Only much later did he come to see his conversation with Sparkman as a piece of high Washington comedy.

"I came back to New York that night feeling that I had been given a very clear message," Steinberg said later. In fact, that day, with the realization that the national powers of government as well as those of business were solidly aligned against him, Steinberg decided on surrender. The following morning, he went as scheduled to his third meeting with Chemical's top officers. As things turned out, it was to be his last such meeting. Again let us hear two versions:

Steinberg: "I came into the meeting with a public statement in my pocket—a surrender statement. I told them I'd been in Washington the previous day, and I told them whom I'd met. I said I'd concluded as a result of those conversations that the only way we could proceed with a tender offer was with Chemical's great enthusiasm for the merger, and I wasn't sure even that would help. I waited a few moments. To put it mildly, nobody from Chemical expressed great enthusiasm. Then I said that in half an hour I was going to release a statement of withdrawal. I pulled the statement from my pocket and read it to the Chemical men. You could sense the relief—almost touch it. There was a kind of quiet pandemonium. Everybody shook hands. I haven't seen any of them since then."

Renchard: "Steinberg came in with a couple of henchmen. He said he'd decided it wasn't the time to pursue the matter, and he was going to make an announcement to that effect later that day. It was a very friendly and satisfactory meeting."

The announcement that Steinberg released later—which, in view of the fact that its last part largely negates a philosophy that he had expressed previously and would reaffirm later, suggests that he had been temporarily brainwashed—read as follows:

GREAT NECK N.Y., February 20, 1969—Saul P. Steinberg, chairman of Leasco Data Processing Equipment Corporation, stated today that he has no plans to acquire control of the Chemical New York Corporation. Without the support and enthusiasm of the management, Leasco has no interest in pressing for an affiliation with Chemical.

Mr. Steinberg observed that hostile takeovers of money-center banks were against the best interest of the economy because of the danger of upsetting the stability and prestige of the banking system and diminishing public confidence in it.

It was presumably with satisfaction that the directors of Chemical that afternoon read the following telegram:

PLEASED TO REPORT LEASCO HAS ANNOUNCED WITHDRAWAL OF PLANS TO PRESS FOR AFFILIATION WITH CHEMICAL

BILL RENCHARD

So it was over, just two weeks after it had formally begun. "They"—the Chemical Bank, most of the banking business, the Cravath law firm, a cross section of Wall Street power and influence, the leading proxy solicitors, the governor and legislature of New York State, the members of the Federal Reserve Board and the Senate Banking and Currency Committee, and sundry more or less related forces—had combined to beat Saul Steinberg of Leasco, and apparently to cause him to lose his nerve at the last moment. (He and Leasco came back—gamely, although disastrously from a financial point of view—to take over control that summer of Pergamon Press, a British publishing giant.)

And yet it wasn't really quite over; for American business and society alike, it had reverberations, some perhaps beneficial, others certainly purgative and self-revelatory. Renchard said later, "I took the whole thing very seriously, although a lot of people I know didn't. At the bank we're more on the alert now for that kind of thing. I took a lot of kidding about it. If Steinberg had gone ahead, it could have resulted in quite a fight. I'm not saying we would have been defeated. I still think we could have successfully fought them off. I'm just as glad not to have had to go through the process, though."

What Steinberg, for his part, chiefly remembers about the whole episode is the aura of hysteria that seemed to prevade so many people's reactions to it. "Nobody was objective," he says. "I wanted objective opinions, and I couldn't get them. All through those two weeks, bankers and businessmen I'd never met kept calling up out of the blue and attacking us for merely thinking about taking over a big bank. . . . Months after we'd abandoned our plans, executives of major corporations were still calling up and ranting, 'I feel it was so *wrong,* what you tried to do—' And yet they could never say why. We'd touched some kind of nerve center. I still don't know exactly

what it was. Once, at a party, the head of a huge corporation asked me if there had been any anti-Semitism in the campaign against us. I said, not that I knew of. There are bankers and businessmen who are anti-Semitic, but it was more than that. I think now it would have been a good thing if we'd done a hostile takeover, and then there had been Congressional hearings, to get all those rancid emotions out in the open air."

Ruefully, Steinberg summed up his emotional reaction when he said, immediately after his surrender, "I always knew there was an Establishment—I just used to think I was a part of it." As for the Establishment, perhaps *its* last word on the affair was the apothegm allegedly pronounced on it by an officer of a lordly commercial bank, who is supposed to have said, with a lordly mixture of misinformation, illogic, and sententiousness, "Never trust a fat man."

CHAPTER 8

REVELRY BEFORE WATERLOO

While Steinberg was finding out that he did not belong to the Establishment, and that in its old age it was neither too gentlemanly nor too toothless to fight, the investment revolution of the nineteen sixties was all but completed, and the era was having its last great speculative fling.

By 1969, institutional investors had effectively taken over the New York Stock Exchange business. At the beginning of the decade their share in it had been less than a third; now they had 54 percent of total public-share volume and 60 percent of total public-dollar volume. The mutual funds, the fastest-growing of the investing institutions, now held assets of some $50 billion, and were moving in and out of the market at a turnover rate of 50 percent, or half of their portfolios per year, as against less than 20 percent as recently as 1962.

The market was beginning to unravel in earnest. The Dow, after peaking out at 1970 in May—only a few points below the all-time high of January 1966—went into a steep three-month decline that left it just above the 800 mark late in July. The Federal Reserve, worried about accelerating inflation, kept constricting the money supply, driving interest rates through the roof without apparently accomplishing its purpose, and there came to be the specter—confounding

to classical economists—of a recession accompanied by runaway inflation, the worst of two apparently opposing worlds. The failure of the blue-chip Dow to reflect the true situation was becoming more pronounced all the time; the advance guard of the former high flyers were already crashing not 20 percent like the Dow but 50 to 75 percent, and even more.

A particularly ominous foreshadowing of things to come was to be found in the abrupt decline in brokerage-firm profits. Trading volume, the source of brokerage revenue, was diminishing rapidly. Meanwhile the huge expansion downtown of personnel and facilities to meet the volume rise of the previous year had raised brokerage costs enormously.

The omens were everywhere; doom hung in the air, and a tomorrow-we-die, night-before-Waterloo mood was pandemic. The national climate was just right for a binge. The country, tired of riots and crime and liberalism, and with a new conservative Republican administration in Washington, was moving politically to the right, which in economic terms meant toward the newer forms of laissez faire. Mergers went on increasing at a fantastic rate, and so, as a result, did capital concentration: billion-dollar corporations had, in only a decade, enlarged their share of total national assets from 26 to 46 percent. "Creative accounting" continued to flourish, and accounting authorities to shrug. Deal-making brokers, meanwhile, had learned how to bring together the two great new forces in the stock market—the conglomerates and the mutual funds—in a way that all but constituted a conspiracy to deceive the public. The deal-maker would propose and promote a merger, in the process salting away for himself large blocks of the stock of the merging companies. Next, he would sell the companies' stock to funds on the basis of the secret merger plans; then when the merger was announced, the accountants would work their bottom-line magic; the merger-mad, bottom-line-loving public would bid up the stock, the insiders would unload, and the public would be left holding as big and empty a bag as in the more naïve market manipulations of the nineteen twenties.

Still, the victims of such schemes were comparatively few. Tens of millions of investors who had been lucky or shrewd enough to avoid the most popular conglomerates, and the other go-go stocks of the most-actively-traded list, were sitting pretty. Most of these handsome profits would largely evaporate within the coming year, but nobody knew that, and in mid-1969 the profits were gratifyingly there, on

paper, to make the small investor feel confident and rich, and to put him in a spending mood. Catching the mood of Wall Street itself, the investing public was living as if there were no tomorrow.

The rise of institutional investing had brought into being a new kind of high-risk brokerage operation, the block positioner. A time had come when a large mutual or pension fund might suddenly want to buy or sell at a single stroke a block of 100,000, 500,000, or even a million shares. Traditionally, the responsibility for matching up buyers and sellers in such an order, and rounding it out by using his own capital on one side or the other when necessary, fell on the specialist on the Exchange floor; but now with such huge sums involved in mammoth transactions the specialists' capital was often ludicrously inadequate to the task. The firm that most spectacularly and successfully moved in to fill this crack in Wall Street's crumbling edifice of traditional procedure was Salomon Brothers, formerly Salomon Brothers and Hutzler, founded in 1910, a leading institutional trader for years not in stocks but in bonds. Indeed, so great was this firm's reputation in bond trading that at one time the Wall Street definition of a marketable bond was one on which Salomon would make a bid. In the mid-sixties, when Goldman, Sachs and Bear, Stearns had the lion's share of the new and expanding business of block positioning of stocks for institutions, the partners of Salomon Brothers, headed by canny, soft-spoken William R. (Billy) Salomon, experienced a revelation. Block positioning in stocks, they mused, was not basically different from doing the same thing in bonds. In both cases, you had to know your customers, the institutional investors. Salomon Brothers knew them already from trading bonds with them for years. You had to have the resources and the nerve to assume huge capital risks. Salomon Brothers for years had been king of the plungers in the bond market; why not, then, move into the wholesale stock business?

Beginning in 1964-65, they did, and by 1968 were the unquestioned leaders in it. Their star stock trader came to be Jay Perry, a fast-talking and fiercely competitive man in his early thirties, from Hot Springs, Arkansas, who had previously been a bond trader. In Salomon Brothers' noisy trading room at 60 Wall Street, Perry would be asked by a big institution for a price on so many hundred thousand shares of a certain stock—a block worth, say, $30 or $40 million. After consulting the firm's executive committee, he would shout into the phone a bid a little under the current market, but—and

369

here was the nub of the matter—not nearly so far under it as would be the case if the shares were thrown directly onto the mercy of a capital-weak floor specialist. Then, working at a 120-key telephone console connecting them to all the major funds in the country (an amenity denied to the floor specialist, who was forbidden to deal directly with institutions), Perry and the rest of the Salomon organization would begin trying to round up buyers for parts of the huge block available for sale. Quite often the number of shares they could find bids for would fall short of the offered block by a couple of hundred thousand shares. That was where the positioning came in. Salomon Brothers would obligingly buy those residual shares for its own account, completing the deal, and collecting commissions from both the seller and the various buyers. Then would come the hairy part: unloading the shares Salomon had taken, and didn't really want to tie up its capital with, over a period that might drag out to as much as a couple of months, with tens of millions of capital at stake. "We'll bid for almost anything," said Salomon blandly, "and we take many baths." The risks his firm took through seat-of-the-pants plunges in stocks of companies it knew little about was balanced, and more than balanced, by the enormous commissions it could count on from both sides of its executed deals.

As for Salomon Brothers' "baths," one of the wettest and most prolonged of them occurred over the first three months of 1968, in the stock of Fairchild Camera and Instrument, one of the market's most spectacular performers of 1965. On December 21, 1967, Salomon Brothers, evidently in a free-spending Yuletide mood, bought from an investing institution 52,000 shares of Fairchild at 88, for a capital commitment of about $4.5 million. Later the same day, the firm sold off 22,500 shares at 90 5/8, thereby turning a quick profit of $58,000. That left almost 30,000 Fairchild shares in Salomon's inventory. Eight days later, on December 29, 1967, the firm bought 41,000 more Fairchild shares at 88½ from another investing institution, and on January 22, 1968 —by which time the market for Fairchild had gone distinctly sour, and Salomon Brothers had decided it was a real bargain—the firm absorbed another block of 31,000 Fairchild shares at 78, thus raising its inventory to 102,000 shares at an average cost of $85, for a capital commitment of almost $9 million.

Day followed day, and Fairchild did not recover. On the contrary, it continued dropping—quite possibly speeded on its way by hedge funds that, knowing of the huge Salomon block hanging over the

market, may have made short sales to take advantage of the situation. The days stretched out to weeks, and Fairchild stock showed no signs of recovery, and at last Billy Salomon and his partners decided that they had simply been wrong. On March 1, they unloaded 2,000 Fairchild shares at 66; on March 2, 17,400 at prices down to 59½; on March 6 to 9, 25,500 additional shares at prices down to 55⅝; and finally, between March 10 and 31, the rest of the block at prices down to 52—which turned out to be just about Fairchild's low for the year. Salomon Brothers' profits on the whole series of transactions, including the December 21 capital gain and commissions, were $105,000; its losses were $2,878,000, leaving a net loss of $2,773,000.

But why worry? Next week, or next month, there would be a new block trade that would result in a *profit* of $3 million or more, as attested by Salomon Brothers' consistently gratifying annual results.

There were other, less salutary, developments. Many of the mutual funds themselves were taking advantage of the permissive climate by indulging in a form of sleight-of-hand—perfectly legal at the time—that gave their asset value the same kind of painless, instant, and essentially bogus boost as merger accounting could give to conglomerate earnings. Asset value was to a mutual fund what earnings per share were to a conglomerate: its advertisement, its bait for new capital, the formal measure of its success or failure. The sleight-of-hand involved the use of what was called "letter stock," and was, in the late nineteen sixties, freely indulged in by many mutual-fund magicians. The one who had the bad luck to become associated with letter stock in the public mind was Frederick S. Mates.

It may or may not be considered paradoxical that Mates, in 1968, had a well-deserved reputation as one of the most high-minded and socially concerned, as well as one of the most successful, young fund managers in Wall Street. Born in Brooklyn, a graduate of Brooklyn College, class of 1954, he had married a Barnard College psychology teacher, been a teacher briefly himself at a Brooklyn yeshiva, and then spent several years with the brokerage firm of Spingarn, Heine before launching his own Mates Investment Fund in August 1967. The fund was an instant success—so great a success that Mates could soon afford to integrate his social ideals into his business operations. For the Mates Fund portfolio he bought no stocks of companies manufacturing armaments, cigarettes, or products that he considered to be pollutants of the environment.

He called his office "the kibbutz on William Street" and his young staff "the flower children." His seemed to be an operation entirely in tune with his times. Whether despite or because of these policies, objectives, and attitudes, by the summer of 1968 the Mates Fund was the new sensation of the mutual-fund industry, its asset value up almost 100 percent in its first year, and new money coming in at such a rate—a million and a half dollars a day, far exceeding the previous record set by Fred Carr's Enterprise Fund—that, in June, Mates had to close the sales window temporarily to keep his facilities from being overwhelmed.

It was in September 1968 that Mates made the investment that he, and eventually much of the fund industry, would have cause to regret. A tiny conglomerate called Omega Equities privately sold the Mates Fund 300,000 shares of common stock at $3.25 a share. Omega was then selling on the over-the-counter market at around 25, so the price was apparently an almost unbelievable bargain. But only apparently. The Omega shares that Mates bought were not registered with the S.E.C., and therefore could not legally be resold until they had been through such registration; for practical purposes, they were unmarketable. They had been sold to Mates —legally—through an investment letter (whence the term "letter stock") in which these terms were set forth and the buyer agreed not to resell pending registration. So now the Mates Fund had in its portfolio 300,000 shares of Omega; the question was, what value were they to be assigned in calculating the fund's assets?

Mates did what was the common practice in accounting for letter stock: he took the market price as his base, marked it down by one-third to allow for the shares' nonregistration, and carried them at $16 a share. It will be noted that this was almost five times as much as he had just paid for them. With no change in the market price of Omega stock, then, and with no particular good news as to Omega's business prospects, the Mates Fund had made what appeared on the books it displayed proudly to the investing public to be an investment yielding an instant profit of almost 500 percent.

The layman will have no trouble recognizing this as a form of cheating. The startling thing is not that Mates did it, but that it was being done all the time in 1968, by mutual funds and hedge funds, and that not until late 1969 did the S.E.C. get around to a mild crackdown on mutual funds' letter-stock investments, and subsequent arbitrary up-valuations of them. What made Mates a

scapegoat was some untimely ill fortune that shortly overtook Omega. Early in December 1968, the Mates Fund assets, partly on the basis of the Omega deal, were up an eye-popping 168 percent for the year, making Mates, by a wide margin, the nation's leading fund performer in the greatest of all fund performance years. Then, on December 20, the S.E.C. abruptly suspended trading in all Omega stock on grounds that it was being traded "on the basis of incomplete and inaccurate information." The immediate result was as disastrous for Mates as it was predictable. Many Mates Fund shareholders demanded redemption of their shares in cash, and this demand, because of the unmarketability of all Omega shares, was one that the fund could not possibly meet. Technically, it had failed. But the S.E.C. was in no mood to force it out of business and thus damage its 3,300 stockholders. Mates hastily applied to the S.E.C. for permission to suspend redemptions for an indefinite period, and the S.E.C. hastily and meekly complied.

The fund industry shuddered. This was purest heresy; the fundamental right of share redemption without question at any time was the cornerstone of the whole $50-billion business, analogous to the right of a bank depositor to draw from his checking account; now the cornerstone was cracked, the letter-stock deception stood suddenly exposed, and dozens of other funds came under suspicion of having similar concealed weakness. Mates, cornered, acted as bravely and honorably as he could. He immediately valued his Omega holding down to his cost of $3.25 per share, ruining Mates Fund's preeminent performance record for the year. He vowed to resume redemptions just as soon as possible. That was cold comfort to his shareholders; but a leading Wall Street fund man commented with sympathy and candor, "After all, Fred Mates is only one of many." In February 1969, an S.E.C. official seemed to be remarkably calm about the whole matter when he said, reflectively, "The Mates situation really puts the problem in bold relief." That July, Mates finally made good his promise to resume redemptions—with Omega marked down to fifty cents a share. He was hoping eventually to find a way to sell his 300,000 shares for much more; early in 1972, however, the Mates Fund still had them, and was carrying them at a value of one nickel each.

Perhaps his story may be seen as raising the arresting dilemma, which is worse in a time of national crisis: a young swinger who speculates with his investors' money but pursues high-minded in-

vestment policies, or a more conservative codger who keeps his clients in the comfortable blue-chip stocks of corporations that fuel the wars and foul the rivers and the air?

And there were other shows playing to paying customers that year Off-Wall Street; the further their remove from New York's financial district, the less they resembled moral drama and the more the repertoire suggested musical comedy or farce.

If some *farceur* with more imagination than restraint had written the story of Great American Management and Research, or Gramco, as fiction, he would surely have been accused of painting with too broad a brush. Short of a corporation president conducting his enterprise from a baby's playpen, Gramco's founder and boss Keith Barish seemed to be the ultimate manifestation of the youth revolution in finance. At eighteen, while a student at the University of Miami, Barish had helped start a bank in Hialeah, of racetrack fame; because he was legally under age, his seat at directors' meetings had been regularly occupied, on his behalf, by his mother. In 1967, when he was twenty-two and had already amassed a small fortune, he founded Gramco as a mutual fund that would invest chiefly in American real estate, rather than in American stocks. Thus he would bring to his investors the benefits of the apparently endless upward trend in land and property values. The S.E.C. frowned on such funds because of real estate's inherent lack of liquidity, but no matter; Barish planned to "invent" a new thing called "liquid real estate"; and besides, he proposed to escape the disapproving surveillance of the S.E.C. entirely by setting up his fund in the Bahamas and selling its shares only outside the United States, presumably to non-Americans. And that, briefly, was what he did. Nassau became Gramco's official domicile, London its operating base, Panama, Curaçao, and the Grand Duchy of Luxembourg its tax shelters, and most of the world ex-U.S.A. its selling territory.

Barish took as his partner a dispossessed Cuban just over thirty named Rafael G. Navarro, who had some mutual-fund experience. He took on others, without such experience, to other purpose. One summer, during the administration of John F. Kennedy, Barish as a teen-ager had served as a "summer intern" at the White House and had evidently spent his time well among the authorities he found striding in and around its corridors. To apply the magical Kennedy aura, so powerful in so many distant lands, to the selling of Gramco

shares, Barish hired as Gramco officers and directors a group of old New Frontiersmen; most visibly, the portly, amiable, highly visible former Kennedy press secretary and later U.S. Senator from California, Pierre Salinger.

"Economics have never been my strong point," Salinger once confessed disarmingly, but no matter; Salinger was made titular head of the Gramco sales organization, which came to comprise some six hundred salesmen in fifty countries, and by May 1969 had brought in investments in Gramco of more than $100 million, a figure that would be doubled before the end of that year. The money was invested in such U.S. real estate ventures as the Americana Fairfax Apartments outside Washington, the Clermont Towers in New York City, Harbor House in Chicago, the LTV Tower in Dallas, and a shopping center in Oklahoma City. Meanwhile, those within the Gramco organization with more of a penchant for economics were ensuring that Gramco itself got its share of the proceeds. By charging fund customers the usual stiff mutual-fund sales commissions and management fees while serving as their own brokers in these transactions (and collecting commissions accordingly), and buying real estate on credit, in the first three and a half years of Gramco's operation, its management took out of the fund for its own profits $43 million, or 17 percent of all the money the customers had entrusted to it. The firm's accountants, meanwhile, were doing their bit to make Gramco's books look simultaneously bearish to the income-tax authorities and wildly bullish to potential investors. Taking advantage of liberal U.S. depreciation guidelines for real estate, the accountants would report on their U.S. tax returns that the properties Gramco had bought were dropping in value. At the same time, reporting to shareholders and potential shareholders abroad on the fund's asset value, they would record, on the same property at the same time, substantial increases in value. What was going down in Oklahoma City and Chicago, the accountants seemed to be saying, was simultaneously rising and shining in Nassau, Panama, and the Grand Duchy of Luxembourg.

In May 1969, Gramco followed the crowd and went public: a million shares were issued, priced at $10 each. Again, everybody was rich, except, by some oversight, the far-flung investors who had put their trust in the Kennedy aura and a good bit of their money, inadvertently, into the pockets of former Kennedy men. Surely the old New Frontiersmen were finding exciting new frontiers indeed,

on a new trail blazed by the stripling they had first taken a liking to that summer at the White House.

To round out this sampling of the various symptoms of dementia that afflicted the 1968-69 stock market, there were the hot new issues, the "shooters," that shot up on their first day of trading from 10 to 20 or from 5 to 14, and later went to 75 or 100, oblivious of the fact that the companies they represented were often neither sound nor profitable: the garbage stocks that everyone could make money on just so long as, and no longer than, everyone could contrive to hold his nose and avert his eyes and imagine that the garbage was actually nourishing and palatable.

If one fact is glaringly clear in stock-market history, it is that a new-issue craze is always the last stage of a dangerous boom, a warning of impending disaster. If heads could be cooler and memories longer, investors both large and small, professional and amateur, might ward off danger by reading the signs, eschewing the new issues, and lightening their commitments generally. But investors, like other human beings, tragically repeat their mistakes; when the danger signs are plain, the lure of easy money blanks their memories and dissipates their calm. In 1929 the shooters were jerry-built investment trusts like Alleghany, Shenandoah, and United Corporation. In 1961 they were tiny scientific companies put together by little clutches of glittery-eyed young Ph.D.'s, their company names ending in "onics." In 1968-69, what a promoter needed to launch a new stock, apart from a persuasive tongue and a resourceful accountant, was to have a "story"—an easily grasped concept, preferably related to some current national fad or preoccupation, that *sounded* as if it would lead to profits. Such stories, like most stories, were best told quickly and concisely, and best of all within the name of the company itself. Were the new government Medicare and Medicaid programs pouring millions into the care of elderly persons? A cunning investor could presumably get a piece of that action by buying stocks called Four Seasons Nursing Centers or United Convalescent Homes. Were people's recreational expenditures soaring? Hardly coincidentally, there turned out to be a stock called International Leisure. Was concern about the environment a popular passion of the moment? Why, look here—a stock called Responsive Environments! Was weight watching in the wind? One might grow rich while growing thin, perhaps, with

Weight Watchers International. Finally, it may be assumed that there were some investors who, so far as company names were concerned, didn't want to be bothered with the suggestion of any particular product or service, and just wanted a stock whose name made it sound like a winner. For them, there was Performance Systems, Inc., not to mention Bonanza International.

And then there was National Student Marketing Corporation, whose "story" was the youth market. The young man who set out in the biggest way to exploit the youth market, or at least to convince Wall Street that he was doing so, was Cortes Wesley Randell. Randell was about to turn thirty when, in 1965, he founded National Student Marketing Corporation in Washington as headquarters for a string of part-time student representatives on campuses whose job it was to distribute samples and employment guides, do market research, and sell fad items like posters and paper dresses. The enterprise took off like a bird. By early 1968—just in time for the great national speculative fever—Randell had nearly six hundred campus reps and was ready to take N.S.M.C. public. And Wall Street was more than ready to receive it. The solid old-line brokerage house of Auchincloss, Parker and Redpath became N.S.M.C.'s underwriter for the stock issue; its lawyers were Covington and Burling, its accountants Arthur Andersen and Company. Buoyed by this parlay of glamour and apparent respectability, the stock, offered to the public on April 24, 1968, at a price of 6, went to 14 the same day and by early June was selling at 30.

And so, armed with a red-hot stock appraised by the market at a price-to-earnings multiple of 100, Randell set out to make his company a giant through acquisitions, including school-bus companies, low-cost-travel guides, even some companies scarcely related to the youth market. Before the year was out, N.S.M.C. stock had skyrocketed on the over-the-counter market from the original price of 6 to a 1968 high of 82. Meanwhile, Randell had moved his headquarters from Washington to New York, to be where the financial action was. Significantly, the corporate style he fostered was anything but countercultural. N.S.M.C. executives wore dark suits and narrow ties, and kept their shoes shined. In simple truth, N.S.M.C. was not primarily selling goods and services to youth, at all—it was selling stock to Wall Street.

Its astonishing success in that particular enterprise is a crucial sign of the times in Wall Street. Bankers Trust, Morgan Guaranty,

the Continental Illinois of Chicago, and the State Street Fund of Boston bought N.S.M.C. stock; so did the Harvard and Cornell endowment funds, the General Electric pension fund, and the University of Chicago. There seemed to be scarcely any investment citadels left for Randell to conquer.

And the stockbrokers—did they doubt Randell's glowing accounts of N.S.M.C.'s present and future? He was able to arrange things so that they could hardly afford to; before long a number of them were working for him, beating the bushes to find companies for N.S.M.C. to acquire so that it could keep increasing its earnings, and being paid off handsomely for their efforts with batches of N.S.M.C. stock. Sometimes the brokerage firms apparently found it possible to sweeten up the deal with a recommendation of N.S.M.C. stock to their customers.

So the money factory was a closed chain, infallible so long, and just so long, as the chain remained unbroken. The weak link was, of course, the disparity between Cort Randell's promises and his company's real results, which, closely scrutinized, were unspectacular. The first serious test of his credibility in Wall Street came late in 1969. N.S.M.C.'s report for the fiscal year ended that summer showed net profit of around $3.5 million, duly fulfilling Randell's projections. But to achieve the figure, the company's accountants had been obliged, among other strokes of creativity, to defer until a future year product development and start-up costs of $533,000, even though the money had already been spent; to include as income $2.8 million of "unbilled receivables," which was to say, money that had not been received because it had not even been asked for; and—perhaps more egregiously—to include as net income more than $3 million attributable to the profits of N.S.M.C. subsidiaries that N.S.M.C. had not yet acquired at the close of the year being reported on. With the elimination of that item, which was explained to investors in a small mumbled footnote, N.S.M.C.'s 1969 profit would have been all but wiped out.

N.S.M.C. stock dropped briefly after the report appeared—only to rise again to the 100-times-earnings range. But a few Wall Streeters seem to have read the footnotes; stock analysts and investing institutions began asking N.S.M.C. executives pointed questions for the first time late in 1969.

In early February, N.S.M.C.'s financial vice president gave a dumbstruck group of company executives the jolting news that the

actual result for the quarter just ended would be a loss. By February 17, Randell's ebullience had been dampened at last, at least to the extent that, in a speech to the St. Louis security analysts that day, he said merely that N.S.M.C.'s first 1970 quarter would be "profitable." His partial concession to reality was too little and too late. The following day, amid panic in the councils of N.S.M.C., Randell resigned as president; a week later, a first-quarter loss of $1.2 million was announced, and two days after that, the company shamefacedly admitted that there had been a "mechanical error in transferring figures from one set of books to another," and that the actual loss was more like $1.5 million. By this time the market for the stock had understandably caved in; having sold at 140 as recently as late December, it was down to 50 and sinking fast; by July it would stand at 3½, a loss of more than 97 percent from its peak seven months before. As for Cort Randell, he would by then have vanished into the obscurity of his Potomac palace, with a few million dollars intact from stock sales made in time—one more stock-market rocket of youth's short era, rich and burned out at thirty-five.

Well and good. But the question remains, how could he have fooled the Morgan Guaranty, the Bankers Trust, Harvard and Cornell, the whole brains trust of institutional investing, for as long as he did—and, of course, taken the innocent investing public along with them? The answer appears to be painfully simple: that he was plausible and they were gullible as well as greedy; that, in times of speculative madness, the wisdom and experience of the soundest and soberest may yield to a hysteria induced by the glimpse of fool's gold dished by a young man with a smile on his lips and a gleam in his eye.

CHAPTER 9

THE 1970 CRASH

In terms of the analogy between the nineteen twenties and the nineteen sixties with which this chronicle began, the beginning of the year 1970 corresponds roughly to the late spring of 1929. In each case, there were warning signals across the land of a coming economic recession, possibly a full-scale depression, and an uneasy Republican administration, only a year or so in office, was wondering

what to do for its best friend and principal political client, the business community. In each case a steep decline in second-rate stock issues—a sort of hidden crash, since it didn't show up in the popular averages—was already under way. In each case speculation continued to flourish, and money was historically tight; and in each case the Federal Reserve, torn between trying to dampen speculation and inflation on the one hand and trying to head off recession on the other, was frantically pressing its monetary levers to little effect.

But there was at least one big difference. Where in 1929 the stock market became the national craze as it had never quite been since, and interest in it was actually increased by its disintegration, in 1970 the investor mood was one of fatalism, and the decline in trading volume would become as great a problem for Wall Street as the decline in stock prices.

The chairman of the New York Stock Exchange in 1970, who was fated to be the key man in Wall Street's near-fatal convulsions that year, was Bernard J. Lasker, always called Bunny, a tall, athletic-looking man of fifty-nine with the semi-distant yet curiously vulnerable air of command of a tough regular-army top sergeant.

Like so many self-made men in America, big, bluff Bunny Lasker was a bellicose conservative, ever eager to praise the free-enterprise environment that had gravitated him from Wall Street runner into Stock Exchange management. Indeed, one is tempted to describe him as a Republican by instinct or even by religion. On the whole, his faith in the Grand Old Party and its members seemed to stand him in good stead. It certainly did in his relations with Richard Nixon, with whom he first became associated as a fund-raiser in the 1960 Presidential campaign. The following year, when the defeated candidate was visiting New York, he called up Lasker to thank him for his efforts in the campaign and to suggest that, since they had never met, they do so now. The two men met at the Plaza and hit it off immediately. Then, after Nixon had hit political bottom with his 1962 defeat in the California gubernatorial election and had temporarily abandoned politics to come to New York to practice law, Lasker and his wife more or less took their friends in hand: Lasker helped the Nixons find an apartment, Mrs. Lasker helped Mrs. Nixon find a dressmaker, and the two couples frequently dined together. It was in 1964, though, that Lasker without conscious intention put the future President most deeply in his debt. Nixon would say later that Lasker, in helping to talk him out of making the Presidential race

again in that overwhelmingly Democratic year, had had a large hand in saving his political career.

So when Lasker came to the Stock Exchange chairmanship in 1969, the Stock Exchange had a friend at court. Lasker began drawing on his Washington connections on April 29—the day of the Cambodia invasion, and another day of steadily declining stock prices —when, at Lasker's suggestion and with Nixon's approval, he and a group of other Wall Street leaders met at the White House with a group of top government officials including Economic Advisers Council Chairman Paul McCracken. Each side reassured the other that everything was under control; but nevertheless, as Donald Regan, chairman of Merrill Lynch, reported later, "the tone of the meeting was dejected." Still, it served to open a wire between Wall Street and Washington that would be crucial in the weeks to come.

In early May, matters on Wall Street went from bad to worse. Trading volume was still relatively low. It was not a panic but a funk—"a kind of neurosis," as George Shultz, then Nixon's Bureau of Management and Budget chief, said. Shultz did not add that the neurosis seemed to have been brought about in good part by the actions of the Nixon administration in noneconomic fields. Cambodia and Kent State, on top of everything else, had stunned the nation. Nothing could be discerned ahead but more futile overseas war and domestic violence. The last thing people felt like doing was buying stocks.

Lasker, having decided that the time had come to play his ace, now sought a personal interview with Nixon, who, he felt, was simply neglecting the stock market and its consequences in his preoccupation with foreign affairs and inflation. On the afternoon of May 20, he was notified that the President would see him the following morning at eleven o'clock.

What the two men decided on, as an immediate step, was the scheduling, with due fanfare, of a large White House dinner for top officials of government, Wall Street, and business, to be tailored specifically to show the nation that the government was indeed concerned about the stock-market situation and was prepared to do what could be done to remedy it.

Lasker went back to Wall Street the same day, well satisfied with his White House audience. Yet the stock market went on dropping. On May 22, the averages hit a new low since early 1963, and Merrill Lynch had to call for $11.5 million in new margin money from its customers who had bought stock partially on credit. The weekend

break brought no surcease, and on Monday, May 25, the Dow dropped 20.81 points—the biggest one-day drop since the Kennedy assassination in 1963—to finish just above 640. Economic analyst Eliot
Janeway had begun talking about a bottom of 500.

Midnight seemed to be at hand. Panic lurked in the wings. On
Monday afternoon, after the market closed, the brokerage and investment community learned of the planned White House dinner from
an announcement carried on the Dow news tape. The dinner was to
be held that Wednesday the twenty-seventh and was to be attended
by sixty or more leading figures from business and finance. But the
studied implication of Presidential concern for the fortunes of Wall
Street had disappointingly little immediate effect. The next day,
Tuesday, the Dow dropped nine more points, to 631. Then on Tuesday evening through television news reports, and on Wednesday
morning through newspaper coverage and comment, the significance
of the coming event seemed to sink in. In one of the great prepran-
dial celebrations of American history, a cocktail hour of staggering
economic importance, the Dow on Wednesday the twenty-seventh
leaped upward 32.04 points for the biggest one-day gain in Stock Exchange history.

The dinner itself, taking place when the announcement of it had
already largely fulfilled its purpose, was something of an anti-climax,
with certain overtones of farce. In the White House's State Dining
Room the full panoply of government, business, and financial power
was duly arrayed. The proceedings seem to have been solemn, por-
tentous, and in some ways rather horrifying. The President spoke
first. Referring to a huge map of Southeast Asia that had been set up
behind him, he characterized the three-week-old Cambodian invasion as the best-executed American military coup since MacArthur's
landings at Inchon in Korea in 1950. Why, the President wanted to
know, did Wall Street look upon such a national triumph as an occasion for selling stocks? On the contrary, he said, it ought to be considered highly bullish. On the domestic front, he predicted resumed
economic growth and a cooling of inflation in the second half of the
year. Lasker, speaking next, urgently insisted that a substantial stock
recovery was dependent on three government actions: strict adher-
ence to the announced plans for withdrawal of American troops from
Cambodia, clear evidence that the Federal Reserve would support
the price of government bonds, and further steps by the Fed to increase the money supply. Chairman Burns of the Fed, arising next,

assured those present that his institution was fully aware of the magnitude and significance of the Wall Street crisis, and declared flatly, and most satisfactorily, that the Fed was prepared to fulfill its responsibilities as a lender of last resort. This, as it happened, was the only concrete reassurance of constructive economic action to be uttered by a government official all evening.

Following Burns's remarks, Nixon called for questions. There was a question as to how the President proposed to deal with the nation's young people and their campus revolts, to which the President replied, apparently to everyone's satisfaction, that junior faculty members at universities ought to show "more guts" in dealing with student protesters. According to one account, "he added that he had not become President of the United States to witness the liquidation of all our alliances and to see us lose our place of primacy in the hierarchy of nations."

And then came the bombshell. A guest named Isidore Cohen, who was entirely unknown to almost everybody present, arose with a "question" that swiftly evolved into a slashing ten-minute attack on the administration's policies. As Cohen went on, heatedly and implacably, and it became clear that there was a cuckoo in this nest of the business-financial-government complex, there was general consternation and dismay. When at last Cohen had finished his tirade and resumed his seat, the President coolly picked up where he had left off, almost as if nothing had happened; and a few minutes later the meeting broke up to general applause.

What had happened? Who was Izzy Cohen and what was he doing there? "What was he doing there?" Bunny Lasker asked later, with rhetorical indignation. "Why, he's a Democrat!" At least as much to the point, Cohen was by no means a businessman of comparable stature to the others present. In fact, he was a principal of Joseph Cohen and Sons, a men's clothing manufacturer based in New York and Philadelphia that had recently merged with Rapid-American, the conglomerate headed by the one-time Israeli Meshulam Riklis—who had not been favored by a Presidential invitation. Cohen was there, in a word, because someone involved in the planning of the dinner had blundered. We may be grateful to the anonymous blunderer, and to Cohen himself, for making the President's dinner into something both more human and more representative of the nation than anyone had intended.

History is full of ironies, and it is just barely possible that the

United States was saved from "another 1929" by this White House non-event. The reports of the dinner that circulated in Wall Street the next day emphasized Burns's reassurances rather than Cohen's contrariety, and the market rose. It bounded up 21 more points that day, and on the following day, a Friday, it climbed above 700. Early in June a fresh decline began, and threatened to turn into a rout when, on the twenty-first, the supposedly unshakable Penn Central Railroad Company, suffering from management that in retrospect would appear to have been inept beyond belief, suddenly collapsed into bankruptcy. With the Penn Central's paper in default, the danger was that the unfortunate companies that had lent tens of millions to the Penn Central might themselves be unable to meet their obligations, and that other commercial-paper lenders might suddenly refuse to renew their loans, leading to a chain reaction ending in a classic national money panic and, of course, a stock-market collapse. But the Federal Reserve, this time, was on its toes; warned in advance of impending danger, it applied the classic remedy to the classic dilemma, opening wide its usually carefully restricted loan window and suspending the banks' usual interest-rate ceilings, thereby releasing a flood of money into the market and preventing the chain reaction from starting. Fast footwork by the often heavy-footed Fed kept the Penn Central failure an isolated tragedy instead of a national disaster; early in July, the Dow began a long, fairly steady rise that would carry it by the end of the year to above 840.

Having compared 1929 and 1970 as to sequence of events and attitudes toward events and found the similarities at least as striking as the differences, we will do well to compare the hard figures. From the September 1929 peak to the nadir of the Great Depression in the summer of 1932, the Dow industrial average dropped from 381 to 36, or just over 90 percent. From the December 1968 peak to the May 1970 bottom, the same index dropped from 985 to 631, or about 36 percent. By that standard, a pistol shot as against a mortar barrage. But, as we have had occasion to note before, that standard really will not do. As measured by the performance of the stocks in which the novice investor was most likely to make his first plunges, the 1969-70 crash was fully comparable to that of 1929.

And again, measured by the number of people affected and the gross sums of money they lost, 1969-70 was strikingly *worse* than 1929-32. In 1929 there were, at the most, four or five million Ameri-

cans who owned stock; in 1970, by the New York Stock Exchange's own proud count, there were about 31 million. As to the sums of money lost, between September and November 1929 around $30 billion eroded from the paper value of stocks listed on the New York Stock Exchange, and a few billion more from that of stocks traded elsewhere; the 1969-70 loss, including issues listed on the two leading exchanges and those traded over-the-counter, totaled in excess of $300 billion, ten times the former amount.

Losses, then, of $300 billion in a year and a half, spread over more than 30 million investors—such were the bitter fruits of the go-go years: of the conglomerates and their promoters' talk of synergism and of two and two making five; of the portfolio wizards who wheeled and dealt with their customers' money; of the works of bottom-line fiction written by the creative accountants; of the garbage stock dumped on the market by two-a-week underwriters; of the stock salesmen who acted as go-betweens for quick commissions; of the mutual funds that got instant performance by writing up the indeterminate value of unregistered letter stock. But the fact remains that the human and social damage that resulted from the more recent crash was immeasurably less. In a nation far richer in real terms than it had been in 1929, the market losers of 1969-70 could better absorb their losses, and moreover, more intelligent and conscientious federal regulation in the later era shielded the losers from the worst consequences of their gullibility and greed.

What resulted, in fact, was a middle-class crash, productive of severe discomfort rather than disaster. If one heard of investor hardship in 1970, but not of lost homes, shattered lives, and suicides, much of the credit must go to that key piece of New Deal reform legislation, the Securities Exchange Act of 1934, which (among many other things) gave the Federal Reserve its power to regulate stock-market credit. At the very time when old-style liberalism was being widely reviled and ridiculed, a key measure of old-style liberalism, little noticed or honored, was serving as a small but significant piece of evidence that in forty years the country had learned something, after all.

And of course, not so much because of more enlightened government policies as because of the enormous industrial strength of the nation, the 1970 crash, unlike that of 1929, was not followed by a catastrophic depression. It was, however, followed by a serious one. To the layman, signs of recession late in 1970 were everywhere plain

to see. In October, the Bureau of Labor Statistics reported that, with national unemployment at 5.2 percent of the work force, the figure for male black teen-agers in urban areas stood at 34.9 percent. At about the same time the tide of recession began spreading upward in the economic spectrum. It never did soak, or even dampen, the rich—corporate chieftains went right on drawing astronomical salaries, and banks in particular actually flourished because of continuing tight money—but in the autumn of 1970 the recession wave swamped the middle class. An organizer of the United Steelworkers told Studs Terkel, chronicler of the Great Depression of the nineteen thirties, "When a guy is cashing his biweekly check at the neighborhood bar, every check for the last few years has been $300, $400. Now he brings home $150 to $170."

In October, the airlines, anticipating collective losses of at least $100 million on the year's operations, were cutting back luxury services. The same month, the Department of Labor identified thirty-five separate major labor areas with "substantial or persistent" unemployment; the Council of Better Business Bureaus estimated that there were 400,000 currently unemployed executives; and large companies began making across-the-board cuts of executive and white-collar paychecks.

There was talk of stockbrokers working as cab drivers, art directors taking jobs as layout artists, and accountants accepting sharp salary cuts and for the first time in their lives paying agency fees. That winter in Manhattan, for-hire limousines were in supply rather than in demand; for the first time in the memory of many opera patrons, there were empty seats at almost every Metropolitan Opera performance; many former Saks Fifth Avenue customers were patronizing Klein's or Alexander's, and many former taxi riders were riding buses and subways. In December, placement counselors at colleges began telling seniors of a sharp drop in job offers, and warning them that the days when they could take their pick of starting jobs were over.

And so it went. There were no breadlines or applesellers, but bread was being eaten instead of cake, apples instead of baked Alaska. And the reaction of worried politicians to the deteriorating situation called forth more sardonic echoes of the past. As the year 1970 ran out with the gross national product down for the first time since 1958, and with industry limping along at three-quarters of capacity, the President, with the concurrence of Congress, began applying that old Herbert Hoover standby, the trickle-down theory of

trying to save old jobs and create new ones through federal handouts to business. By the end of the year, Congress had voted the Lockheed Aircraft Corporation a $250-million loan guarantee in a financial rescue operation intended principally to save the jobs of 60,000 employees by saving the company from bankruptcy; the bankrupt Penn Central was on the way to a $125-million federal loan guarantee to keep its passenger trains running and its employees working; a new governmental corporation, Amtrak, was being established to operate all of the nation's intercity trains; and government shipbuilding subsidies were in the process of being greatly increased. It looked like Hoover's famous breadline for business, the Reconstruction Finance Corporation, all over again, with the difference that the R.F.C. had usually driven a harder bargain with its petitioners than the Nixon administration did now.

Week by week and month by month, new parallels kept appearing. In 1971, Nixon repeatedly rejected the idea of direct federally sponsored job programs, just as Hoover had done in 1930 and 1931. Week by week and month by month, the dollar grew weaker in the international markets. When the United States had finally been forced to abandon its pledge to redeem dollars with gold on April 18, 1933, it had been three and a half years after the beginning of the 1929 stock-market crash. This time, the triumph of political necessity over national honor came sooner. When the gold default of 1933 was repeated down to all but the smallest details in August 1971, it was hardly more than a year after the height of the 1970 crash.

History, in its economic aspect, seemed to have become a recurring nightmare from which the United States could not awake. But for Wall Street, the nightmare this time had a new dimension. In the second half of 1970, Wall Street itself, as distinguished from its hapless customers, came within a hair of plunging into bankruptcy, and the American securities market into full-fledged socialism.

CHAPTER 10

SAVING GRACES

If Wall Street can lay claim to special expertise in any particular field, that field is the raising and management of capital. Bringing together, presumably in an orderly and mutually beneficial way,

companies that need new money to run their businesses and investors who wish to hire out some of their money at reasonable risk, is Wall Street's work — the social justification of its existence. By and large, over the years, it has performed this function well. Yet in the latter nineteen sixties the capital structure of Wall Street itself became unsafe and unsound to a degree that, when hard times struck, was revealed as nothing less than a scandal.

Matters had not always been thus. The celebrated post-1929 suicide victims had been for the most part customers rather than brokers. The brokers' yachts were scarce by 1932, but their firms had come through that crisis still solvent, partly because most of them had been conservatively financed with the personal resources of careful Puritanical partners, partly because the brokerage business in those days had been of manageable size, and not least because the terrible drop in stock prices had occurred on such unprecedentedly high trading volume as to enable brokers to recoup on commissions much of their losses on stocks they owned.

But in the nineteen sixties, when the securities business had broadened to become mass business for the first time, brokerage houses financed themselves not by adopting the mass-business methods they understood so well and so often urged on others, but by merely adding new and dubious twists to the traditional methods of what had been, by the standards of American Telephone or General Motors, a cottage industry. Not until 1970, for example, did the first Wall Street firm raise money for its operations from outside by selling its own stock to the public, and it took a change in the New York Stock Exchange's constitution to make such a sale possible. Like most bad business practices, Wall Street's obsolete and unsound capital-raising methods worked well enough in good times; it required only a little misfortune to expose them as the jerry-built mechanisms they were.

That misfortune, utterly unanticipated, consisted of the simultaneous drop in stock prices and trading volume in 1969 and the first half of 1970.

Let us look, in brief and simplified form, at a brokerage firm's typical capital structure in 1969-70, as administered by the New York Stock Exchange and grudgingly but nonetheless leniently approved by the S.E.C.

The Stock Exchange requires that the ratio between a firm's aggregate indebtedness and its "net capital" be at no time higher than twenty

to one, and the Stock Exchange, through a system of surprise audits, undertook to see that its members complied with this rule. And what was the nature and source of the "net capital" required under the rules? Its basic and soundest forms were the traditional ones—the cash investments of general partners, entitling them to stated shares in the profits, and the cash loans of other backers, entitling them to interest. But that was only the beginning, and, by the end of the nineteen sixties, only a small percentage of the capital of many firms consisted of such unassailable assets. There were other less substantial but still permissible forms of "capital" that, after the great expansion of 1967-68, came to predominate over the traditional ones. One of these consisted of the loan of securities by an investor to a broker—a fair enough form of capital except that, unlike cash, the securities might abruptly decline in dollar value, thus abruptly reducing the amount of capital that they represented. Also qualified for inclusion as capital were a firm's accounts receivable, which sometimes consisted of such birds-in-the-bush as anticipated tax refunds and possibly uncollectable cash debts from customers. Then there were secured demand notes. Anyone owning a batch of securities— no matter how volatile and speculative—could pledge them as collateral on a paper loan to a brokerage firm and thus technically contribute to the firm's capital. No money would actually change hands, nor would the investor actually give up the benefits of his pledged securities; there would merely be, for the firm, a cheering new capital entry on its balance sheet, and for the lender, the pleasure of regularly collecting interest on money he had never parted with and at the same time collecting dividends, were any paid, on his stocks. As if this were not a pleasant enough arrangement, under the terms of some such notes it was explicitly agreed that the lender would not have to part with any money or any securities, except in the all but unthinkable event that the brokerage firm should become insolvent, unable to meet its day-to-day obligations, or not in compliance with the net capital rule.

Shakiest of all, there were subordinated loans. Any securities-holding customer of a brokerage firm in need of additional capital could simply sign a paper headed "Event of Subordination Agreement." In this magic instrument, the customer did no more than agree, in the event of the firm's liquidation, to subordinate his claims to those of other customers and creditors; in exchange, he was allowed to go on collecting dividends on his stocks and simultaneously

collecting interest on his "loan"—which, of course, had involved no actual money—while the brokerage firm was allowed to enter on its books the market value of the securities, less a reasonable discount, as new capital. Here, then, was "capital" that the beneficiary could *never* lay his hands on—unless he went broke, and even in that case the hands laid on it would be not his but those of his creditors.

The net of these perhaps rather abstruse ground rules is that the S.E.C. and the Stock Exchange allowed Wall Street firms to comply with the net capital rule—imposed for the protection of the firms themselves as well as that of their customers—with capital that was essentially a mirage. It was money that could not be seen, or rubbed together, or jangled in the hand, or, more to the point, used in the operation of a brokerage business; essentially, it was money that would become available, if at all, too late to do any good. Finally, contributors of the palpable and useful forms of brokerage capital, equity cash and debt cash, were entitled to withdraw any and all of their money at any time on only ninety days' notice, whenever for some reason they didn't like the way things were going. In 1969 and 1970 few investors in brokerage houses liked the way things were going, with the quite logical and rational consequence that there was an enormous and nearly catastrophic outflow of working capital from the nerve center of world capitalism.

Capital troubles began to crop up in the backlash of the 1968 paperwork crisis, and one small firm, Pickard and Company, actually failed that year as a result of too much business too inefficiently handled. The Exchange, to its credit, was ready to deal with the plight of Pickard's customers. In 1964, following the collapse of Ira Haupt and Company resulting from the infamous salad-oil swindle, it had set up a $25 million Special Trust Fund, paid for by subscription of Stock Exchange member firms, and reserved specifically for restoring the lost holdings of the unlucky customers of any member firm that should go broke. Pickard's being the first member-firm failure since Haupt, the trust fund had never been drawn upon; now it was tapped for some $400,000 and Pickard's 3,500 customers were reimbursed—or, in the legal expression, "made whole."

Well and good: an isolated case, everyone supposed, in which the machinery had worked exactly as planned. But in the late spring of 1969, when stock prices and trading volume began to sink in unison, the squeeze on brokerage profits was on in earnest, leaving the firms' rickety capital structures increasingly exposed.

Early in 1970, as the continuing decline in prices and volume made the situation for brokers progressively worse, a wave of brokerage mergers arose—frantic, hastily arranged shotgun marriages dictated not by love but by the need for survival. During a dreadful March, there were two more member-firm failures and a quasi-failure. McDonnell and Company, in spite of high social prestige and close ties with the Ford family of Detroit, closed its doors (cost to the Special Trust Fund: $8.4 million); Baerwald and DeBoer went into liquidation (cost to the fund: about $1 million); and out in Los Angeles, the former hottest deal-maker of them all, Kleiner, Bell, found the going so rocky that it simply withdrew from the brokerage business. Then, on March 16, Bache and Company reported that for fiscal 1969 it had incurred the largest annual operating loss in the annals of American brokerage, $8,741,000. Shock waves followed the announcement; investors began to experience the chills of panic, and on March 23, Robert Haack, president of the Exchange, felt called upon to refute wayward rumors by stating that all of the twenty-five largest Stock Exchange firms were in compliance with the capital rules.

Whether or not Haack knew it at the time, this was quite wide of the truth, as subsequent events would more than demonstrate. In fact, five Stock Exchange firms were at that moment in liquidations that would end up costing the Exchange's Special Trust Fund $17 million of its $25 million total; yet another member firm, Dempsey-Tegeler, was in its death throes, and its liquidation would eventually cost the trust fund over $20 million; and, worst of all, Hayden, Stone and Company, an eighty-four-year-old giant not far from the core of the Wall Street Establishment, with some 90,000 brokerage customers and a major share of the underwriting business, had lost nearly $11 million the previous year and was now losing money at a rate in excess of a million dollars a month. Hayden, Stone's affairs were shortly to erupt into the first phase of the crisis that almost brought Wall Street low for good.

At the end of May—at just about the time of the White House dinner that got credit for turning the market around—Stock Exchange Chairman Bernard J. Lasker and some of his fellow governors of the Exchange decided that the time had come to form a special committee to maintain surveillance over member firms' financial affairs.

It was Robert L. Stott, Jr., a well-known floor specialist, who came

to Lasker and suggested that a committee of governors be formed forthwith. Responding enthusiastically, Lasker appointed to the new committee—formally named the Surveillance Committee, but usually thereafter called the Crisis Committee—himself; Ralph DeNunzio, executive vice president of Kidder, Peabody and vice chairman of the Exchange; Stott; Stephen M. Peck, senior partner in Weiss, Peck and Greer; Solomon Litt, senior partner in Asiel and Company; and Felix George Rohatyn, a partner in Lazard Frères and Company.

The chairman of the committee was Rohatyn, and it was he and Lasker, working in tandem, who would bear the brunt of its work over the months ahead. Rohatyn had been born in Vienna in 1928, and he and his Polish-Jewish parents had arrived in the United States as refugees from Hitler in 1942, after an interim stay in France. He had graduated in 1948 from Middlebury College, in Vermont, with a B.A. in physics, gone directly to Lazard, and never left again except for a spell of military service during the Korean war. As a young acolyte making the transition from natural science to the intricate and unnatural science of corporate finance, Rohatyn at Lazard had had the good luck to become a protégé of one of the leading masters of corporate deal-making, the French-born, publicity-shy, tough old wizard of Wall Street, André Meyer. Under such Cordon Bleu tutelage, sous-chef Rohatyn flourished. "Nobody has a record quite as spectacular as Felix's," a partner in a rival investment-banking house said of him in 1970. The record consisted of having become one of Wall Street's most ingenious experts in corporate acquisition and reorganization. That is to say, Rohatyn had become, like his mentor, a master merger-maker, and one of the firms for which he arranged intricate, multimillion-dollar acquisitions was the Lazard client International Telephone and Telegraph, on whose board of directors he sat.

In 1972, Rohatyn would come to national prominence, of a sort, as the banker for I.T.T. who the previous year had had a series of private meetings with then Acting Attorney General Richard G. Kleindienst to argue, on public-policy grounds, for a favorable settlement of the Justice Department's antitrust suit against I.T.T. Disclosure of those meetings involved Rohatyn in considerable controversy, since Kleindienst would later deny, for a time, that he had had anything to do with the settlement. (It was never alleged that Rohatyn had any knowledge of or involvement in the famous I.T.T. financial commitment to the Republicans for their 1972 national convention.) What-

ever the facts of that matter, Rohatyn in 1970 was quite possibly the most brilliant, and certainly among the most dedicated and energetic, men in Wall Street at a time when Wall Street badly needed brains, talent, and energy to save it from its own folly. Rich enough at forty-two, married to a daughter of the well-known author and Union-with-Britain advocate Clarence Streit, beginning to be spoken of as heir apparent to Meyer as boss of Lazard Frères, Felix Rohatyn in 1970 was riding the crest.

The Surveillance Committee started out by meeting once a week, for lunch on Thursdays, in a committee room on the sixth floor of the Stock Exchange building. According to Rohatyn and Lasker—both of whom later talked to me at length about the committee and its work—its first job consisted chiefly of trying to exercise due diligence as to the use of the trust fund in current liquidations, and of trying to set up an early warning system as to other firms that were heading for trouble. To their horror, the committee members began to see that weakness was the rule rather than the exception. "It was like a nightmare," Rohatyn said later. "You pushed here, you pushed there, at random, and wherever you pushed, you found softness."

Early in June, when the committee had been in existence for only a few weeks, it faced the first of three heroic challenges: the impending collapse of Hayden, Stone and Company. That venerable firm had been in serious trouble since 1968, as the Exchange had ample occasion to know; in that year—a banner business year in which Hayden, Stone's gross income was at an all-time high of $113 million—its record-keeping situation had become so bad that it had literally called on the Coast Guard for help, hiring members of that service to moonlight in the back office. As early as the spring of 1969, investors in Hayden, Stone were getting the message that the good days were gone, and accordingly they began withdrawing their capital in huge amounts.

In September 1969, matters were hardly improved when the Stock Exchange imposed restrictions on Hayden, Stone's operations and fined the firm $150,000 for rule infractions during the previous year. At all events, the firm started out 1970 in technical capital compliance only on the basis of such gossamer assets as a tax refund claim that, far from having been approved by the Internal Revenue Service, had not yet even been filed.

By late May, when the Crisis Committee came into existence, Hayden, Stone was a huge black cloud on Wall Street's horizon, a

storm latent but brewing. Its roster of branch offices had shrunk from eighty at the beginning of the year to sixty-two, and its back-office expenses had been drastically curtailed through mass firings, but, even so, it continued to lose approximately $1 million a month on current operations. Meanwhile though, its capital problems had apparently been solved, at least temporarily and technically, at a single stroke. On Friday, March 13—of all dates—a group of Oklahoma businessmen signed demand notes lending Hayden, Stone $12.4 million, pledging stock in their own companies as collateral. They included Bill Swisher of CMI corporation, who pledged 165,000 shares then worth $4,372,500; Jack E. Golsen of LSB Industries, who pledged 200,000 of his firm's shares worth $1.2 million; and—most unfortunately, as it turned out—Jack L. Clark of Four Seasons Nursing Centers, who pledged 120,000 shares of his firm's high-flying stock with a March market value just short of $5 million. All told, the collateral added up to $17.5 million, apparently an ample sum to cover the $12.4 million demand note and give Hayden, Stone a rosy capital future. A rosy present income for the Oklahomans was assured by an interest rate on their "money" of around seven percent.

However, as the reader will have no trouble discerning, this was a classic case of phantom capital, created by a shuffle of papers and used to maintain formal compliance with a rule of the Stock Exchange's that the Exchange had no stomach for enforcing. Hayden, Stone, which so desperately needed capital, could not get its hands on a cent.

Then the shaky structure cracked. In mid-May, the S.E.C. suddenly suspended trading in Four Seasons Nursing Centers, which shortly thereafter expired in bankruptcy. Down the drain went $5 million in Oklahoma collateral on $3.3 million of Hayden, Stone capital. And the prices of the other Oklahoma stocks were dropping—20, 30, 40 percent—along with the rest of the market. By the beginning of June, when the Crisis Committee was hardly a week old, the market value of the Oklahoma collateral had declined from $17.5 million to around $9 million, and as a result Hayden, Stone was plainly in violation of the capital rule, as a routine surprise audit would confirm a few days later. Things were in a worsening mess now; but what, the committee members asked themselves, could the Stock Exchange do? As Lasker and Rohatyn saw the matter, the Exchange had only one course—to find new capital to save Hayden, Stone, or to admit to the public that Wall Street could no longer be relied upon.

As a first step, the Exchange found some capital in a curious place. The Special Trust Fund was more than doubled by transferring into it $30 million that the Exchange had squirreled away as a building fund. The Special Trust Fund, as we have seen, was clearly intended for the single purpose of rescuing the customers of bankrupt member firms. But these were parlous times, and the language of the Special Trust Fund provisions was conveniently vague. So the Exchange's governors, on recommendation of the Crisis Committee, now voted to lend $5 million of their constitutents' money to Hayden, Stone to keep it in business. It was just a matter of saving the broker in order to save the customers, they rationalized. Thus, on July 2, Hayden, Stone was restored to capital compliance—this time with real money, albeit money obtained in a most peculiar way.

But the reprieve was short-lived. By now, houses were crumbling from one end of Wall Street to the other. In mid-August, the Exchange, through President Haack, announced for the first time the names of ten brokerage firms that were in bankruptcy or liquidation, and gave soothing reassurances that the augmented trust fund, now theoretically amounting to $55 million, was adequate to make their customers whole. Nevertheless, by the last week of August it was generally known in the Street that the fund was again depleted.

Meanwhile, Hayden, Stone went on losing money. The Oklahomans were screaming bloody murder at what was happening to their investment, and the loudest screamer was Jack Golsen. The conduct of Hayden, Stone's affairs, as it was now being gradually revealed, seemed to Golsen to be a public scandal. "In my business, if we are missing inventory, we stop everything and look for it," he complained. "In Wall Street, if they're missing seven million dollars, they just accept it as part of the game." The representations that the officers of the firm had made to him, in asking for the loan, now appeared to him to have been false; it seemed to him that Hayden, Stone's talk about its capital assets represented "dealings not in realities but in the abstract."

Early in August there was an attempt, prompted by the Exchange, to save Hayden, Stone through a merger with Walston and Company, but the deal fell through. The next merger candidate was Cogan, Berlind, Weill and Levitt (the same firm, with a name change, that had so profitably brokered the Leasco-Reliance merger in 1968). C.B.W.L., still doing well, was a small firm eager to expand, and the merger with Hayden, Stone would be a quick path to expansion. Un-

fortunately, it might also be a quick path to financial and operational chaos, since its new partner was virtually bankrupt. Knowing full well that it would have to sweeten the deal, the Stock Exchange offered $7.6 million to C.B.W.L. in exchange for its assuming the Hayden, Stone mess—a $7.6 million that the Exchange didn't have just then, in its trust fund or anywhere else, but that it believed it could raise from its membership. And that did it. At last agreement was reached that the Hayden, Stone offices would be divided between C.B.W.L. and Walston. The surviving firm was to be named CBWL-Hayden, Stone, Inc.

The whole thing almost fell through in what for the Crisis Committee was a hair-raising sequence of events on September 2 and 3. On the afternoon of the second, the Chicago Board of Trade, the nation's largest commodity exchange, suddenly announced that it planned to suspend Hayden, Stone for insolvency. Such a suspension would force the New York Stock Exchange to take similar action the next day, and that would be the ball game. At the last minute, the suspension order was revoked in consideration of Hayden, Stone's putting up a half a million dollars in escrow. And *that* crisis was surmounted. But there remained a single crucial detail to be carried out—that of getting approval of the merger from every last one of Hayden, Stone's 108 subordinated lenders. It was, indeed, a delicate situation. Since they all apparently stood to lose most of their money anyway, their egos could have free play, unfettered by financial considerations. Meanwhile, they found themselves in the satisfying position of being able to hold up the Wall Street Establishment—for revenge, for publicity, or for principle—by simply refusing to sign and thus forcing Hayden, Stone out of business.

All the persuasive powers of the Stock Exchange authorities were brought to bear. Haack flew to London to get one lender's signature, and got it. Others at first refused to sign, then allowed themselves to be persuaded. But time was running out; the Exchange could not go on ignoring its capital rule forever, and at last, under S.E.C. pressure, a deadline had to be set: the deal would be consummated by 10:00 A.M. on Friday, September 11 or Hayden, Stone would go into suspension, its 90,000 customers would be left out in the cold, and public confidence in Wall Street would end, possibly forever. By the morning of September 10, all of the subordinated lenders had signed except Golsen.

He stood firmly on principle. "I'm interested in justice being

done," he said. "I want an example made. The only way to make it is to go to a liquidation and let the Exchange lose twenty-five million or so. I want this crime to be brought to the attention of the public."

So for a day Golsen, in Oklahoma, held Hayden, Stone's and perhaps Wall Street's fate in his hand, while Lasker, from his office at the Exchange and his suite uptown at the Carlyle, pleaded repeatedly by phone. Lasker finally, at almost literally the last minute, won. It has been said that his clincher, delivered in the middle of the night of September 10, was a suggestion—or a threat—to have Richard Nixon himself call Golsen. Lasker vehemently denies that he went any further than to tell Golsen in general terms that he knew the President was very much concerned about the Wall Street situation and its effect on the national economy. Rather, Lasker attributes his success with Golsen to a homely coincidence. On the evening of September 10, Lasker says, an old friend and Wall Street colleague of his—Alan C. Greenberg, of Bear, Stearns and Company—called him unexpectedly and said, "Bunny, I hear you want a favor from Jack Golsen. I've known Golsen all my life. We were kids together in Oklahoma and, before we were both married, I used to date his wife and he used to date mine. You want me to call him?"

Reflecting that God must be on the side of the Stock Exchange, Lasker said yes. Greenberg called Golsen and said, "Bunny Lasker is an honest man and a good friend of mine, and I want you to do what he wants because I ask you."

Not to save Wall Street or the economy, then, or to obey the President of the United States, but for the sake of friendship. Whatever the case, something prevailed on Golsen, the Oklahoma outsider with a loaded gun pointed directly at Wall Street's head. After waiting melodramatically until ten minutes before deadline time on Friday the eleventh, Golsen signed; at ten o'clock sharp the CBWL-Hayden, Stone merger was announced, and the Hayden, Stone crisis was over.

"Hayden, Stone blooded us," Rohatyn says. "After that, the Crisis Committee had some idea what it was up against." The case accomplished something else, perhaps more important: it welded Rohatyn and Lasker, both of whom would spend the rest of 1970 devoting themselves virtually full-time to Crisis Committee work, into a team. These two highly diverse, imperfect men made common cause. They were together, for example, in being highly dissatisfied with the

Exchange's staff work on member-firm finances. Right after the resolution of the Hayden, Stone crisis, John Cunningham, the Exchange's executive vice president, assured a meeting of the board of governors that this was the end—no more problems with member firms' finances could be expected. Rohatyn, appalled, jumped up to say that Cunningham was crazy—it was nowhere near the end.

Later, Rohatyn would say that he felt that autumn as if he and Lasker had lived in a foxhole together, and that, different as the two were in many ways, he had come out of the experience thinking of Lasker as "a true friend, a man who reached beyond himself when he was under pressure." Emphatically, it was not over; and the last and in some respects most harrowing phase of the crisis was to be complicated by an acrimonious controversy within the ranks of the Stock Exchange itself.

The last act concerned the Wall Street investment firm of Francis I. du Pont and Company, and it marked the point when the crisis involved not just the New York financial Establishment but the national one. F. I. du Pont was a part of the fief of America's oldest and perhaps most powerful business barony. More than a century and a half had passed since Eleuthère Irénée du Pont had come with his family to America from France on an erratically wandering clipper ship and had begun setting up a gunpowder works on the Brandywine near Wilmington, Delaware. In the early years of the twentieth century, Eleuthère du Pont's great grandson, Francis I. du Pont, had been a brilliant maverick within the family, generally regarded as the most talented chemist the company had ever had, and, more surprisingly, also well known at one time as a single-tax radical. But Francis I. was restless in Wilmington and environs. Fascinated by the gyrations of the stock market during and after the 1929 crash, he embarked in middle life on a whole new career. In 1931, at the age of fifty-eight, he started his own Stock Exchange firm, first handling the investments of a few relatives, and then branching out to deal with the public as well. By the early nineteen sixties—by which time Francis I. du Pont was dead, but his firm was still solidly controlled by members of his family and was managed by his son, Edmond— F. I. du Pont and Company was, as to retail business, the second-largest brokerage house in the country.

By 1969 it had dropped to third, after Merrill Lynch and Bache; it operated ninety-five branch offices. But the 1969 audit, completed in September, disclosed an impermissible capital-to-debt ratio

of 1:32 (1:19 was the Exchange's approved figure), representing a capital shortage of some $6.8 million. But the Exchange was prevailed upon by the du Pont partners to take no precipitate action and, by the time the report reached the S.E.C. in December, the partners had found enough new capital to restore the firm to compliance. So F.I. du Pont staggered through the year 1969, but not without incurring an operating deficit, before tax recoveries, of $7.7 million.

Knowing that the firm was sick and probably getting sicker, the Stock Exchange early in 1970 urged it to strengthen itself through a merger. It did, at least, make a merger. On July 1, it joined forces with two other brokerage houses, Glore, Forgan and Staats and Hirsch and Company, to form a new organization to be called F.I. du pont-Glore, Forgan and Company. Making the announcement, Edmond du Pont commented ebulliently, "This is what I would call a true case of synergism in which the resulting entity should add up to a lot more than the sum of the parts." Or so he hoped. In truth, it was a case of the drowning trying to rescue the drowning, since at the time of the merger Glore, Forgan and Staats was itself out of control. Some members of the Crisis Committee, Rohatyn among them, were appalled that the merger was effected without an accompanying audit. By mid-summer, Haack went to Wilmington to plead with various members of the du Pont clan—among them Lammot du Pont Copeland, then chairman of the board of E.I. du Pont de Nemours, but soon to resign in the aftermath of his son's spectacular personal bankruptcy—that they buttress their floundering brokerage firm with an infusion of $15 million in new capital. Haack's request was refused; moreover, by some later accounts, the du Ponts seemed to be affronted that the request had even been made.

Through the Hayden, Stone crisis, the du Pont situation simmered. It could not simmer forever, and it began to boil at the start of November. The du Ponts realized not only that a time had come when their brokerage firm definitely needed new capital to stay in business, but that they were no longer able to raise that capital within the family. They further realized that they had on their payroll a man with both the motive and the ready cash to be the new investor they so desperately needed. In July, in a resolute attempt to straighten out their tangled back office, they had commissioned Electronic Data Systems, of Dallas, to handle all of their electronic data processing requirements at a cost that was expected to average around $8 million a year. The head of E.D.S. was the quixotic Texan,

Henry Ross Perot, whose well-publicized financial situation was such that a few million dollars would apparently be hardly more than a drop in the bucket.

By taking on the du Pont computer contract, Perot had put E.D.S. into the Wall Street crisis perhaps more deeply than he realized or intended. The contract made du Pont one of E.D.S.'s largest customers; a du Pont failure now would mean not only lost revenue to E.D.S. but a severe blow to its reputation, and possibly a severe drop in the price of its stock, the source of Perot's immense wealth. So to some extent the du Ponts had already tangled Perot in their web; it might be cheaper for him to lend them a few millions than for him not to do so. Realizing the leverage that this handed them, the du Ponts went to Perot in early November and asked him for a $5 million loan to keep F.I. du Pont-Glore, Forgan and Company afloat.

Broadly speaking, it was Hayden, Stone all over again: another faltering old-line Wall Street firm going to the back country to find a rough and ready rescuer, with the Stock Exchange doing what it could to make the rescue possible in the interest of the innocent investors and, ultimately, of its own skin. But this time, there was a new element that changed the human equation. That factor was the du Ponts, and the fact that they *were* du Ponts: no parochial Wall Street bigwigs like the partners of Hayden, Stone, but—du Ponts! Why, after all, should they, wearers of the Wilmington purple, give quarter to a moralizing Texan or to the minions of the Stock Exchange? Used to getting their way, accustomed to living and having their business in a state that they ruled like a barony, these worthies seemed on occasion to the Stock Exchange representatives during the negotiations to treat the securities industry itself as a far-flung part of their personal preserve.

Dozens of du Ponts were investors in F.I. du Pont—some of them female relatives who had never seen Wall Street and never would see it—but two of the most august and imperturbable conducted most of the negotiations with Perot's group and with the Stock Exchange. The chief representative in the early stages was Edmond du Pont. In his middle sixties, a Princeton and Oxford man, a yachtsman and leading Episcopal layman, he was of commanding bearing, often spoken of as the handsome du Pont, just as his cousin Henry Francis, founder of the Winterthur Museum, was spoken of as the artistic one. Time after time over the months ahead, the du Ponts would meet the Crisis Committee, along with Perot and his group of Texans.

Rohatyn and Lasker generally found the du Pont family representatives hard to deal with. Perot, horse trader that he was by training and instinct, strove to drive a hard bargain for his money; in exchange for a loan to F.I. du Pont he wanted the guarantee of as large an equity in the brokerage firm as he could obtain. The du Ponts, in turn, seemed to regard Perot as a hip-shooting high-binder with his eye on the main chance, attempting to get the best of them by threatening to let their firm fail and its customers lose their money—using Wall Street itself as a hostage. Seeing Perot as the prototypical *nouveau riche*—and accurately, since he was certainly one of the newest-richest persons in all history—the du Ponts *père et fils* bitterly resented the necessity of being rescued by him at all. But there it was; perhaps they could hold their noses and take his money. Perot, for his part, regarded the du Ponts as pompous ingrates. The Stock Exchange men were in the middle. When they would point out to the du Ponts that their firm was all but insolvent, they would talk about its "going concern value" and yield little or nothing to Perot. To hear Rohatyn tell it, all through the negotiations the du Pont representatives were inclined to be cocky and intransigent, apparently unwilling to acknowledge any responsibility for the welfare of Wall Street, the national economy, or even the customers of their firm.

"The du Ponts are a great and public-minded family, but most of them seem to have been essentially in the dark as to what was at stake in the troubles of their brokerage firm. We had to sort of rap their representatives' knuckles all the time. The representatives seemed to be arrogant without having much to be arrogant about. There was an air of sullen defiance. They seemed to have no conception of what it meant, in terms of responsibility, to have over three hundred thousand customers' money in your hands. As a result, some of the meetings were nightmarish. Of course, Tony du Pont had a hard problem—he had been the firm's chief capital-raiser for the past couple of years, scraping up additional funds from the various relatives. And now he was faced with the distasteful prospect of having to tell his relatives that the money he had wheedled out of them was down the drain," Rohatyn said later.

Three highly diverse factions, then: a hard-trading Texan motivated by goodwill, or the hope of profit, or perhaps something of each; bred-in-the-bone Wall Streeters struggling to save the club; and a group of Delaware aristocrats whose *noblesse* seemed unwilling to *oblige*. And while they thrashed things out and Wall Street's

fate hung, once again, in the balance, Robert Haack very nearly blew everything apart.

Later he would say that his timing had been bad; there is little question that his motives were good. At all events, he chose November 1, at the height of the du Pont crisis, to make a speech at a din-'ner of the Economic Club of New York in which he called for prompt abolition of the Stock Exchange's age-old system of fixed commissions on brokerage transactions and its replacement with a system of freely negotiated rates. He added, as if to be certain to enrage all Stock Exchange conservatives, "Whatever vestiges of a private-club atmosphere remain at the New York Stock Exchange must be discarded." "Private club": the classic red cape to the old bulls (and for that matter the old bears) of Wall Street, the expression used previously to goad them by S.E.C. chairmen William Douglas in 1937 and William Cary in 1962. Most unforgivable, in the view of traditionalists, Haack made his remarks without first clearing them with any member of the board of governors whose paid employee he was. If rage was what Haack had wanted, he got it. Lasker issued a tight-lipped public statement: "Under the constitution of the New York Stock Exchange, policy is made by the board of governors and not by the president, who is responsible for the administration." Rohatyn pointedly criticized Haack for speaking without first consulting the governors.

Haack's speech meant that the du Pont-Perot accommodation was in trouble. Freely negotiated commissions meant lower commissions and thus meant that investment in brokerage firms would be less attractive; so Haack seemed to be attacking Wall Street's profitability at the very moment when it was dying for lack of profits. The Crisis Committee was terrified that Perot would be so upset by the reduced prospects for brokerage profits, and disgusted by this unseemly squabbling within Wall Street, that he would simply pull out and leave F.I. du Pont to fail.

Then, on November 23, came further reason for Perot to be upset. Distressing new information was forthcoming as to the state of F.I. du Pont's finances. For many men it would have been the last straw. But not Perot. He saw that development as a new call to arms; he saw the greater weakness on the other side as a chance to strike a better bargain. As he put the matter in his best country-boy manner, "My father always used to say, 'If you can't give me cash, give me chickens.'" And so, after recovering from his initial fit of anger at the

apparently casual treatment Wall Street was giving him, he coolly set about seeing how many chickens he could get out of F.I. du Pont and the Stock Exchange for the $10-million figure the du Ponts now claimed to need to keep their firm operating.

It was in this particular endeavor that he fell afoul not only of the du Ponts but of much of Wall Street as well. By the end of November, when news of the du Pont negotiations had begun leaking out in Wall Street, Perot had replaced Haack as the chief center of controversy. What was the true character of the Texan? Was he a ruthless bounty hunter and scalper taking advantage of well-mannered gentlefolk in temporary distress, as he was now regarded by the du Ponts, many of the Stock Exchange staff, and perhaps a majority of the investment community at large? Or was he an almost unbelievably long-suffering and public-spirited citizen willing to endure appalling financial sloppiness, and to put huge sums of his own money at risk for the good of the country? In truth, it was a perfect Perot moral situation, of precisely the sort he had been drawn into, or perhaps created for himself, for years. He was characteristically outraged when people suggested that he was interested in the du Pont deal chiefly for what it might bring him. "From a businessman's point of view, I just don't want to invest!" he raged, complaining bitterly that the ungrateful du Ponts, facing the prospect of annihilation, were accusing him of trying to "steal" their firm. "I'm being treated like a raider when I'm trying to help!"

At the start of December, Wall Street hung by its fingertips. Roughly one hundred Stock Exchange firms had vanished over the past two years through merger or liquidation. Forty thousand customer accounts were involved in the thirteen cases of liquidation, and most of them were still tied up, the customers unable to get their cash or securities. Commitments to the Stock Exchange's trust fund from its member firms were approaching the $100-million mark, and some member firms had had about enough. Legislation to create a Federal Securities Investor Protection Corporation, on the model of the Federal Deposit Insurance Corporation to protect bank depositors, was before Congress; it had no chance of passage until the present mess in Wall Street was cleared up, and thus, while it might help in future crises, it was powerless in this one.

Worst of all, the du Pont deal and another operation to save the floundering firm of Goodbody were interrelated. In its contract to take over Goodbody, Merrill Lynch had insisted on a provision to the

effect that, should any other major firm fail before the Merrill Lynch-Goodbody merger became final several months later, then the Merrill Lynch-Goodbody merger would be canceled.

So a du Pont failure would mean a Goodbody failure; the arch deprived of its keystone would fall, more than half a million customer accounts would be tied up, many perhaps never to be redeemed, and public confidence in Wall Street would end for years to come, if not forever. In the retrospective opinion of those best situated to know, the fall of the arch would have meant much more than that. Haack said at the time that the consequence of Goodbody's failure alone would be "a panic the likes of which we have never seen." Lasker said later: "If du Pont and Goodbody had gone down, a market crash would have occurred, but that would have been only the beginning. There would have been a run on the resources of brokerage firms—partners wanting their capital, customers wanting their cash and securities—causing many new failures. There would have been no federal investor-protection legislation. Mutual fund redemptions would have been suspended, putting fund investors in the same situation as customers of bankrupt brokerage houses. Undoubtedly the Stock Exchange would have ben forced to close. All in all, millions of investors would have been wiped out, and as for Wall Street, it would have marked the end of self-regulation. The government would have moved in and taken over."

It did not happen. Three times round—Hayden, Stone; Goodbody; du Pont—went the more or less gallant, more or less decrepit ship of Wall Street, and it did not sink to the bottom of the sea. Through the early days of December the negotiations continued, and at last, on December 16, a deal was announced. Two of Perot's associates hand-carried to Lasker a certified check for $10 million, payable to F.I. du Pont and Company; in exchange, the Perot group would get the right to convert part of their loan into 51 percent of du Pont stock, thus taking control out of du Pont hands for the first time in the company's history. Edmond du Pont would resign as managing partner, and the firm's remaining partners would undertake to raise promptly an additional $15 million in capital.

Wall Street seemed to be saved. It wasn't, really, because the arrangement soon came apart, and the last phase of the rescue stands as a kind of gigantic, grotesque footnote. Far from putting up or raising more capital, in the early months of 1971 the F.I. du Pont partners and investors took millions more of the previously committed

capital *out*. A group of the firm's investors, led by Anthony du Pont, showed that they had no taste for the original accommodation in any case, and set about trying to salvage what they could for themselves, whether at the cost of the firm's liquidation or not. Meanwhile, further errors in the du Pont books were found. By February 1, 1971, it appeared that the amount needed from the Perot group was not $5 million, or $10 million, but considerably more. At last, on April 23, the appalling fact came to light: the rescue would require somewhat in excess of $50 million.

"I want out!" Perot shouted over the telephone from Dallas; now he had been pushed too far. But the Crisis Committee would not let him out. Rohatyn would later call it a game of chicken, with each side, the du Ponts and the Perot group, using the threat of the firm's failure and the terrible social and economic consequences as a lever to improve its bargaining position. Through it all, despite the gravity of the matter, humor of a sort seems to have survived. Once, after many hours of hot-and-heavy negotiations, Lasker took Perot to dinner at the posh Côte Basque restaurant.

"I'll bet you want a big drink, after all that," Lasker said.

"You bet I do!" Perot replied, in heartfelt tones; and commanded the hovering proprietor, "Bring me the biggest ginger ale in the house!"

Matters came to a head in mid-April; there were daily and nightly sessions in Dallas, at the Stock Exchange, at Lasker's suite, finally at the S.E.C. offices in Washington. Perot did not carry out his threat to withdraw; the negotiations succeeded. In the last week of April an agreement was reached that would stick: Perot and his colleagues to lend $55 million, in exchange this time for at least 80 percent control of F.I. du Pont; and the Stock Exchange, through assessment of its members, to indemnify Perot against resulting losses up to the sum of $15 million.

For the reader who has been numbed by the size of the sums tossed around, and the surrealistic ease with which they escalated, let a single figure serve as summary and conclusion: over two years, it would eventually appear, the errors and miscalculations in the account books of F.I. du Pont had amounted to somewhere in the neighborhood of $100 million.

Wall Street was saved now, and the go-go years were about over. The Perot deal went through, and F.I. du Pont continued operations

under the briskly competent management of Morton H. Meyerson, a young Perot lieutenant. "My objective is for du Pont to become the most respected firm in the securities business," said Perot, in the sober pear-shaped tones of many Wall Streeters before him, and it was at least possible that he would reach his objective. Lasker, Rohatyn, and their colleagues could begin to catch up on their sleep, and on their private business affairs. Albert H. Gordon, chairman of Kidder, Peabody, wrote to Lasker, "If you had once lost your nerve, we would have gone down with all hands lost." Surely no one could deny that Lasker had kept his nerve, done what of all things in the world he could do best: as a conservative, he had superbly filled the role of conservator.

Perot had come out probably the largest single investor in Wall Street and certainly the biggest man in its looming automated future; for all his outback ways a man of complexity and paradox: an idealist and yet a pragmatist, a passionate believer and yet conceivably a bit of a faker, and in Wall Street an Early American—such a leader as Wall Street might have had in 1870—called to answer a Late American problem in 1970. In the nineteen sixties, finance capitalism as practiced in America had once again, through its own folly, dug itself an almost inescapable grave and then dug itself right out—had once again survived, but just barely. The architects of its survival, men like Lasker, Rohatyn, and Perot, had shown courage, persistence, and self-sacrifice amounting almost to heroism. The question remained: Was the heroism in a good cause? Was the old system that could produce "creative" accounting, manipulation of stock prices, victimization of naïve investors, and mind-boggling messes in brokerage firms really worth saving? There are those, a few of them in Wall Street itself, who thought and still think not—who believe that Hayden, Stone, Goodbody, and du Pont should have been allowed to go under so that the resulting bloodbath would cleanse Wall Street and bring about a government takeover to humble Wall Street's pride and set it on the path of righteousness. It goes without saying that those people do not include Lasker, Rohatyn, or Perot—and that, when all was said and done, in the 1970 crisis it was they rather than their opponents who had the vitality and the faith to win the day. How long the day would remain won was another matter.

And so this chronicle ends, as it began, with Henry Ross Perot, the extraordinary man who, metaphorically speaking, won the money game and used his winnings to buy Wall Street.

CHAPTER 11

THE GO-GO YEARS

S ome epitaphs for the go-go years: In mid-October 1970, the week before Gramco Management suspended redemptions and sales of its collapsed offshore-fund, Director Pierre Salinger sat perched on the desk of his London office and said amiably to a reporter, "The offshore business is a dead duck." Gramco stock, which had once sold at 38, was then available for 1½.

Between the end of 1968 and October 1, 1970, the assets of the twenty-eight largest hedge funds declined by 70 percent, or about $750 million. (Theoretically, hedge funds alone among financial institutions were ideally structured to survive a market crash or even to profit from one. But only theoretically. Structure is not genius; even for the exclusive hedge funds, genius turned out to have been a rising market. In practice, their managers, as carried away by the go-go spirit as anyone else, had simply forgotten to hedge in time. One of the most heralded of them had had the spectacular bad luck—or bad judgment—to begin large-scale short selling on May 27, 1970, the very day the market turned around and made a record gain.) Among the heavy losers in one such fund, which closed down in 1971, were Laurence Tisch, head of Loews Corporation; Leon Levy, partner in Oppenheimer and Company; Eliot Hyman, former boss of Warner Brothers Seven Arts; and Dan Lufkin, co-founder of Donaldson, Lufkin and Jenrette. The dumb money could take bitter comfort in the company it had among the smartest of the *formerly* smart money.

A study of mutual funds by Irwin Friend, Jean Crockett, and Marshall Blume of the faculty of the Wharton School of Finance and Commerce, published in August 1970, resulted in the startling conclusion that "equally weighted or unweighted investment in New York Stock Exchange stocks would have resulted in a higher rate of return than that achieved by mutual funds in the 1960–1968 period as a whole." More simply stated, the pin-the-tail-on-the-donkey system of stock selection would, according to the authors' figures, have worked better than the system of putting one's trust in expert portfolio management.

If that conclusion suggests that gunslinger performance had been a fantasy born of mass hysteria, an item in *Forbes* magazine in early 1971 suggested that corporate profit performance—presumably the bedrock beneath the boom—had been another. By *Forbes*'s method

of reckoning, Saul Steinberg's Leasco, the king of all the go-go stocks, over the years of its stock-market glory had not earned any aggregate net profit at all.

Reform follows public crises as remorse follows private ones. Before the dust had settled on the 1969–70 Wall Street crisis—indeed, before its last phase was over—reform began. In December 1970, Congress passed and President Nixon signed into law a bill creating a Securities Investor Protection Corporation, "Sipic" for short—a federally chartered membership corporation, its funds provided by the securities business, which would henceforth protect customers against losses when their brokers went broke, up to $50,000 per customer. Every customer hurt by a brokerage failure over the years 1969–70 was eventually going to end up whole again, the Stock Exchange now announced. But what with lawsuits and the law's delays, it would take time. In midsummer of 1971, some eighteen thousand customers of liquidated firms were still waiting for their securities and money. By the end of 1972, virtually everyone had been paid.

Just as in the nineteen thirties, the Stock Exchange set about reforming itself internally. In March 1972, its members voted to reorganize its governing structure along more democratic lines by replacing the old thirty-three-man heavily insider-dominated board with a new board comprising twenty-one members, ten of them from outside Wall Street, and a new salaried chairman to supersede the traditionally unpaid, nominally part-time chairman of the past, such as Lasker. In the spirit of reform, the new board, at its maiden meeting in July, selected as its first paid chairman James J. Needham, not a Wall Streeter but an accountant and S.E.C. man. The first new "public" representatives to be elected to the board were mostly rich industrialists scarcely likely to share the point of view of the small investor, suggesting that the job of reform was not done yet. Still, the change unmistakably represented progress.

But if Wall Street's nineteen sixties were in many ways a replay of its nineteen twenties—refuting the optimism of those who believe that reform can make social history into a permanent growth situation rather than a cyclical stock—its go-go years were also utterly characteristic of the larger trends of their own time, reflecting and projecting all the lights and shadows of a troubled, confused, frightening decade the precise like of which had never been seen before and surely will not be seen again. Consider, for example, the subtle shift

in the aspirations of the moneymakers who have dominated the various stages of this chronicle. Edward M. Gilbert, at the beginning of the decade, was a throwback to the vanished American style, originally canonized in the nineteen twenties, of personal and social irresponsibility elevated to the status of principle. Gerald Tsai —reaching his apogee in 1964 and 1965, the period of calm between the storms of John Kennedy's assassination and the upheavals of 1967 and after—aspired to and largely achieved a more rational American dream dating back to more stable times, that of the poor immigrant using his wits to make good in the land of the free. Saul Steinberg in 1968 and 1969 was the financial world's version of a figure familiar in the larger national scene at that moment, the young and brash outsider setting out to join the insiders by overthrowing them—and, like other contemporaneous American rebels, ending up largely gaining his objective by ironically being defeated and then admitting his mistake. Finally, the two figures who dominated Wall Street at the decade's end, Lasker and Perot, dutifully reflected a national turn toward the more conservative and conventional forms of social responsibility. Unabashedly loving their country because it had provided such a complaisant arena for their personal ambitions, they set out to do what they could to reciprocate—Lasker by throwing his heart and soul and mind into the saving of the New York Stock Exchange, Perot by throwing huge sums of his own money into the same enterprise, and, in his futile attempt to rescue American prisoners in North Vietnam, riding off in all directions like a modern Don Quixote with a Boeing 707 as his Rosinante.

What then of the customer, the little investor, Wall Street's "consumer"? To begin with, there can be little question that, by and large, he was a big loser in the nineteen sixties market. It is entirely possible that as of July 1970, when the Exchange distributed its stockholder census, people's capitalism had left at least 10 million American investors, or one-third of all American investors, poorer by an aggregate sum of many billions of dollars.

The man or woman of the nineteen sixties who—in quest of a third car or a Caribbean vacation, or to pay a private-school bill, or merely to try to stay even with inflation—invested in Ling-Temco-Vought, or Leasco, or the Mates Fund, or even National Student Marketing Corporation, had one measurable advantage over the unfortunate who in 1929 had taken an equally disastrous flyer in Radio or

Shenandoah or Alleghany. Thanks to the Securities Acts and the S.E.C., the nineteen sixties investor was technically protected from corporate deception by federal requirements of full disclosure. But the key word, of course, is "technically." The question is whether or not an amateur investor, with affairs of his own to attend to and limited time and attention to give to the ins and outs of the stock market, might reasonably be expected to have understood what was disclosed. Was he not entitled to rely on the investment skill and integrity of his broker and his mutual-fund manager—especially when their judgment was so often confirmed by that of the greatest professional investing institutions, the national banks, the huge mutual and pension funds, the insurance companies and foundations? In sum, had the game of stock investing really been made fair for the amateur?

Indeed it had not—not when the nation's most sophisticated corporate financiers and their accountants were constantly at work finding new instruments of deception barely within the law; not when supposedly cool-headed fund managers had become fanatical votaries at the altar of instant performance; not when brokers' devotion to their customers' interest was constantly being compromised by private professional deals or the pressure to produce commissions; and not when the style-setting leaders of professional investing were plunging as greedily and recklessly as any amateur.

Thus the amateur investor remains and probably will remain at a certain disadvantage in relation to the professional. Perhaps his best protection lies in the knowledge of that fact itself.

All that notwithstanding, Wall Street is changing in a democratic direction, and will surely change more: the public will be better represented in the councils of the New York Stock Exchange (perhaps tied in with the Amex and the smaller regional exchanges), the commissions on more and more trades will be determined by free-market negotiation rather than by fiat of the securities industry, mutual-fund charges and operations will be better regulated. But perhaps the biggest change is not strictly financial, but rather social and cultural.

After it graduated, around the beginning of this century, from being chiefly an arena for the depredations of robber barons and the manipulations of sharp traders in railroad bonds, Wall Street became not only the most important financial center in the world but also a national institution. In the nineteen twenties it was in a real sense what Wall Streeters always cringed to hear it called, a private

club—and not just any private club but probably the most important and interesting one in the country, a creator and reflector of national manners and a school for national leaders. In the nineteen sixties, despite declining aristocratic character and political influence, it was still those things, playing out week by week and month by month its concentrated and heightened version of the larger national drama. But after the convulsion with which the decade and that particular act in the drama ended, its days in the old role seemed to be numbered. Wall Street as a social context is apparently doomed not by reform but by mechanization. Already in the early nineteen seventies, a significant proportion of stock trading is being conducted not face to face on a floor under a skylight but between men sitting in front of closed-circuit television screens in offices hundreds of thousands of miles apart. There is a growing movement, forced by Wall Street's increasingly obvious inability to handle a vastly expanded national securities business, to abolish stock certificates and replace them with entries in computer memory units. The head of the nation's biggest brokerage firm—Regan of Merrill Lynch —predicted in 1972 that "by 1980 Wall Street will have lost lots of its distinctive flavor. . . . The Street will be the scene of a lot less colorful action than we have witnessed in the past few years. . . . Early to go, I imagine, will be that decorative piece of paper [the stock certificate]. . . . When all the electronic gear is in place, will we still need a New York Stock Exchange? Probably not in its present form."

Good-bye, then, to the private club. The twin forces that hold Wall Street together as a social unit are the stock certificate, the use of which calls for geographical unity because it must be quickly and easily conveyed from seller to buyer, and the stock-exchange floor, which gives stock trading a visible focal point. If the certificate and the floor go, Wall Street will have moved a long way toward transforming itself into an impersonal national slot machine—presumably fairer to the investor but of much less interest as a microcosm of America. The private-club aspect, however deplorable from the standpoint of equity and democracy, is necessary to the social ambiance; the wishes of a reformer and those of a social historian must be at odds. If the private club goes, with it, perhaps, will go that tendency of Wall Street's of which I have spoken: to be a stage for high, pure moral melodrama on the themes of possession, domination, and belonging. This may be, conceivably, one of the last books to be written about "Wall Street" in its own time.

COSELL

A condensation of the book by

HOWARD COSELL

CHAPTER 1

THE 20TH OLYMPIAD

I never dreamed it would turn out to be the worst time of my life—a time when all kinds of doubts would be renewed about the meaning of the Olympic Games. The 20th Olympiad. The Germans had organized it brilliantly. The Olympic needle rose above the stadium. The torch was lighted. And the Games—Willy Brandt called them "the joyous games"—opened with a flourish of mountain horns and the release of thousands of doves, the music of massed bands playing modern, spirited tunes instead of anthems.

And then another note was introduced. Bavarian bullwhips cracked and exploded and echoed in the clear, sunlit August air. The sound was unnervingly like gunfire.

I can't explain what I felt. But standing on the infield of the stadium, surrounded by 80,000 people, with hundreds of millions watching on TV, the sound of the whips unsettled me. It was as though they were symbolic, an echo of things past and, somehow, a precursor of things to come.

As the days passed it seemed that I was enmeshed in every controversy the Games produced—and they were epidemic. But I never expected to be a reluctant observer of what became the biggest, cruelest news story of the year.

Harry Curtis knocked at my door at the München Sheraton Hotel at seven o'clock, the morning of September 5. Harry, my radio engineer, said almost casually, "Did you hear the news?"

"No, what?"

"Arab commandos got into the Village, took over the Israeli building, shot some of them dead and are holding the rest hostage."

I stared at him. "Harry, don't kid about a thing like that."

"Howard, it happened. It's absolutely true."

My head whirled. "Good God," I said. "I've had an uneasy feeling ever since I got to Germany. It's almost as if I were back in the age of Hitler. I can't describe this damned feeling."

I called Roone Arledge, the president of ABC Sports and the moving force behind our Olympic coverage.

"Roone, you heard—"

"Yes. Get right over to the Village. Jennings is already there for news. Get over to the Village and hold the fort there. We'll get a camera crew to you in the Village."

"Okay." I looked at my wife, Emmy. What the hell do you say at a time like that?

All over Munich, people were waking up that morning to the horror of this news. So grotesque, so remote from the spirit of the Games, as though it had happened on some other planet.

In the press dormitories at the Olympic complex, German orderlies moved efficiently through the halls. They knocked on the doors of ABC technical personnel and awakened them:

"There's a problem in the Olympic Village. You're needed at the ABC bungalow." Our whole Olympic broadcast contingent was about to rejoin the real world.

We raced to the company bungalow just outside the entrance to the Village, where we were met by Marv Bader of ABC Operations. Quickly he told us that there was only one entrance we could get through, far around the other side of the Village. Bader also said we had one film crew already inside and that it was for the use of Peter Jennings, the young film producer John Wilcox, and me.

We drove around to the entrance to which Bader had directed us. No way to get in. Especially, no reporters. So I divested myself of all identification—the ABC jacket, everything. The others did the same. I was now in a shirt, tieless, wearing Puma tennis shoes. We found another entrance. In we went. We didn't even look back, for fear they were going to stop us. We headed straight for the scene behind the Israeli quarters, Building 31—which in its way was about to become the same sort of tragic landmark as the Texas School Book Depository Building in Dallas.

It was now 8:30 A.M., Munich time. I found Wilcox and Jennings and the crew, not at Building 31 but in an area immediately behind the Italian and Burmese buildings. Both overlooked Building 31, which was under the control of the Arab terrorists and roped off by a

massive West German police guard. Jennings was assiduously getting all the data then available, by walkie-talkie, from the Associated Press and the United Press International. The facts as known were these: Shots had broken the quiet of the Village at approximately 4:30 A.M., only a few minutes after ABC had completed its feed of the previous night's coverage back to the States. The Arabs, in disguise—at least one as a woman—had climbed a wall, slipped past the flimsy security at the main gate, and forced their way into the Israeli building. The unarmed Israeli athletes awakened to that dreadful sound of other years—the pounding on the door in the middle of the night. Two were murdered as they resisted. Nine were taken hostage. Some escaped.

And now the vigil began. We watched all day. We fed reports. Jennings sneaked into the Italian building—how he got past the police I'll never know—and situated himself on an upper floor, from which he had a perfect view of the Israeli building and the events taking place in front of it.

In the early afternoon John Wilcox disguised himself in an Olympic sweat suit and darted into the Burmese building carrying a walkie-talkie. He wound up in a room no more than 10 or 15 feet away from the very Arab guarding the hostages. He could look directly into his eyes.

On the balcony of the building, one could now see furtive figures in stocking masks.

Meanwhile, I was based about 20 yards from an underpass that separated the Italian and Burmese buildings and led to the Israeli quarters. All day long, hour after hour, that underpass was a beehive of activity.

At one point ambulances arrived. They took out some stretchers. The plainclothesmen, even while in their street clothes, could be seen putting submachine guns over their shoulders, partly hidden under the backs of their jackets.

During all of this battle—call it frenzy—I learned that a close friend of one of the slain Israelis was at the other side of the underpass, just outside the roped-off area in front of Building 31. I ran around and induced him to come back with me for an interview.

At two o'clock I learned that athletic events were still going on. Even as two Israeli athletes lay dead, even as time was running out on the lives of nine others, as the anguish and torment mounted with each hour, crowds cheered at soccer and field hockey and volleyball

417

matches. It all seemed a bad dream. At the Boxhalle, heavyweight Duane Bobick, the U.S. hope for a gold medal, was meeting Teofilo Stevenson of Cuba. The day before it had seemed important. There was no way I would cover it now.

I thought it was obscene for the Games to continue while the Olympic Village was being turned into a deathtrap. It was insane, the tired old men of the IOC debating whether or not to postpone, or even interrupt, their precious pageant, even as blood still bathed the steps of Building 31. They would, finally, suspend the competition around four o'clock.

As the vigil continued, more cars pulled into the underpass. German police garbed in athletes' uniforms poured out of them, their submachine guns and pistols plainly visible, and vanished into the buildings adjacent to the Israeli quarters. Snipers, equipped with rifles and telescopic lenses, climbed to the nearest rooftops. One sensed they would attempt to rush the Arabs.

Yet no one moved. The Germans were playing for time. No one wanted to risk a misstep that might panic these men and lead to the slaughter of the helpless Israeli hostages.

Now dusk came—and with it the eeriest scene I have ever witnessed. I did my last film piece on the back slope of a hill. I had them turn the cameras on a spot 300 yards away where hundreds and hundreds of athletes had congregated, held back by police guards and ropes. The number grew as the day wore on. Athletes of every country, male and female, watching and waiting. It was like the Roman arena of ancient days. They waited for a shoot-out that would not come until hours later—and then not in the Village but at an airport miles away.

You wished you could turn off your mind. But the thoughts kept coming until there did not seem to be room for them in your brain. The games seemed remote, distant. Yet 500 yards from where we stood I could see athletes casually moving around the recreation area, playing chess and shuffleboard and Ping-Pong. I cursed them for their indifference and callousness.

We paced aimlessly on small patches of grass, tortured by thoughts. What must the Israelis be thinking? Of their homes, their families? Were they wondering, all this time, what the world was doing about them?

Well, you're not human if your life doesn't spring before your eyes. I'm a man born of Jewish parents who grew up in Brooklyn. My

father was old-worldish. I myself had received no formal religious training. I married a Protestant girl. My older daughter married a Catholic boy. So I'm a hybrid character. But I did grow up in Brooklyn, of Jewish parents, in the age of the Depression and the threat of Hitler. I had never felt so intensely Jewish as when I watched this scene: two Israelis already dead; more to die here in Germany, where Hitler inflicted his scars; the Arabs, incredibly, this tiny coterie of desperadoes, holding forth. I found myself wanting to scream at the German authorities: "YOU DIRTY BASTARDS!"

I wasn't being rational or really fair. No one wanted things to be right more than the West Germans. They were driven by a desire to erase the awful memories of World War II; what happened was the last thing on earth they wanted. Another point ought to be made. There is a limit to security and a limit to control. Even with infinitely more security the same tragedy might have occurred. Who's to say?

The day turned to night and the shoot-out hadn't come. We were all exhausted. But then there was a sudden scurrying. Cars moved out. The police emerged from the buildings and scattered in all directions. Some were changing back out of the sweat suits and into their uniforms. We could no longer film because of the lighting factor, but were still unable—emotionally and by training—to leave the scene. Near us was a plaza over which flew the flags of all the nations in the Olympics. Now the police began to rope it off.

I approached the head police official and asked, "What goes on here?"

"A deal," he said. "A deal has been made. The helicopters will be here. In moments they come."

I reported it on the air. But the helicopters didn't land, not for 15 minutes, not for 30. The helicopters came more than an hour later but not there, not at the plaza. They landed in a field behind the Village. The rest is part of the history of our times.

When it ended all of the Israelis were dead. They had died in the flames and gunfire on the runway at Furstenfelder Airport, as German soldiers attempted, in vain, to pick off the Arab terrorists. The shoot-out had indeed come. Bound and blindfolded, the Israelis never had a chance. A confusion of news bulletins—it was at first reported they had survived—only heightened the final horror.

Later that morning we went to the Olympic Stadium for the memorial services that were being held in honor of the slain Israelis. I almost couldn't get Emmy in. Admission was being granted only to

those who came with tickets for the athletic events that were to have been held that day. I was outraged. One would have thought that we were going to just another entertainment.

But the outrage was nothing compared to the disgust and indignation that overwhelmed us as we listened to Avery Brundage, the president of the International Olympic Committee, speak. No thought or suggestion of suspending the games. Instead, unbelievably, an apparent attempt to equate the murder of the Israelis with the issue that had preceded the Games—whether or not Southern Rhodesia should be admitted. "The Games of the Twentieth Olympiad," Brundage declared grimly, "have been subjected to two savage attacks. We lost the Rhodesian battle to naked political blackmail. . . . I am sure that the public will agree that we cannot allow a handful of terrorists to destroy the nucleus of goodwill and cooperation. . . . The Games must go on."

He then declared a day of mourning. Incredibly, he made it retroactive to 4:00 P.M. the day of the tragedy. Why? So the games could resume quicker? The effect could not have been more stunning.

There is no way I can describe Avery Brundage. I have known him since 1956. He is, in some ways, one of the most remarkable men I've ever known. By his precepts he is a completely principled man. The only trouble with Avery Brundage is that he believes in all the wrong things. He loves having power. He loves it! He believes in pomp and circumstance. He believes in superficial things. He has a curious unconcern about what is going on in the world in terms of people, and the legitimate hopes and aims and aspirations of people. I don't suppose he ever showed it more than the day after the tragedy, at the ceremonies.

For me, the Olympics died with the Israelis.

CHAPTER 2

JACKIE, YOU TAUGHT US ALL

There are certain people in American sports who are now valid figures in this nation's history books. Jackie Robinson is one. Muhammad Ali is another. The Joe Namaths of the world are meaningless. They come and go, fleeting figures of passing glamour. You'll find them in the sports tomes but not in the history books.

You'll find Robinson there because of the bloodless social revolution he created. Now, as a consequence of the case of the United States vs. Muhammad Ali, you'll find Ali there. Curt Flood's attack on baseball's reserve clause will place his name in the lawbooks as well as in the history texts.

I do not weep for Jackie Roosevelt Robinson. But I mourn the injustices imposed upon all of the great black players who have come into baseball since he pried open the door. And of course I equally mourn the superb black players of another era like Satchel Paige, Josh Gibson, Buck Leonard, and all of the others consigned for so many years to languish in the old black leagues.

Robinson's emergence took place 26 years ago, years of sweeping and dramatic changes in this country, and still we hear that they are looking for a "qualified" black to manage.

Now, anyone who is over the age of 12, who has ever been exposed to the sports scene, who has ever met a major-league manager, knows that this is pure and total hogwash. Any 12-year-old knows that all they do is play musical chairs with a bunch of anonymous mediocrities as managers. In fact, the longer you are around baseball and the more conversant you become with their hypocrisy in this area, the more you begin to get the feeling that there are certain preeminent qualifications to managing a major-league baseball club: You must be white and either a heavy drinker or a cardplayer. The most regaled manager I have known was at least two of the three.

Now that's not true in all cases. There are exceptions. Fred Hutchinson was a great man. Gil Hodges was a fine man. Ralph Houk is a strong, astute individual. Others could be named. But in general, as a class, baseball managers have been notoriously inept. What an absurdity to try to tell the American people, in the year 1973, that they are still searching for a qualified black.

Jackie Robinson came upon the scene in 1947 and they haven't found one yet. Good Lord. Forget the fact that they seldom hire qualified whites. What are they trying to say? That Bill White, who played for the Cardinals and the Phillies, who made the dean's list at Hiram College, isn't qualified? Or the articulate and voluble Maury Wills, immensely personable and attractive and terribly bright; a black Leo Durocher, but with more character. And Frank Robinson, a man who has studiously prepared himself to manage by performing that job in the Puerto Rican winter leagues. Only white managers, it seems, require no experience.

Yet there are those in major-league baseball who will tell you privately that the "problem" is not in the *hiring* of a black manager but rather in the *firing*. Their implication is clear—that they fear, in the event of such a firing, adverse reaction by black pressure groups that would do undue harm to the "game." Equally clear is the fact that this is the cheapest kind of cop-out, an alibi that could be used forever to stop a black man from becoming a major-league manager. One might note in this regard that when Lenny Wilkins (the black, former player/coach of Seattle in the National Basketball Association) was released from his job, the matter went almost unnoticed.

One major-league operator was on the verge of a breakthrough with a black manager, but it never came to pass. He was Michael Burke of the Yankees, and the time was the summer of '72. The Yankees were floundering, and the fans were booing Ralph Houk (possibly the best manager in baseball) mercilessly. Burke told me that if things didn't get better he would have to let Houk go. His first choice was Billy Martin who was managing the Tigers. If he couldn't get Billy he planned to bring in Frank Robinson. The Yankees did a turnabout, got into the pennant race and, quite properly, Burke signed Ralph to a new three-year contract. But the Burkes are few and far between, and Mike, in the immortal words of presidential press secretary Ron Ziegler, has been rendered "inoperative" by the new Yankee ownership which took over in late 1972.

Yet during all of those years I did not find Jackie Robinson to be embittered. I would describe him as realistic. In my opinion Jackie had as much capacity to be a great manager as any man who ever lived. His achievements as a human being, not just as a baseball player, are recorded now for all of history. He was an extraordinary man whose mere presence filled a room wherever he went. He was straightforward, outspoken, honest.

I remember standing in front of the church in Brooklyn on the day of Gil Hodge's funeral, a block away from where my grandmother lived when I was a child. And one by one the "boys of summer," as Roger Kahn called them in his superb book of that name, appeared. Pee Wee Reese arrived. And Roy Campanella, Carl Furillo, Don Newcombe, and Joe Black. But not Jackie. The crowd watched them all come in, and there were ripples from the youngsters and from the older people of my generation. And then, suddenly, around the corner, walking so painstakingly that it was hard to believe that body had once been so taut and quick, hanging onto the arm of Ralph

Branca, came Jackie Robinson. You could hear, abruptly, the whispers. The thing that struck me first was that it was youngsters, kids under 15: "There's Jackie Robinson. . . ."

In later years, to my shock and consternation, when Jackie retired some wrote blithely about what he owed to baseball. Good Lord! What this man went through. What he did for the sport is impossible to measure. He gave it the only good and honest image it has in the United States of America today. What has been its image since Jackie? Carpetbagging across the land, pretending to be the national pastime, deserting the nation's capitol for little Arlington, Texas. Who is kidding whom?

The refrain against Jackie went like this: (1) He owed it to the writers to give them the story, and (2) How could he knock baseball? *Look what the game did for him.*

What did baseball do for Jackie Robinson? I'll tell you. It tortured him, tormented him. What he had to live with was the greatest debasement of a proud human being in my lifetime. But he gave baseball the appearance of being a democratic business—that's what he did for baseball—and he gave it a place in American history by his mere presence. And one of the great tragedies of American sports journalism is that often you read it the other way—that Jackie Robinson left a debt to baseball.

He was a very important figure in my career. When Gil Hodges died, Jackie knew ABC was doing a Monday-night special on his old teammate, and so we had arranged for him to drive back to Manhattan in a limousine with me, with a camera crew in the front seat. We did the last interview we ever did together—and, assuredly, I did over 100 interviews with Jackie Robinson in his lifetime. We sat in that car and we reviewed his life. One eye was completely gone, the other eye was milky white. He had diabetes, high blood pressure, and had survived two coronaries. He had suffered through the problems of Jackie, Jr.—crime, rehabilitation, Vietnam, drug addiction, rehabilitation. He exulted in the superb work by the youngster at the Daytop Drug Rehabilitation Center in Seymour, Connecticut—the very work the youngster was doing for the center on the night he was driving home, exhausted, at two in the morning, when he lost control of his car, crashed, and was killed.

While I was in the car we reviewed every one of those things, and I asked Jackie if he felt that God had singled him out for the most untoward adversity I'd ever seen befall a man. He said that he and

Rachel had talked about it often. His wife is a glorious lady. She was an utterly beautiful woman who, quite frankly, has been ravaged now by the weight of events. But she remains a remarkable lady who was on the Yale faculty as a clinical psychologist. They both felt, said Jackie, that, yes, he had been given a cross to bear.

My last question to him, in this last interview, was how would he characterize his life.

He looked at me with those eyes that could hardly see and he said, "Oh, we've had a great life." And he wasn't being heroic. It was just an interview in the back of a limousine. "We've accomplished so much," he added.

As long as I knew him he never said "I." It was always "we." Without Rachel he was nothing and he knew it. He said, "We've accomplished so much, there's so much more to be done I guess we'll not have the chance to do it. Oh, what a great life we've had."

Jackie Robinson was a remarkable man. The day he was admitted to the Hall of Fame we sent a camera crew to his home in North Stamford, Connecticut. I was doing a special on him, called "New Man at Cooperstown." We sat on the steps of his church, a Presbyterian church some 400 yards from his property, a classic old New England church. We talked about religion—how he viewed his place in the society—what it meant to him. We went into his billiard room and shot pool and we talked about his origins in baseball, the black leagues, his relationship with Branch Rickey.

We walked down by his lake, and we talked about the neighbors who did not want the Robinsons in that plush section. We talked about his children and how they were reacting to all of the hardships they had faced. You know, it is a great hardship for a child who is white to be the son or daughter of a famous father. Translate that into what it means to be black and the child of a famous father and you begin to understand what had happened to Jackie Robinson, Jr. The same name. The high expectations. People never left him alone.

I don't think there was anything about life that we didn't talk about that day. I think there is only one word that describes Jackie Robinson. Unconquerable. He was the most unconquerable human being I have ever known. I loved him.

Of course, we had our run-ins. I'm a volatile man, and so was he. One of our disagreements was the result of a *Wide World of Sports* show I had to do after Ali's fight with Ernie Terrell. It was not an easy one to do because Ali, in my opinion, had behaved very badly

in that fight and had, indeed, turned on me in the ring interview afterward. He turned on everyone. He knew—he later admitted it to me privately—that he had been needlessly cruel to Terrell. So there he was, three days later in the studio, and three or four New York writers were present.

It was a tense scene in that room because I knew I had a job to do and, quite frankly, I was upset at always being the one who had to do the tough shows, the issue shows that would produce a great diversity of reaction. And I did a very tough show with Muhammad Ali. It was later characterized in a profile of me in *Sports Illustrated* as a shouting contest. It wasn't that, but it was a very hard-hitting show, and subsequently I got flooded with mail. I was no longer a nigger-loving Jew bastard as I usually was in any adverse mail that reaches my office. I was the black-hater. I actually got, for the first time in my life, a letter signed by a whole dormitory in Michigan State telling me I was anti-black.

None of which really mattered. What did matter was an angry phone call from Jackie Robinson. "Howard," he said, "that just wasn't you. What's happened to you?"

I said, "Jack, we're just not going to see eye to eye on this." I explained my position to him, and he said, "I just don't agree."

I said, "Jack, I'm sorry, but that's the way it is. I think I'm right. You think you're right. I did what I had to do in my mind and my heart as a journalist. I don't apologize for a bit of it." So there was some coolness in that conversation. We had others like it.

For a brief time Jackie and I worked together as part of ABC's broadcasting team for the major-league show *Game of the Week*. Few remember that the first time a black man appeared on a sports network as a broadcaster was with ABC, and that Roone Arledge did it. We had Chris Schenkel, Leo Durocher, Keith Jackson, Jackie, and myself. I remember flying home one day with Chris and Jackie, and I was discussing something he had said on the air. In my usual tactful way I began, "Now, Jack, I think you should have—"

"Howard," he stopped me, "you're not the greatest man who ever lived, and I can remember when you weren't so darned good. I admit I'm not. . . ."

It was a flash of insecurity about his performance. Losing would enrage him. In that respect he was like Vince Lombardi.

I don't think there is any need here to embellish *The Boys of Summer*. But it is true that the Brooklyn Dodgers were all of baseball

to all of the world. They really became the American dream when Jackie Robinson joined them. And so the Brooklyn Dodgers have a place unique in the history of sports in the United States. I think the whole thing was epitomized when I was doing *New Man at Cooperstown*. I wanted to return Jackie Robinson to where Ebbets Field had been.

That was baseball, and I wanted to go back with Jackie because they had torn it all down and were building a housing development. We walked into the project. It was a skeletal thing then, and we walked to the area where second base had been. They had marked off a place where a plaque was to be implanted. The words were written out: "Jackie Robinson stood here." (I'll go back there someday, to see if they ever did put the plaque in.)

At that time they called the project The Ebbets Field Apartments. Now they are called The Jackie Robinson Apartments.

CHAPTER 3

LOMBARDI: ASK HIS PLAYERS

I have never known a man who left more of himself in those close to him, whose lives he touched, than Vincent Thomas Lombardi. The men who moved in his orbit—the players and the coaches and those like myself, who were merely passing through —were equally influenced by him. No man has ever had a greater impact on me.

Looking back, it is odd that it turned out that way. On the surface we seemed to have little in common. Lombardi was a political conservative, an establishment man. He was also a man of discipline and maxims, of principle and unbending character, with the mind of a classical scholar. He had—and this might surprise some—a gift of humor. He like to drink, to play cards. He cared deeply about people. He cared about excellence, about winning, and he cared about being remembered. He had a positive obsession about being the first coach in the National Football League to win three championships in a row. The fact that those championships would encompass two Super Bowl victories was incidental.

I'm not certain why Vince and I hit it off so well. But I respected his values. He trusted me, and I believed in him. When he left the

Packers and joined the Redskins, a Washington writer asked him why he allowed me into his training camp with my film crew when he would not allow others. "Howard is a moral man," he replied, "he would never break his word." Family meant everything to Vince, apart from football, family and loyalty to old friends.

So Vince was basically a simple man, just as his football teams played simple football. "Don't give me any fancy offenses or new tricks on defense," he would bark. "You block better, you tackle better than the other guy, you win the football game." And Lombardi, as no other coach in the history of professional football, made that dictum work. Every other team knew what was coming when the Green Bay Packers played them. The power sweep, with either Hornung or Taylor carrying, with Jerry Kramer and Fuzzy Thurston leading the charge. They knew it was coming but they couldn't stop it. That was the key play in "the Green Bay offensive category," as Vince put it, and it set up every other play in the Packer offensive scheme.

I knew Vince slightly when we were at college, he at Fordham, as one of the Seven Blocks of Granite, and I at NYU, but we never became friends really until 1964. On occasion I would see him at West Point when he was on Colonel Blaik's coaching staff, and later when he was the offensive coach of the Giants. In those days he never had the security, the command presence that later became one of his trademarks. But even then you could see that he was something special as a football coach.

He literally worshiped Colonel Blaik and patterned himself after him. Until he died, the friendship between them was a beautiful thing to see. Blaik had been pictured by many as a martinet, a dictator and a tyrant, unapproachable and cold. Never mind Blaik's successes as a football coach, they would say, look at him as a man. He's mean. In later years, at the peak of his coaching career, Lombardi would hear the same things said about himself.

I suppose some of my early affection for Lombardi stemmed from my feeling for Colonel Blaik. Back in the late Fifties when I was doing a nightly network sports show, Blaik was holding forth at West Point. I hardly knew him. I was a nobody trying to become a somebody. I felt it would be a feather in my cap if I could get an interview with him. I mentioned this to Lombardi, who was then with the Giants. "Call Joe Cahill at the academy," Vince snapped. "I'll bet the colonel will see you."

I called Joe Cahill, a fine man who was the sports information di-

427

rector at West Point. To my amazement Cahill called back and said that Blaik would be glad to do it. We made a date for the next morning at the Battle Monument on the Plains. I have wondered ever since if Vince called the colonel.

In any event, when I got to the Point the next day, there was Blaik, right on time and cordial to a fault. I was scared to death. The man is the image of the late General Douglas MacArthur, the two were best friends, and as the story goes, Blaik did not introduce two-platoon football at the academy until he got clearance from the general who was then on duty in the Phillipines. I asked the colonel about his relationship with MacArthur, and then I asked him all the direct, personal questions about himself: the unbending image, the stern authoritarianism. Blaik couldn't have been more responsive. When we got done he said, "That's a fine interview, young man. I've been wanting to do that for a long time." I left West Point on cloud nine. Ever since then, Blaik and I have been good friends. When his book *You Have to Pay the Price,* written with Tim Cohane, was published, I received a copy in the mail. It was inscribed, "From this old pro with respect for a great pro in his own field, Earl Blaik." To this day I'm as proud of that inscription as any I have ever received. And I know that my feeling for the colonel carried over to Vince Lombardi. A matter of instinct.

Shortly after the Blaik incident Vince moved on to Green Bay as head coach. I was then doing color on a six-game pro-football package that ABC had acquired. It consisted of four pre-season games and two regular-season games. Green Bay was playing in one of the preseason games at Bowman Gray Stadium in Winston-Salem, North Carolina. I talked with Vince before the game. He was right on. "I've got a tough situation. Long way to go. McHan will be my quarterback as of now, but I want to look at this kid Starr. He may have something." Starr sure did. Under Vince he became the winningest quarterback in the contemporary history of professional football. And Bart would be the first to tell you that he could never have done it without Lombardi.

There were little incidents like that, where Vince was always helpful to me. Then, as I have noted, we became close in 1964, and that was because of a fine writer named W.C. "Bill" Heinz. I have characterized Bill Heinz as the greatest boxing writer I have ever read. I should have said he is one of the greatest writers I have ever read. Boxing, football, cancer surgeons (he did great writing in this area),

you name it. Bill Heinz worked with Vince on Vince's book—a classic now—*Run to Daylight*.

I was at Bill's house in Stamford, Connecticut, along with Red Smith and Vince, the night the book was entitled. Bill wanted to call it *Six Days and Sunday*. That sounded fine to me, but Betty Heinz, who had read the text, said, "I like that phrase 'run to daylight.'"

Vince jumped in and growled, "So do I." And that was it. Immediately it became Vince's idea.

Lombardi's book was published and it was a hit. This was at a time when I was producing documentaries for WABC-TV in New York. It was at a time when professional football was entering its golden age, with Lombardi the golden figure. It was at a time when Paul Hornung was coming back from a year's suspension for betting on games. Topically, there could not have been a better time to adapt Vince's book to television. And wonder of wonders, the publishers, Prentice-Hall, agreed. Vince also agreed, and so I made a deal with them for next to no money. Money didn't matter to Vince. Quality did. I have no illusions as to why they agreed. They agreed because of their faith in Bill Heinz, who would write the adaptation. Bill was the heart and soul of *Run to Daylight*, and I owe him as much for that show as I owed to Vince himself.

I have never been so excited about any show before or since. I couldn't wait to get to Green Bay. It was the first time anybody would be allowed to shoot Lombardi as he greeted the rookies, as he oversaw the medical exams, as he addressed his men for the first time, as he consulted with his coaching staff, and as he lived his professional life. Bill Heinz had mapped the whole thing out. He had a complete shot list prepared, and he had scheduled Vince moment by moment for shooting purposes over a four-day period. Bill himself got to Green Bay a couple of days before I arrived with my director and my crew.

The next morning, right on schedule, we were at Vince's office and started doing audio tape with him to adduce some of the very lines that were in *Run to Daylight*, magnificent, descriptive lines on Paul Hornung, Bart Starr, Dave "Hawg" Hannah, Henry Jordan, and others in the Packers coterie. Lombardi could not have been more cooperative, more thoughtful, more winning in his considerateness. After that we moved out onto the campus of little Saint Norbert's College, in West De Pere, Wisconsin, where the Packers live during training. There we shot the opening scene of the show, Lombardi

walking down a tree-shaded mall, thoughtful, alone, and then bumping into two of the nuns on the faculty, greeting them, continuing on. He did it so naturally, I thought to myself, "The guy's an actor, too."

We went from there to the steps of Sensenbrenner Hall, the dormitory where the team lived. The rookies were due to arrive. This was when I saw how absorbed Lombardi could be, and how nervous he could get. He kept talking to his personnel man, Pat Peppler, and kept reciting the names of the expected rookies over and over again. Finally a bus arrived, and out poured the youngsters, who were far more nervous than Lombardi. They formed a line and announced their names to Vince, who shook hands with each of them and got off a little quip relating to each of their personal backgrounds.

After lunch came the physical exams. Watching Lombardi with his players—some of the veterans were already in, including Hornung—you got caught up with the way he regarded his young men. The running back, Tom Moore, for instance: Lombardi smacked him on the shoulders, put his arm around him, and as Bill Heinz wrote it, "You could see him remembering that big run against the Lions." Around and around the room he went, a word here, a word there, the memory uncanny. The rookies frightened, respectful, almost in awe. The seasoned ones glad to be back but knowing the moments of laughter would be few.

Dinnertime came, and the hazing of the rookies began. One of the amazing things about pro-football training camps is how men can become boys. Lombardi himself did. He loved those rookie hazings. "It's good for them," he would say. "Embarrasses them a little, but relieves them a lot. Makes them part of the group." After dinner he delivered the first address to the troops.

As Hornung said later, "The old boy never loses his touch."

That touch was the ability to communicate with young men to a greater degree than anyone I had ever seen. I left the room with the maxims ringing in my ears: "You've got to give everything you've got, on every play, because any single play can determine the outcome of an entire game." "You can't play fatigued. Fatigue makes cowards of us all." "Sure I want to win. I'm here, you're here, we're all here only if we win. If we lose, we're gone. And we only want winners."

Two-a-day practices began the next day. We were there bright and early with our cameras. The work began almost instantly. Calisthenics and more calisthenics. Mobility drills. Breakdowns into units

for the respective coaches. Lombardi everywhere. Watching. Shouting. Criticizing. Applauding. The field commander in action.

Our cameras were out on that practice field, in blistering heat, taking tight shots of the faces of the men as they were working. Suddenly I heard Lombardi screaming, "Get the hell out of here, will ya! Get out of here with your damn people. You're all the same, give you an inch, you want a mile. Get out of here."

I realized he was talking to me, and I said to Bill Heinz, "That's it, I'm getting out. This man's crazy. I won't take that from anybody."

I told the crew to start packing up and I was getting ready to leave when Lombardi came over and said, "What the hell's the matter with you? What are you doing?"

I said, "Vince, that's not part of our deal. I can't accept from you what you just did."

He said, "What are you talking about? What did I do?"

I told him. And then he said, "You know better. I get so absorbed, I don't even know what I'm saying. Don't leave now. Anything you want is yours, you know that."

I realized that the man was so totally lost in concentration that he wasn't the slightest bit aware of what he had said. Football chewed him up. For him, football was work and preparation. It was all-consuming. From that moment on, Lombardi was just incredible in the way he cooperated. What was equally astonishing was the way his players cooperated. They did it for Lombardi. They wanted to show how they felt about him.

There was a day when I was in Hornung's room. Hornung said, "Want a lift? I'm driving over to practice." Sure, any time.

A few minutes later Bart Starr popped his head in. "Coach says everybody in the bus in five minutes."

Hornung got up from his chair. I asked him where he was going. "To the bus," he answered.

"But I thought you were giving me a lift."

Hornung then said, "Didn't you listen? The coach wants everyone in the bus in five minutes. I'll be in the bus. If he said everyone walks to practice, I walk. If he says everyone runs to practice, I run. If he says everyone swims the Fox River to practice, I swim the damned river."

That's the way he felt about Vince, and as much as I like Paul I have often wondered how he could have hurt Vince so when he was betting on games. On the other side of the coin, Paul was Vince's

all-time favorite, even after he came back. Vince would say of Paul, "Inside the twenty-yard line he becomes the greatest football player I have ever seen. He smells the goal line."

Vince's widow, Marie, is a splendid lady, and Emmy and I are very fond of her. We see her often. Once, in an interview, she told me that, deep down, Vince would have liked to have been Paul Hornung. As I said, there was a lot of fun in Lombardi, and a little bit of rogue, too. Yes, he wanted to be Paul, with that golden-boy charm and that life-is-a-cabaret outlook, but he wanted to be what he was much more.

What he did have was a streak of sentimentality. He would cry easily. When I was shooting *Run to Daylight*, it was clear that Jerry Kramer was unwell. His weight had dropped steadily, and he suffered internal pains. Still, he was trying to play. Lombardi talked with me about it. He was enormously distressed. At first he thought Jerry had been faking. Now he knew better. The feeling was that Kramer had cancer. "I'm afraid of the worst," Lombardi mourned. "But you can't tell the big guy to stop."

They finally opened Kramer up, found slivers from an old accident on a ranch that had been undetected in prior surgeries, and Jerry got well again—well enough to make the most famous block in football history on Jethro Pugh of Dallas, the one that Bart Starr followed into the end zone to give the Pack another title and led to Jerry's book *Instant Replay*. But too soon after the operation Jerry went hunting for polar bears. Vince had a fit.

Kramer was one of the last people I spoke with when I left Green Bay. We had done a radio show together. "Now maybe you know the truth about Vince Lombardi," he said.

Lombardi was sorely tried when he had to let a player go who was not good enough to make the team but who had given everything he had in his effort to make the team. He sat with me along the bank of the Fox River and he said, "When a kid has given you the best he has to give, and you have to tell him it wasn't good enough, that's when you ache inside and think maybe there's a better way to make a living, maybe football isn't worth it. But when you tell a man he's through, and you know he has the talent to stick but hasn't put it to work, then you don't feel sorry at all. He's got it coming. Maybe the worst of all is when you have to give the word to a veteran, a man who's been with you for years, a man who's given you everything, who's part of you. You can't face him, you don't know how to tell

him, but you have to. I've had to do that, and I don't mind telling you, I've cried." Anybody who has ever said Lombardi was a cruel man didn't know him.

When I left Lombardi in Green Bay in 1964, his final words were, "How do you think it'll come out?" I told him I thought it would be a good show but we'd only know when it had been edited. "I hope it's a good show," he said. "But above all, make it an honest show. Show me as I am. Don't try to make me look good as long as you don't try to make me look bad. Just show me as I am." I think we did. *Run to Daylight* may still be the most highly regarded sports documentary yet done.

In later years Vince and I did a number of shows together. We did a half-hour interview called a "Self Portrait." After the interview he said, "Boy, you sure did put me on the spot. But you were right to do it." I had probed him about Jimmy Taylor, who was playing out his option; words had grown harsh between Vince and Jimmy. Then we did a "Super Bowl Analysis" of the Jets' victory over the Colts, and that's when I first knew how much Vince would have liked to coach Joe Namath. We did so many shows together, in fact, that once Lombardi said, "I'm making you famous."

I told him, "You're beginning to sound like Muhammad Ali." Vince didn't like that.

In the beginning Lombardi never gave any thought to becoming a football coach. He wavered between law and accounting and wound up in law school. But he decided law was not for him and quit law school. He didn't let his father know until he had a job, and he grabbed the first job he could get—teaching at Saint Cecelia's High School in Englewood, New Jersey. The football coach at Saint Cecelia's was an old friend, Andy Palau, who had quarterbacked the Fordham team with the Seven Blocks of Granite. One night there was a knock on the door of the Lombardi apartment. It was Palau. He had been having a romance with a girl from North Carolina, and the love affair was in danger of busting up. Palau told Vince, "I'm going to North Carolina. Here's a bottle of gin to celebrate. You're the new coach at Saint Cecelia's." With that he shoved the bottle of gin into Vince's hand and left. And so Vince's coaching career began, and that's how he got the bug.

It was no surprise when Lombardi quit as Packer coach. More surprising was the fact that his sensitivity to sportswriters was one of the factors that caused him to quit. This man, who was supposed to be so

tough, really was vulnerable to the adverse things written about him. This was particularly true of a piece in *Esquire* magazine written by Leonard Shecter. Once again, I know, because Vince spoke to me on the phone about it. It upset him terribly for two reasons. The first was that he didn't believe the piece was accurate and he felt it was maliciously inspired. Second, his mother had read the piece and had called him in an emotional state saying, "This is not my son, this is not my son. What are they doing to you?" It was during the phone conversation with me that Lombardi told me he'd had about enough, that he didn't want to go through this kind of thing anymore.

It would be equally absurd to conclude that Vince stepped down as coach only because of the writers, and in particular because of Shecter's piece. He was tired. He had worked relentlessly. He wanted to play golf, to stop driving himself. Still, five minutes after he announced his retirement he knew he had made a terrible mistake. He wondered almost instantly what he was going to do with himself, how he could stay away from the field, how he could get along without his players. That's what Lombardi's life was truly all about, how he felt about his players, how they felt about him.

During the year he was general manager but not coach of the Pack, his whole personality changed. Marie told me he was miserable.

At the end of the year he got offers. While in Miami for the Jets-Colts Super Bowl game, I was with him at the Kenilworth Hotel when Bill Sullivan, president of the New England Patriots, arrived. He was meeting with Vince to make a tremendous offer to get Vince to take over the Patriots—again, not just a salary offer, but a partial ownership offer. Vince turned him down. Then came the offer from the Washington Redskins. By this time Vince knew he had to get back on that field, had to work with the young ones, had to live by those damned yard markers and yard lines. Washington appealed to him. The national capital. Close to New York. The people in Green Bay were wonderful, but Marie had never found the climate tolerable. Washington had years of gridiron futility behind it. It seemed a whole new challenge, a whole new stimulus. He still had a contract with the Packers though. What about that? Well, through the years he had resisted other offers, kept his loyalty to Green Bay, and what a job he had done for them. The Pack was the most glamorous team in football, Green Bay was the football capital of the nation—indeed, not just Green Bay, but Superior, Racine, Ashland, Sheboygan, Madison, Milwaukee, the whole state. Lombardi had fulfilled his

mission, had paid his debt and then some. He spoke to the Packer president, Dominic Olejniczak, and to the board members. He got released from his contract and went with Washington. He had a chance to live again.

And then he got it. He got it from a group of writers, the very men he was so sensitive to. Lombardi, the man of principle, had a double standard, they wrote. One for players, another for himself: Players should be bound to contracts, but not coaches. Was that Lombardi's philosophy? He had no right to leave the Pack. Vince grew sick over this, literally sick. In his mind he could not have acted more honorably. But he had to take the punishment. He faced up to it. By the time he began working with the Redskins at Dickinson College in Carlisle, Pennsylvania, he almost had it beat—almost. He would never completely defeat it despite that tough exterior, not with that soft Italian sentimentality.

When Vince started training camp with the Redskins I was there, along with my crew. He was a man reborn, perhaps more joyous than I had ever seen him. As always he was all over the practice field, yelling here, cajoling there. When I interviewed him his manner could not have been more hearty. Did he realize, I asked him, what he had to live up to in terms of the record he had created? "Yes," he answered, "but I'm too young to be a legend, and I never was one really." The conversation moved along, covering the new team he had taken over. I asked him about tight end Pat Richter's broken nose. He became Lombardi, vintage '66, put back his head, and roared, "It's nothing at all, Howard. I broke my nose seventeen times when I was playing."

Later, when I spoke with Richter, Richter told me, "The coach is right, it's nothing. What matters is, he makes us all feel like men."

It made me think of Henry Jordan's classic remark when we did *Run to Daylight.* That's when Henry told us, "Coach Lombardi treats us all the same, like dogs." That was a great line by Henry, but it was uttered in jest. Lombardi treated 40 men 40 different ways. He would chew Hornung out. But he would baby Bart Starr. He knew the differences in the makeup of people.

He had something else: a sense of proportion, a sure instinct for the things that mattered. He preached discipline and lived by it. But some things were more important than rules. Quality for instance.

He watched approvingly as the Redskins reported to him for the first time in training camp. Sonny Jurgensen came in. Charley Taylor

arrived. And then a car pulled up and out jumped a mod kid with hair down to his shoulders and a guitar under his arm. Lombardi looked at him with suspicion and spat out to his assistant, "Who the hell is *that*?" The assistant said, "That's Jerry Smith, the tight end."

Lombardi, who had been studying Redskins' game films all winter and spring, nodded. "He can play. Let him keep the hair and guitar."

During that interview at Carlisle, the pride in Lombardi was busting out all over. Sam Huff had come out of retirement to play for him. Vince remembered Sam. Sam, along with the old Giants kicker Don Chandler, had left the Giants camp when they were rookies. He and Don thought they couldn't make it. The man who caught up with them, stopped them before they left town, and brought them back was a fellow named Lombardi.

One other thing sparked Lombardi in that interview. "Don't forget, Howard, I've got the quarterback. A real, first-class, National Football League quarterback." And with that his eyes wandered over to where Sonny Jurgensen was hunched over the center, eyes scanning the defense, barking the signals, backpedaling, and releasing the football. This would be different for Vince from Green Bay. With the Pack he had to take an unknown youngster, seventeenth-round draft choice from Alabama, and mold him, patiently, tirelessly, into the Bart Starr who will be a Hall of Famer. But Jurgensen came packaged, ready-made.

Finally, the key question. What about the newsmen, some of whom were already firing the old darts at him. For the first and only time Lombardi made a public admission about them. "I know what they're writing," he said, "and I know it's not true. You know, as well as anyone, that what they used to write was one of the reasons I retired from coaching at Green Bay. But that won't happen again. I'm back where I belong, and as far as I'm concerned, they'll never get to me again. If you really want to find out, ask my players about me."

Lombardi's first year with Washington was successful. The Redskins finished above 500 in the won-and-lost percentages for the first time in years. The second season would be even better; the foundation had been laid. But for Vince it never came. Something else did. Cancer. Increasingly he had been having those pains. Then loss of weight, almost imperceptible. Marie never knew how sick he felt. He kept it from her. Then, finally, to the hospital. And three days later she knew. It was hard to look at him. His players knew. The NFL players were on strike then, but the Redskins were practicing

on their own, at a local Washington field. Vince struggled out to look at them. Pat Richter told me, "We looked over at him on the sideline. We tried to work the way he wanted us to work. When he left we stopped and cried."

The last game he saw, and he never should have gone, was between the Redskins and Colts rookies. He almost passed out going up the steps of the stands. He went back to the hospital, and Marie told me that no man should have to suffer the way he suffered. He would prepare himself for visits, because the way he was, he had to prepare. He didn't want his players to see him cry. But he did. He couldn't help it. You don't always measure a man's strength by the toughness of his talk. Sometimes you can measure it in tears. Paul Hornung would visit Vince and then go to a local pub to drink it off. "I can't stand seeing what's happening to him," he said. And off he would go in tears.

They had the funeral services at Saint Patrick's on Labor Day 1970. There was a black player sitting in the row in front of Emmy and me. He had his head in his hands and was trying to cover his eyes. He lost his battle with himself. The tears poured out. Emmy asked me his name. I told her it was Larry Brown. Larry Brown. An eighth-round draft choice from Kansas State. Nobody ever heard of him. Lombardi found him at the Redskins camp. Looked at him closely. Thought he had ability. But something was wrong, Lombardi found out. He was hard of hearing, couldn't catch the signals quickly enough. So a hearing aid was installed in his helmet. There is no finer running back in football than Larry Brown now. And Brown will never forget Vince Lombardi.

The funeral services ended, and the overflow crowd dispersed. I went to have coffee with Emmy. Not a word between us. My thoughts went back to the previous Friday night. Vince had died, and I had to put on a memorial special on his life. It was like the Jackie Robinson show. Scenes from *Run to Daylight* and from Carlisle, Pennsylvania. Statements from his great stars at Green Bay.

Paul Hornung said: "He saved my life."

Jerry Kramer said: "He was a beautiful man."

Willie Davis said: "He was all the man there is."

Bart Starr said: "He meant everything to me."

I thought about these young men and about Vince. About how they had grown because of him. About what has happened to so many of the Packers who played for him. As a group they are the most suc-

cessful alumni I have ever known in sports. What Lombardi taught them about life—not about football but about life—how he helped to mold them, has to be part of the reason.

I thought about Lombardi. About how in his later years he tried to relate his whole philosophy about football to the full sweep of the society itself. About how he came to understand that even for him football was not everything. About how overjoyed he was when for the first time the American Management Asssociation asked him to address them. ("Maybe I'm not just an Xs and Os guy," he said.) About how much he wanted to do that kind of thing, to reach more and more people, and to evidence the simple fact that he was a whole man, educated, sensitive, and caring.

Like Jackie Robinson he died before his time. But he went knowing that he had become more, much more, than a football coach; that in his latter years government had sought him out, and industry, and educators; that he had proved, in a strange way, that some of the old virtues are infinite—like honesty, hard work, and loyalty; and that his fundamental credo was correct: "Individual commitment to a group effort, gentlemen, that's what makes a team work, a company work, a society work, a civilization work."

And he went knowing that a lot of us loved him.

Ask his players.

CHAPTER 4

THE UNMAKING OF A BROOKLYN LAWYER

Arrogant, pompous, obnoxious, vain, cruel, persecuting, distasteful, verbose, a show-off. I have been called all of these. Of course, I am.

I am asked about my drive. I do work very hard. I always have and I always will. A couple of days off for me is like poison. I go stir crazy. Surely a lot of my drive stems from the way I grew up—in Brooklyn, during the Depression, Jewish, fighting a group of Studs Lonigans and running away from them, to get to school safely.

It was the age of Hitler, and that hovered over anyone who was Jewish. And times were difficult for my dad. I remember the electricity being turned off in our house for nonpayment of rent and my dad fighting with the janitor to try and get it turned back on.

And so I guess that growing up this way, with all of the insecurities attendant to it, you develop a drive or you simply cease to exist. I think your basic instinct is for financial and emotional security. That is your quest. You don't ever want to have happen to you what you have seen happening in your home.

My father, Isadore Cohen, was two years old when his parents emigrated to the United States. They were fleeing the pogroms of Poland and Europe. My dad traveled most of his life, as an accountant for a credit clothing chain. They were living in Winston-Salem, North Carolina, when I was born on March 25, 1920. It is a piece of biographical data I now find curious; no one thinks of me as a southerner. We were in Raleigh briefly, then moved, before my third birthday, to Brooklyn. We—my brother Hilton and I—were raised basically by my mother; dad was always on the road. My mother made sacrifice after sacrifice, and it told upon her health.

I became determined to succeed in the material sense. Later I realized that material success is only one kind of success—the American kind, I hate to say. But if you have a mind and an education, some degree of culture, of literacy, of sensitivity, you discover early on that money is not the answer. You discover that life is in your home, your family. And that's where I've been successful.

My marriage to Mary Edith (Emmy) Abrams was undertaken under adverse circumstances, she being Protestant, the daughter of a very well-known industrialist who wound up in the Eisenhower administration, and I being Jewish, though not formally reared as such, not even bar mitzvahed. But my folks recoiled at the thought of their son marrying a *shikse*.

So it wasn't easy. For two years my wife and her father did not speak. Her mother sneaked into Brooklyn to visit us. And suddenly, for the first time in her life really, Emmy came upon prejudice and rejected it. All of which probably bound us more tightly together.

Emmy's my life. She has been for 29 years. I go nowhere without her. I wouldn't do *Monday Night Football*, I wouldn't travel, I wouldn't cross the Triboro Bridge without Emmy. We've been very fortunate in our two daughters, Jill and Hilary. Jill is married to a fine young man, Peter Cohane, the son of Tim Cohane, the writer. They have two lovely sons—our Justin and Jared. And Hilary is a very much with-it girl, very liberal, a highly intellectual young woman. She does her thing. We know she's an independent but family-oriented girl. So we're lucky.

This may sound like the scenario for one of those World War II movies they turned out like sausages in the early Forties, starring June Allyson (whom Emmy resembles). It so happens that we met—and courted—in the Army. Together.

I had enlisted as a private. In two and a half years I was promoted to major, one of the youngest in the Army Service Forces in World War II. In fact, my initial recommendation for promotion to the field-grade rank of major was balked by the War Department on the grounds that I was being advanced too rapidly, for my age. Air Force officers could become majors, or higher, when very young. (The standing gag: "Twenty-two, and *only* a major.") But I wasn't flying a plane. That objection was surmounted, and I got promoted.

I enlisted in the Army a few months after Pearl Harbor. I was assigned, by God, to Brooklyn. I commuted every morning on the Sea-Beach Express; I was a Sea-Beach commando. But I wanted out of Brooklyn, I wanted more from my military experience.

So I went to OCS, to the Transportation Corps School at Mississippi State. I got down there in time to see Chuck Conerly and Ole Miss beat State College. I finished OCS, and, I'll be damned, they sent me back to the Brooklyn docks, to the New York Port of Embarkation. I never left there the entire war except for the three months I spent at Mississippi State.

The New York Port of Embarkation was the largest stateside command post in the Army. It had five staging areas and three ammunition backup points. I was in charge of all manpower, including a pool of 50,000 civilians. I was 24.

Emmy came into the Port with the first contingent of WAC's. She was assigned as a secretary to a major named Bob Lewiston, and I'll never forget the first day I saw her. I was walking past Bob's office and I saw this cute, pudgy blonde. I did a double take, an about-face, and went in, presumably to engage in some badinage with Lewiston, but all the while I was looking at her and putting on a show in my own way, playing the big man. I saw a twinkle in her eye and for weeks I wanted to date her. I knew she was interested.

Finally I went to the commanding general and got written permission to date her. We began to see each other, and I knew I was in love with her. She wrote a "Dear John" letter to the Kentucky squire she had been engaged to, and we got married. Her parents were at the wedding; they were shocked, as were mine. We were married by a judge, in chambers, and moved immediately into a studio apart-

ment in Brooklyn Heights. It was charming and overlooked the harbor. We ignored the constant threat of mice and roaches.

In the beginning Norman Ross Abrams didn't want me in the family. He was respectful of my Army accomplishments, I think. He was proud of his own Army career and had, in fact, persuaded Emmy to join on the grounds of patriotism. But when I left the Army and no longer had the rank, he became coldly indifferent. Emmy quarreled with him. Nasty things were said, and they went two years without talking.

The war ended. The guns grew quiet. The troops came home. And I thought the world was waiting for me to come out of the Army, that I would immediately become the biggest man in industry, or in labor relations. I got the shock of my life. They didn't credit my military experience as being worth a tinker's damn. I had juggled a working force of 65,000—civilian and military. I had negotiated with the International Longshoremen's Association. But it wasn't industry. And I had nowhere to turn. I had Emmy and a baby daughter, Jill. And I had a law degree. So, with the encouragement of Emmy, I opened my own law office—up the establishment!

We went heavily into debt. It has long since been paid back, every cent, but we struggled. I was a lawyer, living and working within a few miles, a few minutes, of the neighborhood where I had spent most of my years. Was this all there is?

The day after I got out of the Army I arranged to meet a fraternity brother from my college days at NYU. His name was Stanley Kramer, like me fresh out of the service, destined for a brilliant career as a motion-picture producer. We spent a weekend in Philadelphia, one night watching Ray Bolger in *Three to Make Ready*, when he introduced the old soft-shoe routine; the next night watching NYU beat Temple at Convention Hall, in what was then the big challenge for both teams. We were rabid NYU fans.

We were at dinner that first night when Stanley announced, "I'm gonna make movies. I can make them cheaper and better than anybody in Hollywood." Kramer was already thinking ahead. "What do you think I ought to do?" he asked. "Arthur Laurents' *Home of the Brave*, or *Focus* by Arthur Miller?"

Automatically I said, *"Focus,"* which had an anti-Jew theme.

Stanley shook his head. "No way," he said. "They've already made *Gentleman's Agreement*. I'm gonna make *Home of the Brave*, but I'll make the Jewish boy black and I'm gonna deal with the great prob-

lem of America to come. The black problem." That's what he did.

I grew up on *Studs Lonigan* by James T. Farrell. It was light reading—until the age of Hitler. And then, *then* you began to take it seriously. As young as you were you knew, by God, that you were Jewish, and you knew every restrictive boundary and every thoughtless slight.

Sports was the one luxury you had in those days. I attended P.S. 9 in Brooklyn, fifteen blocks from Ebbets Field. School was dismissed at 3:00 P.M. The Dodger games began at 3:15. They didn't have numbers on their backs then, as we lay on our stomachs, peering under the center-field fence, but we *knew* our ballplayers. I lived on Eastern Parkway and I'd hear the roar of the crowd and I would shout to my brother, "Camilli has done it again."

But what of my own career? The future seemed to offer little excitement. I was just beginning to get somewhere as an attorney, just coming into money, when suddenly came this freakish radio opportunity. A radio career had been on my mind the moment I got out of the Army, but an audition at WOR painfully convinced me that I just didn't have an announcer's voice. So I had given up any idea of it.

I was making nearly $30,000 a year as an attorney, when that was a helluva lot of money, what with different tax rates and almost no inflation compared to what we have now. And of course my income was growing every year.

So what did I do? I accepted a network offer from ABC Radio to do ten five-minute sports shows a weekend for $25 a show. Less than scale. It began, in the most curious way, with a Little League panel show that I had moderated without pay. (I had drawn a charter for Little League baseball in New York, and ABC asked me to furnish the kids to interview athletes.) Even with that show we made news.

When ABC offered me a six-week deal—by God, what security, six weeks!—I told Emmy I wanted to give up my law practice and go into broadcasting. Me, the one without the voice, who had already been told he couldn't make it as an announcer. Emmy, ignoring the fact that I was finally providing a decent living, told me to go ahead. As always, she was stalwart.

My father was horrified. Right down to the day he died, in 1957, he would say to Emmy, "Please, dear, have him go back to the profession." It meant so much to him for his son to be a professional man, a lawyer.

But I was infected with my desire, my resolve, to make it in broad-

casting. I knew exactly what I wanted to do, and how. Not having a name or a reputation, I knew that I had to have the biggest names I could get. My first weekend I had Eddie Arcaro; it was the weekend of Nashua's last ride. Phil Rizzuto had quit baseball—no, Stengel had fired him—and I interviewed Rizzuto. I was probably the first reporter to carry his own tape recorder everywhere he went. The damned thing weighed 30 pounds and I wore it on my back. I must have looked like Edmund Hillary carrying his knapsack.

There were frequent days, in those years, when I would begin in the early morning with a fighter at his training camp—a Floyd Patterson—then hurry out to the racetrack to catch an Arcaro, and then wind up at Ebbets Field. Or the Polo Grounds.

I'd go to spring training and cover every camp in Florida in five days, still lugging that tape recorder. Some of the local announcers laughed at me. But not the professionals. I learned quickly that they respected a man who worked. "You're like shit," Ralph Houk told me, "you're everywhere." That line, I can say with certain mixed feelings, has survived to this day.

I was putting into practice my theory of what the sporting public wanted to hear. That was the era of the rip-and-reader—the sportscaster who would tear copy off the wire machine and read it verbatim:

For the Dodgers: six runs, twelve hits, no errors. For the Braves: five runs, ten hits, and one error. The winning pitcher: Clem Labine, who came on in the eighth in relief of Don Newcombe.

That was their idea of a sportscast. Not mine. I had my own notion about the business. I felt that the field was wide open for anyone willing to develop the sources and get to the scene. I wanted to bring to sports broadcasting the idea of developing a story in depth; I wanted to explore the issues. The world of sports was about to explode in America. Great changes in technology were coming; an increase of leisure time; the exodus to the suburbs to escape from the great cities. The whole pattern of society was changing, and sports would become ever more important. The influx of black athletes had begun. A whole new set of smoldering problems would emerge. Could we keep giving the country line scores as news?

There was nothing being done in depth, a total absence of commentary and little in the way of actuality. I had the background for it. First, the legal training, which gives a man the ability to interrogate,

to bring out things in an orderly manner. One develops an orderly mind when one studies law. I had another advantage—a basic feel for language. The abstract interview, replete with provocative questions concerning human personality, produces answers that are timeless. Good yesterday, good today, good next year, good forever.

When I came into the business, one of the people I admired was the writer Walter "Red" Smith. I got to know him, and he gave me two words of advice: "Be there." Ralph Houk's line in Florida indicated that I was trying.

I made it a point to be there. I established friendships and connections that became news sources, without which a reporter is useless.

The first network interview Jimmy Brown ever did was with me. And Paul Hornung. And Alex Karras. In 1955 Karras was a big, heavy, pudding-faced kid out of Iowa visting New York as a member of *Look* magazine's All America team. Nobody suspected that he had comic potential. He told me, with honestly moist eyes, the story of how he had quit school and returned to his home in Gary, Indiana. He was too fat and too slow and they had booted him off the Iowa team. His mother threw him out of the house. "You go back there and be a man," she ordered. "You get that weight off and you play football."

It was one hell of an interview. Alex hasn't forgotten it either. Today he's a smart-assed broadcaster and movie star. Alex has come a long way from the fat kid who was afraid of his mother.

By 1958 we had moved to Pound Ridge, and almost every morning I drove into the city with Giant defensive end and defensive Captain Andy Robustelli, a neighbor in North Stamford. We didn't drive in alone; we were joined often by another fellow then with the Giants, a defensive coach named Tom Landry. He had created something called the 4-3 defense. We would talk about it driving in, about how Tom had the front four blocking to the outside, giving the rookie middle linebacker a clear shot at the ball carrier. The rookie linebacker was Sam Huff, and that maneuver made Huff famous out of proportion to his ability. Sam was a fine player, but, in truth, Landry's defense allowed him to make the tackles while the others were doing their job.

I once did a radio show in which I explained exactly that point. Sam heard it, and he didn't resent it; he respected it. That's one lesson I've learned in sports. Some want only to hear the good things. But the real men, the people who matter, accept the truth.

Early on, as I broke into local television, I did half-hour specials with Wilt Chamberlain, Lombardi, Brown, Houk, Pancho Gonzales, Julie Boros, Tony Lema. They were kind and cooperative, and each, in his way, became important to me. I came to admire a man like Del Crandall, the catcher who had good seasons with the Braves. He had retarded children, and his life was a study in strength and love.

You make news contacts by going on the beat, by meeting people in their very beginnings, taking an interest, showing them you care, being willing to listen to their problems and never, not ever, forsaking their trust. You can't replace integrity.

And so it began by seeking out the story, by interviewing the people involved in making things happen. I still have those early tapes, as part of a personal tape library that numbers in the thousands.

The people at ABC liked what I was doing. It was the first time they had ever gotten personal, incisive actualities on the radio in sports. Now it's the accustomed thing. And now, of course, I've moved more into the field of commentary.

Still, I was terribly insecure in those early years. Don Durgin, now a top executive at NBC Television, ran ABC Radio at the time and he was convinced that I was a poor risk. He went along with me only because of a man named Ray Diaz, the program head for the radio network. Durgin was convinced that I couldn't make it because of what he considered the nasal abrasiveness of my voice. But I believed in the content of what I was doing, and slowly I saw that I was having an impact. I learned, not by accident, how to use my voice, as an actor does, with variety of tone and mood.

We were soon living in Peter Cooper Village, along with a rather creative group of young Army veterans. The group included John Forsythe, Karl Malden, and Tony Randall. We were all friendly, all sports fans. I'd take them to some of the events I covered. It was a good place to live and dream. Down the street a young lawyer named John Lindsay lived at Stuyvesant Town, a less expensive apartment complex.

Karl Malden was already a superb actor, appearing in *The Desperate Hours* and in *Streetcar Named Desire.* John Forsythe, who had grown up with me on Eastern Parkway in Brooklyn and had been for a time the public-address announcer at Ebbets Field, was beginning to make it. He was starring in *Teahouse of the August Moon.* I watched John take lessons to develop voice variety, because in those days everyone cast him as a lower-case Henry Fonda. He had no

identity of his own. By osmosis I learned something about the use of the voice: the gradations of the decibels, when to speak loudly, when to cut back.

So I lost some of my insecurity, and my career began to proceed apace. But, of course, I do not now—and never will—feel totally secure. Nothing in my life has conditioned me for it; certainly not in broadcasting. It is a colossal jungle. No one is ever safe in it.

CHAPTER 5

A HOLE IN THE SUBWAY

There is a quality about boxing that attaches to no other sport. Well, maybe not boxing; maybe the men who fight, rather than the science itself. They are the most interesting of all athletes, for they seem to have the deepest feelings about life. Theirs is a lonely sport, at times ugly, brutal, naked. You have to get inside a ring to appreciate how small it is. You wonder how men can ever escape.

Boxing has been infested with corruption and gangsterism from the day it began, yet it engages our basic emotions like no other athletic activity. Somehow it touches the men of letters and art and culture. When great writers are drawn to sports they turn irresistibly to the ring. Ernest Hemingway did. Budd Schulberg did. So did Norman Mailer.

It is also a fact that while movies with sports themes almost invariably fail at the box office, the exceptions have been movies with a boxing plot. John Garfield was memorable in *Body and Soul*. Kirk Douglas burst into public prominence with *Champion*. Jack Palance was acclaimed in *Requiem for a Heavyweight*. And, of course, there was *The Harder They Fall*, Budd Schulberg's opus.

I have discovered that sooner or later the great writers who turn to boxing fall in love with a fighter. For Mailer and Schulberg, for instance, there were Muhammad Ali and José Torres. For Roger Kahn, unaccountably, it was the momentarily glamorous Swede, Ingemar Johansson. Which only proves that each writer romanticizes in his own way.

My own interest in boxing developed because of three men: Floyd Patterson, Cus D'Amato, and Bill Heinz.

In my view Heinz is the greatest boxing writer who has ever lived.

He had a feeling for the sport like no one I have ever known, and it showed itself in the way he wrote. Somehow he could get inside a fighter's head—and his heart—from the champion to the lowliest pug, and there would emerge an earthy insight into the whole being of the fighter.

It was Bill Heinz who would sit and talk with me about Lew Jenkins. (His piece on Lew in the *Fireside Book of Boxing* may be the all-time boxing classic. Bill, incidentally, edited that book.) He would take me back to Fritzie Zivic, stir my memories on Maxie Baer, Jack Sharkey, Max Schmeling, Joe Louis, Archie Moore, and Rocky Marciano. The more Bill Heinz talked, the more fascinated I became with boxing. And then it was the age of Floyd Patterson. Bill liked Floyd. He never thought he was a great fighter, but he liked him. In fact, in those days I didn't know anybody who did not like Floyd Patterson. He was a sociologist's dream, and a psychologist's guinea pig.

Many people know Patterson's background. A product of the Brooklyn ghetto. Overly sensitive, overly shy as a result, he turned ever inward and found a nest, a hole in the subway where he would sit, alone, afraid, watching the trains go by.

He wound up in the Wiltwyck School, then located in Aesopus, New York, a school for disturbed children. At the Wiltwyck School Floyd discovered the countryside. He fell in love with it for the rest of his life. He loves quiet, he loves peace, he loves to walk alone, to hear the birds, to pick up a twig, to throw a stick in the air, to watch the ripples in the stream when he tosses a rock in. Wiltwyck School was right for him. It was there that Floyd Patterson began to emerge from his shell.

He came back home and attended a special school in Manhattan. This kind of school was called a "600" school. It was programmed for young men with the kind of background Floyd had.

How odd that one with such a background should wind up in a profession of violence, a profession where, notwithstanding one's own sensitivity, one seeks to impose pain upon another. But strangely, in apparent contradiction of his whole personality, Floyd Patterson did.

The "600" school he attended was not far from Fourteenth Street—Union Square if you will. Almost just around the corner, upstairs in a seedy, broken-down building on Fourteenth Street, was a place called the Gramercy Gym. What it really was was a fleabag.

Nobody in his right mind would visit there. It was stark and empty except for the fact that in the middle of the floor—it was an old-time loft—there was a boxing ring. And over in a corner, there was a cot. There was also a dog, a vicious-looking German shepherd, always muzzled, and there was a man who lived there, slept on that cot—a man with a vigorous body, crew-cut white hair, a man who spoke in an educated fashion, the sentences grammatically correct, the speech interestingly literate. The only problem was that he spoke in terms of mystery, of devious plots against him, suspicious figures lurking everywhere who were out to get him. The plain truth was, you could never tell what the hell he was talking about. His name was Cus D'Amato, and he was a boxing manager.

Whether or not you could understand Cus when he talked about "his enemies," when he talked about boxing it was another thing. On this subject he was clear and explicit. And he could get young fighters to come to his gym. Two of Floyd Patterson's older brothers would go there. And Floyd, at age 14, would leave the "600" school and go there to watch his brothers. It was inevitable that he would start to train, to learn how to fight. And so Floyd's dream was born early: to become a professional fighter and use the money he would make to help his family.

In Helsinki, Finland, in 1952 he won the gold medal as a middleweight in the Olympics. He was Cus's boy, with a special style of fighting that Cus had taught him, the "peekaboo," the gloves up high, in front of the chin, to afford better defense and yet be so positioned as to be able to deliver blows with greater quickness than the opponent. At least that was the theory.

He came back from Finland, and his professional career began, under Cus's careful tutelage. Those were the days when I became friendly with Floyd and Cus. Those were my early days in radio. Repeatedly both of them guested for me. I developed an almost fatherly affection for Patterson. And I was sympathetic to Cus's drive against the IBC—the International Boxing Club—an octopus-like organization, headed up by the late Jim Norris, that controlled boxing and, as was later documented, was gangster influenced.

I would go up to Greenwood Lake, New York, and watch Patterson train. I had begun to learn much about boxing, and it was clear that Floyd was an exceptional young fighter. The one drawback seemed to be his size, or the absence thereof. He had become a heavyweight, but looked to be more like a light heavyweight.

I became absorbed with Floyd—with his personal life, his softness, both of manner and voice, the way he would express interest in a variety of things—religion, family, and hobbies. He converted to Catholicism and seemed utterly at peace with himself. He was that way then as a fighter. "If Cus says I can win, then I can win," he would say.

And he kept winning. Until finally, on November 30, 1956, Patterson knocked out Archie Moore in the fifth round at the Chicago Stadium to become the heavyweight champion of the world. He was only 21, the youngest champion in history. The following Sunday at ten in the morning our doorbell rang. It was Cus, ebullient, enthusiastic, and eager to savor the fruits of victory. He brought with him a bottle of 100-year-old Armagnac brandy as a gift. "Take it," he insisted, "you've been with us all the way."

Once he became champion, there was no tangible change in Patterson. He was as quiet as ever, as shy as ever. He had a home in Rockville Centre, Long Island, was married to a girl named Sandra, and they had a baby daughter named Seneca. My own daughters, Jill and Hilary, were crazy about him. They worried every time he fought. Emmy was much the same way. Floyd had become a personal thing. Out of nowhere he would drop in to visit us in Pound Ridge. Or we would visit him in the isolation of his training camp and watch him work out.

I found myself no different from the writers. I had fallen in love with a fighter. So had my family. Part of his charm for all of us was his apparent vulnerability. Even when he was champion he was somehow a figure of sympathy, which he has been in the public mind ever since.

As for boxing, Cus was more than cautious with Patterson's career. Floyd faced one stiff after another. Finally, there was to be a championship defense in New York against Ingemar Johansson, a Swedish heavyweight who had knocked out Eddie Machen in the first round in a bout held in Sweden. Everyone remembered that Johansson had been disqualified in the 1952 Olympics for "not fighting." Everyone thought that Ingemar was just another handpicked patsy for Floyd to beat.

The Patterson-Johansson fight was the first I ever broadcast. It was in June 1959 and it was to be broadcast on the ABC Radio Network. It would also be seen on theater television and would set the pattern for many major heavyweight-championship broadcasts to

come—radio network to the home, and theater TV for those who wanted to see it. Our broadcast was being sponsored by United Artists and the Mirisch Brothers to promote a new movie of theirs called *The Horse Soldiers*. The stars of that movie were John Wayne and William Holden, and they were to broadcast with me and Les Keiter.

Holden came into town several days before the broadcast, and I visited both training camps with him. Patterson was training in Summit, New Jersey, but wasn't even there when we appeared. That finished off Patterson as far as Holden was concerned, despite every excuse I made for Floyd. Then we went to visit Johansson at Grossinger's, in upstate New York, and because he was there, and was most amiable, Holden responded to him instantly. As a matter of fact, Ingo, who has always had a good eye for the buck, was on tenterhooks waiting for Holden. Ingo thought he should be in the movies and that Holden could help show him the way. Bill did nothing to discourage him. Holden's eyes had fastened upon Birgit Lundgren, Johansson's fiancée, who also nurtured Hollywood visions and who hardly seemed antipathetic to the vision of Holden himself. It's altogether possible that Bill could have been reciprocal to Birgit's apparent interest, but a look at Johansson in fighting trunks deterred him.

On the way back to New York, Holden said, "Howard, Johansson will beat Patterson."

We got along very well. He was a down-to-earth guy, and so for that matter was John Wayne when he joined us. The two of them really enjoyed the fight, which proved to be one of the big upsets in boxing history. Holden led the cheering as Johansson's right got to Patterson in the third, and Patterson went down *seven* times before they finally stopped it. At that moment Ingo had made believers out of all of us. Suddenly there was truth in what his manager, Edwin Ahlquist, had told us all at a press conference a week earlier. "Dere is toonder in his right. You vill see." We had all laughed.

In the ring after the fight Cus D'Amato said to me, "Floyd Patterson will become the first heavyweight champion ever to regain his title." Having lost the fight, Patterson went into seclusion at his home in Rockville Centre.

A few days after the fight I got a call from Cus. He told me that Floyd was still in a deep depression and that he was worried about him. He asked if I would go out to see him to try to cheer him up. I said, "Sure, but why don't I take Jackie Robinson along?" I knew

that Floyd, though he had never met Jackie, respected him enormously. Cus thought it was a great idea, cleared it with Floyd, and the next morning at nine o'clock Jackie and I were at Floyd's house.

From the outside it looked unoccupied. All the blinds were drawn. We rang, and rang again. And again. Finally Sandra appeared and let us in. Floyd was unmarked, but he tried to avoid looking us in the eye. I could only suppose that the terrible shame he felt derived in some way from his whole background. It was as if he were sitting in that little hole in the subway all over again.

Robinson talked to Floyd at length. He told him about his own life, about the comebacks he had had to make and how Floyd could do it more quickly than Jackie had ever done it, because he was so much younger. Patterson seemed visibly encouraged by the time we left. This, by the way, was the beginning of a long-term friendship between Patterson and Robinson. Years later Robinson was to go to Alabama at a time when Bull Connor, the sheriff, was turning the dogs loose on the blacks of Birmingham. Patterson went with him. There was a time when the two were in the Deep South, when Patterson, no longer diffident and sheepish, would in the presence of southern whites go up to the two water fountains in the center of town, one marked "black" and the other "white," and deliberately drink from the fountain labeled "white." Then he turned around, faced the whites and said, in his quiet, laconic way, "Tastes like the same water."

There was a rematch clause; Patterson was to fight Johansson again. The day before the fight—it was June 19, 1960—I was alone with Patterson taping the prefight show. It was then that I could see the fury in the man. For a whole year he had been seething inside. He didn't like Johansson and he had for the first time in his life felt hate. It was amazing that he had been able to disguise his feelings so well. He told me that he would nullify Johansson's right and beat him with his left hook.

June 20, 1960, made boxing history. It was at the old Polo Grounds, and in the fifth round Patterson hit Johansson with as strong and as clean and as pulverizing a left hook as I had ever seen. Johansson lay there on the canvas, unconscious, his right foot twitching, blood pouring out of his mouth. I interviewed Patterson briefly and then went over to where Johansson still lay, on the canvas, still out cold, the blood still coming out of his mouth. Whitey Bimstein, his trainer, was leaning over him.

"For God's sake, Whitey," I said, "is he dead?"

Whitey, a colorful relic of boxing's heyday, looked up at me and answered, "The son of a bitch should be. I told him to look out for the left hook."

That was the zenith of Floyd Patterson's career, but only the beginning of the vicissitudes in our relationship that were to follow.

I realized Patterson was not an outstanding fighter after his third bout with Johansson, which came a year later in Miami. Johansson was overweight, out of shape, bloated, had virtually no movement in the ring. Yet Patterson was defenseless against Ingo's right and went down several times. Ingo finally went down one more time than Patterson and stayed there, so Floyd retained the title. But he had made it utterly clear that he could not defend against a right hand and that he went down with unbecoming ease. The more I listened to Floyd talk after that fight, the more I began to wonder about him. On the surface he was still the same—diffident, almost timid. But things were happening. He had broken with Cus D'Amato, the very man who had made him, who had carefully selected his opponents and who, even though D'Amato never would admit it, knew Patterson's limitations as a fighter.

It seemed to me that, forever after, Patterson was helpless without D'Amato. Yet his public image was never higher. He was the "good guy" and Sonny Liston, the "looming threat," was definitely a bad guy. And always, somehow, Floyd got you involved in his personal psychiatry. He could not be vicious against Johansson in the third fight, he said, because he had been so vicious in the second fight and he never wanted to be that way again. "It's wrong to hate the way I hated," he said.

Then the new tack started to develop. "I keep getting knocked down, but I keep getting up. That's the test." As if it were now the mark of a champion to be knocked to the canvas even by a Tom McNeely, as long as one managed to regain one's feet.

I often wonder what Cus D'Amato would have done about Sonny Liston, whether he could have kept Floyd away from Liston. But Cus D'Amato or no, the pressures were building on Patterson to meet Sonny Liston. The newspapers were headlining Liston's successes, speculation was rife as to when the two would meet. Even at the White House, President Kennedy in a meeting with Floyd inquired about a fight with Liston.

So the fight was set, for September 1962 in Chicago. I was certain

it would be no fight at all. In my talks with Floyd I sensed a preac-
ceptance of defeat. On my prefight show he openly said, "I wonder
how it will be when I come out."

Yes, he wondered—but not too much. Remember, he had a disguise ready, which he adopted to escape town. The fight lasted 2
minutes and 11 seconds. In the ring after the fight Patterson told me,
"Sonny started too fast for me tonight." My instinctive feeling was
that he was relieved that it ended so quickly.

Patterson became a recluse again, ashamed and alone, but there
was to be a rematch the following year at Las Vegas. In the buildup
for that, the word was that Floyd had fought Liston's fight the first
time, that he had gone at Liston and should have used his superior
foot speed, moved around and outboxed him. This time it would be
different.

This time it took 2 minutes and 16 seconds. And Liston told me in
the ring, "I said it would be a rerun."

It was at this point that Liston looked down at ringside, picked out
the young Cassius Clay, and pointed, "You're next, big-mouth." It
was the summer of '63.

Patterson's next big fight was in the fall of '65, against Muhammad
Ali, who had become the champion. Floyd insisted on calling him
Cassius Clay, and I didn't like that one bit; it seemed to me a deliberate attempt by Floyd to cast himself in the role of the good guy. He
did something else in this fight. He went into it with a bad back, a
fact he never disclosed, and he should not have been in that ring that
night.

A few days later, in New York City, I did a *Wide World of Sports*
show on the fight with Muhammad Ali. It was during the taping of
this show that Ali admitted that he *carried* Floyd Patterson. According to Ali, he "didn't want to kill him." Also according to Ali, he was
damned if he did and damned if he didn't. "When I knock a man out
I'm cruel. When I don't I can't punch."

At the moment when Ali confessed that he carried Patterson, I
stopped the taping. I asked Chuck Howard, the producer, and Lou
Volpicelli, the director, to come down from the control booth. I
wanted them to be present while I advised Ali of the implications of
what he had just said. I said, "You might lose your license to fight
because of what you are saying. In effect you have admitted that you
didn't put forth your best effort."

"I don't care," Ali retorted, "it's the truth and I want to say it."

It wasn't long after that that an article appeared in *Esquire* magazine, by Floyd Patterson, with Gay Talese, the writer. Gay had been close to Floyd for as long as I had. Indeed, Floyd was one of the principals in a book by Gay called *The Overreachers,* so Talese was very familiar with the singular quirks and fancies of Floyd.

In the piece, Patterson wrote in effect that "Howard Cosell, who used to be my friend," had gotten Ali to say that he had carried him. In the first place, that was untrue. In the second place, a ventriloquist couldn't put words in Ali's mouth. In the third place, friendship has nothing to do with reporting.

The next time I saw Floyd Patterson he couldn't look me in the eye. I challenged him about what he had written, and he tried to avoid the subject. More and more, as the years passed, Floyd would be receptive to those who had most recently written or spoken well of him.

He always knew how to appeal to the public. The impact he had made upon the public reached its apex on the night of March 8, 1971. Madison Square Garden. The fight of the century. Perhaps the most extravagant sports event of the age. *Frazier* versus *Ali.* One by one the great champions of the past were introduced: Dempsey; Louis; Tunney; Sugar Ray; Archie Moore. Then another name echoed from the loudspeakers: Floyd Patterson. People stood, heads swiveling. They screamed his name. They searched for him. They gave him the loudest ovation of the night. He wasn't even there.

It was a perfect tribute to a man whose career had been a fantasy.

But that was all the opportunists at the Garden had to see and hear. They realized Floyd was still box office. Quickly they promoted a match for him with Oscar Bonavena, which Patterson won on a disputed decision.

And that led to a rematch with Ali, who was now fighting anyone and everyone as he waited, and existed, to meet Frazier again. I was preparing to leave for Munich and the 20th Olympiad when the match between Patterson and Ali was announced. I went on the air to say, unequivocally, that the fight should not be licensed.

When I returned from Munich I learned that *Wide World of Sports* would be carrying the Ali-Patterson fight. I was assigned to it. It was just what I expected—a grotesque mismatch. For five rounds Ali did nothing, absolutely nothing. In the fourth he had held his hands at his sides the entire round and merely bobbed and weaved and slipped punches; poor Patterson could do nothing with him. Then

in the sixth Ali went to work, and, in nothing flat, blood gushed from a cut over Patterson's eye. They had to stop the fight.

In the ring interview Floyd told me he was going to make his move in the next round. He said he wanted a rematch, "if the public will buy it." That speaks for itself.

To this day I give Floyd Patterson credit for this much: his love of boxing, I'm convinced, is sincere. With the passing years I grew ever more disillusioned and disenchanted, until I discovered what I felt was an ultimate truth about this strange and moody and complicated man: that he lives off self-martyrization and sympathy.

I think I understand him. It took a long time.

CHAPTER 6

HIS NAME IS MUHAMMAD

The first time I met him he was a brash, lippy kid from Louisville, Kentucky. He was a descendant of slaves, and his very name bespoke the fact. Cassius Marcellus Clay. His namesake had been a Kentucky senator, a relative of Henry Clay, and a slave owner. I had no reason then to suspect that he would become a dominant figure in my career, and an historical one in sports.

This was August 1962, about a month before Liston was to meet Patterson for the title at Comiskey Park in Chicago. I did my first interview with the young Clay, then engaged in a long-range campaign to draw attention to himself. It was very easy to be charmed by him, and I was no different from anyone else. He was attractive, outgoing, full of nonsense. He didn't know who Howard Cosell was. Nor did he care. He knew me only vaguely as the guy who did the fights on radio. There was an appealing gaiety and irresponsibility about him.

I watched him gradually develop under the shrewd handling of Angelo Dundee, beating poor old Archie Moore, and then taking on Henry Cooper in England. As director of sports for ABC Radio I arranged to have the fight carried in the States. It was deliciously broadcast by a pair of British commentators. Clay won, but in the process was decked by Cooper, an inferior fighter who had been described by the British press as having "a great capacity for public suffering." Ali's defenses were not then refined to the level of precision they would reach within two years.

When Clay returned to New York I had him delivered straight from the airport to our studios, where he went on live with me on a local television news show over Channel 7. This, I think, really touched off our whole relationship and the series of dialogues yet to come.

I happened to know that he was waiting for an advance from Madison Square Garden and I asked him about it. He was startled. "Gee," he said, "you really know this boxing business, don't ya?" I did not disagree. Then we went on the air and we kidded back and forth. By this time, of course, Liston was the champion, and all Clay wanted, he kept insisting, was "the Big Black Bear, the Big Black Bear."

I needled him: "Cooper knocked you down. What's Liston gonna do to you?"

He said airily, "No contest, not a chance."

That interview attracted some notice. There was an instant rapport between us, not just because I found him a natural entertainer but because instinctively he sensed that the two of us made a very good pair in reaching the public.

Finally he was signed to fight Sonny Liston in 1964 in Miami. I distinctly remember a show I did on the radio network the day before I was to visit Clay in the Fifth Street Gym where he trained. In it I described what Liston would do to him, how Clay had to be frightened of him, and how he was trying to cover with a youthful kind of braggadocio that would vanish when he stepped into the ring.

So I got to the Fifth Street Gym the next morning and at the sight of me Clay broke into a grin as broad as Atlantic Avenue. A feigned stricken look then contorted his face, "I'm gonna—just gonna collapse when I get into the ring against that Big Black Bear!" And I knew he had heard the show. "There is no way," he went on, "that young Cassius can fight that man . . . he is a terror."

He made a mockery of everything I had said on the air. I surrendered. He wasn't angry, just having a great deal of fun with it, and instantly I began thinking, "My God, maybe it's not false bravado; the guy really thinks he can beat Sonny Liston. . . . "

I was one of the many who subscribed to the Liston mystique. The baleful stare, the huge head wrapped in the towel, all the rest. At that point I opened my tape recorder and explained to Clay that this was for the prefight show, that no one would hear it until he was in the ring; he could speak freely. I said, "Now, I want you to assume

that you're about to leave the dressing room. You start walking toward the ring. What do you think your mental processes will be as you make that walk?"

He nodded, and in a voice that was barely above a whisper he began: "I'm leaving the dressing room, about to go against the Big Black Bear. This terrible man. Cassius Clay is frightened. Cassius Clay is ready to run. I keep walking toward the ring and, all the time, even while I'm so frightened that I'm almost afraid to look at him with that terrible look he gives you, I'm thinking—YOU POOR OLD MAN!"

I left there still not giving him a chance to win but now convinced that the guy was totally unafraid. I learned early in the game that Cassius Clay is one of the most confusing men in the world; just being in his company one can undergo a series of conflicting impressions. He has the instinct of a honeybee, darting from flower to flower, always looking for the pollen.

The next day came the famous scene at the weigh-in, like something out of the Mad Hatter. Sugar Ray Robinson, restraining him. Drew Brown, one of his handlers, who called himself Bundini, restraining him. All the while, Clay going through this act of apparent insanity, gesturing and screaming at Liston, leaping around the room. The blood pressure was way up. Everyone who saw him wondered if he had truly popped his cork out of fear.

So now what did I think about this curious young man? I had been with him the previous day when he manifested nothing but assurance. Now I saw this crazed behavior and I thought, "Well, he fooled me yesterday . . . the guy *is* scared to death." But somewhere deep in the cabinet of my mind I began to understand that here was one terrific actor.

This was utterly confirmed when I arrived at the Miami Beach Convention Hall that night to do the fight. While the preliminaries were on, as I mixed with friends in the crowd, I suddenly discovered Clay standing in the semidarkness in the back of the hall. His brother was about to fight in the next prelim. He motioned to me. "You watch Rudy," he whispered. "He'll show you something."

I did a double take. He was the most composed guy in the place. "Wha—what was all that this afternoon?" I stammered.

He looked at me, winked, and said, "I wanted Liston to know I was crazy. Only a fool isn't scared of a crazy man. You'll see tonight."

Now the fight began. We got to the third round. Clay was boxing

Liston all over the ring, and Sonny couldn't get to him. The Liston left arm that used to seem as long as a lamppost couldn't even reach him, because Clay was circling steadily, swiftly, to his left, staying out of range. And he did it so quickly, so continuously, that he was always free to respond with his own combinations, beginning with the left. Liston was slow and ponderous, and suddenly I was in the process of seeing the Big Black Bear exposed.

Later a lot of people wanted to know if I thought the fight was fixed, if Liston just quit or what. They still want to know. To a degree Liston did quit, but he was a beaten old man, and in my opinion that fight was completely legitimate. To explain how I became totally convinced of that, I take you back to the third round. In those years Clay had a technique of turning his punches at the moment of impact, and it would be almost like a knife. It would just slit a man's face open.

With it he slashed the left side of Liston's face. Now, Sonny had a flabby face, except that no one ever noticed it because he was so all-powerful. After all, he had the two quick first-round knockouts of Patterson, a sinister history, and people were petrified of him. Except for one blow by Cleveland Williams, he had never been really hit hard enough to stagger.

Now out of nowhere the left side of Liston's face was just slit from the eye down to the lip. It was like a zipper, and out gushed the blood, which he tasted. Rocky Marciano, who was doing the fight with me, leaned over and said, "Jesus Christ, Howie, he's become an old man."

Clay was in complete command and appeared to have the fight won. But no, in Liston's corner some liniment was picked up on the gloves, got into Clay's eyes and temporarily blinded him. It is true that he would not have come out for the fifth round if Angelo Dundee hadn't pushed him to the ring. But there was nothing Liston could do, because Clay instinctively kept moving his legs, circling to the left. And then, as the eyes cleared, it was all over.

In the ring afterwards, in my interview with him, Clay went berserk. He taunted the writers at ringside. "I told ya, I told ya," he laughed at them, "I'm the greatest, the Big Black Bear, I'm the greatest, I told ya. . . ."

The next day the mood suddenly, almost melodramatically, turned somber. He appeared at a press conference as the new heavyweight champion of the world. And he told them, defiantly, "Yes, the rumors

are true. My name is Muhammad Ali. I'm a Black Muslim now."

Everyone had heard the rumors. Everyone knew that Malcolm X and Clay had been meeting. Perhaps what some didn't know was that Rudolph Valentino Clay had *already* become a Black Muslim and had a major influence on his brother's thinking. It meant nothing to me because I felt it was the man's own business. I was amused by the fact that it mattered so much to the Old World sportswriters who have their own vision of America, which is planes flying over a stadium at half time and raising the flag and singing the anthem.

I said that I was "amused" at the reaction of much of America and in particular some of the writers. I was—at first. Later I grew angry and finally furious. Didn't these idiots realize that Cassius Clay was the name of a slave owner? What intelligent proud black in the 1960's would wish to bear the name of a white Kentucky senator who, before the Civil War, bought and sold black flesh? Had I been black and my name Cassius Clay, I damned well would have changed it! The insinuations and objections of whites, in particular the ones that appeared in the press, can best be called racist snarls. What should I say about the likes of Patterson and Ernie Terrell? They didn't know any better.

This was 1964, and now the dialogues between us really began. We would tape virtually every Ali fight, bring him into the studio, talk over the film, and have our conversations. And I would challenge him, as no one else would, because reporting was still involved in our exchanges. Invariably he would bang back. The fans argued over whether we were friends, enemies or what, a confusion that exists to this day. Some expected Ali, at any moment, to punch me in view of the cameras. If he ever had, of course, I would have broken every bone in his body.

Muhammad Ali immediately knew that I was on the side of justice. Only one person in the media called him by the name he had adopted. I did this instantly. I could not have cared less what the public's reaction would be toward me, and in some corners of the country I was already labeled a "White Muslim." I'm born and raised at law, and under the law a man is entitled to be known by the name of his choice, unless by that change of name he seeks to avoid payment of lawfully inculcated debts to creditors.

How selectively we apply our righteous indignation. Nobody calls Betty Perske by that name. She's Lauren Bacall. Cary Grant was a stilt walker at Coney Island named Archie Leach. Ever hear anyone

call him Archie? As part of the sickness of the decade, and as part of the dugout mentality of a certain portion of the press, they would ceaselessly refer to Ali as Cassius Clay. But he knew my position and respected me for it.

(Coincidentally, I wonder how many people would know Howard Cosell as Howard William Cohen? And for the record, Cosell—once spelled with a K—*is* the family name. It was changed back not for show-biz reasons but by the family, to comply with the wishes of our late father. As a Polish refugee, my grandfather had been unable to make his name clear to a harried immigration inspector. The official simply compromised on Cohen and waved him through. So I understood, better than most, that names are not necessarily engraved on marble tablets, never to be disturbed.)

Ali knew now that I would back him. Whenever he came to New York he would either call or just walk in on me unannounced. He'd get a kick out of strolling down the street with me, and he reacted to the stares we attracted. Our kidding would be very racial. He would say, "Call me nigger in front of these people. They'll think we hate one another. . . ."

By early 1964 it was clear that he was totally under the control of the Muslims. The syndicate of Louisville businessmen who gave him his start was now an object of the past. It should be said that the Louisville group did well by Ali; started a trust fund for him, were sincerely concerned for his long-term well-being, and then faded out rather gracefully. Now Ali couldn't make a move without Herbert Muhammad, the son of the Grand Prophet, Elijah Muhammad. This wasn't an easy situation for Angelo Dundee, but he kept trying to do his job.

So there was a suggestion of tension around Ali, leading up to what was to be the rematch with Liston in Lewiston, Maine.

To this day people ask me, "Was it fixed?" I still don't know. Was I suspicious of it? I was then and I am now. I never saw the knockout punch. The reports from ringside were mixed. Jimmy Cannon, the veteran boxing writer, said he was situated exactly right when the knockout occurred. He told me later, on the air, "I was sittin' right there. I saw the punch, and it couldn't have crushed a grape."

We may never know for certain what happened. My most vivid memory of the whole episode was of Jersey Joe Walcott, the referee, staggering around the ring and the late Nat Fleischer stopping it when the count had reached about 24. The entire moment was sur-

real. The kids from Bates College were pouring down the aisles and screaming, "FIX—FIX—FIX." It was an unbelievable scene in this little Saint Dominick's Arena in Lewiston, Maine, and I can't forget the two fighters leaving the ring. There was a look of absolute relief on Liston's face. I don't think I ever saw Sonny appear so content in his life, and I wondered about that. Was he glad just to have it over? Or just to be alive? There had been wild talk about rival Muslim factions and possible gunplay directed at either fighter, or both. Cannon had kept the story bubbling. Jimmy is the last of the Damon Runyon era of Broadway sports columnists, and melodrama was his meat. He had murder-by-implication hanging in the air. He swelled eagerly on the presence of Muslims in the crowd at Liston's camp. It lent even more strangeness to the occasion, and it lent credibility to the rumors—that Liston's life was threatened, that he lay down, that it was fixed.

I can't explain the expression of total release on Liston's face when the fight ended. Or Ali, leaving the arena, spotting me and winking. Was it a dump? That was not then and is not now provable. If there is a secret to the story of Lewiston, Maine, it went to the grave with Sonny Liston.

We showed the film of the fight in stop-action on *Wide World of Sports*. It was more ludicrous than ever, the mistiming of the count, the confusion in which it ended, the phantom punch. I brought in Rocky Marciano and Jimmy Cannon as part of a panel to review the footage. Rocky insisted he never saw the punch. Cannon made his public declaration that it wouldn't have crushed a grape.

Ali called it his "anchor" punch, and claimed that he had gotten it from Stepin Fetchit, the old, shuffling, black character actor. That was something I never understood about Muhammad. He included in his entourage this comic figure who symbolized all the old darky stereotypes, all the things Ali himself did not represent. It was a poetic turn, I thought, when Ali announced that the invisible punch was taught him by Stepin Fetchit. The fight was a fiasco.

I ended my show that night with the statement, "If boxing can survive this, it can survive anything." And it has, more or less.

The next public moment was the Patterson fight, and I began to get an index to the fact that Muhammad Ali could be a terribly cruel man. He didn't like Floyd. He considered him an Uncle Tom. He resented deeply the fact that the public loved Patterson and that he himself had become controversial because of his Muslim position.

461

He did not respect Floyd as a man. He said to me, curious, "You like Patterson, don't you?"

I said, "Yes, very much," and I explained why, how I had become interested in him.

He shook his head. "He's not a good man and he's no fighter at all. I can do what I want with him."

I had the awful sense then that he was really planning to punish Patterson. He did so, savagely, needlessly, to my total disgust. But at the same time I had begun to grow uneasy about Floyd Patterson —the two embarrassing bouts with Liston, the departure with the beard, the constant humility, the obsession with saying the right thing to please the most number of people at a given time—so my own feelings were confused about the two men. Nevertheless, there was no need for Ali to have dealt so contemptibly with him. He just tortured him.

And so, for the first time, I went after Ali in a *Wide World* interview, establishing that he had, indeed, been needlessly vicious. He could have finished him at any time, but he kept Floyd on his feet. This was when he admitted that he carried Patterson. As it turned out, there were no repercussions from the New York State Boxing Commission, or any other.

Public disapproval of Ali had not yet reached the stage of hysteria, but it would shortly. His draft board suddenly elected to reopen his case. He was reclassified as 1-A. Ali greeted the news with the deathless words, "I ain't got no quarrel with them Viet Cong." It was an attitude many in this country would come to share, but not then, not in 1965.

He signed to fight Ernie Terrell in Illinois, but the commission there no longer wanted it. Not a state in the Union did. He was suddenly poison in his own country.

Ali was now forced to fight overseas. In May 1966 he traveled to Britain to meet Henry Cooper. I found him a moodier young man but still open and receptive to the love the British people lavished on him. He was a hero in another land. It was at this point that he came to understand that he was a world figure, unlike any other American athlete.

I doubt that he had ever, at the beginning, anticipated what would happen to him in America, between his public embracing of the Black Muslims and his resistance to the draft. Now he was getting a taste of it. Yet through all of the troubles he would endure in the next

five years he was, in one sense, the most extraordinary human being I have ever known.

He grew homesick in England, troubled by the uncertainty about when he would fight again in America. But the homesickness soon disappeared. Everywhere he walked on the streets of London, the crowds knew him and surrounded him. He had a taste of what it was to be an elegant, almost foppish figure of means. Once he even affected the top hat and tails and striped diplomat's trousers. He made a speech in Hyde Park. He could hardly have been in a gayer mood.

To open the telecast of the fight, producer Chet Forte had prepared a half-hour show, a film creatively done of Ali in various London scenes, all laid against the lyrics of Roger Miller's tune: "England swings like a pendulum do, bobbies on bicycles, two by two. . . ."

ABC was to carry the fight live by satellite, and we had rolled about five minutes of the film package when Jimmy Ellis knocked out his opponent in the first round of the last preliminary. Under the British system the fighters were to enter the ring within two minutes of the prior match, but if they did, our half-hour show on Ali would be down the drain. So we were in serious trouble. Chet screamed at me, "Howie, you gotta hold up the fight."

Chris Schenkel was calling the blow-by-blow. I was to handle the color with Rocky Marciano. Everyone turned toward me. I retreated a step, raised a hand, and said, "Look, I'm in a foreign country. I couldn't do it in America, much less England. There must be another way."

Chet said, "No there isn't, Howard. You know Ali. You gotta get him to hold up this fight."

There was no time to argue. I leaped from my seat and started racing toward the dressing rooms. I really had no idea what I would say when I got there. I ducked into the dressing room, knowing that at any second the ring attendants were coming for Ali to make his entrance. Ali was sitting on the training table, relaxed, ready to go. He was telling stories to the bobbies, amusing them—and himself—with yarns about his boyhood scrapes with the police in Louisville.

Angelo Dundee looked up and said, "What the hell are you doing in here?"

I tried to catch my breath. "Angie," I panted, "hold everything. You can't send him out yet."

His jaw dropped. "What the hell is the matter with you, Howard?

Are you crazy? My man's got a title defense. The other guy ain't a bad left-hooker. He knocked him down once. Cooper can do a job, ya know. Get out of here before you upset—"

Ali heard us arguing. "What's the matter?"

I said, "Muhammad, remember the great footage we shot of you walking around London—the way the people here feel about you —how much you want the people in the United States to see this now, with all your troubles?"

He nodded. I said, "It's on the air right now. Just started. We won't be able to show it if you go out there now. They're going to be coming in for you any second. If you go with them there's just no way we'll get the whole show on. It's critical."

He was thinking this over when they knocked on the door. A British ring official stuck his head in the doorway: "Aw right. It's time to go."

Instantly Ali was on his feet, shadowboxing. "How much time you need?" he asked me in a whisper. I told him 18 minutes would do it.

He started dancing around the room, bobbing and weaving. "I won't be out for 18 minutes," he announced. "Nobody tells the champ when to go."

I patted him on the shoulder. "Great work, champ." And out I went, tearing back to ringside to report to Forte. "I don't know what's going to happen in this arena, Chet, but he isn't coming out for another 18 minutes."

By now the place was in total darkness, and the crowd was just sitting there. It was incredible, but Ali held fast. And finally the time passed. Abruptly a white spotlight cut the darkness and out came Cooper, who had refused to appear until Ali left his dressing room. And, at last, here was Ali. He had held up a championship fight for 18 minutes—long, labored minutes—in order for the American public to see a film we had prepared of him moving about London.

The fight began, and Ali quickly sliced Cooper to ribbons. It was over, and a riot broke out. I climbed into the ring, catching an occasional ricochet from some of the wildly swinging fans. But I was basically protected, and I proceeded to interview Ali.

He started off by thanking everybody in the world, and he began to go through his litany about the Muslims and the Grand Prophet.

I cut him off. "We've been through all that before, Muhammad," I said. "How about thanking the President of the United States?"

And he said, "Oh, yes, yes. Him, too."

I would recall that moment with irony in the months to come—as Ali took on the weight and power of the United States government—as I would later reflect on so many of our meetings and exchanges and stages shared.

What were my feelings then and now about Ali? What kind of man, at bottom, did I find him to be? These are the questions I have been most often asked in my lifetime in sports. I'm not sure they can be answered in the abstract.

He is a chameleon—a man of many moods. Open, expansive, gay, and charming. Full of fun and mischief. Gregarious. Born to perform. But sullen, petulant, and sometimes cruel. Without formal education but with native brightness and vocally quick. A very short attention span. A practical joker. A man of inordinate courage; how else to explain the willingness to have a career destroyed, to give up millions of dollars, to defy the authority of the United States, to risk the abuse of multimillions of people? A man of unquestioned sincerity in his religious belief. A man with an inborn need for that belief. A man who does not hate whites, but a man who would rather not be with them. A man reluctant to discuss his religion with whites. A mercurial man, impenetrable, a man who will always puzzle and confuse me. But, always, a salesman.

I was present at what I would regard as his denouement, against Ken Norton, when in the throes of inexplicable defeat and humiliation and pain, his only words to me were a final attempt at humor. To the end, he played a part.

CHAPTER 7

THE LIMBO

The summer of 1966 marked the beginning of what, in retrospect, would be the last sweet days of Muhammad Ali as a fighter. He would soon enter a three-and-a-half year limbo in which Uncle Sam would be his only opponent. It was a battle that would cost him dearly and erode his great skills, which now, I felt, had only begun to mature.

I am of the opinion that the finest fighter of my lifetime was Muhammad Ali—until, to all intents and purposes, his career was terminated by 42 months of enforced idleness. He was a picture

fighter. Watching him in action I got a sense of watching an artist work with oils, hearing Beverly Sills sing an aria, listening to Rubinstein at the piano. First of all, Ali had that superb size, that marvelous body. Second, while not a one-punch knockout fighter, he had the blow that could slit open a man's face. Third, few could touch him—not even with his hands held mockingly at his sides. His speed, for a heavyweight, was not approached by any fighter who has yet lived. And he had that same speed with his fists. He could land combinations with such swiftness that an adversary—any adversary—could only wonder where the punches were coming from. He was an extraordinary athlete. But the skills vanished—as they had to—at the very peak of his boxing life. In so sedentary a sport as baseball, Curt Flood could not make it back after being away for one year. How then, in the most demanding sport of all, could Ali recapture the old skills after three and a half years?

In August 1966 he was still, in effect, in exile, driven abroad to earn the living. that was denied him in America. He had to keep fighting; the legal bills were beginning to look like the budget for the Pentagon. So it was back to England for a quick joust with Brian London, at an historic London arena called Earl Lord's Court.

The fight itself was noteworthy largely for what happened in the ring afterward. Ali had knocked London unconscious in the third round, and he began our interview once again by spouting his gratitude-to-the-Muslims speech. I cut him off: "Awright, Muhammad, I think we've been through that enough, once and for all, do you understand? Now back to the fight."

I flew back to New York the next morning with Ali and Herbert Muhammad. Ali started right in. "Do you know what you said to me in the ring last night? When I was talking about Elijah and Herbert?"

"Yeah, I know what I said."

Herbert broke in: "Howard was exactly right. He had to say that. You've just got to stop doing that."

Photographers and reporters were waiting when the plane landed at Kennedy Airport. And that was when Roger Sharp, the ABC correspondent, asked him: "After what he said to you in the ring last night, when are you going to fight Howard Cosell?"

Ali answered, "Why, Howard Cosell is my man. We ain't never gonna fight." Pause. "No, on second thought, I'm gonna whup him."

Ali was now taking on every match he could get. He was a man

running out of time, trying to squirrel away a few nuts for what would be a long winter. His third opponent in four months would be the German southpaw Karl Mildenberger, at Frankfurt. It was to be a fight of many diverse and intriguing elements. It would be the first color telecast of a sports event to be transmitted by satellite, and the first fight I had ever done alone. We filmed a dramatic interview with Ali on the banks of the Frankfurt am Main River, with boats and whistles as the backdrop and German urchins waiting around to get Ali's autograph. The night of the fight would witness the reunion of Max Schmeling and Joe Louis at ringside.

Ali needed 12 rounds to knock out Karl Mildenberger, who was tough and game and put up the fight of his career. Ali fought badly. He completely ignored the instructions Angelo Dundee had given him. Instead of fighting his normal fight and circling steadily to his left, he worked it out in his mind that because Mildenberger was a southpaw he should circle the other way. He just got himself totally fouled up.

In Chet Forte's room after the fight, Dundee joined us for a card game. He was so disgusted with Ali's performance he refused to discuss it. The famous cardplayer's lament, "Shut up and deal," could be heard until four in the morning.

Ali had now effectively cleaned out the European heavyweight division. As his date with the Army—or the federal attorney—drew closer, a few promoters emerged who were willing to risk the wrath of the superpatriots in return for the fat box office that Ali's presence assured. The likeliest shelter was the Astrodome, in Houston, where ironically his draft case would be decided. Ali wasn't exactly playing with a cold deck. Bob Arum, one of his attorneys, and Fred Hofheinz, whose father operates the Astrodome, were partners in Top Rank, a closed-circuit-television company.

So Ali signed to fight Cleveland "Big Cat" Williams under the vast acrylic bubble on the night of November 16, 1966. Williams is a story in his own right, a once powerful puncher of the kind the contenders always avoided, gunned down by a Texas deputy and apparently finished, then managed by a man named Hugh Benbow, the Elmer Gantry of boxing. Benbow owned a farm at a town called—so help me—Yoakum, Texas, a half hour from Houston, and Williams trained there for his comeback against Ali. In those years we always filmed a fight preview for *Wide World of Sports*, and so we—myself and Chet Forte—chartered a small plane to fly us there.

We got there and couldn't find the damned airstrip. Finally, the pilot spotted it and we landed. It was about 100 yards long, in the most isolated place this side of the Amazon River. A car was supposed to meet us but there was absolutely nothing in sight, except one pole with a pay telephone on it. Forte walked over and called New York to get the point spread on the pro football games.

There we were on a Sunday morning in Yoakum, Texas, getting the line on the pro games at this remote airstrip in the heart of nowhere, when at last a car appeared, and we drove to Benbow's farmhouse to meet the great evangelist. Incredibly he had people pouring in from the wide-open spaces to actually watch Williams train. And the only interesting thing about the Big Cat was the gunshot wound in his belly.

We came out of it with a remarkable film piece. We moved in close on the scar and had Williams tell his story: how he was stopped on a dark country road, ticketed for speeding, shot, and nearly killed when, in a panic, he tried to get away. We used Benbow's speech to the crowd, how Williams was going to upset Ali.

Of course, the fight lasted only three rounds and Ali destroyed him. Williams was no real opponent, but it was vintage Ali, probably the best anyone will ever see him. He chose this night to introduce a move he called the "Ali Shuffle," a kind of dance step that was right out of vaudeville. It was almost a quick fox-trot, a sleight-of-foot movement that, against the helpless Williams, worked. Later, on *Wide World*, he demonstrated it on me. I found it as bewildering as had Williams.

Three months later he returned to the Astrodome—on February 6, 1967—to meet tall Ernie Terrell, who had won the World Boxing Association title in a process that can best be compared to a secret ballot. Ali couldn't wait to reunite the two halves of the heavyweight title.

The Terrell fight was Ali at his ugliest, a throwback—and more—to his performance against Floyd Patterson. He despised Terrell, thought him a whiner and complainer. Ernie had been critical of Ali's stand on the draft and persisted in calling him Cassius Clay. Ali taunted Terrell all through the fight. With each shattering blow he challenged him with "What's my name? . . . What's my name?" The question was clearly audible at ringside. It was a mean game that Ali played that night. I felt there was lust in the way he tortured and humiliated Terrell for 15 rounds. At times he laughed out loud.

The moment the fight ended I was in the ring to interview him. He turned on me with a meanness I hadn't seen before. "I'm sick and tired," he bellowed, "of talking to you and taking your stuff. . . ." He kept up the tirade until we went off the air. I walked away without comment.

The next morning I again saw the contradictory nature of Muhammad Ali. I was with him at the Hotel America in Houston, and he said, almost sheepishly, "I was really bad last night, wasn't I? With you—with everything."

I said, "You sure as hell were. You made an ass out of yourself."

He said, "Well, when I go into the press conference I'll make up for it."

A few minutes later he faced a roomful of reporters and could not have been more charming. This is the most vacillating man, in terms of mood, I've ever known. He complimented Terrell and appeared rather contrite.

Around the country, speculation was now building over what Ali's response would be to his draft call. One by one his attorneys had lost their appeals to have his status reclassified. Would he accept induction and serve his time in the kind of soft, cushiony, showcase job the military had found for Joe Louis and others in the last war? Or would he refuse to serve, risking the contempt and abuse of his countrymen and even jail?

Ali's last fight before his moment of public decision was set for March 22, a month after his baiting of Terrell. He would meet Zora Folley in Madison Square Garden in an odd fight in which he would have little interest and little spirit. He knew he could beat Zora, a man he liked and for whom he could work up no anger. So the scene was set for a routine, dull exercise that saw Ali knock him out with regret. It was quite a contrast from the Terrell fight.

Now the odyssey of Muhammad Ali drew Ali back to Houston, to 4800 San Jacinto Street, the Federal Customs Building—and a confrontation with the United States Army. The date was April 28, 1967. I took a camera crew to the Federal Building to shoot whatever footage we could get. Ali arrived, climbed out of his car, and started moving quickly up the steps. I was right behind him, a microphone in my upraised hand and the camera crew at my heels.

"Are you," I yelled after him, "going to take the step, Muhammad? Are you going—to take—the step?"

Just as we were about to enter the building, he flashed me a quick grin and said, "Howard Cosell—why don't *you* take the step?"

"I did," I snapped back. "In Nineteen forty-two."

So now we moved through the crowd and proceeded to an assembly room upstairs, there to wait for that symbolic moment when the recruiting officer asks the inductees to take one step forward. The moment came. Ali stood fast. Within seconds he had been whisked into a private office, where a federal marshal read his rights to him. He reappeared, passed out a statement prepared by the Muslims, and would not say one word to the press.

Within a matter of minutes after Ali chose not to step forward, Edwin Dooley, the politically appointed boxing commissioner of New York State, stripped him of his championship and of his license to fight—in short, of his right to earn a living.

Mr. Dooley, a former congressman, was doing the popular thing. But there had been no arraignment, no grand-jury hearing, no indictment, no trial, no conviction, no appeal to a higher court. And, in a matter such as this, with the Supreme Court likely to hear the case, there had been no appeal to the court of last resort. In other words, due process of law had not even been initiated, let alone exhausted. Under the Fifth Amendment, no person may be deprived of life, liberty, or property without due process of law. Yet every state in the Union adopted the action of the New York Commission. Now here was Ali: unable to fight anywhere in America; stripped of his right to leave the country, hence unable to fight overseas either.

Yet during the years of his idleness, New York and other states were licensing men who had been deserters from the Army. Ironically two of the major stories of 1972 would involve the boxing careers of convicted murderers: Ron Lyle was pardoned to become a professional fighter; Bobby Lee Hunter, through special arrangement with his warden, emerged as a sentimental favorite while fighting.

But this unsettling, confusing, sometimes arrogant young man was dealt with, punished, locked out, while an overwhelming majority of the press and public gloated.

We were still in contact during the troubled months and years ahead, and still I found him utterly unperturbed. I saw him on the campuses and in New York and during his rehearsals for an Off-Broadway play called *Buck White*, part of a wave of black-relevant productions then developing in stage and film.

I attended his opening night. Who should be sitting next to me but

Floyd Patterson, exercising again his habit of appearing unannounced at the unlikeliest of times. For reasons of his own
—curiosity, perhaps—there he was at Ali's opening night. At the end
of the show, as Muhammad was on the stage taking bows, he looked
down and included in his final lines a welcoming quip to me. I
pointed to Patterson, and a flicker of surprise registered in Ali's eyes.
"My friend, Floyd Patterson," he said gently, "has come to see me."

And suddenly they were enemies no longer. At least for a time.

It was during this period that James Earl Jones had revived the
legend of Jack Johnson in a Broadway hit called, aptly, *The Great
White Hope*. Ali identified with Johnson, who in an earlier time had
been persecuted and hounded for a life-style white America could
not accept. He saw the play and, emotionally, went backstage to visit
Jones, who had portrayed Johnson. "That's me," Ali told him.
"That's about me."

He also recounted an anecdote that had been passed down to him
by his grandfather, who had seen the old champion in his heyday.
Johnson, driving one of the long, sleek fast cars he favored, was
flagged down by a country sheriff as he roared through Kentucky. He
asked how much the fine was. "Fifty dollars," he was told.

Easily, he peeled off two fifties and handed them to the surprised
lawman. "I'm coming back," he explained.

It was all symbolic to Ali. He almost reveled in it. To many it now
seemed certain that he faced imprisonment. I never thought so; I
contended from the first that the courts would uphold him. But I
often wondered how people could ask me, during these years, if he
was really sincere. My God, the man gave up three or four million
dollars. He was pilloried by ignorant fans and sportswriters and
politicians. He gave up a deal offered by the federal government that
would have made him a hero, a deal even cozier than Joe Louis had
had. I was advised by Army sources that if he would agree to be
drafted, Ali would spend 30 days overseas entertaining the troops,
and then return to the States and a rematch against Patterson, with a
fortune in money for him and a chunk of the receipts to charity.

Every few months during this period a rumor would surface that a
boxing commissioner somewhere had sucked up his nerve and was
about to license Ali to fight again. But time after time, pressure from
the American Legion or the Boy Scouts or local politicians would
send everyone scurrying under their rocks.

It was during this period of inactivity that a subtle change in na-

tional sentiment toward Ali began to occur, tied to the growing frustration over American policies in Indochina. Ali had become the continuing story of a man adrift; a latter-day Philip Nolan; a man who could not find a friendly port. He was, in a way, tormented by hope and anticipation and promises. Austin. Detroit. Seattle. Las Vegas. Pittsburgh. Tampa. Hot Springs. In town after town promoters hustled to make him offers that could not be fulfilled.

His draft-induction case was moving laboriously through the corridors of justice. Would he go to prison? Would he ever fight again? Would he have any skills left if he did?

Meanwhile, Ali's attorneys had initiated their own action to have his boxing license restored in the state of New York—a case totally unrelated to the federal government's pursuit of him. This separate action by Ali came before the Southern District Federal Court, in October 1970, in the very state where his persecution had begun.

Judge Walter Mansfield determined that Ali had been denied his rights under the Fourteenth Amendment of the Constitution, which provides equal protection under the law. The judge explained in his decision that the New York State Athletic Commission had been granting boxing licenses to deserters from the military. How, then, could Ali's license be denied constitutionally?

So Ali now had his license back. But he had lost a commodity no one could restore. He had lost time. Now, three and one-half years later, he began a frantic comeback that would lead him ultimately into the ring against Joe Frazier, the inheritor of his title. His first tune-up would be with Jerry Quarry, in Atlanta. These negotiations had been in progress and the promoters insisted it would be held. Now the federal-court ruling by Judge Mansfield gave the fight new momentum.

Yet still unanswered was the most vexing question of all: Would he go to prison?

CHAPTER 8

THE FALL

Judge Walter Mansfield's decision, which in effect restored Ali's license to fight in the state of New York, was warmly greeted by that astute protector of civil rights, Edwin B. Dooley, the

chairman of the New York State Athletic Commission. With a magnificent gesture of hypocritical largesse, Dooley piously intoned that Muhammad would be welcomed back into the ring in New York. Dooley's cycle of cheap expediency had run full. If this doesn't teach you something about boxing, nothing will—and about politics in sports.

But Ali's mind was now on Jerry Quarry. One had to wonder how wise it was to have selected Quarry as the first man to go against after the long layoff. As a fighter Quarry is many things, mostly bad. But he can punch, he can take a punch, and he is always unafraid.

Quarry has a number of other things going for him. He is white. He has an effective way of alibiing his defeats. He occasionally looks impressive. And always, there is the Madison Square Garden Boxing Department. They will keep Jerry alive. This, then, was the man Ali was to meet, fighting for the first time in three and a half years. What a marvelous situation for Quarry, if he could pull it off.

Atlanta, Georgia, was a happening the night they fought. The soul people came in from everywhere. Their clothes were a knockout, the costumes so garish, so colorful, that the artist LeRoy Neiman had a field day. It was like Van Gogh discovering the vineyards. They came to rejoice. The king was back. Long live the king.

The king looked like his old self in the very first round. He did not look so good in the second round. But Ali did open a severe cut over Quarry's eye, and they stopped the fight after the third round. Few noticed that Ali, after the first round, did not do much; that the old hand and foot speed seemed diminished. Few conjectured about what might have happened had Quarry not been cut.

But Ali did. Whatever he lost in boxing skills during the long layoff, he lost nothing in the way of promotional ability. Cunningly he told me after the fight that Quarry was entitled to another chance, that the cut eye was just a stroke of bad luck for Jerry. In fact, on *Wide World* that week we set up a split-screen phone conversation during which Ali promised Quarry another chance. This was October 1970. Quarry would get his other chance in June 1972.

But now step number one on the road to Joe Frazier was out of the way. Step number two would be the clumsy Argentine heavyweight, Oscar Bonavena. It was while Muhammad was preparing for the Bonavena fight that the changes within him became visible. They were mental as well as physical. He no longer had a taste, even an urge, for training, the way he once did. His preparation was slovenly.

His body seemed flaccid. And it showed in the fight itself; he was sluggish throughout. Often Bonavena would bull him about the ring. But clearly Ali was on his way to a decision, when suddenly, in the last round, he connected with a left that finished Bonavena. Ali, ever the instant promoter, grabbed the microphone from me in the ring and pronounced, "I have done what Joe Frazier couldn't do. I have knocked out Oscar Bonavena. Now where is he? I want Frazier."

And so the scene was set for what would be the biggest money bout in history. Joe Frazier had come into his own. During Ali's long absence Joe had become the recognized heavyweight champion of the world. He had beaten everyone, and he got championship recognition when he literally pulverized Jimmy Ellis, the WBA champion, with a series of devastating left hooks.

The Ali-Frazier fight was set for March 1971 at the Garden. The fighters were to share an incredible five-million-dollar guarantee. There were multimillions potentially to be made from theater, television and the public—the general public, which had waited so long for this fight—would be virtually shut out from viewing it. In the name of free enterprise.

This was a fight that needed no promotion. But it got it. Every day, or so it seemed, Ali would spout off. He was going to do this to Frazier, he was going to do that to Frazier. Frazier said little. He was training as he had never trained before. Ali was not. Angelo Dundee was working as hard with Ali as he could, but Ali was not running in the mornings, the way he should have been; he was not conditioning his body for 15 rounds, the way he should have been; and there was telltale flab about his midriff. I asked his doctor, Ferdie Pacheco, about this and he shrugged and said, "He'll be in the best shape possible for a man his age who lost three and a half years of fighting."

I watched Ali closely during this time, and I became more convinced than ever of two things: first, that he could not recapture the old speed; second, that he took Frazier too lightly, that he thought he had more than enough left to beat Joe.

After an incident at Miami Beach in January 1971, I became absolutely convinced of the latter point. I was down there for the Baltimore-Dallas Super Bowl game. Ali, of course, was training at the Fifth Street Gym. There came a day at the Americana Hotel, where Emmy and I were staying, when, lying at poolside, we suddenly heard Ali approaching. He was screaming, attracting everyone's attention. "Where is he? Where is he? Where's that white fella who

gives me so much trouble? Where's Cosell?" And then, his new jingle: "When I'm finished with Frazier, at the sound of the bell, I'll jump through the ropes and take care of Cosell."

Then Ali turned to Emmy and said, "I want your husband. I want to take him with me. I want to show him it's only fifteen minutes from heaven to hell." To my sore chagrin, Emmy said, "Take him. He's yours."

I protested. Ali insisted. "I know what you've been saying about me. I'm not in shape, my speed is gone. Well, I'm gonna take care of you." And off we went to his car.

Driving across the Seventy-ninth Street Causeway to Miami, Ali said, "I'm going to take you to the ghetto, to meet my people. You'll see what life is really like."

"I've seen Harlem and I've seen Watts," I told him. "It won't be news to me." And then with a quick grin I added, "After all, remember what the vice-president said: 'If you've seen one you've seen them all.' "

Then Ali grew serious. First he talked about the fight, explained why Frazier was no match for him, how he would box his ears off. After all the years I had spent with Ali I knew when he was talking honestly about a fight. There was no question of his confidence. I cautioned him about taking Frazier too lightly. He laughed it off. I cautioned him about his physical condition and his training. He laughed it off.

By now we had gotten to the Miami ghetto. His first stop was at a pool parlor. We jumped out of the car and went in, with Ali yelling, "Here he is, here's the white guy who gives me all that trouble on television."

It was a dingy, smelly place filled with what were doubtless habitués. The shades were drawn, the only lights those above the tables. The scene looked like one of those dust jackets on books about junkies.

"Knock it off," I whispered. "These guys might take you seriously." But nothing would contain him. He kept egging them on as they gathered around him and me, and I began to get more and more nervous. Then, abruptly, in that manner so characteristic of him, he threw an arm around my shoulder and said, "I'm only kidding. He's my friend." And then he leaned into my ear and said, "Call me nigger." No way. I may have a few years left.

From the pool parlor, we went to a barbershop which he had fre-

quented years earlier, in his early professional boxing days when he lived in Miami. Unlike the pool parlor it was clean and cheerful, a place to go and shoot the breeze. A very big guy—he looked like a fighter himself—started throwing not-so-soft punches at Ali. Muhammad blocked and slipped the punches, dancing about, laughing, never hitting the other man. He handled what might have become an ugly situation with his usual extraordinary grace.

But then he turned and grabbed me, forcing me down in a barber chair. "Let's give Howard a haircut," he laughed. "Howard needs a haircut bad, don't he?"

"Lay off me, Muhammad!" I was squirming to get out of the chair. "I have little enough hair as it is." I wasn't wearing my toupee.

The next stop was out of the ghetto—the house he had lived in those many years before. He introduced me to the people with whom he had lived, and once again performed his act. Finally we were on the way back to the Americana. His last words to me were: "It's no contest. No contest." Then he added, "I'm glad you met my people."

Emmy was waiting for me in the hotel room. "What did he want?" she asked me.

"It was strange," I answered. "Somehow he felt he wanted to be with me. Maybe because he's coming up to the fight of his life, and because we've been together so long. Maybe because he feels kind of lonely, with so many writers picking Frazier. And he did want me to see the ghetto, where he had hung out when he first came under Angie's wing."

"As long as you know him, you'll never really know him," she said. As usual, she was right.

The days moved swiftly leading up to the fight. I was with Ali in the Fifth Street Gym for his last training session. It was a Saturday. The fight would be on Monday. I was doing a last-minute preview of the fight for exhibition that very afternoon. I had already videotaped Frazier, who was as tight-lipped and determined and physically ready as any fighter I have ever seen. I watched Ali intently in this last workout. I didn't like what I saw. He didn't seem in any sense to be the old Ali. He seemed tired. In one respect he was unchanged: his self-assurance looked to be as high as ever.

We did the show after he finished the workout. I picked Joe Frazier to knock out Muhammad Ali somewhere between the tenth and twelfth rounds. I had been saying this on the air continually

from a month before the fight until the day of the fight. Ali knew it. All he said was, "Cosell, you're wrong. You're always wrong."

The rest is ring history. It was a great fight, a truly great fight. As always in Ali fights there were curiosities: the way Ali would rest against the ropes, gloves together in front of his face, expecting Frazier to punch himself out; the way Frazier came ceaselessly at him; the way Ali would show flashes of what he once was—an utterly superb machine; the way Frazier seemed, with that nonprotecting style of his, a human punching bag. For ten rounds Ali amazed me. I had him ahead at that point. In the eleventh Frazier got him with a left hook, and Ali wandered aimlessly about the ring. Some still think he was playacting. I don't. I think that blow in the eleventh turned the fight for Frazier. I believe Joe won the twelfth, thirteenth, and fifteenth, when he floored Ali. I scored the fight 8-6-1 for Frazier.

But the punishment Joe took was unbelievable. His manager, Yancy Durham, and his handlers virtually carried Frazier to his dressing room. His face was a hideous pulpy mess. And then Emmy and I waited in the aisle as Muhammad walked out. *Walked out.* His right jaw was swollen, as if he had an apple in it, but he had all his senses. As he went past he spotted me—and he winked! He actually winked. He would never change.

They talked about that fight for weeks. The following Saturday Frazier and Ali were to be on *Wide World* with me. Only Ali came. Frazier was in the hospital. He didn't get out for three weeks. Ali had taken the defeat the night of the fight with good grace. He had told the press, as he held his jaw, "I guess I'm not pretty any more."

I look back on that fight often. I have studied the films. Under the circumstances it may have been the greatest fight Ali ever fought. Why? Because he was going against a very good, very tough fighter. He had lost three and one-half years at the peak of his skills. Those skills were no longer supreme. His physical condition was not what it had been in those earlier years. Only on rare occasions in the fight could he move with the speed of yore. He had to rest against the ropes, to conserve himself, in order to go the distance. Yet he did go the distance, and in the process he inflicted untold physical damage upon Frazier, who ever since that day has shown no sign of being the very good fighter that he had been. In my view the Frazier fight was an authentication of Ali's greatness as a fighter.

Now all the talk would be of a rematch. But, in the first place,

there could only be a rematch if Ali were available. The government's action against him was before the Supreme Court. He had been convicted in the federal district court, and the circuit court of appeals had upheld the conviction. If the Supreme Court of the United States upheld the conviction, then jail beckoned. Ali remained uperturbed. Whenever I was with him he would talk only of fighting again, and of fighting Joe Frazier again. His battle with the government hardly seemed to be on his mind.

The Supreme Court ruled on his case in May 1971. It was now as much a conservative court—based upon Nixon appointments—as a liberal court. But it didn't matter. They all voted alike. By a count of eight to nothing the conviction was reversed. The court simply decided that Muhammad was sincere in his religious convictions. And so Ali was a free man.

Ali had won the biggest fight he would ever fight. This is why he is a figure for the history books, not just the sports-history books. His case proved again the truth of the old adage: What is popular is not always right; what is right is not always popular. But nobody could give him back the three and a half years that had been taken from him. Nobody.

Later Ali would confide to me that the decision was a load off his mind. It had to be. Despite all the cover, all the bluster, he is human, and the specter of incarceration had to have taken its toll on him.

And so it was back to fighting, to stay in shape for the return match with Frazier. Ali's next bout would be against Jimmy Ellis, his former sparring partner. Ali put him away in laconic fashion.

Next was the fiasco in the Houston Astrodome in November 1971—Ali against Buster Mathis. Mathis went down from sheer fatigue, the fatigue of trying to move his huge body around the ring for 12 rounds. So Ali won by a knockout.

In June 1972 it was Jerry Quarry's turn again at Las Vegas, Nevada. Ali's body looked better conditioned than it had for a long time. He really gave it to Quarry this time. Mercifully they stopped that fight in the seventh. After Emmy and I had left the arena I was accosted by a woman who screamed at me, "Why did they stop it? Jerry was still on his feet. He could have beaten that bum."

We looked at her as if she were crazy. "Who are you?" I asked.

"I'm Jerry's aunt," she replied.

"Do you want him to get killed?" I asked her. And we walked away, disgusted.

In August 1972 I was doing the finals of the Olympic Boxing Trials at West Point. Arledge hired Ali to do the color with me. That was the day he saw our Olympic heavyweight, Duane Bobick, for the first time. Never one to miss a trick, Ali started to promote him at once. A new "White Hope." Ali was counting the potential gate two years hence. He was too optimistic, in light of what happened to Duane at the Olympics.

Another interesting sidelight occurred that day. Muhammad had signed to fight Floyd Patterson again at the Garden in September. "You're saying that this fight shouldn't be licensed, aren't you?" he asked me.

"Yes," I answered, "I don't want you to hurt him."

"I won't hurt him," he promised. "But Patterson's broke, he needs money."

"What? I thought Floyd, of all fighters, had kept his money. I thought he was in good shape for the rest of his life."

"No," Ali told me. "His taxes were all mixed up and the Internal Revenue has got all of it." I was astonished, and later called Bob Arum, Ali's attorney and, incidentally, a good tax man. He confirmed what Ali had told me. So there may be another factor in why Floyd keeps fighting.

After Patterson came Bob Foster and Joe Bugner. Foster cut Ali over the eye, and Bugner survived 12 rounds—both facts not very subtle indexes to Ali's decline as a fighter. Still, at the time when Ali fought Bugner, many believed that Ali could defeat the new heavyweight champion, George Foreman, who had destroyed Frazier at Kingston, Jamaica, in January 1973. One of those who thought so was the famous oddsmaker, Jimmy "the Greek" Snyder. I did a show with Jimmy in March wherein he said he would make Ali a six-to-five favorite over Foreman if the two fought within the next year. This was just a couple of weeks before Ali fought a man named Ken Norton in San Diego, California.

When Emmy and I landed in San Diego on the afternoon of March 30, Jerry Gross, a San Diego sports announcer, was waiting at the airport to do a news spot with me. "What do you think of the fight, Howard?" Jerry asked me.

"What fight?" I answered.

He laughed. "Ali-Norton," he said.

"It's a farce," I said. (I never go out on a limb.)

I got my first shock that evening. We went over to the hotel where

Ali was staying. I looked at him. In the six weeks since the Bugner fight he had ballooned terribly. He looked flabby. But I never gave it a second thought; there seemed no way he could lose to Ken Norton. Angie Dundee had told me all about Norton. "He's tailor-made for Ali," Angie had said. "He's wide open for a left, he has no right, kind of chops with it, his only good punch is a left hook to the belly, and he has an open stance and drags one leg." With that assessment from Angie one couldn't expect any kind of fight at all. And obviously Ali didn't. It was the night before the fight and he was all over that coffee shop, laughing and talking, here and there, swarmed over by people. Not a moment's rest.

I had to go back to the hotel the next morning to get the tickets. It was about 9:45. The scene hadn't changed. Ali was on center stage, regaling 15 or 20 people around him with story after story. He saw me and came over. "Look," he said, "I want you to know this for the telecast. When we're both in the ring, being introduced, I'm going to start waving my hands in front of him, slowly, like this, as if I'm hypnotizing him. You'll be able to explain what I'm doing for the people at home."

The fight was to begin at 2:30 in the afternoon. I was to tape an interview with Ali in his dressing room at 2:15. This was not uncommon; we had done this on many past occasions. But this time an odd situation developed. The lights were out in Ali's dressing room, and the guard told us he was sleeping and could not be disturbed. This was just 20 minutes before the fight. Three minutes later I got the guard to let me in. We were fighting a desperate time problem. The room was pitch-dark, and I called to Muhammad.

"I'm not ready yet, Howard," came the voice. "I'm having an important conversation with Herbert."

All that time Ali had not been sleeping! He had been talking with Herbert Muhammad about heaven knows what. What a time for a conference. Suddenly the whole situation seemed eerie. Outside of Ali's dressing room I found Dundee. "Do you think Muhammad and you are taking Norton too lightly?" I asked him.

"Not at all," said Angie. "He's tailor-made."

Two minutes later we were all allowed in. Quickly I did the interview. Ali no longer seemed at ease, no longer was he so casual. He seemed strangely tense. Yet Dundee showed me the inside of Ali's glove, where Ali had written, "KO 3." He would knock Norton out in the third round.

480

The interview done, I scrambled back to ringside to open the telecast. Ali came into the ring late. He never did do the hypnosis thing he had spoken to me about that morning.

The fight began. I had Yancey Durham sitting to my left, Joe Frazier to my right. In the first round Ali seemed transfixed. Virtually no blows were struck by either fighter, but of the minimal scoring there was, Ali had the better of it.

In the second round Ali did absolutely nothing. Norton began to land some blows. None seemed in any sense damaging, but clearly Norton had won the round.

In the third round—the round marked down in Ali's glove for the knockout—Ali came out dancing. He was all over the ring, Norton couldn't even find him, and this was the first sign of the Ali that everyone expected. He didn't come close to knocking Norton out but he won the round easily.

At the end of the round Durham said, "He'll put him away in the next round."

Ali did nothing the next round. All movement stopped. Norton won the round, again with blows that seemed to do no damage. During that round, on microphone, I asked Dundee what was wrong with his fighter. "Nothing," Angie assured me. "It's going according to plan. He's just letting Norton punch himself out."

The fifth came and went, and so did the sixth. Nobody was doing much of anything, though in the sixth I felt that a Norton right had hurt Ali. It landed on Ali's left jaw. I asked Dundee again what was wrong with Muhammad. "Nothing at all," Angie said again. "Look at the way he's fighting now."

That's exactly what I was looking at. It was inexplicable.

"What round is coming up?" Durham asked me.

"The seventh," I said.

"He'll put Ken away in this round," Durham predicted.

Nothing happened. But Frazier was openly rooting for his old sparring partner, saying on the air to me that Norton was a good fighter, very much underrated.

As Ali sloughed around the ring, Joe leaned over and said to me, "Maybe they'll talk now about how much I took out of him, instead of what he took out of me." Make no mistake about it. Frazier despises Ali.

The eighth round came. This was when I detected that Ali's mouth looked curious, twisted. And I spotted just a little bit of blood at the

left corner of his mouth. I conjectured in my commentary that he might have a loose tooth.

The fight droned on. Suddenly, in the eleventh, Ali showed the movement he had shown in the third. He won the round easily.

Going into the twelfth I asked Durham and Frazier how they scored the fight. Each had it even.

Norton beat Ali all over the ring in the twelfth. In this round he hit him on the left jaw, hard and clean, at least twice and maybe three times. Ali was clearly hurt. Norton had won the fight.

The whole thing seemed like a fantasy. Frazier was exultant. Durham was anything but. I jumped into the ring.

The decision took an interminable length of time. While I was waiting, Dundee ran over to me and said that Ali's jaw had been broken in the first round. I was thunderstruck. I couldn't remember a single right that had landed on Ali's left jaw in the first round.

We left San Diego for the National Football League annual spring meeting at Phoenix. It was good to get away. Remembering Ali as he had been, at the beginning, in his prime, remembering the way he had held together during the three and a half years of inactivity, remembering the classic bout against Frazier, remembering him for the artist he had been, it seemed such a shabby way to go out. I recalled one day when he looked at me and laughed, "When I'm done, you won't even remember who I was. I'll be just another ex-champ." Not in my book. Never. He was special.

No one will ever really understand that fight, or when Ali's jaw was broken. Ali, Dundee, and Ferdie Pacheco were supposed to appear on television with me the following Saturday. Ali's jaw was wired, and so they canceled out. Instead we brought in Dr. William Lundeen, the chief attending physician at ringside. We played the key rounds of the fight, at regular speed, and some in slow motion. Dr. Lundeen drew the conclusion that Ali's jaw was definitely not broken in the first round. It could have been, he deduced, in the second, fourth, or sixth. Finally we agreed that it had probably been the sixth, and that certainly the break had been intensified in the twelfth.

There was also a story after the fight about Ali's ankle. Apparently he had visited the trainer of the San Diego Chargers football team for treatment of a sprained ankle about a week before the fight. The films showed no evidence of Ali being hampered by such a sprain. As Dr. Lundeen noted, Ali showed real foot movement as late as the eleventh round.

Muhammad Ali is already fighting again. He and his people are busy propagating the notion that the first Norton fight was a "warning to him from God"; that he now stays in hard training; that he will again become the old Ali. People will pay to see him. He is box-office magic. I think it is unfortunate, even sad. Watching him now will be like listening to Sinatra when Frank can only croak.

I don't know how much money Ali has. As I've said, he is a terrific spender. He owns a home in Cherry Hill, New Jersey, and property near Reading, Pennsylvania, where he has built a training camp. He recently sold a second home in Philadelphia, the proceeds of which he applied toward the purchase of a new home for his mother in Louisville. He also owns automobiles, sometimes more than you can count, and has owned two Rolls-Royces at one time, plus a 1901 Oldsmobile, a colorful antique that Ali loves to drive around the neighborhood. Bob Arum tells me that Ali has no tax problems, that they have managed to save about $300,000 for him. Bob also says that, contrary to popular opinion, the Muslims have not taken his money. "He just spends it," says Bob. "It was all we could do to put aside the three hundred thousand."

Muhammad may need it.

But he will never look for help, not this descendant of slaves who stood tall and proud, even against the government and against most of the people. He will look at those around him, long in the future, and he will say, "I was right, and I won. Ask your grandchildren. They read about me in American history. My name is Muhammad Ali."

CHAPTER 9

MONDAY NIGHT FOOTBALL

With a voice that had all the resonance of a clogged Dristan bottle, sportscaster Howard Cosell made pro football addicts of more than 25 million viewers on Monday nights. . . ."

The above quote could conceivably have originated with a television critic or a sportswriter. But it did not. It might have been the brainchild of the ABC Publicity Department. But it was not. Believe it or not, the above quote appears in the Encyclopedia Britannica Year Book—1973. In what I can only view as the ultimate in mis-

placed emphasis, I have been biographied in the most distinguished of all world books. *Monday Night Football* is the reason.

We are now in our fourth year of *Monday Night Football*. It continues to be a television phenomenon, a sensation in the television ratings, and, in financial terms, the most successful sports package in history. It is a phenomenon because it has changed the social habits of America on Monday nights in the autumn. The movie business has gone to hell on those nights. The bars aren't doing business, either.

Many restaurants shut down on Monday nights. And the department stores complain about a sharp drop in sales. ABC does not share that complaint. In its first year, *Monday Night Football* was sold out at $65,000 per minute of commercial time. Now it is sold out at $80,000 per minute. And there are sponsors waiting on line.

This is how it all began.

In the spring of 1970, at a time when I was doing a nightly local television show, I got an urgent phone call. It was from Chuck Howard. Could I get right over to the National Football League office with a film crew? I knew at once that the negotiations had been completed, that ABC had purchased the right to telecast professional football in prime entertainment time on Monday nights. I picked up my crew and shot over to interview Pete Rozelle and Roone Arledge.

How different the reaction was then. CBS and NBC quietly—no, not so quietly—snickered. CBS had twice tried pro football in prime time. It hadn't worked, not even with the Green Bay Packers of Vince Lombardi as the attraction. The problem, according to most industry thinking, was women. Women watched television at night. They dominated the sets in use. They would not watch football. Privately, some at ABC agreed. But ABC had to do something. Its ratings on Monday nights languished terribly. They were not remotely competitive to the other two networks.

Thus, when Pete Rozelle came up with the idea of *Monday Night Football*—and it was *his* idea—he found a willing listener in Arledge.

Weeks passed after it was announced that there would be *Monday Night Football* at ABC. I personally gave little thought to the idea that I would be part of the package. Then one night I did my local television show with Pete Rozelle. Subsequently, we went over to the Tavern on the Green in Central Park for a cocktail. This was when Pete said that he hoped I would do the color commentary on the games. I was frankly surprised, because while I had always liked

and respected Rozelle, I did not fit his mold, nor the traditional NFL mold. That mold had been carefully stamped out through all the years of NFL telecasts: You get a play-by-play announcer, add one former NFL player for "expertise and analysis," and you've got the telecast. In my own opinion, every telecast sounded like every other.

But Rozelle understood this. He felt that a new approach was needed in prime time to capture a new type of audience. However, he could only think about it. He had nothing to do with selection of announcers. So it would be up to Arledge.

The way Roone works, events take on an erratic flow. You may not see him or hear from him for many days. Then suddenly he is all over you, and you begin to hope that he will vanish again. Thus, out of nowhere, on a hot June day, I was lunching with friends at Jimmy Weston's, when I was paged. Roone wanted to see me immediately. I went directly to his office and, in that carefully mild, understated way of his, he said, "Hey, we've got to talk about the pro football package."

"What about it?" I asked.

"How would you feel about working with Don Meredith?" Roone asked me. "We'd use him on replays."

I said fine. I had known Don for a lot of years, only superficially, but had always enjoyed his company.

"Well," said Arledge, "Frank Gifford recommended him. And I think it's a hell of a thing because Frank wanted this job himself." The Giff was then under contract to CBS. Meredith got the job.

Then, in the days that followed, Arledge developed his approach to the telecasts. A different approach. One that would excite all kinds of press. One that would draw enormous attention to the package. He wanted three men in the broadcast booth. It was his conviction that the play-by-play announcer should serve really as a public address announcer, that he should be on quickly with the basic information, and then quickly off, as Dandy and I were to pick up with color and analysis, and hopefully some candor, some humor, and some human insights into the athletes so that they would become more than face masks, shoulder pads, and numbers.

Keith Jackson was the man Roone hired for play-by-play. I was delighted. Keith is all competence, all work, and all man. So that was our broadcast team.

Chet Forte was named producer-director of the telecasts. He was an ideal choice. This little former basketball All-American from Co-

lumbia is a volatile man, emotional, sometimes even tempestuous, but when a broadcast begins he is all business and he knows his business as well as anyone in the industry. He also knows sports —including football—inside out.

Now we were all set. We were to do a trial run. We would tape a preseason game between Detroit and Kansas City just as though it were a regular telecast, but it would never air. Keith, Dandy, and I met in Detroit and the three of us drove to the Lions training camp to watch them work out and to move among the players. Dandy knew the Lions, of course. He had worked often enough against them. And I knew most of them from my coverage of the beat.

We did the test-run game but Don was painfully ill at ease. He wasn't really sure of his role in the telecast. Keith was first-rate. I made some observations that pleased Arledge. Not that they were anything brilliant, but they were the very kind of observations that had been studiously eschewed in the telecasting of NFL games in the past.

But it was all new to Meredith, and he was not, after all, a professional. We went back to New York and studied the tape with Arledge and Forte. Roone and Chet pointed out to Don the areas where he could do better, and what was expected of him. Dandy is a sensitive man to begin with, and at the time he was struggling with a tremendous personal depression and concern. His little daughter, Heather, born blind and retarded, was about to be institutionalized. Against that, football could not have been less important.

So Don was wrestling with himself and his emotions got the better of him. He stood up and said, "Let's face it, fellows. I'm not qualified for this. I don't even know that much about football. I just know the Xs and Os that Landry taught me."

"Don," I said, "in my opinion you'll be making the biggest mistake of your life if you even think about leaving us. You're going to come out of this a hero. Middle America will love you. Southern America will love you. And there are at least forty sportswriters in this country who can't wait to get at me. You'll benefit thereby. Don't worry about me, though, because in the long run it will work for the old coach, too. You'll wear the white hat, I'll wear the black hat, and you'll have no problems from the very beginning."

Dandy lifted his drink. "By golly," he said, "I'm with you, coach. All the way." And off he went to Dallas. He didn't know it then but he was only 20 weeks away from winning an Emmy. And I didn't

know it then, but I was going to reach a point where I would lose my perspective, and begin to feel sorry for myself. Only in my case it would take a lot less than 20 weeks. And I would learn that I still had a lot to learn about myself, and some more growing up to do.

Keith and Dandy and I did our first on-air game together in Pittsburgh. It was a preseason game that promised to have a maximum of disinterest. About the only interest we could conjure up was the fact that Terry Bradshaw, the Li'l Abner-type character from Louisiana Tech, would be making his debut as the Pittsburgh quarterback on national television.

Arledge recognized the situation. He wanted to grab some national attention for us despite the unattractive match-up. So he suggested that we try to put a mike on Fran Tarkenton, the Giants' quarterback, who would not be playing that night because of a pulled muscle in the groin.

So I talked to Fran, who was most agreeable on the condition that his coach, Alex Webster, would agree to it. Webster, as nice a man as you would want to meet, was agreeable too. Thus we started the game with Fran wearing a live microphone.

He was outstanding. Dandy would talk to him during a lull in the action—which was almost all night long—and say, "Son of a preacher man, what do you think of that young blond-haired boy from my part of the country, that there quarterback from Louisiana Tech?"

And Francis would chuckle and then answer. I had my own series of quips going back and forth with Tark, and we all felt good in the booth because we had a whole new thing going. But overall, I was not happy with the telecast because of the way it was formatted. I opened the show on the field and interviewed Terry Bradshaw. We were six minutes into the game before I even got to the booth. And then, I was concerned about the three men in the booth, trying to feel my way with Keith and Don. I left the stadium feeling that this whole thing was wrong for me. I was now the way Don had been after the trial-run game.

I expected what would happen after that telecast and it did. The sportswriters were up in arms. There was Cosell again, breaching all the rules. How dare I wire Tarkenton? So the New York writers called Rozelle and demanded that they be allowed to sit on the bench with the team during the game if ABC was going to put a live microphone on Giant players. Rozelle had no taste for the idea either, but he knew we were just trying to juice up our first telecast.

For myself, I wondered when someone other than me would tell the truth. What right did the writers have to demand this? Their newspapers don't pay one red cent for the right to cover the games. Their writers sometimes travel and eat at team expense, thus defying one of the fundamental laws of journalism and creating a clear conflict of interest. ABC, on the other hand, paid millions of dollars for the right to broadcast the games, and each announcer was paid by ABC, not the National Football League. We also slept and ate at ABC's expense, and we traveled at ABC's expense. But no, in the peculiar and often sick structure of "sports print journalism" I was to be the whipping boy. I even considered doing a commentary demanding that newspapers pay for the right to have their reporters cover the games.

So I got it from many of them, all across the country. "Cosell is at it again," they wrote. "He makes himself bigger than the event." As if a preseason game between the Giants and Pittsburgh (which won only one game that year) was a major circumstance in this nation's history. Frankly, I was disgusted. But then I got mad. I called Arledge, I told him I wanted to stay on the package, and I couldn't wait to start the regular season.

Our first regular season game was to match the New York Jets and the Cleveland Browns at Cleveland. We felt that it was a break for us, for two reasons: First, Cleveland is always a solid team; and second, the Jets had the biggest draw in pro football—Joe Willie Namath. I never have been better prepared for a show in my life than I was for that first *Monday Night* game.

I was very close to the Jet players and, of course, I was particularly close to Joe Willie Namath. Meredith knew little about the Jets. He knew about Cleveland, because the Browns had always had a hex on Dallas and had defensed Meredith very well throughout the years. But to Don, the American Football League had never existed.

So I took Meredith with me much of that week preparatory to the game—to the Jets' dressing room, out to the practice field, and, finally, to Joe Namath's apartment. There Joe sat with a projector and ran the films again and again for us of the Cleveland defenses. He explained the basics of what the Jets were going to do. The main element of the ground game was to go against young Jerry Sherk, a rookie defensive lineman from Oklahoma State. And, indeed, when the game took place that's exactly what they did.

Namath then explained to Don and me exactly how he would try

to crack the Cleveland zone defense. Don related to Joe the troubles he had suffered through the years with the Cleveland secondary. "They're a funny kind of team," Don told him. "They bend, but they don't break. Just when you think you've got them, they'll come up with the key interception."

Namath couldn't have been more honest with us or more thorough in his evaluations. In fact, in our three years of *Monday Night Football*, nobody has treated us more openly or fully. When we left, Meredith said, "I'm glad I spent this time with him. He's not at all like they write about him."

When I got to Cleveland, I spent most of Sunday with Bill Nelsen, the quarterback of the Browns. Bill is another direct guy, who told me exactly what the Browns were going to do. Not that there was any mystery about it. The key to the Jets' secondary had always been the fine strong safety, Jim Hudson. But Hudson had bad knees, which the public knew about, and also a bad back, which the public didn't know. So, obviously, Bill was going to test Hudson immediately. It would be Hudson's task to cover one of the best tight ends in football, Milt Morin. Naturally, he would resort to other familiar aerial tactics, including his favorite play when near the end zone, the post pattern to Gary Collins. He would also, of course, balance the attack, if he could, with the running of Leroy Kelly and Bo Scott.

The whole flow of the game tied neatly to our preparation for it. We pointed out that the Jets gained more than 500 yards, but that when the chips were down the Cleveland defense would not break; it would only bend, as Don had said to Namath.

In the course of the game we were each fitting into the roles expected of us. Keith was right on. Dandy was humorously cornpone. I was wisecracking, second-guessing, and leading Dandy. Examples: After a pass interference call I asked Don to explain the rule. After a couple of false starts Dandy nonchalantly cornponed, "Don't know what that there rule is, Ha'rhd, but whatever happened down there was a no-no."

Another highlight of the telecast was Dandy Don's irreverent reference to the colorful name of the Cleveland rookie wide receiver, Fair Hooker. Keith and I had no rejoinder.

So *Monday Night Football* had made its debut; a new treatment for television and professional football. A new hero had been born: Dandy Don Meredith. And a new goat: Howard Cosell.

Leaving the stadium that night, we all felt pretty good about the

telecast. It had been a fine game. There had been a definite rhythm among the three of us. We were on our way. Until the next day. Then I found out that I might be on *my* way—out. Looking back now, you have to wonder about the whole seedy business, how and why there could have been such a storm surrounding me. But at the time, despite all I had told Dandy about how I would be ripped, the damned thing got to me. I felt I had fallen into all six of Nixon's crises at once—and Watergate was yet to come.

Instantly, the flood of letters began, addressed both to ABC and to me directly. Only a minimal amount of it—out of literally thousands of letters—favored me. That was the first wave of a building, critical, first reaction to my part in the *Monday Night* debut.

In the midst of all this furor Emmy and I escaped—to Puerto Rico, where I was to do the live telecast of the lightweight championship fight between Ismael Laguna and Kenny Buchanan. This assignment came at exactly the right time. We planned to revisit the statehouse where I shot the opening scene of *Bananas*, to have lunch on the patio of El Convento where we had lunched with Woody Allen, and to try to forget the whole mess. The only trouble was I honestly couldn't. It was chewing me up inside.

Then a call from Chet Forte helped me a great deal. He told me that he and Roone had studied the tape of the telecast, and had graded me "very good." They had graded Keith similarly and had marked Dandy as "raw but very promising." Then he told me about the mail. "More than half of it, Howard," he said, "doesn't even relate to the telecast. It's about you and Muhammad Ali." I knew instinctively what he meant. It was a pattern with which I was painfully familiar: "Get that nigger-loving Jew bastard off the air. Football is an *American* game."

Then he said, "Some of it says you can't criticize the players, you never played the game."

Another refrain I had heard throughout much of my career, carefully propagated over a long span of years as an aftermath of the networks' continued use of ex-athletes as announcers. I had long had strong feelings about the policy of using ex-jocks as announcers. I think it is perfectly proper to use them limitedly, for "analysis," under the guidance and leadership of a professional. I think it is a desperately wrong thing, and a debasement of my profession, to take a man off the diamond, or off the gridiron, or off the basketball court, and put him on a news show as a so-called reporter.

The reasons are obvious. In the first place, the man has had no training whatsoever in journalism, in communications, and in speech and delivery. In the second place, he doesn't begin to know the nuts and bolts of reporting, the who, what, when, where, how, and why of a story. In the third place, participating in one sport doesn't remotely make a man knowledgeable in any other sport. Quite the contrary, it often inhibits his knowledgeability. In the last place, the ex-athlete is, in a journalistic sense, hampered by divided loyalties, because of old ties and old loyalties to the management for which he worked, to the sport in which he participated, and to all of the teams and teammates with whom and against whom he played.

Thus, by my precepts, the employment of Dandy Don was exactly right. He was being used for a specific purpose, in a specific way, without any pretense that he was a trained professional. I also want to make it clear that ex-athletes of long broadcast experience must be regarded as professional broadcasters—men like Frank Gifford and Pat Summerall. This is not to say that it was right to hire them as all-purpose sports reporters in the first instance—and that's the way they were hired. But it is to say that they are highly intelligent men and, given the opportunity, have worked and studied hard through the years. This is why they are professionals now.

All of this, and a great deal more, was on my mind as we idled away the hours in Puerto Rico. I guess, in times of stress, people always tend to become philosophical. But I had made up my mind to one thing: I was going to do one helluva fight broadcast. I was going to open that show with absolute confidence in my performance. I wasn't going to let anybody, either in the public or in the press, think that I had been reached by the static crackling around me at home.

CHAPTER 10

A MONDAY KIND OF LOVE

As our plane touched down at Friendship Airport in Baltimore my spirits were still soaring. The tempest I had left behind in New York five days earlier seemed an incidental part of a distant past.

But I was soon reinfected with the whole doleful situation. While I was away certain National Football League owners had objected to

my presence on the *Monday Night* package. Some of my friends thought I was in trouble. I didn't need to be told this. I could read it in their faces.

We were to be met at the terminal by Don Klosterman, the general manager of the Baltimore Colts. As Emmy and I approached the airport bar, we spotted Don whispering to Jim Mahoney, a Beverly Hills public-relations man whose clients included Frank Sinatra. I knew Don was telling Jim about the flow of events following the first *Monday Night* game. I said so to Emmy.

"Let's not go through that again," she begged. "Forget the whole thing. Don't let anyone know that it bothers you."

I said I'd try. But I could feel myself crashing. Stop the world. I wanted to get off.

We had a quick drink and left for Don's home, where we were to spend the weekend. My mood was subdued. I was sick to death of the whole silly affair. My dilemma was: Do I quit now, tell them all to go to hell? Who needs to be bothered with petty people who live their lives in thimbles? What I had done was to bring a few decent lines to a pro-football telecast, and the reaction against me, as far as I could see, was a reflection of the whole seedy structure of the sports business and the phony sports legends. On the other hand, if I didn't stick it out I'd be giving in to everything that in my mind was wrong and unfair. I talked it through with Emmy at Klosterman's. Finally we looked at each other and laughed. I made the choice I knew I'd make from the beginning. To stick it out.

Before I knew it we were at the stadium for the second game of *Monday Night Football*. Roone Arledge was quite aware of the enormous flack surrounding me and the tensions I was under. He suggested that I cut back a little, that I go easy and ride this thing out. All of which made sense to me.

I opened with a joint interview with John Unitas and Len Dawson, the two great veterans. In that interview I asked Unitas the question that was foremost in the minds of football people. He was aging, having trouble with his arm. I asked if he could still throw the long ball. He met it head on, the way he always does. Would you believe that at least 15 columns followed that interview, denouncing me for daring to ask such an impertinent question of the greatest quarterback "who ever played the game." You see, I had never played the game.

During the course of the game I started to lay back a little as Ar-

ledge had suggested. But early on, Mike Garrett was hurt, and when he went out our camera zeroed in tight on him. I said, feeling as confident by now as I always feel on a telecast, "Dandy, there's little Mike on the sidelines." And just then you could pick up Garrett's voice on our sideline microphones, and the TV audience heard him ask a teammate, "Wonder what Cosell is sayin' tonight?"

I couldn't resist a chuckle. "Tough little cookie," I commented offhandedly. "He'll be back."

Whereupon Roone spat out from the truck, over my intercom: "There you go, Howard. That's the very kind of thing that's going to get you in trouble because they're looking to sock you. What if he doesn't come back?"

I was shocked. What if he didn't come back? So what? It was a throwaway line, a passing comment. What the heck. I had known Mike Garrett and had been friendly with him since his junior year at USC. I knew his physical capacities. It didn't really matter whether Hank Stram returned him to the game or not. I knew Mike would be willing.

Well, I then decided to just shut up. I virtually remained mute for the rest of the night. I was upset about everything, but mostly about Arledge having snapped at me. And yet I understood. He was uptight, under pressure from higher-ups in the company with respect to me. And he had handpicked me as the key man in the package. (Incidentally, Roone was proven right. The one remark the writers did seize on from the telecast was my statement that Mike would be back! In a telecast where I was accused on the one hand of shilling by my very silence, the Garrett comment was held up as another example of Cosell's ignorance. I never played the game.)

Coming up to the third week of *Monday Night Football*—Chicago at Detroit—I was really down, more depressed, professionally, than I have ever been in my life. Everywhere I went in that damned ABC building I felt the eyes of people. I was imagining whispers about getting rid of me. Only later did I learn that Leonard Goldenson had called Elton Rule every Tuesday morning to ask, "What about Howard? What are you going to do about him?"

And Rule, even though he knew Goldenson was getting pressure from the board of directors, stood firm. "Nothing," he would say. "Howard works for Arledge."

I did a helluva job on the Chicago-Detroit game. Arledge said, "Keep that up and there's no way they can touch you." But the let-

ters kept pouring in, fomented by the still critical columns that were appearing in papers all over the country. I made it a point to study them all. And to read every letter. The columnists would take a single line out of an entire telecast and pounce on it. Sometimes a word. There was no way I could defend myself.

The mail was a different thing. A literate, cultured Miami department-store executive was critical. I took that letter seriously, because he reflected a certain common reaction: *I had never played the game.* To this man's credit, before the season ended, he wrote a letter to the president of ABC apologizing, saying, "I have learned much about football, and even more about the men who play the game, from a man who never played the game."

Green Bay at San Diego was next. I couldn't wait for this game. I really couldn't. No man alive knew more about the Green Bay Packers than I did. No man was closer to the players than I was. (Remember *Run to Daylight?*) I opened the show with an interview with Bart Starr. I will never forget what Bart Starr did. He knew the travail I was going through. At the end of the interview, still on the air, he deliberately said, "Howard, I want you to know that every member of the Green Bay Packers thanks you for the remarkable memorial you paid to Mr. Lombardi when he died. Every man on the team asked me to tell you this."

One thing Roone said to me on the flight from San Diego stayed with me. "I think," he mused, "that the country is beginning to catch on to what we're trying to do."

God knows, I hoped he was right. And there was good reason to believe he was. I began to take stock. Our ratings up to that point were outstanding, far better than we had expected. We were achieving better than 30-percent share of the audience. ABC had never come close to this on Monday night.

The press attention—good and bad—we were getting was simply incredible. I personally had been reviewed in *Newsweek, Sports Illustrated, Time,* and even *Life* magazine. Virtually every sports columnist in the country had been writing about me, most of them calling me "abrasive," but some of them now beginning to write that I was bringing a new look to the game, that I was a perfect offset to Meredith. My byplay with Dandy was no longer a shock, an inside joke. Many people didn't really know whether we were friends or not, but they were beginning not to care. They would just enjoy it when I would say, as I looked down at Bart Starr, "Of course, Starr

494

will be remembered for his excellence, Dandy for his futility under crisis conditions."

And Dandy would shoot back: "What would you know about that, Ha'hrd? You never played the game."

I learned so much about Meredith that first year. I learned that he was not what some represented him to be, a dim-witted Texas corn pone. I learned that he's a highly intelligent, sensitive man who has gone through a great deal of personal hardship in his life. I learned that his aspirations go far beyond football. And I learned a fundamental thing—that we both look at life in very much the same way; that we both take our private relationships very seriously; that we both enjoy humor and a good time, but that we're both always very much aware of that which is going on in the world.

I was staying at the Marriott Hotel in Bloomington, Minnesota, when I bumped into Don Weiss of Rozelle's staff. All the frustration suddenly came gushing out of me. I had just read again that I didn't know football. I began to ruminate all over again, this time at the expense of the hapless Weiss. At that moment he seemed to represent the football establishment, which was exactly what I felt most of the football writers did with their treasured nonsense: "He never played the game." What the hell was it anyway? Was it invented by Enrico Fermi and refined by Werner Von Braun? Hardly. On the contrary, except for the lexicon it has created, that tired litany of mystical cliches, it is the same game you played in the streets: Send the tall guy out against a short guy, a fast guy out against a slow guy; hook to your left at the fire hydrant.

So I poured it all out to Weiss, a fine, sensitive, quiet fellow. And then I behaved badly, boyishly, monosyllabically all day, with Forte, with Dandy, with Keith, with all of them.

Just before the telecast was to begin, Arledge came to see me in the booth and said, "Howard, this may be the most important game we have yet done. It's a big game. Two teams with a real chance for the title, Los Angeles and Minnesota. And you've got everybody unnerved, everybody, the way you're acting."

Arledge looked at me hard. "If you want to quit after this game—fine. If you want to talk it over tomorrow—fine. But give us all a break and do your thing tonight."

I knew he was right. "Don't worry about it," I said.

The telecast went fine.

But let's face it. I had become a pain in the ass. To everyone, including myself. The night after the Minnesota-Los Angeles game Pete Rozelle dropped by our apartment for a cocktail. Don Weiss had told him of my outburst, and Pete was concerned. He addressed himself first to Emmy. "Look," he said, "I just wanted to come here and talk as a friend and tell you that Howard is taking this thing much too seriously. He should have fun with the *Monday Night* games. I think he has been, on the air, but deep inside apparently he's still being troubled. It's ridiculous. Howard"— and he turned to me—"just have fun with the game."

We went to Milwaukee—Baltimore was to play Green Bay. The telecast was in its early stages and Dandy was breezing along, as he had been through the whole series. He was telling one anecdote after another. Arledge was in New York for this one. Suddenly Chet spoke to Dandy from the truck. "Dandy," he said, "Roone just called. He wants you to stop with the anecdotes. He says they're getting silly."

Meredith looked at me. "Did you hear that?" he asked. "I've had it. I'm going back to New York with you to have it out with all of them. I'm getting out of this thing."

The spiral was still spinning. Now it was Meredith who was going to quit. One or the other of us was leaving the package each week. Keith was our only contribution to sanity.

Later, when we got back to the hotel, I assumed the unlikely role of peacemaker. I told Chet he had hurt Dandy's feelings. "What was I to do?" he responded. "Arledge called and he was right. The stories *were* getting silly."

"Well," I said, "he's a sensitive guy."

He resolved his problem with Roone and it was back home for Dandy, back to the scene, back to Dallas. The Cowboys were to meet the Cardinals, and Meredith would come unglued. As for me, I dreaded the trip. Dallas to me was the heart of hard-core conservatism. It was the city where John F. Kennedy, whom I had admired so much, had been killed. Besides, I had been through so much trash in the first six weeks of the season, my mood was still unsettled.

But they held an affair in Dallas at noon on the day of the game and they labeled it "The Why I Hate Howie Luncheon." They had a turnaway crowd, and Sam Blair wrote about it in the next day's *Dallas Morning News*, ending with the words: "Hate Howard Cosell? Hell, no. This was a Monday kind of love."

The people in Dallas, it developed, were wonderful to me, and my reception there has grown each year. In 1971 they drew 1,800 at the old Adolphus Hotel and had to open a separate ballroom to seat everyone. The guests there couldn't even see me, but they could hear, and they didn't complain.

What happened *after* the game that first year, which the Cardinals won by a crushing 38-0, was more confusing than a Japanese morality play. Meredith went wild in the booth over the performance of his old team. He couldn't understand their absolute futility and he all but exploded with personal emotions.

Every week was now a happening in every town. The spin-offs, the reactions, the people, all formed a kind of hazy panorama. And then came Philadelphia.

I don't really remember much about the Giants-Eagles game that Monday night. I only really saw a quarter and a half of it. What I do remember is how cold and vicious that day and night were, and all the events leading up to the now historic was-he-sick-or-was-he-crocked episode.

I started the day feeling queasy. I had lunch with Leonard Tose, the new owner of the Eagles, and Pete Retzlaff, his general manager. Tose arranged to have a limousine take me to Franklin Field in late afternoon to do half-time highlights. We were in for a treat when we reached the stadium. The power was out. No lights, no heat, nothing. I sat there for two and a half hours in the winter chill. Finally they raised sufficient power to transmit the highlight show.

We went directly from the stadium to the athletes' lounge and dining room at the University of Pennsylvania, where Tose was throwing a party for us and the press. It was now nearly 6:30. I was beginning to feel slightly fevered, clammy, uncomfortable, with occasional dizziness. I stayed about three-quarters of an hour. Then I returned to the field to prepare for the opening interview, with Ron Johnson of the Giants, which we were to videotape. The moment I hit the open air I began to get chills all over again. It was even colder than it had been before. This was late November. The wind had razor blades in its teeth. As I started toward the field someone slapped me on the shoulder, almost knocking me down. "Hey, buddy," I heard him say. I turned around. It was John Carlos, then on the taxi squad of the Eagles.

"John," I said, "I'm freezing. It's terrible."

"Well," he suggested, "let's run, buddy."

So, like a nut, there I was, running wind sprints with the former Olympian, John Carlos, on the cinder track surrounding the field. It must have been quite a spectacle.

I finished the Johnson interview in short order, returned to the party just long enough to say my good-byes, and then Dandy and I climbed up to the press level, down a winding stairwell, and across rickety wooden steps to reach the broadcast booth. The booth at Franklin Field is an overhanging one, and getting there is to take your life in your hands.

The booth was open to the cold. Keith Jackson was ready. He had bought a brand new overcoat for the occasion, and I kidded him about it as the show opened. I was really feeling a little better, from the sheer exhilaration of performing. As the game got under way I had a great time with Dandy. I was all over him that night, crediting him with statements about different players that he had never made. Dandy would wail, "Now, Ha'hrd, I don't know where you got that. I never said anything like it. I don't even know that little fellow from Bowling Green."

Arledge later said to me that the first quarter and a half of that game was our best job of the year. But midway through the second quarter I began to sink. I was beginning to sense a loss of balance. I was uncommonly light-headed and was having trouble articulating. By the half-time break they knew in the truck that something was wrong with me. My voice had become thick, I could not say Philadelphia, and all of this happened on camera. If anyone ever looked like an on-camera drunk, I did.

Immediately after getting off camera I threw up in the booth—all over Dandy's cowboy boots. Then, with the help of a policeman, I staggered out of the booth, was led out of the stadium, and got into a taxi for the airport. I don't remember anything about the drive to the airport. I only dimly remember that my secretary had told me of a late night flight to New York. When I got to the airport I staggered to the ticket counter and somehow mumbled to the agent that I wanted the late plane to New York. She told me that the flight had been discontinued.

Some things you do remember. And it's funny the way you remember them. With all the dimness of my mind, I suddenly thought, "My God, I'm going to die in Philadelphia." And then, oddly, I thought of W. C. Fields's epitaph.

I stumbled out of the airport and into another cab. "Please take me

to New York," I said. The driver said it would cost a lot of money. "I don't care," I said, "just get me there."

The next thing I knew, the driver was telling me we were in New York. I thickly mumbled my address to him. Finally I was home. I remember paying the driver $92 for the ride. It was about 3:45 A.M. I fumbled at the door to my apartment, and Emmy ran to meet me. She had been terrified.

My body was still shaking with chills, as though I had the ague. I couldn't keep my balance at all. Emmy helped me into bed and wrapped me in blankets. At 6:30 in the morning I called my doctor, who agreed to come right over.

Somehow, I'm almost embarrassed to recall it today, but I even managed to mumble out my morning radio show. The show must go on, and all that theatrical baloney. Here I thought I might be dying and I had to get my last five-minute radio trick on the air.

An electrocardiograph established that my heart was okay. What I suffered from, it developed, was toxic vertigo, an infection in the inner ear that causes loss of balance and, sometimes, thickness of speech. It is a terrible thing to get and terribly difficult to get rid of. To this day I have vestiges of it. I will wake up in the morning, on occasion, get out of bed, and totally lose my balance, tumbling back into bed.

During the course of that next day the phone rang incessantly. I knew I had become a whole new *cause célèbre*. As Roone Arledge told me on the phone, the whole country "thinks you were drunk last night."

"That's bullshit, Roone," I snapped, "and you know it. I've never been drunk in my life."

"I know that," Arledge answered, "and that's what I've told the brass."

The days of the week that followed were torture for Emmy and me. We went up to our home at Pound Ridge, and I just lay in bed for most of the week. I simply couldn't get my strength back, and I simply couldn't shake the damned dizziness. In the meantime the inevitable columns were appearing—all over again. Some of them mocking, some of them gloating, most of them contemptuous. A battle I thought I had clearly won was in danger of being permanently lost. Indeed, *Sports Illustrated* carried an item saying I was "out."

The next *Monday Night* game was at Atlanta—the Dolphins against the Falcons. I still felt ill and debated not going. I also didn't

want to face the press. I was tied up in a knot, a knot of anger, of shame and self-pity. I talked to Arledge about it, and he told me to make my own choice.

I flew to Atlanta the morning of the game. I had made up my mind to one thing: I would open that game lightheartedly and I would be myself. I wouldn't let the press know how I felt inside.

So I opened the show and I felt the comforting sympathy of Dandy and Keith. Garo Yepremian kicked off for Miami. Quickly I told the story of how Yepremian, when he was with Detroit, had kicked six field goals in one game to defeat Minnesota. And how, after that game, a scribe asked Van Brocklin, then coaching the Vikings but now at Atlanta, how he thought one could handle Yepremian.

"Tighten the immigration laws," Van Brocklin snapped.

And with that Dandy and Keith roared and we were on our way. It was a fine telecast, and Arledge and I flew back to New York together. I felt strong and clean and good.

Our final *Monday Night* game that first year was Detroit at Los Angeles. We had a great telecast, it was a fine, exciting game, Dandy was loose and easy, singing on the air, and Keith, Dandy, and I had really become a triumvirate. Each knew the others' moves, we had good timing, perfect rhythm. And we had behind us the most extraordinary and the most exaggerated series of individual experiences that the imagination could invent. We had lived through a 13-week fantasy. We had all emerged as national personalities. We had achieved a marvelous success in the ratings. *The Carol Burnett Show* would have to move to a night other than Monday on CBS. There had been talk of moving *All in the Family* to Monday night. It would now stay in its Saturday time slot. ABC had now become competitive, and then some, in Monday-night prime-time television.

I said good-bye to Dandy and Keith. Jim Mahoney drove Emmy and me to the airport. As I was getting into the car a couple of fans spotted me and shouted as we were driving off, "Hey, Howie baby. Were you really drunk in Philadelphia?"

I chuckled. And so did Jim Mahoney. Then he said, "They bum-rapped you the whole damned season, and they wound up making a star our of you. *Monday Night Football* is the biggest hit in the country."

This from the man who represents Sinatra.

As I ducked into the plane I knew two things: There was no more talk about quitting. Dandy, Keith, and I would never sit at the Pon-

chartrain again, looking at ourselves and cursing our fates. We had proved something, and we all wanted to come back. Two of us would. (Keith was later replaced by Frank Gifford.)

The other thing I knew was that I had been a damned fool. I had behaved with emotional immaturity. That would never happen again.

The writers never laid a glove on me. And they never will.

CHAPTER 13

MYTH OF THE FAN

L ike millions of others, Emmy and I were in front of the television set when Bobby Kennedy was shot. Like millions of others, we recoiled in horror. Like millions of others, we stayed up most of the night, waiting for word on whether or not Bobby Kennedy would live. We thought about the Kennedy family, about the unbelievable tragedies in their lives, about all the Kennedy children. And then, I think quite understandably, we thought about and talked about our own two daughters, Jill and Hilary, about the kind of society they were growing up in, a society where assassination had become commonplace.

We have a liberal home. John Kennedy had meant much to us. So had Martin Luther King. So had Robert Kennedy. But if we had had opposite political views it would not have mattered. It seemed to us the American society had gone berserk, that we were in danger of utter chaos. Three times in a decade. When I studied American history and read of the assassination of Lincoln, and of Garfield, and of McKinley, it seemed somehow remote, abstract, part of history, but the kind of thing that could not happen in contemporary society. Now I knew better. Oh, how I knew better.

I suspect that when future generations read the history of the 1960's they'll regard it in an abstract way, too. The whole mess of the era. The apparently endless war in Vietnam. The ecology. The racial anguish. The drug abuse. But it existed then, and most of it exists now, including the crisis of the great cities, and somehow all of it meshed and related to the disorder of many minds, the kind of disorder that could produce assassination.

In any event, at seven o'clock in the morning after Bobby Kennedy was shot I had to do my regular morning network radio show,

"Speaking of Sports." I simply could not speak of sports that morning. I felt that I had to reevaluate that which I do in life, come to grips with myself, and make it clear that the microcosm of sports is of small consequence in the full sweep of the society. I couldn't have faced my daughters otherwise. They were stricken with grief, with disbelief, and with doubts and fears about the whole civilization around them.

So I went on the air that morning and said, "This is Howard Cosell, but this morning I cannot speak of sports." I then explained that there would be no ball scores, no routine sports items. Instead I talked of Robert Kennedy, of the three assassinations in a decade, and why I had to think about what I do and why I do it, and I suggested that it might be the time for everyone to do just that because clearly there was a terrible sickness in the society.

I never dreamed what the response would be. Hundreds of letters, many of them vicious, denouncing me for not giving the sports news. "Don't tell me how to live," one said, "just give us the scores. That's what you're paid for." That was the theme of most, with profanities running through many of the letters.

I was stunned. My instant reaction: What hope is there for the country if this is the thinking? And then the attempt at rationalization. After all, there are over 200 million people in the United States, and these letters can't be the majority. But then, as the thought processes continued, the realization that it didn't matter whether or not they were a majority. What mattered was that there were, obviously, a very large number of people in the United States who didn't want their normal routines interrupted on any count, for any reason, to whom hearing a baseball score was more important than some introspective thought about the state of the nation, about the kind of society in which their children were growing up, about how three assassinations could take place in the United States within five years, and about what was wrong and what one could do about it.

I began to wonder if that "fan" kind of thinking is one of the things that makes us so prone to assassination (and assassination attempts, e.g., George Wallace) in this country. Maybe there is such an absence of intellect and sensitivity in the United States today that only violence is understandable and acceptable. The matter is deeply psychological and complex, and hardly susceptible of resolution, especially in a book about the life of a sports commentator. But one thing emerged as certain: If one has any kind of mind, one has to

wonder about the people—the "fans"—who wrote those letters. I even got scurrilous phone calls: "Don't preach to us." Only their language wasn't that clean. What made it even worse, they felt they were right and within their rights. After all, they were "fans," and through all the years that I have been in sports, the "fan," generally speaking, has been sanctified by most sportswriters and sports broadcasters. I think it's time for that nonsense to stop.

The popular notion has been that since the fan pays his money, he is entitled to say or do almost anything he wants. Absurd. The payment of an admission price to a stadium does not carry with it a license to engage in disorderly conduct, unseemly behavior, and the utterance of profanities that are offensive to others. This all results from the disproportionate emphasis placed upon sports in America in which people get so bound up with an event, with winning or losing, that their whole sense of values is discarded in the transitory escape from real life that the event provides. Life hardly begins or ends when Miami beats Washington in the Super Bowl, yet many act as if it does.

Sometimes it doesn't even take an event as important as the Super Bowl to arouse the "fans." As I have explained elsewhere in this book, we have had a television miracle with *Monday Night Football*. But within the basic miracle a second miracle emerged—the half-time highlights. Roone Arledge felt that the public was tired of watching local high-school bands perform at half time—indeed, research had established the audience decline at half time—and he felt that it would be an audience disaster in prime time to employ such programming. So he dreamed up the notion of playing the highlights of key, or exciting, NFL games of the previous Sunday afternoon. It is a tough thing to do, logistically, because the films of the Sunday games have to be sent to Philadelphia, where NFL Films is located, and then the film must be developed and edited to time, and then transmitted to the stadium where *Monday Night Football* is taking place. This is usually done a couple of hours before the game, barring technical problems, and as the film is fed in I ad-lib over it.

The half-time highlights quickly became a "thing." Audiences stay glued to the television set, and, of course, in every city the fans hope to see their team in action. The hope cannot be fulfilled. We have five to six minutes available for the highlights, and twelve games are played every Sunday. So, as practical fact, the most we can deal with are four or five games. The games have been picked by our co-

producers, Chet Forte and Dennis Lewin, with very simple criteria employed in the selection. They go for games that have the most meaning in the standings, but also the games that have the most exciting plays visually. They also have to be concerned about the number of viewers. In other words, if the two New York teams are blacked out in New York on a Sunday, and Los Angeles is similarly blacked out, it becomes important to show those teams because so many millions of viewers are involved, far more than if Denver or Miami were blacked out. All of this has been made perfectly clear to the fans during the three years past of *Monday Night Football*.

The fans couldn't care less. Thus, in our second year of *Monday Night Football*, there came a day when Washington crushed St. Louis. It was a lousy football game, no excitement, but Washington was unbeaten at the time. Forte and Lewin elected not to use highlights from this game. The reaction was extraordinary. I began to get calls from Washington announcers and sportswriters demanding statements from me as to the cause of my prejudice against the Redskins. Then the mail! Hundreds upon hundreds of letters. "Get Cosell off the air. He hates Washington." We were amused and, in a sense, delighted. It showed the impact of the half-time show. Then I got word that the "fans" were hanging me in effigy in the nation's capital. As I laughingly explained to the members of the media who called, I had nothing to do with the selection of the highlights, only the performance of them. I pointed out that every week as I lead into the highlights I say on the air, "Now, yesterday's highlights as selected by the producers of *Monday Night Football*." The fans in Washington, every time I go there, still want to know why I hate the Redskins.

Why should they be different? Let me tell you about Miami. In 1972 the Dolphins came of age. They proved they were a truly great football team, winning 17 straight games. Their fans went wild. But they were not on the half-time highlights every week. Suddenly, out of nowhere, I began getting vile mail. The letters this time mounted into the thousands. What did I have against Miami? ABC should take action against me.

While all this was going on I was advising media people in Miami of what I told the people in Washington—that I had nothing to do with selection of half-time highlights. I gave them Chet Forte's name. Now Forte started to get the mail, and I started to enjoy his discomfiture. "It's not funny," he said, "these people are nuts. Read

some of this stuff." I told him I didn't have to. I was quite familiar with it.

When we got to Miami for our *Monday Night* game there, the papers were full of the "war between the fans and the ABC broadcast team." Dandy Don said, "What the hell do they mean, broadcast team? I'm no part of this. Cosell's the guy." I always said Dandy had a great sense of humor.

To our astonishment, Forte and I learned that the one man who had been stirring up the population against us most was a sports announcer on our own Miami affiliate station. We were incredulous. He had been telling the people to write me, write Roone Arledge, write Chet Forte, get the Dolphins on every half time. We bumped into this guy at a dinner, Forte did an interview with him explaining how the half-time highlights were picked, and then Chet asked me to talk to him. I did, reluctantly, and there was acid in my voice. Later Chet and I watched the interviews on television and we could not believe it when the man wound up his show saying, "Cosell and Forte are staying at the Sonesta Beach Hotel." This was one of the most professionally scurrilous acts I've ever witnessed. Within seconds after he said it Forte and I started to receive ugly, profane, threatening calls. We had our phones turned off.

By now my wife was both disturbed and disgusted with the whole series of events. I wasn't happy. And Meredith was saying, "Damn, you're unbelievable, Howard. You don't have anything to do with picking the damned highlights, and the silly business is becoming a national story." Indeed, papers around the country were writing about my life being threatened, special security was to be provided for me at the game, and all the rest.

The night of the game could not have been more uneventful. Miami won easily, as expected. There was only one thing worthy of note. The gridiron was encircled by a cordon of police, each policeman holding a vicious-looking German shepherd by the leash. The dogs were deterrents, or supposedly so, to the "fans," who had a propensity for rushing onto the field during the course of play. The fans were not deterred. Some went onto the field anyway, and one even picked up the football before the ball was snapped by the center. Fortunately none of the dogs got loose or there could have been a serious aftermath. Forte did not put his cameras on the scene for fear it would lead to similar exhibitionism around the country, but Dandy and I described the situation, and Dandy said, "You know

there are really some nutty people down here." Yes, indeed. But some nice ones, too. Lots of them. After we left Miami I got stacks of mail from people in the Miami area apologizing for those who had been plaguing Forte and me.

You look back on stories like these with high humor, but at some point you have to wonder again about the distortion of emphasis on sports in the United States, and wonder how grown people can take so seriously something so unimportant as 45 seconds of action footage at half time.

Then you think about some of the great athletes you've known, and you remember their involvement with the "fans."

Early Wynn, for instance, was one of the greatest pitchers I have ever seen and he's recently been elected to the Baseball Hall of Fame. I remember sitting with this very characterful and interesting man near the end of his career when he was struggling to win his 300th career game—he could no longer win with the consistency he had once enjoyed—and he started talking about what was happening to him inside. He said, "It now becomes very hard for me to go out on the field. . . . They boo me. They boo me the minute I appear." He continued, "I think I'm a tough man. I think my whole career has proved that. I know I have no physical fear, but something happens to me. Those fools, they don't even know what they're booing. They're booing a man who's done his very best, who's never done anything less than his very best through all of the years—and I think my record will get me into the Hall of Fame—but right now I just want that three-hundredth victory and they won't let me alone. I'm beginning to think I'm never going to get it, because I can't stand what they're doing to me."

I saw the hair fall out of Roger Maris's head. I was extremely close to Roger Maris during the year 1961. I saw his hands begin to shake and I knew what was going on inside him, and still the fans booed him. Why? Because Mantle was their hero, not Maris, and it began to get to him. I believe that was part of the reason the hair was falling out. It was the whole undoing of his baseball life in New York. Sure, the 61 home runs haunted him, but what haunted him even more was when he would sit and say to me unendingly, "Do you hear them? I don't even want to go out there anymore." They destroyed Roger Maris in New York, and he couldn't wait to get away. And now he sits, a fat man in Jacksonville, with his beer distributorship, and when he thinks back to baseball what does he think about? He

thinks not about the 61 home runs, but mainly about the fans in New York, and you can't really get him to talk about baseball anymore.

This very day, as Henry Aaron, one of the finest men and players in the game, approaches Babe Ruth's sacred home-run record, he is getting the most vicious kind of mail, with the "nigger" element thrown in. There can be only one Babe Ruth, say the letter writers, and no "black bastard" has any right to challenge his record.

These are fans?

One could go on and on with stories like these. Once I saw Mickey Mantle in actual physical jeopardy as he was literally mobbed by "fans," young and old, for his autograph. When Mickey finally broke free of them they shouted, almost in unison, "Where would you be without us, you bum? Who pays your salary anyway?"

All of the above will undoubtedly be taken by some to mean that I am complaining about being in the public eye, and that athletes complain about the same thing, or that all fans are wild and unruly. Not at all. I think any person who performs in the public arena, as I do, as athletes do, has to expect some manifestation of public fervor during the course of his life. The question is to what degree, and in what ways? Does my wife have to sit at a table at Emily Shaw's Inn in Pound Ridge, New York, and have a man come up to her to say, "I hate your husband's guts. He's a no good son of a bitch"? I think not. On the other side of the coin, I now enjoy a degree of recognition in the country that is almost ridiculous, and for every person who will invade your privacy or turn on you at the slightest opportunity, there is the person who'll make you feel good. When you walk down a street in Wichita or San Diego and a stranger recognizes you and calls out, "Hey, Howie baby, keep it up, you're doing a good job," it's only human to feel a sense of elation. That's one of the great rewards of performing.

Finally, when I think about the "fan," I inevitably must think about three and a half years of my life and the life of Muhammad Ali; about the tens of thousands of letters directed to me, beginning with the general refrain, "You nigger-loving Jew bastard . . . "; and about the phone calls, some of which would begin, "We're gonna get you. We know where you're at, and we're gonna get you." Once again it's easy to laugh all this off with the rationalization that such "fans" are in the minority, but there are too many of them and they are part of the general group termed "fans" whose interests so many seem dedicated to protecting.

To be identified with Ali was to catch the full sweep of the fans' mentality. Once, in early 1971, after I had repeatedly defended Ali's right to earn a living, I was confronted by a group of hard-hats. They were doing construction work on Fifty-second Street, across from Mike Manuche's, where I often have lunch.

As I approached, one of them said, "Here he is, the Jew who loves Clay." They quickly encircled me. He continued, "We know you, Cosell. What is with you and that traitor, that black son of a bitch? The guy should never be allowed to fight again."

His name, I soon found out, was Johnny. He seemed to be the leader. He was a big, rough, potbellied guy. I looked at him and collected my thoughts. As it happened Ali was in New York that very afternoon and staying at the Hilton Hotel. "Now wait a minute," I said, as they crowded closer. "I know how we can settle this. Clay is just around the corner at the Hilton. We can go over there right now, and you—" I jabbed a finger at Johnny "—can lay that son of a bitch low."

He looked at me with suspicion. "Are you serious?" he demanded.

"Of course," I shot back. "Look at your body. You can handle him. I'm with you all the way. He's around the corner in Room nineteen ten. He's up there right now. We'll go over—you bring the other guys along—and you can have a piece of him. You can whip his ass."

So then the other hard-hats picked up the chant. "Yeah, that's right, Johnny. You can take care of him. You can whip him. Come on. Let's go."

He raised his hands to quiet them down. "What the hell is the matter with you guys?" he asked. "You crazy? The guy is a professional fighter. Gimme a hammer and I'll go over there, maybe."

I said, "Hell, you don't need a hammer to take care of a yellow traitor who wouldn't fight for his country. Just go over there and beat his ass."

The others were telling him to put up or shut up. Johnny looked at me for a long while and finally he said, "Aw, let's go back to work. You know, Howie ain't all that bad. He loved Lombardi."

I quickly ducked inside Manuche's, and my heart was palpitating. Although I had enjoyed agitating Johnny, the experience had been a distasteful one. I felt that it could just as easily have gone another way and become physically unpleasant. By great verbal dexterity I had managed to extricate myself and win them over.

But I wasn't through with Johnny the Hard-Hat. Over the next few days he grew friendlier each time I passed. One afternoon I stopped

and said, "Johnny, tell you what. They're going to announce the signing of the Ali-Frazier fight next week at Toots Shor's. After the signing I'll bring him over to meet you. You might like him."

"Aw, don't you start that," he said.

I smiled. "No problem," I said.

The next week, after the signing, I persuaded Ali to take a walk with me. I led him to Fifty-second Street and found Hard-Hat Johnny at work with his friends.

"Hey, Johnny."

"Oh, hey, Howie, how are ya?"

"I want you to meet Muhammad Ali," I announced, "you know, the black son-of-a-bitch traitor." I had prepared Ali on the whole story. He was looking ferocious.

"Now, wait a minute, Champ," stammered Johnny. "Wait a minute, Champ. You got to understand Howie, ya know?"

"Did you call me a black son-of-a-bitch traitor?" Ali stepped toward him.

"Champ, you don't understand. Kidding. You know, kidding."

In the middle of this Ali started to laugh. Within moments, he was regaling them with stories, telling them what he was going to do to Frazier, dancing and shadowboxing. The hard-hats were laughing, and hanging on every word. Johnny slapped me on the shoulder. "Hey," he shouted in my ear, *This is some guy!* They done him wrong. This guy is awright." And as we walked down the street the hard-hats were still there, grinning, waving, wishing Ali luck.

Of course, the fickleness of the fans is a subject on which Joe Willie Namath could write another book. On January 12, 1969, Namath engineered the greatest upset in the history of pro football. It was a victory that changed the very face of the sport. He was truly the toast of Broadway, the overlord of Manhattan Island. For not quite 12 months.

In December, when the Jets lost the American Football Conference title to Kansas City, the Shea Stadium fans booed him off the field. *Sic transit gloria mundi.*

In my view, the "fan" does deserve certain things. With the reminder that he voluntarily pays admission to an event—no one puts a gun to his head—I think he is entitled to a clean, comfortable, and safe ball park. I think he is entitled to the assurance that the ownership is doing everything it can legitimately do to produce a product of excellence—in the case of sports, a winning team. I think he is en-

titled to the assurance that, if the product is good (not great) and if the fan supports it so that the owner shows a reasonable profit, the owner will not desert him by moving the franchise to another city. I think he is entitled to the assurance that the athletes he pays to see will give of themselves to the utmost in their performances within the arena, and I think a reporter, like myself, with large-scale public recognition, has the same obligation to the fan that he has to his employer—namely, to do the best reporting job possible, to relay the most information, provide total accuracy, deliver the most responsible journalism, and yet deliver it in the most attention-getting manner possible. Also to deliver commentary that is probative and responsible.

If the fan gets all these things, he is getting what he is entitled to. He is also entitled to courtesy from each and every one of us, owners, athletes, reporters. But he is not entitled to impinge upon our privacy, endanger our safety, demean our dignity. Personally I feel I have lived by my responsibility to the public.

I know of no better evidence than the way I have sought to expose the carpetbaggers in baseball, nor do I know of a better way to protect the interests of the fan. I am not at all sure that many of the fans even understand, or want to be protected. This is their right, but it is just another reason why they should not be celebrated as a sacrosanct body always to be served.

There is a final reason why the fan should not be unduly celebrated—the most compelling reason of all—and that is the basic obligation to be a journalist. It is an easy thing to appeal to the fan in order to achieve his quick approval. It would have been an easy thing to have called Muhammad Ali "Cassius Clay," and to have extolled the fact that he had been barred from professional boxing. That would have been the popular thing to do. But not the right thing. To repeat what I have said elsewhere, what is popular is not always right, and what is right is not always popular. Oddly, that maxim has to be learned by Americans in every generation. I think I have practiced it throughout my career. It is a course guaranteed to cause one countless frustrations, but in the face of them you sometimes gather strength from unlikely sources.

There was a night when I felt abused by an unruly audience at the annual dinner of the Long Island Athletic Club. I had emceed this affair for five years as a personal favor to Gene Ward, a sports columnist for the *New York Daily News.*

510

You have to understand the climate of your typical sports banquet. It is the celebration of a season just beginning, or ending; a joining of people—usually men—with a common loyalty; a chance to hear coaches and athletes and people who inhabit the very world that so excites them. In short, it is a dream night for the fan. The fellowship is strong. So is the booze. There is often about it the roughhouse aura of a stag party.

This night the crowd, always roisterous, grew disorderly and discourteous to the point of being obnoxious. In other years this crowd had booed Allie Sherman mercilessly. It had behaved rudely during a speech by Vince Lombardi. Tonight I listened to their jeers and watched their misbehavior until I had my fill of it. I told them their conduct was inexcusable. They'd had me for the last time. At the end of the evening I refused a gift the sponsors had provided for me, and I left, to drive an hour and a half through a midwinter snow to my home.

Later that night I described my disgust and disappointment to Emmy. And the next day I was handed a letter, neatly typed, by my daughter Hilary, then 17. It was dated February 5, 1970, and I read it hungrily.

Dear Daddy,
This afternoon Mom told me about what happened at the dinner in Garden City. I wanted to let you know how sorry I am. We are all very proud of you and what you do; your courage in always speaking the truth, and your willingness to stand up for these truths. We are also admittedly proud of the adjective "controversial" which is always coupled with your name. At the same time we tend to forget that the burden of being controversial is not a light one, and that you ultimately are the one who must shoulder it. Never forget though that we are ready to help if we can.

You and I frequently talk about what a strange and sick time we live in. While sometimes we disagree about the cause and the remedy, both of us are firm in our stand that the remedy must be found and the disease cured. The only way that this will ever happen is by people telling the truth, no matter how ugly and unpalatable it may be. Your truths, though not so immediately significant as those of a Martin Luther King or a John Kennedy, are important. It doesn't really matter if the particular truth concerns poverty, Muhammad Ali or Joe Willie's knees. What I believe is important now is the realization that at this particular period in our country the truth, while rarely easy to swallow, is now impossible to choke down. Nearly every American knows that there is something terribly wrong with our society. Though they may differ in their opinion of the cause of the problem, they are

all alike in their desire to hear their anxieties explained away by pat phrases, worn-out rhetoric, and half-truths. You well know, and I am slowly learning, that there is no place in such a world for those few who will not lie or compromise with soothing half-truths. You are one of those few.

I'm glad that you stayed at the dinner and showed them that it takes more than behavior like theirs to stop those who tell the truth.

When I heard of this ugly occurrence I remembered a tape I saw of Robert Kennedy speaking at Kansas University during the campaign. Those students wanted to hear pleasant lies about themselves and their country. But Bobby told them the ugly facts about poverty, war and racism. And they booed him and jeered him. They wouldn't let him finish a sentence. He stood up to them and told them that they had better listen and change their attitudes because there was a very real possibility that they might be the last generation to have the chance to change things before it was too late.

It must have been humiliating for him then, as it was for you last night. But he had every right to be proud of himself. And I'm sure that his family was proud of him too. No matter how that audience, or any audience, treated him he knew he spoke the truth. No one, not even Sirhan Sirhan, could rob Robert Kennedy or his family of that knowledge and the strength it gives. And while I in all honesty cannot, despite the greatness you possess, attribute to you all the greatness of the Senator, I can compare you. There is much that is comparable. And coming from me, you know that that is the highest praise I can give.

Peace.

Much love,

Hilary Jennifer

Raising a daughter capable of such feelings gives meaning to a man's life. Hilary's letter is with me always. She is one fan I want forever.